BEN WALSH

OCR
GCSE Modern World History

Third Edition

THE
HARRODIAN SCHOOL

SEP 2011

Year book purchased:

YEAR	PUPIL	FORM	CONDITION
2011/12	Eva Carroll	14k	New
2012/13	Gabriel Scott	14 st	bit ropey.

DYNAMIC LEARNING

HODDER
EDUCATION
AN HACHETTE UK COMPANY

The Publishers would like to thank the following for permission to reproduce copyright material:
Photo credits: Please see page 502 – Acknowledgements.

Acknowledgements Laszlo Beke: extracts from *A Student's Diary: Budapest October 16–November 1, 1956* (Hutchinson, 1957), reprinted by permission of Penguin Group USA; Malcolm Brown: extracts on the Battle of the Somme, reprinted by permission of the author; Jason Burke: extracts from *Al Qaeda: The True Story of Radical Islam* (Penguin Books, 2007); Billy Congreve: diary entries from *Armageddon Road: A VC's Diary 1914–1916 Billy Congreve*, edited by Terry Norman (William Kimber, 1982); Countee Cullen: 'For A Lady I Know' from *On These I Stand: An Anthology of the Best Poems of Countee Cullen* (Harper and Bros., 1947), copyrights held by Amistad Research Center, Tulane University, Administered by Thompson and Thompson, reprinted by permission; *The Daily Mirror*: extract from *The Daily Mirror* (October 23rd 1962), reprinted by permission of the publisher; Niall Ferguson: extracts from an article on Vietnam from the *New York Times* (4 May 2008), © Niall Ferguson, reprinted by permission of The Wylie Agency (UK) Ltd; Gilbert Frankau: extract from 'The Voice of the Guns' from *The Poetical Works of Gilbert Frankau, Vol 1 (1901–1916)* (Chatto & Windus, 1923), reprinted by permission of A.P. Watt Ltd on behalf of Timothy d'Arch Smith; Michael Hickey: extracts from *Gallipoli: A Study in Failure* (John Murray, 1995); Adolf Hitler: extracts from *Mein Kampf*, translated by Ralph Manheim (Hutchinson, 1969), reprinted by permission of The Random House Group UK; Richard Holmes: extract from *Tommy: The British Soldier on the Western Front* (HarperCollins, 2004); Victor Klemperer: diary entries from *I Shall Bear Witness: The Diaries of Victor Klemperer, 1931–41, Vol. 1* (Phoenix, 1999), reprinted by permission of The Orion Publishing Group; Craig Mair: extract from *Britain at War, 1914–1919* (John Murray, 1989), reprinted by permission of the publisher; Henrik Metelmann: extracts from *Through Hell for Hitler* (Spellmount Publishers, 2002); J. Enoch Powell: 'I seem to see "The River Tiber foaming with much blood"' – from a speech in Birmingham (20 April 1968), reprinted by permission of Lord Howard; Dominic Sandbrook: extracts from *White Heat: A History of Britain in the Swinging Sixties* (Little, Brown & Company, 2006); Kim Sengupta: article, Enoch Powell still haunts immigration debate from *The Independent* (21 April 2008), reprinted by permission of the publisher; Robert Service: extracts from *A History of Modern Russia: From Nicholas II to Putin* (Penguin Books, 2003); Peter Simkins: extract from an article entitled 'The Events of the "Last Hundred Days" 1918' from *Journal of the Royal United Services Institute for Defence Studies*, Vol. 143, No.6 (The Royal United Services Institute, December 1998), reprinted by permission of the author; Robert Winder: extracts from *Bloody Foreigners: A History of Immigration to Britain* (Little, Brown & Company, 2004), reprinted by permission of the publisher; Neil Young: song lyrics from '*Ohio*' (Crosby, Stills, Nash and Young, 1970).

Every effort has been made to establish copyright and contact copyright holders prior to publication. If contacted, the publisher will be pleased to rectify any omissions or errors at the earliest opportunity.

Although every effort has been made to ensure that website addresses are correct at time of going to press, Hodder Education cannot be held responsible for the content of any website mentioned in this book. It is sometimes possible to find a relocated web page by typing in the address of the home page for a website in the URL window of your browser.

Hachette UK's policy is to use papers that are natural, renewable and recyclable products and made from wood grown in sustainable forests. The logging and manufacturing processes are expected to conform to the environmental regulations of the country of origin.

Orders: please contact Bookpoint Ltd, 130 Milton Park, Abingdon, Oxon OX14 4SB. Telephone: (44) 01235 827720. Fax: (44) 01235 400454. Lines are open 9.00–5.00, Monday to Saturday, with a 24-hour message answering service. Visit our website at www.hoddereducation.co.uk

©Ben Walsh 1996, 2001, 2009
First published in 1996 by
Hodder Education,
An Hachette UK Company
338 Euston Road
London NW1 3BH

Second edition published in 2001
This third edition published in 2009

Impression number   5
Year   2013 2012 2011

Cover photos *Front Cover:* A fallen statue of Stalin, © David Turnley/Corbis; *Back cover:* Adolf Hitler, c. 1930s, © Popperfoto/Getty Images; Prime Minister Winston Churchill makes the victory sign, © Bettmann/Corbis; Chairman of the Palestine Liberation Organisation Yasser Arafat attends a manifestation celebrating the 13th anniversary of the Palestinian Revolution, 1977, © Claude Salhani/Sygma/Corbis.
Illustrations by Oxford Designers & Illustrators
Typeset in Garamond Light Condensed 10.5pt by 2idesign Ltd
Printed in Dubai

A catalogue record for this title is available from the British Library.

ISBN: 978 0340 981832

Other titles in the series:
- *OCR GCSE Modern World History Teacher's Resource Book* (with CD) 978 0340 986677
- *GCSE Modern World History 1 International Relations Dynamic Learning* 978 1444 117608
- *GCSE Modern World History 2 Depth Studies Dynamic Learning* 978 1444 117776
- *GCSE Modern World History 3 Twentieth Century British History Dynamic Learning* 978 1444 117783
- *OCR GCSE Modern World History Revision Guide* 978 0340 992203.

Contents

Introduction
How will this book help you succeed?

What worries **most candidates** when they take the OCR Modern World History exam?

I'm worried that I will forget everything in the exam and dry up.

Candidates most worry about not knowing enough, and it's true that the OCR Modern World History course has a lot of History to take in. To tackle the questions in the OCR exam you need to have a good knowledge of the main events and you also need to use facts and figures to show the examiner you know your stuff. So you will be glad this book is written by an experienced teacher and examiner who knows what you need and also what you find hard.

This book tells you what you need to know

It thoroughly covers the OCR Modern World History specification – the Focus Points and the Specified Content (ask your teacher if you are not sure what this means).

But we don't just cover it by droning on about one event after another. The author text helps you to understand and investigate issues and to establish important links and relationships between events. This is important in the OCR exams which don't only ask you to describe or explain events. They also ask you to make connections, express your own opinions, to investigate issues and to draw your own conclusions from the history you study.

We try to make it memorable.
Wherever we can we tell the story through the actions or views of real people. We try to describe and explain big concepts and ideas in terms of what they might have meant to individuals living through those events at the time.

If you had been a 16-year-old Aryan living in Nazi Germany you would probably have been a strong supporter of Adolf Hitler. The Nazis had reorganised every aspect of the school curriculum to make children loyal to them.
   At school you would have learned about . . .

There are lots of brilliant sources.
History is at its best when you can see what people said, did, wrote, sang, watched on film, laughed about, cried over and got upset about (and a few other things as well!). You'll see a lot of cartoons like this one, but many other types of sources as well. OCR exam questions usually ask you to explain historical sources, so we give you lots of help to do that effectively.

SOURCE **23**

A cartoon from the *Daily Mail*, 29 October 1962.

Factfile

The terms of the Treaty were announced on 7 May to a horrified German nation. Germany was to lose:

➤ 10 per cent of its land.
➤ All of its overseas colonies.
➤ 12.5 per cent of its population.
➤ 16 per cent of its coalfields and almost half of its iron and steel industry.
➤ Its army was reduced to 100,000 men. It could have no air force, and only a tiny navy.

The book is packed with **hard facts and examples** which support the points that are made – no vague generalisations. In OCR papers the examiners like this. For example in a question on the Versailles Treaty a statement like 'Germans were upset because they lost land' is correct but it's vague – it's a low level answer (probably a D grade). Add some facts and figures like these and you'll go up a grade or two.

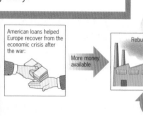

Increased employment

American loans helped Europe recover from the economic crisis after the war:

More money available

Rebuilt industry

Increased international trade

Increased profits

Sales

We use lots of diagrams. OCR candidates over many years have told us that they like the way these diagrams help them to understand important events.

What worries **most examiners** when they read your answers?

While candidates must worry about drying up, examiners have a different worry. They regularly comment that most candidates know enough, they just don't know how to use it! They often wander off the point of the question and drift into irrelevant answers. We help you with this issue too.

> *This person clearly knows enough but they aren't using it!*

This book also tells you how to use what you know

The main way is the Focus Tasks which you will find throughout this book. These help you to focus your writing on the exact issue itself rather than rambling about the whole topic. This is not easy – it is not a skill that you will suddenly develop during the examination. You have to practice studying the issue, deciding what you think and then selecting and deploying your knowledge to back up your views on the issue. The only way to develop this skill is through practice. The Focus Tasks give you the practice you need.

If you have tackled the Focus Tasks you will find your mind is already thinking along the same lines as the examiner. You will be using what you know to consider issues, not just 'learning stuff'! The Focus Tasks directly tackle each Focus Point which make up the OCR specification.

An example from the British Depth Study 1890–1918

Focus Task

How did women contribute to the war effort?

It is 1918. Use the information and sources on pages 428–29 to write a report for the Prime Minister. Your report is designed to convince him that the contribution of women to the war effort means they should get the vote. You should mention the role of women in:
- recruitment
- freeing up men to fight
- munitions
- putting up with prejudice
- continuing with 'men's work'.

> This title is a **focus point** from the OCR specification.

> **The key skill** in this task is the selection and deployment of information. First you select information from the text and sources and then deploy.

> **The bullet points guide** you to the broad areas of content which the examiner wants to see in an answer. You then have to decide which points belong under which of the headings – this will force you to get your thinking and your writing organised.

> You then have to **use this information** for something. You have to argue the case for female suffrage, pointing out which type of contribution was most important. This will force the kind of thinking that will help you in the exam. Where you may have to examine links between women's war work and their campaign to win the vote.

So, every Focus Task is designed to prepare you better for your exam. Then at the end of each section we give you some more specific advice on exam skills and we analyse some good answers which show how to use your Focus Task learning in an examination.

Section 1

OCR Paper 1 Core Content:
International Relations, 1919–2005

1

Were the peace treaties of 1919–23 fair?

The Paris Peace Conference

SOURCE 1

Allied soldiers and officials watch the signing of the Treaty of Versailles.

Source 1 was taken at the signing of the Treaty of Versailles at the Paris Peace Conference. It was a spectacular occasion and a momentous event. Months of hard negotiation, argument and compromise ended when the two German representatives who had been summoned to sign the Treaty did so on 28 June 1919.

When the treaty terms were announced the Germans complained that it was unfair. Many historians have criticised it since. To understand why the treaty was so controversial (and still is among historians) we need to start by looking at the mood in 1919.

The mood in 1919

When the leaders of Britain (Lloyd George), France (Clemenceau) and the USA (Wilson) arrived in Paris in January 1919 to draw up a treaty, they were already under pressure to deal severely with Germany. The people of the victorious countries, particularly in France and Britain, felt strongly that Germany was responsible for the war and should be punished.

There was also a strong feeling that Germany should pay for all the damage and destruction caused by the war. Apart from the USA, all of the countries that had fought in the war were exhausted. Their economies and their industries were in a bad state. Millions of young men had been killed or injured on both sides. Total British and French casualties, killed or injured, probably amounted to over 9 million. Ordinary civilians had faced shortages of food and medicine. Villages and towns in large areas of Belgium and France had been devastated.

1 You are a reporter for a Belgian newspaper. Write a caption to go with Source 2. Your caption should aim to persuade the Allied leaders to punish Germany.

SOURCE 2

An aerial photograph of Ypres in Belgium showing the almost complete destruction of the town by four years of heavy gun bombardment.

SOURCE 3

British Empire Union cartoon, 1919. The BEU was a pressure group which campaigned for people to buy British Empire goods.

Although no fighting took place on British soil, the huge casualties left their mark on public opinion in Britain. Almost every family had lost a member in the fighting. In the British general election campaigns of 1918 politicians knew they could rely on the support of the British people if they demanded a harsh peace settlement with Germany.

SOURCE 4

If I am elected, Germany is going to pay . . . I have personally no doubt we will get everything that you can squeeze out of a lemon, and a bit more. I propose that every bit of [German-owned] property, movable and immovable, in Allied and neutral countries, whether State property or private property, should be surrendered by the Germans.

Sir Eric Geddes, a government minister, speaking to a rally in the general election campaign, December 1918.

The case for treating Germany harshly was strengthened when it became public how harshly Germany had treated Russia in the Treaty of Brest-Litovsk in 1918 (see page 318). The Treaty stripped Russia of huge amounts of land and 25 per cent of its population. From the point of view of the Allies this was further proof of the evil ambitions of the German regime. The Allies felt that this was what Germany would have done to Britain and France if it had won.

Although the war and the fighting had ended in November 1918, the bitterness, hatred and enmity between the warring countries was far from over.

SOURCE 5

To the Allied Powers the Treaty of Brest-Litovsk was almost as significant as to the Russians and Germans who signed it. The naked and brutal policy of annexation [take-over of land] as practised by a victorious Germany weakened the arguments of well-meaning but misguided pacifists in the countries of the Entente.

An extract from Purnell's *History of the War*, written in 1969.

2 Explain in your own words what Source 3 is trying to say about 'the German'.
3 Read Source 5. What sort of treaty do you think the 'well-meaning but misguided pacifists' might have wanted?

Activity

1 Source 4 comes from a speech in the 1918 British general election campaign. Write an extra paragraph for the speech giving reasons for this harsh treatment of Germany.
2 At the end of the speech Geddes is holding a question time. What questions do you think might be asked, or what criticisms or comments might be made?

The aims of the leaders at the Paris Peace Conference

As soon as the Paris Peace Conference began, there was disagreement about what the Conference was aiming to do.

- Some felt that the aim was to punish Germany.
- Others felt that the aim was to cripple Germany so that it could not start another war.
- Many felt that the point of the Conference was to reward the winning countries.
- Others believed that the aim of the Conference should be to establish a just and lasting peace.

> 1 If you had been there to advise the Big Three, in what order of priority would you put the four aims described on the right?

Profile

Georges Clemenceau
(Prime Minister of France)

Background
➤ Born 1841 (he was aged 77 when the Paris Conference began).
➤ First entered French politics in 1871.
➤ Was Prime Minister from 1906 to 1909. From 1914 to 1917 he was very critical of the French war leaders. In November 1917 he was himself elected to lead France through the last years of the war.

Character
A hard, tough politician with a reputation for being uncompromising. He had seen his country invaded twice by the Germans, in 1870 and in 1914. He was determined not to allow such devastation ever again.

SOURCE 6

Sometimes people call me an idealist. Well, that is the way I know I am an American . . . America is the only idealist nation in the world.

President Wilson in 1918.

Focus Task

What were the aims of the Big Three at the Paris Peace Conference?

Using the information and sources on pages 2–5, draw up a chart like the one below summarising the aims of the three leaders at the Paris Peace Conference.
NB Leave the fifth column blank. You will need it for a later task.

Leader	Country	Attitude towards Germany	Main aim	

Georges Clemenceau (France)

France had suffered enormous damage to its land, industry, people – and self-confidence. Over two-thirds of the men who had served in the French army had been killed or injured. The war affected almost an entire generation. By comparison, Germany seemed to many French people as powerful and threatening as ever.

Ever since 1870, France had felt threatened by its increasingly powerful neighbour, Germany. The war increased this feeling. German land and industry had not been as badly damaged as France's. France's population (around 40 million) was in decline compared to Germany's (around 75 million). Clemenceau and other French leaders saw the Treaty as an opportunity to cripple Germany so that it could not attack France again. The French President (Poincaré) even wanted Germany broken up into a collection of smaller states, but Clemenceau knew that the British and Americans would not agree to this. Clemenceau was a realist and knew he would probably be forced to compromise on some issues. However, he had to show he was aware of public opinion in France. He demanded a treaty that would weaken Germany as much as possible.

Woodrow Wilson (USA)

Wilson has often been seen as an idealist whose aim was to build a better and more peaceful world from the ruins of the Great War. This is partially true, but Wilson did believe that Germany should be punished. However, he also believed that the treaty with Germany should not be too harsh. His view was that if Germany was treated harshly, some day it would recover and want revenge. Wilson's main aim was to strengthen democracy in the defeated nation so that its people would not let its leaders cause another war.

He believed that nations should co-operate to achieve world peace. In January 1918 he published his Fourteen Points to help achieve this. The most important for Wilson was the fourteenth. In this he proposed the setting up of an international body called the League of Nations.

Wilson was not a politician who could be pushed around. For example, he refused to cancel the debts owed to the USA by Britain and its Allies so that he could put pressure on them to accept his ideas. He also believed in self-determination (the idea that nations should rule themselves rather than be ruled by others). He wanted the different peoples of eastern Europe (for example, Poles, Czechs and Slovaks) to rule themselves rather than be part of Austria–Hungary's empire.

Profile

Woodrow Wilson
(President of the USA)

Background
➤ Born 1856.
➤ Became a university professor.
➤ First entered politics in 1910.
➤ Became President in 1912 and was re-elected in 1916.

Character
An idealist, and a reformer. As President, he had campaigned against corruption in politics and business. However, he had a poor record with regard to the rights of African Americans. He concentrated on keeping the USA out of the war. Once the USA had joined the war, he drew up the Fourteen Points as the basis for ending the war fairly, so that future wars could be avoided. Once he made his mind up on an issue he was almost impossible to shift. This irritated Clemenceau and Lloyd George. So did the fact that Wilson felt the USA was morally superior to the European powers.

Profile

David Lloyd George
(Prime Minister of Britain)

Background
➤ Born 1863.
➤ First entered politics in 1890. A very able politician who became Prime Minister in 1916 and remained in power until 1922.

Character
A realist. As an experienced politician, he knew there would have to be compromise. Thus he occupied the middle ground between the views of Wilson and those of Clemenceau.

THE FOURTEEN POINTS

1 No secret treaties.

2 Free access to the seas in peacetime or wartime.

3 Free trade between countries.

4 All countries to work towards disarmament.

5 Colonies to have a say in their own future.

6 German troops to leave Russia.

7 Independence for Belgium.

8 France to regain Alsace–Lorraine.

9 Frontier between Austria and Italy to be adjusted.

10 Self-determination for the peoples of eastern Europe (they should rule themselves).

11 Serbia to have access to the sea.

12 Self-determination for the people in the Turkish Empire.

13 Poland to become an independent state with access to the sea.

14 League of Nations to be set up.

Many people in France and Britain did not agree with the ideas contained in Wilson's Fourteen Points. They seemed impractical. Take self-determination, for example. It would be very difficult to give the peoples of eastern Europe the chance to rule themselves because they were scattered across many countries. For example, 25 per cent of the population of the new state of Czechoslovakia were neither Czechs nor Slovaks. Some people were bound to end up being ruled by people from another group with different customs and a different language. Some historians have pointed out that while Wilson talked a great deal about eastern and central Europe, he did not actually know very much about the area.

David Lloyd George (Great Britain)

At the peace talks Lloyd George was often in the middle ground between Clemenceau and Wilson. He wanted Germany to be justly punished but not too harshly. He wanted Germany to lose its navy and its colonies because Britain thought they threatened the British Empire. However, like Wilson, he did not want Germany to seek revenge in the future and possibly start another war. He was also keen for Britain and Germany to begin trading with each other again. Before the war, Germany had been Britain's second largest trading partner. British people might not like it, but the fact was that trade with Germany meant jobs for them.

SOURCE 7

We want a peace which will be just, but not vindictive. We want a stern peace because the occasion demands it, but the severity must be designed, not for vengeance, but for justice. Above all, we want to protect the future against a repetition of the horrors of this war.

Lloyd George speaking to the House of Commons, before the Peace Conference.

Like Clemenceau, Lloyd George had real problems with public pressures at home for a harsh treaty (see Sources 3 and 4 on page 3). Even his own MPs did not always agree with him and he had just won the 1918 election in Britain by promising to 'make Germany pay', even though he realised the dangers of this course of action.

Activity

Sources 8–10 are all comments on the Paris Peace Conference.

1 Choose one cartoon and on your own copy annotate it to explain the key features of the cartoon.
2 Which of the three cartoons do you think would most appeal to each of the Big Three?
3 All the cartoons come from the same magazine, *Punch*. Why do you think they take different viewpoints?

SOURCE **8**

GIVING HIM ROPE?

German Criminal (*to Allied Police*). "HERE, I SAY, STOP! YOU'RE HURTING ME! [*Aside*] IF I ONLY WHINE ENOUGH I MAY BE ABLE TO WRIGGLE OUT OF THIS YET."

SOURCE **9**

SOURCE **10**

THE FINISHING TOUCH.

Disagreements and compromises

As the talks at Versailles went on, it became clear that the very different objectives of the three leaders could not all be met. Clemenceau clashed with Wilson over many issues. The USA had not suffered nearly as badly as France in the war. Clemenceau resented Wilson's more generous attitude to Germany. They disagreed over what to do about Germany's Rhineland and coalfields in the Saar. In the end, Wilson had to give way on these issues. In return, Clemenceau and Lloyd George did give Wilson what he wanted in eastern Europe, despite their reservations about his idea of self-determination. However, this mainly affected the other four treaties, not the Treaty of Versailles.

Clemenceau also clashed with Lloyd George, particularly over Lloyd George's desire not to treat Germany too harshly. For example, Clemenceau said: '. . . if the British are so anxious to appease Germany they should look overseas and make colonial, naval or commercial concessions.' Clemenceau felt that the British were quite happy to treat Germany fairly in Europe, where France rather than Britain was most under threat. However, they were less happy to allow Germany to keep its navy and colonies, which would be more of a threat to Britain.

Wilson and Lloyd George did not always agree either. Lloyd George was particularly unhappy with point 2 of the Fourteen Points, allowing all nations access to the seas. Similarly, Wilson's views on people ruling themselves were somewhat threatening to the British government, for the British Empire ruled millions of people all across the world from London.

Activity

How did the Big Three feel about the Fourteen Points and each other?

1 Work in groups. Draw up a table to show what views:
  a) Clemenceau
  b) Lloyd George
  would have expressed on points 2, 4, 5, 8, 10 and 14 of President Wilson's Fourteen Points. You can find them on page 5.
2 On your own, write a letter from one of the two leaders to Wilson summarising your view of the Fourteen Points.
3 Copy the following diagram and use it to summarise the attitudes of the three leaders to each other.

Wilson

Clemenceau

Lloyd George

The Treaty of Versailles

None of the Big Three was happy with the eventual terms of the Treaty. After months of negotiation, all of them had to compromise on some of their aims, otherwise there would never have been a treaty.

The main terms can be divided into five areas.

The terms of the treaty

Focus Task

Why did the victors not get everything they wanted?

1 Work in threes. Look back at the profiles of Clemenceau, Wilson and Lloyd George on pages 4–5. Choose one each. Study the terms of the treaty on these two pages. Think about:
 ◆ which terms of the Treaty would please your chosen person and why
 ◆ which terms would displease him and why
 ◆ how far he seemed to have achieved his aims.
 Report your findings to your partners.
2 Look back at the chart you compiled on page 4. There should be a blank fifth column. Put the heading 'How they felt about the Treaty' and fill it in for each leader with a one-sentence summary.
3 a) Choose one of the following phrases to finish off this sentence:

 The victors did not all get what they wanted because . . .
 ◆ Clemenceau bullied Wilson and Lloyd George into agreeing to a harsh treaty
 ◆ the leaders' aims were too different – they could not all have got what they wanted and someone was bound to be disappointed
 ◆ public opinion in their home countries affected the leaders' decisions.
 b) Write a paragraph to explain why you chose that sentence.
 c) Write two more paragraphs to explain whether there is evidence to support the other two.

1 War guilt

This clause was simple but was seen by the Germans as extremely harsh. Germany had to accept the blame for starting the war.

2 Reparations

The major powers agreed, without consulting Germany, that Germany had to pay reparations to the Allies for the damage caused by the war. The exact figure was not agreed until 1921 when it was set at £6,600 million – an enormous figure. If the terms of the payments had not later been changed under the Young Plan in 1929 (see page 32), Germany would not have finished paying this bill until 1984.

3 German territories and colonies

Germany's overseas empire was taken away (see Source 11). It had been one of the causes of bad relations between Britain and Germany before the war. Former German colonies became mandates controlled by the League of Nations, which effectively meant that France and Britain controlled them.

Germany's European borders were very extensive, and the section dealing with former German territories was a complicated part of the Treaty (see Source 12). In addition to these changes, the Treaty also forbade Germany to join together with its former ally Austria.

SOURCE **11**

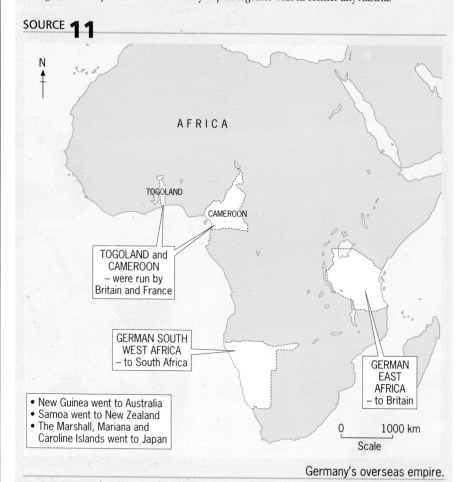

- New Guinea went to Australia
- Samoa went to New Zealand
- The Marshall, Mariana and Caroline Islands went to Japan

Germany's overseas empire.

4 Germany's armed forces

The size and power of the German army was a major concern of all the powers, especially France. The Treaty therefore restricted German armed forces to a level well below what they had been before the war.

- The army was limited to 100,000 men.
- Conscription was banned – soldiers had to be volunteers.
- Germany was not allowed armoured vehicles, submarines or aircraft.
- The navy could build only six battleships.
- The Rhineland became a demilitarised zone. This meant that no German troops were allowed into that area. The Rhineland was important because it was the border area between Germany and France (see Source 12).

SOURCE **12**

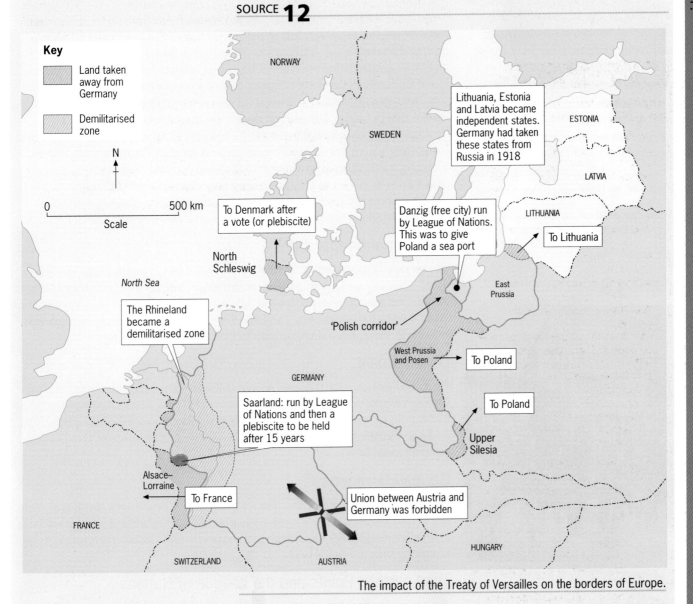

Key

Land taken away from Germany

Demilitarised zone

NORWAY

SWEDEN

ESTONIA

LATVIA

LITHUANIA

Lithuania, Estonia and Latvia became independent states. Germany had taken these states from Russia in 1918

To Lithuania

To Denmark after a vote (or plebiscite)

Danzig (free city) run by League of Nations. This was to give Poland a sea port

North Schleswig

North Sea

East Prussia

'Polish corridor'

The Rhineland became a demilitarised zone

GERMANY

West Prussia and Posen

To Poland

To Poland

Saarland: run by League of Nations and then a plebiscite to be held after 15 years

Upper Silesia

Alsace–Lorraine

To France

Union between Austria and Germany was forbidden

FRANCE

SWITZERLAND

AUSTRIA

HUNGARY

0   500 km
Scale

The impact of the Treaty of Versailles on the borders of Europe.

5 League of Nations

Previous methods of keeping peace had failed and so the League of Nations was set up as an international 'police force'. You will study the League in detail in Chapter 2. Germany was not invited to join the League until it had shown that it was a peace-loving country.

SOURCE 13

Today in the Hall of Mirrors the disgraceful Treaty is being signed. Do not forget it! The German people will, with unceasing labour, press forward to reconquer the place among the nations to which it is entitled.

From *Deutsche Zeitung* (German News), on the day the Treaty was signed.

SOURCE 14

The mistake the Allies made, and it did not become clear until much later, was that, as a result of the armistice terms, the great majority of Germans never experienced their country's defeat at first hand. Except in the Rhineland, they did not see occupying troops. The Allies did not march in triumph into Berlin, as the Germans had done in Paris in 1871. In 1918 German soldiers marched home in good order, with crowds cheering their way; in Berlin, Friedrich Ebert, the new president, greeted them with 'no enemy has conquered you!'

From *Peacemakers*, by Professor Margaret Macmillan of the University of Toronto, published in 2001.

SOURCE 15

Germans demonstrate against the Treaty, May 1919. The placard reads, 'We foreign Germans protest against the forced peace and against the robbery of our private property'.

1 How would you describe the tone of Source 13?
2 How does Source 14 help to explain the attitude shown in Source 13?

German reactions to the Treaty of Versailles

The terms of the Treaty were announced on 7 May to a horrified German nation. Germany was to lose:

- 10 per cent of its land
- all of its overseas colonies
- 12.5 per cent of its population
- 16 per cent of its coalfields and almost half of its iron and steel industry.

Its army was reduced to 100,000 men. It could have no air force, and only a tiny navy.

Worst of all, Germany had to accept the blame for starting the war and should therefore pay reparations.

The overall reaction of Germans was horror and outrage. They certainly did not feel they had started the war. They did not even feel they had lost the war. In 1919 many Germans did not really understand how bad Germany's military situation had been at the end of the war. They believed that the German government had simply agreed to a ceasefire, and that therefore Germany should have been at the Paris Peace Conference to negotiate peace. It should not have been treated as a defeated state. They were angry that their government was not represented at the talks and that they were being forced to accept a harsh treaty without any choice or even a comment.

At first, the new government refused to sign the Treaty and the German navy sank its own ships in protest. At one point, it looked as though war might break out again. But what could the German leader Ebert do? He consulted the army commander Hindenburg, who made it clear that Germany could not possibly win, but indicated that as a soldier he would prefer to die fighting.

Ebert was in an impossible position. How could he inflict war and certain defeat on his people? Reluctantly, he agreed to accept the terms of the Treaty and it was signed on 28 June 1919.

War guilt and reparations

The 'war guilt' clause was particularly hated. Germans felt at the very least that blame should be shared. What made matters worse, however, was that because Germany was forced to accept blame for the war, it was also expected to pay for all the damage caused by it. The German economy was already in tatters. People had very little food. They feared that the reparations payments would cripple them. As Source 17, shows, there was little sympathy for them among their former enemies.

Disarmament

The disarmament terms upset Germans. An army of 100,000 was very small for a country of Germany's size and the army was a symbol of German pride. Despite Wilson's Fourteen Points calling for disarmament, none of the Allies disarmed to the extent that Germany was disarmed in the 1920s. It is no great surprise that Adolf Hitler received widespread approval for his actions when he rebuilt Germany's armed forces in 1935.

German territories

Germany certainly lost a lot of territory. This was a major blow to German pride, and to its economy. Both the Saar and Upper Silesia were important industrial areas. Meanwhile, as Germany was losing land, the British and French were increasing their empires by taking control of German and Turkish territories in Africa and the Middle East.

The Fourteen Points and the League of Nations

To most Germans, the treatment of Germany was not in keeping with Wilson's Fourteen Points. For example, while self-determination was given to countries such as Estonia, Latvia and Lithuania, German-speaking peoples were being divided by the terms forbidding *Anschluss* with Austria or hived off into new countries such as Czechoslovakia to be ruled by non-Germans.

Germany felt further insulted by not being invited to join the League of Nations.

SOURCE 16

A German cartoon published in 1919. The German mother is saying to her starving child: 'When we have paid one hundred billion marks then I can give you something to eat.'

SOURCE 17

THE RECKONING.

PAN-GERMAN. "MONSTROUS, I CALL IT. WHY, IT'S FULLY A QUARTER OF WHAT *WE* SHOULD HAVE MADE *THEM* PAY, IF *WE'D* WON."

A cartoon from *Punch* magazine, 1919.

SOURCE 18

ALLIES STERN REPLY TO HUNS.
Terms of Peace Treaty Better Than Germany Deserves.
WAR-MAKERS MUST BE MADE TO SUFFER
RANTZAU AND OTHER ENVOYS GO TO SPA FOR ORDERS.

The Allies have made a stern and uncompromising reply to Rantzau's pleas that German industry will be ruined and her population rendered destitute by the economic terms of the Peace Treaty.

The reply points out that the terms have been determined by Germany's capacity to pay, not by her guilt; and the Huns are reminded that as they were responsible for the war they must suffer the consequences as well as other nations.

The German Delegation has left for Spa to consult with their Government, probably with the idea of arranging a means for 'saving their face', as it is now believed they will sign the Treaty.

From the British newspaper the *People*, 25 May 1919.

'Double standards'?

German complaints about the Treaty fell on deaf ears. In particular, many people felt that the Germans were themselves operating a double standard. Their call for fairer treatment did not square with the harsh way they had treated Russia in the Treaty of Brest-Litovsk in 1918 (see page 318). Versailles was much less harsh a treaty than Brest-Litovsk.

There was also the fact that Germany's economic problems, although real, were partly self-inflicted. Other states had raised taxes to pay for the war. The Kaiser's government planned to pay war debts by extracting reparations from the defeated states.

SOURCE 19

The Allies could have done anything with the German people had they made the slightest move toward reconciliation. People were prepared to make reparations for the wrong done by their leaders . . . Over and over I hear the same refrain, 'We shall hate our conquerors with a hatred that will only cease when the day of our revenge comes.'

Princess Bleucher, writing in 1920. She was an Englishwoman married to a member of the German royal family.

Focus Task

Why did the Germans react so angrily to the Treaty of Versailles?

Imagine that you are in an exam and you have to answer the above question. You only have time to explain two of the points below in your answer. Decide which two points you would choose and then hold a vote to see if the rest of the class agrees.
◆ The Germans were not aware of the situation in 1919
◆ War guilt and reparations
◆ Disarmament
◆ German territories
◆ The Fourteen Points
◆ The League of Nations.

The impact of the Treaty on Germany

In 1919 Ebert's government was very fragile. When he agreed to the Treaty, it tipped Germany into chaos. You can read about this in detail on pages 252–54. Ebert's right-wing opponents could not bear the Treaty and they attempted a revolution against him.

This revolution, called the Kapp Putsch, was defeated by a general strike by Berlin workers. The strike paralysed essential services like power and transport. It saved Ebert's government but it added to the chaos in Germany – and the bitterness of Germans towards the Treaty.

Worse was yet to come. Germany fell behind on its reparation payments in 1922, so in 1923 French and Belgian soldiers entered the Ruhr region and simply took what was owed to them in the form of raw materials and goods. This was quite legal under the Treaty of Versailles.

The German government ordered the workers to go on strike so that they were not producing anything for the French to take. The French reacted harshly, killing over 100 workers and expelling over 100,000 protesters from the region. More importantly, the strike meant that Germany had no goods to trade, and no money to buy things with.

The government solved this problem by simply printing extra money, but this caused a new problem – hyperinflation. The money was virtually worthless so prices shot up. The price of goods could rise between joining the back of a queue in a shop and reaching the front (see page 257)! Workers needed wheelbarrows to carry home their wages – billions of worthless marks. Wages began to be paid daily instead of weekly.

The Germans naturally blamed these problems on the Treaty. But the truth is more complex. Some say the French acted too harshly (even if the Treaty gave them the right). Others say that the Germans brought the problems on themselves by failing to pay reparations.

SOURCE 20

People coming from the bank with millions of paper marks in suitcases or wheelbarrows. People paying for seats at a theatre with eggs or pats of butter . . . Money that lost half its value in 12 hours. People who had been wealthy trying to sell watches or jewellery for food or articles instead of that hated money. A woman I knew had saved year by year, to assure her son's welfare. Her capital would have bought enough furniture for a decent house. Three months later it would not pay her tram fare.

An Englishman who before the war had lent £6,000 in marks; when they were repaid, they were worth about 87p in English money. The middle class was wiped out in a matter of weeks.

A German woman describes her problems in 1923; from Vernon Bartlet, *Nazi Germany Explained.*

Activity

What was the impact of the Treaty of Versailles on Germany?

It is New Year's Eve 1923. You are a German living in Berlin. As a civilian you survived the shortages and the starvation of the war. You are writing to a friend in America describing what your life has been like since the war ended.

In your letter, tell your friend about:
* the general strike in Berlin in 1920
* the French and Belgians taking over the Ruhr in 1923
* the awful inflation of 1923.

Explain how each of these problems has been caused by the Treaty of Versailles and how each problem has affected your life. Sources 16–21 will help you. You can also find out a lot more about these events on pages 253–58.

SOURCE 21

Hände weg vom Ruhrgebiet!

A German cartoon of 1923. The woman represents France. The text means 'Hands off the Ruhr!'

Verdicts on the Treaty of Versailles

The Treaty of Versailles is one of history's most controversial events. It was bitterly criticised by most Germans in 1919 and as Source 22 shows, they were still bitter about it five years later.

SOURCE 22

A cartoon from the German magazine *Simplicissimus*. It was published in February 1924 just after the death of Woodrow Wilson. It shows Wilson being judged and sent to Hell.

But it was not just the Germans who disliked the Treaty. There were plenty of critics in Britain as well (see Source 29 on page 15 for example).

Even the Big Three who drew up the Treaty were not satisfied with it.

- Clemenceau's problem was that it was not harsh enough for the French people who wanted to punish Germany. In 1920 he was voted out in a French general election.
- Lloyd George received a hero's welcome when he returned to Britain. However, at a later date he described the Treaty as 'a great pity' and indicated that he believed another war would happen because of it.
- Wilson was very disappointed with the Treaty. He said that if he were a German he would not have signed it. However, in a letter to his wife he said 'Well, it is finished, and, as no one is satisfied, it makes me hope that we have made a just peace; but it is all in the lap of the gods'. The American Congress later refused to approve the Treaty.

Hindsight

Looking back at the Treaty from the present day we know that the Treaty helped to create the cruel Nazi regime in Germany and helped cause a second world war. We call this hindsight – when you look back at an historical event and judge it knowing its consequences. You would expect hindsight to affect historians' attitudes to the Treaty and it has – but maybe not exactly as you might expect.

Some historians side with critics of the Treaty and its makers. Others point out that the majority of people outside Germany thought that the Treaty was fair and that a more generous treaty would have been totally unacceptable to public opinion in Britain or France. They highlight that the peacemakers had a very hard job balancing public opinion in their own countries with visions of a fairer future. Some say that the Treaty may have been the best that could be achieved in the circumstances.

Focus Task

Could the Treaty of Versailles be justified at the time?

1 Study Sources 22–29 carefully. Match one source to each of these headlines:
   ◆ The best that could be achieved in the circumstances
   ◆ They did what the people wanted
   ◆ A death warrant for Europe
   ◆ Betrayal

2 For each source, decide whether you think it is a critical, positive or balanced view of the Treaty.
   Then mark the sources on to a diagram like this.

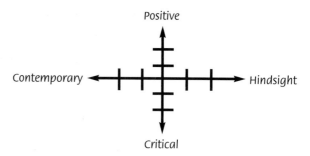

3 Compare your diagram with others in your class. Then write a paragraph explaining how far you agree with this statement: 'The views of the Treaty with hindsight are generally kinder than the views expressed at the time.'

Here is a range of sources – some from the time of the Treaty, some with hindsight.

SOURCE 23

The historian, with every justification, will come to the conclusion that we were very stupid men ... We arrived determined that a Peace of justice and wisdom should be negotiated; we left the conference conscious that the treaties imposed upon our enemies were neither just nor wise.

Harold Nicolson, British diplomat, 1919. He was one of the leading British officials at the Conference.

SOURCE 24

Severe as the Treaty seemed to many Germans, it should be remembered that Germany might easily have fared much worse. If Clemenceau had had his way ... the Rhineland would have become an independent state, the Saar would have been annexed [joined] to France and Danzig would have become a part of Poland ...

British historian W Carr, *A History of Germany*, 1972.

SOURCE 25

PEACE AND FUTURE CANNON FODDER

The Tiger: "Curious! I seem to hear a child weeping!"

A cartoon by the artist Will Dyson, first published in the *Daily Herald*, 13 May 1919. The 1940s class represents the children born in the 1920s who might die in a future war resulting from the Treaty.

SOURCE 26

The peacemakers of 1919 made mistakes, of course. By their offhand treatment of the non-European world they stirred up resentments for which the West is still paying today. They took pains over the borders in Europe, even if they did not draw them to everyone's satisfaction, but in Africa they carried on the old practice of handing out territory to suit the imperialist powers. In the Middle East they threw together peoples, in Iraq most notably, who still have not managed to cohere into a civil society. If they could have done better, they certainly could have done much worse. They tried, even cynical old Clemenceau, to build a better order. They could not foresee the future and they certainly could not control it. That was up to their successors. When war came in 1939, it was a result of twenty years of decisions taken or not taken, not of arrangements made in 1919.

Extract from *Peacemakers* by Professor Margaret Macmillan of the University of Toronto, published in 2001.

SOURCE 27

. . . a fair judgment upon the settlement, a simple explanation of how it arose, cannot leave the authors of the new map of Europe under serious reproach. To an overwhelming extent the wishes of the various populations prevailed.

Winston Churchill, speaking in 1919. He had been a member of the government and a serving officer during the war.

SOURCE 28

Looking at the conference in retrospect there is much to approve and much to regret. It is easy to say what should have been done, but more difficult to have found a way for doing it.

To those who are saying that the Treaty is bad and should never have been made and that it will involve Europe in infinite difficulties in its enforcement, I feel like admitting it. But I would also say in reply that empires cannot be shattered and new states raised upon their ruins without disturbance. To create new boundaries is always to create new troubles. The one follows the other. While I should have preferred a different peace, I doubt whether it could have been made, for the ingredients for such a peace as I would have had were lacking at Paris.

An extract from the diary of Edward House, one of Wilson's top officials, 29 June 1919.

SOURCE 29

A cartoon from the British newspaper the *Daily Herald*, 30 June 1919.

1 Explain the following features in Source 29:
  • the figure with wings
  • the stance of the Big Three
  • the iron ball
  • the people in the bottom left corner.
2 Now, without our help, do a similar analysis of Source 22. Note all the symbolic features and explain their meaning.
3 If you were trying to find out whether the bitterness of the Germans over the Treaty faded with time, how would Source 22 help you?

The other peace settlements

All Germany's allies also had to disarm and pay reparations. The four treaties that dealt with this (see below) were not negotiated by the Big Three but by officers and diplomats working with the foreign ministers of the Allied powers. The treaties were made in consultation with representatives of the nationalities in eastern and central Europe (except those of the defeated countries). Because the empire of Austria–Hungary collapsed in 1918, the treaties made eastern Europe a 'patchwork' of new states.

SOURCE 30

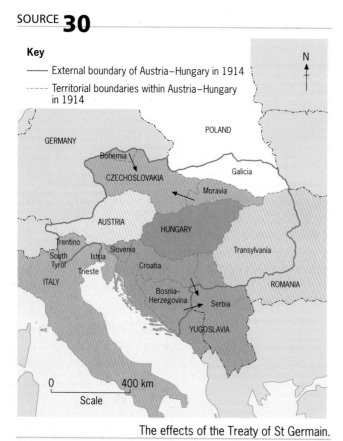

The effects of the Treaty of St Germain.

Treaty of St Germain, 1919 – dealt with Austria

This treaty separated Austria from Hungary and confirmed that Austria was no longer a leading power. Under the treaty, Austrian territories were divided as follows:

Territory	From Austria to
Bohemia and Moravia	new state of Czechoslovakia
Bosnia and Herzegovina, Croatia	new state of Yugoslavia (which also included the former kingdom of Serbia)

Austria also lost Galicia to Poland and land to Italy. Its army was restricted to 30,000 and it was forbidden ever to unite with Germany.

The old Austrian Empire had already collapsed by 1918 and many new states had already been set up. The Treaty of St Germain was really about sorting out a chaotic jumble of territories into new states rather than punishing Austria. One state that was not entirely happy, however, was Italy, which felt it should have received more land. On the other hand, many millions in eastern Europe were given self-determination and freedom to rule themselves.

Austria suffered severe economic problems after the war, as much of its industry had gone to Czechoslovakia. Other areas also suffered, because they were suddenly part of foreign states. Whereas once their markets had been in one empire, now they were in different countries.

SOURCE 31

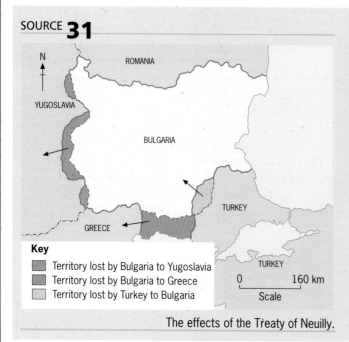

Key
- Territory lost by Bulgaria to Yugoslavia
- Territory lost by Bulgaria to Greece
- Territory lost by Turkey to Bulgaria

The effects of the Treaty of Neuilly.

Treaty of Neuilly, 1919 – dealt with Bulgaria

Bulgaria did well compared to Germany, Austria and Hungary. However, it lost lands to Greece, Romania and Yugoslavia and its access to the Mediterranean. It, too, had to limit its armed forces to 20,000 and pay £100 million in reparations. Bulgaria had played a relatively small part in the war and was treated less harshly than its allies. Nevertheless, many Bulgarians were governed by foreign powers by 1920.

SOURCE 32

Key

——— Frontier of Hungary before war

- - - - - Frontier of Hungary after war

The effects of the Treaty of Trianon.

Treaty of Trianon, 1920 – dealt with Hungary

This treaty was not signed until 1920 but, like that of St Germain, its main terms involved the transfer of territories.

Territory	From Hungary to
Transylvania	Romania
Slovakia, Ruthenia	Czechoslovakia
Slovenia, Croatia	Yugoslavia

A number of other territories went to Romania.

Hungary lost a substantial amount of its territory and its population. (Three million Hungarians ended up in other states.) Its industries suffered from the loss of population and raw materials. It was due to pay reparations, but its economy was so weak it never did.

SOURCE 33

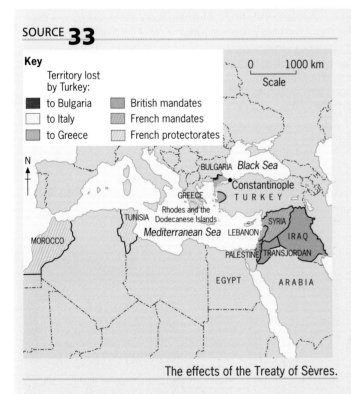

Key

Territory lost by Turkey:

- ■ to Bulgaria
- □ to Italy
- ▨ to Greece
- ▨ British mandates
- ▨ French mandates
- ▨ French protectorates

The effects of the Treaty of Sèvres.

Treaty of Sèvres, 1920 – dealt with Turkey

The last of the treaties to be arranged was the Treaty of Sèvres with Turkey. Turkey was important because of its strategic position and the size of its empire. Its territorial losses are shown in the table below.

Territory	From Turkey to
Smyrna	Greece
Syria	Mandate under French control

Turkey also effectively lost control of the straits running into the Black Sea.

The Turks had formally to accept that many countries of their former empire, such as Egypt, Tunisia and Morocco, were now independent or were under British or French protection. In practice, this was already true, but under the treaty Turkey had to accept and agree to this.

It was not a successful treaty. Turks were outraged by it. Turkish nationalists led by Mustafa Kemal challenged the terms of the treaty by force when they drove the Greeks out of Smyrna. The result was the Treaty of Lausanne (1923) which returned Smyrna to Turkey.

There were other criticisms of the Treaty of Sèvres. The motives of Britain and France in taking control of former Turkish lands were suspect. The Arabs who had helped the British in the war gained little. Palestine was also a controversial area and remains a troubled region to the present day.

Focus Task

How fair were the peace treaties of 1919–23?

In this chapter you have investigated a number of different treaties. Choose two treaties and give them a score on a scale of 1 to 5 for fairness: 1 is very fair, 5 is very unfair.

For each of the two treaties, write a paragraph to explain why you gave it the score you did.

2 To what extent was the League of Nations a success?

Focus

Horrified by the suffering of the First World War, many people in Europe wanted a lasting peace. The League of Nations was supposed to help keep the peace. In the 1920s it had some successes. But by 1937 it had become irrelevant, ignored even by its main members, Britain and France. In 1939, despite the efforts of the League, the world was once again plunged into war.

2.1 covers the League of Nations in the 1920s.
◆ You will investigate some of the League's successes and failures in the 1920s.
◆ You will look at the organisation of the League and consider whether there were weaknesses in it.
◆ You will investigate whether the world was a more peaceful and secure place at the end of the 1920s than it had been at the beginning.

2.2 looks at the League in the 1930s.
◆ You will discover how worldwide economic depression of the 1930s made the League's work much more difficult.
◆ You will investigate how two crises, in Manchuria and Abyssinia, contributed to the League's failure in the 1930s.

1919–39

The period 1919–39 is a complex one. The timeline below gives you an overview of the main events of this period that you will be studying in Chapters 2 and 3.

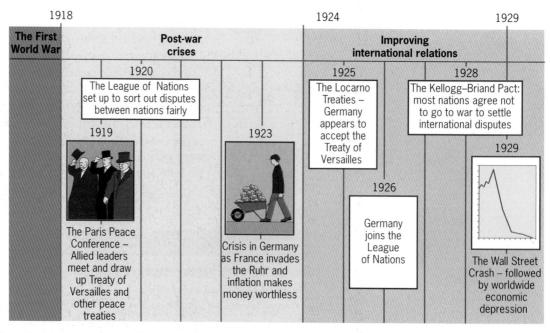

1918

The First World War

Post-war crises

1924

Improving international relations

1929

1920
The League of Nations set up to sort out disputes between nations fairly

1919
The Paris Peace Conference – Allied leaders meet and draw up Treaty of Versailles and other peace treaties

1923
Crisis in Germany as France invades the Ruhr and inflation makes money worthless

1925
The Locarno Treaties – Germany appears to accept the Treaty of Versailles

1926
Germany joins the League of Nations

1928
The Kellogg–Briand Pact: most nations agree not to go to war to settle international disputes

1929
The Wall Street Crash – followed by worldwide economic depression

18

SOURCE **2**

A family from Macedonia about to board a train which they hope will take them home after the First World War. Thousands of people were driven from their homes during the fighting in the First World War. There were also huge numbers of prisoners of war who needed to be returned home. The disruption of war wrecked food supplies and transport systems leading to disease. Some 20 million died from a deadly flu epidemic which broke out in 1918.

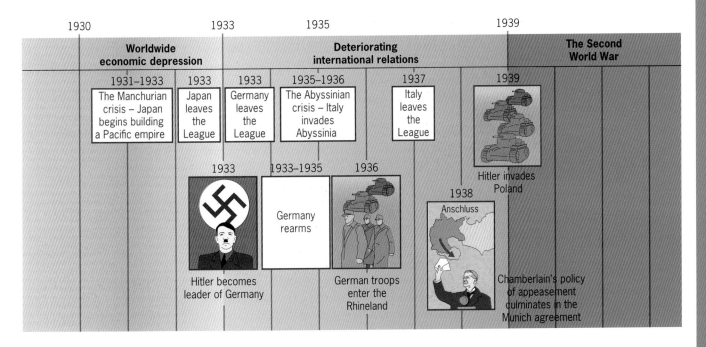

1930		1933		1935		1939	
Worldwide economic depression			**Deteriorating international relations**			**The Second World War**	

1931–1933	1933	1933	1935–1936	1937	1939
The Manchurian crisis – Japan begins building a Pacific empire	Japan leaves the League	Germany leaves the League	The Abyssinian crisis – Italy invades Abyssinia	Italy leaves the League	Hitler invades Poland

1933 — Hitler becomes leader of Germany

1933–1935 — Germany rearms

1936 — German troops enter the Rhineland

1938 — Anschluss — Chamberlain's policy of appeasement culminates in the Munich agreement

19

2.1 How successful was the League in the 1920s?

The birth of the League

SOURCE **2**

The front page of the *Daily Express*, 27 December 1918. Following the Allied victory in the First World War, President Woodrow Wilson was given a rapturous reception by ordinary people wherever he went in Europe.

SOURCE **3**

Merely to win the war was not enough. It must be won in such a way as to ensure the future peace of the world.

President Woodrow Wilson, 1918.

1 Which of the three kinds of League proposed by the Allies do you think would be the best at keeping peace?

SOURCE **4**

[If the European powers] had dared to discuss their problems for a single fortnight in 1914 the First World War would never have happened. If they had been forced to discuss them for a whole year, war would have been inconceivable.

President Wilson speaking in 1918.

2 You have probably studied the causes of the First World War in history. If so, do you agree with Wilson (Source 4)?

After the First World War everyone wanted to avoid repeating the mass slaughter of the war that had just ended. They also agreed that a League of Nations – an organisation that could solve international problems without resorting to war – would help achieve this. However, there was disagreement about what kind of organisation it should be.

- President Wilson wanted the League of Nations to be like a world parliament where representatives of all nations could meet together regularly to decide on any matters that affected them all.
- Many British leaders thought the best League would be a simple organisation that would just get together in emergencies. An organisation like this already existed. It was called the Conference of Ambassadors.
- France proposed a strong League with its own army.

It was President Wilson who won. He insisted that discussions about a League should be a major part of the peace treaties and in 1919 he took personal charge of drawing up plans for the League. By February he had drafted a very ambitious plan.

All the major nations would join the League. They would disarm. If they had a dispute with another country, they would take it to the League. They promised to accept the decision made by the League. They also promised to protect one another if they were invaded. If any member did break the Covenant (see page 24) and go to war, other members promised to stop trading with it and to send troops if necessary to force it to stop fighting. Wilson's hope was that citizens of all countries would be so much against another conflict that this would prevent their leaders from going to war.

The plan was prepared in a great hurry and critics suggested there was some woolly thinking. Some people were angered by Wilson's arrogant style. He acted as if only he knew the solutions to Europe's problems. Others were worried by his idealism. Under threat of war, would the public really behave in the way he suggested? Would countries really do what the League said? Wilson glossed over what the League would do if they didn't.

Even so, most people in Europe were prepared to give Wilson's plans a try. They hoped that no country would dare invade another if they knew that the USA and other powerful nations of the world would stop trading with them or send their armies to stop them. In 1919 hopes were high that the League, with the United States in the driving seat, could be a powerful peacemaker.

A new age?

SOURCE 5

For the first time in history the counsels of mankind are to be drawn together and concerted for the purpose of defending the rights and improving the conditions of   rking people – men, women, and children – all over the world. Such a thing as that was never dreamed of before, and what you are asked to discuss in discussing the League of Nations is the matter of seeing that this thing is not interfered with. There is no other way to do it than by a universal league of nations, and what is proposed is a universal league of nations.

Extract from a speech by President Woodrow Wilson to an American audience in 1919.

3 Source 5 may not sound the most riveting of speeches but maybe that explains why Wilson sometimes got people's backs and up failed to convince people of his point of view. If you were a modern spin doctor asked to spice up this speech what would you add or take away? (You can read the full speech on the internet at the Spartacus Educational website.)

SOURCE 6

British cartoon from 1919.

SOURCE 7

Fireworks display celebrating the opening of the League of Nations in 1920.

SOURCE 8

OVERWEIGHTED.

President Wilson. "HERE'S YOUR OLIVE BRANCH. NOW GET BUSY."
Dove of Peace. "OF COURSE I WANT TO PLEASE EVERYBODY ; BUT ISN'T THIS A BIT THICK ?"

Cartoon from the magazine *Punch*, March 1919. Punch was famous for its political cartoons.

Activity

Optimistic or pessimistic?

Work in pairs. One of you work with Source 6 and the other work with Source 8.
1 What is the message of your cartoon? Make sure that you explain what details in the cartoon help to get this message across.
2 Is your cartoon optimistic or pessimistic about the League of Nations? Give reasons.
3 Compare your ideas with your partner's, then write a paragraph comparing the two cartoons.

How successful was the League?

50% successful

50% failure

4 Make your own copy of this diagram, but with one difference. Redraw the segments to predict how successful you think the League is going to be. If you think it will have as many successes as failures draw your two segments equal. If you predict successes are going to outweigh failures then draw your left segment bigger.
At the moment you can only guess, but as you study this chapter, you will re-draw this diagram to show how the League is doing at this point.

1 Study Source 9. Write a ten-word slogan summarising each reason for opposing the USA's membership of the League.
2 Look at Source 11. What reasons are given for opposition to the League in the USA?
3 Study Source 10. Explain how the bridge in the cartoon might have been seen by
 a) supporters
 b) opponents of the League.

A body blow to the League

Back in the USA, however, Woodrow Wilson had problems. Before the USA could even join the League, let alone take a leading role, he needed the approval of his Congress (the American 'Parliament'). And in the USA the idea of a League was not at all popular, as you can see from Source 9.

SOURCE 9

The league was supposed to enforce the Treaty of Versailles yet some Americans, particularly the millions who had German ancestors, hated the Treaty itself.

If the League imposed sanctions (e.g. stopping trade with a country that was behaving aggressively) it might be American trade and business that suffered most!

Some feared that joining the League meant sending US soldiers to settle every little conflict around the world. No one wanted that after casualties of the First World War.

Some feared that the League would be dominated by Britain or France – and would be called to help defend their empires! Many in the US were anti-empires.

Reasons for opposition to the League in the USA.

SOURCE 10

An American cartoon re-printed in the British newspaper the *Star*, June 1919.

SOURCE 11

U.S. SENATE AND HOME RULE.

SUSPICIONS OF THE LEAGUE.

FEAR OF OLD WORLD ENTANGLEMENTS.

(FROM OUR SPECIAL CORRESPONDENT.)

WASHINGTON JUNE 7

Headline from the *Times*, 9 June 1920. Home Rule refers to the movement for independence in Ireland. By 1920 Republicans in Ireland were fighting for an end to British rule there. Many Americans had Irish roots and these Irish Americans were an influential group. Old World means Europe (America was the New World).

Together, the groups in Source 9 put up powerful opposition to the League. They were joined by Wilson's many political opponents. Wilson's Democratic Party had run the USA for eight troubled years. Its opponents saw the League as an ideal opportunity to defeat him. Wilson toured the USA to put his arguments to the people, but when Congress voted in 1919 he was defeated.

In 1920 Wilson became seriously ill after a stroke. Despite that, he continued to press for the USA to join the League. He took the proposal back to Congress again in March 1920. Source 12 shows you the outcome.

SOURCE 12

The New York Times.

"All the News That's Fit to Print."

THE WEATHER
Snow or rain today; Sunday, fair and slightly warmer; increasing shifting winds.
For full weather report see Page 13.

VOL. LXIX...No. 22,701   NEW YORK, SATURDAY, MARCH 20, 1920.   TWO CENTS Metropolitan District 50 Mile Radius | THREE CENTS Within 200 Miles | FOUR CENTS Elsewhere

SENATE DEFEATS TREATY, VOTE 49 TO 35; ORDERS IT RETURNED TO THE PRESIDENT; GERMAN DISORDERS GROW, HUNDREDS SLAIN

RED ARMY CAPTURES ESSEN
City Surrenders After Violent Fighting with

Police Trail Kaiser in Walks, Only a Few Steps Removed
AMERONGEN, March 19 (Associated Press).—Evidence that an extremely close guard has been placed by the Dutch Government on former

INDICT A. D. PORTER, ENRIGHT'S DEPUTY, IN VICE INQUIRY

Japan Spurs Shantung Parley; Ready for Big Concessions
TOKIO, March 12 (Associated Press).—It is understood here that the Government has instructed

MAYOR OF CORK IS SHOT DEAD BY MASKED MEN

Lodge Is Willing to Take Treaty Into Campaign; Hitchcock Glad That Reservations Are Nullified
Special to The New York Times.
WASHINGTON, March 19.—After the adjournment of the

LACK 7 VOTES TO RATIFY
28 Republicans and 21

The front page of the *New York Times*, 20 March 1920.

SOURCE 13

Focus Task

Why did the USA not join the League of Nations?

You are the special correspondent in Washington for *The Times*. Write an article for your newspaper in about 150 words which explains why the USA has not joined the League. Use Source 12 to help you.

THIS LEAGUE OF NATIONS BRIDGE WAS DESIGNED BY THE PRESIDENT OF THE U·S·A·

BELGIUM·FRANCE   ENGLAND·ITALY   KEYSTONE USA

A British cartoon from 1920. The figure in the white top hat represents the USA.

Activity

Look back to your diagrams from the activity on page 21. Do you want to change your prediction at all?

Still the Democrats did not give up. They were convinced that if the USA did not get involved in international affairs, another world war might follow. In the 1920 election Wilson could not run for President – he was too ill – but his successor made membership of the League a major part of the Democrat campaign. The Republican candidate, on the other hand, campaigned for America to be isolationist. His slogan was to 'return to normalcy', by which he meant life as it was before the war, with the USA isolating itself from European affairs. The Republicans won a landslide victory (see page 341).

So when the League opened for business in January 1920 the American chair was empty. The USA never joined. This was a personal rebuff for Wilson and the Democrats, but it was also a body blow to the League.

How did the League of Nations work?

The aims of the League

A Covenant set out the aims of the League of Nations. These were:

- to discourage aggression from any nation
- to encourage countries to co-operate, especially in business and trade
- to encourage nations to disarm
- to improve the living and working conditions of people in all parts of the world.

Focus Task

What were the aims of the League?

Design a placard for the rally shown in Source 14. It should summarise the League's aims in ten words or less.

Factfile

The League of Nations

➤ The League's home was in Geneva in Switzerland.
➤ Despite being the brainchild of the US President, the USA was never a member of the League.
➤ The League was based on a Covenant. This was a set of 26 Articles or rules which all members of the League agreed to follow.
➤ Probably the most important Article was Article 10. 'The members of the League undertake to preserve against external aggression the territory and existing independence of all members of the League. In case of threat of danger the Council [of the League] shall advise upon the means by which this obligation shall be fulfilled.'
➤ Article 10 really meant collective security. By acting together (collectively), the members of the League could prevent war by defending the lands and interests of all nations, large or small.
➤ One of the jobs of the League was to uphold and enforce the Treaty of Versailles.
➤ Forty-two countries joined the League at the start. By the 1930s it had 59 members.

SOURCE 14

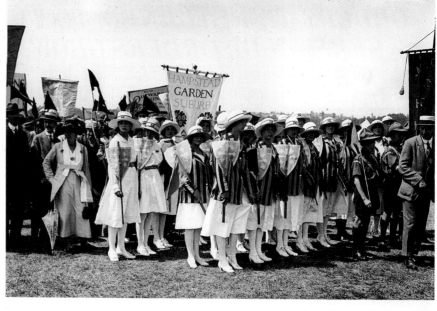

A League of Nations Union rally in Hyde Park, London, in 1921.

SOURCE 15

From a menu card for a banquet given by the League of Nations Assembly. It shows the hopes for the League with one of its most influential figures, Briand, as Moses, leading the statesmen of Europe to 'the promised land'. The sunrise is labelled 'The United States of Europe'.

Membership of the League

In the absence of the USA, Britain and France were the most powerful countries in the League. Italy and Japan were also permanent members of the Council, but throughout the 1920s and 1930s it was Britain and France who usually guided policy. Any action by the League needed their support.

However, both countries were poorly placed to take on this role. Both had been weakened by the First World War. Neither country was quite the major power it had once been. Neither of them had the resources to fill the gap left by the USA. Indeed, some British politicians said that if they had foreseen the American decision, they would not have voted to join the League either. They felt that the Americans were the only nation with the resources or influence to make the League work. In particular, they felt that trade sanctions would only work if the Americans applied them.

For the leaders of Britain and France the League posed a real problem. They were the ones who had to make it work, yet even at the start they doubted how effective it could be.

SOURCE 16

The League of Nations is not set up to deal with a world in chaos, or with any part of the world which is in chaos. The League of Nations may give assistance but it is not, and cannot be, a complete instrument for bringing order out of chaos.

Arthur Balfour, chief British representative at the League of Nations, speaking in 1920.

Both countries had other priorities. British politicians, for example, were more interested in rebuilding British trade and looking after the British Empire than in being an international police force.

France's main concern was still Germany. It was worried that without an army of its own the League was too weak to protect France from its powerful neighbour. It did not think Britain was likely to send an army to help it. This made France quite prepared to bypass the League if necessary in order to strengthen its position against Germany.

SOURCE 17

1 List the strengths and weaknesses of Britain and France as leaders of the League of Nations.
2 France proposed that the League should have an army of its own. Why do you think most people opposed this?
3 Think back to Wilson's ideas for the League. What problems would be caused by the fact that
   a) the USA
   b) Germany
   were not members of the League?

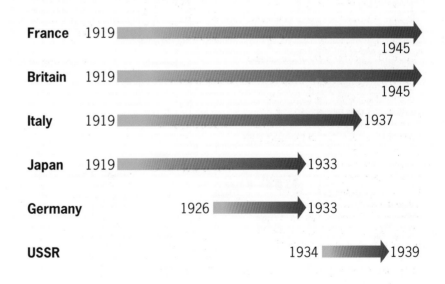

France	1919	1945
Britain	1919	1945
Italy	1919	1937
Japan	1919	1933
Germany	1926	1933
USSR	1934	1939
USA	never joined	

Membership of the League of Nations. This chart shows only the most powerful nations. More than 50 other countries were also members.

The structure of the League of Nations

The Covenant laid out the League's structure and the rules for each of the bodies within it – see Source 19 below.

1 Study Source 19. Which part of the League would deal with the following problems:
a) an outbreak of a new infectious disease
b) a border dispute between two countries
c) accidents caused by dangerous machinery in factories
d) complaints from people in Palestine that the British were not running the mandated territory properly?

SOURCE **18**

A

B

SOURCE **19**

The Assembly
The Assembly was the League's Parliament. Every country in the League sent a representative to the Assembly. The Assembly could recommend action to the Council and could vote on:
● admitting new members to the League
● appointing temporary members of the Council
● the budget of the League
● other ideas put forward by the Council.
The Assembly only met once a year. Decisions made by the Assembly had to be unanimous – they had to be agreed by all members of the Assembly.

The Council
The Council was a smaller group which met more often, usually about five times a year and in case of emergency. It included:
● permanent members. In 1920 these were Britain, France, Italy and Japan.
● temporary members. They were elected by the Assembly for three-year periods. The number of temporary members varied between four and nine at different times in the League's history.
Each of the permanent members of the Council had a veto. This meant that one permanent member could stop the Council acting even if all other members agreed. The main idea behind the Council was that if any disputes arose between members, the members brought the problem to the Council and it was sorted out through discussion before matters got out of hand. However, if this did not work, the Council could use a range of powers:
● Moral condemnation: they could decide which country was 'the aggressor', i.e. which country was to blame for the trouble. They could condemn the aggressor's action and tell it to stop what it was doing.
● Economic and financial sanctions: members of the League could refuse to trade with the aggressor.
● Military force: the armed forces of member countries could be used against an aggressor.

The Secretariat
The Secretariat was a sort of civil service. It kept records of League meetings and prepared reports for the different agencies of the League. The Secretariat had specialist sections covering areas such as health, disarmament and economic matters.

The Permanent Court of International Justice
This was meant to be a key part of the League's job of settling disputes between countries peacefully. The Court was based at the Hague in the Netherlands and was made up of judges from the member countries.
If it was asked, the Court would give a decision on a border dispute between two countries. It also gave legal advice to the Assembly or Council.
However, the Court was not like the courts which carried out the law within member countries. It had no way of making sure that countries followed its rulings.

The International Labour Organisation (ILO)
The ILO brought together employers, governments and workers' representatives once a year. Its aim was to improve the conditions of working people throughout the world. It collected statistics and information about working conditions and it tried to persuade member countries to adopt its suggestions.

C

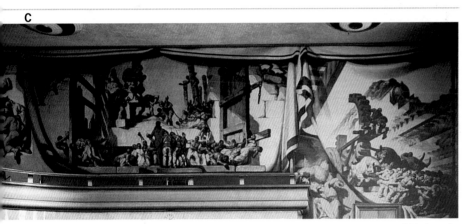

Details of the murals painted on the walls of the Assembly Room of the League of Nations in Geneva by José Maria Sert in the 1930s.

The League of Nations Commissions

As well as dealing with disputes between its members, the League also attempted to tackle other major problems. This was done through commissions or committees such as:

The Mandates Commission
The First World War had led to many former colonies of Germany and her allies ending up as League of Nations mandates ruled by Britain and France on behalf of the League. The Mandates Commission made sure that Britain or France acted in the interests of the people of that territory, not in its own interests.

The Refugees Committee
This helped to return refugees to their original homes after the end of the First World War.

The Slavery Commission
This worked to abolish slavery around the world.

The Health Committee
The Health Committee attempted to deal with the problem of dangerous diseases and to educate people about health and sanitation.

The organisation of the League of Nations.

Focus Task

Were there weaknesses in the League's organisation?

Here is a conversation which might have taken place between two diplomats in 1920.

> Peace at last! The League of Nations will keep large and small nations secure.

> I'm not sure. It might look impressive but I think there are weaknesses in the League.

Work in pairs.

Choose one statement each and write out the reasons each diplomat might give for his opinion.

In your answer make sure you refer to:

- the membership of the League
- what the main bodies within the League can do
- how each body will make decisions
- how the League will enforce its decisions.

Activity

1 Look at Source 18. These murals symbolise the work of the League. Prepare an entry for the League of Nations visitors' guidebook explaining what aspects of the League's work they represent.
2 Go back to your diagram from page 21 and see if you want to change your predictions.

SOURCE **20**

The new Yugoslav–Italian border ran along this river, splitting a village in half. The villagers had to drive their carts through the river to avoid the frontier control.

The League and border disputes in the 1920s

The treaties signed at the Paris Peace Conference had created some new states and changed the borders of other existing states. However, putting a dotted line on a map was a lot simpler than working out where the boundaries actually lay on the ground. These new boundaries might split a community, putting some people in one state and the rest in another.

It was the job of the League to sort out border disputes. From the start there was so much for the League to do that some disputes were handled by the Conference of Ambassadors. Strictly speaking, this was not a body of the League of Nations. But it had been set up to sort out problems arising from the post-war treaties and was made up of leading politicians from the main members of the League – Britain, France and Italy – so it was very closely linked to the League.

SOURCE **21**

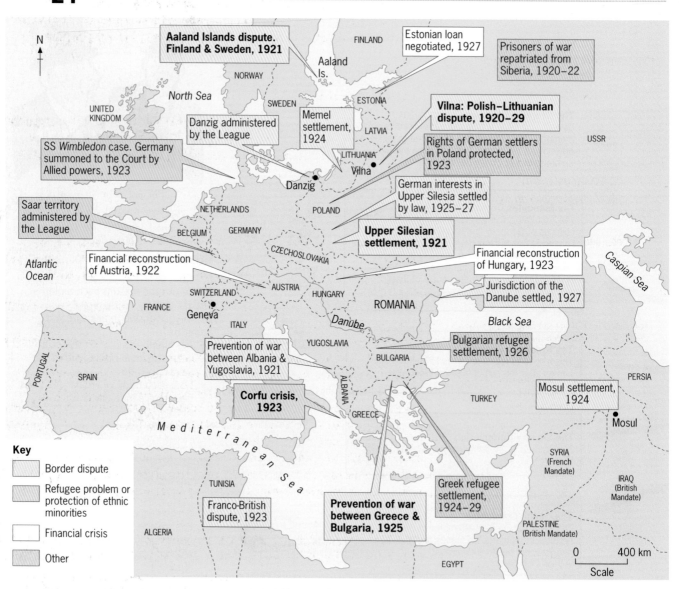

Problems dealt with by the League of Nations in the 1920s. The problems in bold text are described on pages 29–30.

Focus Task

Did weaknesses in the League's organisation make failure inevitable? (Part 1)

Five of the problems shown in Source 21 are described on pages 29–30. They are highlighted in bold text on the map on page 28. As you read about each one, score the League's success on a scale of –5 (a total failure) to +5 (a great success).

(Focus Task continued on page 30.)

SOURCE **22**

The League had been designed to deal with just such a dangerous problem as this. It had acted promptly and fairly and it had condemned the violence of the Italians. But it had lost the initiative. The result was that a great power had once again got away with using force against a small power.

Historians Gibbons and Morican referring to the Corfu crisis in *The League of Nations and the UNO*, 1970.

SOURCE **23**

The settlement of the dispute between Italy and Greece, though not strictly a League victory, upheld the principles on which it was based.

From J and G Stokes, *Europe and the Modern World*, 1973.

1 Sources 22 and 23 are referring to the same event. How do their interpretations differ?
2 Could they both be right? Explain your answer.
3 'The main problem in the Corfu crisis was not the League's organisation but the attitude of its own members.' Explain whether you agree.

Vilna, 1920

Poland and Lithuania were two new states created by the post-war treaties. Vilna (now Vilnius) was made the capital of the new state of Lithuania, but its population was largely Polish. In 1920 a private Polish army simply took control of it.

Lithuania appealed for help. This was a crucial first 'test case' for the League. Both countries were members of the League. Poland was clearly the aggressor, though many people could see its case. The League protested to Poland, but Poland did not withdraw. The League was now stuck. According to the Covenant it could have sent British and French troops to force the Poles out of Vilna. But it did not. The French were not prepared to upset Poland because they saw it as a possible ally against Germany in the future. Britain was not prepared to act alone and send troops right to the other side of Europe.

In the end the League did nothing. The Poles kept Vilna.

Upper Silesia, 1921

Upper Silesia was an industrial region on the border between Germany and Poland. It was inhabited by both German and Polish people. Both Germany and Poland wanted control of it, partly because of its rich iron and steel industry. In 1920 a plebiscite was organised for Silesians to vote on which country they wished to join. French and British troops were sent to keep order at the polling booths.

The industrial areas voted mainly for Germany, the rural areas mainly for Poland. The League therefore divided the region along these lines, but it built in many safeguards to prevent future disputes. It safeguarded rail links between the two countries and made arrangements for water and power supplies from one side of the border to be supplied to the other. Both countries accepted the decision.

Aaland Islands, 1921

Both Sweden and Finland wanted control of the Aaland Islands, which were midway between the two countries. Both countries were threatening to fight for them. They appealed to the League. After studying the matter closely, the League said the islands should go to Finland. Sweden accepted the League's ruling and war was avoided.

Corfu, 1923

One of the boundaries which had to be sorted out after the war was the border between Greece and Albania. The Conference of Ambassadors was given this job and it appointed an Italian general called Tellini to supervise it. On 27 August, while they were surveying the Greek side of the frontier area, Tellini and his team were ambushed and killed.

The Italian leader Mussolini was furious and blamed the Greek government for the murder. On 29 August he demanded that it pay compensation to Italy and execute the murderers. The Greeks, however, had no idea who the murderers were. On 31 August Mussolini bombarded and then occupied the Greek island of Corfu. Fifteen people were killed. Greece appealed to the League for help.

The situation was serious. It seemed very like the events of 1914 which had triggered the First World War. Fortunately, the Council was already in session, so the League acted swiftly. By 7 September it had prepared its judgement. It condemned Mussolini's actions. It also suggested that Greece pay compensation but that the money be held by the League. This money would then be paid to Italy if, and when, Tellini's killers were found.

Officially, Mussolini accepted the League's decision. However, behind the scenes, he got to work on the Conference of Ambassadors and persuaded it to change the League's ruling. The Greeks had to apologise and pay compensation directly to Italy. On 27 September, Mussolini withdrew from Corfu boasting of his triumph.

Activity

Go back to your diagram from page 21. You have done your predictions. Now you are finding out what actually happened. How will you show the balance of success and failure at this stage?

The Geneva Protocol

The Corfu incident demonstrated how the League of Nations could be undermined by its own members. Britain and France drew up the Geneva Protocol in 1924, which said that if two members were in dispute they would have to ask the League to sort out the disagreement and they would have to accept the Council's decision. They hoped this would strengthen the League. But before the plan could be put into effect there was a general election in Britain. The new Conservative government refused to sign the Protocol, worried that Britain would be forced to agree to something that was not in its own interests. So the Protocol, which had been meant to strengthen the League, in fact weakened it.

Bulgaria, 1925

Two years after Corfu, the League was tested yet again. In October 1925, Greek troops invaded Bulgaria after an incident on the border in which some Greek soldiers were killed. Bulgaria appealed for help. It also sent instructions to its army (see Source 24).

The League condemned the Greek action. It ordered Greece to pull out and pay compensation to Bulgaria. Faced with the disapproval of the major powers in the League, the Greeks obeyed, although they did complain that there seemed to be one rule for the large states (such as Italy) and another for the smaller ones (such as themselves).

SOURCE 24

Make only slight resistance. Protect the refugees. Prevent the spread of panic. Do not expose the troops to unnecessary losses in view of the fact that the incident has been laid before the Council of the League of Nations, which is expected to stop the invasion.

A telegram from the Bulgarian Ministry of War in Sofia to its army commanders, 22 October 1925.

1 Read Source 24. Why do you think Bulgaria was so optimistic about the League?
2 Look at Source 25. What impression of the League does this cartoon give you?
3 Look back at the Focus Task on page 27. If the diplomats had met up again in 1925, which of the events described on pages 29–30 would each one have used to show that he had been correct?

Focus Task

Did the weaknesses in the League's organisation make failure inevitable? (Part 2)

Can you find evidence to support or challenge each of the following criticisms of the League's organisation:
♦ that it would be slow to act
♦ that members would act in their own interests, not the League's
♦ that without the USA it would be powerless?
Use a table like this to record your answers:

Criticism	Evidence for	Evidence against

Focus first on the Bulgarian and Corfu crises. These will be most useful for your exam. Then look for evidence from the other crises.

Keep your table safe. You will add to it in a later task on page 42.

Once you have completed your table look at the balance of evidence. Does this suggest to you that the League could have succeeded, or not?

SOURCE 25

BALKANDUM AND BALKANDEE.

"JUST THEN CAME DOWN A MONSTROUS DOVE
WHOSE FORCE WAS PURELY MORAL,
WHICH TURNED THE HEROES' HEARTS TO LOVE"

A cartoon about the Bulgarian crisis in *Punch*, 11 November 1925. The characters are based on Tweedledee and Tweedledum, from the children's book *Alice's Adventures in Wonderland*, who were always squabbling.

How did the League of Nations work for a better world?

The League of Nations had set itself a wider task than simply waiting for disputes to arise and hoping to solve them. Through its commissions or committees (see page 27), the League aimed to fight poverty, disease and injustice all over the world.

SOURCE 26

A

B

Two League of Nations' projects.

4 Study Sources 26A and 26B. What aspects of the League's work do you think they show?

5 Why do you think the founders of the League wanted it to tackle social problems?

6 The work of the League's commissions affected hundreds of millions of people, yet historians write very little about this side of its work. Why do you think this is?

• **Refugees** The League did tremendous work in getting refugees and former prisoners of war back to their homelands. It is estimated that in the first few years after the war, about 400,000 prisoners were returned to their homes by the League's agencies. When a refugee crisis hit Turkey in 1922, hundreds of thousands of people had to be housed in refugee camps. The League acted quickly to stamp out cholera, smallpox and dysentery in the camps.

• **Working conditions** The International Labour Organization was successful in banning poisonous white lead from paint and in limiting the hours that small children were allowed to work. It also campaigned strongly for employers to improve working conditions generally. It introduced a resolution for a maximum 48-hour week, and an eight-hour day, but only a minority of members adopted it because they thought it would raise industrial costs.

• **Health** The Health Committee, which later became the World Health Organization, worked hard to defeat the dreaded disease leprosy. It started the global campaign to exterminate mosquitoes, which greatly reduced cases of malaria and yellow fever in later decades. Even the USSR, which was otherwise opposed to the League, took Health Committee advice on preventing plague in Siberia.

• **Transport** The League made recommendations on marking shipping lanes and produced an international highway code for road users.

• **Social problems** The League blacklisted four large German, Dutch, French and Swiss companies which were involved in the illegal drug trade. It brought about the freeing of 200,000 slaves in British-owned Sierra Leone. It organised raids against slave owners and traders in Burma. It challenged the use of forced labour to build the Tanganyika railway in Africa, where the death rate among the African workers was a staggering 50 per cent. League pressure brought this down to four per cent, which it said was 'a much more acceptable figure'.

Even in the areas where it could not remove social injustice the League kept careful records of what was going on and provided information on problems such as drug trafficking, prostitution and slavery.

Activity

Revisit your pie chart from page 21. How should it look now?

International agreements of the 1920s

- ➤ **1921 Washington Conference:** USA, Britain, France and Japan agreed to limit the size of their navies.
- ➤ **1922 Rapallo Treaty:** The USSR and Germany re-established diplomatic relations.
- ➤ **1924 The Dawes Plan:** to avert a terrible economic crisis in Germany, the USA lent money to Germany to help it to pay its reparations bill (see page 33).
- ➤ **1925 Locarno treaties:** Germany accepted its western borders as set out in the Treaty of Versailles.
- ➤ **1928 Kellogg–Briand Pact:** 65 nations agreed not to use force to settle disputes. This is also known as the Pact of Paris.
- ➤ **1929 Young Plan:** reduced Germany's reparations payments.

Disarmament

In the 1920s, the League largely failed in bringing about disarmament. At the Washington Conference in 1921 the USA, Japan, Britain and France agreed to limit the size of their navies, but that was as far as disarmament ever got.

The failure of disarmament was particularly damaging to the League's reputation in Germany. Germany had disarmed. It had been forced to. But no other countries had disarmed to the same extent. They were not prepared to give up their own armies and they were certainly not prepared to be the first to disarm.

Even so, in the late 1920s, the League's failure over disarmament did not seem too serious because of a series of international agreements that seemed to promise a more peaceful world (see Factfile).

- • **The Locarno agreements** in 1925 were greeted with terrific enthusiasm, particularly in France. When news of the agreements was announced, church bells were rung, fireworks were set off and celebrations carried on into the night. The agreements seemed to resolve some of the problems left over from the First World War. France felt that at last it was being given some guarantee of border security. Germany had shown more goodwill towards France than ever before. The agreements paved the way for Germany to join the League of Nations. Germany was granted entry into the League in 1926. Now the Soviet Union was the only major European power not in the League.

SOURCE **27**

A

A LEAGUE TRIUMPH.
WITH MR. PUNCH'S CONGRATULATIONS TO THE BRITISH COMMISSIONAIRE.

B

—AND NOW THE NEXT STEP!

British cartoons from 1925. In **A** Fräulein Gretchen stands for Germany.

1 Look at Sources 27A and B. Are these sources making the same point about Locarno? Explain your answer.
2 Describe fully the contrasting moods shown in the cartoons.

- • Three years after Locarno, the **Kellogg–Briand Pact** marked the high point of international relations in the 1920s. Sixty-five nations agreed to condemn war as a means of solving international disputes. There was nothing in the Pact about what would happen if a state broke the terms of the agreement. Nor did the agreement help the League of Nations with disarmament. The states all agreed that they had to keep their armies for 'self-defence'. However, at the time, the Pact was greeted as a turning point in history. If you had asked any observer in 1928 whether the world was a safer place than it had been in the early 1920s, the answer would almost certainly have been yes.

How did economic recovery help the League?

Another reason for optimism in 1928 was that, after the difficult days of the early 1920s, the economies of the European countries were once again recovering. The Dawes Plan of 1924 had helped to sort out Germany's economic chaos and had also helped to get the economies of Britain and France moving again (see Source 28). The recovery of trading relationships between these countries helped to reduce tension. That is why one of the aims of the League had been to encourage trading links between the countries. When countries were trading with one another, they were much less likely to go to war with each other.

SOURCE **28**

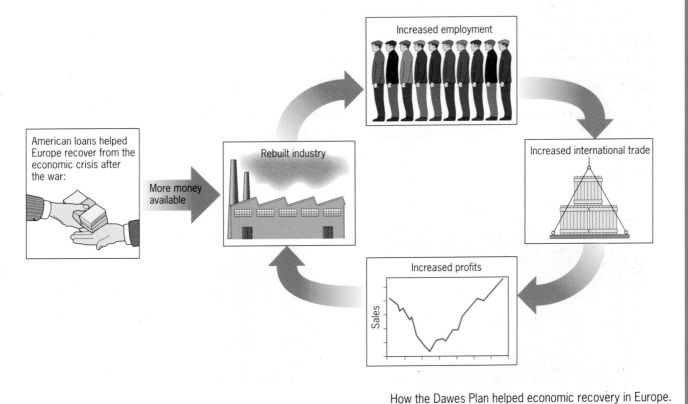

How the Dawes Plan helped economic recovery in Europe.

Focus Task

How successful was the League in the 1920s?

The League had four objectives. These are shown on the file cards on the left.

- to discourage aggression from any nation

- to encourage countries to co-operate, especially in business and trade

- to encourage nations to disarm

- to improve the living and working conditions of people in all parts of the world

1 Put the objectives in order, according to how successful the League was in achieving them. Put the objective you think was achieved to the greatest extent at the top, and that which was achieved least at the bottom. Write a paragraph to explain your order and support it with evidence from this chapter.
2 It is 1929. Suggest one change the League could make to be more effective in each of its objectives. Explain how the change would help.
3 Now think about the overview. Look again at your diagram from page 21. Do you want to revisit it again?
4 Which of the following statements do you most agree with?
  - 'The League of Nations was a great force for peace in the 1920s.'
  - 'Events of the 1920s showed just how weak the League really was.'
  - 'The League's successes in the 1920s were small-scale, its failures had a higher profile.'
  Explain why you have chosen your statement, and why you rejected the others.

2.2 Why did the League fail in the 1930s?

Historians do not agree about how successful the League of Nations was in the 1920s. However, in contrast, they almost all agree that in the 1930s the League of Nations was a failure. In the second part of this chapter you are going to investigate the factors and events that led to the failure of the League of Nations in the 1930s.

SOURCE **1**

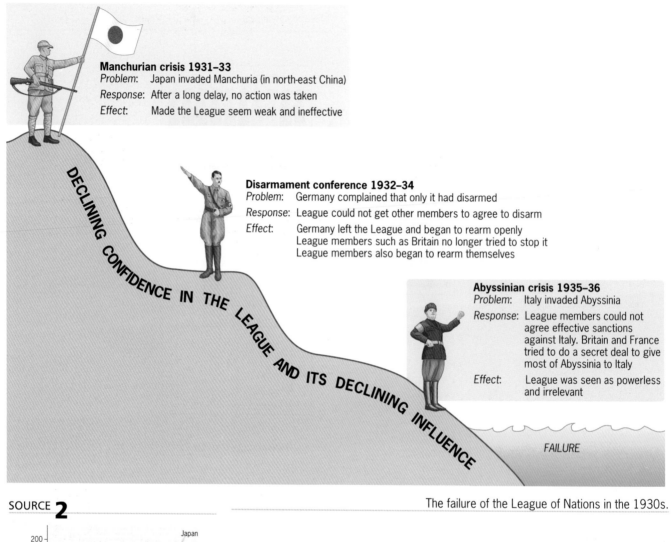

Manchurian crisis 1931–33
Problem: Japan invaded Manchuria (in north-east China)
Response: After a long delay, no action was taken
Effect: Made the League seem weak and ineffective

DECLINING CONFIDENCE IN THE LEAGUE AND ITS DECLINING INFLUENCE

Disarmament conference 1932–34
Problem: Germany complained that only it had disarmed
Response: League could not get other members to agree to disarm
Effect: Germany left the League and began to rearm openly
League members such as Britain no longer tried to stop it
League members also began to rearm themselves

Abyssinian crisis 1935–36
Problem: Italy invaded Abyssinia
Response: League members could not agree effective sanctions against Italy. Britain and France tried to do a secret deal to give most of Abyssinia to Italy
Effect: League was seen as powerless and irrelevant

FAILURE

The failure of the League of Nations in the 1930s.

SOURCE **2**

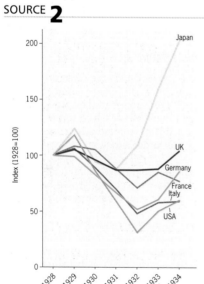

The rise and fall in industrial production in selected countries, 1928–34.

How did the economic depression harm the work of the League?

In the late 1920s there had been a boom in world trade. The USA was the richest nation in the world. American business was the engine driving the world economy. Everyone traded with the USA. Most countries also borrowed money from American banks. As a result of this trade, most countries were getting richer. You saw on page 33 how this economic recovery helped to reduce international tension. However, one of the League's leading figures predicted that political disaster might follow if countries did not co-operate economically. He turned out to be right.

In 1929 economic disaster did strike. In the USA the Wall Street Crash started a long depression that quickly caused economic problems throughout the world (see page 371). It damaged the trade and industry of all countries (see Source 2). It affected relations between countries (see Source 3). It also led to important political changes within countries (see Source 3). Much of the goodwill and the optimism of the late 1920s evaporated.

SOURCE 3

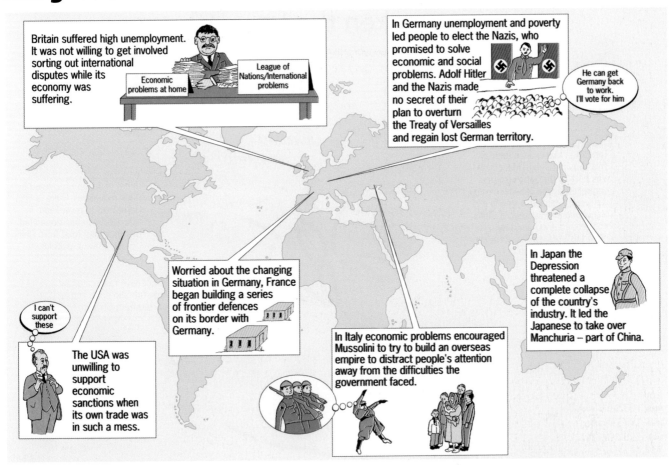

The effects of the Depression within various countries.

Focus Task

How did the Depression make the work of the League harder?

Study these statements:
- ◆ I have not worked since last year.
- ◆ I will support anyone who can get the country back to work.
- ◆ If we had our own empire we would have the resources we need. Economic depressions would not damage us so much.
- ◆ Reparations has caused this mess.
- ◆ The bank has closed. We've lost everything!
- ◆ We need tough leaders who will not be pushed around by the League of Nations or the USA.
- ◆ We should ban all foreign goods. That will protect the jobs of our workers.

Now
a) suggest which country (or countries) they would have been made in during the Depression – USA, Britain, France, Germany, Japan or Italy
b) suggest why these views would worry the League of Nations.

1 Compare Source 4 with Source 28 on page 33. What has changed?

SOURCE 4

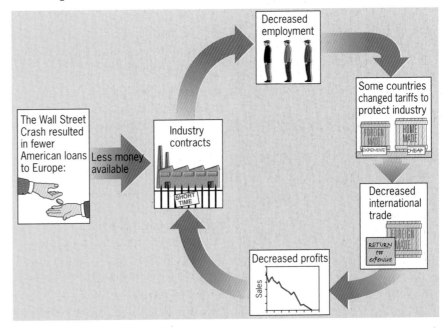

The effects of the Depression between countries.

Activity

Revisit your pie chart from page 21. How should it look now?

How did the Manchurian crisis weaken the League?

The first major test for the League came when the Japanese invaded Manchuria in 1931.

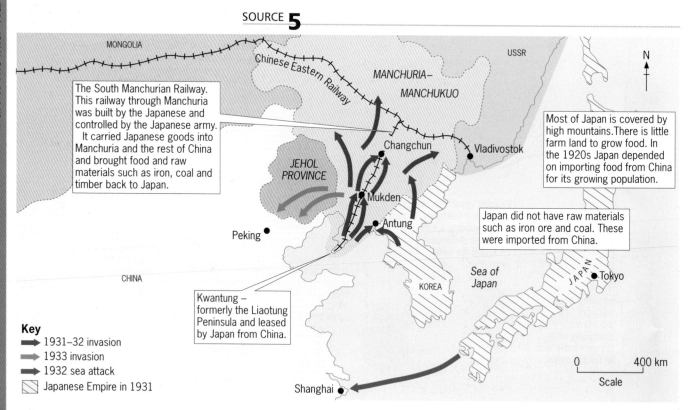

The South Manchurian Railway. This railway through Manchuria was built by the Japanese and controlled by the Japanese army. It carried Japanese goods into Manchuria and the rest of China and brought food and raw materials such as iron, coal and timber back to Japan.

Most of Japan is covered by high mountains. There is little farm land to grow food. In the 1920s Japan depended on importing food from China for its growing population.

Japan did not have raw materials such as iron ore and coal. These were imported from China.

Kwantung – formerly the Liaotung Peninsula and leased by Japan from China.

Key
→ 1931–32 invasion
→ 1933 invasion
→ 1932 sea attack
▨ Japanese Empire in 1931

The railways and natural resources of Manchuria.

Japanese troops in action in Manchuria.

Since 1900 Japan's economy and population had been growing rapidly. By the 1920s Japan was a major power.

- It had a very powerful army and navy – army leaders often dictated government policy.
- It had a strong industry, exporting goods to the USA and China in particular.
- It had a growing empire which included the Korean peninsula (see Source 5).

The Depression hit Japan badly. Both China and the USA put up tariffs (trade barriers) against Japanese goods. The collapse of the American market put the Japanese economy in crisis. Without this trade Japan could not feed its people. Army leaders in Japan were in no doubt about the solution to Japan's problems – they wanted to build up a Japanese empire by force.

In 1931 an incident in Manchuria gave them the opportunity they had been looking for to expand the Japanese Empire. As you can see from Source 5, the Japanese army controlled the South Manchurian Railway. In September 1931 they claimed that Chinese soldiers had sabotaged the railway. In retaliation they overran Manchuria and threw out all Chinese forces. In February 1932 they set up a puppet government in Manchuria – or Manchukuo, as they called it – which did exactly what the Japanese army told it to do. Later in 1932 Japanese aeroplanes and gunships bombed Shanghai. The civilian government in Japan told the Japanese army to withdraw, but its instructions were ignored. It was clear that it was the army and not the government that was in control of Japanese foreign policy.

China appealed to the League. Japan claimed it was not invading as an aggressor, but simply settling a local difficulty. The Japanese argued that China was in such a state of anarchy that they had to invade in self-defence to keep peace in the area. For the League of Nations this was a serious test. Japan was a leading member of the League. It needed careful handling. What should the League do?

1 Why did it take so long for the League to make a decision over Manchuria?
2 Look at Sources 7 and 8. What criticisms are the cartoonists making of:
   a) Japan
   b) the League?
3 Did the League fail in this incident because of the way it worked or because of the attitude of its members?

There was now a long and frustrating delay. The League's officials sailed round the world to assess the situation in Manchuria for themselves. It was September 1932 – a full year after the invasion – before they presented their report. It was detailed and balanced, but the judgement was very clear. Japan had acted unlawfully. Manchuria should be returned to the Chinese.

However, in February 1933, instead of withdrawing from Manchuria the Japanese announced that they intended to invade more of China. They still argued that this was necessary in self-defence. On 24 February 1933 the report from the League's officials was approved by 42 votes to 1 in the Assembly. Only Japan voted against. Smarting at the insult, Japan resigned from the League on 27 March 1933. The next week it invaded Jehol (see Source 5).

The League was powerless. It discussed economic sanctions, but without the USA, Japan's main trading partner, they would be meaningless. Besides, Britain seemed more interested in keeping up good relationships with Japan than in agreeing to sanctions. The League also discussed banning arms sales to Japan, but the member countries could not even agree about that. They were worried that Japan would retaliate and the war would escalate.

There was no prospect at all of Britain and France risking their navies or armies in a war with Japan. Only the USA and the USSR would have had the resources to remove the Japanese from Manchuria by force and they were not even members of the League.

SOURCE 7

A cartoon by David Low, 1933. Low was one of the most famous cartoonists of the 1930s. He regularly criticised both the actions of dictators around the world and the ineffectiveness of the League of Nations.

SOURCE 9

I was sad to find everyone [at the League] so dejected. The Assembly was a dead thing. The Council was without confidence in itself. Beneš [the Czechoslovak leader], who is not given to hysterics, said [about the people at the League] 'They are too frightened. I tell them we are not going to have war now; we have five years before us, perhaps six. We must make the most of them.'

The British elder statesman Sir Austen Chamberlain visited the League of Nations late in 1932 in the middle of the Manchurian crisis. This is an adapted extract from his letters.

SOURCE 8

A French poster of 1932.

Activity

Look again at your pie chart from page 21. Do you want to revise it?

All sorts of excuses were offered for the failure of the League. Japan was so far away. Japan was a special case. Japan did have a point when it said that China was itself in the grip of anarchy. However, the significance of the Manchurian crisis was obvious. As many of its critics had predicted, the League was powerless if a strong nation decided to pursue an aggressive policy and invade its neighbours. Japan had committed blatant aggression and got away with it. Back in Europe, both Hitler and Mussolini looked on with interest. Within three years they would both follow Japan's example.

To make myself perfectly clear, I would ask: is there anyone within or without Germany who honestly considers the present German regime to be peaceful in its instincts . . . Germany is inhibited from disturbing the peace of Europe solely by its consciousness of its present military inferiority.

Professor William Rappard speaking to the League in 1932.

Why did disarmament fail in the 1930s?

The next big failure of the League of Nations was over disarmament. As you saw on page 32, the League had not had any success in this area in the 1920s either, but at that stage, when the international climate was better, it had not seemed to matter as much. In the 1930s, however, there was increased pressure for the League to do something about disarmament. The Germans had long been angry about the fact that they had been forced to disarm after the First World War while other nations had not done the same. Many countries were actually spending more on their armaments than they had been before the First World War.

In the wake of the Manchurian crisis, the members of the League realised the urgency of the problem. In February 1932 the long-promised Disarmament Conference finally got under way. By July 1932 it had produced resolutions to prohibit bombing of civilian populations, limit the size of artillery, limit the tonnage of tanks, and prohibit chemical warfare. But there was very little in the resolutions to show how these limits would be achieved. For example, the bombing of civilians was to be prohibited, but all attempts to agree to abolish planes capable of bombing were defeated. Even the proposal to ban the manufacture of chemical weapons was defeated.

It was not a promising start. However, there was a bigger problem facing the Conference – what to do about Germany. The Germans had been in the League for six years. Most people now accepted that they should be treated more equally than under the Treaty of Versailles. The big question was whether everyone else should disarm to the level that Germany had been forced to, or whether the Germans should be allowed to rearm to a level closer to that of the other powers. The experience of the 1920s showed that the first option was a non-starter. But there was great reluctance in the League to allow the second option.

This is how events relating to Germany moved over the next 18 months.

Mariannes Papagei
Le perroquet de Marianne | Madame La France's Parrot | Il pappagallo di Marianna

A German cartoon from July 1933 commenting on France's constant call for more security when it was already well armed. The parrot represents France.

July 1932
Germany tabled proposals for all countries to disarm down to its level. When the Conference failed to agree the principle of 'equality', the Germans walked out.

September 1932
The British sent the Germans a note that went some way to agreeing equality, but the superior tone of the note angered the Germans still further.

December 1932
An agreement was finally reached to treat Germany equally.

January 1933
Germany announced it was coming back to the Conference.

February 1933
Hitler became Chancellor of Germany at the end of January. He immediately started to rearm Germany, although secretly.

May 1933
Hitler promised not to rearm Germany if 'in five years all other nations destroyed their arms'.

June 1933
Britain produced an ambitious disarmament plan.

October 1933
Hitler withdrew from the Disarmament Conference, and soon after took Germany out of the League altogether.

1 Look at Source 12. Explain what Low is saying about:
   a) ordinary people
   b) political leaders.
2 In what ways were each of the following to blame for the failure of the Disarmament Conference:
   a) Germany
   b) Britain
   c) the League itself?

By this stage, all the powers knew that Hitler was secretly rearming Germany already. They also began to rebuild their own armaments. Against that background the Disarmament Conference struggled on for another year but in an atmosphere of increasing futility. It finally ended in 1934.

SOURCE **12**

David Low's cartoon commenting on the failure of the Disarmament Conference in 1934.

The Conference failed for a number of reasons. Some say it was all doomed from the start. No one was very serious about disarmament anyway. But there were other factors at work.

It did not help that Britain and France were divided on this issue. By 1933 many British people felt that the Treaty of Versailles was unfair. In fact, to the dismay of the French, the British signed an agreement with Germany in 1935 that allowed Germany to build up its navy as long as it stayed under 35 per cent of the size of the British navy. Britain did not consult either its allies or the League about this, although it was in violation of the Treaty of Versailles.

It seemed that each country was looking after itself and ignoring the League.

SOURCE **13**

3 Look at Source 13.
   a) Describe the attitude of each country to France's proposals.
   b) Is this cartoon optimistic or pessimistic about peace in Europe? Give reasons.

A cartoon from the *Daily Express*, 19 July 1934, by Sidney Strube. The singer is supposed to be France. France had proposed an alliance with the USSR known as 'Eastern Locarno'.

Activity

Look again at your pie chart from page 21. Do you want to revise it?

How did Mussolini's invasion of Abyssinia damage the League?

The fatal blow to the League came when the Italian dictator Mussolini invaded Abyssinia (now Ethiopia) in 1935. There were both similarities with and differences from the Japanese invasion of Manchuria. Like Japan, Italy was a leading member of the League. Like Japan, Italy wanted to expand its empire by invading another country. However, unlike Manchuria, this dispute was on the League's doorstep. Italy was a European power. It even had a border with France. Abyssinia bordered on the Anglo-Egyptian territory of Sudan and the British colonies of Uganda, Kenya and British Somaliland. Unlike events in Manchuria, the League could not claim that this problem was in an inaccessible part of the world. Some argued that Manchuria had been a special case. Would the League do any better in this Abyssinian crisis?

SOURCE 14

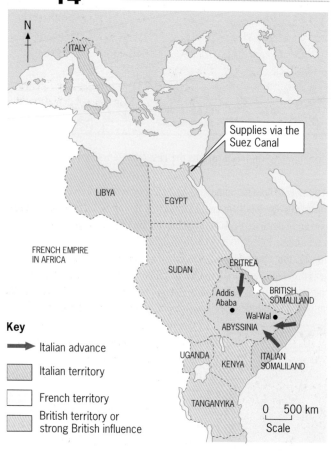

British, French and Italian possessions in eastern Africa.

SOURCE 15

A cartoon from *Punch*, 1935. *Punch* was usually very patriotic towards Britain. It seldom criticised British politicians over foreign policy.

Background

The origins of this crisis lay back in the previous century. In 1896 Italian troops had tried to invade Abyssinia but had been defeated by a poorly equipped army of tribesmen. Mussolini wanted revenge for this humiliating defeat. He also had his eye on the fertile lands and mineral wealth of Abyssinia. However, most importantly, he wanted glory and conquest. His style of leadership needed military victories and he had often talked of restoring the glory of the Roman Empire.

In December 1934 there was a dispute between Italian and Ethiopian soldiers at the Wal-Wal oasis – 80 km inside Abyssinia. Mussolini took this as his cue and claimed this was actually Italian territory. He demanded an apology and began preparing the Italian army for an invasion of Abyssinia. The Abyssinian emperor Haile Selassie appealed to the League for help.

Phase 1 – January 1935 to October 1935: the League plays for time

In this period Mussolini was supposedly negotiating with the League to settle the dispute, while at the same time he was shipping his vast army to Africa and whipping up war fever among the Italian people – he was preparing for a full-scale invasion of Abyssinia.

To start with, the British and the French failed to take the situation seriously. They played for time. They were desperate to keep good relations with Mussolini, who seemed to be their strongest ally against Hitler. They signed an agreement with him early in 1935 known as the Stresa Pact which formalised a protest at German rearmament and a commitment to stand united against Germany. At the meeting to discuss this, they did not even raise the question of Abyssinia. Some historians suggest that Mussolini believed that Britain and France had promised to turn a blind eye to his exploits in Abyssinia in return for his joining them in the Stresa Pact.

However, as the year wore on, there was a public outcry against Italy's behaviour. A ballot was taken by the League of Nations Union in Britain in 1934–35. It showed that a majority of British people supported the use of military force to defend Abyssinia if necessary. Facing an autumn election at home, British politicians now began to 'get tough'. At an assembly of the League, the British Foreign Minister, Hoare, made a grand speech about the value of collective security, to the delight of the League's members and all the smaller nations. There was much talking and negotiating. However, the League never actually did anything to discourage Mussolini.

On 4 September, after eight months' deliberation, a committee reported to the League that neither side could be held responsible for the Wal-Wal incident. The League put forward a plan that would give Mussolini some of Abyssinia. Mussolini rejected it.

Phase 2 – October 1935 to May 1936: sanctions or not?

In October 1935 Mussolini's army was ready. He launched a full-scale invasion of Abyssinia. Despite brave resistance, the Abyssinians were no match for the modern Italian army equipped with tanks, aeroplanes and poison gas.

This was a clear-cut case of a large, powerful state attacking a smaller one. The League was designed for just such disputes and, unlike in the Manchurian crisis, it was ideally placed to act.

There was no doubting the seriousness of the issue either. Source 16 shows the view of one cartoonist at the time. The Covenant (see Factfile, page 24) made it clear that sanctions must be introduced against the aggressor. A committee was immediately set up to agree what sanctions to impose.

Sanctions would only work if they were imposed quickly and decisively. Each week a decision was delayed would allow Mussolini to build up his stockpile of raw materials. The League imposed an immediate ban on arms sales to Italy while allowing them to Abyssinia. It banned all loans to Italy. It banned all imports from Italy. It banned the export to Italy of rubber, tin and metals.

However, the League delayed a decision for two months over whether to ban oil exports to Italy. It feared the Americans would not support the sanctions. It also feared that its members' economic interests would be further damaged. In Britain, the Cabinet was informed that 30,000 British coal miners were about to lose their jobs because of the ban on coal exports to Italy.

1 Look at Source 16. What has Mussolini let out?

SOURCE 16

A cartoon by David Low published in October 1935. The figure taking off the lid is Mussolini.

SOURCE 17

Yes, we know that World War began in Manchuria fifteen years ago. We know that four years later we could easily have stopped Mussolini if we had taken the sanctions against Mussolini that were obviously required, if we had closed the Suez Canal to the aggressor and stopped his oil.

British statesman Philip Noel Baker speaking at the very last session of the League in April 1946.

1 Explain in your own words:
   a) why the Hoare–Laval deal caused such outrage
   b) how it affected attitudes to the League
   c) how the USA undermined the League.
2 Look at Source 18. What event is the cartoonist referring to in 'the matter has been settled elsewhere'?
3 Look back at your chart from page 30. Do a similar analysis for the crises in Manchuria and Abyssinia.

SOURCE 18

A German cartoon from the front cover of the pro-Nazi magazine *Simplicissimus*, 1936. The warrior is delivering a message to the League of Nations: 'I am sorry to disturb your sleep but I just wanted to tell you that you should no longer bother yourselves about this Abyssinian business. The matter has been settled elsewhere.'

More important still, the Suez Canal, which was owned by Britain and France, was not closed to Mussolini's supply ships. The canal was the Italians' main supply route to Abyssinia and closing it could have ended the Abyssinian campaign very quickly. Both Britain and France were afraid that closing the canal could have resulted in war with Italy. This failure was fatal for Abyssinia.

Equally damaging to the League was the secret dealing between the British and the French that was going on behind the scenes. In December 1935, while sanctions discussions were still taking place, the British and French Foreign Ministers, Hoare and Laval, were hatching a plan. This aimed to give Mussolini two-thirds of Abyssinia in return for his calling off his invasion! Laval even proposed to put the plan to Mussolini before they showed it to either the League of Nations or Haile Selassie. Laval told the British that if they did not agree to the plan, then the French would no longer support sanctions against Italy.

However, details of the plan were leaked to the French press. It proved quite disastrous for the League. Haile Selassie demanded an immediate League debate about it. In both Britain and France it was seen as a blatant act of treachery against the League. Hoare and Laval were both sacked. But the real damage was to the sanctions discussions. They lost all momentum. The question about whether to ban oil sales was further delayed. In February 1936 the committee concluded that if they did stop oil sales to Italy, the Italians' supplies would be exhausted in two months, even if the Americans kept on selling oil to them. But by then it was all too late. Mussolini had already taken over large parts of Abyssinia. And the Americans were even more disgusted with the ditherings of the French and the British than they had been before and so blocked a move to support the League's sanctions. American oil producers actually stepped up their exports to Italy.

Mussolini 'obtains' Abyssinia

On 7 March 1936 the fatal blow was delivered. Hitler, timing his move to perfection, marched his troops into the Rhineland, an act prohibited by the Treaty of Versailles (see page 9). If there had been any hope of getting the French to support sanctions against Italy, it was now dead. The French were desperate to gain the support of Italy and were now prepared to pay the price of giving Abyssinia to Mussolini.

Italy continued to defy the League's orders and by May 1936 had taken the capital of Abyssinia, Addis Ababa. On 2 May, Haile Selassie was forced into exile. On 9 May, Mussolini formally annexed the entire country. The League watched helplessly. Collective security had been shown up as an empty promise. The League of Nations had failed. If the British and French had hoped that their handling of the Abyssinian crisis would help strengthen their position against Hitler, they were soon proved very wrong. In November 1936 Mussolini and Hitler signed an agreement of their own called the Rome–Berlin Axis.

SOURCE 19

Could the League survive the failure of sanctions to rescue Abyssinia? Could it ever impose sanctions again? Probably there had never been such a clear-cut case for sanctions. If the League had failed in this case there could probably be no confidence that it could succeed again in the future.

Anthony Eden, British Foreign Minister, expressing his feelings about the crisis to the British Cabinet in May 1936.

Activity

1 Revise your pie chart from page 21 for the last time, showing your final view of how successful the League was.
2 Compare your chart with the one you made at the start. How accurate were your predictions?

4 From Sources 20–24 make a list of ways in which the Abyssinian crisis damaged the League.

A disaster for the League and for the world

Historians often disagree about how to interpret important events. However, one of the most striking things about the events of 1935 and 1936 is that most historians seem to agree about the Abyssinian crisis: it was a disaster for the League of Nations and had serious consequences for world peace.

SOURCE 20

The crises of 1935–6 were fatal to the League, which was not taken seriously again . . . it was too late to save the League. Instead, it began the emotional preparation among the democracies for the Second World War . . .

Written by historian JR Western in 1971.

SOURCE 21

The implications of the conquest of Abyssinia were not confined to East Africa. Although victory cemented Mussolini's personal prestige at home, Italy gained little or nothing from it in material terms. The damage done, meanwhile, to the prestige of Britain, France and the League of Nations was irreversible. The only winner in the whole sorry episode was Adolf Hitler.

Written by historian TA Morris in 1995.

SOURCE 22

After seeing what happened first in Manchuria and then in Abyssinia, most people drew the conclusion that it was no longer much use placing their hopes in the League . . .

Written by historian James Joll in 1976.

SOURCE 23

The real death of the League was in 1935. One day it was a powerful body imposing sanctions, the next day it was an empty sham, everyone scuttling from it as quickly as possible. Hitler watched.

Written by historian AJP Taylor in 1966.

SOURCE 24

If new accounts by historians show that statesmen were able to use the League to ease tensions and win time in the 1920s, no such case appears possible for the 1930s. Indeed, the League's processes may have played a role in that deterioration. Diplomacy requires leaders who can speak for their states; it requires secrecy; and it requires the ability to make credible threats. The Covenant's security arrangements met none of those criteria.

Extract from *Back To The League of Nations* by Susan Pedersen, Professor of History at Columbia University.

Activity

Work in pairs. Write a caption for one of the two cartoons in Source 25, showing people's feelings about the League after the Abyssinian crisis.

Your teacher can tell you what the original captions were.

SOURCE 25

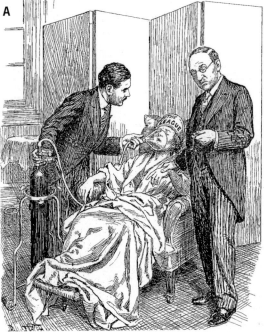

Two cartoons from *Punch*, 1938. The doctors in **A** represent Britain and France.

Why did the League of Nations fail in the 1930s?

Here is a diagram summarising the failure of the League of Nations. Complete your own copy of the diagram to explain how each weakness affected Manchuria and Abyssinia. We have filled in one point for you. There is one weakness that you will not be able to write about – you will find out about it in Chapter 3.

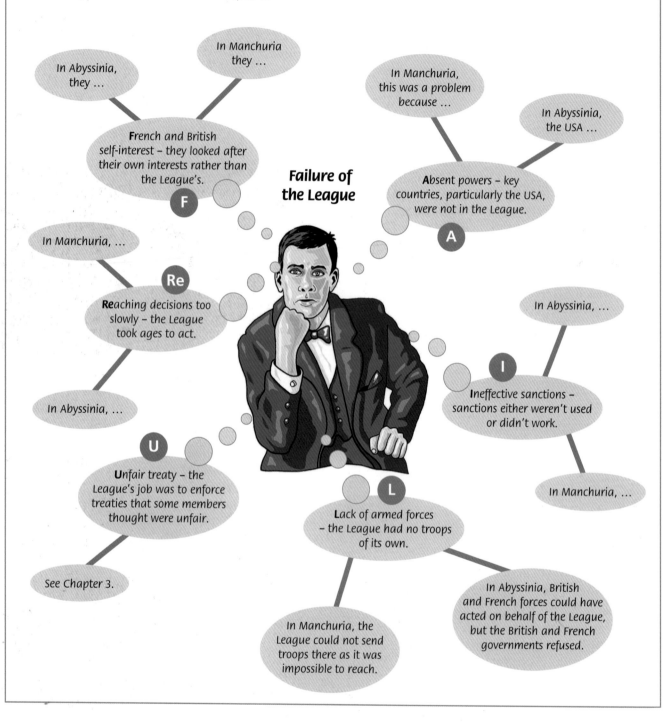

In Abyssinia, they …

In Manchuria they …

French and British self-interest – they looked after their own interests rather than the League's.
F

In Manchuria, …

Reaching decisions too slowly – the League took ages to act.
Re

In Abyssinia, …

Unfair treaty – the League's job was to enforce treaties that some members thought were unfair.
U

See Chapter 3.

Failure of the League

In Manchuria, the League could not send troops there as it was impossible to reach.

Lack of armed forces – the League had no troops of its own.
L

In Manchuria, this was a problem because …

In Abyssinia, the USA …

Absent powers – key countries, particularly the USA, were not in the League.
A

In Abyssinia, …

Ineffective sanctions – sanctions either weren't used or didn't work.
I

In Manchuria, …

In Abyssinia, British and French forces could have acted on behalf of the League, but the British and French governments refused.

Why had international peace collapsed by 1939?

From foot-soldier to führer

Focus

Tension between countries rose dramatically in the 1930s. Hitler was rearming Germany and openly defying the Treaty of Versailles. Dictatorships in other countries became more and more powerful and the democracies seemed either unwilling or unable to stop them. Finally, in 1939 war once again broke out in Europe.

In this chapter you will investigate why Britain and France declared war on Germany in September 1939. You will make up your own mind as to how far Hitler's own policies were to blame for the war and whether other factors were equally important.

You will consider:
◆ whether Britain's policy of appeasing Hitler could be justified
◆ how weaknesses in the First World War peace treaties had long-term consequences for international relations
◆ the consequences of the failure of the League of Nations in the 1930s
◆ how important the Nazi–Soviet Pact was in causing the war.

SOURCE 1

Adolf Hitler (right) during the First World War.

SOURCE 2

Adolf Hitler is welcomed by a crowd of Nazi supporters in 1933.

SOURCE 3

Any account of the origins and course of the Second World War must give Hitler the leading part. Without him a major war in the early 1940s between all the world's great powers was unthinkable.

British historian Professor Richard Overy, writing in 1996.

Less than twenty years separates Sources 1 and 2. Between 1918 and 1933 Adolf Hitler rose from being an obscure and demoralised member of the defeated German army to become the all-powerful Führer, dictator of Germany, with almost unlimited power and an overwhelming ambition to make Germany great once again. His is an astonishing story which you can read about in detail on pages 264–75. Here you will be concentrating on just one intriguing and controversial question: how far was Hitler responsible for the outbreak of the Second World War. Is Source 3 right?

Hitler's plans

Hitler was never secretive about his plans for Germany. As early as 1924 he had laid out in his book *Mein Kampf* what he would do if the Nazis ever achieved power in Germany. His three main aims are described below.

Abolish the Treaty of Versailles!

Like many Germans, Hitler believed that the Treaty of Versailles was unjust.

He hated the Treaty and called the German leaders who had signed it 'The November Criminals'. The Treaty was a constant reminder to Germans of their defeat in the First World War and their humiliation by the Allies. Hitler promised that if he became leader of Germany he would reverse it.

By the time he came to power in Germany, some of the terms had already been changed. For example, Germany had stopped making reparations payments altogether. However, most points were still in place. The table in the Focus Task on page 47 shows the terms of the Treaty that most angered Hitler.

Expand German territory!

The Treaty of Versailles had taken away territory from Germany. Hitler wanted to get that territory back. He wanted Germany to unite with Austria. He wanted German minorities in other countries such as Czechoslovakia to rejoin Germany. But he also wanted to carve out an empire in eastern Europe to give extra *Lebensraum* or 'living space' for Germans.

SOURCE 4

We demand equality of rights for the German people in its dealings with other nations, and abolition of the Peace Treaties of Versailles and St Germain.

From Hitler's *Mein Kampf*, 1923–24.

1 From the evidence of Sources 4 and 5, why might Czechoslovak leaders be concerned about Hitler's plans?

SOURCE 5

We turn our eyes towards the lands of the east . . . When we speak of new territory in Europe today, we must principally think of Russia and the border states subject to her. Destiny itself seems to wish to point out the way for us here.

Colonisation of the eastern frontiers is of extreme importance. It will be the duty of Germany's foreign policy to provide large spaces for the nourishment and settlement of the growing population of Germany.

From Hitler's *Mein Kampf*.

Defeat Communism!

A German empire carved out of the Soviet Union would also help Hitler in one of his other objectives – the defeat of Communism or Bolshevism. Hitler was anti-Communist. He believed that Bolsheviks had helped to bring about the defeat of Germany in the First World War. He also believed that the Bolsheviks wanted to take over Germany.

SOURCE 6

We must not forget that the Bolsheviks are blood-stained. That they overran a great state [Russia], and in a fury of massacre wiped out millions of their most intelligent fellow-countrymen and now for ten years have been conducting the most tyrannous regime of all time. We must not forget that many of them belong to a race which combines a rare mixture of bestial cruelty and vast skill in lies, and considers itself specially called now to gather the whole world under its bloody oppression.

The menace which Russia suffered under is one which perpetually hangs over Germany. Germany is the next great objective of Bolshevism. All our strength is needed to raise up our nation once more and rescue it from the embrace of the international python . . . The first essential is the expulsion of the Marxist poison from the body of our nation.

From Hitler's *Mein Kampf*.

Activity

It is 1933. Write a briefing paper for the British government on Hitler's plans for Germany. Use Sources 4–6 to help you. Conclude with your own assessment on whether the government should be worried about Hitler and his plans.

In your conclusion, remember these facts about the British government:

- Britain is a leading member of the League of Nations and is supposed to uphold the Treaty of Versailles, by force if necessary.
- The British government does not trust the Communists and thinks that a strong Germany could help to stop the Communist threat.

Hitler's actions

This timeline shows how, between 1933 and 1939, Hitler turned his plans into actions.

DATE	ACTION
1933	Took Germany out of the League of Nations Began rearming Germany
1934	Tried to take over Austria but was prevented by Mussolini
1935	Held massive rearmament rally in Germany
1936	Reintroduced conscription in Germany Sent German troops into the Rhineland Made an anti-Communist alliance with Japan
1937	Tried out Germany's new weapons in the Spanish Civil War Made an anti-Communist alliance with Italy
1938	Took over Austria Took over the Sudetenland area of Czechoslovakia
1939	Invaded the rest of Czechoslovakia Invaded Poland

War

When you see events leading up to the war laid out this way, it makes it seem as if Hitler planned it all step by step. In fact, this view of events was widely accepted by historians until the 1960s.

In the 1960s, however, the British historian AJP Taylor came up with a new interpretation. His view was that Hitler was a gambler rather than a planner. Hitler simply took the logical next step to see what he could get away with. He was bold. He kept his nerve. As other countries gave in to him and allowed him to get away with each gamble, so he became bolder and risked more. In Taylor's interpretation it is Britain, the Allies and the League of Nations who are to blame for letting Hitler get away with it – by not standing up to him. As you examine Hitler's actions in more detail, you will see that both interpretations are possible. You can make up your own mind which you agree with.

Focus Task

Hitler and the Treaty of Versailles

1 Draw up a table like this one to show some of the terms of the Treaty of Versailles that affected Germany.
2 As you work through this chapter, fill out the other columns of this 'Versailles chart'.

Terms of the Treaty of Versailles	What Hitler did and when	The reasons he gave for his action	The response from Britain and France
Germany's armed forces to be severely limited			
The Rhineland to be a demilitarised zone			
Germany forbidden to unite with Austria			
The Sudetenland taken into the new state of Czechoslovakia			
The Polish Corridor given to Poland			

47

SOURCE **7**

I am convinced that Hitler does not want war . . . what the Germans are after is a strong army which will enable them to deal with Russia.

British politician Lord Lothian, January 1935.

1 Design a Nazi poster to present the information in Source 10 to the German people.
2 Fill out the first row of your 'Versailles chart' on page 47.
3 What factors allowed Hitler to get away with rearming Germany?

Rearmament

Hitler came to power in Germany in 1933. One of his first steps was to increase Germany's armed forces. Thousands of unemployed workers were drafted into the army. This helped him to reduce unemployment, which was one of the biggest problems he faced in Germany. But it also helped him to deliver on his promise to make Germany strong again and to challenge the terms of the Treaty of Versailles.

Hitler knew that German people supported rearmament. But he also knew it would cause alarm in other countries. He handled it cleverly. Rearmament began in secret at first. He made a great public display of his desire not to rearm Germany – that he was only doing it because other countries refused to disarm (see page 38). He then followed Japan's example and withdrew from the League of Nations.

In 1935 Hitler openly staged a massive military rally celebrating the German armed forces (see Source 8). In 1936 he even reintroduced conscription to the army. He was breaking the terms of the Treaty of Versailles, but he guessed correctly that he would get away with rearmament. Many other countries were using rearmament as a way to fight unemployment. The collapse of the League of Nations Disarmament Conference in 1934 (see pages 38–39) had shown that other nations were not prepared to disarm.

Rearmament was a very popular move in Germany. It boosted Nazi support. Hitler also knew that Britain had some sympathy with Germany on this issue. Britain believed that the limits put on Germany's armed forces by the Treaty of Versailles were too tight. The permitted forces were not enough to defend Germany from attack. Britain also thought that a strong Germany would be a good buffer against Communism.

Britain had already helped to dismantle the Treaty by signing a naval agreement with Hitler in 1935, allowing Germany to increase its navy to up to 35 per cent of the size of the British navy. The French were angry with Britain about this, but there was little they could do.

SOURCE **8**

German soldiers and armaments on show at the Proclamation of Freedom to Rearm Rally in 1935.

SOURCE **9**

Year	per cent
1935	7.4
1936	12.4
1937	11.8
1938	16.6
1939	23.0
1940	38.0

The proportion of German spending that went into armaments, 1935–40.

SOURCE 10

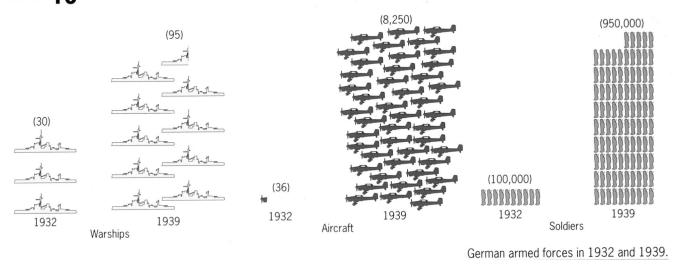

German armed forces in 1932 and 1939.

The Saar plebiscite

The Saar region of Germany had been run by the League of Nations since 1919 (see page 28).

In 1935 the League of Nations held the promised plebiscite for people to vote on whether their region should return to German rule. The vote was an overwhelming success for Hitler. Around 90 per cent of the population voted to return to German rule. This was entirely legal and within the terms of the Treaty. It was also a real morale booster for Hitler.

SOURCE 11

Following the plebiscite in 1935, people and police express their joy at returning to the German Reich by giving the Nazi salute.

Remilitarisation of the Rhineland

In March 1936, Hitler took his first really big risk by moving troops into the Rhineland area of Germany.

The demilitarisation of the Rhineland was one of the terms of the Treaty of Versailles. It had also been accepted by Germany in the Locarno Treaties of 1925 (see page 32). Hitler was taking a huge gamble. If he had been forced to withdraw, he would have faced humiliation and would have lost the support of the German army (many of the generals were unsure about him, anyway). Hitler knew the risks, but he had chosen the time and place well.

France had just signed a treaty with the USSR to protect each other against attack from Germany (see Source 13). Hitler used the agreement to claim that Germany was under threat. He argued that in the face of such a threat he should be allowed to place troops on his own frontier.

Hitler knew that many people in Britain felt that he had a right to station his troops in the Rhineland and he was fairly confident that Britain would not intervene. His gamble was over France. Would France let him get away with it?

SOURCE **12**

Scale 0 — 100 km

North Sea

NETHERLANDS

GERMANY

• Cologne

BELGIUM

LUXEMBOURG

FRANCE

Rhine

SWITZERLAND

ITALY

Key

January 1935: Saar returned to Germany after a plebiscite

March 1936: German forces re-enter the Rhineland

The Rhineland.

1 Fill out row 2 of your 'Versailles chart' on page 47.

SOURCE **13**

An American cartoon entitled 'Ring-Around-the-Nazi!' published in March 1936 showing the encirclement of Germany by France and the USSR.

SOURCE **14**

German troops marching through the city of Cologne in March 1936. This style of marching with high steps was known as goose-stepping.

SOURCE 15

At that time we had no army worth mentioning . . . If the French had taken any action we would have been easily defeated; our resistance would have been over in a few days. And the Air Force we had then was ridiculous – a few Junkers 52s from Lufthansa and not even enough bombs for them . . .

Hitler looks back on his gamble over the Rhineland some years after the event.

SOURCE 16

Hitler has got away with it. France is not marching. No wonder the faces of Göring and Blomberg [Nazi leaders] were all smiles.

Oh, the stupidity (or is it the paralysis?) of the French. I learnt today that the German troops had orders to beat a hasty retreat if the French army opposed them in any way.

Written by William Shirer in 1936. He was an American journalist in Germany during the 1930s. He was a critic of the Nazi regime and had to flee from Germany in 1940.

As the troops moved into the Rhineland, Hitler and his generals sweated nervously. They had orders to pull out if the French acted against them. Despite the rearmament programme, Germany's army was no match for the French army. It lacked essential equipment and air support. In the end, however, Hitler's luck held.

The attention of the League of Nations was on the Abyssinian crisis which was happening at exactly the same time (see pages 40-43). The League condemned Hitler's action but had no power to do anything else. Even the French, who were most directly threatened by the move, were divided over what to do. They were about to hold an election and none of the French leaders was prepared to take responsibility for plunging France into a war. Of course, they did not know how weak the German army was. In the end, France refused to act without British support and so Hitler's big gamble paid off. Maybe next time he would risk more!

SOURCE 17

THE GOOSE-STEP.

"GOOSEY GOOSEY GANDER,
WHITHER DOST THOU WANDER?"
"ONLY THROUGH THE RHINELAND—
PRAY EXCUSE MY BLUNDER!"

A British cartoon about the reoccupation of the Rhineland, 1936. *Pax Germanica* is Latin and means 'Peace, German style'.

2 Does Source 13 support or contradict Hitler's argument that Germany was under threat? Explain your answer.

3 What do Sources 15 and 16 disagree about? Why might they disagree about it?

4 Why has the cartoonist in Source 17 shown Germany as a goose?

5 Look at the equipment being carried by the goose. What does this tell you about how the cartoonist saw the new Germany?

6 Would you regard reoccupation of the Rhineland as a success for Hitler or as a failure for the French and the British? Explain your answer by referring to the sources.

The Spanish Civil War

These early successes seemed to give Hitler confidence. In 1936 a civil war broke out in Spain between Communists, who were supporters of the Republican government, and right-wing rebels under General Franco. Hitler saw this as an opportunity to fight against Communism and at the same time to try out his new armed forces.

In 1937, as the League of Nations looked on helplessly, German aircraft made devastating bombing raids on civilian populations in various Spanish cities. The destruction at Guernica was terrible. The world looked on in horror at the suffering that modern weapons could cause.

SOURCE **18**

Le peuple basque assassiné
par les avions allemands
GUERNICA MARTYRE _ 26 Avril 1937

A postcard published in France to mark the bombing of Guernica in 1937. The text reads 'The Basque people murdered by German planes. Guernica martyred 26 April 1937'.

Focus Task

What were the consequences of the failure of the League in the 1930s?

In Chapter 2 you studied the failures of the League of Nations. You are now in a position to evaluate the impact of those failures on Hitler's actions.
1 Look back over pages 48–52. Look for evidence that the weakness of the League of Nations in the 1930s allowed Hitler to achieve what he did.
2 Write a paragraph describing the effect of each of the following on Hitler's actions:
   ◆ the Manchurian crisis
   ◆ the failure of disarmament
   ◆ the Abyssinian crisis.

The Anti-Comintern Pact, 1936–37

The Italian leader Mussolini was also heavily involved in the Spanish Civil War. Hitler and Mussolini saw that they had much in common also with the military dictatorship in Japan. In 1936, Germany and Japan signed an Anti-Comintern Pact. In 1937, Italy also signed it. Anti-Comintern means 'Anti-Communist International'. The aim of the pact was to limit Communist influence around the world. It was particularly aimed at the USSR. The new alliance was called the Axis alliance.

Anschluss with Austria, 1938

With the successes of 1936 and 1937 to boost him, Hitler turned his attention to his homeland of Austria. The Austrian people were mainly German, and in *Mein Kampf* Hitler had made it clear that he felt that the two states belonged together as one German nation. Many in Austria supported the idea of union with Germany, since their country was so economically weak. Hitler was confident that he could bring them together into a 'greater Germany'. In fact, he had tried to take over Austria in 1934, but on that occasion Mussolini had stopped him. Four years later, in 1938, the situation was different. Hitler and Mussolini were now allies.

There was a strong Nazi Party in Austria. Hitler encouraged the Nazis to stir up trouble for the government. They staged demonstrations calling for union with Germany. They caused riots. Hitler then told the Austrian Chancellor Schuschnigg that only *Anschluss* (political union) could sort out these problems. He pressurised Schuschnigg to agree to *Anschluss*. Schuschnigg asked for help from France and Britain but was refused it. So he called a plebiscite (a referendum), to see what the Austrian people wanted. Hitler was not prepared to risk this – he might lose! He simply sent his troops into Austria in March 1938, supposedly to guarantee a trouble-free plebiscite. Under the watchful eye of the Nazi troops, 99.75 per cent voted for *Anschluss*. *Anschluss* was completed without any military confrontation with France and Britain. Chamberlain, the British Prime Minister, felt that Austrians and Germans had a right to be united and that the Treaty of Versailles was wrong to separate them. Britain's Lord Halifax had even suggested to Hitler before the *Anschluss* that Britain would not resist Germany uniting with Austria.

1 Explain what each of the cartoons in Source 19 is saying about the *Anschluss*.
2 Complete row 3 of your 'Versailles chart' on page 47.

SOURCE 19

GOOD HUNTING

Mussolini. " All right, Adolf—I never heard a shot "

Two cartoons commenting on the *Anschluss*, 1938.
A is from *Punch*. **B** is a Soviet cartoon showing Hitler catching Austria.

Once again, Hitler's risky but decisive action had reaped a rich reward – Austria's soldiers, weapons and its rich deposits of gold and iron ore were added to Germany's increasingly strong army and industry. Hitler was breaking yet another condition of the Treaty of Versailles, but the pattern was becoming clear. The Treaty itself was seen as suspect. Britain and France were not prepared to go to war to defend a flawed treaty.

Why did Britain and France follow Appeasement in the 1930s?

Britain signed the naval agreement with Germany in 1935. For the next three years, Britain followed a policy of giving Hitler what he wanted – a policy that became known as Appeasement. Neville Chamberlain is the man most associated with this policy (see Profile, page 57), although he did not become Prime Minister until 1937. Many other British people, including many politicians, were also in favour of this policy. See Source 20 for their reasons.

SOURCE **20**

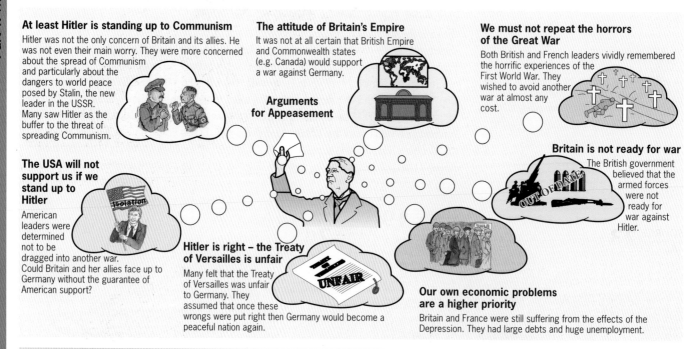

At least Hitler is standing up to Communism
Hitler was not the only concern of Britain and its allies. He was not even their main worry. They were more concerned about the spread of Communism and particularly about the dangers to world peace posed by Stalin, the new leader in the USSR. Many saw Hitler as the buffer to the threat of spreading Communism.

The attitude of Britain's Empire
It was not at all certain that British Empire and Commonwealth states (e.g. Canada) would support a war against Germany.

Arguments for Appeasement

We must not repeat the horrors of the Great War
Both British and French leaders vividly remembered the horrific experiences of the First World War. They wished to avoid another war at almost any cost.

The USA will not support us if we stand up to Hitler
American leaders were determined not to be dragged into another war. Could Britain and her allies face up to Germany without the guarantee of American support?

Hitler is right – the Treaty of Versailles is unfair
Many felt that the Treaty of Versailles was unfair to Germany. They assumed that once these wrongs were put right then Germany would become a peaceful nation again.

Britain is not ready for war
The British government believed that the armed forces were not ready for war against Hitler.

Our own economic problems are a higher priority
Britain and France were still suffering from the effects of the Depression. They had large debts and huge unemployment.

What was wrong with Appeasement?

Britain's leaders may have felt that they had no option but to appease Hitler, but there were obvious risks to such a policy. Some of these were stated at the time (see Sources 22–24). Others became obvious with hindsight (Source 21). You will return to these criticisms in the Task on page 66. You may even be able to add to this list from what you have already studied.

SOURCE **21**

It encouraged Hitler to be aggressive
With hindsight, you can see that each gamble he got away with encouraged him to take a bigger risk.

Arguments against Appeasement

It allowed Germany to grow *too* strong
With hindsight, you can see that Germany was not only recovering lost ground: it was also becoming much more powerful than Britain or France.

It put too much trust in Hitler's promises
With hindsight, you can see that Hitler often went back on his promises. Appeasement was based on the mistaken idea that Hitler was trustworthy.

It scared the USSR
With hindsight, you can see how the policy alarmed the USSR. Hitler made no secret of his plans to expand eastwards. Appeasement sent the message to the Soviet Union that Britain and France would not stand in Hitler's way.

1 Look at Source 22. What does the cartoonist think Appeasement will lead to?
2 Most people in Britain supported Appeasement. Write a letter to the London *Evening Standard* justifying Appeasement and pointing out why the cartoonist in Source 22 is mistaken. Use the points given in Source 20.

SOURCE **22**

A cartoon by David Low from the London *Evening Standard*, 1936. This was a popular newspaper with a large readership in Britain.

SOURCE **23**

THE BLESSINGS OF PEACE
or
MR. EVERYMAN'S IDEAL HOME

A cartoon from *Punch*, November 1937. *Punch* was deeply critical of the British government's policies that allowed Hitler to achieve what he wanted in the 1930s. The magazine was an important influence on public opinion, particularly among educated and influential people. It had a circulation of about 120,000 copies per week during the 1930s.

SOURCE **24**

David Low cartoon commenting on the *Anschluss*, 1938.

Activity

Why Appeasement?

1 Read the explanations in Source 20 of why Britain followed a policy of Appeasement.
2 Make notes under the following headings to summarise why Britain followed a policy of Appeasement:
 • Military reasons
 • Economic reasons
 • Fear
 • Public opinion
 • Other
3 Use your notes to help you to write a short paragraph to explain in your own words how each of these reasons influenced the policy of Appeasement.

The Sudetenland, 1938

After the Austrian *Anschluss,* Hitler was beginning to feel that he could not put a foot wrong. But his growing confidence was putting the peace of Europe in increasing danger.

SOURCE **25**

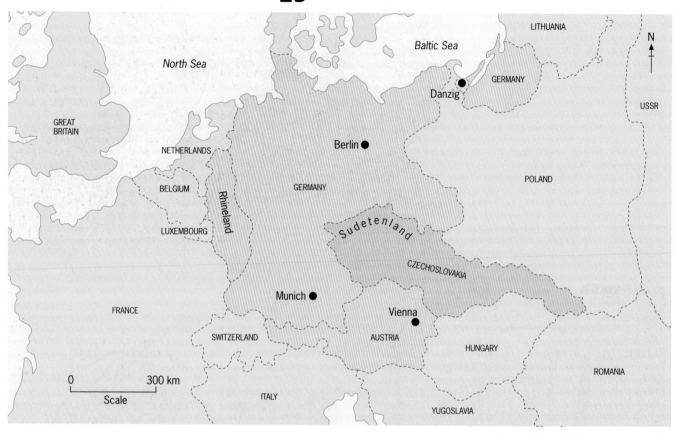

Central Europe after the *Anschluss*.

SOURCE **26**

I give you my word of honour that Czechoslovakia has nothing to fear from the Reich.

Hitler speaking to Chamberlain in 1938.

Unlike the leaders of Britain and France, Edward Beneš, the leader of Czechoslovakia, was horrified by the *Anschluss*. He realised that Czechoslovakia would be the next country on Hitler's list for takeover. It seemed that Britain and France were not prepared to stand up to Hitler. Beneš sought guarantees from the British and French that they would honour their commitment to defend Czechoslovakia if Hitler invaded. The French were bound by a treaty and reluctantly said they would. The British felt bound to support the French. However, Chamberlain asked Hitler whether he had designs on Czechoslovakia and was reassured by Hitler's promise (Source 26).

Despite what he said to Chamberlain, Hitler did have designs on Czechoslovakia. This new state, created by the Treaty of Versailles, included a large number of Germans – former subjects of Austria–Hungary's empire – in the Sudetenland area. Henlein, who was the leader of the Nazis in the Sudetenland, stirred up trouble among the Sudetenland Germans and they demanded to be part of Germany. In May 1938, Hitler made it clear that he intended to fight Czechoslovakia if necessary. Historians disagree as to whether Hitler really meant what he said. There is considerable evidence that the German army was not at all ready for war. Even so the news put Europe on full war alert.

Unlike Austria, Czechoslovakia would be no walk-over for Hitler. Britain, France and the USSR had all promised to support Czechoslovakia if it came to war. The Czechs themselves had a modern army. The Czechoslovak leader, Beneš, was prepared to fight. He knew that without the Sudetenland and its forts, railways and industries, Czechoslovakia would be defenceless.

All through the summer the tension rose in Europe. If there was a war, people expected that it would bring heavy bombing of civilians as had happened in the Spanish Civil War, and in cities around Britain councils began digging air-raid shelters. Magazines carried advertisements for air-raid protection and gas masks.

SOURCE 27

How horrible, fantastic, incredible it is that we should be digging trenches and trying on gas masks here because of a quarrel in a far away country between people of whom we know nothing. I am myself a man of peace to the depths of my soul.

From a radio broadcast by Neville Chamberlain, September 1938.

Profile

Neville Chamberlain

➤ Born 1869.
➤ He was the son of the famous radical politician Joseph Chamberlain.
➤ He was a successful businessman in the Midlands before entering politics.
➤ During the First World War he served in the Cabinet as Director General of National Service. During this time he saw the full horrors of war.
➤ After the war he was Health Minister and then Chancellor. He was noted for his careful work and his attention to detail. However, he was not good at listening to advice.
➤ He was part of the government throughout the 1920s and supported the policy of Appeasement towards Hitler. He became Prime Minister in 1937, although he had little experience of foreign affairs.
➤ He believed that Germany had real grievances – this was the basis for his policy of Appeasement.
➤ He became a national hero after the Munich Conference of 1938 averted war.
➤ In 1940 Chamberlain resigned as Prime Minister and Winston Churchill took over.

SOURCE 28

Digging air raid defences in London, September 1938.

In September the problem reached crisis point. In a last-ditch effort to avert war, Chamberlain flew to meet Hitler on 15 September. The meeting appeared to go well. Hitler moderated his demands, saying he was only interested in parts of the Sudetenland – and then only if a plebiscite showed that the Sudeten Germans wanted to join Germany. Chamberlain thought this was reasonable. He felt it was yet another of the terms of the Treaty of Versailles that needed to be addressed. Chamberlain seemed convinced that, if Hitler got what he wanted, he would at last be satisfied.

On 19 September the French and the British put to the Czechs their plans to give Hitler the parts of the Sudetenland that he wanted. However, three days later at a second meeting, Hitler increased his demands. He said he 'regretted' that the previously arranged terms were not enough. He wanted all the Sudetenland.

SOURCE 29

The Sudetenland is the last problem that must be solved and it will be solved. It is the last territorial claim which I have to make in Europe.

The aims of our foreign policy are not unlimited . . . They are grounded on the determination to save the German people alone . . . Ten million Germans found themselves beyond the frontiers of the Reich . . . Germans who wished to return to the Reich as their homeland.

Hitler speaking in Berlin, September 1938.

To justify his demands, he claimed that the Czech government was mistreating the Germans in the Sudetenland and that he intended to 'rescue' them by 1 October. Chamberlain told Hitler that his demands were unreasonable. The British navy was mobilised. War seemed imminent.

With Mussolini's help, a final meeting was held in Munich on 29 September. While Europe held its breath, the leaders of Britain, Germany, France and Italy decided on the fate of Czechoslovakia.

On 29 September they decided to give Hitler what he wanted. They announced that Czechoslovakia was to lose the Sudetenland. They did not consult the Czechs, nor did they consult the USSR. This is known as the Munich Agreement. The following morning Chamberlain and Hitler published a joint declaration (Source 31) which Chamberlain said would bring 'peace for our time'.

SOURCE 30

People of Britain, your children are safe. Your husbands and your sons will not march to war. Peace is a victory for all mankind. If we must have a victor, let us choose Chamberlain, for the Prime Minister's conquests are mighty and enduring – millions of happy homes and hearts relieved of their burden.

The *Daily Express* comments on the Munich Agreement, 30 September 1938.

SOURCE 31

We regard the Agreement signed last night . . . as symbolic of the desire of our two peoples never to go to war with one another again. We are resolved that we shall use consultation to deal with any other questions that may concern our two countries, and we are determined to continue our efforts to assure the peace of Europe.

The joint declaration of Chamberlain and Hitler, 30 September 1938.

1 Study Sources 30–36. Sort them into the following categories:
   a) those that support the Munich Agreement
   b) those that criticise the Munich Agreement.
2 List the reasons why each source supports or criticises the agreement.

Activity

Write extracts from the diaries of some of the main parties affected by the Sudetenland crisis, e.g. Chamberlain, Hitler, Beneš or one of the diplomats who was involved in making the agreement, or of an ordinary Briton or an ordinary Czech.

Hitler had gambled that the British would not risk war. He spoke of the Munich Agreement as 'an undreamt-of triumph, so great that you can scarcely imagine it'. The prize of the Sudetenland had been given to him without a shot being fired. On 1 October German troops marched into the Sudetenland. At the same time, Hungary and Poland helped themselves to Czech territory where Hungarians and Poles were living.

The Czechs had been betrayed. Beneš resigned. But the rest of Europe breathed a sigh of relief. Chamberlain received a hero's welcome back in Britain, when he returned with the 'piece of paper' – the Agreement – signed by Hitler (see Profile, page 57).

SOURCE 32

A

"Horrible and Fantastic, that a quarrel in a faraway country between two peoples of whom we know nothing .. ho hum!"

CZECH

DOOR TO EUROPEAN AND BRITISH DOMINATION

B

CZECH CRISIS

PEACE

WAR

Two British cartoons commenting on the Sudetenland crisis of 1938.

A triumph or a sell-out?

What do you think of the Munich Agreement? Was it a good move or a poor one? Most people in Britain were relieved that it had averted war, but many were now openly questioning the whole policy of Appeasement. Even the public relief may have been overstated. Opinion polls in September 1938 show that the British people did not think Appeasement would stop Hitler. It simply delayed a war, rather than preventing it. Even while Chamberlain was signing the Munich Agreement, he was approving a massive increase in arms spending in preparation for war.

SOURCE 33

By repeatedly surrendering to force, Chamberlain has encouraged aggression . . . our central contention, therefore, is that Mr Chamberlain's policy has throughout been based on a fatal misunderstanding of the psychology of dictatorship.

The *Yorkshire Post*, December 1938.

SOURCE 34

We have suffered a total defeat . . . I think you will find that in a period of time Czechoslovakia will be engulfed in the Nazi regime. We have passed an awful milestone in our history. This is only the beginning of the reckoning.

Winston Churchill speaking in October 1938. He felt that Britain should resist the demands of Hitler. However, he was an isolated figure in the 1930s.

SOURCE 35

A British cartoon from 1938.

SOURCE 36

The front page of the *Daily Sketch*, 1 October 1938.

Activity

Write a selection of newspaper headlines for 30 September – the day after the Munich Agreement. Your selection might include headlines for:

- different British newspapers
- a neutral American newspaper
- a German newspaper
- a Czech newspaper
- a Polish newspaper.

For each newspaper decide whether the Agreement would be seen as a triumph or a sell-out.

For one of the headlines write a short article describing the Agreement. You can use quotations from Sources 30, 33 and 34.

3 Complete row 4 of your 'Versailles chart' on page 47.

The end of Appeasement

Czechoslovakia, 1939

Although the British people welcomed the Munich Agreement, they did not trust Hitler. In an opinion poll in October 1938, 93 per cent said they did not believe him when he said he had no more territorial ambitions in Europe. In March 1939 they were proved right. On 15 March, with Czechoslovakia in chaos, German troops took over the rest of the country.

SOURCE **37**

Key

■ October 1938 Teschen taken by Poland

□ November 1938 to March 1939 Slovak border areas and Ruthenia taken by Hungary

■ October 1938 Sudetenland region given to Germany in the Munich Agreement

■ March 1939 Remainder of Czechoslovakia taken under German control

— German border in 1939

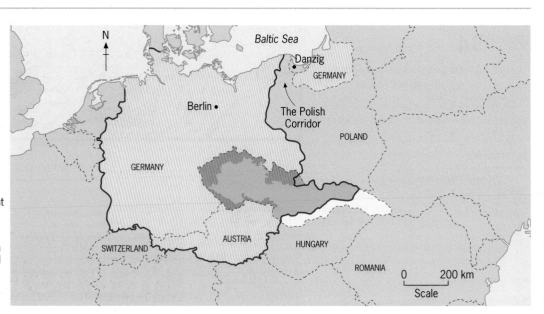

The take-over of Czechoslovakia by 1939.

SOURCE **38**

German troops entering Prague, the capital of Czechoslovakia, in March 1939.

1 Choose five words to describe the attitude of the crowd in Source 38.

There was no resistance from the Czechs. Nor did Britain and France do anything about the situation. However, it was now clear that Hitler could not be trusted. For Chamberlain it was a step too far. Unlike the Sudeten Germans, the Czechs were not separated from their homeland by the Treaty of Versailles. This was an invasion. If Hitler continued unchecked, his next target was likely to be Poland. Britain and France told Hitler that if he invaded Poland they would declare war on Germany. The policy of Appeasement was ended. However, after years of Appeasement, Hitler did not actually believe that Britain and France would risk war by resisting him.

The Nazi–Soviet Pact

Look at your 'Versailles chart' from page 47. You should have only one item left. As Hitler was gradually retaking land lost at Versailles, you can see from Source 37 that logically his next target was the strip of former German land in Poland known as the Polish Corridor. He had convinced himself that Britain and France would not risk war over this, but he was less sure about Stalin and the USSR. Let's see why.

Background

Stalin had been very worried about the German threat to the Soviet Union ever since Hitler came to power in 1933. Hitler had openly stated his interest in conquering Russian land. He had denounced Communism and imprisoned and killed Communists in Germany. Even so, Stalin could not reach any kind of lasting agreement with Britain and France in the 1930s. From Stalin's point of view, it was not for want of trying. In 1934 he had joined the League of Nations, hoping the League would guarantee his security against the threat from Germany. However, all he saw at the League was its powerlessness when Mussolini successfully invaded Abyssinia, and when both Mussolini and Hitler intervened in the Spanish Civil War. Politicians in Britain and France had not resisted German rearmament in the 1930s. Indeed, some in Britain seemed even to welcome a stronger Germany as a force to fight Communism, which they saw as a bigger threat to British interests than Hitler (see page 54).

Stalin's fears and suspicions grew in the mid 1930s. He signed a treaty with France in 1935 that said that France would help the USSR if Germany invaded the Soviet Union. But Stalin was not sure he could trust the French to stick to it, particularly when they failed even to stop Hitler moving into the Rhineland, which was right on their own border.

The Munich Agreement in 1938 increased Stalin's concerns. He was not consulted about it. Stalin concluded from the agreement that France and Britain were powerless to stop Hitler or, even worse, that they were happy for Hitler to take over eastern Europe and then the USSR.

SOURCE 39

It will be asked how it was possible that the Soviet government signed a non-aggression pact with so deceitful a nation, with such criminals as Hitler and Ribbentrop . . . We secured peace for our country for eighteen months, which enabled us to make military preparations.

Stalin, in a speech in 1941.

SOURCE 40

A British cartoon from 1937. The figures on the left represent Britain and France. The figure on the right is Molotov, the Soviet Foreign Minister.

SOURCE 41

A Soviet cartoon from 1939. CCCP is Russian for USSR. The French and the British are directing Hitler away from western Europe and towards the USSR.

2 What does Source 41 reveal about Soviet attitudes to Britain and France?
3 How might a British politician justify the Munich Agreement to Stalin?

1 Look at Source 44. What point is the cartoonist making about the Nazi–Soviet Pact?

2 Do you agree with his view of the Pact?

SOURCE 42

Hitler regarded the Pact as his master stroke. Although he had promised the Russians eastern Poland, Finland, Estonia and Latvia, he never intended to allow them to keep these territories.

Stalin did not expect Hitler to keep his word either. He was sure he could only gain from a long war in which Britain, France and Germany exhausted themselves. Seldom have two countries entered an alliance so dishonestly.

From *The Modern World since 1870*, a school textbook by LE Snellgrove, published in 1980.

SOURCE 43

Why did Britain and France help Hitler to achieve his aims? By rejecting the idea of a united front proposed by the USSR, they played into the hands of Germany. They hoped to appease Hitler by giving him some Czech territory. They wanted to direct German aggression eastward against the USSR and the disgraceful Munich deal achieved this.

[In 1939] the USSR stood alone in the face of the growing Fascist threat. The USSR had to make a treaty of non-aggression with Germany. Some British historians tried to prove that this treaty helped to start the Second World War. The truth is it gave the USSR time to strengthen its defences.

Soviet historian Kukushkin, writing in 1981.

3 What do Sources 39, 42 and 43 agree about?

4 What do they disagree about?

Activity

Was the war all Hitler's fault?

Imagine that Hitler is on trial. He is facing the charge that he deliberately planned and started the Second World War.

1 What evidence would the prosecution bring forward?

2 What evidence would be put forward by the defence?

3 Take a vote with your class as the jury. Do you find Hitler guilty or not guilty?

SOURCE 44

A British cartoon from 1939.

Despite his misgivings, Stalin was still prepared to talk with Britain and France about an alliance against Hitler. The three countries met in March 1939, but Chamberlain was reluctant to commit Britain. From Stalin's point of view, France and Britain then made things worse by giving Poland a guarantee that they would defend it if it was invaded. Chamberlain meant the guarantee as a warning to Hitler. Stalin saw it as support for one of the USSR's potential enemies.

Negotiations between Britain, France and the USSR continued through the spring and summer of 1939. However, Stalin also received visits from the Nazi foreign minister Ribbentrop. They discussed a rather different deal, a Nazi–Soviet Pact.

In August, Stalin made his decision. On 24 August 1939, Hitler and Stalin, the two arch enemies, signed the Nazi–Soviet Pact and announced the terms to the world. They agreed not to attack one another. Privately, they also agreed to divide Poland between them.

Why did Stalin sign? It was probably a combination of factors that led to the Pact.

- Stalin was not convinced that Britain and France would be strong and reliable enough as allies against Hitler.
- He also had designs on large sections of eastern Poland and wanted to take over the Baltic states, which had been part of Russia in the Tsar's day.
- He did not believe Hitler would keep his word, but he hoped for time to build up his forces against the attack he knew would come.

War

The Pact was perhaps the pinnacle of Hitler's triumphs. It cleared the way for Germany's invasion of Poland.

On 1 September 1939 the German army invaded Poland from the west. On 17 September Soviet forces invaded Poland from the east. Poland soon fell.

If Hitler was planning ahead at all, then in his mind the next move would surely be an attack against his temporary ally, the USSR. He was certain that Britain and France would not go to war over Poland. But Hitler's triumph was spoilt by a nasty surprise. Britain and France did keep their pledge. On 2 September they declared war on Germany.

Hitler had started a war, but it was not the war he had in mind. It was too soon and against the wrong opponents. Hitler had taken one gamble too many.

Did Chamberlain follow the w
policy?

Chamberlain certainly believed in Appeasement. In June 1938 he wrote in a letter to his sis
completely convinced that the course I am taking is right and therefore cannot be influenced by the
attacks of my critics.' He was not a coward or a weakling. When it became obvious that he had no
choice but to declare war in 1939 he did.

On page 54 you studied the main reasons Chamberlain followed this policy and the reasons why
people opposed him. However, remember that Chamberlain was not alone. There were many more
politicians who supported him in 1938 than opposed him. It looked pretty clear to them in 1938 that
the balance fell in favour of Appeasement.

Yet when Hitler broke his promises and the policy did not stop war, the supporters of Appeasement
quickly turned against the policy, some claiming that they had been opposed all along. Appeasers
were portrayed as naïve, foolish or weak – Source 45 is one of hundreds of examples which parody
the policy and the people who pursued it. Historians since then and popular opinion too have judged
Chamberlain very harshly. Chamberlain's 'Peace for our time' speech is presented as self-deception
and a betrayal. Chamberlain and his cabinet are seen as 'second rate politicians' who were out of
their depth as events unfolded before them. On the other hand the opponents of Appeasement such as
Winston Churchill are portrayed as realists who were far sighted and brave.

SOURCE 45

'*Remember . . . One More Lollypop, and Then You All Go Home!*'

A cartoon by the American artist Dr Seuss published on 13 August 1941 (before the USA
entered the Second World War).

5 What is Source 45 trying to say about the policy of Appeasement?
6 Make a list of the reasons why Appeasement has generally been seen in negative terms.
7 Churchill once remarked to President Roosevelt 'History will judge us kindly because I shall write the history'. Read Source 46. How should this affect our viewpoints on Appeasement?

SOURCE 46

The Gathering Storm has been one of the most influential books of our time. It is no exaggeration to claim that it has strongly influenced the behaviour of Western politicians from Harry S. Truman to George W. Bush.

. . . It is a good tale, told by a master story-teller, who did, after all, win the Nobel prize for literature; but would a prize for fiction have been more appropriate?

Professor John Charmley of the University of East Anglia writing about Churchill's account of the 1930s called *The Gathering Storm.*

It really has been a very one-sided debate. Yet this debate matters because the failure of Appeasement
to stop Hitler has had a profound influence on British and American foreign policy ever since. It is
now seen as the 'right thing' to stand up to dictators. You will find an example of this in Chapter 9
when you study the Iraq War. This is a lesson that people have learned from history. One of the
reasons why people study history is to avoid making the same mistakes from the past but before we
leap so quickly to judgement on this issue, let's run this argument through two different checks.

Check 1

If Chamberlain had stood up to Hitler in 1938 what would have happened?

The historian Professor Niall Ferguson of Harvard University has set out some 'counter-factual' scenarios – suggesting what might have happened if particular policies were followed. In particular, he has argued that confronting Hitler in 1938 instead of appeasing him 'would have paid handsome dividends. Even if it had come to war over Czechoslovakia, Germany would not have won. Germany's defences were not yet ready for a two-front war.'

Professor Ferguson then had the chance to test his scenario by playing a computer game! *The Calm and the Storm* is a powerful simulation which allows users to make decisions and then computes the possible impact of those decisions.

SOURCE 47

So how did my pre-emptive strategy stand up to a computer stress test? Not as well as I had hoped, I have to confess. The Calm & the Storm made it clear that lining up an anti-German coalition in 1938 might have been harder than I'd assumed. To my horror, the French turned down the alliance I proposed to them. It also turned out that, when I did go to war with Germany, my own position was pretty weak. The nadir [low point] was a successful German invasion of England, a scenario my book rules out as militarily too risky.

Professor Niall Ferguson in an article for the *New York Magazine*, 16 October 2006.

SOURCE 48

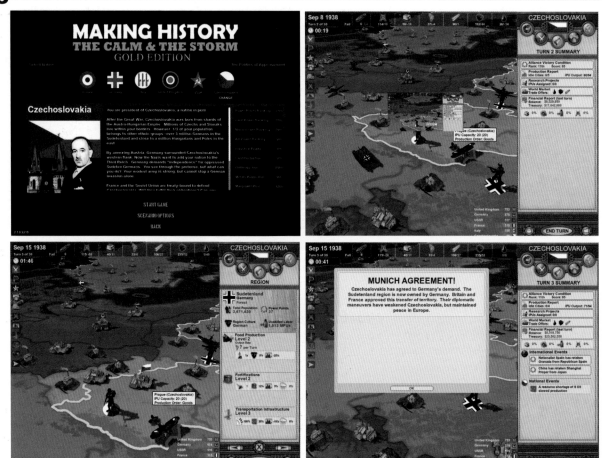

Screen Shots from the computer simulation mentioned in Source 47, *The Calm and the Storm*. In this instance the player is taking the role of Czechoslovakia.

Professor Ferguson believes that using computer simulations could help leaders of the future make key decisions in times of crisis. Maybe you don't trust a computer game to teach you anything about history! But you might trust some hard statistics. So try check 2.

Check 2

Did Appeasement buy time for Chamberlain to rearm Britain?

One of the strongest arguments for Appeasement was that in 1938 Britain simply was not equipped to fight a war with Germany. So did Appeasement allow Britain to catch up?

In the 1960s British historian AJP Taylor argued that Chamberlain had an exaggerated view of Germany's strength. Taylor believed that German forces were only 45 per cent of what British intelligence reports said they were.

But Taylor was writing in 1965 – not much help to Chamberlain in the 1930s. Britain had run down its forces in the peaceful years of the 1920s. The government had talked about rearmament since 1935 but Britain only really started rearming when Chamberlain became Prime Minister in 1937. Chamberlain certainly thought that Britain's armed forces were not ready for war in 1938. His own military advisers and his intelligence services told him this.

So did Appeasement allow Britain the time it needed to rearm? Source 49 will help you to decide.

SOURCE **49**

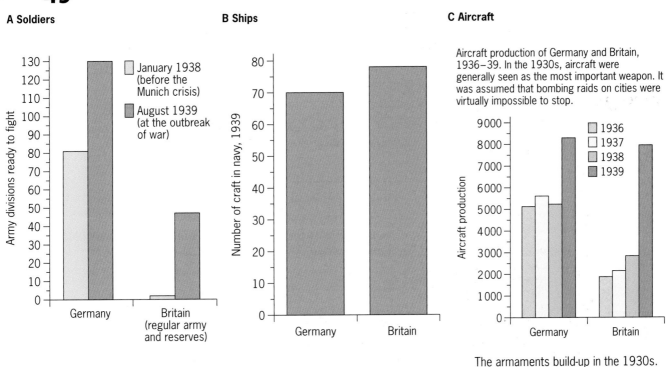

A Soldiers

January 1938 (before the Munich crisis)

August 1939 (at the outbreak of war)

Army divisions ready to fight

Germany / Britain (regular army and reserves)

B Ships

Number of craft in navy, 1939

Germany / Britain

C Aircraft

Aircraft production of Germany and Britain, 1936–39. In the 1930s, aircraft were generally seen as the most important weapon. It was assumed that bombing raids on cities were virtually impossible to stop.

Aircraft production

1936 / 1937 / 1938 / 1939

Germany / Britain

The armaments build-up in the 1930s.

1 Study carefully graphs A–C in Source 49.
  a) What evidence do they provide to support the view that Britain's armed forces caught up with Germany's between 1938 and 1939?
  b) What evidence do they provide to oppose this view?

Activity

Look back at your work in the Activity on page 62. Does reading this section change your verdict?

Focus Task

Was the policy of Appeasement justified?

◆ The right policy at the right time.
◆ The wrong policy, but only with hindsight.
◆ A betrayal of the people of Czechoslovakia.
◆ A risky policy that purchased valuable time.

1 Work in pairs or groups. Collect evidence from pages 54–65 to support each of the above views.
2 Choose one viewpoint that you most agree with and write some well argued paragraphs to explain your choice:
  a) what the viewpoint means – in your own words
  b) what evidence there is to support it
  c) what evidence there is against it and why you have rejected that evidence
  d) your conclusion as to why this is a good verdict.

Focus Task

Why had international peace collapsed by 1939?

Work in groups of six.

1 Each of you take one of the following topics. Write it large at the top of a blank sheet of paper.
  ◆ Hitler's actions
  ◆ The policy of Appeasement
  ◆ The problems caused by the peace treaties
  ◆ The Nazi–Soviet Pact
  ◆ The failures of the League of Nations
  ◆ The Depression
2 On your sheet, summarise the ways in which this factor helped lead to war in 1939.
3 Stick the six sheets on to a larger sheet of paper.
4 Draw lines between the causes to show how they are connected to one another.
5 Discuss with your group whether, if you took any of these causes away, there would have been a war.
6 Now, on your own, write an essay on the topic 'Why had international peace collapsed by 1939?' You can use the structure below:

Paragraph 1:

(This is the place to explain how resentment against the Versailles Treaty brought Hitler to power in the first place and guided his actions in the 1930s.)

There were important long-term factors which help to explain why war broke out in 1939. One factor was the Versailles Treaty. It was important because . . .

_____

_____

Paragraph 2:

(Here you should explain how the failure of the League encouraged Hitler and made him think he could achieve his aims.)

The failure of the League of Nations in the 1930s also contributed towards the outbreak of war. This was because . . .

_____

_____

_____

Paragraph 3:

(Here you should explain how the Depression was an underlying cause of the failure of the League, Japan's aggression and Hitler's rise to power.)

Economic factors also played an important role. The worldwide economic Depression . . .

_____

_____

_____

Paragraph 4:

(Here you should briefly describe what Appeasement was, and how instead of stopping Hitler it encouraged him. You could also point out the links between Appeasement and the Depression.)

Another factor which helps to explain the outbreak of war was the policy of Appeasement. Appeasement . . .

_____

_____

Paragraph 5:

(Here you should explain how the Nazi–Soviet Pact led to the invasion of Poland and how that in turn led to war. You could also point out that these short-term factors probably could not have happened if there had not been a policy of Appeasement.)

There were also key short-term factors which actually sparked off the war. One of these was . . .

_____

_____

_____

Paragraph 6:

(Here you should indicate which factor(s) you think were most important. This is where you should bring in any of the factors you discussed in stage 5 of the Focus Task.)

All of these factors played important roles. However, [INSERT YOUR CHOICE OF FACTOR(S)] was / were particularly important because . . .

_____

_____

4 Who was to blame for the Cold War?

The beginnings of the Cold War: 1945–49

Focus

In May 1945 American troops entered Berlin from the west, as Russian troops moved in from the east. They met and celebrated victory together. Yet three years later these former allies were arguing over Berlin and war between them seemed a real possibility. What had gone wrong?

In this chapter you will consider:
- how the wartime alliance between the USA and the USSR broke down
- how the Soviet Union gained control over eastern Europe and how the USA responded
- the consequences of the Berlin Blockade in 1948.

Finally, you will make up your own mind as to whether the USA or the USSR was more to blame for the outbreak of the Cold War.

Activity

This timeline summarises the key events you will be looking at in this chapter. As you study the chapter, add details to your own copy of the timeline. First of all extend your timeline back to 1917 and use the information on these two pages to mark any events that might affect relationships between the USA and the Soviet Union.

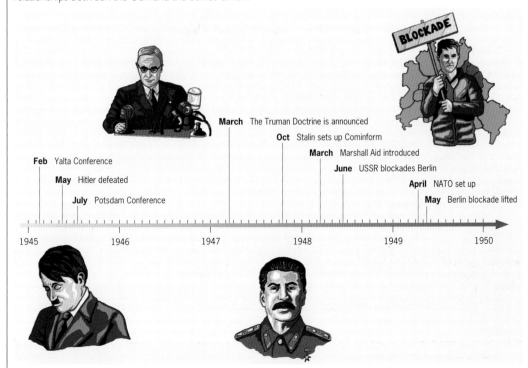

March The Truman Doctrine is announced
Oct Stalin sets up Cominform
March Marshall Aid introduced
June USSR blockades Berlin
Feb Yalta Conference
May Hitler defeated
July Potsdam Conference
April NATO set up
May Berlin blockade lifted

1945   1946   1947   1948   1949   1950

How strong was the wartime alliance?

ПРИВЕТ ГЕРОЙСКИМ ВОИНАМ СОВЕТСКОГО СОЮЗА ОТ БРИТАНСКИХ СОЮЗНИКОВ БОРЮЩИХСА С НИМИ

МЫ ВСЕГДА С ВАМИ В ЧДАЧАХ И НЕЧДАЧАХ ВМЕСТЕ ДОБЬЕМ РАЗГРОМИМ ЧНИЧТОЖИМ НАЩЕГО ВРАГА

A British government poster from 1941. The Russian caption reads, 'Greetings to the heroic warrior of the Soviet Union from British allies fighting with him.'

Allies against Hitler

In the latter stages of the Second World War the British people were bombarded with images like Source 1, showing friendly co-operation between American, British and Soviet forces and peoples.

In fact the real story is probably more like Source 2. Hitler is shown as Cupid – a god of love – bringing the otherwise distrustful leaders together. Hitler was the common danger which united President Roosevelt (USA), Winston Churchill (Britain) and Communist leader Josef Stalin of the Soviet Union (the USSR). It was a strategic wartime alliance not a bond of brotherhood. This becomes clear when we look back further into history.

A British cartoon from 1941, with the caption 'Love conquers all'.

Thirty years earlier

The USSR had been a Communist country for more than 30 years. The majority of politicians and business leaders in Britain and the USA hated and feared Communist ideas (see the Factfiles on page 69). Soon after the Communists took power in Russia in 1917 they faced a civil war. During this civil war British and American troops were sent to fight against the Communists (see page 318). As you can imagine, the experience of the civil war made the USSR wary of Britain and the USA. So the two sides were enemies long before they were allies.

In the 1920s the fear of Communism created a Red Scare in the USA (see Source 3). Thousands of immigrants to the USA who held radical political views were arrested, harassed and often deported. In 1926 the British government reacted fiercely to a General Strike by British workers. One of the reasons for this harsh reaction was that the British government was convinced that the Strike was the work of agents of the USSR.

1 Explain the message of each of the sources 1 and 2. Remember to explain the points being made and how the details of the cartoon get these points across.
2 Explain why Source 2 presents a more realistic view of the alliance than Source 1.
3 Spot the loaded language! What words and phrases in Source 3 tell us that this source is hostile to Communism and the USSR?

. . . Like a prairie-fire, the blaze of revolution was sweeping over every American institution of law and order a year ago. It was eating its way into the homes of the American workmen . . . crawling into the sacred corners of American homes . . .

Robbery, not war, is the ideal of Communism . . . Obviously it is the creed of any criminal mind, which acts always from motives impossible to understand for those with clean thoughts.

Extract from a statement by Mitchell Palmer, Attorney General of the USA, April 1920.

Ten years earlier

Relations between Britain and the USSR were harmed in the 1930s by the policy of Appeasement (see page 54). It seemed to Stalin that Britain was happy to see Germany grow in power so that Hitler could attack him.

So in many ways the surprising thing is that the old enemies managed a war-time alliance at all. But they did and the course of the war in Europe was decisively altered when the Soviets mounted a fierce defence of their country against the power of the German forces from 1941 to 1945. Churchill was full of respect for the Soviet achievement saying that the Soviets 'tore the heart out of the German army'. It was Soviet determination and Soviet soldiers that turned the tide of the European war against Germany.

Clash of ideologies

So why did Britain and America have these underlying concerns about Communism? One key reason was that the Allies had political and economic systems based on completely different ideologies (see the Factfiles below). Despite these differences they had managed to work together against Hitler. The next big question was whether this friendship would last once he was defeated.

Factfile

The USA

➤ The USA was a democracy. Its government was chosen in free democratic elections.
➤ It was capitalist. Business and property were privately owned.
➤ It was the world's wealthiest country. But, as in most capitalist countries, there were extremes – some great wealth and great poverty as well.
➤ For Americans, being free of control by the government was more important than everyone being equal.
➤ Americans firmly believed that other countries should be run in the American way.
➤ Many Americans were bitterly opposed to Communism and were alarmed by Communist theory which talked of spreading revolution.
➤ Americans generally saw their policies as 'doing the right thing' rather than serving the interest of the USA.

Factfile

The USSR

➤ The USSR was a Communist state.
➤ It was a one-party dictatorship. Elections were held, but all candidates belonged to the Communist Party.
➤ It was an economic superpower because its industry had grown rapidly in the 1920s and 1930s, but the general standard of living in the USSR was much lower than in the USA. Even so, unemployment was rare and extreme poverty was rarer than in the USA.
➤ For Communists, the rights of individuals were seen as less important than the good of society as a whole. So individuals' lives were tightly controlled.
➤ Soviet leaders believed that other countries should be run in the Communist way.
➤ Communist writers believed that the role of a Communist state was to encourage Communist revolutions worldwide. In practice, the USSR's leaders tended to take practical decisions rather than be led by this ideology.
➤ Many people in the USSR were bitterly opposed to capitalism.

USSR – COMMUNIST

 ELECTIONS

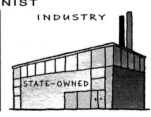 INDUSTRY
STATE-OWNED

INDIVIDUAL RIGHTS

USA – CAPITALIST AND DEMOCRATIC

 ELECTIONS

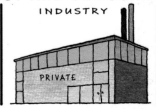 INDUSTRY
PRIVATE

INDIVIDUAL RIGHTS

4 Make your own copies of the diagrams on the right and then use the Factfiles to make notes around them summarising the two systems.

The Yalta Conference, 1945

In February 1945 it was clear that Germany was losing the European war, so the Allied leaders met at Yalta in the Ukraine to plan what would happen to Europe after Germany's defeat. The Yalta Conference went well. Despite their differences, the Big Three – Stalin, Roosevelt and Churchill – agreed on some important matters.

- Stalin agreed to enter the war against Japan once Germany had surrendered.
- They agreed that Germany would be divided into four zones: American, French, British and Soviet. Since the German capital, Berlin, was deep in the Soviet zone, it was agreed that Berlin itself would also be divided into four zones.
- As Allied soldiers advanced through Germany, they were revealing the horrors of the Nazi concentration camps. The Big Three agreed to hunt down and punish war criminals who were responsible for the genocide.
- They agreed that as countries were liberated from occupation by the German army, they would be allowed to hold free elections to choose the government they wanted.
- The Big Three all agreed to join the new United Nations Organisation, which would aim to keep peace after the war.
- The Soviet Union had suffered terribly in the war. An estimated 20 million Soviet people had died. Stalin was therefore concerned about the future security of the USSR. The Big Three agreed that eastern Europe should be seen as 'a Soviet sphere of influence'.
- The only real disagreement was about Poland. Stalin wanted the border of the USSR to move westwards into Poland (see Source 20 on page 74). Stalin argued that Poland, in turn, could move its border westwards into German territory. Churchill did not approve of Stalin's plans for Poland, but he also knew that there was not very much he could do about it because Stalin's Red Army was in total control of both Poland and eastern Germany. Roosevelt was also unhappy about Stalin's plan, but Churchill persuaded Roosevelt to accept it, as long as the USSR agreed not to interfere in Greece where the British were attempting to prevent the Communists taking over. Stalin accepted this. It seemed that, although they could not all agree, they were still able to negotiate and do business with one another.

SOURCE 4

We argued freely and frankly across the table. But at the end on every point unanimous agreement was reached ... We know, of course, that it was Hitler's hope and the German war lords' hope that we would not agree – that some slight crack might appear in the solid wall of allied unity ... But Hitler has failed. Never before have the major allies been more closely united – not only in their war aims but also in their peace aims.

Extract from President Roosevelt's report to the US Congress on the Yalta Conference.

SOURCE 5

I have always worked for friendship with Russia but, like you, I feel deep anxiety because of their misinterpretation of the Yalta decisions, their attitude towards Poland, their overwhelming influence in the Balkans excepting Greece, the difficulties they make about Vienna, the combination of Russian power and the territories under their control or occupied, coupled with the Communist technique in so many other countries, and above all their power to maintain very large Armies in the field for a long time. What will be the position in a year or two?

Extract from a telegram sent by Prime Minister Churchill to President Roosevelt in May 1945.

Activity

SOURCE **6**

A publicity photograph of the Big Three at the Yalta Conference February 1945.

1 Imagine you were describing the scene (in Source 6) for a radio audience in 1945. You can use the internet to find examples of radio broadcasts from the period. Describe for the listeners:
- the obvious points (such as people you can see)
- the less obvious points (such as the mood of the scene).

2 Source 6 presents a friendly, positive scene. Look through the information on the Yalta Conference from the previous page and list facts, points and evidence which support this view of the Conference.

3 Now list any facts, points and evidence that this view of the Conference is not the whole story (you can use the next two pages as well).

4 Suggest a new caption for Source 6 which tells readers a little more about Yalta.

Focus Task

What was going on behind the scenes at Yalta?

The war against Hitler had united Roosevelt, Stalin and Churchill and at the Yalta Conference they appeared to get on well. Source 7 illustrates the 'public' face of Yalta. But what was going on behind the scenes? Sources 8–17 will help you decide.

1 Use a table like this to analyse the sources.

Evidence for disagreement	Evidence for agreement	Reasons why the source is reliable or unreliable

SOURCE 7

I want to drink to our alliance, that it should not lose its . . . intimacy, its free expression of views . . . I know of no such close alliance of three Great Powers as this . . . May it be strong and stable, may we be as frank as possible.

Stalin, proposing a toast at a dinner at the Yalta Conference, 1945.

SOURCE 9

In the hallway [at Yalta] we stopped before a map of the world on which the Soviet Union was coloured in red. Stalin waved his hand over the Soviet Union and exclaimed, 'They [Roosevelt and Churchill] will never accept the idea that so great a space should be red, never, never!'

Milovan Djilas writing about Yalta in 1948.

SOURCE 11

The Soviet Union has become a danger to the free world. A new front must be created against her onward sweep. This front should be as far east as possible. A settlement must be reached on all major issues between West and East in Europe before the armies of democracy melt.

Churchill writing to Roosevelt shortly after the Yalta Conference.

SOURCE 13

[At Yalta] Churchill feared that Roosevelt was too pro-Russian. He pressed for a French zone to be added to the other three to add another anti-Russian voice to the armies of occupation.

Written by Christopher Culpin in a school textbook, *The Modern World*, 1984.

SOURCE 8

Perhaps you think that just because we are the allies of the English we have forgotten who they are and who Churchill is. There's nothing they like better than to trick their allies. During the First World War they constantly tricked the Russians and the French. And Churchill? Churchill is the kind of man who will pick your pocket of a kopeck! [A kopeck is a low value Soviet coin.] And Roosevelt? Roosevelt is not like that. He dips in his hand only for bigger coins. But Churchill? He will do it for a kopeck.

Stalin speaking to a fellow Communist, Milovan Djilas, in 1945. Djilas was a supporter of Stalin.

SOURCE 10

Once, Churchill asked Stalin to send him the music of the new Soviet Russian anthem so that it could be broadcast before the summary of the news from the Soviet German front. Stalin sent the words [as well] and expressed the hope that Churchill would set about learning the new tune and whistling it to members of the Conservative Party. While Stalin behaved with relative discretion with Roosevelt, he continually teased Churchill throughout the war.

Written by Soviet historian Sergei Kudryashov after the war.

SOURCE 12

A Soviet cartoon. Churchill is shown with two flags, the first proclaiming that 'Anglo-Saxons must rule the world' and the other threatening an 'iron curtain'.

SOURCE 14

OPERATION UNTHINKABLE
REPORT BY THE JOINT PLANNING STAFF
We have examined Operation Unthinkable. As instructed, we have taken the following assumptions on which to base our examination:

Great Britain and the United States have full assistance from the Polish armed forces and can count upon the use of German manpower and what remains of German industrial capacity . . .

Owing to the special need for secrecy, the normal staff in Service Ministries have not been consulted.

OBJECT
The overall or political object is to impose upon Russia the will of the United States and British Empire. The only way we can achieve our object with certainty and lasting results is by victory in a total war.

Extract from a top secret document called *Operation Unthinkable*. It was presented by the Army Chiefs to Churchill in May 1945 but the research and planning had been taking place during the Yalta Conference. Churchill rejected the idea.

SOURCE 15

One night Stalin stung Churchill when proposing a toast by reminding Churchill of his failures at Gallipoli in the First World War.

Another night Churchill declared (whilst slightly drunk) that he deserved a medal for teaching the Soviet army to fight so well through the intervention at Archangel.

The Soviet Foreign Minister Molotov writing about Yalta. In 1915 Churchill had been responsible for a failed attack at Gallipoli (see page 245). In 1918 Churchill had supported the British decision to send troops to Archangel to help in the fight against the Communists in the Russian Civil War (see page 318).

SOURCE 16

One could see that Churchill had left a deep impression on the Soviet leaders as a farsighted and dangerous statesman – although they did not like him.

Milovan Djilas comments, in 1948, on Stalin's assessment of Churchill.

SOURCE 17

[In May 1945] Churchill ordered Montgomery to keep the German arms intact, in case they had to be used against the Russians.

Written by historian Hugh Higgins in *The Cold War*, 1974.

2 Draw a diagram like this and use Sources 7–17 to summarise what each of the leaders thought of the other.
3 Is it possible to tell from these extracts what Stalin and Churchill really felt about each other? Explain your answer.
4 How do Sources 7–17 affect your impression of the Yalta Conference?
5 Write three sentences to sum up the main concerns of each of the Big Three at Yalta. Use the text and Sources 7–17.

The Potsdam Conference, July–August 1945

In May 1945, three months after the Yalta Conference, Allied troops reached Berlin. Hitler committed suicide. Germany surrendered. The war in Europe was won.

SOURCE **18**

American and Soviet soldiers shake hands in April 1945.

1 Source 18 is to be used in a newspaper in April 1945. Write a caption to go with it.

SOURCE **19**

This war is not as in the past; whoever occupies a territory also imposes on it his own social system. Everyone imposes his own system as far as his army has power to do so. It cannot be otherwise.

Stalin speaking, soon after the end of the Second World War, about the take-over of eastern Europe.

SOURCE **20**

Poland has borders with the Soviet Union which is not the case with Great Britain or the USA. I do not know whether a truly representative government has been established in Greece. The Soviet Union was not consulted when this government was being formed, nor did it claim the right to interfere because it realises how important Greece is to the security of Great Britain.

Stalin, replying to Allied leaders about his plans for Poland in April 1945. Britain had helped to prop up an anti-Communist government in Greece (see page 76).

2 Read Source 19. At Yalta, Churchill and Roosevelt had agreed with Stalin that eastern Europe would be a Soviet 'sphere of influence'. Do you think Source 19 is what they had in mind?

3 Would they agree with Stalin's views expressed in Sources 19 and 20? Explain your answer.

4 Explain how each of the three developments described in the text might affect relationships at Potsdam.

A second conference of the Allied leaders was arranged for July 1945 in the Berlin suburb of Potsdam. However, in the five months since Yalta a number of changes had taken place which would greatly affect relationships between the leaders.

1 Stalin's armies were occupying most of eastern Europe

Soviet troops had liberated country after country in eastern Europe, but instead of withdrawing his troops Stalin had left them there. By July, Stalin's troops effectively controlled the Baltic states, Finland, Poland, Czechoslovakia, Hungary, Bulgaria and Romania, and refugees were fleeing out of these countries fearing a Communist take-over. Stalin had set up a Communist government in Poland, ignoring the wishes of the majority of Poles. Britain and the USA protested, but Stalin defended his action (see Source 20). He insisted that his control of eastern Europe was a defensive measure against possible future attacks (see Source 23).

2 America had a new president

On 12 April 1945, President Roosevelt died. He was replaced by his Vice-President, Harry Truman. Truman was a very different man from Roosevelt. He was much more anti-Communist than Roosevelt and was very suspicious of Stalin. Truman and his advisers saw Soviet actions in eastern Europe as preparations for a Soviet take-over of the rest of Europe.

3 The Allies had tested an atomic bomb

On 16 July 1945 the Americans successfully tested an atomic bomb at a desert site in the USA. At the start of the Potsdam Conference, Truman informed Stalin about it.

Focus Task

Why did the USA–USSR alliance begin to breakdown in 1945?

Under the following headings, make notes to summarise why the Allies began to fall out in 1945:
- Personalities
- Actions by the USA
- Actions by the USSR
- Misunderstandings

Disagreements at Potsdam

The Potsdam Conference finally got under way on 17 July 1945. Not surprisingly, it did not go as smoothly as Yalta.

In July there was an election in Britain. Churchill was defeated, so half way through the conference he was replaced by a new Prime Minister, Clement Attlee. In the absence of Churchill, the conference was dominated by rivalry and suspicion between Stalin and Truman. A number of issues arose on which neither side seemed able to appreciate the other's point of view.

- **They disagreed over what to do about Germany.** Stalin wanted to cripple Germany completely to protect the USSR against future threats. Truman did not want to repeat the mistake of the Treaty of Versailles.
- **They disagreed over reparations.** Twenty million Russians had died in the war and the Soviet Union had been devastated. Stalin wanted compensation from Germany. Truman, however, was once again determined not to repeat the mistakes at the end of the First World War and resisted this demand.
- **They disagreed over Soviet policy in eastern Europe.** At Yalta, Stalin had won agreement from the Allies that he could set up pro-Soviet governments in eastern Europe. He said, 'If the Slav [the majority of east European] people are united, no one will dare move a finger against them.' Truman became very unhappy about Russian intentions and soon adopted a 'get tough' attitude towards Stalin.

The 'iron curtain'

5 How do Sources 22 and 23 differ in their interpretation of Stalin's actions?
6 Explain why they see things so differently.

The Potsdam Conference ended without complete agreement on these issues. Over the next nine months, Stalin achieved the domination of eastern Europe that he was seeking. By 1946 Poland, Hungary, Romania, Bulgaria and Albania all had Communist governments which owed their loyalty to Stalin. Churchill described the border between Soviet-controlled countries and the West as an iron curtain (see Source 22). The name stuck.

SOURCE 21

A British cartoon commenting on Churchill's 'Iron Curtain' speech, in the *Daily Mail*, 6 March 1946.

SOURCE 22

A shadow has fallen upon the scenes so lately lighted by the Allied victory. From Stettin on the Baltic to Trieste on the Adriatic, an iron curtain has descended. Behind that line lie all the states of central and eastern Europe. The Communist parties have been raised to power far beyond their numbers and are seeking everywhere to obtain totalitarian control. This is certainly not the liberated Europe we fought to build. Nor is it one which allows permanent peace.

Winston Churchill speaking in the USA, in the presence of President Truman, March 1946.

SOURCE 23

The following circumstances should not be forgotten. The Germans made their invasion of the USSR through Finland, Poland and Romania. The Germans were able to make their invasion through these countries because, at the time, governments hostile to the Soviet Union existed in these countries. What can there be surprising about the fact that the Soviet Union, anxious for its future safety, is trying to see to it that governments loyal in their attitude to the Soviet Union should exist in these countries?

Stalin, replying to Churchill's speech (Source 22).

1 Study Source 24 and make a list of the actions that Communists took to achieve power in eastern Europe.
2 Explain how each factor helped.

Soviet expansion into eastern Europe

In the years following the Second World War, Stalin was determined that he would not be attacked again through eastern Europe. Source 24 shows how he extended Soviet power across eastern Europe.

SOURCE 24

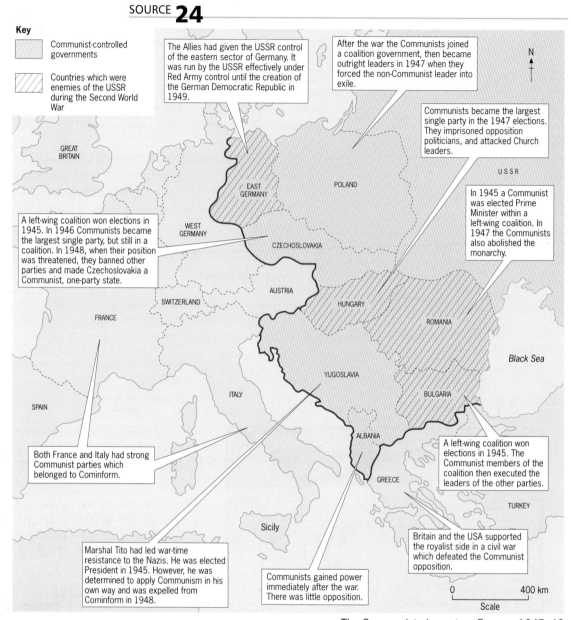

Key

Communist-controlled governments

Countries which were enemies of the USSR during the Second World War

The Allies had given the USSR control of the eastern sector of Germany. It was run by the USSR effectively under Red Army control until the creation of the German Democratic Republic in 1949.

After the war the Communists joined a coalition government, then became outright leaders in 1947 when they forced the non-Communist leader into exile.

Communists became the largest single party in the 1947 elections. They imprisoned opposition politicians, and attacked Church leaders.

In 1945 a Communist was elected Prime Minister within a left-wing coalition. In 1947 the Communists also abolished the monarchy.

A left-wing coalition won elections in 1945. In 1946 Communists became the largest single party, but still in a coalition. In 1948, when their position was threatened, they banned other parties and made Czechoslovakia a Communist, one-party state.

A left-wing coalition won elections in 1945. The Communist members of the coalition then executed the leaders of the other parties.

Both France and Italy had strong Communist parties which belonged to Cominform.

Marshal Tito had led war-time resistance to the Nazis. He was elected President in 1945. However, he was determined to apply Communism in his own way and was expelled from Cominform in 1948.

Communists gained power immediately after the war. There was little opposition.

Britain and the USA supported the royalist side in a civil war which defeated the Communist opposition.

0   400 km
Scale

The Communists in eastern Europe, 1945–48.

Focus Task

How did the USSR gain control of eastern Europe by 1948?

It is 1948. Produce a briefing paper to update President Truman on the situation in eastern Europe. Your report should mention:

◆ the Communist successes in eastern Europe between 1945 and 1948 and the reasons for them
◆ Stalin's plan for eastern Europe
◆ the methods being used by Stalin to control eastern Europe
◆ whether you think the USA should be worried.

Stalin tightens his control

With Communist governments established throughout eastern Europe, Stalin gradually tightened his control in each country. The secret police imprisoned anyone who opposed Communist rule, or might oppose it at a later date.

In October 1947, Stalin set up the Communist Information Bureau, or Cominform, to co-ordinate the work of the Communist Parties of eastern Europe. Cominform regularly brought the leaders of each Communist Party to Moscow to be briefed by Stalin and his ministers. This also allowed Stalin to keep a close eye on them. He spotted independent-minded leaders and replaced them with people who were completely loyal to him. The only Communist leader who escaped this close control was Tito in Yugoslavia. He resented being controlled by Cominform and was expelled for his hostility in 1948.

Unless Russia is faced with an iron fist and strong language another war is in the making. Only one language do they understand – 'how many [army] divisions have you got?' . . . I'm tired of babying the Soviets.

President Truman, writing to his Secretary of State in January 1946.

SOURCE 26

After all the efforts that have been made and the appeasement that we followed to try and get a real friendly settlement, not only is the Soviet government not prepared to co-operate with any non-Communist government in eastern Europe, but it is actively preparing to extend its hold over the remaining part of continental Europe and, subsequently, over the Middle East and no doubt the Far East as well. In other words, physical control of Europe and Asia and eventual control of the whole world is what Stalin is aiming at – no less a thing than that. The immensity of the aim should not betray us into thinking that it cannot be achieved.

Extract from a report by the British Foreign Secretary to the British Cabinet in March 1948. The title of the report was 'The Threat to Civilisation'.

3 What is your overall impression of Source 25:
   • a reasonable assessment of Stalin's aims based on the facts
   • an overreaction to Stalin's aims based on fear and prejudice against the USSR?
   Use extracts from the source to support your view.
4 Source 26 is a British source. Does it seem likely that similar documents were being produced by the American government?
5 Write your own definition of the term 'Cold War' as it might appear in a historical dictionary.
6 Make a list of the criticisms of the USA in Source 27.

Why did the tensions between the Allies turn into a Cold War?

You can see from Source 25 that by 1946 the wartime friendship between the Allies had broken down. As Source 26 shows, by 1948 it had been replaced by suspicion and accusation. The distrust between the USA and the USSR was soon so great that leaders were talking in public about the threat of war between the two countries. Instead of running down arms expenditure after the war, as you would expect them to, the two sides actually increased their stock of weapons.

SOURCE 27

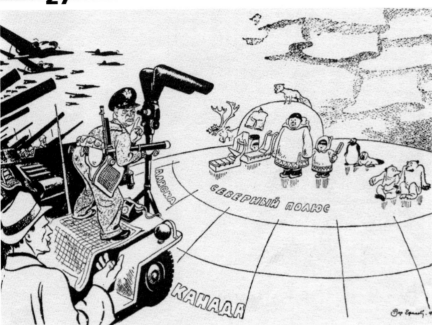

A Soviet cartoon of 1947. The 'ordinary American' is asking the American General Eisenhower why there is so much American military activity focused in an uninhabited area. The General says: 'Can't you see the enormous concentration of enemy forces right here?'

Each side took every opportunity to denounce the policies or the plans of the other. A propaganda war developed. In this atmosphere of tension and recrimination, people began to talk about a Cold War. This Cold War was going to last for 30 years and would dominate relations between the countries for much of that time.

But why did it happen this way? As you have seen, there was tension and suspicion in the 1920s and 1930s but there had not been a Cold War. The differing beliefs of the USA and the USSR were important, of course, but there were some other important differences between the 1940s and those earlier periods.

The USA and the USSR had emerged from the war as the two 'superpowers'. In the 1930s, other countries such as Britain and France had been as important in international affairs. However, the war had finally demoted Britain and France to a second division. They were not big enough, rich enough or strong enough to exercise real international leadership. Only the USA and the USSR were able to do this. They were the superpowers.

The USA was well aware that a responsibility was attached to being a superpower. In the 1930s, the USA had followed a policy of isolation – keeping out of European and world affairs. The Americans might have disapproved of Soviet Communism, but they tried not to get involved. However, by the 1940s the USA had learned a lesson. They did not want to repeat the mistakes they had made before the Second World War. Roosevelt had set the Americans firmly against a policy of isolation. In March 1945 he said to the American Congress that America 'will have to take the responsibility for world collaboration or we shall have to bear the responsibilities for another world conflict'. There would be no more appeasement of dictators. From now on, every Communist action would meet an American reaction.

The reaction of the USA

The Western powers were alarmed by Stalin's take-over of eastern Europe. Roosevelt, Churchill and their successors had accepted that Soviet security needed friendly governments in eastern Europe. They had agreed that eastern Europe would be a Soviet 'sphere of influence' and that Stalin would heavily influence this region. However, they had not expected such complete Communist domination. They felt it should have been possible to have governments in eastern Europe that were both democratic and friendly to the USSR. Stalin saw his policy in eastern Europe as making himself secure, but Truman could only see the spread of Communism.

1 Do Sources 28 and 29 have the same message?

SOURCE **28**

A French cartoon commenting on Stalin's take-over of eastern Europe. The dancing figure is Stalin.

SOURCE **29**

An American cartoon commenting on Stalin's take-over of eastern Europe. The bear represents the USSR.

By 1948, Greece and Czechoslovakia were the only eastern European countries not controlled by Communist governments. It seemed to the Americans that not only Greece and Czechoslovakia but even Italy and France were vulnerable to Communist take-over. Events in two of these countries were to have a decisive effect on America's policy towards Europe.

Greece

When the Germans retreated from Greece in 1944, there were two rival groups – the monarchists and the Communists – who wanted to rule the country. Both had been involved in resistance against the Nazis. The Communists wanted Greece to be a Soviet republic. The monarchists wanted the return of the king of Greece. Churchill sent British troops to Greece in 1945 supposedly to help restore order and supervise free elections. In fact, the British supported the monarchists and the king was returned to power.

In 1946, the USSR protested to the United Nations that British troops were a threat to peace in Greece. The United Nations took no action and so the Communists tried to take control of Greece by force. A civil war quickly developed. The British could not afford the cost of such a war and announced on 24 February 1947 that they were withdrawing their troops. Truman stepped in. Paid for by the Americans, some British troops stayed in Greece. They tried to prop up the king's government. By 1950 the royalists were in control of Greece, although they were a very weak government, always in crisis.

Activity

Look at Sources 28 and 29. Design or describe a Soviet cartoon or poster commenting on the USSR's actions. It could either:
- attack the attitudes of the West, or
- justify and explain Soviet actions.

SOURCE **30**

I believe that it must be the policy of the United States to support free peoples who are resisting attempted subjugation by armed minorities or by outside pressures . . . The free peoples of the world look to us for support in maintaining those freedoms. If we falter in our leadership, we may endanger the peace of the world.

President Truman speaking on 12 March 1947, explaining his decision to help Greece.

Activity

Make a poster summarising the Truman Doctrine in Source 30. Include a short caption.

The Truman Doctrine

American intervention in Greece marked a new era in the USA's attitude to world politics, which became known as 'the Truman Doctrine'.

Under the Truman Doctrine, the USA was prepared to send money, equipment and advice to any country which was, in the American view, threatened by a Communist take-over. Truman accepted that eastern Europe was now Communist. His aim was to stop Communism from spreading any further. This policy became known as containment.

Others thought containment should mean something firmer. They said that it must be made clear to the Soviet Union that expansion beyond a given limit would be met with military force.

The Marshall Plan

Truman believed that Communism succeeded when people faced poverty and hardship. He sent the American General George Marshall to assess the economic state of Europe. What he found was a ruined economy. The countries of Europe owed $11.5 billion to the USA. There were extreme shortages of all goods. Most countries were still rationing bread. There was such a coal shortage in the hard winter of 1947 that in Britain all electricity was turned off for a period each day. Churchill described Europe as 'a rubble heap, a breeding ground of hate'.

SOURCE **31**

Homeless people

Cost of rebuilding damaged homes

Damage caused by war to infrastructure (roads, bridges, etc.)

Debts from cost of war effort

Refugees

Shortage of food and clothing

Shortage of fuel

Problems in post-war Europe.

Marshall suggested that about $17 billion would be needed to rebuild Europe's prosperity. 'Our policy', he said, 'is directed against hunger, poverty, desperation and chaos.'

In December 1947, Truman put his plan to Congress. For a short time, the American Congress refused to grant this money. Many Americans were becoming concerned by Truman's involvement in foreign affairs. Besides, $17 billion was a lot of money!

Czechoslovakia

Americans' attitude changed when the Communists took over the government of Czechoslovakia. Czechoslovakia had been ruled by a coalition government which, although it included Communists, had been trying to pursue policies independent of Moscow. The Communists came down hard in March 1948. Anti-Soviet leaders were purged. One pro-American Minister, Jan Masaryk, was found dead below his open window. The Communists said he had jumped. The Americans suspected he'd been pushed. Immediately, Congress accepted the Marshall Plan and made $17 billion available over a period of four years.

2 Which of the problems shown in Source 31 do you think would be the most urgent for Marshall Aid to tackle? Explain your choice.
3 Explain how events in both Greece and Czechoslovakia affected American policy in Europe.

1 Draw a diagram to summarise the aims of Marshall Aid. Put political aims on one side and economic aims on the other. Draw arrows and labels to show how the two are connected.

On the one hand, Marshall Aid was an extremely generous act by the American people. On the other hand, it was also motivated by American self-interest. They wanted to create new markets for American goods. The Americans remembered the disastrous effects of the Depression of the 1930s and Truman wanted to do all he could to prevent another worldwide slump.

Stalin viewed Marshall Aid with suspicion. After expressing some initial interest, he refused to have anything more to do with it. He also forbade any of the eastern European states to apply for Marshall Aid. Stalin's view was that the anti-Communist aims behind Marshall Aid would weaken his hold on eastern Europe. He also felt that the USA was trying to dominate as many states as possible by making them dependent on dollars.

SOURCE **32**

An American cartoon, 1949.

SOURCE **33**

A Soviet cartoon commenting on Marshall Aid. The rope is the 'Marshall Plan' and the lifebelt is 'Aid to Europe'.

SOURCE **34**

2 Do Sources 32–34 support or criticise Marshall Aid?
3 Do you think the sources give a fair impression of Marshall Aid? Explain your answer.

Focus Task

How did the USA react to Soviet expansion?

You are an adviser to Stalin. Write a briefing paper on the USA's plans for Europe. Your report should mention:
- President Truman's plans for Europe
- the methods being used by Truman to resist the spread of Communism
- whether you think the USSR should be worried.

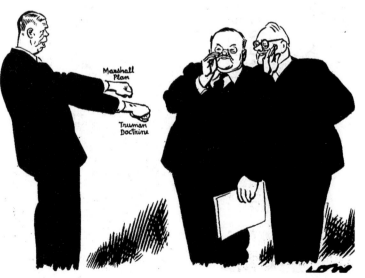

A cartoon by David Low, June 1947. The figure on the left is Marshall. The figure nearer to him is Molotov, the Soviet Foreign Minister. Marshall is asking 'Which hand will you have, Comrade?'

Why did the Soviet Union blockade Berlin?

Despite all the threatening talk of the early years of the Cold War, the two sides had never actually fired on one another. But in 1948 they came dangerously close to war.

SOURCE 35

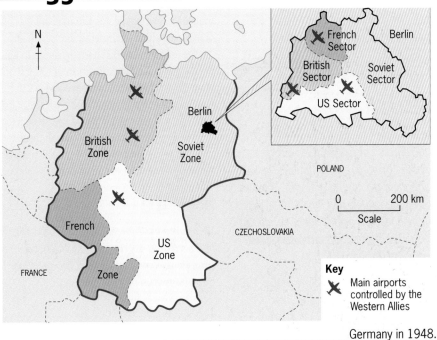

Germany in 1948.

4 Look at the cartoons in Source 36. Do they make the same point?

Germany had become a real headache for the Western Allies. After the destruction of war, their zones were in economic chaos. Stalin feared a recovering Germany and wanted to keep it crippled. But it was clear to the Allies that Germany could not feed its people if it was not allowed to rebuild its industries. Although they themselves were wary of rebuilding Germany too quickly, Britain, France and the USA combined their zones in 1946 to form one zone (which became known in 1949 as West Germany; see page 83). In 1948 they reformed the currency and within months there were signs that Germany was recovering.

SOURCE 36

Two cartoons from 1949. **A** is Soviet and **B** is British. In **A**, the documents on the ground are headed 'Occupation statutes' and 'Bonn constitution'. The caption to **B** is: 'If we don't let him work, who's going to keep him?'

SOURCE 37

On 23 June the Soviet authorities suspended all traffic into Berlin because of alleged technical difficulties . . . They also stopped barge traffic on similar grounds. Shortly before midnight, the Soviet authorities issued orders to . . . disrupt electric power from Soviet power plants to the Western sectors. Shortage of coal was given as a reason for this measure.

US Government report, June 1948.

SOURCE 38

The Berlin air-lift was a considerable achievement but neither side gained anything from the confrontation. The USSR had not gained control of Berlin. The West had no guarantees that land communications would not be cut again. Above all confrontation made both sides even more stubborn.

Historian Jack Watson writing in 1984.

SOURCE 39

The crisis was planned in Washington, behind a smokescreen of anti-Soviet propaganda. In 1948 there was danger of war. The conduct of the Western powers risked bloody incidents. The self-blockade of the Western powers hit the West Berlin population with harshness. The people were freezing and starving. In the Spring of 1949 the USA was forced to yield . . . their war plans had come to nothing, because of the conduct of the USSR.

A Soviet commentary on the crisis, quoted in P Fisher, *The Great Power Conflict*, a textbook published in 1985.

1 Read Source 37. What reasons did the Soviet Union give for cutting off West Berlin?
2 Why do you think the USA did not believe these were genuine reasons?
3 How do Sources 38–40 differ in their interpretation of the blockade?
4 Which do you think is the most useful source for a historian studying the Berlin Blockade?
5 Which source do you think gives the most reliable view of the blockade?

Stalin felt that the USA's handling of western Germany was provocative. He could do nothing about the reorganisation of the western zones, or the new currency, but he felt that he could stamp his authority on Berlin. It was deep in the Soviet zone and was linked to the western zones of Germany by vital roads, railways and canals. In June 1948, Stalin blocked all these supply lines, cutting off the two-million strong population of West Berlin from western help. Stalin believed that this would force the Allies out of Berlin and make Berlin entirely dependent on the USSR.

It was a clever plan. If US tanks did try to ram the road-blocks or railway blocks, Stalin would see it as an act of war. However, the Americans were not prepared to give up. They saw West Berlin as a test case. If they gave in to Stalin on this issue, the western zones of Germany might be next. Truman wanted to show that he was serious about his policy of containment. He wanted Berlin to be a symbol of freedom behind the Iron Curtain.

The only way into Berlin was by air. So in June 1948 the Allies decided to air-lift supplies. As the first planes took off from their bases in West Germany, everyone feared that the Soviets would shoot them down, which would have been an act of war. People waited anxiously as the planes flew over Soviet territory, but no shots were fired. The planes got through and for the next ten months West Berlin was supplied by a constant stream of aeroplanes bringing in everything from food and clothing to oil and building materials, although there were enormous shortages and many Berliners decided to leave the city altogether. By May 1949, however, it was clear that the blockade of Berlin would not make the Western Allies give up Berlin, so Stalin reopened communications.

SOURCE 40

We refused to be forced out of the city of Berlin. We demonstrated to the people of Europe that we would act and act resolutely, when their freedom was threatened. Politically it brought the people of Western Europe closer to us. The Berlin blockade was a move to test our ability and our will to resist.

President Truman, speaking in 1949.

SOURCE 41

Coal being unloaded from a plane at Berlin airport, 1948. For ten months, planes landed every three minutes throughout the day and night.

A divided Germany

As a result of the Berlin Blockade, Germany was firmly divided into two nations. In May 1949, the British, French and American zones became the Federal Republic of Germany (known as West Germany). The Communist eastern zone was formed into the German Democratic Republic (or East Germany) in October 1949.

A powerful symbol

Germany would stay a divided country for 41 years. Throughout that time Berlin would remain a powerful symbol of Cold War tensions – from the American point of view, an oasis of democratic freedom in the middle of Communist repression; from the Soviet point of view, an invasive cancer growing in the workers' paradise of East Germany.

SOURCE **42**

A 1958 Soviet cartoon. A Soviet doctor is injecting the cancer (the 'Occupation regime' of the Western Allies) with a medicine called 'Free City Status for West Berlin'.

A flashpoint

Berlin was more than a symbol, however. It was also a potential flashpoint. As you study the story of the Cold War, you will find that the USA's and the USSR's worries about what might happen in Berlin affected their policies in other areas of the world. You will pick up the story of Berlin again in Chapter 7.

A pattern for the Cold War

Most importantly, the Berlin Blockade set out a pattern for Cold War confrontations. On the one hand, the two superpowers and their allies had shown how suspicious they were of each other; how they would obstruct each other in almost any way they could; how they would bombard each other with propaganda. On the other hand, each had shown that it was not willing to go to war with the other. The Berlin Blockade established a sort of tense balance between the superpowers that was to characterise much of the Cold War period.

Focus Task

It is difficult to give an exact date for when the Cold War actually started. Some might say that it was at Yalta, as Stalin, Churchill and Roosevelt argued over Poland, others that it started in 1948 with the Berlin Blockade. There are other possible starting dates as well between 1945 and 1948.

What do you think? As a class, list all the possible starting dates you can think of. Then choose three to compare. Whatever your choice, support it with evidence from this chapter.

SOURCE 43

Article 3: To achieve the aims of this Treaty, the Parties will keep up their individual and collective capacity to resist armed attack.

Article 5: The Parties agree that an armed attack against one or more of them in Europe or North America shall be considered an attack against them all.

Extracts from the NATO Charter.

SOURCE 44

The Soviet government did everything it could to prevent the world from being split into two military blocks. The Soviet Union issued a special statement analysing the grave consequences affecting the entire international situation that would follow from the establishment of a military alliance of the Western powers. All these warnings failed, however, and the North Atlantic Alliance came into being.

Stalin commenting on the formation of NATO, 1949.

Why was NATO set up?

During the Berlin Blockade, war between the USSR and the USA seemed a real possibility. At the height of the crisis, the Western powers met in Washington and signed an agreement to work together. The new organisation they formed in April 1949 was known as NATO (North Atlantic Treaty Organisation).

SOURCE 45

A cartoon by David Low, 1949, entitled 'Your play, Joe'. Western leaders wait to see how Stalin will react to the formation of NATO.

SOURCE 46

A 1963 Soviet cartoon. The dog's teeth are labelled NATO. He is about to attack the German Democratic Republic (East Germany; see page 83).

SOURCE 47

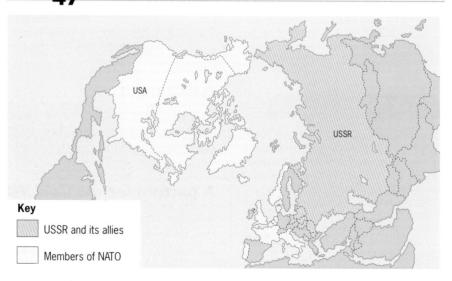

Key

USSR and its allies

Members of NATO

NATO and the Soviet satellites of eastern Europe. With the establishment of NATO, Europe was once again home to two hostile armed camps, just as it had been in 1914.

---

1 What evidence is there in Sources 43–47 to indicate that NATO was a purely defensive alliance?
2 Read Source 44. What 'grave consequences' do you think Stalin had in mind?

Focus Task

Who was more to blame for the Cold War?

Work in small groups. Five people per group would be ideal.
You are going to investigate who was to blame for the Cold War. The possible verdicts you might reach are:

A The USA was most to blame.
B The USSR was most to blame.
C Both sides were equally to blame.
D No one was to blame. The Cold War was inevitable.

This is our suggested way of working.

1 Start by discussing the verdicts together. Is one more popular than another in your group?
2 a) Each member of the group should research how one of the following factors helped to lead to the Cold War:
   ◆ the situation before the Second World War (pages 68–69).
   ◆ the personal relationships between the various leaders (pages 67–77).
   ◆ the conflicting beliefs of the superpowers (pages 75–76).
   ◆ the war damage suffered by the USSR (pages 70 and 75).
   ◆ Stalin's take-over of eastern Europe (pages 74–76).
   ◆ Marshall Aid for Europe (pages 79–80).
   You can start with the page numbers given. You can introduce your own research from other books or the internet if you wish.
   b) Present your evidence to your group and explain which, if any, of the verdicts A–D your evidence most supports.
3 As a group, discuss which of the verdicts now seems most sensible.
4 Write a balanced essay on who was to blame, explaining why each verdict is a possibility but reaching your own conclusion about which is best.

Who won the Cuban Missile Crisis?

Background 1: What was containment?

Although the USA was the world's most powerful nation, in 1950 it seemed to President Truman that events were not going America's way.

- As you have seen in Chapter 4 from 1946 to 1948 most of eastern Europe had fallen under the influence of the USSR.
- In 1949 Communist forces under Mao Zedong defeated the Chinese Nationalist forces and took control of China. This was a bitter blow: the USA had given vast amounts of money and weapons to Mao's opponents and a Communist China was now a serious potential threat to America's business interests in Asia.
- Also in 1949 the Soviet leader Stalin announced that the USSR had developed its own atomic bomb. The USA was no longer the world's only nuclear power.
- In 1950, Communist North Korea invaded the USA's ally, South Korea. After three years of warfare US forces pushed the North Koreans (who were aided by Communist China) back to their original borders but could make no further progress.

These events shocked the USA and led to furious discussion about how it should react. The result was the American policy of containment which meant trying to contain or stop Communism from spreading. In practice the policy had two main features: Allies and Arms.

Focus

The USA was strongly opposed to Communism. It seemed to the American government that Communism might spread all around the world unless it did something to stop it. So from the 1950s to the 1970s, American foreign policy was largely directed to trying to stop the spread of Communism. In the next two chapters you will study two examples of this policy – and judge how well it worked.

Chapter 5 focuses on the Cuban Missile Crisis of 1962 when the USA and USSR went to the very brink of nuclear war over Cuba.

In this chapter you will:
- investigate how the USA reacted to the communist revolution in Cuba
- consider why the Soviet Leader Khrushchev decided to put nuclear missiles on Cuba
- examine how President Kennedy of the USA reacted to this move and why he did what he did
- try to decide whether there was a winner in this crisis.

Coming soon in the Cold War ...

The Cuban Missile Crisis was only one incident in the Cold War (see the map below). This crisis lasted just thirteen days. In Chapter 6 you are going to examine a much more complex example of cold war rivalries: The Vietnam War which lasted nearly twenty years.

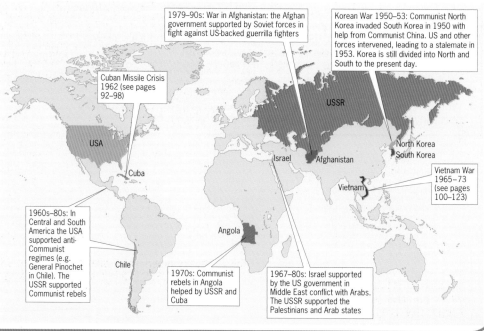

1979–90s: War in Afghanistan: the Afghan government supported by Soviet forces in fight against US-backed guerrilla fighters

Korean War 1950–53: Communist North Korea invaded South Korea in 1950 with help from Communist China. US and other forces intervened, leading to a stalemate in 1953. Korea is still divided into North and South to the present day.

Cuban Missile Crisis 1962 (see pages 92–98)

USSR

USA

North Korea
South Korea

Israel   Afghanistan

Vietnam War 1965–73 (see pages 100–123)

Vietnam

Cuba

1960s–80s: In Central and South America the USA supported anti-Communist regimes (e.g. General Pinochet in Chile). The USSR supported Communist rebels

Chile

Angola

1970s: Communist rebels in Angola helped by USSR and Cuba

1967–80s: Israel supported by the US government in Middle East conflict with Arabs. The USSR supported the Palestinians and Arab states

ALLIES

To contain communism even a nation as powerful as the USA needed allies. US Secretary of State Dulles set up a network of anti-Communist alliances around the world (see Source 1). You have already seen how NATO was set up in 1949 (see page 83). The South-East Asia Treaty Organisation (SEATO) was formed in 1954. The Central Treaty Organisation (CENTO) was formed in 1955. To help keep these allies the USA gave them money and practical support.

The **Soviet Union** responded by establishing its own alliance. It felt very threatened by the American alliances and accused the USA of trying to encircle the Communist world. In 1955, therefore, the Warsaw Treaty Organisation (better known as the Warsaw Pact) was set up between the USSR and all the Communist east European countries except Yugoslavia.

SOURCE **1**

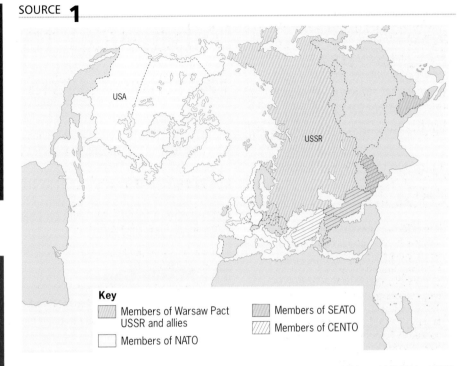

Key

Members of Warsaw Pact USSR and allies

Members of NATO

Members of SEATO

Members of CENTO

Membership of organisations allied to the USA and USSR in 1955.

1   Look at Source 1. Would you agree that the Communist world was encircled?

ARMS

The **USA** also built up a large arsenal of nuclear weapons, and strengthened their conventional forces. They kept soldiers and weapons constantly ready for action. For example, the American Strategic Air Command kept a fleet of 12 B52 bombers armed with nuclear weapons in the air 24 hours a day. They supplied arms and soldiers to friendly allies and sited some of their own nuclear weapons in friendly countries.

The **Soviet Union** responded by building up its own conventional and nuclear forces. Through the 1950s the USA and USSR competed with each other to build bigger, more powerful, quicker and cleverer nuclear weapons. Turn over to find out more about the arms race.

2   Study Source 2. Why do you think the USA based missiles in Europe?

3   What action would you expect a Soviet leader to take in response?

SOURCE **2**

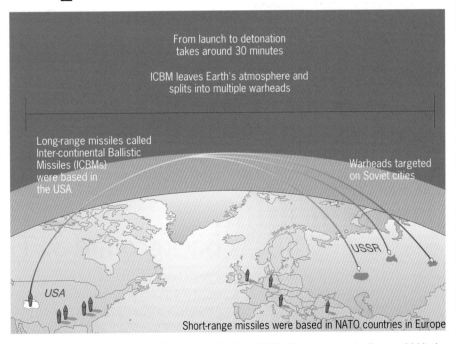

From launch to detonation takes around 30 minutes

ICBM leaves Earth's atmosphere and splits into multiple warheads

Long-range missiles called Inter-continental Ballistic Missiles (ICBMs) were based in the USA

Warheads targeted on Soviet cities

Short-range missiles were based in NATO countries in Europe

The location of American missiles trained on the USSR. Short-range missiles could hit the USSR in minutes. Long-range ones from the USA would take 30 minutes.

Khrushchev, around that period, came to the conclusion that missiles were the weapons of the future, and that warships were getting obsolete, bombers were getting obsolete. That we should concentrate everything on missiles, and as he said somewhere that, 'We are on the point of producing missiles like sausages.'

Oleg Troyanovski, an adviser to
Khrushchev in the 1950s.

Senate Majority Leader Lyndon Johnson could hardly have had a more opportune week to start his Senate Subcommittee investigation of the state of the nation's defences. In Moscow Nikita Khrushchev, in his latest ploy of missile oneupmanship, boasted that the USSR now had assembly-line production of intercontinental ballistic missiles with pinpoint accuracy 'to any part of the globe'.

... Back in the Senate, it was Chief Witness McElroy who dropped the week's bombshell ... he told the Senators that in the early 1960s the USSR will be ahead of the US in operational ICBMs by a substantial margin, perhaps 3 to 1.

McElroy took pains to stress that the ICBM gap will be temporary, and that while it lasts it will not mean a real defense gap. The US, he pointed out, has and will have a 'diversified' arsenal, with various means of delivering nuclear retaliatory power including bombers and submarines.

Extract from an article in the American
magazine *Time*, 9 February 1959.

Activity

Create your own set of definitions for the following terms:
• Arms Race
• ICBM
• Missile Gap
• Polaris.
Aim to keep your definitions as short as possible.

Background 2: The nuclear arms race

You have just seen on page 87 how the USA and USSR built up stockpiles of nuclear bombs in the early 1950s. This was serious enough when these weapons were to be dropped by bomber planes, but missiles were far more deadly. The Soviets took the lead in missile technology in the 1950s, building on the achievements of their successful space programme. The new Soviet leader Nikita Khrushchev was a strong supporter of the space and missile programmes. He convinced his colleagues in the Communist Party that nuclear missiles were the key to the USSR's future security. Engineers from all over the Soviet Union were brought together in a remote location in Kazakhstan to build the top-secret rocket base of Baykonyr. On 15 May 1957, they began testing the world's first Intercontinental Ballistic Missile (ICBM). This technology allowed the Soviets to launch a missile into space and then bring it down on a specific target in the USA. At that time Khrushchev was a relatively new arrival as leader of the USSR and there were still some powerful figures in the Communist Party who were unsure about him. The successes of the space and missile programmes were important in helping Khrushchev to silence his critics.

The Missile Gap

These technological advances by the USSR rocked public opinion in the USA. The US public was alarmed by the fear that the USSR had many more nuclear missiles than the USA. The idea of the 'Missile Gap' was widely reported in the American media (see Source 4) during the 1950s.

With hindsight, we now know that the Missile Gap was a myth. Of course, Khrushchev was not going to admit this because he would look foolish and it would help his critics inside the USSR. At the same time, the American military commanders were happy to go along with the claims that there was a missile gap because it helped them to get funding from the government to pay for the development of new weapon systems. President Eisenhower was concerned about the cost of these new systems but he was in a difficult position too. By the early 1960s Eisenhower knew the Missile Gap was a myth because he had an important source in the Soviet military who had defected to the CIA. However, because this contact was still in the USSR, Eisenhower could not admit he knew how many missiles the Soviets actually had without revealing his source. When John F Kennedy became President in January 1961 he faced the same problem.

Meanwhile, myth or not, the USA had been forging ahead with its own missile production programme to 'narrow the Missile Gap'.

• By 1959 the Americans developed their own ICBM systems. Atlas and Minuteman missiles would be able to reach the USSR as quickly and as accurately as Soviet missiles could reach the USA. They soon had far more of these long-range missiles than the USSR.

• A further American technological development was the introduction of Polaris missiles. These could be fired from submarines which were virtually undetectable.

• In addition, the USA had medium-range missiles stationed in Europe and in Turkey which could reach the USSR in just a few minutes.

By the early 1960s the USA was pulling ahead in the arms race.

Background 3: The fear factor

What did this arms race mean for the average Soviet or American citizen? Naturally, both feared the spectre of nuclear war. Information was very tightly controlled in the USSR so it is hard to find evidence of what the average Soviet citizen knew about the threat of nuclear war or what they felt. However there are plenty of sources which give insights of what American people might have felt.

Throughout the 1950s Americans had been warned of the terrible dangers of nuclear attack. Bert the Turtle had warned children to 'Duck and Cover'. Americans young and old had also been through drills like Source 7.

SOURCE 5

The War of The Worlds was one of the most successful films in 1953. It painted a picture of a world where America and all it stood for were under attack from Martian invaders and even nuclear weapons could not keep the invaders at bay.

SOURCE 6

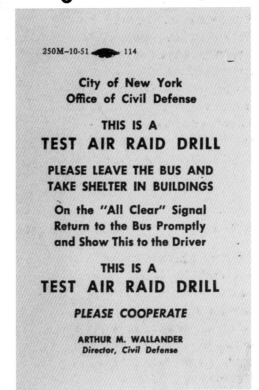

A notice of an air raid drill in New York, November 1951.

SOURCE 7

A

There was a turtle by the name of Bert
And Bert the Turtle was very alert
When danger threatened him he never got hurt
He knew just what to do.
He'd Duck and Cover, Duck and Cover
He did what we all must learn to do
Me and you and you and you –
Duck and Cover.

A The opening song from the film.

B Bert The Turtle.

C Children following Bert's advice to Duck and Cover.

Extracts from *Duck And Cover*, a very well-known and widely broadcast information programme designed to warn children about what to do in a possible nuclear attack.

Activity

1 Here is a fearometer:
   Use Sources 5–7 and your own internet research to decide where on this fearometer you would place the people of the USA in the 1950s.
   For your internet research you could use search words like 'Duck and Cover', 'Reds under the bed' and 'Hollywood B-Movies'.

2 Historians find sources like these very useful in studying how people felt in past situations. However, they often find it difficult to decide whether the sources reflect the fear that people had or whether the sources actually created those fears in the first place. What do you think? Discuss this question in your class.

Very afraid

Relaxed

SOURCE **8**

A American TV reporter Walter Cronkite

We considered it part of the United States practically, just a wonderful little country over there that was of no danger to anybody, as a matter of fact it was a rather important economic asset to the United States.

B President Kennedy speaking in 1963

I believe there is no country in the world . . . whose economic colonisation, humiliation and exploitation were worse than in Cuba, partly as a consequence of US policy during the Batista regime. I believe that, without being aware of it, we conceived and created the Castro movement, starting from scratch.

American attitudes towards Cuba during Batista's rule.

---

1 Does Source 9 support the view that Castro had support in Cuba? Explain your answer.
2 Apart from the caption in Russian, how else can you tell that the cartoon in Source 10 is a Soviet cartoon?

SOURCE **10**

A 1960 Soviet cartoon. The notice held by the US Secretary of State says to Castro in Cuba: 'I forbid you to make friends with the Soviet Union.'

How did the USA react to the Cuban Revolution?

The Batista regime

Cuba is a large island just 160 km from Florida in the southern USA. It had long been an American ally. Americans owned most of the businesses on the island and they had a huge naval base there (see Source 19 on page 93). The Americans also provided the Cuban ruler, General Batista, with economic and military support. Batista was a dictator. His rule was corrupt and unpopular. The Americans supported Batista primarily because he was just as opposed to Communism as they were.

Enter Fidel Castro

There was plenty of opposition to Batista in Cuba itself. In 1959, after a three-year guerrilla campaign, Fidel Castro overthrew Batista. Castro was charming, clever and also ruthless. He quickly killed, arrested or exiled many political opponents. Castro was also a clever propagandist. He was very charismatic, and he had a vision for a better Cuba which won over the majority of Cubans.

The USA responds

The USA was taken by surprise at first and decided to recognise Castro as the new leader of Cuba. However, within a short period of time relations between the two countries grew worse. There were two important reasons:

- There were thousands of Cuban exiles in the USA who had fled from Castro's rule. They formed powerful pressure groups demanding action against Castro.

- Castro took over some American owned businesses in Cuba, particularly the agricultural businesses. He took their land and distributed it to his supporters among Cuba's peasant farmer population.

SOURCE **9**

A rally in the Cuban capital of Havana celebrating the successful Cuban Revolution of January 1959.

SOURCE 11

By October 1962 the historic friendship between Cuba and the USA was gone. Behind this change was the story of the betrayal of the Cuban people. It began with Fidel Castro triumphantly entering Havana in 1959. Castro promised democracy and freedom and for a time it appeared to most Cubans that they were liberated. But it soon became apparent that Castro had sold out to Premier Khrushchev of the Communists. By 1961 Castro's policy had led to a formal break between the United States and Cuba.

Commentary from an American TV programme made in 1962. This section was read out over film footage of the rally shown in Source 9.

SOURCE 12

I think he [Khrushchev] did it [was so aggressive] because of the Bay of Pigs. He thought that anyone who was so young and inexperienced as to get into that mess could be beaten; and anyone who got into it and didn't see it through had no guts. So he just beat the hell out of me.

If he thinks I'm inexperienced and have no guts, until we remove those ideas we won't get anywhere with him.

Kennedy speaking after a meeting with Khrushchev in 1961 in which Khrushchev had been very aggressive towards Kennedy.

As early as June 1960, US President Eisenhower authorised the US Central Intelligence Agency (CIA) to investigate ways of overthrowing Castro. The CIA provided support and funds to Cuban exiles. They also investigated ways to disrupt the Cuban economy, such as damaging sugar plantations. American companies working in Cuba refused to co-operate with any Cuban businesses which used oil or other materials which had been imported from the USSR. The American media also broadcast a relentless stream of criticism of Castro and his regime (see Source 11 for example).

Castro responded to US hostility with a mixed approach. He assured Americans living in Cuba that they were safe and he allowed the USA to keep its naval base. He said he simply wanted to run Cuba without interference. However, by the summer of 1960 he had allied Cuba with the Soviet Union. Soviet leader Khrushchev signed a trade agreement giving Cuba $100 million in economic aid. Castro also began receiving arms from the Soviet Union and American spies knew this.

To invade or not to invade, that is the question!

In January 1961 the USA's new President, John F Kennedy, broke off diplomatic relations with Cuba. Castro thought that the USA was preparing to invade his country. The Americans did not invade directly, but Kennedy was no longer prepared to tolerate a Soviet satellite in the USA's 'sphere of influence'. The plans to overthrow Castro which were begun under Eisenhower began to take shape.

The Bay of Pigs

Rather than a direct invasion, President Kennedy supplied arms, equipment and transport for 1,400 anti-Castro exiles to invade Cuba and overthrow him. In April 1961 the exiles landed at the Bay of Pigs. They were met by 20,000 Cuban troops, armed with tanks and modern weapons. The invasion failed disastrously. Castro captured or killed them all within days.

The impact of the invasion

The half-hearted invasion suggested to Cuba and the Soviet Union that, despite its opposition to Communism in Cuba, the USA was unwilling to get directly involved in Cuba. The Soviet leader Khrushchev was scornful of Kennedy's pathetic attempt to oust Communism from Cuba.

Historians too argue that the Bay of Pigs fiasco further strengthened Castro's position in Cuba. It suggested to the USSR that Kennedy was weak. It also made Castro and Khrushchev very suspicious of US policy.

Focus Task

How did the USA respond to the Cuban revolution?

1 The President has asked his advisers how he should deal with Cuba. Here are some suggestions they might have made:

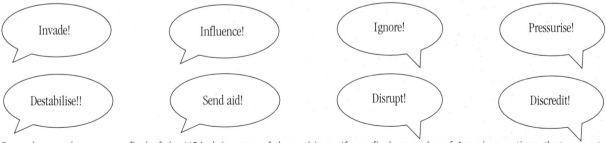

Invade!   Influence!   Ignore!   Pressurise!

Destabilise!!   Send aid!   Disrupt!   Discredit!

Record examples you can find of the USA doing any of these things. If you find examples of American actions that are not covered by these words record them too.

2 Place these actions on a 'containment continuum' like this:

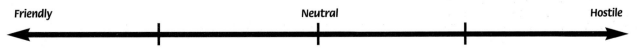

Friendly   Neutral   Hostile

The Missile Crisis, 1962

After the Bay of Pigs fiasco, Soviet arms flooded into Cuba. In May 1962 the Soviet Union announced publicly for the first time that it was supplying Cuba with arms. By July 1962 Cuba had the best-equipped army in Latin America. By September it had thousands of Soviet missiles, plus patrol boats, tanks, radar vans, missile erectors, jet bombers, jet fighters and 5,000 Soviet technicians to help to maintain the weapons.

The Americans watched all this with great alarm. They seemed ready to tolerate conventional arms being supplied to Cuba, but the big question was whether the Soviet Union would dare to put nuclear missiles on Cuba. In September Kennedy's own Intelligence Department said that it did not believe the USSR would send nuclear weapons to Cuba. The USSR had not taken this step with any of its satellite states before and the US Intelligence Department believed that the USSR would consider it too risky to do it in Cuba. On 11 September, Kennedy warned the USSR that he would prevent 'by whatever means might be necessary' Cuba's becoming an offensive military base – by which, everyone knew, he meant a nuclear missile base. The same day the USSR assured the USA that it had no need to put nuclear missiles on Cuba and no intention of doing so.

The October crisis

On Sunday, 14 October 1962, an American spy plane flew over Cuba. It took amazingly detailed photographs of missile sites in Cuba. To the military experts two things were obvious – that these were nuclear missile sites, and that they were being built by the USSR.

More photo reconnaissance followed over the next two days. This confirmed that some sites were nearly finished but others were still being built. Some were already supplied with missiles, others were awaiting them. The experts said that the most developed of the sites could be ready to launch missiles in just seven days. American spy planes also reported that twenty Soviet ships were currently on the way to Cuba carrying missiles.

SOURCE 13

[Estimates were that the] missiles had an atomic warhead [power] of about half the current missile capacity of the entire Soviet Union. The photographs indicated that missiles were directed at certain American cities. The estimate was that within a few minutes of their being fired 80 million Americans would be dead.

President Kennedy's brother, Robert Kennedy, describing events on Thursday 18 October in the book he wrote about the crisis, *13 Days.*

SOURCE 14

Photograph of Cuban missile sites taken in October 1962. The labelling was added by the Americans.

Why did Khrushchev put nuclear missiles on Cuba?

The USSR had supplied many of its allies with conventional weapons but this was the first time that any Soviet leader had placed nuclear weapons outside Soviet soil. Why did Khrushchev take such an unusual step? There are probably several reasons.

- One reason was the Missile Gap. Khrushchev was extremely aware of the fact that the USA had far more long-range nuclear missiles than the USSR. The USA also had missiles based in Western Europe and Turkey. Putting nuclear missiles in Cuba would help Khrushchev to restore the nuclear balance. Medium-range missiles could reach most of the USA from Cuba (see Source 19). The USSR had many more medium-range missiles than the USA. Medium-range missiles were much less difficult and expensive to develop.

1 Compare Source 2 on page 87 with Source 19. Describe how the Soviet missiles on Cuba changed the Cold War balance of power.

SOURCE 15

From the territory of the Soviet Union, the medium-range missiles couldn't possibly reach the territory of the USA, but deployed on Cuba they would become strategic nuclear weapons. That meant in practical terms we had a chance to narrow the differences between our forces.

General Anatoly Gribkov, commander, Soviet forces, Cuba.

SOURCE 16

I immediately appreciated the strategic importance of the presence of those missiles in Cuba. By that time, the Americans had already transported similar missiles to Turkey. I thought: If we expected the Soviets to fight on our behalf, to run risks for us, and even involve themselves in a war for our sake, it would be immoral and cowardly on our part to refuse to accept the presence of those missiles here.

Fidel Castro.

SOURCE 17

In addition to protecting Cuba, our missiles would have equalized what the West likes to call the 'balance of power'. The Americans had surrounded our country with military bases and threatened us with nuclear weapons, and now they would learn just what it feels like to have enemy missiles pointing at you …

Khrushchev writing in his memoirs in 1971.

SOURCE 18

We did that purposely to make Castro pay more attention to that than to causing trouble in Latin and Central America. But the Cubans and the Russians, they told us later, believed that the United States really did intend to attack Cuba and therefore Castro kept saying, 'I need some help'.

General Smith, a high ranking US military official, commenting on the practice invasion of Cuba carried out in the spring of 1962.

SOURCE 19

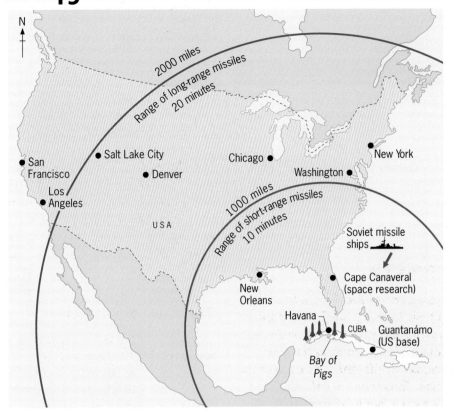

Map showing the location of Cuba and the range of the Cuban missiles.

- Khrushchev probably hoped to strengthen his own position in the USSR by forcing Kennedy to allow the missiles or at least get Kennedy to give some concessions. Khrushchev had already had some success against Kennedy in 1961 (see Source 13). Also, the superiority of the USA in nuclear missiles undermined Khrushchev's credibility inside the USSR. His critics pointed out that he was the one who had urged the USSR to rely on nuclear missiles.

- Khrushchev was also very anxious to defend Cuba. It was the only Communist state in the Western hemisphere, and it had willingly become Communist rather than having become Communist as a result of invasion by the Red Army. In addition, Cuba was in 'Uncle Sam's Backyard'. As Castro himself put it: 'The imperialists cannot forgive that we have made a socialist revolution under the nose of the United States'. Just by existing, Castro's Cuba was excellent propaganda for the USSR. It also made an ideal base to support Communist movements in South America. The Americans were so concerned about Cuba being used in this way that in the spring of 1962 they carried out a practice invasion of Cuba involving 40,000 US Marines. They thought this would deter Castro from trying to support Communists in South America. In fact the exercise had a much more dramatic effect (see Source 18).

Focus Task

Why did Khruschev put nuclear missiles on Cuba?

The text on pages 92–93 suggests a number of reasons why Khruschev put the missiles on Cuba.
1 Summarise each of the motives in a headline or phrase and write each on a separate card.
2 Add to the card any evidence from the text or Sources 13–18 to support it.
3 Some of these motives are connected. Draw lines between the cards to show how they are connected.
4 Now put your motives in rank order according to how important you think it was to Khruschev – the most important motive should be rated 1. You can reject any motives that you think are not supported by the evidence.
5 Write a paragraph of explanation for your top motive and for any motive that you have rejected.

How did President Kennedy deal with the crisis?

On Tuesday 16 October, President Kennedy was informed of the discovery. He formed a special team of advisers called Ex Comm. They came up with several choices.

Activity

Work in groups. You are advisers to the President. You have to reduce the five options to just two for the President to choose between.

When you have made your decision explain why you have rejected the three you have.

Option 1 Do nothing?

For:
The Americans still had a vastly greater nuclear power than the Soviet Union. The USA could still destroy the Soviet Union, so – the argument went – the USSR would never use these missiles. The biggest danger to world peace would be to overreact to this discovery.

Against:
The USSR had lied about Cuban missiles. Kennedy had already issued his solemn warning to the USSR. To do nothing would be another sign of weakness.

Option 2 Surgical air attack?

An immediate selected air attack to destroy the nuclear bases themselves.

For:
It would destroy the missiles before they were ready to use.

Against:
1 Destruction of all sites could not be guaranteed. Even one left undamaged could launch a counter-attack against the USA.
2 The attack would inevitably kill Soviet soldiers. The Soviet Union might retaliate at once.
3 To attack without advance warning was seen as immoral.

Option 3 Invasion?

All-out invasion of Cuba by air and sea.

For:
An invasion would not only get rid of the missiles but Castro as well. The American forces were already trained and available to do it.

Against:
It would almost certainly guarantee an equivalent Soviet response, either to protect Cuba, or within the Soviet sphere of influence – for example, a take-over of Berlin.

Option 4 Diplomatic pressures?

To get the United Nations or other body to intervene and negotiate.

For:
It would avoid conflict.

Against:
If the USA was forced to back down, it would be a sign of weakness.

Option 5 Blockade?

A ban on the Soviet Union bringing in any further military supplies to Cuba, enforced by the US navy who would stop and search Soviet ships. And a call for the Soviet Union to withdraw what was already there.

For:
It would show that the USA was serious, but it would not be a direct act of war. It would put the burden on Khrushchev to decide what to do next. The USA had a strong navy and could still take the other options if this one did not work.

Against:
It would not solve the main problem – the missiles were already on Cuba. They could be used within one week. The Soviet Union might retaliate by blockading Berlin as it had done in 1948.

What happened next?

President Kennedy is informed of the missile build-up. Ex Comm formed.

Kennedy decides on a blockade of Cuba.

Kennedy announces the blockade and calls on the Soviet Union to withdraw its missiles. 'I call on Chairman Khrushchev to halt and eliminate this reckless and provocative threat to world peace . . . He has the opportunity now to move the world back from the abyss of destruction . . . withdrawing these weapons from Cuba.'

SOURCE 20

Good Evening, My Fellow Citizens:

This government, as promised, has maintained the closest surveillance of the Soviet military build-up on the island of Cuba. Within the past week, unmistakable evidence has established the fact that a series of offensive missile sites is now in preparation on that imprisoned island. The purpose of these bases can be none other than to provide a nuclear strike capability against the Western Hemisphere. . . .

Acting, therefore, in the defence of our own security and of the entire Western Hemisphere, and under the authority entrusted to me by the Constitution as endorsed by the resolution of the Congress, I have directed that the following initial steps be taken immediately:

First: To halt this offensive build-up, a strict quarantine on all offensive military equipment under shipment to Cuba . . . Second: I have directed the continued and increased close surveillance of Cuba and its military build-up. . . . I have directed the Armed Forces to prepare for any eventualities . . . Third: It shall be the policy of this nation to regard any nuclear missile launched from Cuba against any nation in the Western Hemisphere as an attack on the United States, requiring a full retaliatory response upon the Soviet Union.

Extract from President Kennedy's TV broadcast to the American people on 22 October 1962.

Kennedy receives a letter from Khrushchev saying that Soviet ships will not observe the blockade. Khrushchev does not admit the presence of nuclear missiles on Cuba.

SOURCE 21

WHY CUBA HAS TOUCHED AMERICA ON THE RAW
SUDDENLY ON THEIR DOORSTEP, A COMMUNIST THREAT WHERE THEY SAW IDEALISM . . .
Cuba exerts a powerful tug at American nerves and emotions. Astounding as it may be to British minds tonight, Americans regard it as a natural, desirable thing to have a showdown with Castro.

I have not met a single American who was not itching to 'get it over with' – to attack Cuba and demolish the 'commie' regime and restore a republic friendly to the United States . . . You might think it ridiculous that little Cuba should present such a threat to so huge and strong a nation as the United States. But it is not ridiculous to Americans. Conditioned for a very long time to the idea that the Soviets want world conquest, they see the threat of these missile bases on nearby Cuban soil.

And they see Russia enjoying the tactical advantage and contemplating attack – with Cuban rockets as the immediate weapon to fall on their heads. They read that other clever electronic Russian installations in Cuba can detect and even sabotage all American launching operations from Cape Canaveral.

Almost any American you meet tonight will say that Castro has become a stain on US honour and should be removed by military means.

This may seem very odd but it is true.

Extract from an article in the *Daily Mirror*, 23 October 1962.

Timeline (left margin):

Tue 16 October

Sat 20 October

Mon 22 October

Tue 23 October

Questions (left column):

1 What words and phrases in Source 20 reveal how serious Kennedy believed the situation was in October 1962?

2 Kennedy was renowned as a skilled communicator. How does he convince his audience that he is in the right?

3 President Kennedy knows the risks of nuclear war but he also knows the strength of public opinion. Before you turn to the next page work in pairs to discuss what you think Kennedy should do next.

Wed 24 October

The blockade begins. The first missile-carrying ships, accompanied by a Soviet submarine, approach the 500-mile (800 km) blockade zone. Then suddenly, at 10.32 a.m., the twenty Soviet ships which are closest to the zone stop or turn around.

SOURCE **22**

"INTOLERABLE HAVING YOUR ROCKETS ON MY DOORSTEP!"

A cartoon by Vicky (Victor Weisz) from the *London Evening Standard*, 24 October 1962.

British Cartoon Archive, University of Kent © Solo Syndication/Associated Newspapers Ltd.

1 Source 22 is a British cartoon. Pretend you did not know this. Explain why it is unlikely to be an American or Soviet cartoon.
2 What is its attitude to the two sides in the crisis?
3 Kennedy described Wednesday 24 October and Saturday 27 October as the darkest days of the crisis. Use the information on this page to explain why.

Thu 25 October

Despite the Soviet ships turning around, intensive aerial photography reveals that work on the missile bases in Cuba is proceeding rapidly.

Fri 26 October

Kennedy receives a long personal letter from Khrushchev. The letter claims that the missiles on Cuba are purely defensive, but goes on: 'If assurances were given that the USA would not participate in an attack on Cuba and the blockade was lifted, then the question of the removal or the destruction of the missile sites would be an entirely different question.' This is the first time Khrushchev has admitted the presence of the missiles.

Sat 27 October a.m.

Khrushchev sends a second letter – revising his proposals – saying that the condition for removing the missiles from Cuba is that the USA withdraw its missiles from Turkey.
 An American U-2 plane is shot down over Cuba. The pilot is killed. The President is advised to launch an immediate reprisal attack on Cuba.

Sat 27 October p.m.

Kennedy decides to delay an attack. He also decides to ignore the second Khrushchev letter, but accepts the terms suggested by Khrushchev on 26 October. He says that if the Soviet Union does not withdraw, an attack will follow.

SOURCE **23**

It was a beautiful autumn evening, the height of the crisis, and I went up to the open air to smell it, because I thought it was the last Saturday I would ever see.

Robert McNamara talking about the evening of 27 October 1962. McNamara was one of Kennedy's closest advisers during the Cuban Crisis.

Sun 28 October

Khrushchev replies to Kennedy: 'In order to eliminate as rapidly as possible the conflict which endangers the cause of peace . . . the Soviet Government has given a new order to dismantle the arms which you described as offensive and to crate and return them to the Soviet Union.'

4 Study Source 24. What is the single most important announcement made by Kennedy in this source? Would you agree that he tries to hide it in amongst other statements?

5 On which day in the crisis between 16 and 28 October do you think Source 26 was published? Give your reasons – based on the detail in the source and what you know about the crisis. Your teacher can tell you the correct date.

SOURCE 24

I have been informed by Chairman Khrushchev that all of the Soviet nuclear bombers in Cuba will be withdrawn within 30 days. Inasmuch as this goes a long way towards reducing the danger which faced this hemisphere four weeks ago, I have this afternoon instructed the Secretary of Defence to lift our naval quarantine. We will not abandon the political, economic and other efforts of this hemisphere to halt subversion from Cuba. It is our purpose and hope that the Cuban people shall someday be truly free. But these policies are very different from any intent to launch an invasion of Cuba.

Kennedy announces the end of the Cuban Crisis.

SOURCE 25

Much of the evidence tends to support the view that, despite the many unpredictable elements in the decision making process, in crucial instances the leaders on both sides chose courses of action which were both non-provocative and allowed room for retreat from exposed positions . . .

Richard Crockatt, Senior Lecturer in American History at the University of East Anglia, writing in 2000.

SOURCE 26

A cartoon from the *Daily Mail*.

Focus Task

Why did Kennedy act as he did in the Cuban crisis?

Now that you know what Kennedy did through each stage of the crisis you are going to use the sources to explain *why* he acted as he did. Here are four important decisions he made:

◆ April 1961: rather than a full scale invasion he sent a poorly equipped mercenary army to invade Cuba.
◆ 20 October 1962: he ordered a blockade to prevent Soviet missiles arriving in Cuba.
◆ 27 October 1962: he delayed an air attack on Cuba.
◆ 28 October 1962: he trusted Khrushchev's word.

1 Choose one decision and explain why you think Kennedy did this – was he escalating the conflict or de-escalating it. You will need to consider:
   ◆ what else he could have done
   ◆ whether he chose the more risky option; or the less risky option?

2 Compare your ideas with others who have considered a different decision then discuss whether you agree with the historian in Source 25.

Making connections – a challenge!

3 Remember what you found out about the policy of Appeasement in 1938. How would this lesson from history help someone making decisions in the case of the Cuban Missile Crisis? President Kennedy was very interested in this.

   When Kennedy was a university student in 1941 he wrote a book called *Why England Slept*. This was about Appeasement in the 1930s, particularly the Munich Crisis of 1938. He researched the issues carefully and he was helped by the fact that his father had been the US Ambassador in Britain at the time! Kennedy argued that Britain was forced to make a deal with Hitler in 1938 because it was too weak to stand up to Germany. As President of the USA he was determined that he would never be forced to appease an enemy the way Chamberlain had to in 1938 (see Chapter 3, pages 63–65).

   Now that you know what Kennedy did, do you think he put these ideas into action in 1962 or was he a bit more pragmatic and flexible? For each decision you studied, which influence seems to be stronger?

Focus Task

Who won the Cuban Missile Crisis?

Here are three contestants, Kennedy, Castro and Khrushchev, and a podium. Who are you going to put in each position and why? Read the information on these two pages then make your decision. Write a paragraph to explain it. Make sure you include evidence from the sources and text in this chapter in your explanation. You should refer to:

◆ the information and sources on pages 98–99
◆ your work on the Cuban Revolution
◆ your work on the US reaction to the Cuban Revolution
◆ your work on Khrushchev's aims
◆ your work on Kennedy's actions.

Above all, think about which leader was closest to achieving his original aims.

Who won?

SOURCE 27

[In 1961] we increased our military aid to Cuba. We were sure the Americans would never agree to the existence of Castro's Cuba. They feared, and we hoped, that a Socialist Cuba might become a magnet that would attract other Latin American countries to socialism. We had to find an effective deterrent to American interference in the Caribbean.

The Caribbean Crisis was a triumph of Soviet foreign policy and a personal triumph in my own career. Today Cuba exists as an independent socialist country right in front of America. Cuba's very existence is good propaganda.

We behaved with dignity and forced the United States to demobilise and to recognise Cuba.

Khrushchev was forced from power in 1964. This extract comes from his memoirs written in 1971.

1 Source 27 is a source written by Khrushchev praising Khrushchev! What words and phrases make you doubtful about its value as a source?
2 Is there anything in Source 24 (on the previous page) which backs up Khrushchev's views in Source 27?
3 Is there anything in your own knowledge which supports Source 27?

SOURCE 28

Even after it was all over [the President] made no statement attempting to take credit for himself or for his administration for what had occurred. He instructed all [his staff] that no interview should be given, no statement made, which would claim any kind of victory. He respected Khrushchev for properly determining what was in his own country's interests and in the interests of mankind. If it was a triumph, it was a triumph for the next generation and not for any particular government or people.

Written by Robert Kennedy in *13 Days*.

SOURCE 29

President Kennedy will be remembered as the President who helped to bring the thaw in the Cold War. This was always his aim but only after Cuba did he really act. That crisis left its mark on him; he recognised how frightening were the consequences of misunderstandings between East and West.

President Kennedy was shot dead by a gunman in Texas in November 1963. This is from his obituary in the British newspaper, the *Guardian*.

SOURCE 30

The whole world was under the impression that Khrushchev had lost because he'd given in to the pressure of a strong president. That he'd taken everything out of Cuba, but got nothing in return. No one knew about the agreement regarding the missiles in Turkey. If you ask who won or who lost, I'd say neither Kennedy nor Khrushchev.

Anatoly Dobrynin, Soviet ambassador to the United States.

SOURCE 31

There is no question that if it hadn't been solved, and we had invaded Cuba, we would have been in a nuclear war and the number of people who would have been killed around the world in that nuclear war would have been absolutely disastrous. That was the biggest crisis of the 20th century, and the fact that Kennedy solved it with Khrushchev is absolutely important, because then we were moving into a totally different world.

Pierre Salinger, press secretary to President Kennedy.

The outcomes …

For the USA

- Kennedy came out of the crisis with a greatly improved reputation in his own country and throughout the West. He had stood up to Khrushchev and had made him back down.
- Kennedy had also successfully stood up to the hardliners in his own government. Critics of containment had wanted the USA to invade Cuba – to turn back Communism. However, the Cuban Missile Crisis highlighted the weakness of their case. Such intervention was not worth the high risk.
- Kennedy did have to remove the missiles from Turkey. This was slightly awkward for him as technically the decision to remove them was a decision for NATO. His NATO allies were unhappy that Kennedy had traded them during the Cuban Missile Crisis but clearly this was much better than a nuclear war.
- Kennedy also had to accept that Castro's Cuba would remain a Communist state in America's backyard. The USA still has trade and other economic restrictions in place against Cuba today.

For the USSR

- In public Khrushchev was able to highlight his role as a responsible peacemaker, willing to make the first move towards compromise.
- There was no question that keeping Cuba safe from American action was a major achievement for the Soviets. Cuba was a valuable ally and proved a useful base to support Communists in South America.
- Khrushchev did also get the USA to withdraw its nuclear missiles from Turkey. However, Khrushchev had to agree that this withdrawal was to be kept secret so he was unable to use it for propaganda purposes.
- The crisis also exposed the USA to criticism amongst some of its allies. Newspaper articles in Britain, for example, felt that the USA was unreasonable to have missiles in Turkey and then object to Soviet missiles in Cuba.
- On the other hand, there was no denying the fact that Khrushchev had been forced to back down and remove the missiles. The Soviet military was particularly upset at the terms of the withdrawal. They were forced to put the missiles on the decks of their ships so the Americans could count them. They felt this was a humiliation.
- Khrushchev's actions in Cuba made no impact on the underlying problem of the Missile Gap. The USSR went on to develop its stockpile of ICBMs at a huge financial cost, but it never caught up with the USA.
- In 1964 Khrushchev himself was forced from power by his enemies inside the USSR. Many commentators believe that the Cuban Missile Crisis contributed to this.

For the Cold War

- Historians agree that the Cuban Missile Crisis helped to thaw Cold War relations between the USA and the USSR. Both leaders had seen how their game of brinkmanship had nearly ended in nuclear war. Now they were more prepared to take steps to reduce the risk of nuclear war. A permanent 'hot line' phone link direct from the White House to the Kremlin was set up. The following year, in 1963, they signed a Nuclear Test Ban Treaty. It did not stop the development of weapons, but it limited tests and was an important step forward.
- Although it was clear the USSR could not match US nuclear technology or numbers of weapons, it was also clear that this was not necessary. The Soviet nuclear arsenal was enough of a threat to make the USA respect the USSR. It is noticeable that for the rest of the Cold War the Superpowers avoided direct confrontation and fought through their allies where possible (see Source 30).

For Castro's Cuba

- Castro was very upset by the deal which Khrushchev made with America but he had little choice. He needed the support of the USSR.
- Cuba stayed Communist and highly armed. The nuclear missiles were removed but Cuba remained an important base for Communist supporters in South America. Cuban forces also intervened to help the Communist side in a civil war in Angola (in South-West Africa) in the 1970s.
- Castro also kept control of the American companies and other economic resources he nationalised during his revolution. This remains a source of dispute between Cuba and the USA today but Castro has never backed down.

6 Why did the USA fail in Vietnam?

The origins of the Vietnam War

Focus

Although many Americans regarded the Cuban Missile Crisis as a victory for the USA, it did not reduce their fear of Communism and it did not lessen their enthusiasm to prevent the spread of Communism around the world. In this chapter you are going to look at how this policy dragged America into a war which still scars the country today. You will:

◆ investigate why the USA became increasingly involved in Vietnam
◆ examine the different methods and tactics used by the USA and its allies and the Communists
◆ decide which side's tactics were the most effective
◆ investigate why the USA eventually pulled out of Vietnam.

Activity

1 Sources 1A and 1B both show US troops in Vietnam in 1965 and 1968. Work in pairs and make a list of the differences between the two images.
2 In 1965 the USA was the world's most powerful country and its forces were facing an underground army helped by North Vietnam, a small and poor country. In pairs or small groups, suggest reasons why the US forces had not succeeded in defeating their enemies after three years. Keep a list of your ideas and see if they turn out to be right as you work through the chapter.

SOURCE 2

A poor feudal nation had beaten a great colonial power . . . It meant a lot; not just to us but to people all over the world.

Viet Minh commander Vo Nguyen Giap commenting on the victory over France in 1954.

SOURCE 1A

US Marines land at da Nang in Vietnam 1965. These were the first official US combat troops in Vietnam, although US 'advisers' had been there for some years before.

SOURCE 1B

US troops in action in January 1968.

Fighting the Japanese

Vietnam had a long history of fighting outsiders.

Before the Second World War Vietnam (or Indochina as it was called then) was ruled by France. During the war the region was conquered by the Japanese. They ruled the area brutally and treated the Vietnamese people savagely. As a result, a strong anti-Japanese resistance movement (the Viet Minh) emerged under the leadership of Communist Ho Chi Minh. Ho was a remarkable individual. He had lived in the USA, Britain and France. In the 1920s he had studied Communism in the USSR. In 1930 he had founded the Indochinese Communist Party. He inspired the Vietnamese people to fight for an independent Vietnam. When the Second World War ended, the Viet Minh controlled the north of the country and were determined to take control of the whole country. The Viet Minh entered the city of Hanoi in 1945 and declared Vietnamese independence.

Fighting the French

The French had other ideas. In 1945 they came back wanting to rule Vietnam again but Ho was not prepared to let this happen. Another nine years of war followed between the Viet Minh and the French. Ho was supported by China, which became a Communist state in 1949 under Mao Zedong. The Americans saw the Viet Minh as the puppets of Mao and the Chinese Communists so they helped the French by pouring $500 million a year into the French war effort. Despite this the French were unable to hold on to the country and pulled out of Vietnam in 1954. A peace conference was held in Geneva and the country was divided into North and South Vietnam until elections could be held to decide its future.

SOURCE **3**

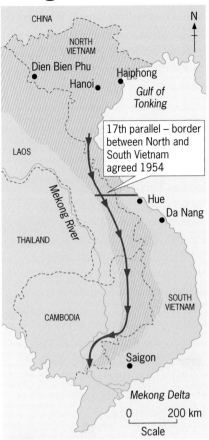

Key

▨ Communist-controlled areas in the mid 1960s

➤ Ho Chi Minh trail

The location of Vietnam.

1 Many neutral observers in Vietnam were critical of US policy. Explain why.
2 Explain how US politicians would have defended their policies.

How did American involvement in Vietnam escalate?

Under the terms of the ceasefire between the French and the Viet Minh, elections were to be held within two years to reunite the country. You will remember how the USA criticised Stalin for not holding free elections in Soviet-controlled eastern Europe after the war (see page 75). In Vietnam in 1954 the USA applied a different rule. It prevented the elections from taking place because it feared that the Communists would win.

In 1955 the Americans helped Ngo Dinh Diem to set up the Republic of South Vietnam. They supported him because he was bitterly anti-Communist and was prepared to imprison or exile Communists. He belonged to the landlord class, which treated the Vietnamese peasants with contempt. He was a Christian and showed little respect for the Buddhist religion of most Vietnamese peasants (see Source 5 on page 102). Diem's regime was also extremely corrupt. He appointed members of his family or other supporters to positions of power and refused to hold elections, even for local councils. The Americans were concerned and frustrated by his actions, but as Dulles said, 'We knew of no one better.' The USA supported Diem's regime with around $1.6 billion in the 1950s. Diem was overthrown by his own army leaders in November 1963, but the governments that followed were equally corrupt. Even so, they also received massive US support.

SOURCE **4**

It was generally agreed that had an election been held, Ho Chi Minh would have been elected Premier . . . at the time of the fighting, possibly 80 per cent of the population would have voted for the communist Ho Chi Minh as their leader.

President Eisenhower writing after the Vietnam War.

The actions of these anti-Communist governments increased opposition to the South Vietnam government among ordinary people and among influential Buddhist priests (see Source 5). The government's actions also increased support among the ordinary peasants for the Communist-led National Front for the Liberation of South Vietnam, set up in December 1960. This movement was usually referred to as the Viet Cong. It included South Vietnamese opponents of the government, but also large numbers of Communist North Vietnamese taking their orders from Ho Chi Minh. Peasants who did not support the Viet Cong faced intimidation and violence from them.

The Viet Cong also started a guerilla war against the South Vietnamese government. Using the Ho Chi Minh trail (see Source 3), the Viet Cong sent reinforcements and ferried supplies to guerrilla fighters. These fighters attacked South Vietnamese government forces, officials and buildings, gradually making the countryside unsafe for government forces. They also attacked American air force and supply bases.

By 1962 President Kennedy was sending military personnel (he always called them 'advisers') to fight the Viet Cong. He supported policies such as the Strategic Hamlet Programme (see Source 11).

In 1963 and 1964 tension between North and South Vietnam increased and so did American involvement (11,500 troops by the end of 1962; 23,000 by the end of 1964). However, Kennedy said he was determined that the USA would not 'blunder into war, unclear about aims or how to get out again'.

President Kennedy was assassinated in 1963. His successor, Lyndon Johnson, was more prepared than Kennedy to commit the USA to a full-scale conflict in Vietnam to prevent the spread of Communism. His resolve would soon be tested. In August 1964, North Vietnamese patrol boats opened fire on US ships in the Gulf of Tonkin. In a furious reaction, the US Congress passed the Tonkin Gulf Resolution. The Resolution gave Lyndon Johnson the power to 'take all necessary measures to prevent further aggression and achieve peace and security'. It effectively meant that he could take the USA into a full-scale war if he felt it was necessary, and very soon that was the case. On 8 March 1965, 3,500 US marines, combat troops rather than advisers, came ashore at Da Nang. America was at war in Vietnam.

SOURCE 5

Quang Duc, a 73-year-old Buddhist priest, burns himself to death in protest against the attacks on Buddhist shrines by the government of South Vietnam in 1963.

Focus Task

Why did the USA get increasingly involved in Vietnam?

1 Draw a timeline of the period 1945–65.
2 Mark on it increasing American involvement using the following headings:
    ◆ No direct American involvement
    ◆ Financial support
    ◆ Political involvement
    ◆ Military involvement
3 Write annotations to show the date on which each of these phases started and what events triggered the increasing involvement.
4 Choose two events that you think were critical in increasing the USA's involvement in the war in Vietnam. Explain your choice.
5 American governments and the American public were traditionally 'isolationist' i.e. very wary of getting involved in foreign wars. The diagram opposite summarises the attitudes and factors that made them act against these traditional instincts in the case of Vietnam. An isolationist meets an interventionist from the 1960s. What might they say to each other?

SOURCE 6

First is the simple fact that South Vietnam, a member of the free world family, is striving to preserve its independence from Communist attack. Second, South East Asia has great significance in the forward defence of the USA. For Hanoi, the immediate object is limited: conquest of the south and national unification. For Peking, however, Hanoi's victory would only be a first step towards eventual Chinese dominance of the two Vietnams and South East Asia and towards exploitation of the new strategy in other parts of the world.

Robert McNamara, US Defence Secretary, explaining in 1964 why he supported the policy of sending US troops to Vietnam.

Containment

Containment meant stopping the advance of Communism wherever it looked like it was gaining ground. So for example, the USA supported the French in Vietnam because they thought the Vietnamese were allied to Communist China. The USA also supported the French in Vietnam because they wanted to keep the support of France against Communism in Europe. Look back to Chapter 4 and you will see that the Cold War was also in full swing there, with the Soviet domination of Eastern Europe, the Berlin Blockade and many other tense events.

Domino Theory

This was closely linked to the policy of containment. President Eisenhower and his Secretary of State JF Dulles were convinced that China and the USSR were planning to spread Communism throughout Asia. The idea was often referred to as the Domino Theory. If Vietnam fell to Communism, then Laos, Cambodia, Burma, Thailand, and possibly even India might also fall – just like a row of dominoes. The Americans were determined to resist the spread of Communism in Vietnam which they saw as the first domino in the row.

Why did the USA become increasingly involved in Vietnam?

American politics

Political issues back in the USA also played a role in American involvement in Vietnam, particularly at election time. The Americans elect a new President every four years. In the 1950s and 1960s for all candidates it was a sure vote winner to talk tough about Communism and a sure vote loser to look weak on Communism. So for example in his 1960 election campaign, John F Kennedy promised to continue the tough policies of President Eisenhower.

The military–industrial complex

Another controversial view held by some historians is that powerful groups within the USA wanted a war. In 1961 President Eisenhower himself warned that America had developed a powerful 'military–industrial complex'. The government gave huge budgets to the military commanders. These budgets were spent on weapons contracts which went to huge corporations. Thus, both the military and big business actually gained from conflict. Eisenhower did not accuse business and military leaders of anything, but in his last speech as President he warned the American people not to let these groups become too influential. Some historians believe that this was a factor in American involvement in Vietnam but it is hotly disputed by others.

Activity

1 List all the evidence in Sources 7–12 to support the view that the Americans were not adequately prepared to fight in Vietnam.
2 Now go over your list again and decide which of these points could have been predicted at the time, and which can only be seen with hindsight.

Were the Americans ready for the Vietnam War?

With hindsight it is easy to see that the American decision to get fully involved in the war was a huge gamble. True, their firepower and technology were totally superior to the Communist forces, but they were fighting a war in a distant land, to support a government which had lost the support of many of its own population, against an enemy who had already won the hearts and minds of many ordinary Vietnamese people. But did the Americans know that at the time?

SOURCE 7

In 1963 the military did not anticipate being in Vietnam for a long haul. They expected to withdraw the force of 16,000 military advisers by the end of '65, and that the first unit of withdrawal would be completed within 90 days, by the end of December 1963.

Robert McNamara, US Defence Secretary under President Kennedy and then President Johnson.

SOURCE 8

I have today ordered to Vietnam the Air Mobile Division, and certain other forces which will raise our fighting strength from 75,000 to 125,000 men almost immediately. Additional forces will be needed later, and they will be sent as requested.

President Johnson announces the arrival of US combat troops in Vietnam in 1965. In reality US military 'advisers' were already fighting on the ground and US pilots were flying regular missions to support the South Vietnamese army.

SOURCE 9

We were all kind of hot to go, hot to get into something, do something that was other than train and drill and, um, there was a kind of a feeling, I don't know if anybody ever said this – a sort of feeling that being U.S. Marines, our mere presence in Vietnam was going to terrify the enemy into quitting.

Philip Caputo, US Marine in Vietnam.

SOURCE 10

This was the type of war that we'd had no experience with before, and we were on a learning curve … and some of our policies were kind of trial and error in character.

General William Westmoreland, commander, US Forces, Vietnam.

SOURCE 11

In reality, the Strategic Hamlet Programme often converted peasants into Viet Cong sympathisers. In many places they resented working without pay to dig moats, plant bamboo stakes and erect fences against an enemy that did not threaten them. Many were angered by corrupt officials, who pocketed the money which was meant for seed, fertiliser and irrigation, as well as medical care, education and other social benefits.

Extract from *Vietnam – A History* by S. Kamow, published in 1994. Since 1962 the South Vietnam government had been pursuing a programme called the Strategic Hamlet Programme. This involved moving peasant villages from Viet Cong-controlled areas to areas controlled by the South Vietnam government. The Americans supplied building materials, money, food and equipment for the villagers to build new improved farms and homes.

SOURCE 12

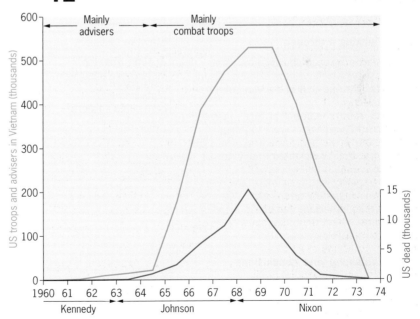

US troops and deaths in Vietnam, 1960–74. US troops were not the only foreign soldiers in the war. About 46,000 Australian and New Zealand troops fought too.

War in Vietnam: Troops, tactics and technology

If the USA thought that its soldiers would win an easy victory, it was soon proved wrong. American technology and firepower were totally superior, but as time wore on it became clear that the USA needed more than technology and dollars to win this kind of war. On the next six pages you will compare Viet Cong and US tactics in more detail to see why the US army could not win. The timeline opposite will help you put these sources into context. The Focus Task below will direct your reading.

Focus Task

Part 1

What were the different ways that the USA and the Communists fought the war?

On pages 106–9 there is information and evidence (visual and written sources) about the tactics of the two sides. Work in pairs or groups and study either the Communists (pages 106–7) or the USA (pages 108–9). Remember also that the internet has a wealth of material on the Vietnam War that could help you with your research if you want to look deeper. Your teacher can suggest some sites to help you begin.

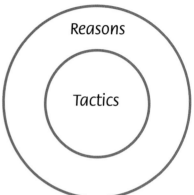

Create a diagram like the one on the right.
- In the inner circle record all you can find out about the tactics that they used.
- In the outer circle record reasons why they used these tactics.
- Draw lines between the inner and outer circles if there are specific links that you can see.

Compare your diagrams. Add to your diagram anything that you can learn from the evidence your partner has gathered.

Part 2

Whose tactics were the most effective – the USA's or the Communists'?

Stage 1: Gathering the evidence

1 Make your own copy of this chart:
2 Using pages 106–9, make notes in columns 2 and 4 to record how far each side had each quality.
3 Add other rows if you wish to.

Stage 2: Thinking it through

4 Next, in each row of column 3, draw some scales to show which way the balance falls for this quality. Did the USA or the Viet Cong have the advantage?
5 Now think about the overall picture – how the strengths and weaknesses work together.
   a) Were the armies finely balanced or was the balance strongly weighted to one side or the other?
   b) Which quality was most important in determining who won the war? Was one feature so important that being ahead in that area meant that other advantages or disadvantages did not matter?

Qualities of a successful army	The US army	⟋⟍ or ⟋⟍	The Viet Cong
Well-trained soldiers			
The right technology			
Reliable supplies and equipment			
Effective tactics			
Support from the Vietnamese population			
Motivated and committed soldiers			
Other			

Stage 3: Explaining your conclusions

6 Now write up your answer. You could use this structure:
   a) Describe how the failure of the US army was a combination of its own weaknesses and Viet Cong strengths.
   b) Give balanced examples of US strengths and weaknesses.
   c) Give balanced examples of Viet Cong strengths and weaknesses
   d) Choose one American weakness and one Viet Cong strength that you think were absolutely vital in preventing the USA from beating the Viet Cong and explain the significance of the points you have chosen.

Timeline: Vietnam War

DATE		ACTION
1954		Vietnam is divided into North and South Vietnam.
1959		The North Vietnam army creates the Ho Chi Minh Trail to carry supplies down to South Vietnam.
1960		North Vietnam creates the National Liberation Front of South Vietnam (usually called the Viet Cong).
1961		Around 16,000 American 'advisers' help to organise the South Vietnam army.
1962–63		The Viet Cong use guerrilla tactics against South Vietnam's army and government. More American advisers and equipment arrive.
1964		North Vietnamese patrol boats fire on American warships in the Gulf of Tonkin. The American Congress gives President Johnson the authority to do whatever he thinks is necessary.
1965	February	Operation Rolling Thunder – a gigantic bombing campaign against North Vietnam. Factories and army bases are bombed, as well as the Ho Chi Minh Trail and the capital of North Vietnam, Hanoi.
	March	The first American combat troops (3,500 marines) come ashore at Da Nang.
	June–September	A major Viet Cong offensive.
	November	Battle in La Dreng Valley. The Communists suffer heavy losses.
1966		American forces build heavily-armed camps. They control towns. The Viet Cong largely control the countryside.
1967		Continuous running battles between American and Communist forces around the North–South Vietnam border. The Communists are unable to force out American troops.
1968	January	The Tet Offensive: a large-scale Communist attack on over 100 major towns and cities in South Vietnam. Even the American embassy in Saigon is attacked. Some of the fiercest fighting of the war takes place. The city of Hue is almost flattened by intense fighting. Tet is a defeat for the Communists but is also a major shock to the American military and public who thought the war was almost won. Intense fighting continues throughout 1968. Casualties on both sides mount.
	October	Operation Rolling Thunder finishes after three and a half years. More bombs have been dropped on North Vietnam than all the bombs dropped on Germany and Japan during the Second World War.
1969		The USA begins its policy of 'Vietnamisation'. This means building up the South Vietnam army and withdrawing American combat troops. American air power continues to bomb North Vietnam. Intense fighting continues throughout the year. This includes the Battle for Hamburger Hill in May.
1970–71		The fighting spreads to Cambodia. US Secretary of State Kissinger and North Vietnam leader Le Duc begin secret peace talks
1972		Most American forces are now out of Vietnam. A major Communist offensive in March captures much ground. Most land is recaptured by the South Vietnam army by the end of the year. American heavy bombers bomb Hanoi and Haiphong.
1973		Ceasefire signed in Paris and end of draft in the USA. The last US troops leave Vietnam.
1974		Major North Vietnam Army offensive against South Vietnam.
1975		South Vietnam capital Saigon falls to Communists; US officials are evacuated by helicopter.

Vietcong tactics 1964–68

In early 1965 the Viet Cong and North Vietnamese Army (NVA) had about 170,000 soldiers. They were well supplied with weapons and equipment from China and the USSR, but they were heavily outnumbered and outgunned by the South Vietnamese forces and their US allies. The Communist forces were no match for the US and South Vietnamese forces in open warfare. In November 1965 in the La Dreng Valley, US forces killed 2000 Viet Cong for the loss of 300 troops. This did not daunt Ho Chi Minh. He believed that superior forces could be defeated by guerrilla tactics. He had been in China and seen Mao Zedong use guerrilla warfare to achieve a Communist victory there. Ho had also used these guerrilla tactics himself against the Japanese and the French. The principles were simple: retreat when the enemy attacks; raid when the enemy camps; attack when the enemy tires; pursue when the enemy retreats.

SOURCE 13

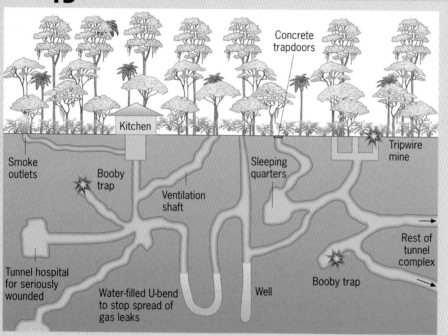

A Viet Cong tunnel complex. To avoid the worst effects of American air power, the Viet Cong built a vast network of underground tunnels, probably around 240 km of them.

SOURCE 14

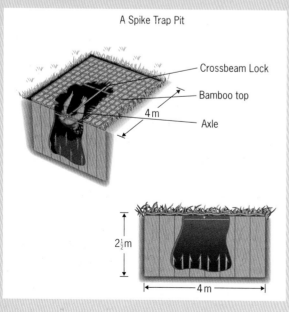

A Spike Trap Pit

A diagram showing one type of booby trap. A trap pit is a large trap box with a bamboo top. Stakes are made of sharpened bamboo or barbed spikes and used to line the box. When a man steps on the trap he will fall into the pit. The top turns on an axle; therefore, the trap does not need to be reset to work again. The pit is often prepared as a defensive obstacle and then made safe by locking it in place with a crossbeam (so it can be crossed safely by the enemy) until the desired time of use.

Guerrilla warfare was a nightmare for the US army. Guerrillas did not wear uniform. They had no known base camp or headquarters. They worked in small groups with limited weapons. They were hard to tell apart from the peasants in the villages. They attacked and then disappeared into the jungle, into the villages or into their tunnels (see Source 13).

The aim of guerrilla attacks was to wear down the enemy soldiers and wreck their morale. This was very effective. US soldiers lived in constant fear of ambushes or booby traps. Booby traps could be simple devices such as tripwires or pits filled with sharpened bamboo stakes. Weapons like these were cheap and easy to make and very effective in disrupting US patrols. One of the most unpopular duties in a patrol was going 'on point'. This meant leading the patrol, checking for traps. There were other more sophisticated traps such as the Bouncing Betty land mine. This would be thrown into the air when triggered and would then explode causing terrible injuries to the stomach or groin. Booby traps caused about 11 per cent of US casualties.

Another 51 per cent of casualties were caused by small arms fire in ambushes or 'firefights'. The Viet Cong and NVA quickly learned to fear American air power, so when they did attack they tried to make sure it was close-quarter fighting. This meant that US air power or artillery could not be used because of the danger of hitting their own troops. This tactic was sometimes known as 'hanging on to American belts'.

Ho knew how important it was to keep the population on his side. The Viet Cong fighters were expected to be courteous and respectful to the Vietnamese peasants. They often helped the peasants in the fields during busy periods.

1 One Viet Cong leader said: 'The people are the water. Our armies are the fish.' What do you think he meant?
2 Choose one piece of evidence to show that the Viet Cong had the support of the Vietnamese people.
3 Choose one piece of evidence that suggests that they did not.

However, the Viet Cong could be ruthless – they were quite prepared to kill peasants who opposed them or who co-operated with their enemies. They also conducted a campaign of terror against the police, tax collectors, teachers and any other employees of the South Vietnamese government. Between 1966 and 1971 the Viet Cong killed an estimated 27,000 civilians.

The greatest strength of the Viet Cong fighters was that they simply refused to give in. The Viet Cong depended on supplies from North Vietnam that came along the Ho Chi Minh trail. US and South Vietnamese planes bombed this constantly, but 40,000 Vietnamese worked to keep it open whatever the cost. The total of Viet Cong and North Vietnamese dead in the war has been estimated at 1 million – far higher than US losses. However, this was a price that Ho Chi Minh was prepared to pay. Whatever the casualties, there were replacement troops available.

SOURCE 15

A Viet Cong poster.

SOURCE 16

U.S. Imperialism, Get Out of South Viet Nam!
L'imperialisme americain hors du Sud-Vietnam!
¡Fuera el imperialismo norteamericano del Sur de Vietnam

A Chinese poster commenting on the Vietnam War.

SOURCE 17

In the military respect, it is easier to destroy the puppet troops than the American troops, for the American troops have not had much fighting with us, thus are optimistic and have patriotic pride. The puppet troops [South Vietnamese forces] have lost a lot of battles and now have little enthusiasm to fight. Therefore, our plan is to wipe out the puppet troops.

On the other hand our propaganda will emphasize the slogan 'Find the Americans to kill'. We need to use the methods most suited for destroying the American troops – guerrilla forces encircling the American troops' bases. This upcoming spring and summer, we are aiming for killing about 10,000 Americans as already planned and for the next few years, we should at least kill 40,000 to 50,000 Americans. This is a new goal which will determine our victory. Along with trying to lessen the Americans' strength, we should try to cause great loss of American aircraft, at the same time, curb their activities.

. . . We must not neglect the political war. I just talked about the possibility and necessity to strengthen the political war. Even though the US brings in more troops to Vietnam, they will fail to weaken our political power. In fact, our political power is likely to be enhanced and the US will be isolated and fail miserably. The more troops the US brings in, the more military bases it builds, the larger area it occupies, the more sophisticated weapons it uses, the more B.52 bombs it drops, the more chemical poisons it uses, the worse the conflict between our people and them becomes, the more our people hate them.

Extracts from a letter written in 1965 by Le Duan, Secretary of the North Vietnamese Communist Party and one of Ho Chi Minh's closest associates. The letter was explaining how North Vietnam was planning to react to the large scale arrival of US forces in 1965.

SOURCE 18

. . . Kien knows the area well. It was here, at the end of the dry season of 1969, that his Battalion 27 was surrounded and almost totally wiped out. Ten men survived from the Unlucky Battalion, after fierce, horrible, barbarous fighting.

That was the dry season when the sun burned harshly, the wind blew fiercely, and the enemy sent napalm spraying through the jungle and a sea of fire enveloped them, spreading like the fires of hell. Troops in the fragmented companies tried to regroup, only to be blown out of their shelters again as they went mad, became disoriented and threw themselves into nets of bullets, dying in the flaming inferno. Above them the helicopters flew at tree-top height and shot them almost one by one, the blood spreading out, spraying from their backs, flowing like red mud. The diamond-shaped grass clearing was piled high with bodies killed by helicopter gunships. Broken bodies, bodies blown apart, bodies vaporised. No jungle grew again in this clearing. No grass. No plants.

'Better to die than surrender my brothers! Better to die!' the Battalion Commander yelled insanely; waving his pistol in front of Kien he blew his own brains out through his ear. Kien screamed soundlessly in his throat at the sight, as the Americans attacked with sub-machine-guns, sending bullets buzzing like deadly bees around him. Then Kien lowered his machine-gun, grasped his side and fell, rolling slowly down the bank of a shallow stream, hot blood trailing down the slope after him.

Extract from *The Sorrow of War*. This was a novel by Bao Ninh, a North Vietnamese soldier who fought the Americans in Vietnam in 1969. The novel was based on his experiences.

Focus Task

Use the information and sources in this section to complete the Viet Cong column of the Focus Task on page 104.

US tactics

Bombing

On 7 February 1965 the USA launched Operation Rolling Thunder. Rolling Thunder involved extensive bombing raids on military and industrial targets in North Vietnam. It was the beginning of an air offensive that was to last until 1972. The list of targets was soon expanded to include towns and cities in North and South Vietnam. The list also included sites in Laos and Cambodia along the Ho Chi Minh trail. More bombs were dropped on North Vietnam than were dropped in the whole of the Second World War on Germany and Japan.

To some extent bombing was effective.

- It certainly damaged North Vietnam's war effort and it disrupted supply routes.
- It enabled the USA to strike at Communist forces even when it was reducing US ground forces in Vietnam after 1969.
- From 1970 to 1972, intense bombing campaigns against Hanoi (North Vietnam's capital) and the port of Haiphong forced the North Vietnamese to the negotiating table.

However, US air power could not defeat the Communists – it could only slow them down. The Viet Cong continued to operate its supply lines. Even after major air raids on North Vietnam in 1972, the Communists were still able to launch a major assault on the South.

The cost of the air war was horrendous. The Communists shot down 14,000 US and South Vietnamese aircraft. In 1967 the American *Life* magazine calculated that it cost the USA $400,000 to kill one Viet Cong fighter, a figure that included 75 bombs and 400 artillery shells.

Chemical weapons

The US developed a powerful chemical weapon called Agent Orange. It was a sort of highly toxic 'weedkiller'. It was used to destroy the jungle where the Viet Cong hid. The Americans used 82 million litres of Agent Orange to spray thousands of square kilometres of jungle. Napalm was another widely-used chemical weapon. It destroyed jungles where guerrillas might hide. It also burned through skin to the bone. Many civilians and soldiers were also killed by these chemical weapons.

SOURCE **19**

People in the South Vietnamese city of Hue sort through the wreckage of their homes after a US bombing raid in 1968.

1 'Mixed results.' Is this a fair summary of the effectiveness of bombing in the Vietnam War? Explain your answer.
2 Would you say the US ground forces in Vietnam were more or less effective than the air forces? Explain your answer.

SOURCE **20**

A ten-year-old Vietnamese girl runs naked after tearing her burning clothes from her body following a napalm attack. This photograph became one of the most enduring images of the war.

FactFile

Statistics on the Vietnam War

➤ The Pentagon's estimate of the cost of the Vietnam War was more than $110 billion. This amounts to $2,000 per second over 10 years. In reality the cost was even higher because the US government had to pay large amounts in benefits and pensions to soldiers and their families. The war also had a damaging effect on the US economy, causing inflation and diverting money away from health and welfare programmes.
➤ Almost 5,000 helicopters were destroyed, each costing about $250,000. Over 3,500 fixed wing aircraft were destroyed.
➤ Two-thirds of US bombs were dropped on South Vietnam, which the US was meant to be protecting. Around 50,000 people died in the bombing.
➤ Between 1965 and 1973 US forces and their allies dropped around 20,000 tons of napalm.
➤ Between 1961 and 1970, 100 million lbs of herbicide were dropped in 30,000 missions, destroying four million acres of forest and farm lands and affecting more than 1.3 million people.
➤ About 10,000 shells were fired every day, which cost $1 million at 1970 values.
➤ An American journal, 'The Scientific American', calculated that 'from 1965–71, the area of Indo-China was bombarded by a tonnage of ammunition approximately twice the total used by the USA in all theatres of the Second World War … exploding 13 million tons of ammunition, creating 2.6 million craters'.
➤ An estimated 27,000 tons of munitions remain unexploded in Vietnam today.

Search and destroy

Bombing could not defeat a guerrilla army. The US commander General Westmoreland developed a policy of search and destroy. He established secure and heavily defended US bases in the south of the country and near to the coasts. From here, US and South Vietnamese forces launched search-and-destroy raids from helicopters. They would descend on a village and destroy any Viet Cong forces they found. Soldiers had to send back reports of body counts.

Search-and-destroy missions did kill Viet Cong soldiers, but there were problems.

- The raids were often based on inadequate information.
- Inexperienced US troops often walked into traps.
- Innocent villages were mistaken for Viet Cong strongholds.
- Civilian casualties were extremely high in these raids. For every Viet Cong weapon captured by search-and-destroy, there was a body count of six. Many of these were innocent civilians.
- Search-and-destroy tactics made the US and South Vietnamese forces very unpopular with the peasants. It pushed them towards supporting the Viet Cong.

SOURCE **21**

US troops on a search-and-destroy mission in Vietnam. These were sometimes called 'Zippo raids', after the Zippo cigarette lighters that were often used to burn villages.

Focus Task

Use the information and sources in this section to complete the USA column on page 104.

What problems did the Americans face in Vietnam?

The Americans were fighting against a committed and experienced guerrilla army. But they also had some other problems to deal with.

1 Low morale and inexperience

In the early stages of the war the majority of US troops were professional soldiers who had volunteered for the forces as a career. For the most part morale was good and they stood up well to the conditions. However, after 1967 an increasing number of troops in Vietnam had been drafted.

- Many of these were young men who had never been in the military before. The average age was only 19. Many recruits had just left school. This was their first experience of war. Sixty per cent of the Americans killed in Vietnam were aged 17–21.
- The soldiers knew very little about the country they were fighting for. They often cared little for democracy or communism and just wanted to get home alive. In contrast the Viet Cong were fighting for their own country, and a cause many of them believed in.
- In theory American troops came from all walks of life. In reality the majority of combat troops were from poor and immigrant backgrounds because those privileged enough to be going to university could delay the draft and many were able to use their influence to avoid the draft altogether.
- There were tensions between officers and troops. Many officers were professional soldiers. They wanted to gain promotion. In Vietnam this meant gaining as many kills as possible. Most soldiers on the other hand just wanted to stay alive. There is evidence of 'fragging' – troops killing their own officers. One estimate suggests that three per cent of officer deaths were caused by their own troops.

Many soldiers turned to drugs when they were not fighting. Large numbers of servicemen sold food, drugs and equipment on the black market. Around eighteen per cent of US casualties were caused by factors other than combat, such as illness, car and aircraft crashes, suicide, murder and drug abuse. There were over 500,000 incidents of desertion (although this figure included single individuals who might desert several times). To tackle these problems General Westmoreland introduced a policy of giving troops just a one-year term of service to help morale, although in reality this backfired because as soon as the soldiers gained experience they were sent home.

2 Vietnam's neighbours

Neighbouring countries were sympathetic to the Viet Cong. Political considerations meant that the USA could not send their forces into North Vietnam or neighbouring Cambodia and Laos. This gave the NVA and Viet Cong a huge advantage. They were able to retreat to these other countries to reinforce their losses and get new equipment, ammunition, etc. They also used these states to supply their forces along the Ho Chi Minh trail (see Source 3 on page 101. In fact, the Americans did send unofficial missions into these neighbouring countries and did bomb the Ho Chi Minh Trail and other targets. However, they were never able to officially enter these states with their full force.

3 'Hearts and minds'

From early in the war President Johnson spoke of the importance of winning 'hearts and minds' in Vietnam. Between 1964 and 1968 he mentioned it in 28 speeches! The trouble was that US tactics were based on attrition – killing large numbers of the enemy. This inevitably led to large numbers of civilian casualties. This in turn led the Vietnamese people to support the Viet Cong which caused concern back in the USA. This issue came to a head in one particularly infamous and gruesome event – the My Lai massacre of 1968 which you can study in depth on page 112.

Focus Task

Sources 22–30 are going to be very useful in helping you fill out and analyse the table in the Focus Task on page 104. They are all American sources but they also reveal quite a lot about Viet Cong tactics.

Start by discussing the sources.
1 Which of sources 22–30 would you put under the following headings:
   - morale
   - inexperience
   - neighbours
   - 'hearts and minds'?
   Some sources might belong under more than one heading.
2 Choose one or two sources and discuss:
   - what your sources reveal about Viet Cong tactics
   - what your sources reveal about the effectiveness of Viet Cong tactics
   - what your sources reveal about the effectiveness of American tactics.
3 On your own, look back at your table from the Focus Task on page 104. Add any extra points or examples to the table which have arisen from your discussion. Now complete Stages 2 and 3 of the Focus task.

SOURCE 22

I remember sitting at this wretched little outpost one day with a couple of my sergeants. We'd been manning this thing for three weeks and running patrols off it. We were grungy and sore with jungle rot and we'd suffered about nine or ten casualties on a recent patrol. This one sergeant of mine said, 'You know, Lieutenant, I don't see how we're ever going to win this.' And I said, 'Well, Sarge, I'm not supposed to say this to you as your officer – but I don't either.' So there was this sense that we just couldn't see what could be done to defeat these people.

Philip Caputo, a lieutenant in the Marine Corps in Vietnam in 1965–66, speaking in 1997.

SOURCE 26

Over the years Cambodia, the border area of Cambodia, and, er … and Laos, were used freely by the enemy, but, er, our … by … by virtue of the policy of my government, we could not fight the overt war or deploy troops overtly, military troops, into those countries.

General William Westmoreland, commander, US Forces, Vietnam.

SOURCE 28

An increasing number of recruits scored so low on the standardised intelligence tests that they would have been excluded from the normal peacetime army. The tour of duty in Vietnam was one year. Soldiers were most likely to die in their first month. The large majority of deaths took place in the first six months. Just as a soldier began gaining experience, he was sent home. A rookie army which constantly rotated inexperienced men was pitted against experienced guerrillas on their home ground.

From *Four Hours in My Lai* by Michael Bilton, 1992.

SOURCE 23

The attitude of the enemy was not comparable to what our attitude would have been under the circumstances. He was ready, willing and able to pay a far greater price than I would say we would.

General William Westmoreland, commander, US Forces, Vietnam.

SOURCE 24

My casualties in my company were relatively light and I say relatively light. I lost 17 killed and about 43 wounded so the unit was almost combat ineffective with those kind of casualties, but fortunately we were able to weather that particular piece of the battle.

Lieutenant Colonel George Forrest, US Army, commenting on one battle with Viet Cong fighters.

SOURCE 25

You would go out, you would secure a piece of terrain during the daylight hours, [but at night] you'd surrender that – and I mean literally surrender … you'd give it up, because … the helicopters would come in and pick you up at night and fly you back to the security of your base camp.

Lieutenant Colonel George Forrest, US Army.

SOURCE 27

On one or two occasions, the chiefs recommended US military intervention in North Vietnam and stated that they recognized this might lead to Chinese and/or Soviet military response, in which case, they said, 'We might have to consider the use of nuclear weapons'.

Robert McNamara, US Secretary of Defence.

SOURCE 29

A first aid station in Vietnam in 1966.

SOURCE 30

How do you distinguish a civilian from a Viet Cong? Well of course he shoots at you or he's armed. But how about what happens after a firefight and you find bodies out there, but no weapons? And we were told this is … well, if it's dead and Vietnamese, it's VC. Those were the exact words.

Philip Caputo, US Marine.

SOURCE 31

In the end anybody who was still in that country was the enemy. The same village you'd gone in to give them medical treatment . . . you could go through that village later and get shot at by a sniper. Go back in and you would not find anybody. Nobody knew anything. We were trying to work with these people, they were basically doing a number on us. You didn't trust them anymore. You didn't trust anybody.

Fred Widmer, an American soldier, speaking in 1969.

SOURCE 32

The Quang Ngai area of Vietnam.

1. Do Sources 33 and 34 make the same point?
2. Why do you think it took twelve months for anyone to do anything about the massacre?
3. Why was the massacre so shocking to the American public?

SOURCE 33

We were not in My Lai to kill human beings. We were there to kill ideology that is carried by – I don't know – pawns. Blobs. Pieces of flesh. And I wasn't in My Lai to destroy intelligent men. I was there to destroy an intangible idea . . . To destroy Communism.

From Lieutenant Calley's account of the event, *Body Count*, published in 1970.

Activity

Work in pairs. You are opponents of American involvement in Vietnam. Use the evidence in this chapter to make a poster or a leaflet putting forward your views.

You can include stories and images from pages 100–12. However, you must also include an explanation that will convince the supporters of containment that the policy is not working in Vietnam.

The My Lai massacre

In March 1968, a unit of young American soldiers called Charlie Company started a search-and-destroy mission in the Quang Ngai region of South Vietnam. They had been told that in the My Lai area there was a Viet Cong headquarters, and 200 Viet Cong guerrillas. The soldiers had been ordered to destroy all houses, dwellings and livestock. They had been told that all the villagers would have left for market because it was a Saturday. Most of them were under the impression that they had been ordered to kill everyone they found in the village.

Early in the morning of 16 March, Charlie Company arrived in My Lai. In the next four hours, between 300 and 400 civilians were killed. They were mostly women, children and old men. Some were killed while they worked in their fields. Many of them were mown down by machine-gun fire as they were herded into an irrigation ditch. Others were shot in their homes. No Viet Cong were found in the village. Only three weapons were recovered.

'Something dark and bloody'

At the time, the army treated the operation as a success. The commanding officer's report said that twenty non-combatants had been killed by accident in the attack, but the rest of the dead were recorded as being Viet Cong. The officers and men involved were praised. The event passed into army folklore. All the soldiers knew that it had taken place, but they just took it to be a normal and inevitable part of the war.

However, twelve months later, a letter arrived in the offices of 30 leading politicians and government officials in Washington. It was written by Ronald Ridenhour, an American soldier who had served in Vietnam and who personally knew many of the soldiers who took part in the massacre. He had evidence, he said, of 'something rather dark and bloody' that had occurred in My Lai – or Pinkville as the American soldiers called it. He recounted in detail all the stories he had been told about what had taken place and asked Congress to investigate.

Soon after, *Life* magazine, one of the most influential magazines in the USA, published photographs of the massacre at My Lai that had been taken by an official army photographer.

Investigation

There was an investigation that ended in the trial for mass murder of Lieutenant William Calley. Sources 38–40 are part of the evidence given at that trial. Calley was an officer in Charlie Company. He had personally shot many of the people in the irrigation ditch at My Lai. In September 1969 he was formally charged with murdering 109 people. Ten other members of the company and the commanding officers were also charged. The charges were too much for the army. They placed all responsibility on Calley (see Source 38). They denied that Calley was acting under orders. His senior officers were acquitted. After a long court case surrounded by massive media attention and publicity, in March 1971 Calley was found guilty of the murder of 22 civilians. In August he was sentenced to twenty years' hard labour. In November 1974 he was released.

Aftermath

The revelations about My Lai deeply shocked the American public. It was the clearest evidence that the war had gone wrong.

SOURCE 34

Most of the soldiers had never been away from home before they went into service. And they end up in Vietnam going there many of them because they thought they were going to do something courageous on behalf of their country, something which they thought was in the American ideal.

But it didn't mean slaughtering whole villages of women and children. One of my friends, when he told me about it, said: 'You know it was a Nazi kind of thing.' We didn't go there to be Nazis. At least none of the people I knew went there to be Nazis.

Written by Ronald Ridenhour.

SOURCE 35

A photograph taken at My Lai on 16 March 1968.

SOURCE 36

BRITISH CARTOON ARCHIVE © LESLIE GIBBARD, WITH PERMISSION

A cartoon by Leslie Gibbard from the British newspaper the *Guardian*, 2 April 1971, with the caption 'Woe, oh woe – how could such disregard for life find its way into the army?'

4 What point is being made about the commanders in Source 36?
5 To what extent do Sources 37–39 either support or contradict the view of Source 33?
6 Source 40 was written by someone who worked for the US Army. Does this make it a trustworthy source?

Activity

Before 1968 media coverage of the US war effort in Vietnam was generally positive. Imagine you are a journalist in 1968 who has been reporting the war positively. Write an article explaining how and why your view is changing, and why My Lai in particular has affected your views. You can use the information and sources on pages 114–15 and the internet, especially to search for pictures. Your target word limit is 250 words.

SOURCE 37

US helicopters and troops at My Lai.

SOURCE 38

The testimony from individual members (of Charlie Company) has provided conflicting information concerning the issuance of orders for the operation … the substance of the briefings was considered routine and standard procedures were to be used (i.e. for a search and destroy mission). They did not receive any special instructions on destruction of villages and livestock or on the handling of VC suspects and civilians. Because of their experience from two previous operations in the area, they expected to encounter numerous mines and booby traps … There were exceptions to the above interpretation. Three men, two men from the first platoon, believed they were to shoot anyone in the objective area. Undoubtedly there is some substance to these exceptions. The testimony does not suggest that there was a special effort to prepare the Company for a revenge-type operation.

Extract from the Peers Commission, the official report on the events at My Lai.

SOURCE 39

This was a time for us to get even. A time for us to settle the score. A time for revenge – when we can get revenge for our fallen comrades. The order we were given was to kill and destroy everything that was in the village. It was to kill the pigs, drop them in the wells; pollute the water supply … burn the village, burn the hootches as we went through it. It was clearly explained that there were to be no prisoners. The order that was given was to kill everyone in the village. Someone asked if this meant the women and children. And the order was: everyone in the village, because those people that were in the village – the women, the kids, the old men – were VC … or they were sympathetic to the Viet Cong.

Sergeant Hodge of Charlie Company.

SOURCE 40

I think I was in a kind of daze from seeing all these shootings and not seeing any returning fire. Yet the killing kept going on. The Americans were rounding up the people and shooting them, not taking any prisoners … I was part of it, everyone who was there was part of it and that includes the General and the Colonel flying above in their helicopters … Just as soon as I turned away I heard firing. I saw people drop. They started falling on top of each other, one on top of the other. I just kept on walking. I did not pay any attention to who did it. By that time I knew what the score was. It was an atrocity … I notice this one small boy had been shot in the foot … he was walking toward the group of bodies looking for his mother … then suddenly I heard a crack and … I saw this child flip over on top of the pile of bodies. The GI just stood and walked away. No remorse. Nothing.

Ron Haeberle, the US Army official photographer. His black and white pictures for the Army and his colour photographs taken with his own private camera had a dramatic public impact.

A

B

CBS News journalist Walter Cronkite in Vietnam: **A** speaking to US troops and **B** reporting in February 1968. He was regarded as the most trusted man in America.

The Vietnam War and the media

The Vietnam War was covered extensively by the American and world media, probably in more detail than any previous war.

Early stages of the war

In the early stages of the war, newspaper, radio and TV journalists largely followed the official line of policy. There were some small disagreements when the media reported the Buddhist protests against Diem (see Source 5 on page 102); one US Army spokesman also snapped 'Get on team!' to an American journalist when several US helicopters were shot down at Ap Bac in 1963, but on the whole the media supported the government.

Even when the situation escalated and US forces became directly involved in the war the relationship between the US military and government and the media remained relatively good. The US Army created MACV (Military Assistance Command, Vietnam) to liaise with journalists. Journalists could be accredited by MACV and they would then get transport to war areas, interviews and briefings with commanders, and regular reports. In return they were expected not to reveal any information which would help the enemy. Between 1964 and 1968 only three journalists had their accreditation removed.

Back in the USA editors rarely wanted to publish bad news stories about Vietnam. A major concern was that they did not want to be accused of undermining the war effort. For example, Seymour Hersh, the journalist who broke the story of the My Lai Massacre, had to try several newspapers before he could find one willing to publish the story. There were also commercial considerations. TV networks were reluctant to broadcast off-putting scenes of violence and destruction during peak viewing times because they were worried viewers would switch channels.

Later stages of the war, 1967–8

By 1967–68, however, the tone and content of reporting from Vietnam was beginning to change for two reasons.

- Television was taking over from newspapers as the most important source of news for most Americans. Television can be edited of course but it presents a more raw account of war. Improving technology also meant that TV crews could take lightweight cameras very close to the conflict zones. As early as 1965 the US TV network CBS had shown US Marines using Zippo lighters to set fire to Vietnamese villagers' homes. During the Tet Offensive of 1968 (see pages 118–19) TV viewers saw South Vietnamese police chief Colonel Nguyen Ngoc Loan executing a Viet Cong suspect (see Source 41). To see such casual violence beamed into the living rooms of the USA was deeply shocking to the average American.

A Viet Cong suspect is executed in the street by South Vietnamese police chief Nguyen Ngoc Loan in February 1968.

- At the same time doubts about the whole war effort were intensifying. One of the most famous TV reporters was CBS' Walter Cronkite. He reported throughout the Tet Offensive as US forces devastated large areas of the South Vietnam city of Hue in their efforts to destroy Viet Cong and NVA fighters. It was during the Tet Offensive that Cronkite declared, to his TV audience, that he thought the war was unwinnable. There were others who were quick to agree. President Johnson later remarked that if he lost the support of Cronkite he would lose the support of 'Middle America'.

SOURCE 43

The Marines who carry out patrols like this in the Mekong Delta are convinced they are winning their war against the VC. They point out as evidence of their success the number of VC dead and the number of VC defectors. But to do this they have needed the support of thousands of well trained troops, of barrack ships, helicopter gunships, air support and the river Marine force to contain and destroy what amounts to scattered handfuls of Viet Cong in these parts.

Text of a TV report by a journalist on patrol with US Marines in the Mekong Delta in 1969.

1 Do you think the scene in Source 42 would have been more shocking as a photograph or shown as it happened on TV? Explain your answer.
2 Would you regard the tone of Source 43 as controversial or critical, or fairly neutral? Explain your answer.
3 Study Source 45. Do you agree that veterans are the people best qualified to comment on the impact of the media?

SOURCE 45

The horrors of war entered the living rooms of Americans for the first time during the Vietnam War. For almost a decade in between school, work, and dinners, the American public could watch villages being destroyed, Vietnamese children burning to death, and American body bags being sent home. Though initial coverage generally supported US involvement in the war, television news dramatically changed its frame of the war after the Tet Offensive. Images of the US-led massacre at My Lai dominated the television, yet the daily atrocities committed by North Vietnam and the Viet Cong rarely made the evening news. Moreover, the anti-war movement at home gained increasing media attention while the US soldier was forgotten in Vietnam. Coverage of the war and its resulting impact on public opinion has been debated for decades by many intelligent media scholars and journalists, yet they are not the most qualified individuals to do so: the veterans are.

Extract from a blog called the Warbird's Forum. The author is the daughter of a Vietnam veteran.

What was the impact of the media coverage?

The issue of media coverage has been the subject of intense debate, as you can see from Sources 44 and 45. US Admiral Grant Sharp and General Westmoreland both claimed that the media undermined the war effort. Plenty of other commentators have put forward the view that the media crippled the war effort in Vietnam.

SOURCE 44

What was the effect of television on the development and outcome of the war? The conventional wisdom has generally been that for better or for worse it was an anti-war influence. It brought the 'horror of war' night after night into people's living rooms and eventually inspired revulsion and exhaustion. The argument has often been made that any war reported in an unrestricted way by television would eventually lose public support. Researchers, however, have quite consistently told another story.

Daniel Hallin, Professor of Communications at the University of California, writing on the Museum of TV website.

However before you accept this viewpoint uncritically, here are some alternative arguments.

- American attitudes were turning against the Vietnam War by 1967 anyway. The media reflected the changing views rather than creating them.
- Casualties and war weariness were the reasons why support for the war dropped – not the media.
- Shocking scenes were very rarely shown on TV. Less than 25 per cent of reports showed dead or wounded, and usually not in any detail.
- Research shows that from 1965–70 only 76 out of 2,300 TV reports showed heavy fighting.
- In a sample of almost 800 broadcasts from the time, only 16 per cent of criticisms of government policy came from journalists. The majority of critical comments came from officials or the general public.

Activity

Why is the role of the media in Vietnam a controversial issue?

Study the information and sources on these pages and prepare a presentation on this question. You will need to explain:
- how the reporting angle changed
- the importance and influence of television
- the case that the media undermined the war effort
- the case against this view.
If you are feeling very brave you could decide on which side of the debate you stand! You could also research this issue on the internet, as there is a great deal of debate still going on.

SOURCE 46

This confused war has played havoc with our domestic destinies. Despite feeble protestations to the contrary, the promises of the great society have been shot down on the battlefields of Vietnam. The pursuit of this widened war has narrowed the promised dimensions of the domestic welfare programs, making the poor – white and Negro – bear the heaviest burdens both at the front and at home.

The war has put us in the position of protecting a corrupt government that is stacked against the poor. We are spending $500,000 to kill every Viet Cong soldier while we spend only $53 for every person considered to be in poverty in the USA. It has put us in a position of appearing to the world as an arrogant nation. Here we are 10,000 miles away from home fighting for the so-called freedom of the Vietnamese people when we have so much to do in our own country.

Civil Rights leader Martin Luther King speaking in the USA in April 1968.

The anti-Vietnam War protest movement in the USA

1968 was a year of protest. There were protests on the right campaigning for free speech in universities, civil rights for African Americans (see page 359) and the condition of the poorest people in the USA. There were also massive protests against the Vietnam War. This probably won't surprise you given what you have studied on the previous four pages. Anti-war feeling reached deep into all areas of American society. But two groups were particularly prominent in the anti-war movement.

Civil Rights campaigners

When President Johnson was elected in 1964 he promised to create a 'Great Society'. By this he meant better living standards, health care and other benefits for all Americans. He did manage to deliver on some of his promises but the horrendous cost of the Vietnam War undermined his most ambitious plans.

As Source 46 points out, the Vietnam War had highlighted racial inequality in the USA. There were relatively few African Americans in college in the USA which meant that fewer of them could escape the draft. As a result, 30 per cent of African Americans were drafted compared to only 19 per cent of white Americans. Furthermore, 22 per cent of US casualties were black Americans, even though this group made up only 11 per cent of the total US force. One high profile African American athlete, the boxer Muhammad Ali, made his own stand by refusing to obey the draft on the grounds of his Muslim faith. He was stripped of his world title and had his passport removed. Ali was a follower of the radical Black Power group Nation of Islam. These groups all opposed the draft. How could they fight for a country which discriminated against them at home. As some of them pointed out, 'the Viet Cong never called us nigger'.

Students

One of the most powerful sources of opposition to the war was the American student movement. Many of these young people did not want to be drafted to fight in a war they did not believe in, or even thought was morally wrong. They had seen the media reports from the front line, especially the massacre at My Lai in 1968 (see pages 112–13). Instead of Vietnam being a symbol of a US crusade against Communism, to these students Vietnam had become a symbol of defeat, confusion and moral corruption (see Source 48). Students taunted the American President Lyndon B Johnson with the chant 'Hey, Hey LBJ, how many kids did you kill today?' Thousands began to 'draft dodge' – refusing to serve in Vietnam when they were called up.

The anti-war protests reached their height during 1968–70. In the first half of 1968, there were over 100 demonstrations against the Vietnam War involving 40,000 students. Frequently, the protest would involve burning the American flag – a criminal offence in the USA and a powerful symbol of the students' rejection of American values.

In November 1969, almost 700,000 anti-war protesters demonstrated in Washington DC. It was the largest political protest in American history.

SOURCE 47

"There's Money Enough To Support Both Of You —— Now, Doesn't That Make You Feel Better?"

An American cartoon from 1967.

1 Explain what Source 47 is saying.
2 Which do you think is more effective as a criticism of the Vietnam War – Source 46 or Source 47?

SOURCE 48

One does not use napalm on villages and hamlets sheltering civilians if one is attempting to persuade these people of the rightness of one's cause. One does not defoliate [destroy the vegetation of] the country and deform its people with chemicals if one is attempting to persuade them of the foe's evil nature.

An American commenting on US policy failure in Vietnam.

Anti-war demonstrations often ended in violent clashes with the police. At Berkeley, Yale and Stanford universities, bombs were set off. The worst incident by far came in 1970. At Kent State University in Ohio, students organised a demonstration against President Nixon's decision to invade Vietnam's neighbour, Cambodia. Panicked National Guard troopers opened fire on the demonstrators. Four students were killed and eleven others were injured. The press in the USA and abroad were horrified. Some 400 colleges were closed as two million students went on strike in protest at the action.

SOURCE 49

*Tin Soldiers And Nixon's Bombing
We're Finally On Our Own
This Summer I Hear The Drumming
Four Dead In Ohio*

*Gotta Get Down To It
Soldiers Are Gunning Us Down
Should Of Been Done Long Ago
What If You Knew Her And
Found Her Dead On The Ground
How Can You Run When You Know*

Lyrics to a song by Neil Young commenting on the events at Kent State. There were many protest songs in this period.

SOURCE 50

The Kent State University demonstrations in Ohio, 4 May 1970.

SOURCE 51

"... AND IN VIETNAM MY PRIMARY OBJECTIVE IS TO WIN THE HEARTS AND MINDS OF THE PEOPLE—OF THE U.S.A."

BRITISH CARTOON ARCHIVE, UNIVERSITY OF KENT © DAILY EXPRESS

Cartoon by Garland from the British newspaper the *Daily Telegraph*, 11 January 1967.

Activity

Source 51 is one of a series of cartoons which is to be presented in an online exhibition. Your task is to write a caption for the cartoon which explains the point being made. Your caption needs to be in two parts:
- a brief twenty-word summary
- a more detailed explanation which internet users can select if they want to know more. This should be about 150 words.

You can refer to later events even though this cartoon was published in 1967.

SOURCE **52**

US Marines pinned down by Viet Cong snipers in the city of Hue during the Tet Offensive, January 1968.

SOURCE **53**

Wounded US Marines in Saigon during the Tet Offensive.

SOURCE **54**

Devastation in Saigon towards the end of the Tet Offensive, 1968. Most of the damage was caused by US artillery or aircraft.

The USA looks for a way out of the war

The Tet Offensive

From 1965 to 1967 the official view of the war was that it was going reasonably well. The US and South Vietnamese forces were killing large numbers of Viet Cong. Although they were struggling against guerrilla tactics they were confident that the enemy was being worn down.

This confidence was shattered early in 1968. During the Tet New Year holiday, Viet Cong fighters attacked over 100 cities and other military targets. One Viet Cong commando unit tried to capture the US embassy in Saigon. US forces had to fight to regain control room by room. Around 4,500 Viet Cong fighters tied down a much larger US and South Vietnamese force in Saigon for two days.

In many ways the Tet Offensive was a disaster for the Communists. They had hoped that the people of South Vietnam would rise up and join them. They didn't. The Viet Cong lost around 10,000 experienced fighters and were badly weakened by it.

However, the Tet Offensive proved to be a turning point in the war because it raised hard questions in the USA about the war.

- There were nearly 500,000 troops in Vietnam and the USA was spending $20 billion a year on the war. So why had the Communists been able to launch a major offensive that took US forces completely by surprise?
- US and South Vietnamese forces quickly retook the towns captured in the offensive, but in the process they used enormous amounts of artillery and air power. Many civilians were killed. The ancient city of Hue was destroyed (see Source 19 on page 108). Was this right?
- Until this point media coverage of the war was generally positive, although some journalists were beginning to ask difficult questions in 1967. During the Tet Offensive the gloves came off. CBS journalist Walter Cronkite asked 'What the hell is going on? I thought we were winning this war'. Don Oberdorfer of *The Washington Post* later wrote (in 1971) that as a result of the Tet Offensive 'the American people and most of their leaders reached the conclusion that the Vietnam War would require greater effort over a far longer period of time than it was worth'.

SOURCE **55**

The Tet Offensive was the decisive battle of the Vietnam War because of its profound impact on American attitudes about involvement in Southeast Asia. In the aftermath of Tet, many Americans became disillusioned … To the American public and even to members of the administration, the offensive demonstrated that US intervention … had produced a negligible effect on the will and capability of the Viet Cong and North Vietnamese.

Extract from *The Tet Offensive: Intelligence Failure in War* by James Wirtz.

Activity

Study Sources 52–54 carefully. Choose two sources which you think would improve your presentation in the Activity on page 115. Write a short paragraph explaining this choice.

SOURCE 56A

Sometimes, local editorial writers joined this chorus of doubters. An editorial in the Star, for example, noted the government's 'official' line 'that the Communists have suffered such heavy losses in the offensive' that they clearly experienced a military defeat. 'But,' concluded the editorial, 'what if' this version 'is wrong?' Peggy Howard, editor of the Ball State News, certainly felt that the official story omitted a key fact: 'In spite of claims that the enemy has lost a great number of troops,' she wrote, 'this has been a great psychological victory for North Vietnam'.

SOURCE 56B

But many observers were not sympathetic towards the President. More representative of this sense of pessimism and loss are three other editorial cartoons suggesting administrative mendacity and false optimism. One in the Star showed Johnson in a track suit, running furiously in place with bullets knocking his hat from his head. It was titled: 'We're Advancing on All Fronts'. Johnson here is clearly misleading his public. A Bill Mauldin cartoon in the Ball State News echoed this sentiment from a grunt's point of view. As rockets fall around two soldiers in a foxhole, one says to the other, 'Maybe They Have Had Enough and Are Being Inscrutable about It'. Finally, a cartoon in the press made disillusionment manifest. A sandaled foot named 'Viet Cong Offensive' steps on eyeglasses labelled 'Official US Optimism'. Title: 'Rose Coloured Glasses'.

SOURCE 56C

A substantial body of local opinion supported the option of more force, not less … As early as 2 February, only a few days after the initial Tet assaults, when Saigon was still in chaos and Hue under firm enemy control, the Star offered its own blueprint for military victory in the wake of Tet. It called for 'a declaration of war against North Vietnam; the closing of Haiphong Harbour; invading North Vietnam; destroying all targets of consequence; warning China and Russia that … any attempt to supply [North Vietnam] with arms will be answered militarily'. There was no pessimistic talk of stalemate here.

Extracts from *The Tet Offensive and Middletown: A Study in Contradiction* by Professor Anthony Edmonds of Ball State University in Indiana. This study looked at local newspapers and other sources such as letters to the newspapers and interviews from the time of the Tet Offensive. The author found a mixed response.

President Johnson makes his move

After the Tet Offensive President Johnson concluded that the war could not be won militarily. He reduced the bombing campaign against North Vietnam and instructed his officials to begin negotiating for peace with the Communists. In March 1968 a peace conference began in Paris.

Johnson also announced that he would not be seeking re-election as President. It was an admission of failure. In the election campaign both Republican and Democrat candidates campaigned to end US involvement in Vietnam. The anti-Vietnam feeling was so strong that if they had supported continuing the war they would have had no chance of being elected anyway. It was no longer a question of 'could the USA win the war?' – now it was 'how can the USA get out of Vietnam without it looking like a defeat?'

Focus Task

Why was the Tet Offensive a turning point in the Vietnam War?

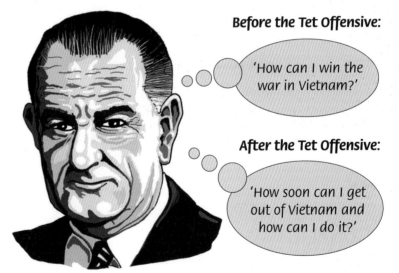

Before the Tet Offensive:

'How can I win the war in Vietnam?'

After the Tet Offensive:

'How soon can I get out of Vietnam and how can I do it?'

Even though the Tet Offensive was a defeat for the Viet Cong and North Vietnamese Army, many historians believe it was the key event that convinced President Johnson the war was unwinnable. From this point on Johnson and his successor Nixon were looking for ways to withdraw American troops from Vietnam.

Your task is to create a presentation to explain why the Tet Offensive had this effect. Use the information and sources on pages 118–19 and further research on the internet if you need to. Your slides should cover:
- what the Viet Cong did
- the outcome of the Tet Offensive in military terms
- how it affected the media
- how it affected American public opinion
- how it affected American politicians
- how the Tet Offensive brought previous concerns to a head and acted as 'the straw that broke the camel's back'.

Ending the war in Vietnam

In November 1968 Richard Nixon was elected President of the United States. From 1969 to 1973 he and his National Security Adviser Henry Kissinger worked tirelessly to end US involvement in Vietnam. This was not easy because the bigger question of how to contain world Communism – the question that had got the USA into Vietnam in the first place – had not gone away. Nixon and Kissinger did not want to appear simply to hand Vietnam to the Communists. They used a range of strategies.

In 1972, the North Vietnamese launched a major offensive but were unable to conquer South Vietnam. In Paris in January 1973, Le Duc Tho, Nixon and the South Vietnamese President Thieu signed a peace agreement (see Source 58). Nixon was jubilant. He described the agreement as 'peace with honour'. Others disagreed, but the door was now open for Nixon to pull out all US troops. By 29 March 1973, the last American forces had left Vietnam.

SOURCE **57**

Pressure on the USSR and China
In 1969 the USSR and China fell out. Indeed late in 1969, it seemed possible that there would even be a war between these two powerful Communist countries. As a result, both the USSR and China tried to improve relations with the USA.

- In 1970 Nixon began Strategic Arms Limitation Talks (SALT) with the USSR to limit nuclear weapons. He asked Moscow to encourage North Vietnam to end the war.
- Nixon also started to improve relations with China. In February 1972 nixon was invited to China. As with the USSR, he asked China to pressure North Vietnam to end the war.

Peace negotiations with North Vietnam
From early 1969, Kissinger had regular meetings with the chief Vietnamese peace negotiator, Le Duc Tho.

'Vietnamisation' of the war effort
In Vietnam Nixon began the process of Vietnamisation – building up South Vietnamese forces and withdrawing US troops. Between April 1969 and the end of 1971 almost 400,000 US troops left Vietnam.

Bombing
Nixon increased bombing campaigns against North Vietnam to show he was not weak. He also invaded Viet Cong bases in Cambodia, causing outrage across the world, and even in the USA.

US strategies to extricate US troops from involvement in Vietnam.

SOURCE **58**

1 *Immediate cease-fire.*
2 *Release of all prisoners of war within 60 days.*
3 *Withdrawal of all US forces and bases.*
4 *Full accounting of men missing in action.*
5 *Self-determination for South Vietnam.*

The main points of the peace agreement of January 1973.

SOURCE **60**

HISTORY OF VIET CONFLICT – MURKY START, UNCERTAIN END

Headline in the *Los Angeles Times*, 24 January 1973.

SOURCE **59**

FOR WHOM THE BELL TOLLS

. . . the nation began at last to extricate itself from a quicksandy war that had plagued four Presidents and driven one from office, that had sundered the country more deeply than any event since the Civil War, that in the end came to be seen by a great majority of Americans as having been a tragic mistake.

. . . but its more grievous toll was paid at home – a wound to the spirit so sore that news of peace stirred only the relief that comes with an end to pain. A war that produced no famous victories, no national heroes and no strong patriotic songs, produced no memorable armistice day celebrations either. America was too exhausted by the war and too chary [cautious] of peace to celebrate.

Reaction to the agreement of January 1973 in the American magazine *Newsweek*, 5 February 1973.

1962 Personally, I find it a rather unrewarding job.

1964 Without the keystone, the whole works would fall.

1966 Hey! That's not in the script.

1967 Butchers!

1968 Meat grinder

1970 Troop withdrawal

1971

1972

A series of cartoons from the *New Republic* magazine, 10 February 1973.

Activity

The author of this book found these cartoons while doing some research. They try to sum up the story of the Vietnam War.

1 Unfortunately the captions of the last two cartoons are missing. Suggest what these captions might be.
2 Explain the story of the eight cartoons in more detail, perhaps using a PowerPoint® presentation or software like Windows Photostory.
3 As a summary of the Vietnam War, how well do you think Source 61 works? Give it a mark out of 100 yourself, and then take a class vote on this question.

SOURCE 62

A 1975 American cartoon commenting on the end of the Vietnam War.

The fall of South Vietnam, 1973–75

It is not clear whether Nixon really believed he had secured a lasting peace settlement. But within two years it was meaningless and South Vietnam had fallen to the Communists.

Nixon had promised continuing financial aid and military support to Vietnam, but Congress refused to allow it. They did not want to waste American money. The evidence was that the South Vietnamese regime was corrupt and lacked the support of the majority of the population. Even more important, Nixon himself was in big political trouble with the Watergate Scandal. In 1974 Nixon was forced to resign over Watergate, but the new President, Gerald Ford, also failed to get the backing of Congress over Vietnam.

Without US air power or military back-up and without the support of the majority of the population, the South Vietnamese government could not survive for long. In December 1974 the North Vietnamese launched a major military offensive against South Vietnam. The capital, Saigon, fell to Communist forces in April 1975.

One of the bleakest symbols of American failure in Vietnam was the televised news images of desperate Vietnamese men, women and children trying to clamber aboard American helicopters and aeroplanes taking off from the US embassy in Saigon, and other areas. All around them Communist forces swarmed through Saigon. After 30 years of constant conflict, the struggle for control of Vietnam had finally been settled and the Communists had won.

SOURCE 63

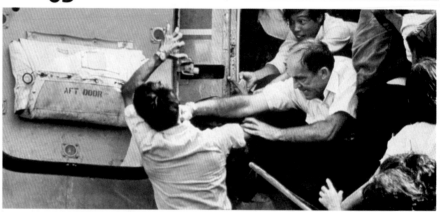

Refugees trying to board a transport plane, April 1975. An American official is punching a man in the face to make him let go of the door.

SOURCE 64

The American military was not defeated in Vietnam –
The American military did not lose a battle of any consequence. From a military standpoint, it was almost an unprecedented performance. This included Tet 68, which was a major military defeat for the VC and NVA.

The United States did not lose the war in Vietnam, the South Vietnamese did –
The fall of Saigon happened 30 April 1975, two years AFTER the American military left Vietnam. The last American troops departed in their entirety 29 March 1973. How could we lose a war we had already stopped fighting? We fought to an agreed stalemate.

The Fall of Saigon –
The 140,000 evacuees in April 1975 during the fall of Saigon consisted almost entirely of civilians and Vietnamese military, NOT American military running for their lives.

There were almost twice as many casualties in Southeast Asia (primarily Cambodia) the first two years after the fall of Saigon in 1975 than there were during the ten years the US was involved in Vietnam.

An extract from a website, www.slideshare.net, 'Vietnam War Statistics', by an American ex-serviceman.

Focus Task

Why did the USA fail in Vietnam?

Look back at your answers to the Focus Task on page 104. You will find them very useful for this summary activity.

1 Whether or not the USA lost the war there is no doubt at all that they failed to win it! You are now going to consider the reasons for this. Make cards like these on the right. On each card write an explanation or paste a source which shows the importance of the reason.
2 Add other cards if you think there are reasons you should consider.
3 Add lines to connect the reasons and write an explanation of the connection.

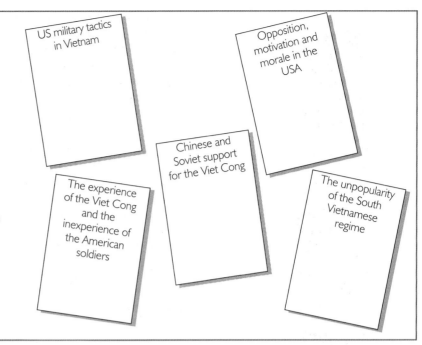

US military tactics in Vietnam

Opposition, motivation and morale in the USA

Chinese and Soviet support for the Viet Cong

The experience of the Viet Cong and the inexperience of the American soldiers

The unpopularity of the South Vietnamese regime

SOURCE 65

Listen to this comment from a high-ranking American official: 'It became clear that if we were prepared to stay the course we could lay the cornerstone for a diverse and independent region. If we falter the forces of chaos would smell victory and decades of strife and chaos would stretch endlessly before us. The choice is clear: we shall stay the course.'

That's not President Bush speaking, it's Lyndon Johnson speaking forty years ago, ordering 100,000 more American soldiers to Vietnam. Here's another quotation: 'The big problem is to get territory and to keep it. That is the big problem. You can get territory today and lose it next week. You have to have enough people to clear it and preserve what you have done.'

That is not President Bush on the need for more forces in Iraq. It is President Johnson in 1966 as he doubled our presence in Vietnam … There was no military solution to that war but we kept trying to find one anyway. And in the end 58,000 Americans died in the search for it. Echoes of that disaster are all around us today. Iraq is George Bush's Vietnam.

US Senator Edward Kennedy speaking on 9 January 2007. He was commenting on President Bush's increase in troop levels in Iraq in 2007, known as 'the surge'.

The lessons of Vietnam

In 2003 US and allied forces went into war in Iraq. Five years later they were still there and many commentators were making comparisons with Vietnam. Study Sources 65 and 66 and consider whether you think the US should have learned lessons from Vietnam.

SOURCE 66

Cartoon in the US newspaper the *Hartford Courant*, 27 June 2005. The figure on the left is George Bush. The one on the right is Lyndon Johnson, US President from 1963–68.

7 How secure was the USSR's control over eastern Europe, 1948–89?

As you saw in Chapter 4, after the Second World War the Communists quickly gained control of eastern Europe. The chaotic situation in many of the countries helped them.

- After the war there was a political vacuum in many countries in eastern Europe. The Soviet leader Stalin helped the Communist parties in them to win power. Through Cominform (see Factfile on page 125) he made sure that these eastern European countries followed the same policies as the Soviet Union. They became one-party states. The Communist Party was the only legal party. Secret police arrested the Communists' opponents.
- There was also a need to restore law and order. This provided a good excuse to station Soviet troops in each country.
- The economies of eastern Europe were shattered. To rebuild them, the governments followed the economic policies of the Soviet Union. They took over all industry. Workers and farmers were told what to produce. Through Comecon (see Factfile on page 125) Stalin made sure that the countries of eastern Europe traded with the USSR. He promised aid to countries that co-operated with the Soviet Union.
- When Soviet control was threatened, the Soviet Union was prepared to use its armed forces to crush opposition (see Source 1).

Focus

By 1948 the Soviet Union controlled most of eastern Europe. The USA saw this as part of Communist plans to dominate all Europe. The Soviet Union saw this area as its buffer from attack by the capitalist West. For the next 40 years eastern Europe was a focus of Cold War tension. In this chapter you will investigate:
- ◆ how effectively the Soviet Union controlled eastern Europe
- ◆ how events in eastern Europe affected relationships between the superpowers.

You will:
- ◆ compare how the Soviet Union dealt with opposition movements in Hungary in 1956 and in Czechoslovakia in 1967
- ◆ consider reasons why the Communists built the Berlin Wall in 1961
- ◆ consider the significance of the Polish trade union Solidarity in weakening Soviet control of eastern Europe
- ◆ investigate why Soviet control of eastern Europe collapsed after Mikhail Gorbachev became leader of the Soviet Union in the 1980s.

1 Stalin used a 'carrot and stick' approach to control eastern Europe. Explain what this means and refer to the information on this page in your answer.

SOURCE 1

"WHO'S NEXT TO BE LIBERATED FROM FREEDOM, COMRADE?"

David Low comments on Stalin's control of eastern Europe, 2 March 1948.

Cominform

➤ Cominform stands for the Communist Information Bureau.
➤ Stalin set up the Cominform in 1947 as an organisation to co-ordinate the various Communist governments in eastern Europe.
➤ The office was originally based in Belgrade in Yugoslavia but moved to Bucharest in Romania in 1948 after Yugoslavia was expelled by Stalin because it would not do what the Soviet Union told it to do.
➤ Cominform ran meetings and sent out instructions to Communist governments about what the Soviet Union wanted them to do.

Factfile

Comecon

➤ Comecon stands for the Council for Mutual Economic Assistance.
➤ It was set up in 1949 to co-ordinate the industries and trade of the eastern European countries.
➤ The idea was that members of Comecon traded mostly with one another rather than trading with the West.
➤ Comecon favoured the USSR far more than any of its other members. It provided the USSR with a market to sell its goods. It also guaranteed it a cheap supply of raw materials. For example, Poland was forced to sell its coal to the USSR at one-tenth of the price that it could have got selling it on the open market.
➤ It set up a bank for socialist countries in 1964.

SOURCE 2

Key

- Territory taken over by USSR at end of Second World War
- Soviet-dominated Communist governments
- Other Communist governments

Eastern Europe, 1948–56.

What did ordinary people in eastern Europe think of Soviet control?

For some people of eastern Europe the Communists brought hope. The Soviet Union had achieved amazing industrial growth before the Second World War. Maybe, by following Soviet methods, they could do the same. Soviet-style Communism also offered them stable government and security because they were backed by one of the world's superpowers. Faced by shortages and poverty after the war, many people hoped for great things from Communism (see Source 3 on page 126).

However, the reality of Soviet control of eastern Europe was very different from what people had hoped for. Countries that had a long tradition of free speech and democratic government suddenly lost the right to criticise the government. Newspapers were censored. Non-Communists were put in prison for criticising the government. People were forbidden to travel to countries in western Europe.

Between 1945 and 1955 eastern European economies did recover. But the factories did not produce what ordinary people wanted. They actually produced what the Soviet Union wanted. Wages in eastern Europe fell behind the wages in other countries. They even fell behind the wages in the Soviet Union. Eastern Europe was forbidden by Stalin to apply for Marshall Aid from the USA (see pages 79–80) which could have helped it in its economic recovery.

Long after economic recovery had ended the wartime shortages in western Europe, people in eastern Europe were short of coal to heat their houses, short of milk and meat. Clothing and shoes were very expensive. People could not get consumer goods like radios, electric kettles or televisions which were becoming common in the West.

In addition, they had little chance to protest. In June 1953 there were huge demonstrations across East Germany protesting about Communist policies. Soviet tanks rolled in and Soviet troops killed 40 protesters and wounded over 400. Thousands were arrested and the protests were crushed. Similar protests in Czechoslovakia, Hungary and Romania were dealt with in the same way.

SOURCE 3

Twenty years ago we jumped head first into politics as though we were jumping into uncharted waters . . . There was a lot of enthusiasm . . . You're like this when you are young and we had an opportunity, which had long been denied, to be there while something new was being created.

Jiři Ruml, a Czech Communist, writing in 1968.

SOURCE 4

1 Study Source 4. Why do you think Tito wished to remain independent of the Soviet Union?
2 Why do you think the Soviet Union was worried about Tito's independence?
3 Look at Source 2 on page 125. Does this help to explain why the Soviet Union allowed Tito to remain independent?

Экспортно-импортный банк США предоставил Тито заё в необычайно короткий срок.

(Из газет).

КУКРЫНИКСЫ-49

Рис. Кукрыниксы.

Тридцать сребреников.

A 1949 Soviet cartoon. Marshal Tito, leader of Yugoslavia, is shown accepting money from the Americans. His cloak is labelled 'Judas' – 'the betrayer'. Yugoslavia was the only Communist state to resist domination by Stalin. The Soviet Union kept up a propaganda battle against Tito. Despite the Cold War, there were more cartoons in the official Communist newspapers attacking Tito than cartoons criticising the USA.

Focus Task

What was Stalin's legacy?

It is 1953. Stalin has died. Write an obituary for him explaining how he gained control of eastern Europe.

The rise of Khrushchev

Stalin was a hero to millions of people in the USSR. He had defeated Hitler and given the USSR an empire in eastern Europe. He made the USSR a nuclear superpower. When he died in 1953, amid the grief and mourning, many minds turned to the question of who would succeed Stalin as Soviet leader. The man who emerged by 1955 was Nikita Khrushchev. He seemed very different from Stalin. He ended the USSR's long feuds with China and with Yugoslavia. He talked of peaceful co-existence with the West. He made plans to reduce expenditure on arms. He attended the first post-war summit between the USSR, the USA, France and Britain in July 1955. He also said he wanted to improve the living standards of ordinary Soviet citizens and those of eastern Europe.

Khrushchev even relaxed the iron control of the Soviet Union. He closed down Cominform. He released thousands of political prisoners. He agreed to pull Soviet troops out of Austria (they had been posted there since the end of the Second World War). He seemed to be signalling to the countries of eastern Europe that they would be allowed much greater independence to control their own affairs.

SOURCE 5

A 1959 Soviet cartoon. The writing on the snowman's hat reads 'cold war'. Khrushchev is drilling through the cold war using what the caption calls 'miners' methods'.

Activity

Look at Source 5.

1 Make a list of the features of the cartoon which show Khrushchev as a new type of leader.

2 Explain:
  a) why he is shown destroying the snowman, and
  b) what this is supposed to suggest about his attitude to the Cold War.

3 Design another cartoon which shows him relaxing the Soviet grip on Eastern Europe. Think about:
  • how you would show Khrushchev
  • how you would represent the states of Eastern Europe (as maps? as people?)
  • how you would represent Soviet control (as a rope? getting looser? tighter?).

You could either draw the cartoon or write instructions for an artist to do so.

SOURCE 6

We must produce more grain. The more grain there is, the more meat, lard and fruit there will be. Our tables will be better covered. Marxist theory helped us win power and consolidate it. Having done this we must help the people eat well, dress well and live well. If after forty years of Communism, a person cannot have a glass of milk or a pair of shoes, he will not believe Communism is a good thing, whatever you tell him.

Nikita Khrushchev speaking in 1955.

Profile

Nikita Khrushchev

➤ Born 1894, the son of a coal miner.
➤ Fought in the Red Army during the Civil War, 1922–23.
➤ Afterwards worked for the Communist Party in Moscow. Was awarded the Order of Lenin for his work building the Moscow underground railway.
➤ In 1949 he was appointed by the Communist Party to run Soviet agriculture.
➤ There was a power struggle after Stalin's death over who would succeed him. Khrushchev had come out on top by 1955 and by 1956 he felt secure enough in his position to attack Stalin's reputation.
➤ Became Prime Minister in 1958.
➤ Took his country close to nuclear war with the USA during the Cuban missile crisis in 1962 (see pages 86–99).
➤ Was forced into retirement in 1964.
➤ Died in 1971.

Activity

Write your own definition of 'de-Stalinisation'. Make sure you include:
• at least two examples
• an explanation of why it was radical.

De-Stalinisation

At the Communist Party International in 1956, Khrushchev made an astonishing attack on Stalin. He dredged up the gory evidence of Stalin's purges (see page 334) and denounced him as a wicked tyrant who was an enemy of the people and kept all power to himself. Khrushchev went on to say much worse things about Stalin and began a programme of 'de-Stalinisation':

• He released more political prisoners.
• He closed down Cominform as part of his policy of reconciliation with Yugoslavia.
• He invited Marshal Tito to Moscow.
• He dismissed Stalin's former Foreign Minister, Molotov.

Those in eastern Europe who wanted greater freedom from the Soviet Union saw hopeful times ahead.

SOURCE 7

Stalin used extreme methods and mass repressions at a time when the revolution was already victorious . . . Stalin showed in a whole series of cases his intolerance, his brutality and his abuse of power . . . He often chose the path of repression and physical annihilation, not only against actual enemies, but also against individuals who had not committed any crimes against the Party and the Soviet government.

Khrushchev denounces Stalin in 1956. For citizens of eastern Europe who had been bombarded with propaganda praising Stalin, this was a shocking change of direction.

The Warsaw Pact

One aspect of Stalin's policy did not change, however. His aim in eastern Europe had always been to create a buffer against attack from the West. Khrushchev continued this policy. In 1955 he created the Warsaw Pact. This was a military alliance similar to NATO (see page 84). The members would defend each other if one was attacked. The Warsaw Pact included all the Communist countries of eastern Europe except Yugoslavia, but it was dominated by the Soviet Union (see Source 2, page 87).

How did the USSR deal with opposition in eastern Europe?

Khrushchev's criticism of Stalin sent a strong signal to opposition groups in eastern Europe that they could now press for changes. The question was: how far would Khrushchev let them go? The first opposition Khrushchev had to deal with as leader was in Poland.

In the summer of 1956 demonstrators attacked the Polish police, protesting about the fact that the government had increased food prices but not wages. Fifty-three workers were killed by the Polish army in riots in Poznan. The Polish government itself was unable to control the demonstrators. Alarmed, Khrushchev moved troops to the Polish border.

By October 1956 Poland was becoming more stabilised. A new leader, Wladyslaw Gomulka, took charge on 20 October. During the Nazi occupation Gomulka had been a popular leader of the Communist resistance (not the main underground army, the AK). However, he was also a nationalist. He had not seen eye to eye with many Polish Communists, who were totally loyal to Stalin. Khrushchev accepted Gomulka's appointment – a popular move in Poland for the next couple of years.

There was also an agreement that the Communists would stop persecuting members of the Catholic Church. The Red Army withdrew to the Polish border and left the Polish army and government to sort things out.

Case study 1: Hungary, 1956

Khrushchev was soon put to the test again in Hungary in October 1956.

Why was there opposition in Hungary?

Hungary was led by a hard-line Communist called Mátyás Rákosi. Hungarians hated the restrictions which Rákosi's Communism imposed on them. Most Hungarians felt bitter about losing their freedom of speech. They lived in fear of the secret police. They resented the presence of thousands of Soviet troops and officials in their country. Some areas of Hungary even had Russian street signs, Russian schools and shops. Worst of all, Hungarians had to pay for Soviet forces to be in Hungary.

Activity

Look at Source 9. The four flags are the flags of:
- Rákosi's government, 1949–56
- the rebels in the 1956 rising
- Kádár's government, 1956–89
- state flag after 1989.
They are not in the right order in Source 9. Work out which one is which.

SOURCE 8

Living standards were declining and yet the papers and radio kept saying that we had never had it so good. Why? Why these lies? Everybody knew the state was spending the money on armaments. Why could they not admit that we were worse off because of the war effort and the need to build new factories? . . . I finally arrived at the realisation that the system was wrong and stupid.

A Hungarian student describes the mood in 1953.

SOURCE 9

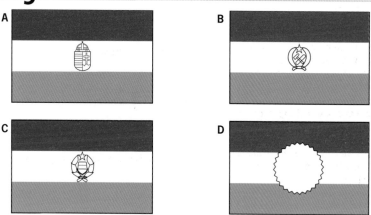

Flags representing different stages of Hungary's position, 1949–89.

In June 1956 a group within the Communist Party in Hungary opposed Rákosi. He appealed to Moscow for help. He wanted to arrest 400 leading opponents. Moscow would not back him. Rákosi's assistant said sarcastically: 'Might I suggest that mass arrests are not reconcilable with our new brand of socialist legality.' The Kremlin ordered Rákosi to be retired 'for health reasons'.

However, the new leader, Ernö Gerö, was no more acceptable to the Hungarian people. Discontent came to a head with a huge student demonstration on 23 October, when the giant statue of Stalin in Budapest was pulled down. The USSR allowed a new government to be formed under the well-respected Imre Nagy. Soviet troops and tanks stationed in Hungary since the war began to withdraw. Hungarians created thousands of local councils to replace Soviet power. Several thousand Hungarian soldiers defected from the army to the rebel cause, taking their weapons with them.

Nagy's government began to make plans. It would hold free elections, create impartial courts, restore farmland to private ownership. It wanted the total withdrawal of the Soviet army from Hungary. It also planned to leave the Warsaw Pact and declare Hungary neutral in the Cold War struggle between East and West. There was widespread optimism that the new American President Eisenhower, who had been the wartime supreme commander of all Allied Forces in western Europe, would support the new independent Hungary.

SOURCE 10

. . . wearing clothes patterned after Western styles, showing interest in Jazz, expressing liberalism in the arts – was considered dangerous in the eyes of the people's democracy. To cite a small example, let us take the case of my university colleague, John. He showed up at lectures one day several weeks before the revolution in a new suit and a striped shirt and necktie, all of which he had received from an uncle in the United States through gift-parcel channels. His shoes were smooth suede and would have cost one month's wages in Hungary. After classes John was summoned by the party officer. He received a tongue-lashing and was expelled.

Written by László Beke, a student who helped lead the Hungarian uprising in 1956, in *A Student's Diary: Budapest October 16–November 1, 1956.*

Focus Task

Why was there opposition to Soviet control in Hungary?

1 Use the text and Sources 8 and 10 to give reasons why the Hungarians disliked Communist control.
2 Which of their demands do you think would be most threatening to the USSR?

How did the Soviet Union respond?

Khrushchev at first seemed ready to accept some of the reforms. However, he could not accept Hungary's leaving the Warsaw Pact. In November 1956 thousands of Soviet troops and tanks moved into Budapest. Unlike in Poland, the Hungarians did not give in. Two weeks of bitter fighting followed. Some estimates put the number of Hungarians killed at 30,000. However, the latest research suggests about 3,000 Hungarians and 7,000–8,000 Russians were killed. Another 200,000 Hungarians fled across the border into Austria to escape the Communist forces. Imre Nagy and his fellow leaders were imprisoned and then executed.

SOURCE 11

In Hungary thousands of people have obtained arms by disarming soldiers and militia men . . . Soldiers have been making friends with the embittered and dissatisfied masses . . . The authorities are paralysed, unable to stop the bloody events.

From a report in a Yugoslav newspaper. Yugoslavia, although Communist, did not approve of Soviet policies.

SOURCE 12

We have almost no weapons, no heavy guns of any kind. People are running up to the tanks, throwing in hand grenades and closing the drivers' windows. The Hungarian people are not afraid of death. It is only a pity that we cannot last longer. Now the firing is starting again. The tanks are coming nearer and nearer. You can't let people attack tanks with their bare hands. What is the United Nations doing?

A telex message sent by the Hungarian rebels fighting the Communists. Quoted in George Mikes, *The Hungarian Revolution*, 1957.

1 How do Sources 11 and 12 differ in the impression they give of the Hungarian uprising?
2 Why do you think they differ?
3 Do the photos in Source 14 on page 131 give the same impression as either Source 11 or Source 12?
4 Write a paragraph explaining the nature of the fighting in Budapest using Sources 11–14.
5 Look back at Source 2 on page 125. Why do you think Hungary's membership of the Warsaw Pact was so important to the Soviet Union?
6 Why do you think the Hungarians received no support from the West?

SOURCE 13

October 27, 1956. On my way home I saw a little girl propped up against the doorway of a building with a machine gun clutched in her hands. When I tried to move her, I saw she was dead. She couldn't have been more than eleven or twelve years old. There was a neatly folded note in her pocket she had evidently meant to pass on through someone to her parents. In childish scrawl it read: 'Dear Mama, Brother is dead. He asked me to take care of his gun. I am all right, and I'm going with friends now. I kiss you. Kati.'

Written by László Beke, a Hungarian student.

Activity

Explain which of these statements you most agree with:

> The speed at which the Red Army crushed resistance in Hungary shows how completely the Soviet Union controlled Hungary.

> The severity of the Red Army in dealing with Hungary in 1956 shows how fragile the Soviet hold on Hungary really was.

The Hungarian resistance was crushed in two weeks. The Western powers protested to the USSR but sent no help; they were too preoccupied with the Suez crisis in the Middle East.

Khrushchev put János Kádár in place as leader. Kádár took several months to crush all resistance. Around 35,000 anti-Communist activists were arrested and 300 were executed. Kádár cautiously introduced some of the reforms being demanded by the Hungarian people. However, he did not waver on the central issue – membership of the Warsaw Pact.

The effects of the uprising in Budapest. **A** shows the scene of destruction outside the Kilian Barracks, where heavy fighting was experienced. **B** shows an armed fifteen-year-old girl.

Case study 2: Czechoslovakia and the Prague Spring, 1968

Twelve years after the brutal suppression of the Hungarians, Czechoslovakia posed a similar challenge to Soviet domination of eastern Europe. Khrushchev had by now been ousted from power in the USSR. A new leader, Leonid Brezhnev, had replaced him.

Why was there opposition in Czechoslovakia?

In the 1960s a new mood developed in Czechoslovakia. People examined what had been happening in twenty years of Communist control and they did not like what they saw. In 1967 the old Stalinist leader was forced to resign. Alexander Dubček became the leader of the Czech Communist Party. He proposed a policy of 'socialism with a human face': less censorship, more freedom of speech and a reduction in the activities of the secret police. Dubček was a committed Communist, but he believed that Communism did not have to be as restrictive as it had been before he came to power. He had learned the lessons of the Hungarian uprising and reassured Brezhnev that Czechoslovakia had no plans to pull out of the Warsaw Pact or Comecon.

The Czech opposition was led by intellectuals who felt that the Communists had failed to lead the country forward. As censorship had been eased, they were able to launch attacks on the Communist leadership, pointing out how corrupt and useless they were. Communist government ministers were 'grilled' on live television and radio about how they were running the country and about events before 1968. This period became known as 'The Prague Spring' because of all the new ideas that seemed to be appearing everywhere.

By the summer even more radical ideas were emerging. There was even talk of allowing another political party, the Social Democratic Party, to be set up as a rival to the Communist Party.

SOURCE 15

In Czechoslovakia the people who were trusted [by the Communist government] were the obedient ones, those who did not cause any trouble, who didn't ask questions. It was the mediocre man who came off best.

In twenty years not one human problem has been solved in our country, from primary needs like flats, schools, to the more subtle needs such as fulfilling oneself . . . the need for people to trust one another . . . development of education.

I feel that our Republic has lost its good reputation.

From a speech given by Ludvik Vaculik, a leading figure in the reform movement, in March 1968.

SOURCE 16

The Director told them they would produce 400 locomotives a year. They are making seventy.

And go look at the scrapyard, at all the work that has been thrown out. They built a railway and then took it down again. Who's responsible for all this? The Communist Party set up the system.

We were robbed of our output, our wages . . . How can I believe that in five years' time it won't be worse?

Ludvik Vaculik quotes from an interview he had with the workers in a locomotive factory run by the Communists.

SOURCE 17

All the different kinds of state in which the Communist Party has taken power have gone through rigged trials . . . There must be a fault other than just the wrong people were chosen. There must be a fault in the theory [of Communism] itself.

Written by Luboš Dubrovsky, a Czech writer, in May 1968.

How did the Soviet Union respond?

The Soviet Union was very suspicious of the changes taking place in Czechoslovakia. Czechoslovakia was one of the most important countries in the Warsaw Pact. It was centrally placed, and had the strongest industry. The Soviets were worried that the new ideas in Czechoslovakia might spread to other countries in eastern Europe. Brezhnev came under pressure from the East German leader, Walter Ulbricht, and the Polish leader, Gomulka, to restrain reform in Czechoslovakia.

The USSR tried various methods in response. To start with, it tried to slow Dubček down. It argued with him. Soviet, Polish and East German troops performed very public training exercises right on the Czech border. It thought about imposing economic sanctions – for example, cancelling wheat exports to Czechoslovakia – but didn't because it thought that the Czechs would ask for help from the West.

In July the USSR had a summit conference with the Czechs. Dubček agreed not to allow a new Social Democratic Party. However, he insisted on keeping most of his reforms. The tension seemed to ease. Early in August, a conference of all the other Warsaw Pact countries produced a vague declaration simply calling on Czechoslovakia to maintain political stability.

Then seventeen days later, on 20 August 1968, to the stunned amazement of the Czechs and the outside world, Soviet tanks moved into Czechoslovakia.

Focus Task

Why was there opposition to Soviet control in Czechoslovakia?

1 According to Sources 15–17, what are the worries of the Czech people?
2 How are they similar to and different from the concerns of the Hungarian rebels (see the Focus Task on page 129)?

SOURCE **18**

Czechs burning Soviet tanks in Prague, August 1968.

1 Explain how and why Sources 19 and 21 differ in their interpretation of the Soviet intervention.

SOURCE **19**

Yesterday troops from the Soviet Union, Poland, East Germany, Hungary and Bulgaria crossed the frontier of Czechoslovakia . . . The Czechoslovak Communist Party Central Committee regard this act as contrary to the basic principles of good relations between socialist states.

A Prague radio report, 21 August 1968.

SOURCE **21**

The party and government leaders of the Czechoslovak Socialist Republic have asked the Soviet Union and other allies to give the Czechoslovak people urgent assistance, including assistance with armed forces. This request was brought about . . . by the threat from counter revolutionary forces . . . working with foreign forces hostile to socialism.

A Soviet news agency report, 21 August 1968.

SOURCE **20**

A street cartoon in Prague.

There was little violent resistance, although many Czechs refused to co-operate with the Soviet troops. Dubček was removed from power. His experiment in socialism with a human face had not failed; it had simply proved unacceptable to the other Communist countries.

Dubček always expressed loyalty to Communism and the Warsaw Pact, but Brezhnev was very worried that the new ideas coming out of Czechoslovakia would spread. He was under pressure from the leaders of other Communist countries in eastern Europe, particularly Ulbricht in East Germany. These leaders feared that their own people would demand the same freedom that Dubček had allowed in Czechoslovakia. Indeed, in 1968 Albania resigned from the Warsaw Pact because it thought that the Soviet Union itself had become too liberal since Stalin had died! Brezhnev made no attempt to force Albania back into the Pact because he did not consider it an important country.

SOURCE **22**

When internal and external forces hostile to socialism attempt to turn the development of any socialist country in the direction of the capitalist system, when a threat arises to the cause of socialism in that country, a threat to the socialist commonwealth as a whole – it becomes not only a problem for the people of that country but also a general problem, the concern of all socialist countries.

The Brezhnev Doctrine.

The Brezhnev Doctrine

The Czechoslovak episode gave rise to the Brezhnev Doctrine. The essentials of Communism were defined as

• a one-party system
• to remain a member of the Warsaw Pact.

Unlike Nagy in Hungary, Dubček was not executed. But he was gradually downgraded. First he was sent to be ambassador to Turkey, then expelled from the Communist Party altogether. Photographs showing him as leader were 'censored'.

SOURCE **23**

A

B

These two photographs show the same scene. In **A**, Dubček is shown by the arrow. How has he been dealt with in photograph **B**?

Before the Soviet invasion, Czechoslovakia's mood had been one of optimism. After, it was despair. A country that had been pro-Soviet now became resentful of the Soviet connection. Ideas that could have reformed Communism were silenced.

Twenty years later, Mikhail Gorbachev, the leader of the USSR, questioned the invasion, and was himself spreading the ideas of the Prague Spring that the Soviet Union had crushed in 1968.

Focus Task

How similar were events in Hungary in 1956 and in Czechoslavakia in 1968?

You are going to compare the two rebellions in Hungary in 1956 and Czechoslovakia in 1968.
For each rebellion consider:

◆ the aims of the rebels
◆ attitude towards Communism
◆ attitude towards democracy
◆ attitude to the USSR
◆ attitude to the West
◆ why the Soviet Union intervened
◆ how each state responded to Soviet intervention.

SOURCE 24

A 1959 Soviet cartoon – the caption was: 'The socialist stallion far outclasses the capitalist donkey'.

1 Look at Source 24. What is the aim of this cartoon?
2 Why might someone living in a Communist country like it or dislike it?

SOURCE 26

West Berlin . . . has many roles. It is more than a showcase of liberty, an island of freedom in a Communist sea. It is more than a link with the free world, a beacon of hope behind the iron curtain, an escape hatch for refugees. Above all, it has become the resting place of Western courage and will . . . We cannot and will not permit the Communists to drive us out of Berlin.

President Kennedy speaking in 1960, before he became President.

3 Which photograph in Source 25 do you think shows East Berlin and which shows West Berlin? Explain your choice and write a detailed description of the differences between the two areas based on the sources and the text.

Case study 3: The Berlin Wall

You have already seen how important Berlin was as a battleground of the Cold War (see pages 81–82). In 1961 it also became the focus of the Soviet Union's latest attempt to maintain control of its east European satellites.

The crushing of the Hungarian uprising had confirmed for many people in eastern Europe that it was impossible to fight the Communists. For many, it seemed that the only way of escaping the repression was to leave altogether. Some wished to leave eastern Europe for political reasons – they hated the Communists – while many more wished to leave for economic reasons. As standards of living in eastern Europe fell further and further behind the West, the attraction of going to live in a capitalist state was very great.

The contrast was particularly great in the divided city of Berlin. Living standards were tolerable in the East, but just a few hundred metres away in West Berlin, East Germans could see some of the prize exhibits of capitalist West Germany – shops full of goods, great freedom, great wealth and great variety. This had been deliberately done by the Western powers. They had poured massive investment into Berlin. East Germans could also watch West German television.

SOURCE 25

A

B

Berlin in the 1950s.

In the 1950s East Germans were still able to travel freely into West Berlin (see Source 27). From there they could travel on into West Germany. It was very tempting to leave East Germany, with its harsh Communist regime and its hardline leader, Walter Ulbricht. By the late 1950s thousands were leaving and never coming back.

SOURCE **27**

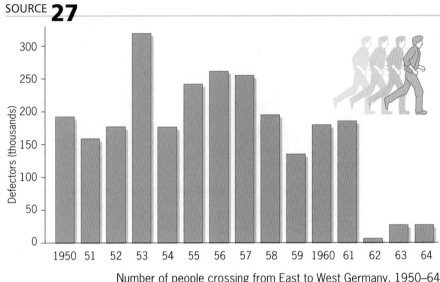

Number of people crossing from East to West Germany, 1950–64.

SOURCE **28**

A

Those who were defecting were very often highly skilled workers or well-qualified managers. The Communist government could not afford to lose these high-quality people. More importantly, from Khrushchev's point of view, the sight of thousands of Germans fleeing Communist rule for a better life under capitalism undermined Communism generally.

In 1961 the USA had a new President, the young and inexperienced John F Kennedy. Khrushchev thought he could bully Kennedy and chose to pick a fight over Berlin. He insisted that Kennedy withdraw US troops from the city. He was certain that Kennedy would back down. Kennedy refused. However, all eyes were now on Berlin. What would happen next?

At two o'clock in the morning on Sunday 13 August 1961, East German soldiers erected a barbed-wire barrier along the entire frontier between East and West Berlin, ending all free movement from East to West. It was quickly replaced by a concrete wall. All the crossing points from East to West Berlin were sealed, except for one. This became known as Checkpoint Charlie.

Families were divided. Berliners were unable to go to work; chaos and confusion followed. Border guards kept a constant look-out for anyone trying to cross the wall. They had orders to shoot people trying to defect. Hundreds were killed over the next three decades.

B

C

Stages in the building of the Berlin Wall. On the sign in **B**, which has been imposed by a photographer wanting to make a point or a question, Ulbricht assures the world that 'no one has any intention of building a wall'.

SOURCE 29

East German security guards recover the body of a man shot attempting to cross the wall in 1962.

SOURCE 30

The Western powers in Berlin use it as a centre of subversive activity against the GDR [the initial letters of the German name for East Germany]. In no other part of the world are so many espionage centres to be found. These centres smuggle their agents into the GDR for all kinds of subversion: recruiting spies; sabotage; provoking disturbances.

The government presents all working people of the GDR with a proposal that will securely block subversive activity so that reliable safeguards and effective control will be established around West Berlin, including its border with democratic Berlin.

A Soviet explanation for the building of the wall, 1961.

The West's reaction to the Berlin Wall

For a while, the wall created a major crisis. Access to East Berlin had been guaranteed to the Allies since 1945. In October 1961 US diplomats and troops crossed regularly into East Berlin to find out how the Soviets would react.

On 27 October Soviet tanks pulled up to Checkpoint Charlie and refused to allow any further access to the East. All day, US and Soviet tanks, fully armed, faced each other in a tense stand-off. Then, after eighteen hours, one by one, five metres at a time, the tanks pulled back. Another crisis, another retreat.

The international reaction was relief. Khrushchev ordered Ulbricht to avoid any actions that would increase tension. Kennedy said, 'It's not a very nice solution, but a wall is a hell of a lot better than a war.' So the wall stayed, and over the following years became the symbol of division – the division of Germany, the division of Europe, the division of Communist East and democratic West. The Communists presented the wall as a protective shell around East Berlin. The West presented it as a prison wall.

SOURCE 31

There are some who say, in Europe and elsewhere, we can work with the Communists. Let them come to Berlin.

President Kennedy speaking in 1963 after the building of the Berlin Wall.

SOURCE 32

ГРАНИЦА ГДР
ДЛЯ ВРАГОВ ЗАКРЫТА!

A Soviet cartoon from the 1960s. The sign reads: 'The border of the GDR (East Germany) is closed to all enemies.' Notice the shape of the dog's tail.

Focus Task

Why was the Berlin Wall built in 1961?

Work in pairs.

Make a poster or notice to be stuck on the Berlin Wall explaining the purpose of the wall. One of you do a poster for the East German side and the other do a poster for the West German side. You can use pictures and quotations from the sources in this chapter or use your own research.

Make sure you explain in your poster the reasons why the wall was built and what the results of building the wall will be.

1 Make your own copy of this graph.
2 Mark on the graph:
   • three developments that improved superpower relations in this period
   • three developments that harmed superpower relations in this period.
3 Compare your graph with those of other people in your class. See if you can produce one combined graph that includes all the developments mentioned on this page and shows the pattern of superpower relations.
4 Now apply this to eastern Europe. What effect do you think these developments will have on Soviet policy towards eastern Europe. As a class write down some predictions.

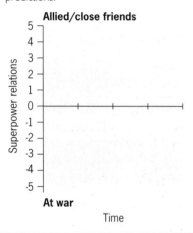

How did superpower relationships change 1970–85?

You will step aside from the story of eastern Europe for a moment and consider the wider picture of the Cold War. The 1970s is considered a period of détente. Détente means 'relaxing of tension'. Following the American humiliation in Vietnam, US presidents worked hard to build better relationships with China and the USSR. They met together. Arms control and human rights were discussed openly. But from the late 1970s there was once again increasing distrust. These two pages summarise those developments and the reasons why the Cold War thawed for a while and then froze again.

1970

Economic problems for the USA and its allies peaked in 1970 when high unemployment and high inflation caused a depression. In such a climate the arms race was very costly. Both superpowers saw this as money that could be spent more wisely on foreign aid to poor countries or improving the conditions of their own people at home.

1972

The Americans withdraw from Vietnam (see page 120).

1981

Ronald Reagan – In 1981, the USA elected the former Hollywood film actor Ronald Reagan as President. Reagan made no secret of his dislike of Communism and the USSR, calling it the Evil Empire. He supported anti-Communist forces in Afghanistan and Nicaragua. Reagan was helped by the fact that many of Europe's leaders at this time (including Britain's Prime Minister, Margaret Thatcher) supported his tough line against the USSR.

His boldest plan was to escalate the arms race in order to end it. He increased US defence spending by $32.6 billion. In 1982, he gave the go-ahead for the Strategic Defense Initiative (popularly known as Star Wars). This was a multi-billion dollar project to create a system using satellites and lasers that could destroy missiles before they hit their targets. Clearly, a weapon such as this could change the whole nature of nuclear war.

1980s and 1990s

Civil wars in Nicaragua and El Salvador and in Angola – Communist rebels (supported by Cuban and Soviet money and expertise) tried to overthrow the governments of these states in South America and Africa. The USA funded the governments against the rebels. In Angola, the USA and the USSR helped to fund a long-running civil war.

1980 and 1984

The Moscow and Los Angeles Olympics – In protest at Soviet involvement in the Afghan War, the USA boycotted the 1980 Olympic games held in Moscow. In retaliation, the USSR and eastern European teams boycotted the Los Angeles Olympics held four years later.

1972

Salt Treaty – Brezhnev and Nixon signed the nuclear arms limitation treaty, SALT 1.

1975 July

High hand shake! American astronauts and Soviet cosmonauts met up and shook hands in space. This was quite literally the high point of détente.

1975 August

Helsinki conference. All countries recognised the borders set out after the Second World War, including the division of Germany. They agreed to respect human rights – e.g. freedom of speech, freedom to move from one country to another.

1976

The biggest ever anti-nuclear protest march took place in Bilbao, Spain. There were anti-nuclear movements in many Western countries.

1979–90

Afghanistan – In 1979 the pro-Soviet regime in Afghanistan was under serious threat from its Muslim opponents, the Mujahideen. To protect the regime, Soviet forces entered Afghanistan on 25 December 1979. Western powers were alarmed that the USSR could get so close to the West's oil supplies in the Middle East. President Carter described the Soviet action as 'the most serious threat to peace since the Second World War'.

The USA secretly began to send very large shipments of money, arms and equipment to Pakistan and from there to the USSR's Mujahideen opponents. The campaign became the Soviet Union's equivalent of the Vietnam War. It was a nightmare campaign, virtually unwinnable for the Soviet forces, although they remained there until the early 1990s.

1979

Revolution in Iran – The Shah of Iran was overthrown in 1979. The USA had supported the Shah because it needed Iran's oil. The new government was strongly anti-American but also strongly anti-Communist. It wanted a society based on Islamic values. The Iranian revolution changed the balance of power in the Middle East and increased tension between the superpowers, who were both worried about how the other would react.

1977

The USA elected a new president Jimmy Carter who criticised the Soviet Union for its abuses of human rights.

1979

Collapse of SALT 2 – The main terms of the SALT 2 agreement had been set out as early as 1974. It was not until June 1979 that SALT 2 was finally signed. By that time, relations between the USA and the USSR had deteriorated so much that the US Congress refused to ratify SALT 2.

1977–79

New nuclear weapons – In 1977 the USSR began replacing out-of-date missiles in eastern Europe with new SS-20 nuclear missiles. The West saw these missiles as a new type of battlefield weapon that could be used in a limited nuclear war confined only to Europe. In response, President Carter allowed the US military to develop the Cruise missile. By 1979 the USA had stationed Pershing missiles in western Europe as an answer to the SS-20s.

Is it any wonder that people are in despair? They must begin queuing outside the butcher's early in the morning and they may still find there is no meat to buy. We want to achieve a free trade union movement which will allow workers to manage the economy through joint control with the government.

Lech Walesa, leader of Solidarity, speaking in 1980.

SOURCE **34**

- *More pay*
- *End to censorship*
- *Same welfare benefits as police and party workers*
- *Broadcasting of Catholic church services*
- *Election of factory managers*

Some of the 21 points.

Profile

Lech Walesa

- ➤ Pronounced Lek Fowensa.
- ➤ Born 1943. His father was a farmer.
- ➤ He went to work in the shipyards at Gdansk.
- ➤ In 1976 he was sacked from the shipyard for making 'malicious' statements about the organisation and working climate.
- ➤ In 1978 he helped organise a union at another factory. He was dismissed.
- ➤ In 1979 he worked for Eltromontage. He was said to be the best automotive electrician. He was sacked.
- ➤ With others, he set up Solidarity in August 1980 and became its leader.
- ➤ He was a committed Catholic.
- ➤ In 1989 he became the leader of Poland's first non-Communist government since the Second World War.

1 Look at Source 35. Make a list of the complaints that appear in this extract.
2 What are the strengths and weaknesses of this source as evidence of attitudes to the Communist Party in Poland?

Case study 4: Solidarity

Throughout the years of Communist control of Poland there were regular protests. However, unlike the protests in both Hungary and Czechoslovakia, they tended to be about wages or food prices. Strikers did not try to get rid of the government or challenge the Soviet Union. They simply wanted to improve their standard of living. The workers were keenly aware that they lagged behind workers in the West. The government for its part seemed aware that it would only survive if it could satisfy the Poles' demands for consumer goods.

During the first half of the 1970s Polish industry performed well. But in the late 1970s the Polish economy hit a crisis: 1976 was a bad year and 1979 was the worst year for Polish industry since Communism had been introduced. This is what happened next.

July 1980	The government announced increases in the price of meat.
August 1980	Workers at the Gdansk shipyard, led by Lech Walesa, put forward 21 demands to the government, including free trade unions and the right to strike (see Source 34). They also started a free trade union called Solidarity. Poland had trade unions but they were ineffective in challenging goverment policies.
30 August 1980	The government agreed to all 21 of Solidarity's demands.
September 1980	Solidarity's membership grew to 3.5 million.
October 1980	Solidarity's membership was 7 million. Solidarity was officially recognised by the government.
January 1981	Membership of Solidarity reached its peak at 9.4 million – more than a third of all the workers in Poland.

Why did the Polish government agree to Solidarity's demands in 1980?

In the light of all you know about the Communist rule of eastern Europe, you might be surprised that the government gave in to Solidarity in 1980. There are many different reasons for this.

- **The union was strongest in those industries that were most important to the government** – shipbuilding and heavy industry. Membership was particularly high among skilled workers and foremen. A general strike in these industries would have devastated Poland's economy.

- **In the early stages the union was not seen by its members as an alternative to the Communist Party.** More than 1 million members (30 per cent) of the Communist Party joined Solidarity.

- **Lech Walesa was very careful** in his negotiations with the government. Behind the scenes he worked with the Communist leader Kania to avoid provoking a dispute that might bring in the Soviet Union.

- **The union was immensely popular.** Almost half of all workers belonged. Lech Walesa was a kind of folk hero, and the movement which he led was seen as very trustworthy (see Source 36).

- **Solidarity had the support of the Catholic Church.** Elsewhere in eastern Europe, Communist governments had tried to crush the Christian churches. In Poland, however, the strength of the Catholic religion meant that the government dared not confront the Catholic Church.

- **The government was playing for time.** As early as 25 August 1980 the government drew up plans to introduce martial law (rule by the army). But to start with, it decided to play for time. It hoped that Solidarity would split into factions just as previous protest movements had.

- **Finally, the Soviet Union had half an eye on the West.** Solidarity had gained support in the West in a way that neither the Hungarian nor the Czech rising had. Walesa was regularly interviewed and photographed for the Western media. Solidarity logos were bought in their millions as posters, postcards and even car stickers throughout the capitalist world. The scale of the movement and the charismatic appeal of Lech Walesa ensured that the Soviet Union treated the Polish crisis cautiously.

SOURCE 35

Inequality and injustice are everywhere. There are hospitals that are so poorly supplied that they do not even have cotton, and our relatives die in the corridors; but other hospitals are equipped with private rooms and full medical care for each room. We pay fines for traffic violations, but some people commit highway manslaughter while drunk and are let off . . . In some places there are better shops and superior vacation houses, with huge fenced-in grounds that ordinary people cannot enter.

Extract from 'Experience and the Future', a report drawn up in 1981 by Polish writers and thinkers who were not members of the Communist Party. They are describing the inequality in Poland between Communist Party members and ordinary people.

---

3 The text describes four problems which led to the government clamp down. Which of these problems do you think would most worry the government?

4 Between August 1980 and December 1981, Solidarity went through some rapid changes. Choose two moments in this period that you think were particularly important in the rise and fall of Solidarity and explain why they were important.

SOURCE 36

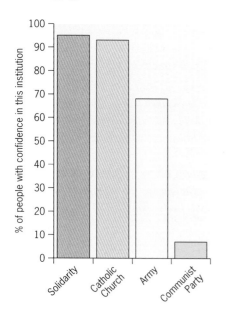

The results of an opinion poll in Poland, November 1981. The people polled were asked whether they had confidence in key institutions in Poland. It is known that 11 per cent of those polled were Communist Party members.

Why did the Polish government clamp down on Solidarity in December 1981?

In February 1981 the civilian Prime Minister 'resigned' and the leader of the army, General Jaruzelski, took over. From the moment he took office, people in Poland, and observers outside Poland, expected the Soviet Union to 'send in the tanks' at any time, especially when the Solidarity Congress produced an 'open letter' saying that they were campaigning not only for their own rights but for the rights of workers throughout the Communist bloc. It proclaimed that the Poles were fighting 'For Your Freedom and For Ours'. Jaruzelski and Walesa negotiated to form a government of national understanding but when that broke down in December, after nine months of tense relationships, the Communist government acted. Brezhnev ordered the Red Army to carry out 'training manoeuvres' on the Polish border. Jaruzelski introduced martial law. He put Walesa and almost 10,000 other Solidarity leaders in prison. He suspended Solidarity. Military dictators are not required to give reasons for their actions. But if they did what might Jaruzelski have to say?

- **Solidarity was acting as a political party.** The government declared that it had secret tapes of a Solidarity meeting setting up a new provisional government – without the Communist Party.
- **Poland was sinking into chaos.** Almost all Poles felt the impact of food shortages. Rationing had been introduced in April 1981. Wages had increased by less than inflation. Unemployment was rising. Strikes were continuing long after the Solidarity leadership had ordered them to stop.
- **Solidarity itself was also tumbling into chaos.** There were many different factions. Some felt that the only way to make progress was to push the Communists harder until they cracked under the pressure.
- **The Soviet Union had seen enough.** It thought the situation in Poland had gone too far. If Poland's leaders would not restore Communist control in Poland, then it would. This was something the Polish leaders wanted to avoid.

In December 1981, looking back on the past 18 months, two things were obvious:

- The Polish people no longer trusted the Communists leadership.
- The only thing that kept the Communists in power was force or the threat of force. When Jaruzelski finally decided to use force, Solidarity was easily crushed. The lesson was clear. If military force was not used, then Communist control seemed very shaky indeed.

Jaruzelski released jailed Solidarity leaders. However, once released they were harassed. Some were murdered. Others were hounded from their jobs. In 1983 Jaruzelski even started a campaign against the Catholic Church. A number of priests were beaten up by the army and some were murdered, including a popular priest called Father Jerzy Popieluszko, who was battered to death by the secret police in 1984. There we leave the story of Solidarity because from 1985 developments in the Soviet Union had as much impact on Poland as events in Poland itself, and the person responsible was the next leader of the Soviet Union.

Focus Task

How important was Solidarity?

Solidarity was important because ...
- it highlighted the failure of Communism to provide good living standards and this undermined Communism's claim to be a system which benefited ordinary people
- it highlighted inefficiency and corruption
- it showed that there were organisations which were capable of resisting a Communist government
- it showed that Communist governments could be threatened by 'people power'

1 Study pages 140–41 and find at least one example to support each statement.

2 Now rearrange the statements in order of importance in your opinion.

And later

Return to this task after you have studied pages 144–49. With the benefit of hindsight, do you think the events of 1985–89 make Solidarity look more or less significant? Explain your answer in a paragraph. You will need to consider:
- Were later events more important than the events in Poland 1980–82?
- Did Solidarity influence events in Eastern Europe 1985–89 (e.g. by inspiring people to protest)?

Profile

Mikhail Gorbachev

- ➤ Born 1931. One grandfather was a kulak – a landowning peasant – who had been sent to a prison camp by Stalin because he resisted Stalin's policy of collectivisation. The other grandfather was a loyal Communist Party member.
- ➤ His elder brother was killed in the Second World War.
- ➤ Studied law at Moscow University in the 1950s. Became a persuasive speaker.
- ➤ Worked as a local Communist Party official in his home area. By 1978 he was a member of the Central Committee of the party and in charge of agriculture.
- ➤ In 1980 he joined the Politburo.
- ➤ He was a close friend of Andropov, who became Soviet leader in 1983. He shared many of Andropov's ideas about reforming the USSR. When Andropov was leader, he was effectively second in command.
- ➤ In 1985 he became leader of the USSR.
- ➤ In October 1990 he was awarded the Nobel Peace Prize.

Dear Mr Gorbachev

So who was this Soviet leader who was to have such an important hand in the fate of Poland and the rest of Eastern Europe? Sources 37–43 are all letters written to Gorbachev in the late 1980s by people from different parts of the world. The fact that these people were writing to him tells us that he was a significant figure in that period. By studying these letters carefully we can build up a picture of the man, his ideas and the influence he had on world affairs in the later 1980s.

Activity

Work in groups.
    Using only the letters on pages 142–43, work out as much as you can about Gorbachev. You could split the work up like this, each person or pair working on one topic:
- What kind of person was Gorbachev?
- What changes did he introduce to the Soviet Union?
- What was his policy on eastern Europe?
- What was his attitude to nuclear disarmament?
- What did he think about human rights?

When you have finished researching, report back to your group. Then consider one last question: How do you think Gorbachev would have reacted if he had been the Soviet leader:
- to the Hungarian crisis in 1956
- to the Czech crisis in 1968
- to the Polish crisis in 1982?

SOURCE 37

Dear Mr Gorbachev

I hope you are feeling well after your journey to Rome to meet Our Leader, Pope John Paul II, with your lovely lady, Raisa. It was indeed a historical and memorable occasion. I want to thank you for all you have done. It is marvellous that . . . the people in Eastern Europe have been granted freedom. It is unbelievable how fast all these wonderful things are happening. We were delighted when the news reached our ears that the people in Russia now have the freedom to practise their faith.

Rosalee (aged 4), John (aged 9), Mary-Lucia (aged 11), Thérèse (aged 12), Majella (aged 13), Patricia (aged 15) and Patrick Furlong (aged 16). Enniscorthy, Co. Wexford, Ireland, December 1989.

SOURCE 38

Dear Mr Gorbachev

. . . I have been deeply moved by the events that have taken place in this country since 9 November 1989 . . . I would like to express my deeply felt thanks for this, for, in the final analysis, it was you, with your policy of perestroika who set the heavy stone of politics in motion.

You can have no idea how many people in Germany revere you and consider you to be one of the greatest politicians of the present age. On that day when the people of East Berlin and of East Germany were able to come to us freely, thousands of people shouted out your name 'Gorbi, Gorbi, Gorbi . . .'

The people fell into each other's arms and wept for joy, because at last they were free after forty-five years of suppression under a communist–Stalinist system. This dreadful wall and border, which was now being opened up and carried away stone by stone, cost many people their life, and was a source of bitter suffering for many families.

Roman von Kalckreuth, Berlin, West Germany, 14 February 1990.

SOURCE 39

Respected Sir

I, a citizen of India, very heartily congratulate you on the giant step you have initiated towards a more human and presidential form of government.

I have already read a lot about glasnost and other policies you have been introducing in your country . . .

Your sincerity, straightforwardness, foresight, capabilities, fearless nature, and eye for minute details will set a shining example for centuries to come and you will go down in the golden annals of history. You are a shining star on the horizon. The sapling which you have sown will become a tree for others to climb.

Naren R Bhuta, Bombay, India,
1 July 1988.

SOURCE 41

Dear Mr Gorbachev

May I offer a few comments on your speech of 2 November, in which you reviewed the history of the Soviet Union? Naturally, I found the discourse of very great interest, and hope that I have understood its significance . . .

May I suggest that in your recasting of the view of Soviet history, there are at least two important things which would make that effort more credible for those people outside of the Soviet Union who have some understanding of that history. One would be to more frankly admit the monstrosity of the tyranny of Stalin – for example, the fact that he killed more communists than anyone else in history. The other would be to give recognition to Leon Trotsky as the person who organised the Red Army and led it to victory in the 1918–21 Civil War.

Professor Robert Alexander, Rutgers
University, New Brunswick, New Jersey,
USA, 5 November 1987.

SOURCE 40

Dear General Secretary Gorbachev

I followed the events of the recent Soviet–American summit with a mixture of uneasy feelings. My one clear feeling was admiration of you – of your intellectual energy, personal strength, and dignity.

Hearing our President's well-intended but often condescending lectures to the Soviet Union's people and political leadership, I was embarrassed for my country . . .

Your term of office, General Secretary Gorbachev, has been marked by a straightforward commitment to address the world we really live in, and to improve it. I admire your combination of pragmatism and idealism.

It seems to me that you face internal obstacles greater than any American leader does, but perhaps the Soviet system has provided more groundwork for perestroika than is clear to Americans.

The 'tightrope' that you yourself are walking, balanced between certain difficult traditions of your society on one side and Western pressures on the other side, seems a great and exhausting challenge. But I ask you to remain strong, and to remember that you are not walking it for yourself alone.

David Bittinger, Wisconsin, USA, 6 June 1988.

SOURCE 42

Dear Mr Gorbachev

I would like to express my appreciation for your efforts to promote peace and understanding between our two countries. As a token of that appreciation, I am enclosing a copy of my book, The Human Rights Movement, *which seeks to promote dialogue between the US and the USSR on human rights . . .*

I agree with you that each country needs to learn more about the other's concepts of human rights – that is we need a lot more listening and a lot less confrontation. This is the basic argument of my book.

Warren Holleman, Baylor College of Medicine, Houston, Texas, USA, 16 June 1988.

SOURCE 43

Dear Gorbaciov and Reagan

We are nine-year-old Italian children, pupils at the Pero elementary school in the province of Milan.

We saw on television and read in the papers about your meeting, during which you came to an important decision: to begin to destroy a small part of your nuclear weapons. We want you to know that we all heaved a sigh of relief, because we think that all the weapons are dangerous, useless, damaging and producers of violence, death, fear and destruction and that their only purpose is to do evil.

We want you to know that we are happy about your initiative, but we also want to tell you that is not enough. For there to be true peace all arms must be destroyed.

Children from Pero (Milan), Italy, 16 December 1987.

How did Gorbachev try to change the Soviet Union?

Gorbachev became leader of the Soviet Union in 1985. Gorbachev was an unusual mix of idealist, optimist and realist.

- The realist in him could see that the USSR was in a terrible state. Its economy was very weak. It was spending far too much money on the arms race. It was locked into a costly and unwinnable war in Afghanistan. There had been almost no new thinking about how to run the Soviet economy since the days of Stalin. Each leader had followed the same policies and had ignored the warning signals that things were going wrong.
- The idealist in Gorbachev believed that Communist rule should make life better for the people of the USSR and other Communist states (see Source 47). In the 1970s he had travelled in western Europe and had seen that there were higher standards of living there than in the USSR. As a loyal Communist and a proud Russian it offended him that goods made in Soviet factories were shoddy and that many Soviet citizens had no loyalty to the government, did not believe what the government said, and resented the way the government controlled their lives. Gorbachev hated the fact that the USSR was the butt of jokes and this was made worse by the fact that US President Reagan was a great collector of anti-Soviet jokes (Source 44).
- The optimist in Gorbachev believed that a reformed Communist system of government could give people pride and belief in their country (see Source 47). He definitely did not intend to dismantle Communism in the USSR and eastern Europe, but he did want to reform it radically.

Glasnost and perestroika

He had to be cautious, because he faced great opposition from hardliners in his own government, but gradually he declared his policies. The two key ideas were glasnost (openness) and perestroika (restructuring). He called for open debate on government policy and honesty in facing up to problems. It was not a detailed set of policies but it did mean radical change.

In 1987 his perestroika programme allowed market forces to be introduced into the Soviet economy. For the first time in 60 years it was no longer illegal to buy and sell for profit.

The Red Army

He began to cut spending on defence. After almost 50 years on a constant war footing, the Red Army began to shrink. The arms race was an enormous drain on the Soviet economy at a time when it was in trouble anyway. Gorbachev was realistic enough to recognise that his country could never hope to outspend the USA on nuclear weapons. He took the initiative. He announced cuts in armament expenditure. Two years later, the USA and the USSR signed a treaty to remove most of their missiles from Europe.

At the same time, Gorbachev brought a new attitude to the USSR's relations with the wider world. He withdrew Soviet troops from Afghanistan, which had become the USSR's Vietnam, consuming lives and resources. In speech after speech, he talked about international trust and co-operation as the way forward for the USSR, rather than confrontation.

SOURCE **44**

A

The Soviet Union would remain a one party state even if the Communists allowed an opposition party to exist. Everyone would join the opposition party.

B

When American college students are asked what they want to do after graduation, they reply: 'I don't know, I haven't decided'. Russian students answer the same question by saying: 'I don't know, they haven't told me'.

Anti-Communist jokes told by US President Reagan to Mikhail Gorbachev at their summit meetings in the late 1980s.

1 Why do you think President Reagan was so fond of jokes like those in Source 44A and B?
2 Do you think it is strange that Gorbachev was upset by these jokes? Explain your answer.

Activity

1 Design a poster promoting one of Gorbachev's reforms: glasnost or perestroika. Your poster should include an explanation of why the reform is needed.
2 Use the information and sources on pages 144–45 to add two to three new points to the Profile of Mikhail Gorbachev on page 142.

SOURCE **45**

US President Reagan and Mikhail Gorbachev at their first summit meeting in Geneva, November 1985. They went on to meet in Reykjavik (October 1986), Washington (December 1987) and Moscow (June 1988).

How did Gorbachev's changes affect eastern Europe?

In March 1985 Gorbachev called the leaders of the Warsaw Pact countries together. This meeting should have been a turning point in the history of eastern Europe. Gorbachev explained to the leaders that he was committed to non-intervention in the affairs of their countries (see Source 46). Gorbachev made it very clear that they were responsible for their own fates. However, most of the Warsaw Pact leaders were old style, hardline Communists like Erich Honecker of East Germany or Nicolae Ceausescu of Romania. To them, Gorbachev's ideas were insane and they simply did not believe he would abandon them to rule themselves.

3 Why do you think the Warsaw Pact leaders did not believe Gorbachev when he told them the Soviet Union would no longer interfere in the internal affairs of other communist countries?

SOURCE 46

The time is ripe for abandoning views on foreign policy which are influenced by an imperial standpoint. Neither the Soviet Union nor the USA is able to force its will on others. It is possible to suppress, compel, bribe, break or blast, but only for a certain period. From the point of view of long-term big time politics, no one will be able to subordinate others. That is why only one thing – relations of equality – remains. All of us must realise this . . . This also obliges us to respect one another and everybody.

Gorbachev speaking in 1987.

SOURCE 47

A

Polish, Hungarian and Romanian dogs get to talking. 'What's life like in your country?' the Polish dog asks the Hungarian dog.

'Well, we have meat to eat but we can't bark. What are things like where you are from?' says the Hungarian dog to the Polish dog.

'With us, there's no meat, but at least we can bark,' says the Polish dog.

'What's meat? What's barking?' asks the Romanian dog.

B

East German leader Erich Honecker is touring East German towns. He is shown a run-down kindergarten. The staff ask for funds to renovate the institution. Honecker refuses. Next he visits a hospital, where the doctors petition him for a grant to buy new surgical equipment. Honecker refuses. The third place on Honecker's itinerary is a prison. This is pretty dilapidated, and here too the governor asks for money to refurbish. This time Honecker immediately pulls out his cheque book and insists that not only should the cells be repainted but that they should be fitted with new mattresses, colour televisions and sofas. Afterwards an aide asks him why he said no to a school and a hospital, but yes to a prison. Honecker says, 'Where do you think we will be living in a few months' time?'

Examples of anti-Communist jokes collected by researchers in eastern Europe in the 1980s.

4 Can jokes really be useful historical sources? Explain your answer.
5 If you think jokes are useful sources, do you think Sources 44 or 47 are more useful? Explain your answer.

SOURCE 48

This meeting was not a sign that Gorbachev thought that communism was doomed in the USSR and eastern Europe. The exact opposite was true. Gorbachev was still at that time a Marxist-Leninist believer: he contended that the Soviet communist order was in many ways already superior to capitalism; he was unshaken in his opinion that the Soviet type of state provided its citizens with better health care, education and transport. The task in the USSR and eastern Europe was consequently to renovate communism so as to match capitalism in other areas of public life. Gorbachev assumed that he would be able to persuade fellow communist leaders in eastern Europe to follow his example. There was to be no repetition of the invasions of Hungary in 1956 and Czechoslovakia in 1968. Renovation had to occur voluntarily. Despite Gorbachev's eloquence, however, the Warsaw Pact leaders did not take him seriously and treated his speech as ceremonial rhetoric (clever speech making).

Extract from *History of Modern Russia* by historian Robert Service, published 2003. In this extract he is commenting on the meeting in March 1985.

In the next few years these leaders would realise they had made a serious error of judgement. As Gorbachev introduced his reforms in the USSR the demand rose for reforms in eastern European states as well. Most people in these states were sick of the poor economic conditions and the harsh restrictions which Communism imposed.

Gorbachev's policies gave people some hope for reform. In July 1988 he made a speech to the Warsaw Pact summit meeting stating his intention to withdraw large numbers of Soviet troops, tanks and aircraft from eastern Europe. He restated these intentions in public in a speech to the Polish Parliament soon afterwards. Hungary was particularly eager to get rid of Soviet troops and when the Hungarians pressed Gorbachev he seemed to confirm that troops would withdraw if Hungary wished. Gorbachev followed up this intention in March 1989. He again made clear to the Warsaw Pact leaders that they would no longer be propped up by the Red Army and that they would have to listen to their peoples. The following months saw an extraordinary turn-about, as you can see from Source 49 on page 146, which led to the collapse of Communism in Eastern Europe.

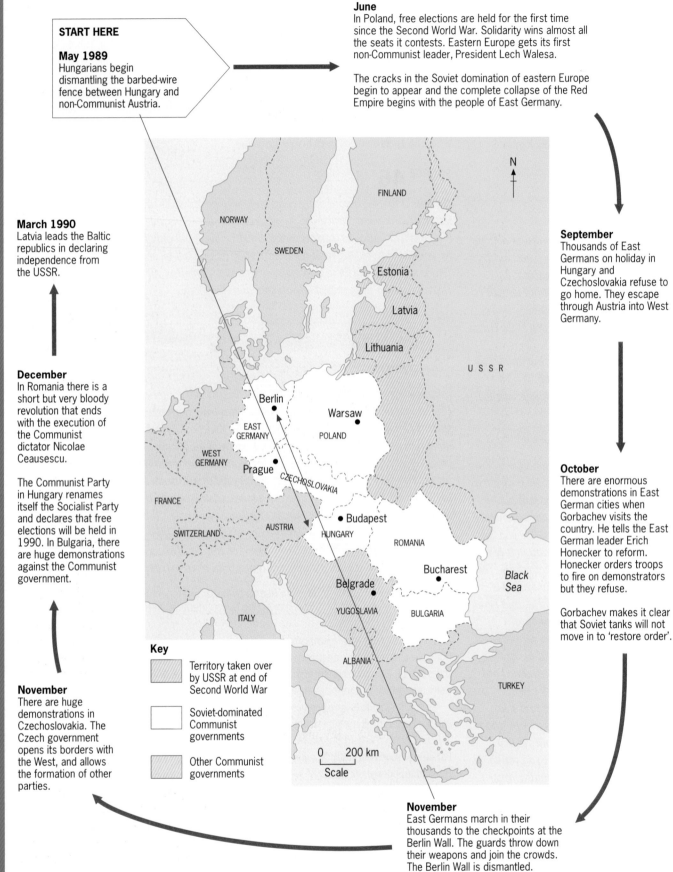

START HERE

May 1989
Hungarians begin dismantling the barbed-wire fence between Hungary and non-Communist Austria.

June
In Poland, free elections are held for the first time since the Second World War. Solidarity wins almost all the seats it contests. Eastern Europe gets its first non-Communist leader, President Lech Walesa.

The cracks in the Soviet domination of eastern Europe begin to appear and the complete collapse of the Red Empire begins with the people of East Germany.

March 1990
Latvia leads the Baltic republics in declaring independence from the USSR.

December
In Romania there is a short but very bloody revolution that ends with the execution of the Communist dictator Nicolae Ceausescu.

The Communist Party in Hungary renames itself the Socialist Party and declares that free elections will be held in 1990. In Bulgaria, there are huge demonstrations against the Communist government.

November
There are huge demonstrations in Czechoslovakia. The Czech government opens its borders with the West, and allows the formation of other parties.

September
Thousands of East Germans on holiday in Hungary and Czechoslovakia refuse to go home. They escape through Austria into West Germany.

October
There are enormous demonstrations in East German cities when Gorbachev visits the country. He tells the East German leader Erich Honecker to reform. Honecker orders troops to fire on demonstrators but they refuse.

Gorbachev makes it clear that Soviet tanks will not move in to 'restore order'.

November
East Germans march in their thousands to the checkpoints at the Berlin Wall. The guards throw down their weapons and join the crowds. The Berlin Wall is dismantled.

Key

- Territory taken over by USSR at end of Second World War
- Soviet-dominated Communist governments
- Other Communist governments

0   200 km
Scale

The collapse of Communism in eastern Europe.

SOURCE **50**

A demonstrator pounds away at the Berlin Wall as East German border guards look on from above, 4 November 1989. The wall was dismantled five days later.

SOURCE **51**

For most west Europeans now alive, the world has always ended at the East German border and the Wall; beyond lay darkness . . . The opening of the frontiers declares that the world has no edge any more. Europe is becoming once more round and whole.

The *Independent*, November 1989.

Reunification of Germany

With the Berlin Wall down, West German Chancellor Helmut Kohl proposed a speedy reunification of Germany. Germans in both countries embraced the idea enthusiastically.

Despite his idealism, Gorbachev was less enthusiastic. He expected that a new united Germany would be more friendly to the West than to the East. But after many months of hard negotiations, not all of them friendly, Gorbachev accepted German reunification and even accepted that the new Germany could become a member of NATO. This was no small thing for Gorbachev to accept. Like all Russians, he lived with the memory that it was German aggression in the Second World War that had cost the lives of 20 million Soviet citizens.

On 3 October 1990, Germany became a united country once again.

Activity

On your own map of eastern Europe, add labels to summarise in your own words how Communism collapsed in each country of eastern Europe.

147

The collapse of the USSR

Even more dramatic events were to follow in the Soviet Union itself.

Early in 1990, Gorbachev visited the Baltic state of Lithuania – part of the Soviet Union. Its leaders put their views to him. They were very clear. They wanted independence. They did not want to be part of the USSR. Gorbachev was for once uncompromising. He would not allow this. But in March they did it anyway. Almost as soon as he returned to Moscow from Lithuania, Gorbachev received a similar demand from the Muslim Soviet Republic of Azerbaijan.

What should Gorbachev do now? He sent troops to Azerbaijan to end rioting there. He sent troops to Lithuania. But as the summer approached, the crisis situation got worse.

In May 1990 the Russian Republic, the largest within the USSR, elected Boris Yeltsin as its President. Yeltsin made it clear that he saw no future in a Soviet Union. He said that the many republics that made up the USSR should become independent states.

In July the Ukraine declared its independence. Other republics followed. By the end of 1990 nobody was quite sure what the USSR meant any longer. Meanwhile Gorbachev was an international superstar. In October 1990 he received the Nobel Peace Prize.

In January 1991 events in Lithuania turned to bloodshed as Soviet troops fired on protesters.

In April the Republic of Georgia declared its independence.

The USSR was disintegrating. Reformers within the USSR itself demanded an end to the Communist Party's domination of government. Gorbachev was struggling to hold it together, but members of the Communist elite had had enough. In **August 1991** hardline Communist Party members and leading military officers attempted a coup to take over the USSR. The plotters included Gorbachev's Prime Minister, Pavlov, and the head of the armed forces, Dimitry Yazov. They held Gorbachev prisoner in his holiday home in the Crimea. They sent tanks and troops on to the streets of Moscow. This was the old Soviet way to keep control. Would it work this time?

Huge crowds gathered in Moscow. They strongly opposed this military coup. The Russian President, Boris Yeltsin, emerged as the leader of the popular opposition. Faced by this resistance, the conspirators lost faith in themselves and the coup collapsed.

This last-ditch attempt by the Communist Party to save the USSR had failed. A few days later, Gorbachev returned to Moscow. He might have survived the coup, but it had not strengthened his position as Soviet leader. He had to admit that the USSR was finished and he with it.

In a televised speech on 25 December 1991, Gorbachev announced the end of the Soviet Union (see Source 56).

Focus Task

How far was Gorbachev responsible for the collapse of the Soviet empire?

You are making a documentary film to explain 'The Collapse of the Red Empire'. The film will be 60 minutes long.
1 Decide what proportion of this time should concentrate on:
   ◆ Solidarity in Poland
   ◆ Gorbachev
   ◆ actions of people in eastern Europe
   ◆ actions of governments in eastern Europe
   ◆ Boris Yeltsin and leaders of Soviet republics
   ◆ other factors.
2 Choose one of these aspects and summarise the important points, stories, pictures or sources that your film should cover under that heading.
   You may be able to use presentation software to organise and present your ideas.

SOURCE **52**

Russian President Boris Yeltsin addressing supporters from the top of a tank after the attempted coup of August 1991.

The end of the Cold War

SOURCE 53

A cartoon by Doonesbury which appeared in the *Guardian* on 13 June 1988.

SOURCE 54

He had no grand plan and no predetermined policies; but if Gorbachev had not been Party General Secretary, the decisions of the late 1980s would have been different. The USSR's long-lasting order would have endured for many more years, and almost certainly the eventual collapse of the order would have been much bloodier than it was to be in 1991. The irony was that Gorbachev, in trying to prevent the descent of the system into general crisis, proved instrumental in bringing forward that crisis and destroying the USSR.

Extract from *History of Modern Russia* by historian Robert Service, published 2003. In this extract he is commenting on the meeting in March 1985.

SOURCE 55

Mikhail Gorbachev after receiving the Nobel Peace Prize, 15 October 1990.

SOURCE 56

A sense of failure and regret came through his [Gorbachev's] Christmas Day abdication speech – especially in his sorrow over his people 'ceasing to be citizens of a great power'. Certainly, if man-in-the-street interviews can be believed, the former Soviet peoples consider him a failure.

History will be kinder. The Nobel Prize he received for ending the Cold War was well deserved. Every man, woman and child in this country should be eternally grateful.

His statue should stand in the centre of every east European capital; for it was Gorbachev who allowed them their independence. The same is true for the newly independent countries further east and in Central Asia. No Russian has done more to free his people from bondage since Alexander II who freed the serfs.

From a report on Gorbachev's speech, 25 December 1991, in the US newspaper the *Boston Globe*.

Focus Task

Mikhail Gorbachev – hero or villain?

Read Source 56 carefully. Here are three statements from the source.
- 'the former Soviet peoples consider him a failure'
- 'History will be kinder'.
- 'His statue should stand in the centre of every east European capital'.

Do you agree or disagree with each statement? For each statement, write a short paragraph to:
a) explain what it means, and
b) express your own view on it.

How effective has terrorism been since 1969?

Focus

Since 1969 modern, powerful states have faced challenges from terrorist groups and have found these groups very difficult to deal with. In this chapter you are going to investigate:
◆ What exactly is meant by terrorism?
◆ The motivation of terrorist groups.
◆ Similarities and differences between terrorist groups.
◆ How governments have reacted to terrorism.
◆ The effectiveness of different terrorist groups.

You will refer to three case studies in particular:
◆ The Irish Republican Army (the IRA)
◆ The Palestine Liberation Organisation (the PLO)
◆ Al-Qaeda.

Activity

The aim of this activity is to see what you already know about terrorism, and in particular the motives of terrorist groups; the methods of terrorist groups; the impact of terrorist groups.
1 Work in pairs or small groups. Using Sources 1–3 and your own knowledge of terrorism draw up a spider diagram to record:
   • what *you already know* about the motives, methods and impact of terrorist groups
   • what *you can definitely tell* about the motives, methods and impact of the IRA, PLO and al-Qaeda from Sources 1–3
   • what *you can infer* about the motives, methods and impact of the IRA, PLO and al-Qaeda from Sources 1–3.
2 a) Draw up a list of questions you would like to investigate about terrorism.
   b) Highlight the questions that you think would help you research the motives, methods and impact of terrorist groups.

SOURCE 1

Smoke pouring from the World Trade Center in New York on 11 September 2001. The terrorist group al-Qaeda hijacked two airliners and flew them into the two towers which later collapsed, killing around 3,000 people.

SOURCE 2

The scene in Enniskillen in Northern Ireland after a bomb planted by the terrorist group the IRA exploded in November 1987. The bomb went off during a Remembrance Day ceremony and killed eleven people.

SOURCE 3

A Palestinian terrorist at the Munich Olympics in 1972. The terrorist group Black September, which was part of the Palestine Liberation Organisation, kidnapped and killed eleven Israeli athletes.

What is terrorism?

Here are three different definitions of terrorism used by US and British organisations.

> **1** The unlawful use of force or violence against persons or property to intimidate or coerce a government, the civilian population, or any segment thereof, in furtherance of political or social objectives.
>
> The American Federal Bureau of Investigation (FBI)

> **2** Premeditated, politically motivated violence perpetrated against non-combatant targets by sub-national groups or clandestine agents, usually intended to influence an audience.
>
> US State Department

> **3** The use or threat, for the purpose of advancing a political, religious or ideological cause, of action which involves serious violence against any person or property.
>
> United Kingdom Government

The problem of definition

How you define terrorism depends on your point of view. If so called terrorists are on your side, or acting for a cause you believe in you might not call them terrorists at all. You would more likely call them 'freedom fighters' or 'protectors'. On the other hand if the terrorist acts are directed against you then you may see them as 'traitors', 'murderers' or just plain 'criminal'. The three groups we feature in this chapter would be regarded as selfless heroes by some, yet brutal psychopaths by others.

SOURCE **4**

My attraction to the IRA was not initially based on the sight or experience of any particular social injustice ... It was the discovery of the tragedies of Irish history, ... and the best part of that history I imbibed alone at home reading books in the family library. It was the pure political injustice of British rule in Ireland against the wishes of the Irish people which fired my anger ...

Shane O'Doherty, an IRA volunteer in the 1970s.

1 How does Source 4 help to explain why terrorism is difficult to defeat?

SOURCE **5**

On one point, at least, everyone agrees: Terrorism is an insulting term. It is a word with intrinsically negative associations that is generally applied to one's enemies and opponents, or to those with whom one disagrees and would otherwise prefer to ignore.

Professor Bruce Hoffman, director of the Centre for the Study of Terrorism and Political Violence at Georgetown University, USA, writing in 2006.

Not surprisingly, terrorists usually reject the labels which their opponents give them. In fact, all terrorist organisations deny that they are terrorists! Terrorists usually see themselves as idealists who have been forced to take up unconventional methods or warfare either to further a good cause or to oppose a brutal and unreasonable enemy.

In 2002 the Organisation of the Islamic Conference, representing 57 Muslim nations, agreed that they condemned terrorism in all its forms. However when it came to defining what actually counted as 'terrorism' they were unable to agree a definition. Middle Eastern delegates, including the Palestinians, objected to a definition of terrorism which included 'any attacks on civilians, including suicide bombings'. The Conference announced 'We reject any attempt to link terrorism to the struggle of the Palestinian people in the exercise of their inalienable right to establish their independent state. We urge the Islamic countries to work toward an international definition of terrorism that distinguishes between terrorism and "legitimate struggles ... against foreign occupation".'

Focus Task

What is terrorism?

Study the definitions of the word 'terrorism' above.
1 First make sure you can understand what they mean! Use a dictionary if necessary.
2 What two important words do they all include?
3 Which of these definitions do you think is the best definition of the word terrorism? Why?
4 What words in these definitions might a terrorist group themselves disagree with?
5 Try to explain to someone else in your class why it is so hard to write a definition of terrorism that everyone agrees with.
6 Could you write a better definition? If you think you can, try it!

Terrorism in the distant past

Terrorism is not a new phenomenon. Terrorism in various forms has been a part of human history since earliest times. In Roman times a Jewish group called the Zealots used terrorist tactics against the Romans. A Muslim terrorist group called the Assassins first operated in the 600s. Since then terrorist groups have fought against governments, monarchs or foreign enemies. The ruler of Russia was killed by a terrorist bomb in 1855. Irish terrorists set off bombs in Britain in the 1860s. The Serbian Black Hand terrorists carried out the assassination which triggered the First World War in 1914 (see page 210). History has shown that terrorist tactics are a very effective way to attack a larger and stronger enemy.

Terrorism in the recent past

Most would agree, however, that terrorism is a much more significant feature of the modern world than it was of the past (see Source 6). Understanding how terrorist organisations work is therefore an important aspect of understanding recent history. If terrorism is a significant feature of modern history then it suggests that terrorist groups find it an effective way of acting. People seldom continue for long with something that fails.

Terrorists aim to bring about political change of one kind or another. They also want to make their cause impossible to ignore and put pressure on governments. They have discovered the power of terrorist acts to achieve this. The most spectacular example was the al-Qaeda attack on New York in September 2001 (see Source 1). In purely statistical terms the attack did very little damage to America, its people or its economy. And yet it had a massive impact on policy and on attitudes in the USA which was felt all around the world and is still being felt today. The fact that governments are expending so much effort to fight terrorism shows how worried they are about terrorism and shows they still see terrorists as a potent force.

The unknown future

Terrorism is unpredictable. Experts around the world study the past and develop views on conflicts which might lead to terrorism, and how terrorists might behave, but they cannot be sure. Throughout history terrorists have surprised their enemies. Sometimes the surprise is when they compromise and make peace when it was least expected. At other times they have surprised their enemies with new tactics or unexpected targets. So the pattern of past terrorist activities does not necessarily guide politicians to understanding the future of terrorism.

Activity

Discussion

The names that terrorist organisations give themselves can reveal something about their aims. For example:
- Freedom or liberation (such as Palestinian Liberation Organisation)
- Regular armies rather than irregular forces (such as Irish Republican Army)
- Movements for protection or self-defence (such as the Ulster Defence Association)
- Righteous vengeance (such as the Palestinian Revenge Organisation).

Other movements are alliances of different groups with varied priorities so they use names which are fairly neutral (for example al-Qaeda, which means 'the base' or 'the foundation').

Study the names around the map in Source 6 opposite.
1 How many of these names fit the characteristics listed above?
2 How useful is Source 6 to someone trying to understand terrorism today?
3 Why do you think an organisation in Israel compiled this list?
4 Would any of the groups listed here object to being on this list?

Research

1 Work in pairs or small groups. Choose one group on this list and see what you can find out about their main aims. Report back to the rest of the class and see if you can find any similarities or differences between the organisations.
2 'Terrorism is one of the key factors in world politics today.' Work in groups and test this statement out for yourselves. Choose one respectable news source (such as the BBC, Al-Jazeera, CNN). Search the site and see how many articles this week cover each of these topics:
  - terrorism
  - the environment
  - the world economy
  - health.
Then as a class decide whether you think the news organisations think terrorism is as important as or more important than these other issues.

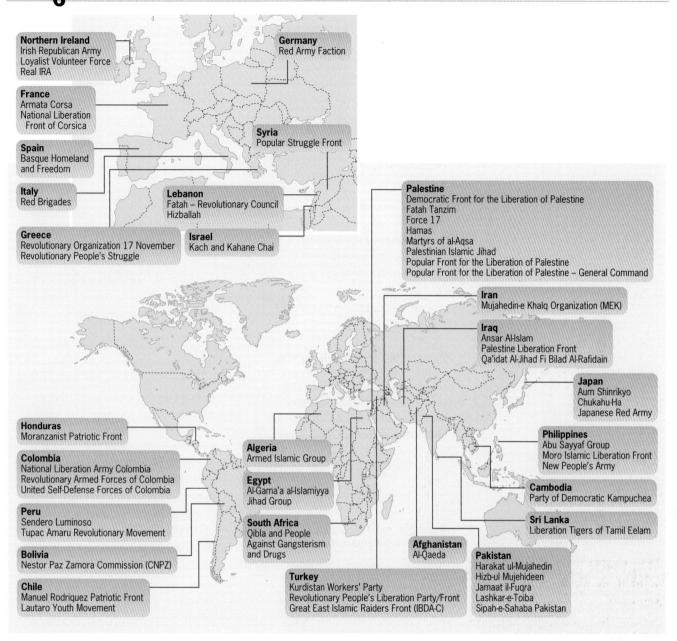

Northern Ireland
Irish Republican Army
Loyalist Volunteer Force
Real IRA

Germany
Red Army Faction

France
Armata Corsa
National Liberation
 Front of Corsica

Syria
Popular Struggle Front

Spain
Basque Homeland
and Freedom

Italy
Red Brigades

Lebanon
Fatah – Revolutionary Council
Hizballah

Palestine
Democratic Front for the Liberation of Palestine
Fatah Tanzim
Force 17
Hamas
Martyrs of al-Aqsa
Palestinian Islamic Jihad
Popular Front for the Liberation of Palestine
Popular Front for the Liberation of Palestine – General Command

Greece
Revolutionary Organization 17 November
Revolutionary People's Struggle

Israel
Kach and Kahane Chai

Iran
Mujahedin-e Khalq Organization (MEK)

Iraq
Ansar Al-Islam
Palestine Liberation Front
Qa'idat Al-Jihad Fi Bilad Al-Rafidain

Japan
Aum Shinrikyo
Chukahu-Ha
Japanese Red Army

Honduras
Moranzanist Patriotic Front

Philippines
Abu Sayyaf Group
Moro Islamic Liberation Front
New People's Army

Colombia
National Liberation Army Colombia
Revolutionary Armed Forces of Colombia
United Self-Defense Forces of Colombia

Algeria
Armed Islamic Group

Cambodia
Party of Democratic Kampuchea

Peru
Sendero Luminoso
Tupac Amaru Revolutionary Movement

Egypt
Al-Gama'a al-Islamiyya
Jihad Group

Sri Lanka
Liberation Tigers of Tamil Eelam

Bolivia
Nestor Paz Zamora Commission (CNPZ)

South Africa
Qibla and People
Against Gangsterism
and Drugs

Afghanistan
Al-Qaeda

Pakistan
Harakat ul-Mujahedin
Hizb-ul Mujehideen
Jamaat il-Fuqra
Lashkar-e-Toiba
Sipah-e-Sahaba Pakistan

Chile
Manuel Rodriquez Patriotic Front
Lautaro Youth Movement

Turkey
Kurdistan Workers' Party
Revolutionary People's Liberation Party/Front
Great East Islamic Raiders Front (IBDA-C)

Known active terrorist organisations in the world today, based on information produced in October 2006 by the International Policy Institute for Counter-terrorism, an organisation based in Israel.

Can terrorism ever be justified?

You do not have to look far to find examples of terrorism being condemned. Terrorism is condemned for its random violence; its cowardly tactics – particularly in targeting innocent civilians; its assault on civilised values or democracy; and for its destructive effects on normal life. Here is a sample from the past thirty years. You can see two other good examples on page 160 (Sources 14 and 15).

In 2005 The Secretary General of the Muslim World League, Dr Abdullah Bin Abul, condemned terrorism.

> He called it 'a barbaric act that has no justification in Islam'. He also claimed that terrorists were trying to create tensions between Muslims and the rest of the world and were even trying to divide Muslims.

In 1972 the PLO kidnapped eleven Israeli athletes at the Munich Olympic Games. After German police tried to rescue them the terrorists killed all of the athletes. King Hussein of Jordan described the PLO action as:

'a savage crime against civilisation perpetrated by sick minds'.

In January 2004 a young female Palestinian suicide bomber killed four Israelis and wounded many others (including Palestinian civilians). The US State Department condemned the attacks. Its spokesman Richard Boucher said:

'Those people are not only killing innocent civilians; they are also killing the dreams and hopes of the Palestinian people . . . You need to end the violence in order to achieve the vision of two states [Israel and Palestine] living side by side.'

These comments make it seem like a simple issue – terrorism is evil. However most terrorists and their supporters do not consider themselves to be terrorists and they do not see their actions as evil. They see each act as a blow against an evil enemy. They see their tactics as justified because it is their only way to beat an opponent who is better armed and resourced.

A common desire of terrorist organisations is to right wrongs being done to 'their' people (even if the people themselves are sometimes not aware of these wrongs). These present day wrongs are often seen as being deeply rooted in the past and this in turn makes the terrorist feel that he or she is part of a deep and meaningful movement. These beliefs are usually reinforced by a strong sense of history, culture, religion, political ideology or all of these factors combined. These factors often make the terrorist a formidable opponent.

SOURCE 7

Terrorists argue that, because of their numerical inferiority, far more limited firepower, and paucity of resources compared with an established nation-state's massive defence and national security apparatus, they have no choice but to operate clandestinely, emerging from the shadows to carry out dramatic (in other words, bloody and destructive) acts of hit-and-run violence in order to attract attention to, and ensure publicity for, themselves and their cause. The bomb in the rubbish bin, in their view, is merely a circumstantially imposed 'poor man's air force': the only means with which the terrorist can challenge – and get the attention of – the more powerful state.

David Whitaker, Senior Lecturer in International Relations at the University of Teesside, writing in 2007. The writer is a specialist in terrorism.

Spot the difference!

Some terrorists argue that their actions are no different from the actions of many governments. For example, during the Second World War Britain and the USA supported resistance movements against the Nazis in countries which they had occupied. These movements used what we today might call terrorist tactics: sabotage, bombing, assassination. In 1945 the USA dropped leaflets on Japanese cities warning them that their cities would be bombed if they did not rise up against their own government. Experts are still debating today over whether these actions should be called terrorism.

The debate is still going on over more recent events. In 2002 the Islamic Conference accused Israel of claiming the PLO were terrorists while at the same time their own forces carried out assassinations of PLO leaders and also drove Palestinian civilians out of their homes in retaliation for PLO attacks.

Similarly in April 1986 the USA launched air strikes against Libya, accusing its leader Colonel Gadaffi of sponsoring terrorism. Gadaffi was indeed an open supporter of both the PLO and the IRA. Then in August 1998 US President Bill Clinton ordered cruise missile strikes against a factory in Sudan (see Source 8) which he claimed was being used by al-Qaeda to develop weapons to supply to terrorists. This was always denied. Many civilians were killed in both of these attacks. Supporters of the terrorist organisations claimed that there was absolutely no difference between a bomb attack by a government and the kinds of attacks which were carried out by the IRA, PLO or al-Qaeda.

SOURCE 8

El Shifa pharmaceutical plant in Sudan after the cruise missile attack. The Sudan government denied there was any al-Qaeda connection with the plant.

SOURCE 9

A cartoon by Rowson published in the *Guardian* newspaper, 14 August 2003. It was commenting on US attempts to stop terrorists from buying missiles or weapons of mass destruction.

SOURCE 10

America is a land of war. That occurred with its help to the Jews for more than fifty years in occupying Palestine, banishing its people and killing them. It is a land of war that attacked and blockaded Iraq, attacked and blockaded Sudan, attacked and blockaded Afghanistan. It has oppressed Muslims in every place for decades and has openly supported their enemies against them.

... There is currently an extermination effort against the Islamic peoples that has America's blessing, not just by virtue of its effective co-operation, but by America's activity. The best witness to this is what is happening with the full knowledge of the world in the Palestinian cities of Jenin, Nablus, Ramallah and elsewhere. Every day, all can follow the atrocious slaughter going on there with American support that is aimed at children, women and the elderly. Are Muslims not permitted to respond in the same way and kill those among the Americans who are like the Muslims they are killing? Certainly! By Allah, it is truly a right for Muslims.

Extracts from a statement made in 2003 by al-Qaeda.

What about the neutrals?

In most conflicts terrorists and their enemies aim to present themselves as reasonable to the neutral observer or to important organisations like the UNO. It is not unknown for some neutral observers to show some sympathy for the viewpoint of terrorist groups as long as they feel that the grievances of the terrorists are legitimate – even if they deeply disapprove the methods used by terrorists. So although terrorism is condemned for the suffering it causes, many neutral observers say that we should also try to understand it and at least see why at least some people feel it may be justified. What do you think?

Focus Task

Can terrorism ever be justified?

When we look at the points raised in this section it is not difficult to put them on the correct side of the scales. Some of them have been done for you! Your task is to consider the strength of the arguments on each side (not necessarily the amount of evidence) and decide which way you think the scales should tip. You could work in groups and prepare a presentation explaining your decision.

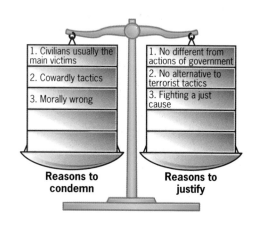

Reasons to condemn	Reasons to justify
1. Civilians usually the main victims	1. No different from actions of government
2. Cowardly tactics	2. No alternative to terrorist tactics
3. Morally wrong	3. Fighting a just cause

Three terrorist organisations: Brief outlines

Source 6 shows some of the terrorist groups operating around the world. You may be relieved to know that you are not going to study all of these organisations and conflicts! As we look at terrorism in this chapter, we are going to focus on case studies of three organisations: The Provisional IRA, the Palestinian Liberation Organisation and al-Qaeda.

Focus Task

Use the information on pages 156–59 to complete your own version of this table. You may wish to do your own extra research as well. Work on rows 1–3 to start with. Some examples have been started for you. You will be adding further rows to this table later in this chapter.

Organisation	IRA	PLO	Al-Qaeda
Origins	*Formed in 1916 to fight in rebellion against English/British control of Ireland.*		
Aims			• *Destroy American influence in all Muslim nations, especially Saudi Arabia.* • *Destroy Israel.* • *Destabilise and overthrow pro-Western governments in Muslim states.*
Key personalities		*Yasser Arafat* • *spent most of his life campaigning for Palestinian rights* • *Founded Fatah in 1958* • *brought the different groups together as PLO in 1969*	

SOURCE **11**

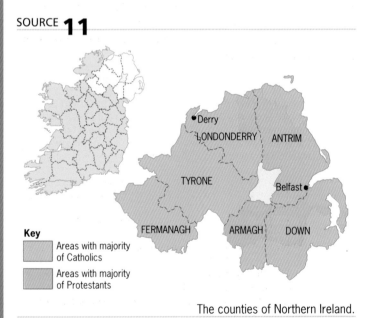

Key

Areas with majority of Catholics

Areas with majority of Protestants

The counties of Northern Ireland.

The Provisional IRA: A brief outline

The roots of the IRA lie in 1916 and to some extent even earlier. From the late 1600s Britain controlled Ireland and there had been various rebellions against British rule which all failed. On Easter Monday 1916 there was another rebellion by Irish militants or Republicans. These Republicans wanted Ireland to be an independent Irish Republic free from British rule. It was also important to them that the Republic should be achieved by armed force – not given to Ireland by the British. The 1916 rebellion was crushed but it sparked off a vicious underground war between Republican forces (the Irish Republican Army) and British forces. In 1921 the two sides signed a Treaty. Twenty-six of Ireland's 32 counties became what is now the Republic of Ireland. However, six counties became Northern Ireland (see Source 11).

Under the Anglo Irish Treaty of 1921 Northern Ireland remained part of the United Kingdom. These counties had a mixed population of Nationalists (mainly Catholic) and Unionists (mainly Protestant). Nationalists generally favoured Northern Ireland becoming part of a united Irish Republic. The more extreme Nationalists were generally known as Republicans. Unionists wanted to keep the Union with Britain. Extreme unionists were usually known as Loyalists. Unionists were the majority group within Northern Ireland as a whole.

Northern Ireland was relatively peaceful until the late 1960s although there were tensions. For example, some Nationalists faced discrimination in areas such as jobs or housing. Even so the IRA virtually disappeared. In 1968 a movement called the Northern Ireland Civil Rights Association began campaigning against the discrimination which some Catholics faced. The Northern Ireland government overreacted to these campaigns and rising tension in the province triggered off massive riots. In August 1969 the British government in London moved British troops into Northern Ireland to prevent Loyalist mobs attacking and burning Nationalist areas in Derry and Belfast. The British troops brought peace for a short while, but tensions remained. Soon relations between the British troops and the Nationalist community began to break down. In this atmosphere the IRA re-formed, aiming to fulfil its traditional aims, as below.

Aims

- to defend Nationalist communities
- to remove British troops from Northern Ireland
- to make the six counties of Northern Ireland part of a united Ireland of 32 counties.

In the early stages of the conflict the IRA actually split into the Official IRA and the Provisional IRA. For most of the conflict any mention of the IRA meant the Provisional IRA.

Throughout the 1970s and 1980s the IRA attacked British troops and the Northern Ireland police force, the RUC (Royal Ulster Constabulary). They also planted bombs in Northern Ireland and on the British mainland. At the same time the Nationalist community was attacked by Loyalist terrorist groups. The death toll in the Northern Ireland conflict was over 3,000, the majority of these being civilians. The IRA was never able to achieve its aims by force, but it proved impossible to defeat by force as well. IRA violence continued in the 1980s and 1990s, but the movement also began to move into politics through its political wing, Sinn Fein. The key Republican leaders, Gerry Adams and Martin McGuinness, were holding secret talks with the British and Irish governments. Slow and painful compromise between the Republicans, the British government and the Unionist majority in Northern Ireland resulted in the Good Friday Agreement of 1998. This effectively ended the conflict although Republican factions did carry out attacks and it took many years to get a new government for Northern Ireland which all parties could work with.

Profile

Gerry Adams

- ➤ Born 1948 in West Belfast into a family with a strong Republican background.
- ➤ Joined the Civil Rights movement in the late 1960s.
- ➤ Interned in 1971 as a suspected IRA member.
- ➤ Released to be part of IRA delegation to meet William Whitelaw in 1972.
- ➤ Re-arrested in 1973 for taking part in escape of IRA prisoners.
- ➤ Responsible for shift in Republican strategy and rise of Sinn Fein in 1980s.
- ➤ Became Sinn Fein MP for West Belfast in 1983.
- ➤ Has always denied IRA membership although few accept this.
- ➤ Survived a Loyalist assassination attempt in 1984, alleging British Army involvement in the attempt.
- ➤ Banned from speaking live on TV or radio in 1988.
- ➤ Held talks with SDLP leader John Hume 1988–93 which paved way for 1994 IRA ceasefire.
- ➤ Given visa to visit USA by Bill Clinton in 1994, against the wishes of the British government.
- ➤ Has frequently managed to convince Republicans to accept changes in policy such as convincing 90 per cent of Sinn Fein delegates to take part in the new Northern Ireland Assembly in 1998.

Profile

Martin McGuinness

- ➤ Born 1950.
- ➤ Joined IRA around 1970 and soon rose to command of Derry brigade.
- ➤ Part of IRA delegation which met British government in 1972.
- ➤ Arrested and imprisoned in the Republic of Ireland in 1973 for terrorist offences.
- ➤ One of the most senior, if not the most senior, IRA commanders.
- ➤ Dominated Republican movement along with Gerry Adams in the 1980s and 1990s.
- ➤ Chief IRA negotiator with the British and Irish governments in the late 1980s and early 1990s.
- ➤ Elected to Northern Ireland Assembly in 1998 and still there as Deputy First Minister.

Profile

Yasser Arafat

➤ Born in Egypt in 1929 to a Palestinian family.
➤ Grew up in Jerusalem.
➤ Fought against the Jews in the Gaza area in 1948.
➤ Studied as an engineer at Faud University (Cairo) but in reality spent most of his time campaigning for the Palestinian cause.
➤ In 1953 he sent a letter to an Egyptian leader written in his own blood which said 'don't forget Palestine'.
➤ Founded the Fatah movement in 1958 and by 1964 was a full-time revolutionary.
➤ By 1969 he had become the undisputed leader of the PLO.
➤ Throughout the 1970s and 1980s he gained worldwide recognition as the leader of the PLO.
➤ Driven out of Jordan in 1971 and then Lebanon in 1982 into exile in Tunis.
➤ Took control of the Intifada (see page 176) in 1987.
➤ Accepted right of Israel to exist in 1988, leading to a long peace process which resulted in the Oslo Accords (see page 177) and a Nobel Peace Prize in 1994.
➤ Became chairman of the Palestinian National Authority in 1996 and remained in power until 2003.
➤ Died in 2004.

Aims of the PLO

• Destroy the state of Israel.
• Re-establish Palestine as the home of the Palestinian Arabs.
• Make the new Palestine part of the wider Arab, Muslim community.

Activity

Go back to the table you created in the Focus Task on page 156 and complete the next column with information on the PLO.

The Palestinian Liberation Organisation: A brief outline

SOURCE **12**

Israel and its neighbours.

The story of the PLO is primarily the story of one land and two people who claim it: the Jews and the Palestinian Arabs. The land in question is Palestine although even the name and the exact borders of Palestine are hotly disputed. The Jews occupied Palestine in ancient times but by the twentieth century Palestine had become part of the British Empire and its population was mainly Muslim Palestinian Arabs who had settled there from the seventh century onwards. In the 1920s and 1930s increasing numbers of Jews came to live in Palestine. Hardline Jews called Zionists wanted to set up a Jewish homeland in what they saw as their traditional lands. The murder of six million Jews by the Nazis during the Second World War strengthened their determination. The aims of the Zionists created tensions between the Jews and the Arabs and there were frequent clashes. In 1947 the British were struggling to control Palestine and handed Palestine over to the control of the United Nations Organisation. The UNO proposed to partition Palestine into two states but the plan failed.

The Zionists then declared the state of Israel to exist. Neighbouring Arab states tried to crush Israel but the Israelis defeated them. Huge numbers of Palestinian Arabs left Palestine as a result of Jewish intimidation or simply to flee the fighting. The majority fled as refugees to Gaza, the West Bank, Jordan, Lebanon, Syria and other Arab states. There were further wars between the Arab states and Israel and in 1967 Israel captured the West Bank of Jordan and the Gaza Strip.

The Palestinian Arabs lived largely in refugee camps which became Palestinian mini-states. They set up various political movements to represent their views, the most important of which was Fatah, led by Yasser Arafat. By 1969 Arafat pulled together the various Palestinian movements under his command and was recognised as the leader of the 'umbrella' movement, the Palestinian Liberation Organisation. The PLO's primary aim was the creation of a Palestinian state. In practice this meant wiping the state of Israel off the map because both peoples claimed the same territory. When open warfare had failed by the late 1960s the PLO began a campaign of terrorist activities against Israel and Israelis. Throughout the 1970s they carried out commando raids into Israel, fired rockets at Israeli towns, hijacked aircraft and also carried out high profile assassinations. The PLO had bases first in Jordan (which kicked out the PLO in 1971) and then in Lebanon (until an Israeli invasion drove them out in 1982).

By the later 1980s the PLO was in decline but there was then a dramatic change. In December 1987 young Palestinians in the Gaza Strip and West Bank began an uprising against Israeli rule which became known as the Intifada. Arafat quickly linked the Intifada to the PLO and this increased his power and status. In December 1988 he accepted that the state of Israel had a right to exist. From here years of hard bargaining and many disappointments followed. In 1993 Israel and the PLO agreed a peace deal (known as the Oslo Accords) which set up a Palestinian authority to run affairs in the Gaza Strip and the West Bank. It was an important step but it was certainly not a final settlement or an end to violence. The question of Palestine is still one of the biggest factors in international politics today. It is also linked to extreme Islamic terrorist movements such as al-Qaeda.

Al-Qaeda: A brief outline

SOURCE **13**

Afghanistan and Saudi Arabia and their neighbours today.

Osama bin Laden

➤ Born March 1957.
➤ Father was a billionaire businessman in Saudi Arabia.
➤ Very large extended family – Osama's father had many wives and around 50 children.
➤ Attended King Abdulaziz University in the late 1970s, studying civil engineering.
➤ While at university he devoted much of his time to religious study.
➤ Left college in 1979 to fight in Afghanistan against the Soviet forces.

Aims of al-Qaeda

• Destroy American influence in all Muslim nations, especially Saudi Arabia.
• Destroy Israel.
• Destabilise and overthrow pro-Western governments in Muslim states.

Activity

Go back to the table you created in the Focus Task on page 156 and complete the next column with information on al-Qaeda.

The roots of al-Qaeda lie in two places: Saudi Arabia and Afghanistan. The story of al-Qaeda is also deeply influenced by the beliefs and experiences of its founder, Osama bin Laden. In 1979 the Soviet Union invaded Afghanistan. At that time the country had a communist government but it was under threat from Afghanistan's Muslim tribal leaders. The Soviets moved in to protect the Communist government and this triggered war. The Afghan tribes were supported by neighbouring Muslim states, particularly Pakistan. The war against the Soviets was funded by the USA (for political reasons) and Muslim Saudi Arabia (for religious reasons) who saw this struggle as a 'jihad' or 'holy war'. Osama bin Laden was one of many young Saudis who joined the war effort. At first he was involved in fundraising but he eventually became a mujahidin fighter. While he was in Afghanistan bin Laden and other Arab volunteers came under the influence of the radical Muslim preacher Abdullah Azzam. Azzam's ideas argued that Islam was under threat from enemies everywhere. Azzam also argued that it was the responsibility of every Muslim to resist these attacks by taking part in jihad. His ideas formed the basis of al-Qaeda's actions: jihad in any form against: the Western democracies; Communism; Jews and the state of Israel; Muslim governments which were not strict enough or co-operate in any way with al-Qaeda's enemies. The greatest enemy of all was the USA.

In 1990 bin Laden returned to Saudi Arabia. By this time Saudi Arabia was divided between those who wished to modernise the country and accept American ideas and values and those who rejected these values and demanded a strict observance of traditional Muslim practices. This division intensified in 1990 when Saddam Hussein, the leader of Iraq, invaded Kuwait and threatened Saudi Arabia. Osama bin Laden offered the services of his fighters to King Fahd but these were rejected. The king accepted the support of the USA and its allies to fight Saddam. Bin Laden was appalled by the arrival of these foreign troops on the sacred soil of Saudi Arabia. He publicly criticised King Fahd. As a result he was forced into exile in Sudan and his family disowned him. He was stripped of his Saudi citizenship in 1994, but he still held control of much of his wealth. He also had allies in the Taliban movement in Afghanistan, and this gave him a base to operate from. Between 1996 and 2001 al-Qaeda developed into the movement which is so well known but not widely understood. In a sense there were three al-Qaeda movements: (1) the hardcore militant organisation which would attack the enemies of Islam (as al-Qaeda saw it), particularly the USA; (2) an organisation which would network with other groups and organisations which shared its views, and provide finance, training and support for them to carry out their own attacks; (3) a rallying point for modern militant Islam, providing inspiration, guidance, publicity and information (or propaganda) about the common aims of militant Islam across the world.

Throughout the 1990 and early 2000s al-Qaeda launched attacks on targets connected with the USA or the West in general. Part of the 'trademark' of al-Qaeda was the use of suicide bombers where the attacker carried the explosive to the target and was killed with it. This was extremely difficult to stop. Firstly, any terrorist prepared to do this was extremely committed to his or her cause. Secondly, the targets had no time to react because the terrorist did not need time to escape. The highest profile was the attack on the World Trade Centre in 2001 (see Source 1). The US government put together a coalition of forces and attacked al-Qaeda and its Taliban allies in Afghanistan. Al-Qaeda has been effectively destroyed as a single organisation, but its aims and influences have filtered down to countless small organisations.

Why do people and organisations resort to terrorism?

After any terrorist attack it is quite common to see images like Sources 14 and 15 in the newspapers. The terrorist attacks seem so appalling that the only way to make sense of them is to assume that the terrorists were deranged, psychopathic murderers. They are often labelled as evil fanatics. Sometimes newspapers highlight the evil leaders of terrorists organisations who mislead others into terrorism. But do terrorists really become terrorists because they are evil psychopaths or deluded fanatics?

SOURCE **14**

A cartoon from the *Sun* newspaper, 23 November 1974.

SOURCE **15**

A cartoon from *the Sun* newspaper, 24 June 1985. It was commenting on a terrorist attack on an Air India jet, thought to be by Sikh extremists. The attack killed 329 people.

Activity

1 Study Sources 14 and 15 carefully. Make a list of:
   • the main points being made about terrorists
   • the ways in which these points are made.
2 Both cartoons are from a newspaper whose readers are generally not very interested in politics. Does this affect how useful the sources are for investigating:
   • the impact of terrorist acts
   • the motivation of terrorists?

Focus Task

The next eight pages contain a lot of information and evidence about the factors that can lead people to terrorism. As you work through pages 162–169 use a diagram like the one below to record examples of these factors at work. You can also add examples from your earlier work or through reading the rest of this chapter or from your own research. Use colour coding and or lines to show connections between factors. Add other bubbles if you think there are other factors that we have missed. You will find a lot more to go in the lower part of the diagram as you study the case studies in the final part of this chapter.

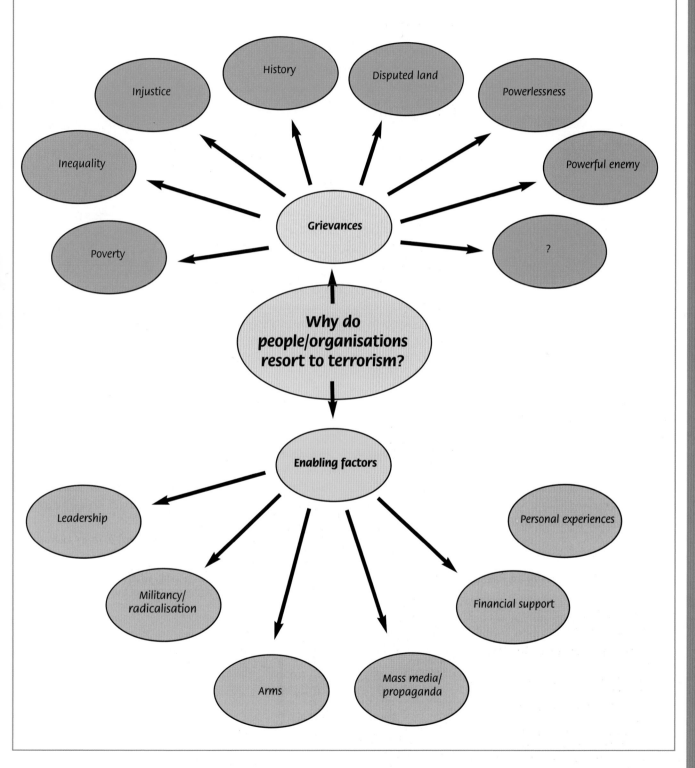

SOURCE 16

Measures to address the conditions conducive to the spread of terrorism.

We resolve to undertake the following measures aimed at addressing the conditions conducive to the spread of terrorism, including (but not limited to): prolonged unresolved conflicts, lack of rule of law and violations of human rights, ethnic, national and religious discrimination, political exclusion, socio-economic marginalisation, lack of good governance. We also recognise that none of these conditions can excuse or justify acts of terrorism.

Extract from the United Nations Organisation Global Counter Terrorism Strategy, issued in 2006. The full strategy can be located from the UNO's website.

Is it about poverty?

Source 16 gives us a clue as to some of the factors which create terrorism. At the heart of most terrorist conflicts we can usually find poverty and inequality.

In Northern Ireland, for example, it is no coincidence that the majority of recruits to the IRA came from the poorer Catholic/Nationalist areas of Northern Ireland's two biggest cities, Belfast and Derry (Catholics usually refer to Londonderry as Derry). Throughout the conflict, unemployment in these areas was generally between 35 per cent and 45 per cent.

It was a similar story for the PLO. Most PLO recruits came from the refugee camps which were set up when over a million Palestinian Arabs left Palestine/Israel in 1948–49. Conditions in these camps were usually very hard and joining the PLO offered status and importance. By the mid 1970s the PLO had around 6,500 fighters and by the early 1980s it was over 11,000, showing it was not hard to find recruits. Israel has always argued that Arab states have deliberately kept the Palestinians in camps because it makes good propaganda against Israel. The Israelis believe Arab oil money could have been used to solve the issue many years ago. They point out that between 1948 and 1972 around 600,000 Jews were forced to leave their homes in Arab and Muslim countries and they were resettled in Israel. The Israelis say that Arab countries could have done the same for the Palestinians, but not surprisingly, few Palestinians or other Arabs have even heard these arguments never mind accepted them.

But what about al-Qaeda? Thanks to Osama bin Laden's fortune and connections the movement was extremely rich. On the other hand, one of bin Laden's complaints against the USA was that it got rich at the expense of ordinary Muslims. For example, in Kuwait US oil companies took Kuwait's wealth and shared it with a few loyal Kuwaiti allies while the ordinary people saw little of this wealth.

Is it about injustice?

Poverty may be a key factor in some cases, but it is not enough on its own. After all, there are many areas of the world which are poor but are not affected by terrorism. As a general rule, terrorist groups emerge because people also have a strong sense of injustice.

For example, the Palestinians lost what they saw as their land. This forced them to live in refugee camps or in densely populated areas of the West Bank or the Gaza Strip. They felt a further sense of injustice because from the 1970s Israeli settlements were established on their lands. The Israeli government did little to stop these settlements.

SOURCE 17

I belong there. I have many memories. I was born as everyone is born.

I have a mother, a house with many windows, brothers, friends, and a prison cell

with a chilly window! I have a wave snatched by seagulls, a panorama of my own.

I have a saturated meadow. In the deep horizon of my word, I have a moon,

a bird's sustenance, and an immortal olive tree.

I have lived on the land long before swords turned man into prey.

I belong there. When heaven mourns for her mother, I return heaven to her mother.

And I cry so that a returning cloud might carry my tears.

To break the rules, I have learned all the words needed for a trial by blood.

I have learned and dismantled all the words in order to draw from them a single word: Home.

A poem called *I Belong There* by the Palestinian poet Mahmoud Darwish. Darwish came from a Palestinian family which was driven out of Israel in 1948. He was an active member of the PLO for many years.

1 Why would Israeli views on the Palestinian camps have little impact on Palestinians or other Arabs?

2 What are the strengths of Source 17 as a source for understanding the aims of the PLO?

3 What are its weaknesses?

4 Does Source 18 support or contradict the view put forward in Source 17? Explain your answer.

SOURCE 18

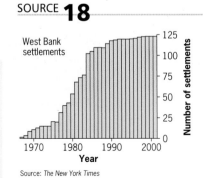

West Bank settlements

Number of settlements

Year

Source: *The New York Times*

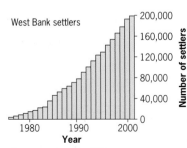

West Bank settlers

Number of settlers

Year

* Data not available before 1976

The development of Israeli settlements in Palestinian areas, 1970 to 2000.

SOURCE 19

I invite all of America's victims to Islam, the religion which rejects injustice and treachery. If they don't convert to Islam, then they should at least take advantage of the Muslims' defensive campaign to repel America's aggression against them and overcome them [the Americans], each in his own way, under his own banner, and with whatever is at his disposal. This is their historic chance because America is reeling from the blows of the mujahidin in Iraq and Afghanistan, thanks to God.

Extract from an interview given by the al-Qaeda second in command Ayman al-Zawahiri in September 2006.

Is it about history?

Sometimes the sense of injustice is identified with a particular historical event. In 1982 Israeli forces and their allies in Lebanon attacked the PLO's bases in Lebanon and drove them out. During this campaign Christian fighters allied to the Israelis entered the Palestinian refugee camps of Sabra and Shatila. They were supposed to be looking for PLO fighters but they simply massacred over 1,000 Palestinian men, women and children. The exact details of the event are hotly disputed by the Israelis and the Palestinians but the reality was that images like Source 20 fuelled support for the PLO.

SOURCE 20

The bodies of Palestinian refugees are collected for burial after the massacres of September 1982.

5 What captions might you find underneath the photograph in Source 20 in: an Israeli newspaper; an American newspaper; a Palestinian newspaper; a moderate Arab newspaper?

6 Try searching picture libraries on the internet and see what images were published at the time and how they were described.

SOURCE 21

At various times over the last 800 years, Irish men and women resisted British rule and attempted to assert Irish independence. Such resistance was repeatedly crushed as the British attempted to subjugate the Irish population.

Between the years 1916 and 1921 Irish nationalists waged a combined political and military campaign against British occupation. In 1920 partition (dividing Ireland into two sections – the 26 southern and the 6 north-eastern counties) was imposed by a British Act of Parliament. The consent of the Irish people was never sought. It was never freely given. The partition of Ireland was merely part of the British government's colonial strategy of divide and rule, used throughout its former empire.

Extract from the Irish history section of the Irish Northern Aid Committee's website. Although it was always denied, this organisation was generally believed to be a fundraising organisation for the IRA.

In Northern Ireland the IRA was motivated by a similar sense of historical injustice. They referred back to events such as the Great Famine of the 1840s (when millions of poor Irish died or left the country due to famine while the British rulers did nothing to help) or more recent events like Bloody Sunday in 1972 when unarmed demonstrators were shot by British troops. To the IRA these were examples of unjust British rule which was discriminatory or harmful to the Irish people. There are certainly plenty of examples of harsh and unjust episodes in British rule, but the Republican tradition has proved very effective in selecting these events and erasing from history the examples of British rule bringing positive benefits. The IRA's version of history has also written out the examples of co-operation and peaceful coexistence between Catholics and Protestants.

These different factors and grivances of poverty and injustice can feed each other. In Northern Ireland, the IRA found it easy to recruit young, discontented unemployed men into the movement. They could be convinced that their poverty and lack of opportunity was the fault of unjust treatment by the British government and the Loyalist community. It was also easy to convince them that they were not unique and that people like them had long suffered injustice.

Is it about powerlessness?

So far on pages 160–164 you have been looking at what historians would call background factors which can feed or breed terrorism. These help to explain why particular groups feel so strongly about particular issues. However, there are many parts of the world where poverty or injustice lead to peaceful protest movements. When we look at areas where these background factors lead to terrorism, we usually find an extra factor – a sense of powerlessness. When a group of people feel that they have no voice or that nobody is listening to that voice they may resort to violence in order to change things.

This was true of the IRA. They operated in a democratic state (the United Kingdom) where, in theory, everyone could have a say in government but they did not see it that way. In their eyes Northern Ireland was doubly biased against them. The British Government would not listen to them, and Northern Ireland's own Parliament was dominated by Unionist politicians who would not listen to them. They saw violence as the way to get what they wanted.

It was also true of al-Qaeda. Within Saudi Arabia there was much debate about how far the country should adopt new customs and ideas such as secular (non-religious) law courts or the education of women. Osama bin Laden and other radical Muslims like him were against this 'westernisation'. They believed that Islam was under attack from non-Muslim opponents. By the 1990s bin Laden and many radicals felt that their views were being ignored. Across the Middle East Muslim governments such as those in Egypt and Turkey were (in al-Qaeda's view) becoming westernised. They were also suppressing traditionalist Islamic viewpoints: in Turkey the army effectively banned Islamic political parties from holding power. Even in Saudi Arabia itself bin Laden felt that traditionalist voices like his were sidelined. When he criticised King Fahd for allying with the USA in the first Gulf War he was expelled from Saudi Arabia. One result was al-Qaeda.

SOURCE 22

The incompetence and authoritarianism of many Muslim and Middle Eastern governments fosters Islamist radicalism. These governments are overwhelmingly unelected, unaccountable, and corrupt; they provide no legitimate outlet for youth discontent. Unsurprisingly, these governments are widely despised by their young people. The old, largely nationalist, ideologies of these governments have failed to deliver either material goods or a sense of dignity either at home or abroad. The half-century failure of Arab states to resolve the Palestinian situation and the inability of Pakistan to ease the lot of Kashmiri Muslims have contributed to the evident corrosion of regimes' legitimacy in the eyes of youth.

An extract from *Examining the Appeal of Islamic Radicals* by Professor Alan Richards of the University of Santa Cruz published in 2003.

Activity

The author of this book strongly believes that simple, clear accounts of history like Source 21 are not good history, because good history is never simple and clear. In pairs or small groups, discuss:
- Do you agree with the author's view generally?
- Do you agree with this view in the case of the IRA and its view of Irish history?
- How would a neutral observer or opponent of the IRA criticise Source 21?

Is it about the strength of the enemy?

What is common to almost all terrorist groups is that they face an immensely powerful enemy. If people feel unjustly treated and ignored they may reach the decision that the best option is to fight, but they know they are never going to survive an all out war.

- In Northern Ireland the IRA was up against a large, modern army alongside a well-organised and dedicated police force.
- The PLO had support from many Arab states but it faced the most powerful and most up-to-date army in the Middle East – supplied by the USA. By the early 1970s it was clear that neither the Arab states or the PLO could defeat Israel in conventional warfare.
- Al-Qaeda was a rich and well-organised terrorist network but it was no match for the leading military power, the USA.

So terrorists use unorthodox military actions like kidnaps, car bombs, etc. because the opponent is too strong to defeat any other way. The aim of the violence is to terrorise or undermine the enemy; to cause chaose; to create anxiety; to sap morale; to drive the enemy away; to force the enemy to listen or compromise; to be noticed.

Sometimes the very strength of their enemy, or the tactics used by their enemy can feed their own organisation. This was the case in Northern Ireland. The British army was originally sent to Northern Ireland to keep peace between Unionists and Nationalists but very soon, through the tactics they used, the army became the target of IRA attack, and a symbol of repression for many Nationalists, as you can see from Source 23.

SOURCE 23

I felt that I was invading the man's home. I felt guilty and ashamed. The place was saturated with CS Gas. Children were coughing. I'm talking now about toddlers, kids of three, four, five.

… I think the major effect of the Falls curfew was that it gave the community in the Lower Falls the opportunity to see the IRA as their saviours and they saw the British Army as the enemy, a foreign occupying force.

… I didn't see myself as a foreign invader and I don't think they did either up until the curfew.

A private in the British Army describing how he and his colleagues searched Nationalist areas in Belfast in the 1970s, looking for arms or terrorists on the run. There were no equivalent searches in Loyalist areas.

SOURCE 24

A British soldier watches a Falls Road resident while other troops search his home, July 1970.

SOURCE 25

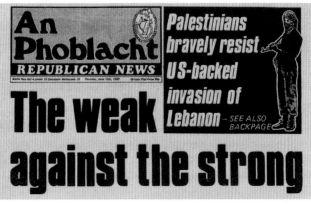

The front page of the IRA newspaper *An Phoblacht,* 10 June 1982. The headline refers to Israel's invasion of Lebanon in 1982 to try and destroy the PLO which was based there.

1 Study Source 24. Write two captions, one which might have appeared in a British newspaper and one which might have appeared in a newspaper supporting the IRA.
2 How does Source 23 help to explain why the Provisional IRA had little trouble finding recruits?
3 What is Source 25 trying to say about the position of the Palestinians?
4 Why would the IRA care about what was happening in Lebanon?

What do terrorists believe in?

So far you have examined some background social, economic and political factors that help breed terrorism. Some historians would argue however that ideology (which simply means a fixed set of beliefs about the world) is an even more powerful motivator of terrorist actions than any of the factors you have so far considered.

Religion

Religious belief can give individuals a sense of purpose. Believers see their duty to God as much more important than anything else – even than their own lives.

The ideals of most religions are against the kind of violence that terrorists use but, even so, terrorists often claim to act in the name of their religion and get support from religious leaders. Terrorist leaders can use the extreme loyalty that religious belief creates for their own purpose.

Some groups make religious claims:
- that God is on their side
- that their opponents are evil
- that their struggle is holy.

Religious belief plays a significant role in al-Qaeda. One of their aims is to ensure all the Muslim countries follow its particular interpretation of Islam. They call their enemy, the USA, the Great Satan.

However, a word of warning: just because a terrorist group uses a religious label it does not mean that religion is their main motivator. The IRA and its supporters were almost all Catholics while the Unionists were almost all Protestant. However it was never part of the IRA's aim to make the Protestants become Catholics. Religion was not *the* issue.

Nationalism

Nationalism is a slippery term. People don't agree about what it means. But in this context nationalism means a sense of identity either as cultural group or a as a nation. Nationalists want their own country where they can run their own affairs for their own benefit without interference from outsiders.

Many terrorists have nationalist ambitions either because they are fighting against an external power who has occupied their country (as claimed by the IRA in Northern Ireland); or because they are hoping to create their own nation (as in Palestine where the PLO are aiming to establish their own homeland in the land currently occupied by Israel). Further in the past we see in the infamous assassination of Archduke Ferdinand that started the First World War that Gavrilo Princip was part of a nationalist movement fighting to free their country from Austrian control.

Nationalism can be a very powerful ingredient in the terrorist recipe. Terrorist leaders can use feelings of national pride to gain support or motivate the members of their organisation to kill for or die for their country. In extreme cases nationalism means terrorists regard anyone from their enemy country as a legitimate target.

Political ideology

All terrorist groups are political in the sense that they are aiming to achieve a shift in power of some sort or another.

However, political ideology is something more precise. A political ideology is a fixed set of beliefs about how society should be organised, for example: Communists (who believe in state control of all aspects of life), Socialists (who believe in sharing wealth to remove inequalities) or Capitalists (who believe in individual freedom to make money). Some terrorist groups are motivated primarily by such ideologies. During the 1970s groups like the German Red Army Faction carried out terror attacks. They were Socialists who believed that German society was corrupt and that its capitalist, democratic system favoured the rich over the poor.

The R in IRA stands for Republican. Republicans believe a country should not be run by a monarch but by an elected government. Many IRA activists also held socialist political ideas and wanted wealth redistributed to improve the lives of ordinary people. They hoped to put these ideas into practice once they removed the British from Northern Ireland.

The complex bit

By now you will be familiar with the fact that History seldom fits into neat boxes. Almost everything in history is connected to almost everything else in some way or other! Some experts have turned what historians have known for a long time into a special theory called Complexity Theory. Terrorism is a good example of this complexity. If you study any of the three groups: the IRA, PLO and al-Qaeda you can quickly see how these different sets of beliefs combine together in rather tricky ways.

For example, Al Qaeda: the ideology of Communism is very anti-religious. In the ideal Communist state religion would have no place because it would divert your attention from serving your country and your fellow workers. Al-Qaeda grew out of the struggle against such atheist Communism ideology in Afghanistan. At that time Communism was the great evil. Al-Qaeda believed that Muslim countries should be run by a religious government not a secular one. Today it targets the Capitalist ideology of the USA and its allies in a similar way. So al-Qaeda combines political ideology and religion – the two are almost interchangeable at times.

What about nationalism? Al-Qaeda is an international movement, not tied to any single state. It operates in dozens of different countries. There is no sense at all that al-Qaeda wants to set up its own nation. So surely nationalism plays no part! Wrong again. Al-Qaeda draws a good deal of power from Arab Nationalism. This is the idea that all Arabs, whether they live in North Africa or the Middle East or elsewhere in the world are part of a single group. Al-Qaeda both feeds and benefits from the sense of identity that spreads across national boundaries.

It's complicated! Bear that in mind as you study the next page.

SOURCE 26

My fellow Muslims,
Jihad is the purpose of your lives, jihad is
your glory, and the substance of your
existence is linked by fate to jihad. Fellow
preachers, you have no value on this earth
beyond that of your destroying the whole
corrupt population of cruel rulers, infidels
and sinners.

Those of the opinion that the religion of
Allah can win without a jihad, without a
battle against the infidels and without
dismembered bodies strewn in every
direction only delude themselves. They do
not understand the true essence of the
Islamic religion.

Extract from the preaching of Abdullah
Azzam, date unknown. It was found by
Israeli troops on a postcard in the
Palestinian territories.

Focus Task

What roles do religion, nationalism and ideology play in terrorism?

1 Study Sources 26–29 carefully. For each source, write a short list of points which emerge. For example, in Source 26 one point might be: *Al-Qaeda – jihad*. Do this for all of the sources.
2 Now place the points you have written down on your own copy of the Venn diagram shown here.
3 Next, search through pages 156–166 for other points which help us to understand what the IRA, PLO or al-Qaeda believe in. Add these points to the Venn diagram.
4 Finally, go back to the table you created on page 156. Add a new row headed 'Beliefs'.

politics

religion   nationalism

SOURCE 27

The ruling to kill the Americans and their allies – civilians and military – is an individual
duty for every Muslim who can do it in any country in which it is possible to do it, in order to
liberate the al-Aqsa Mosque (in Jerusalem) and the holy mosque (in Makka) from their grip,
and in order for their armies to move out of all the lands of Islam, defeated and unable to
threaten any Muslim. This is in accordance with the words of Almighty Allah, 'and fight the
pagans all together as they fight you all together' and 'fight them until there is no more tumult
or oppression, and there prevail justice and faith in Allah'.

Statement by al-Qaeda leader Osama bin Laden in February 1998.

SOURCE 28

The front cover of *The Red Cancer*, written
by Azzam. The book is a bitter attack on
Communism, and includes a chapter
accusing Jews of spreading Communism.

SOURCE 29

Article 1: Palestine is the homeland of the Arab Palestinian people; it is an indivisible part of the
Arab homeland, and the Palestinian people are an integral part of the Arab nation.
Article 4: The Palestinian identity is a genuine, essential, and inherent characteristic; it is
transmitted from parents to children. The Zionist occupation and the
dispersal of the Palestinian Arab people, through the disasters which befell
them, do not make them lose their Palestinian identity and their
membership in the Palestinian community.
Article 8: The phase in their history, through which the Palestinian people are
now living, is that of national (watani) struggle for the liberation of
Palestine. Thus the conflicts among the Palestinian national forces are
secondary, and should be ended.
Article 9: Armed struggle is the only way to liberate Palestine. This is the
overall strategy, not merely a tactical phase.
Article 10: Commando action constitutes the nucleus of the Palestinian
popular liberation war.

Extracts from the Palestinian National Charter of 1968.

SOURCE 30

A mural for Sinn Fein, the political wing of the IRA, in Belfast in
1985. The woman is Erin, representing the spirit of a united
Ireland. The flag is the flag of the Republic of Ireland which the
IRA want Northern Ireland to be part of.

1 What is jihad?
2 According to Azzam, how important is it?
3 What is the message of the image in Source 28?

Personal motives

None of the factors so far determines that someone will *automatically* become a terrorist. It is not like that. The decision to turn to terrorism still comes down to ordinary people taking personal decisions to join a terrorist group or commit a terrorist act. So why do some people, a very few people, decide to follow this path? Experts have studied what terrorists have said and written. Others have interviewed terrorists who have been in prison. Here are some of their findings.

SOURCE 31

Forced to take up arms to protect themselves and their people, terrorists perceive themselves as reluctant warriors driven by desperation – and lacking any viable alternative – to violence against a repressive state, a predatory rival ethnic or nationalist group, or an unresponsive international order.

... Unlike the ordinary criminal or the lunatic assassin, the terrorist is not pursuing purely selfish goals; he is not driven by the wish to line his own pocket or satisfy some personal need or grievance. The terrorist is fundamentally an altruist [acting for the good of others]: he believes that he is serving a 'good' cause designed to achieve a greater good for a wider group – whether real or imagined – which the terrorist and his organisation claim to represent.

... There is a nearly universal element in them that can be described as the 'true believer'. Terrorists do not even consider that they may be wrong and that others' views may have some merit. Terrorists create a polarized 'we versus they' outlook. They attribute only evil motives to anyone outside their own group. This enables the terrorists to dehumanise their victims and removes any sense of doubt from their minds. Another common characteristic of the terrorist is the pronounced need to belong to a group. With some terrorists, group acceptance is a stronger motivator than the stated political objectives of the organisation.

David Whittaker, Senior Lecturer in International Relations at the University of Teesside, writing in 2007. The writer is a specialist in terrorism.

Activity

Source 31 sets out a number of possible characteristics of terrorists. Read Sources 32–34 to see whether they apply to the members of the IRA, PLO and al-Qaeda. Record details in a table like this. There will be gaps in your table.

Characteristics	IRA	PLO	Al-Qaeda
Driven by desperation			
Serving a cause			
Protecting or serving a wider group of people			
Evil enemy who must be fought			
Able to dehumanise enemy			
Belonging to a group			

SOURCE 32

Hughes: My old school was being attacked by loyalist crowds with petrol bombs. One of the IRA men who were there at the time had a Thompson submachine-gun and asked if anybody knew the layout of the school. I did and I went with this fella. Petrol bombs were coming in all over. There was a man on the roof of the school and people were shouting at him to fire into the crowd and he was shouting back that he was under orders to fire over the heads. That's exactly what he did. He fired a Thompson submachine-gun over the heads of the crowd and it stopped the school from being burned down. That was my first contact with the IRA.

Interviewer: What impression did the IRA man with a Thompson submachine-gun have on you?

Hughes: It gave me a sense of pride and a feeling that we had something to protect ourselves with. I wanted to be involved in that too because our whole community felt that we were under attack. I wanted to be part of that defence. From then on in, I got involved with the Movement.

Brendan Hughes, a future IRA Commander, describes the Provisionals in action in 1970. He was being interviewed for a TV series.

SOURCE 33

Those of our Fatah colleagues who did turn to terror were not mindless criminals. They were fiercely dedicated nationalists who were doing their duty as they saw it. I have to say they were wrong, and did so at the time, but I have also to understand them. In their view, and in this they were right, the world was saying to us Palestinians, 'We don't give a damn about you, and we won't care until you are a threat to our interests.' In reply those in Fatah who turned to terror were saying, 'OK, world. We'll play the game by your rules. We'll make you care!' That doesn't justify what they did, but it does explain their thinking and their actions.

Khalad Hassan, a leading member of the PLO commenting in 1984 on the PLO terror campaign of the 1970s.

SOURCE 34

Bin Laden did not kidnap young men and brainwash them. The young men who flocked to Afghanistan to seek military and terrorist training did so of their own free will. As is clear from the testimony of recruits in the training camps run by al-Qaeda in Afghanistan between 1996 and 2001, nobody was kept there against their will. Discipline was tight, but anyone who wanted to leave was allowed to go. Most of the volunteers were dedicated to the cause long before they reached the camps. Indeed many overcame considerable obstacles to reach Afghanistan. Importantly, bin Laden's associates spent much of their time in the 1996–2001 period selecting which of the myriad requests for assistance they would grant. The requests – for money, expertise, advice and other logistical support – came from everywhere, from Morocco to Malaysia. These were not requests for help in building refugee camps or new mosques. They were requests for assistance with bomb attacks, assassinations and murder on a horrific scale. These requests, like the recruits who carried them, originated in the huge swathe of largely young men who were sufficiently motivated to want to devote substantial proportions of their lives and energies to the most extreme end of Islamic militancy.

Extract from *Al-Qaeda* by Jason Burke, published in 2006. The author is a journalist specialising in the Middle East and al-Qaeda.

Focus Task

Why do people or groups resort to terrorism?

For the Focus Task on page 161 you have been creating a diagram to show examples of factors that lead to terrorism.

You now have to take your thinking to a higher level. Your task is to decide how important each of these factors is, and how they are connected to each other. You must then show this in a diagram. You could use one of the following:

◆ a bar graph
◆ a Venn diagram
◆ your own idea.

Make sure your diagram is labelled with plenty of examples and make sure you can explain why you chose your particular diagram. Your teacher may ask you to present and explain your findings.

Poverty

Terrorist groups in action

In this chapter so far you have come across the ideas and aims which underpin three important terrorist organisations. You are now going to look at examples of how they tried to achieve these aims. Not every action they have taken will be considered, but you are going to compare some of these actions.

Aims

The primary aims of the IRA during the conflict in Northern Ireland were:

- Defend Nationalist communities.
- Remove British presence from Northern Ireland.
- Create a united Ireland of 32 counties.

The IRA in the 1970s and 1980s

Strengths

- **Culture and propaganda:** The Republican movement used past and present examples of British injustice towards Irish people in songs, posters, pamphlets and murals.
- **Prisoners:** By 1980 there were hundreds of Republican prisoners in gaols across Northern Ireland. They also became an important propaganda symbol for the IRA.
- **An iron grip on Nationalist areas:** This gave them recruits, information and funds for their campaigns.
- **International support:** The IRA worked hard to link itself to other causes, such as the Palestinian Liberation Organisation. The IRA also had support in the Republic of Ireland. The largest source of funds for the IRA came from the Irish community in the USA. The IRA also received weapons and training from the regime of Colonel Gadaffi in Libya.
- **Effective leadership and organisation:** The two leading figures in the IRA were Martin McGuinness and Gerry Adams. On the military side the IRA reorganised itself into small cells called Active Service Units. These cells never met other cells and knew nothing about each other, so it became much more difficult for the security services to get information about them. Adams also began to recognise the need for the IRA's political wing Sinn Fein to become a more effective political force.

Actions

Throughout the 1970s the IRA used a range of different tactics which were typical of a terrorist organisation.

The main methods used by the IRA were shootings and bombs. The IRA were at their most destructive in the early 1970s but their campaigns continued until their ceasefire in 1996. They killed many soldiers, police and civilians (see Source 35) and set off thousands of bombs. They also targeted businesses in an attempt to disrupt economic life in Northern Ireland. In South Armagh they scouted out Army patrol routes and planted bombs in drains which ran under the roads. These tactics were so effective that South Armagh became known as 'Bandit Country'.

The IRA were also aware of the impact of high profile attacks. In 1979 they killed eighteen British troops in two ambushes at Warrenpoint in County Down and on the same day they killed Lord Mountbatten (a member of the British royal family). In October 1984 they very nearly succeeded in killing the Prime Minister, Margaret Thatcher, by planting a bomb in The Grand Hotel in Brighton. In 1996 they set off huge bombs in London and Manchester which caused devastation and demonstrated that they were a force to be reckoned with.

Other tactics included:

- Kidnapping and hostage taking: This was usually done to raise funds. In the early 1990s the IRA took hostages and forced people to take a bomb into a target area. They were effectively suicide bombs but the IRA gave up this method because opinion within their own supporters was extremely negative towards this tactic.
- Bank robberies and protection rackets to raise funds: The IRA tried to cover up these activities as it did not fit well with their image of themselves as political idealists.

SOURCE 35

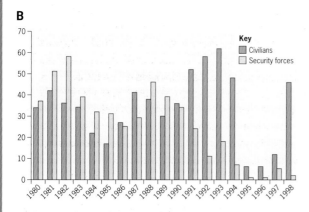

A

B

Deaths caused by IRA actions in the Northern Ireland conflict in **A** 1970s and **B** 1980s and 1990s.

SOURCE 36

The aftermath of the IRA bomb in the Docklands area of London in 1996.

Aims

- Destroy the state of Israel.
- Re-establish Palestine as the home of the Palestinian Arabs.
- Make the new Palestine part of the wider Arab, Muslim community.

The PLO in the 1970s and 1980s

Strengths

- A clever and charismatic leader in Yasser Arafat, accepted by Palestinians as their leader and respected in the Arab world.
- Secure bases in Lebanon: The PLO was originally based in Jordan but fell out with King Hussain in 1971 and was expelled. Lebanon's capital was an ideal place to make contacts (e.g. for arms deals) and also to try and use the world's media to publicise the PLO cause. Lebanon's government was also weak. The Lebanese army was completely unable to stop the PLO launching attacks on Israel from its bases in South Lebanon.
- There had been a large population of Palestinian refugees in Lebanon since 1948. By the 1960s they made up around 10 per cent of the population of the country. This was a powerful base of support for the PLO. By the mid 1970s Arafat had around 6,500 PLO fighters in Lebanon. By the early 1980s there were over 11,000.
- The PLO was able to raise money from expatriate Palestinians working in the USA, Europe, and other parts of the Middle East. Arab states also donated funds to the PLO, particularly Saudi Arabia. Other funding came from bank robberies and kidnappings.
- Arafat built up a Palestinian state within a state. There were courts, schools, hospitals, military training camps and even industrial enterprises.
- The PLO also built up a powerful network of culture and propaganda. Young Palestinians were recruited into the PLO through stories of how their people had been betrayed in 1948.

Actions

From March 1969 to September 1970 the PLO attacked Israel with artillery fire from Jordan on Israeli settlements and military targets. Fatah commandos also attacked civilian targets using typical underground warfare (or terrorist tactics, depending on your point of view). In September 1970 PLO fighters hijacked three airliners in Jordan, demanding the release of Palestinian prisoners in Israel. The passengers were eventually released but the planes were blown up. In 1976 the PLO hijacked another aircraft with over 100 Jewish passengers and flew it to Entebbe airport in Uganda. From the mid 1970s onwards tighter security measures in airports made hijackings more difficult.

An even more high profile attack was carried out by a group called Black September in 1972. Black September was set up by Yasser Arafat to carry out attacks which the official PLO could deny if it suited him. At the Olympic Games in Munich Black September took eleven Israeli athletes hostage and killed them when the German police tried to rescue them. Such actions alienated public opinion in much of the world but the PLO saw them as justified as part of their struggle.

During the 1980s the PLO suffered defeats by Israeli forces which you will look at on pages 176–77. However, in December 1987 events took their own course. A large scale uprising (Intifada) began in the occupied territories of the Gaza Strip and the West Bank (see pages 176–77). The harsh Israeli response to the Intifada (curfews, tear gas and bullets, closing down the school system) probably generated more support for the Palestinian cause than any previous PLO actions.

SOURCE **37**

Burning aircraft after the hijacking in Jordan, September 1970.

Focus Task

How similar were the IRA and the PLO?

The UNO Counter Terrorism Strategy (see Source 20) is investigating past and present terrorist groups to see if there are useful lessons to be learned from their history. You have been asked to do a study on the IRA and the PLO and to give your own view on how similar they were.

Section 1 of your report should be a brief outline of what you have found in this section. You will need to explain:
- the similarities between each movement's aims, strengths, and methods

- the differences between each movement's aims, strengths, and methods.

It is important that you do not simply list these points – you must explain how they are similar or different.

Section 2 of your report should look back at more of the issues you have studied so far. This should provide examples of similarities and differences you have found in:
- the motivation of terrorists from each group
- the conditions which created each organisation
- how people have reacted to their methods
- how they justified their actions.

Al-Qaeda in action

Aims

- Destroy American influence in all Muslim nations, especially Saudi Arabia.
- Destroy Israel.
- Destabilise and overthrow pro-Western governments in Muslim states.

Strengths

- A clear, simple and very powerful set of beliefs – originally set out by the radical preacher Abdullah Azzam and further developed by Osama bin Laden.
- A very difficult movement to combat because it did not want land or anything material. Also very difficult to combat because al-Qaeda was more like a franchise (see below).
- Clever and charismatic leader in Osama bin Laden. He had proved himself as a fighter in Afghanistan and was widely respected as generous to his followers. He was also from an immensely rich family and used his wealth to support the movement. His second in command Ayman al-Zawahiri was also extremely capable.
- A movement that is extremely aware of the potential of technologies such as the internet and mobile phones as tools for running a terrorist organisation.
- Loyal, committed and well-trained operatives who were trained in all aspects of terrorist warfare in training camps in Afghanistan. These techniques were originally taught to Afghan fighters by the Americans to help them fight the Soviets.
- Secure bases: Al-Qaeda was closely allied to the hardline Muslim Taliban movement in Afghanistan and could rely on security and secrecy.
- Generous funding from supporters in Pakistan and Saudi Arabia, along with the drugs trade in Afghanistan.
- Enemies, particularly the USA, who were inadequately prepared to face this type of enemy.

Actions

Al-Qaeda was a terrorist group, but it was also more than that. As you saw on page 159, there were three al-Qaeda movements.

1 A hardcore militant organisation.
2 A network with other groups sharing its views, and providing finance, training and support to carry out their own attacks.
3 An idea or rallying point for modern militant Islam, providing inspiration, guidance, publicity and information (or propaganda) about the common aims of militant Islam across the world.

SOURCE **38**

Any American who pays taxes to his government is our target because he is helping the American war machine against the Muslim nation. Terrorising oppressors and criminals and thieves and robbers is necessary for the safety of people and for the protection of their property.

Extract from an interview by bin Laden given to the American news network ABC early in 1998.

1 Does Source 38 provide convincing evidence that al-Qaeda was an effective organisation?

This made it very difficult to combat because many al-Qaeda attacks were not carried out by al-Qaeda operatives. For example, in 1993 a Pakistani militant called Ramzi Yousef attacked the World Trade Centre in New York with a truck bomb. It killed six people and caused $300 million in damage. Yousef claimed he was inspired by Osama bin Laden's teaching. He was not directly connected to al-Qaeda but he did share their views. He also attended a training camp in Afghanistan. There was a similar attack in Saudi Arabia in November 1995 on the Saudi National Guard and American troops training them. The Saudi security services arrested four men who also claimed to have been inspired by bin Laden. They were later executed.

In 1998 bin Laden announced the formation of a World Islamic Front. He made very clear statements warning of attacks on the USA and hinting at the methods which might be used. Soon afterwards al-Qaeda struck hard. On 7 August 1998 US embassies in Nairobi, Kenya and Dar es Salaam, Tanzania were hit by truck bombs. The Nairobi attack was particularly well planned, with some of the al-Qaeda operatives settling in to the area for years before it and even marrying local women. The attacks were also devastating. The Nairobi attack killed 213 and wounded around 4,600 people. In Dar es Salaam eleven people died and 85 were wounded.

SOURCE 39

Scenes of devastation at the US embassy in Nairobi. The attack was carried out by a suicide bomber in a truck packed with explosives.

2 How far do Sources 40A and B support this view?
3 According to Source 40A, what was different about al-Qaeda tactics?

SOURCE 41

A New York fire-fighter searches for survivors in the ruins of the World Trade Center. (See also Source 1 on page 150.)

SOURCE 40

A

I was shocked. I was astonished by the skill with which these attacks had been carried out. You only had to look at the first few pictures to realise that this was a different kind of terror, that this was terror which aimed at mass casualties in a way that previous attacks never had.

B

I was struck by the scale of the devastation in this bombing and that immediately told me of the capabilities of this organisation. We were not dealing with isolated, small groups of potential extremists. We were dealing with an organisational structure that had planned, thought it out, put all the mechanics in place and successfully carried it out.

Two comments on the bombings of August 1998. **A** from Daniel Benjamin, Director for Counter-Terrorism at the USA's National Security Council, 1998–99 and **B** from Joe Billy, Deputy Director of Counter-Terrorism for the FBI.

USS *Cole* and 9/11

In October 2000 suicide bombers drove a boat packed with explosives into the side of the American warship the USS *Cole*, killing seventeen US sailors. Of course the most significant attack carried out by al-Qaeda was the destruction of the twin towers of the World Trade Center in New York on 11 September 2001. America and the rest of the world were stunned as al-Qaeda operatives hijacked four aircraft. Two were flown into the World Trade Center. One was forced to crash and the fourth hit the Pentagon, the US military headquarters in Washington DC. The attacks killed just under 3,000 people. The vast majority were civilians and a large number were not Americans. It was the most destructive attack ever to hit American soil. While Americans were numb with shock, Islamic militants celebrated what they saw as a great victory. Bin Laden again demonstrated his understanding of the power of modern communications by issuing a video on the attacks, praising the suicide bombers. It was broadcast on the Arabic TV station al-Jazeera although there were some doubts about whether it was genuine.

Focus Task A

Look back at your work in the Focus Task on page 171. Many experts in the UNO believe that al-Qaeda is unlike any other terrorist organisation there has ever been. Your task is to add an extra part to Section 1 of your report explaining whether or not you agree with this view. You will need to explain whether you think al-Qaeda's:
◆ aims
◆ strengths
◆ actions
are unlike the IRA or PLO.

You could also extend Section 2 of your report to compare al-Qaeda with the IRA and PLO:
◆ The motivation of al-Qaeda terrorists.
◆ The conditions which created al-Qaeda.
◆ How people have reacted to al-Qaeda's methods.
◆ How al-Qaeda justified their actions.

Focus Task B

How important are the leaders of terrorist groups?

In many terrorist conflicts leaders of terrorist groups have played a central role. Go back over pages 170–73 and compare the roles and importance of the leaders of the IRA (Adams and McGuiness), PLO (Yasser Arafat) and al-Qaeda (Osama bin Laden). They are also mentioned in many other parts of this chapter so you can track them down there as well.

1 For each leader you should add to the Profiles on pages 157–59 another 5–8 points which explain:
◆ importance to their own movement
◆ abilities (e.g. military, political, organisational)
◆ reputation within the movement
◆ key achievements
◆ how the movement might have been affected if they had been killed or captured.
Your Profile does not need to contain details such as date of birth, death etc. This has already been done for you. This profile is about the importance of the leaders.

2 Hold a class debate and see if you can agree which leader was the most important to his particular movement. You may decide that this question is impossible to answer, but it can be interesting to see!

SOURCE 42

BRITISH CARTOON ARCHIVE, UNIVERSITY OF KENT © DAILY EXPRESS

Cartoon from the *Daily Telegraph* published on 1 February 1994. The man on the ground is Gerry Adams and the 'doctor' is US President Bill Clinton.

SOURCE 43

Cartoon from *Republican News* published in Belfast in 1980. Diplock courts did not have juries because of the problem in Northern Ireland of juries being intimidated. The case was decided by the judge.

Activity

Work in pairs. One of you take Source 43 and the other one take Source 44. Explain what inferences historians can make about the problems of a 'Get Tough' policy.

Get tough or talk? How have governments reacted to terrorism?

Terrorism presents governments with a unique set of problems. This is especially true for democratic governments but the position is similar for non-democratic governments as well. The basic problem is that terrorists are difficult to find. They are also difficult to stop. When faced with terrorism, most people want their governments to get tough. The problem is that when governments do try to get tough then they usually end up restricting the rights and freedoms of people who are not terrorists. They also face the temptation to use illegal methods themselves to tackle terrorism. This brings the danger that in trying to root out terrorism they actually strengthen the terrorists. On the other hand, governments usually get criticised if they do start talking to terrorists. It is a very difficult issue and in this section we are going to examine three different approaches taken by the British government, the Israeli government and the US government.

Case Study 1: The British government and the IRA – Security and politics

Throughout its conflict with the IRA the British government used a combination of Get Tough and Talk approaches. Some of the examples of the Get Tough approach were as follows.

Internment: August 1971

The security forces in Ireland were authorised to arrest and hold anyone suspected of terrorism without charge or trial. It was meant to disrupt IRA activity but it was a disaster. It failed to catch any of the IRA's key leaders. Also, internment was only used against Nationalists, which strengthened the Nationalist view that the state was against them and the IRA was their best protection. It increased support for the IRA in Ireland and in the USA, partly because many of those interned were tortured. Worst of all, internment led to demonstrations which often led to confrontation on the streets. The worst incident was Bloody Sunday, 30 January 1972 when British paratroopers shot dead thirteen unarmed demonstrators. This event was the best kind of recruitment tool the IRA could get.

Focus on security

In 1976 Roy Mason became Secretary of State for Northern Ireland. He saw the IRA purely as a security issue. He increased the level of British forces. He authorised the use of special forces (the SAS) against the IRA and also authorised the use of paid informers. He stopped IRA prisoners being treated as political prisoners and made them go through the same conditions as ordinary criminals (see Source 43). Deaths caused by the IRA fell. In later years IRA leader Martin McGuiness commented that 'Mason beat the crap out of us'.

Covert operations in the 1980s

The Army, SAS, intelligence services and the RUC (Royal Ulster Constabulary) all tried to disrupt IRA operations using informers, technology and ambush techniques based on intelligence. This definitely disrupted IRA operations, prevented many attacks (including a plot to assassinate the Princess of Wales) and led to many arrests. However, there were downsides. In 1982 the RUC shot dead six unarmed IRA suspects in County Armagh, leading to claims of a shoot to kill policy designed to intimidate Nationalists. In 1988 SAS men shot dead three unarmed IRA suspects in Gibraltar. There were claims that the British government was using a policy of political assassination. These claims are still hotly disputed today, but the controversy helped the IRA. For Nationalists who were already suspicious of the British government these actions strengthened their views that the British government was an oppressor and it strengthened support for the IRA. At the same time the British government's decision to let IRA hunger strikers die in prison was seen by even moderate Nationalists as unjust.

The funeral of IRA hunger striker Bobby Sands in May 1981. Funerals and memorials were an important and very powerful form of propaganda. It was estimated that around twenty per cent of the Nationalist population of Northern Ireland attended the funeral. The great majority of these Nationalists were not IRA supporters but they were unhappy with British policies.

Focus Task

Get tough	Talk to terrorists

Get tough or talk?

Imagine you are advising a government which is facing a terrorist threat. Your task is to label this diagram and then give a short presentation with the following title:
Lessons from Northern Ireland: The strengths and weaknesses of Get Tough and Talk to Terrorists policies.

Co-operation with the government of the Irish Republic

In 1985 British Prime Minister Margaret Thatcher signed the Anglo-Irish Agreement with Irish Taoiseach (leader) Garrett Fitzgerald. This increased co-operation between security forces across the border. This made it much more difficult for the IRA to move people, arms and equipment across the border between Northern Ireland and the Republic.

Starving the terrorists of publicity

British governments often claimed that sections of the media were too sympathetic towards the IRA and were also too critical of the government. In the 1980s British Prime Minister Margaret Thatcher banned British radio and TV broadcasters from allowing any member of the IRA or Sinn Fein to be broadcast. The idea was to starve the terrorists of what Thatcher called 'the oxygen of publicity'. With hindsight the policy was a failure. Broadcasters still broadcast the worlds of leaders like Gerry Adams but they got actors to speak his words. If anything, the broadcast ban actually increased interest in the IRA, especially in the USA, and it led to President Bill Clinton inviting Gerry Adams to the USA for talks. It also strengthened Adams' reputation within the IRA.

Talk to terrorists

Although it was usually denied, the British government did in fact talk to the IRA at various stages in the conflict.

- As early as 1972 the British minster in charge of Northern Ireland, William Whitelaw, agreed to secret talks with the IRA leadership but the talks quickly broke down. There was little more contact until the 1980s, when the IRA began to change its tactics.
- Republican leader Gerry Adams became convinced in the late 1970s that the IRA would never win an outright military victory. He made the most of the sympathy generated by the IRA hunger strikes and began to build up the IRA's political wing, Sinn Fein. In June 1983 Adams himself was elected to the Westminster Parliament with 73 per cent of the vote in his West Belfast constituency. Sinn Fein scooped up thirteen per cent of the Northern Ireland vote as a whole. They campaigned using a powerful combination of anti-British statements, Republican aims and criticisms of the poverty and poor housing which affected many working-class Nationalists. Many hardline Republicans were unhappy with the new strategy. They believed that it compromised the IRA's commitment to armed struggle. However, Adams was able to reassure them and point to the benefits which political involvement brought.
- The emergence of Sinn Fein gave the British government an organisation which it could talk to, although the government was bitterly criticised in the British press for talking to terrorists. Even while the British and Irish governments were negotiating the Anglo Irish Treaty, Martin McGuinness and other IRA leaders were in regular discussions with British officials during this period (although it was officially denied).
- In 1993 the British and Irish governments signed the Downing Street declaration. It improved security co-operation but the key element was that the British government declared it had no selfish interest in controlling Northern Ireland. If the majority in Northern Ireland voted for a united Ireland then the British government would not object. Gerry Adams was able to convince the hardline Republicans in his own movement that the British declaration was genuine.
- Adams and McGuinness began to pursue a strategy of negotiation with the British government and other political groups in Northern Ireland, while at the same time trying to convince the rest of the Republican movement they were not selling out. They were helped by having the support of US President Bill Clinton. Adams and McGuinness took a lot of criticism from both sides but by 1998 they were able to get almost all Republicans to sign up to a lasting ceasefire even though Northern Ireland was still part of the UK and British troops were still on Irish soil.

Case Study 2: Israel and the PLO

Get Tough

For most of the conflict between Israel and the PLO the Israeli government's policy has been an uncompromising Get Tough approach. One form of Get Tough policy has been targeted assassinations. These have been used since the 1970s and have included events such as the commando raid in Tunis in 1998 which killed PLO military commander Abu Jihad. More recently these attacks have been carried out using missiles or aircraft. These attacks frequently kill civilians as well as (or instead of) their target and they also open Israel up to claims of using terrorist methods itself.

The Israeli government has also been quite prepared to use full military force. In 1982 Israel launched a full scale invasion of Lebanon to destroy the PLO's bases there. It involved 40,000 troops with tanks and air support. They reached Beirut and subjected the city to a three-month siege. Arafat's Lebanese allies urged the PLO to leave as the Israeli invasion was devastating the country. In a ceasefire plan brokered by the USA around 11,000 PLO fighters were evacuated by sea. The evacuation from Lebanon was a humiliating defeat, but for Yasser Arafat there were small crumbs of comfort:

- The huge civilian casualties had damaged support for Israel around the world. Around 19,000 Palestinians and Lebanese were killed, mostly civilians. The worst event was the massacre of Palestinians in the Sabra and Shatila refugee camps. The massacres even raised concerns from Israelis about their country's actions. Some Israelis began to consider the possibility of trying to reach some kind of deal with Arafat.
- The evacuation of the PLO had been paid for and organised by the USA. The Americans were beginning to take a greater interest in the Palestinian question and began to talk to Arafat about the possibility of setting up a peace process.

The Intifada

In the occupied territories Israeli forces have used a range of security measures. There are checkpoints whenever anyone crosses from Gaza or the West Bank into Israel. These certainly help to restrict the activities of terrorists, and are helpful detecting suicide bombers. On the other hand they cause massive disruption to everyday life and lead to resentment against the Israelis. One of the most common complaints among Palestinians is that it takes them so long to travel short distances because of all the checkpoints.

Measures like these helped to create the Intifada. In December 1987 a large scale uprising (Intifada) began in the occupied territories of the Gaza Strip and the West Bank. It was a protest mostly by young people against Israeli rule. Israeli patrols and bases were stoned or petrol bombed. There was also economic non-cooperation with the Israelis, refusing to work or open shops and businesses. The Intifada was not organised by the PLO. It took them and the Israelis by surprise. The reaction of the Israelis to the Intifada was a harsh clampdown. They placed curfews on Palestinians in the occupied territories. They closed down the Palestinian education system because they claimed it was responsible for radicalising the young Palestinians. Israeli troops used tear gas, rubber bullets and live rounds.

Arafat quickly tried to take control of the Intifada and to link it with the PLO. He recognised that the Israeli clampdown on the Intifada was generating support for the Palestinians. The growing death toll and regular funerals bearing PLO flags saw to this. The events were widely reported across the world, and the impact of Israel's policies was spread across TV screens and newspapers in Europe, the Arab world and the USA. Israel claimed that much of the reporting was one-sided and created a distorted image. The Israeli government tried to control the activities of journalists but with little success. Some journalists were injured and even killed while covering the Intifada, which damaged Israel's reputation further. Much to the frustration of the Israelis, the PLO began to emerge from the news coverage as victims of Israeli oppression. Arafat saw the opportunity which this created to try to establish a Palestinian state in the occupied territories.

He needed American support, because the USA was the only state which Israel really listened to. The USA was sympathetic, but they wanted concessions from Arafat. The most important concession of all was to accept that Israel had the right to exist. In December 1988 Arafat made this important concession. It was not a settlement, but it was an important first step.

1 Draw up your own 50-word definition of 'Intifada'.
2 Explain how scenes like Source 45 would have had a powerful impact on public opinion towards Israel.

SOURCE **45**

A scene from the Intifada in Nablus in the West Bank, January 1988.

Talk to the terrorists

The next few years saw more important developments which pushed Israel and the PLO towards a settlement.

- A new militant Islamic organisation called Hamas was founded in 1988. Hamas was much more hardline than the PLO in terms of Islamic practices and also in terms of its attitude to Israel. In many ways Hamas seemed to be more in tune with the lives of ordinary Palestinians than Arafat and the PLO (see Source 46). The PLO and the Israelis were both concerned about the rise of Hamas.

- In 1990 Saddam Hussein, the leader of Iraq, invaded Kuwait and his army hovered menacingly on the border of Saudi Arabia (see Chapter 9). Saddam was a bitter opponent of Israel and so Yasser Arafat and the PLO expressed their support for him. However, Saddam was defeated by a US-led coalition in 1991. After the war Kuwait and Saudi Arabia withdrew their political and financial support for the PLO.

- By the early 1990s the US President George Bush Senior was keen to establish a peace process in the Middle East. In June 1992 elections in Israel brought a new Prime Minister, Yitzhak Rabin. He was prepared to do a deal with the PLO. He hated Arafat, but he felt that Hamas was a bigger threat than the PLO and believed that a deal would weaken Hamas.

- The sides met in secret talks in Oslo, Norway, in August and September 1993. On 13 September, Arafat and Rabin announced their agreement in Washington.

- A Palestinian Authority was set up to controls aspects of daily life in Gaza and Jericho in the West Bank.

- An armed Palestinian security force was established.

- Israel promised to withdraw troops from the region but in practice they remained to protect Jewish settlers.

- The issue of Jewish settlements was put off.

- Further negotiations in Oslo (sometimes called Oslo II) extended Palestinian authority to most of the rest of the West Bank.

Most Palestinians accepted the deal which Arafat had done but Hamas and some sections of the PLO felt it was a betrayal. Jerusalem was not included in the Oslo Accords, and neither was the issue of Israeli settlements in Gaza and the West Bank. Israeli armed forces were still present in the Palestinian territories and the Palestinians in camps in Jordan and Lebanon gained nothing. Arafat proved unable to control all of the Palestinian factions and attacks were still launched against Israel. In 2001 the Israelis effectively laid siege to his headquarters, demanding action against Palestinian militants. Arafat died in November 2004 at the age of 75. His death did not end the conflict and as this book goes to print in 2009 the Palestinian territories are still hotbeds of discontent.

SOURCE 46

There was always strain between the PLO's foreign-based representatives, with their nice apartments, suits and ties, and their hotel suites in Europe, and the Palestinians in the occupied territories. To them the PLO counselled 'fortitude' or 'steadfastness' ... Arafat may have enjoyed immense personal prestige among the Palestinians as the father of their nation, but his madcap diplomatic gambits had become near irrelevant to the grim experiences of young Palestinians in the occupied territories.

An extract from *Blood and Rage: A Cultural History of Terrorism* by Professor Michael Burleigh, published in 2008.

Activity

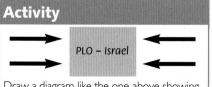

Draw a diagram like the one above showing the factors which pushed the PLO and the Israelis together to reach a deal. Use a larger arrow to represent a more important factor.

Focus Task

Get tough or talk?

Imagine you are advising a government which is facing a terrorist threat. Your task is to label up this diagram and then give a short presentation with the following title:
Lessons from the Israel–PLO conflict: The strengths and weaknesses of Get Tough and Talk to Terrorists policies.
EXTENSION TASK: Prepare a short response to be read to the class on the following question: 'Terrorism always puts governments in a no win situation.' Do you agree?

Case Study 3: The US response to al-Qaeda – The war on terror

In this case study there is no section on talking to terrorists, unless something has been happening behind the scenes which we as historians do not know about. After the USA was attacked on 11 September 2001 (9/11) the US response was swift and devastating. On 20 September the US President George W. Bush issued a demand to the Taliban leader Mullah Omar to turn Osama bin Laden over to the US authorities. The Taliban refused. The US quickly built a coalition of allies, with British Prime Minister Tony Blair playing a key role in this process. US-led forces then joined with Afghan opponents of the Taliban in a massive assault on the country in October 2001.

It began with a huge bombardment using cruise missiles and overwhelming airpower. The Taliban and their al-Qaeda allies had no weapons to match this firepower. Their bases and training camps were soon destroyed. The land campaign began in November 2001. The Taliban and al-Qaeda were no match for the British, American and Northern Alliance opponents. By the middle of November the Afghan capital Kabul, had fallen. The Taliban's home stronghold of Kandahar fell in December, and Mullah Omar fled to Pakistan. Other Taliban and al-Qaeda forces fell back to their mountain strongholds, including the Tora Bora complex. In hard fighting this was taken on 17 December but there was no sign of Osama bin Laden who had probably escaped through the mountains into Pakistan.

SOURCE **47**

The effects of US airpower in Afghanistan: a Taliban base is bombed by US B52 bombers.

SOURCE **48**

Al-Qaeda prisoners on display in Afghanistan, December 2001.

How successful was the war on terror?

On the one hand …

- Al-Qaeda and the Taliban were utterly defeated and a new government was installed in Kabul. The camps which had trained thousands of militants were lost. Most of al-Qaeda's heavy weapons were destroyed or captured. Al-Qaeda also lost all of its archives of information as well as most of its communications and publishing equipment.

- The events of 9/11 also created a new climate in the world. Countries with no great love for the USA became more sympathetic. The horror inspired by 9/11 turned many governments in Asia and the Middle East towards the USA instead of against it. This was partly the result of effective diplomacy by the USA, usually offering aid or economic help but at the same time forcing governments to choose whether they were friends or enemies of the USA. The USA was able to set up bases in places such as Yemen, Somalia and Uzbekistan. These were usually Special Forces and intelligence bases – the kind of warfare which would do most damage to a movement like al-Qaeda. Even Pakistan, traditional ally of the Taliban, supported the US campaign.

- The war also allowed other states such as Russia and Israel to get the support of public opinion to clamp down hard on militants in their areas. Many claims were made about links between al-Qaeda and militants in Chechnya or Palestine, but the evidence for these links is weak.

- Since 2001 security at airports and other facilities has become much tighter. This has made the work of the terrorists much more difficult.

- The USA exported equipment, experts and training to states all over the world which might harbour Islamic militants, again making their work much more difficult. The USA also turned its formidable intelligence network away from the days of the Cold War to now concentrate on terrorism. This meant listening posts, bugging mobile phone communications, spy satellites and of course offering huge cash rewards for the capture of Osama bin Laden or any other terrorist.

- The USA was willing to ignore international criticism about abusing human rights by holding suspected terrorists without trial for years and also flying them to countries where they would be tortured for information.

- Since 2001 there have been no further attacks on the same scale or with the same sophistication as 9/11, although there have been more attacks (see pages 180–81).

SOURCE 49

Graffiti on a wall in a village in Afghanistan 2002. It was found by an American Special Forces team. The people in the Afghan village claimed it showed a native Afghan fighter or mujahidin firing an anti aircraft missile to bring down a Soviet helicopter in the 1980s. The Americans did not believe the villagers. They believed that the graffiti was much more recent. They thought the fighter in the drawing was from the Taliban and that it was an American helicopter being shot down.

SOURCE 50

A young boy chanting anti-US slogans in a rally in Sukkur, Pakistan early in 2003.

1 Study Source 49 and its accompanying information. Why is this useful evidence on why the Americans found it hard to completely defeat the militants?
2 Who is the figure on the banner in Source 50? Is this significant?
3 The President of the USA's press office has called you in and asked you to explain why your newspaper has published the anti-American image in Source 49. What explanation would you give?

Activity

A key feature of an important leader is the ability to make a movement change direction when many of its members are unsure. Each of the case studies on pages 174–79 show examples. Choose one group and explain how and why the leader did this. Turn it into a bullet point to add to one of the Profiles from the Focus Task on page 173.

On the other hand …

- Afghanistan proved very difficult to control. Taliban and al-Qaeda forces continued to mount hit and run attacks on western forces in an insurgency. Since 2001 it has proved very difficult to win the hearts and minds of the Afghan people. They are often caught in the crossfire between Allied forces and the militants and there have been many civilian casualties as well as thousands of refugees from the fighting. Innocent Afghans are often rounded up and interrogated as suspected militants. This has made them reluctant to co-operate with the security forces or provide the intelligence which is so vital in fighting an enemy like al-Qaeda. Heroin production, which actually fell under the Taliban, rose again and Afghanistan now supplies 90 per cent of the world's heroin supply. As this book is being printed in 2009 British, American and other allied forces are still fighting Taliban and al-Qaeda insurgents in remote parts of the country.
- Although many governments in Asia and the Middle East allied with the USA, there was much sympathy for Islamic militancy there. The government of Pakistan, for example, struggle to control elements within its intelligence services and armed forces that are sympathetic towards the Taliban.
- Some American tactics, such as torture and detention, undermined sympathy for the USA and increased support for militancy. It has also caused tension between the media and the governments in Britain and the USA, who feel that the media have been too quick to criticise US forces and too quick to ignore the actions of the terrorists. Reactions have been even more extreme on websites which support the war on terror.
- Osama bin Laden and most of the leading figures in al-Qaeda escaped, probably to Pakistan.

SOURCE 51

In early 2004, when the first revelations about prisoners being tortured by American soldiers at the Abu Ghraib facility in Iraq appeared, the media covered the story on almost a daily basis for months.

In a recent raid on an al-Qaeda safe house in Iraq, US military officials recovered an assortment of crude drawings depicting torture methods like 'blowtorch to the skin' and 'eye removal'.

Along with the images, soldiers seized various torture implements … With this in mind, given the media's fascination with what American soldiers were doing at Abu Ghraib, is it safe to assume that the same level of attention will be given to what our enemy is doing? Or, would that be too much like journalism?

Extract from the US website Newsbusters, a website specifically set up to attack what it saw as a liberal bias in the media. This extract was published in May 2007.

Focus Task

Get tough or talk?

Imagine you are advising a government which is facing a terrorist threat. Your task is to label up this diagram and then give a short presentation with the following title:
Lessons from the al-Qaeda conflict: The strengths and weaknesses of Get Tough and Talk to Terrorists policies.
EXTENSION TASK: Prepare a short response to be read to the class on the following question: 'Terrorism always puts governments in a no win situation.' Do you agree?

The end of Al-Qaeda?

So was al-Qaeda finished? As you have seen many times in your history studies, the answer is both yes and no. In November 2001 Osama bin Laden and the leading figures in al-Qaeda scattered. Bin Laden gave money to any activists who had feasible plans for attacks on the enemies of Islam. We could try and sum up the situation by saying that after 2001 the organisation of al-Qaeda did not exist but its ideas did. In addition, there were thousands of Islamic militants in many parts of the world who had been radicalised and trained in camps in Afghanistan and wanted to play their part in a global jihad. The majority worked in their own countries and they had little or no direct contact with other similar groups. They spread their ideas and expertise so that local groups developed who could not be traced to the original al-Qaeda networks. This made them very difficult to detect. A further factor was the US-led invasion of Iraq in 2003 which generated a new wave of Islamic militant activity (see pages 188–89). Sources 53–56 show examples of further attacks, although it is just a small sample of the many attacks which took place across the world.

SOURCE 52

So what is al-Qaeda? Even well-informed Westerners believe al-Qaeda to be a terrorist organisation founded more than a decade ago by a hugely wealthy Saudi Arabian religious fanatic that has grown into a fantastically powerful network comprising thousands of trained and motivated men, watching and waiting in every city, in every country, on every continent, ready to carry out the orders of their leader, Osama bin Laden, and kill and maim for their cause.

The good news is that this al-Qaeda does not exist. The bad news is that the threat now facing the world is far more dangerous than any single terrorist leader with an army, however large, of loyal cadres. Instead, the threat that faces us is new and different, complex and diverse, dynamic and profoundly difficult to characterise.

… By the middle of 2003 the dominance of the new style of Islamic militancy involving autonomous groups conducting operations independent of any central authority was becoming increasingly clear. Very few of the strikes since 2001 involved the core al-Qaeda figures in any meaningful way. As time passed, not only did the involvement of bin Laden and his associates drop away entirely but so too did the role of the graduates of the Afghan training camps.

Extract from *Al Qaeda* by Jason Burke, published in 2006. The author is a journalist specialising in the Middle East and al-Qaeda.

SOURCE 53

Bali, Indonesia 12 October 2002: Indonesian Islamic militants targeted Western tourists at a night club. There were 202 deaths in this attack.

SOURCE **54**

Istanbul, Turkey 15 November 2003: British Consulate and a British owned bank destroyed along with two synagogues. There were 57 dead and 700 wounded. This is the funeral of one of the victims.

SOURCE **55**

Madrid, Spain 11 March 2004: Ten separate bombs were detonated on the Madrid rail network killing 191 and wounding many. This image is a still taken from Spanish TV news.

SOURCE **56**

London, 7 July 2005: Bombs in tube trains and on a bus (this picture shows the remains of the bus) killed 52 people and injured almost 800. There was no known connection between the Madrid and London attacks but the Madrid attack may have inspired the London one.

Focus Task

How effective was the US response to al-Qaeda?

Your task now is to write a report or create a presentation on whether or not the USA's 'Get Tough' response to al-Qaeda was successful. You need to:

◆ List examples of successes as briefly as possible but identify what you think are the two most significant successes.
◆ List examples of ongoing concerns as briefly as possible and identify what you think are the two most significant areas of concern.
◆ End your report with a conclusion which states whether you think the war on terror was, on balance, successful.

181

Focus Task A

You have now studied a wide range of issues relating to terrorism through three important case studies. In this final section you are going to bring all your work together in a comparison of the three groups.

How effective have terrorist groups been in the period 1969–2005?

It's time to bring these three different studies together. Work in small groups and either take a theme or take a group.

1 Research each group/theme and select examples for each of the boxes in the table below. Some of this you will be able to complete from the work you have done for previous comparative Focus Tasks, e.g. page 156 or pages 171–3.
2 You should also rate each group on a scale of 1–10, with 10 being successful.
3 Now bring your researches together and agree a mark for each section as a group AND select just two examples to support your case.

Themes	IRA	PLO	Al-Qaeda
Aims			
Methods used			
Strengths as a movement			
Ability to withstand actions of opponents			
Qualities and abilities of their leaders			
Overall assessment of how far aims achieved			
Key reasons for success or failure			

Focus Task B

Is terrorism an effective force in the world today?

We also want you to think about the whole issue of whether you think terrorism is an important and effective force in the world today. Look at Source 57 It shows very clearly how much effort governments around the world today are putting into combating terrorism. It also shows how fighting terrorism can also run the danger of actually strengthening terrorism if governments use methods and tactics which neutral observers see as illegal or unfair. It seems that the long history of terrorism is likely to continue – or perhaps you disagree?

Based on your studies of the IRA, PLO and al-Qaeda and your knowledge of the world today, decide whether you think the measures described in Source 57 were successful. Work in pairs or small groups.

1 Study Source 57 carefully and decide which government actions:
   ◆ are new approaches
   ◆ you have seen before
   ◆ you think will succeed
   ◆ you think will fail.
   Report back to the rest of the class, making sure you can support your decisions.
2 Now go back to your groups and discuss the following questions:
   ◆ Do you think terrorist activity will increase or decrease in the future?
   ◆ If you think it will increase, is that because terrorism is ineffective or because there are more situations which contain the preconditions for terrorism (pages 162–65)?
   ◆ If you think it will decrease what factors will cause this?
   ◆ In your view, what parts of the world do you think will give rise to terrorist threats in the future?
   ◆ Why is this a difficult question to answer?

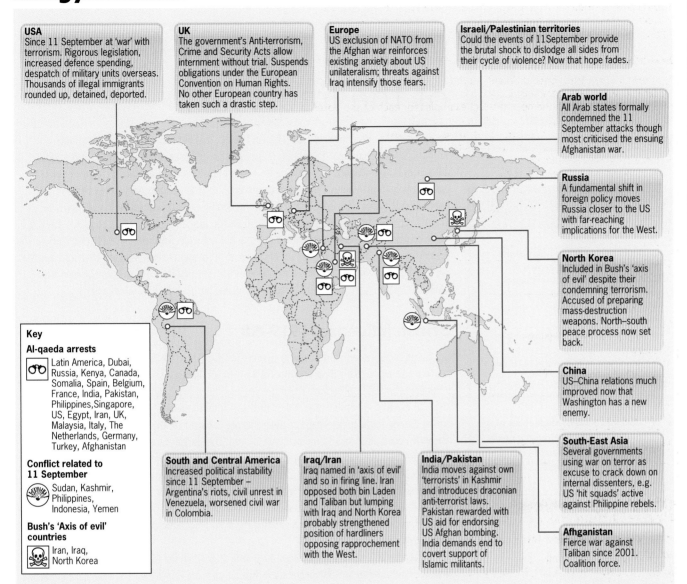

USA
Since 11 September at 'war' with terrorism. Rigorous legislation, increased defence spending, despatch of military units overseas. Thousands of illegal immigrants rounded up, detained, deported.

UK
The government's Anti-terrorism, Crime and Security Acts allow internment without trial. Suspends obligations under the European Convention on Human Rights. No other European country has taken such a drastic step.

Europe
US exclusion of NATO from the Afghan war reinforces existing anxiety about US unilateralism; threats against Iraq intensify those fears.

Israeli/Palestinian territories
Could the events of 11 September provide the brutal shock to dislodge all sides from their cycle of violence? Now that hope fades.

Arab world
All Arab states formally condemned the 11 September attacks though most criticised the ensuing Afghanistan war.

Russia
A fundamental shift in foreign policy moves Russia closer to the US with far-reaching implications for the West.

North Korea
Included in Bush's 'axis of evil' despite their condemning terrorism. Accused of preparing mass-destruction weapons. North–south peace process now set back.

China
US–China relations much improved now that Washington has a new enemy.

South-East Asia
Several governments using war on terror as excuse to crack down on internal dissenters, e.g. US 'hit squads' active against Philippine rebels.

Afhganistan
Fierce war against Taliban since 2001. Coalition force.

India/Pakistan
India moves against own 'terrorists' in Kashmir and introduces draconian anti-terrorist laws. Pakistan rewarded with US aid for endorsing US Afghan bombing. India demands end to covert support of Islamic militants.

Iraq/Iran
Iraq named in 'axis of evil' and so in firing line. Iran opposed both bin Laden and Taliban but lumping with Iraq and North Korea probably strengthened position of hardliners opposing rapprochement with the West.

South and Central America
Increased political instability since 11 September – Argentina's riots, civil unrest in Venezuela, worsened civil war in Colombia.

Key

Al-qaeda arrests
Latin America, Dubai, Russia, Kenya, Canada, Somalia, Spain, Belgium, France, India, Pakistan, Philippines, Singapore, US, Egypt, Iran, UK, Malaysia, Italy, The Netherlands, Germany, Turkey, Afghanistan

Conflict related to 11 September
Sudan, Kashmir, Philippines, Indonesia, Yemen

Bush's 'Axis of evil' countries
Iran, Iraq, North Korea

Examples of how governments reacted to al-Qaeda's attack on the USA in September 2001. The map was published in 2007 in a textbook called *A Terrorism Reader* by David Whittaker, Senior Lecturer in International Relations at the University of Teesside. Whittaker is a specialist in terrorism.

What is the significance of the Iraq War?

People often say history repeats itself. This isn't strictly true but there are often very striking similarities between present day events and past events. Understanding those similarities and the differences is an important part of doing history. Most historians believe that there are issues in the past that help us in dealing with the present particularly when dealing with thorny issues of international affairs. They believe that politicians don't pay enough attention to past events, or alternatively they draw the wrong conclusions based on limited understanding. So as you study this very recent period of history, including a war that has not really finished yet, one of your roles will be to understand the historical context for the invasion of Iraq and to examine how the politicians who launched the invasion in 2003 and the opponents who opposed it used history and learned from it. But first, a quick history of twentieth-century Iraq, and particularly Britain's role in it.

British influence, 1919–58

British forces have a long history of involvement in Iraq. Before the First World War the area we now know as Iraq was actually three provinces of the Turkish Empire. At the end of the war the Turkish Empire was broken up. The three provinces were combined as a League of Nations mandate (see page 20) run by the British. Some of the Kurds and Arabs in the region had allied with the British during the war in the hope of gaining independence at the end of the war. These hopes were dashed when the British effectively set up direct rule of Iraq. They largely ignored the fact that there were huge differences between the Kurdish, Sunni and Shi'ah elements of the country.

Discontent with this British policy led to a major revolt in 1920, mainly involving Shi'ah Arabs. The British crushed the revolt with the help of some of the Arab sheikhs within Iraq who did not support it. Around 500 British troops were killed and around 6,000 Iraqis. British rule was enforced by the military and especially by the power of the Royal Air Force which could attack the strongholds of remote tribes if they caused trouble.

The League of Nations Mandate continued until 1932 when the country became independent. However, British influence did not end there. By that stage the British owned a huge stake in the oil reserves which had been discovered. The British left a divided country behind them.

Focus

Iraq is a country at the heart of the Middle East and at the centre of world affairs today. In this chapter you are going to look at how and why this has happened. You will investigate:

- why the US-led coalition invaded Iraq in 2003
- why there was opposition to the war
- why the invasion was completed so quickly
- what were the consequences of the invasion in Iraq and internationally
- whether the invasion can be regarded as a success.

1. In what ways are Sources 1A and 1B similar?
2. How do they differ?

SOURCE **1**

A

B

British forces in Iraq in 1920 and 2008.

The rise of Saddam Hussein, 1958–79

In 1958 the monarchy was overthrown and Iraq became a republic. From 1968 this republic was dominated by the Ba'ath political party. In 1979 the leader of this party and the ruler of Iraq was Saddam Hussein.

Saddam managed to rise to the presidency of Iraq, despite being the son of a landless peasant. He did this by exploiting family connections, by working hard and by being charming when it suited him. He was careful not to undermine Iraq's ancient network of tribal, religious, ethnic and family loyalties. He built up a network of supporters in the administration, the Ba'ath Party and in the intelligence and security services. He could also be ruthless. He was happy to exploit rivalries between different groups in Iraq to divide his enemies. When he came to power in 1979 he carried out a brutal purge of anyone who might be a threat to him. Around 500 members of his own party were executed. Many more were arrested or fled the country. As well as being clever and ruthless, he was also ambitious. He wanted to make himself the leading figure in the Arab world. In 1979, he thought he saw an opportunity to do this.

3 At the time, the meeting in Source 2 was kept top secret. Why do you think this was?

Activity

The Foreign Office is the government department which represents Britain abroad. Newly declassified documents show that in 1969 British Foreign Office officials met Saddam Hussein for the first time. Their report to London said 'he is a presentable young man with an engaging smile, with whom, if only one could see more of him, it would be possible to do business'. Write an update to this report set in 1988. What would be their assessment after the Iran–Iraq war? Try to keep the report to 100–150 words.

The Iran–Iraq war, 1980–88

As you may have read in Chapter 8, 1979 saw a revolution in neighbouring Iran. The modernising, pro-western Shah of Iran was overthrown in an Islamic revolution by the militant Muslim cleric Ayatollah Khomeini and his followers. This revolution caused great concern throughout the region. Saddam was also concerned that the Shi'ah revolution in Iran would spread to the Arab Shi'ah majority in Iraq. The Gulf States of Saudi Arabia and Kuwait did not want Iran's radicalism spreading to their countries. This concern was shared by the USSR. In addition, the USA was also intensely hostile to Iran because the revolution had overthrown its ally, the Shah.

Saddam saw an opportunity to exploit Iran's weak position. He planned a short, limited war which would force Iran to make concessions, but more importantly would warn Iran that Iraq would not be intimidated or undermined. In September 1980 he launched air attacks and an invasion of Iran, expecting Iran to back down immediately. It was a disastrous miscalculation which bogged his country down in a bloody and brutal war for eight years. Saddam received substantial help from the USA (even though it was supposed to be neutral in the war) and neighbouring Gulf States. The USA and European countries (including Britain and France) supplied Saddam with arms, including the materials and training to make chemical weapons. Some estimates suggest that around 100,000 Iranians were killed by Iraqi chemical weapons during the war. Despite this, the war ended with no obvious advantages to Iraq; around 250,000 Iraqis had been killed and the country was left with a debt of around $80 billion. Some of those dead were Shi'ah and Kurdish opponents of Saddam's regime who had tried to exploit the war to rebel against him. Saddam used poison gas against Kurds in March 1988 (see Source 3).

SOURCE **2**

Donald Rumsfeld, Special Envoy of US President Reagan, shakes hands with Saddam Hussein in December 1983. The US provided money, arms and intelligence resources to help the Iraqi war effort.

SOURCE **3**

A scene from the Kurdish village of Halabja in Kurdish northern Iraq, March 1988. The Iraqi air force attacked the village with a range of chemical weapons including mustard gas and cyanide, killing around 5,000 inhabitants.

The first Gulf War

The Iran–Iraq war left Saddam with $80 billion debt to pay off. The only way he could do this was to increase oil production in Iraq. The problem with this was that Iraq was a member of OPEC (Oil Producing and Exporting Countries). OPEC controlled oil production in order to keep prices high – too much production meant the price dropped. Some leading states in OPEC, particularly Kuwait and Saudi Arabia, refused Saddam's request. Worse still, they demanded repayment of funds given to Iraq during the war. Saddam was never afraid to gamble. In August 1990 he invaded Kuwait. The diagram below shows his thinking.

Once again, Saddam miscalculated spectacularly. The states of the Arab world instantly condemned him. The United Nations Organisation immediately passed resolutions calling on Iraq to withdraw. Most importantly, the US President George Bush Senior would not allow Saddam to threaten one of its major sources of oil. Very soon (January 1991) a US-led coalition of forces removed his troops from Kuwait in a humiliating and devastating defeat. It took a little over a month and Iraqi casualties were horrendous. Bush decided not to invade Iraq and remove Saddam from power. This was because he had no plan for what to do with Iraq if he did invade. He also thought that Saddam's Shi'ah and Kurdish enemies might topple him anyway. They did rise against Saddam but they were brutally suppressed (see Source 4).

SOURCE **4**

Mass graves found in 2003 after the fall of Saddam Hussein. The victims were Shi'ah Muslims from Southern Iraq killed as punishment for the Shi'ah rebellion against Saddam in 1991. Many of the dead were women and children.

Sanctions and inspections, 1991–2003

Although he was left in power, Saddam faced serious restrictions passed by the United Nations.

- **UN Resolution 678** demanded the destruction of all his Weapons of Mass Destruction (WMDs). Saddam had to allow a UN inspection team (UNSCOM) in to investigate all suspected weapon sites and destroy stocks of chemical weapons. He also had to pay reparations to Kuwait. Tough economic sanctions (mainly restrictions on oil sales) were imposed until all the demands were fully met.
- **UN Resolution 688** called on Saddam to stop oppressing his own people. The Kurdish region of Iraq became a safe haven and no-fly zones were declared over northern and southern Iraq to prevent Saddam using his air force against his own people.

Despite these UN resolutions, Iraq continued to present the USA and allies with challenges throughout the 1990s.

- They knew Iraq needed a strong leader to hold together its different peoples. The Americans did not have a friendly Iraqi leader who would be acceptable to all the different factions in Iraq. If Iraq was allowed to break up then that would strengthen Iran, the USA's other big enemy.
- At the same time, the USA and its allies had to ensure that Iraq was no longer a threat to its neighbours (and America's oil supplies). First and foremost, this meant finding and destroying Saddam's Weapons of Mass Destruction (WMDs).

SOURCE 5

A

B

The official Hussein family photograph as seen in Iraq in 1989 and 1996.

1 What differences are there between Sources 5A and 5B?
2 Explain the reason for these differences.

Saddam continued to be awkward and difficult in as many ways as possible. He obstructed and blocked the UN weapons inspectors. In 1997 and 1998 US and British aircraft carried out attacks on Iraqi military installations as punishment, but Saddam was defiant. He made the most of the propoganda value of these attacks. He criticised the USA in the United Nations and in the Iraqi media.

In the later 1990s Saddam tried to build better relations with former enemies. He tried to improve relations with Saudi Arabia and Kuwait. He improved relations with France, Russia and China. Iraq owed France and Russia $17 billion between them, so they were keen to see sanctions ended so that Iraq could sell its oil and they would get their money. China also wanted Iraqi oil. All three of these countries were members of the UN Security Council so they had the power to veto measures against Iraq in the UN. This would make action by the UN difficult as not all members would agree.

Saddam simply did not care about the majority of his people. The economic sanctions imposed on Iraq had little or no impact on Saddam, his family and his loyal followers but they had a devastating effect on ordinary Iraqis. Malnutrition and disease increased dramatically. Infant mortality in Iraq reached its highest level for forty years. Frustrated that innocent Iraqis were bearing the brunt of the sanctions, the UN introduced a programme in 1996 called 'Oil for Food'. Saddam was allowed to sell more oil but the UN would control the money raised and spend it on food and other essentials.

Saddam's hold on power seemed to get stronger rather than weaker. He was extremely clever at exploiting the rivalries between different groups in Iraq, and he used a combination of bribery to ally with some and threats to intimidate other groups. He also made very effective use of the media. He was careful to make sure that close allies and preferably family members held all the key posts in the government. Even here he was prepared to act ruthlessly. In 1996 he had two of his sons-in-law murdered (see Source 5). He also carried out a ruthless campaign against the mainly Shi'ah opponents of his regime in the marshes of southern Iraq. The area was virtually cut off from the rest of Iraq and regularly shelled by the army. Individuals were brutally treated. In 1999, for example, he had Ayatollah Mohammad Sadiq al-Sadr and two of his sons murdered. On a larger scale Saddam began a large project to drain the marshes on which these people depended for survival.

A final frustration was that the many opposition groups in Iraq were small and fragmented. Both the Kurds and the Shi'ah Muslims opposed to Saddam spent as much time in dispute with each other as they did in opposing Saddam. The result was that by the start of the twenty-first century Saddam was as strongly entrenched as ever in Iraq.

Activity

How did Saddam survive for so long as ruler of Iraq?

He was humiliated in 1991, was hated by US Presidents Bush (to 1993) and Clinton (1993–2001) and was hated by many of his people. How did Saddam survive? Use this table to search through the information and sources on these two pages to organise your thoughts on this question.

Keep your table. You will need it for a later Focus Task.

Reasons for the USA to invade Iraq and topple Saddam	Reasons why this did not happen 1991–2000

Reasons for Saddam to be overthrown from within Iraq	Reasons why this did not happen 1991–2000

The invasion of Iraq 2003

In 2001 Saddam was still in power. By early 2003 Iraq had been invaded and Saddam's regime completely overthrown. A multinational force, primarily American and British, invaded Iraq in March 2003 and deposed Saddam within weeks. What had changed by 2003?

1. The USA had a new President

George W Bush, son of George Bush Senior, became President in 2001. Bush Junior was a very different character from President Clinton. He was impatient with the fact that Saddam was still in power. He was also prepared to act unilaterally (i.e. without support or discussion with other countries or organisations) to do what he thought was best for the USA. In his mind what was good for the USA was also morally the right thing. In January 2002 he made a speech in which he described Iraq, along with Iran and North Korea, as countries which made up an 'axis of evil'. Not surprisingly, this attitude was extremely controversial!

2. The anti-Saddam lobby within the USA

There were divided opinions within the different government departments in the USA about what to do over Iraq. By the end of 2002 the neoconservatives (usually called neocons) who favoured tough action had won the power struggle. Men like Donald Rumsfeld, the US Defence Secretary, and Dick Cheney, the Vice President, believed that the best answer to the problem of Iraq was 'regime change'. This meant invading Iraq, taking control of the country for a short time, making it a western style democracy and then leaving behind a friendly, democratic government. Opponents of this plan found themselves marginalised. The neocons also had powerful allies in the media, particularly Rupert Murdoch and his Fox Corporation. Fox News was ferociously anti-Saddam. This helped bring public opinion in the USA in favour of actions against Iraq. Finally, several of the neocons had links with hardline political parties in Israel. Saddam was a bitter enemy of Israel and many politicians in Israel were extremely concerned by his actions.

3. The UK and other allies

Bush had one strong and reliable ally: Tony Blair, the British Prime Minister. Blair was convinced that the best policy for Britain was to be a close ally and supporter of the USA. He developed a close relationship with President Clinton and continued this friendship with George Bush Junior. Blair provided political and diplomatic support as well as military support when the invasion of Iraq began. Other allies who supported the invasion included Australia, Italy, Spain, Poland and Denmark.

4. All efforts to remove Saddam had failed

In 1998 the US Congress passed the Iraq Liberation Act which provided $100 million to Saddam's opponents. By 2002 this had achieved nothing. If anything, Saddam seemed more strongly entrenched. Iraq's economy was actually starting to recover despite sanctions and reparations. Everyday life was even improving (slightly) for ordinary Iraqis. This meant the chances of him being overthrown by his internal opponents were getting smaller all the time.

5. 9/11 and Afghanistan

Terrorist attacks by al-Qaeda on the USA on 11 September 2001, an event known as 9/11 in the USA, convinced American politicians and people that the USA had to take action in the Middle East. There was a strong suspicion that Saddam was somehow involved in 9/11 although this turned out to be completely untrue. After 9/11 US forces and their allies attacked al-Qaeda and its allies in Afghanistan. By early 2002 they had defeated their enemies and placed a friendly government in power. It was assumed that the same quick victory would be possible in Iraq.

6. Saddam's actions

Saddam continued to defy the UN. He began flying aircraft in airspace which was supposed to be out-of-bounds. More seriously, in 1998 he had the UN weapons inspectors removed so nobody knew whether he still had WMDs from the 1980s or even if he had developed new ones since 1998. Defectors fleeing from Saddam's secret police seemed to suggest that there was an on-going programme developing weapons. In 1999 and again in 2001 Saddam refused efforts to get the inspectors back into Iraq. It was another spectacular miscalculation. Saddam defied the UN because in reality he did not have any WMDs. He was much weaker than he had been in 1991. He was putting up a front because he did not want to appear to be pushed around by the USA and he did not want his hostile neighbours, especially Iran, to know that he did not have any WMDs. This was a very effective bluff, but it turned out to be his undoing. The US Congress authorised Bush to use military action as he saw fit. The USA and the UK pushed the UN Security Council for a resolution on the issue and it passed Resolution 1441 on 8 November 2002 (see Source 8).

SOURCE **6**

US troops pull down a statue of Saddam Hussein in Baghdad.

SOURCE **7**

1. Iraq has been and remains in material breach of prior Security Council resolutions.

2. The resolution gives Iraq a final opportunity to comply with its disarmament obligations and establish an enhanced inspections regime. Iraq is obliged to deliver within 30 days (December 8, 2002) a currently accurate, full, and complete declaration of all aspects of its programs to develop weapons of mass destruction and delivery systems.

3. False statements or omissions in declarations required by the resolution and failure by Iraq to comply with and co-operate fully in the implementation of the resolution shall constitute a further material breach of Iraq's obligations.

4. The Council demands that Iraq co-operate immediately, unconditionally and actively with UNMOVIC and IAEA.

5. The Security Council recalled that it has repeatedly warned Iraq that it will face serious consequences as a result of its continued violations of obligations under Security Council resolutions.

Extracts from UN Security Council Resolution 1441, 8 November 2002. UNMOVIC was the new inspection team (United Nations Monitoring, Verifying and Inspection Commission). IAEA is the International Atomic Energy Authority, the UN agency which provides most of the experts for the inspection programme.

1 Study Source 7 carefully. Which section criticises Iraq?

2 What is Iraq required to do?

3 What is Iraq warned not to do?

4 What do you think is meant by 'serious consequences' in section 5?

Focus Task

Why did the multi-national forces invade Iraq in March 2003?

1 Look back at your table from the Focus Task on page 187.
   a) Highlight or circle all the factors that had *not* changed by 2003.
   b) Add an extra column headed 'Factors which had changed by 2003' and then complete the column using the information on these two pages.

2 Prepare a short report or presentation on why the USA led the invasion of Iraq in 2003. Your work should include:
   ◆ at least two long-term factors (with examples and explanations)
   ◆ at least two short-term factors (with examples and explanations)
   ◆ at least one factor which you consider to be decisive (i.e. without this factor or factors the war would not have happened). Make sure you explain this particularly carefully.

Why was there so much opposition to the war?

1 According to President Bush in Source 8, what were the aims of the forces invading Iraq in March 2003?
2 What do sources 9A–F reveal about:
 • the type of people who protested against the war
 • the reason(s) why they were protesting
 • the scale of the protests against the war?

SOURCE **8**

Good morning. American and coalition forces have begun a concerted campaign against the regime of Saddam Hussein. In this war, our coalition is broad, more than 40 countries from across the globe. Our cause is just, the security of the nations we serve and the peace of the world. And our mission is clear, to disarm Iraq of weapons of mass destruction, to end Saddam Hussein's support for terrorism, and to free the Iraqi people.

President Bush announces the invasion of Iraq on US radio, March 2003.

Look closely at Source 8. If you accepted President Bush's view of events in 2003 then there could be no realistic reason for opposing the war. But as Sources 9A–F show, many people did not accept the views of Bush and his ally, Tony Blair. Why were they not prepared to accept the word of the President?

SOURCE **9**

A

B

C

D

E

F

Protests against the Iraq War in 2003: **A** in Moscow, **B** in Los Angeles, **C** in Jordan (an Arab country which had good relations with the USA), **D** in Pakistan, **E** in Paris and **F** in London.

We regard your threats to use force in countries like Iraq, Iran, Lebanon, North Korea, Indonesia and Palestine as reflecting the law of the jungle and believe it will undermine human civilisation . . . We reject your foreign policy, which is based on . . . war and undermining the stability of governments and even overthrowing them. We object to your unilateralism and your inability to participate in the international community as an equal partner . . . You are selective in your application of justice. Israel, a country which regularly challenges international law, kills Palestinians, and possesses weapons of mass destruction, does fit your description of a terrorist state. Your aggression in Iraq will bring on you the wrath of people not only in Saudi Arabia but also in the whole world.

A petition to President Bush signed by Saudi writers and moderate clerics from Saudi Arabia, March 2003.

Concerns in the Muslim and Arab world

The USA's attempts to build a case for war against Iraq caused deep concerns in the Arab world and in Muslim countries more widely. Some of the protests are shown in Sources 9C and 9D. The key issue for many of these countries was the apparent use of different standards for Iraq compared to the USA's ally Israel. Iraq was being attacked because it held WMDs, possibly even nuclear weapons. It was well known that Israel was in possession of nuclear weapons and that neither the USA nor the United Nations had done anything about this. Another ally of the USA in the region was Turkey, but Turkey refused to allow US forces to invade Iraq through its border with northern Iraq because it was unhappy about the case being made for war. Another key ally of the USA was Saudi Arabia. Even the Saudis, who hated Saddam Hussein, had doubts about the legality of the war. They would have supported an overthrow of Saddam by Iraqis but most were opposed to an overthrow by the USA. Eventually they did allow US forces to use their territory as a base from which to invade Iraq but there was a good deal of concern from Saudi citizens about the legality of the war and also the possible consequences of such a war (see Source 10).

Was the invasion illegal?

One of the biggest areas of controversy was over the question of whether the decision to invade Iraq was legal under international law. Look back at Source 7 on page 189. What did you decide was meant by 'serious consequences'? Did all of your class agree? It was a similar situation in the United Nations Organisation. Bush and Blair argued that Resolution 1441 gave them the authority to attack Iraq. Many other states did not agree with this interpretation. Russia and China criticised US actions but the strongest critic of the American action was France. The French disputed that Saddam had links with terrorism as Bush claimed. French President Jacques Chirac argued that Britain and the USA would need a second UN resolution to authorise military action against Iraq. Chirac claimed that the British and Americans refused to try and get a second resolution passed because they knew it would not be supported. We know with hindsight that some of the British government's advisers and even some ministers had doubts about whether the war was legal.

SOURCE **11**

JIM LEHRER (Interviewer): As you know, support for the US position seems to be dropping among nations around the world. Also, recent opinion polls among the American people show the same thing; they want unified action with the UN; they're less enthusiastic about the US going it alone. Does that concern you at all?
COLIN POWELL: Certainly it does. We watch the polls of course, but we have to do what we believe is right, and we believe that if we can make our case to the American people, to the world, that support can be generated; it can be turned around. And I also think that people will understand that if we have to take military action, the United States will not be doing it alone. There will be other nations that will be joining us, whether part of a UN-approved action under a second resolution, or, if that's not possible, and we believe military action is appropriate, there will be other nations that will be joining us. It will not just be the United States and the United Kingdom. I'm also confident that there will be a successful operation, and in the aftermath of that operation, the Iraqi people will be better off, as we would work with coalition partners and international organisations to put in place a new government in Iraq that would be responsive to its people and use the treasure that it has for the benefit of its people and not threaten its people or to threaten its neighbours or to threaten the world.

From an interview on US TV with General Colin Powell, 22 January 2003.

3 According to the interviewer in Source 11, how was US action being viewed abroad?
4 How was US government action being viewed at home in the US?
5 What was Powell's attitude towards a UN Second Resolution?
6 What was Powell's attitude towards the people of Iraq?
7 Choose two statements from this source which you think would have been controversial at the time, and explain why they were.

SOURCE **12**

Cartoon from *The Times* newspaper, 15 July 2003.

Where were the WMDs?

In November 2002 UNMOVIC finally moved into Iraq and began searching for WMDs. To the surprise of many people the head of the inspection team, Hans Blix, reported back that there were no major stockpiles of WMDs in Iraq and there was certainly no nuclear programme. The Americans and the British simply did not believe this. They had intelligence reports which said that there were WMDs in Iraq. Prime Minister Blair told Parliament that Saddam had the ability to deploy these weapons in 45 minutes. All of this information turned out to be wrong, but the real controversy was over what the British and American governments knew, and when they knew it. There was a furious clash between the BBC and the government over a news report which claimed that the government had 'sexed up' the intelligence on Iraq to make it seem more of a threat. After the war was over it was very clear that Saddam did not have stockpiles of WMDs. Blair and Bush admitted this, but continued to justify the action they had taken because they argued that Iraq was a better place for the Iraqi people without Saddam Hussein.

Activity

1 Try to summarise Alistair Campbell's views from Source 13 in about 50 words.
2 What is the message of Source 12? Please try to make your answer as polite as possible!
3 Which of these two statements do you think is most accurate?
   • Sources 12 and 13 prove that the government lied about WMDs.
   • Sources 12 and 13 prove that there was a lot of doubt about the government's statements on WMDs.

SOURCE **13**

Downing Street and the BBC were locked in a ferocious row last night over government intelligence assessments of Iraq's pre-war weapons capabilities after Alastair Campbell apologised for his own mistakes on the 'dodgy dossier', but demanded that the corporation do the same over what he described as their lies. Directly attacking the BBC's defence correspondent, Andrew Gilligan, Mr Campbell denied Mr Gilligan's allegation that he had 'sexed up' the government's earlier September dossier on weapons of mass destruction by inserting, against intelligence advice, the claim that Iraq could have weapons of mass destruction ready within 45 minutes. 'I know we are right in relation to that 45-minute point. It is completely and totally untrue that we sexed it up. It is – I don't use this word lightly – it is actually a lie,' Mr Campbell, Tony Blair's communications director, said during a three hour televised grilling by the Commons foreign affairs select committee.

Far from sexing it up he had 'actually sexed it down in places'. And, contrary to Mr Gilligan's claims, the 45 minute point had been in the first draft. 'I simply say in relation to the BBC story it is a lie . . . that is continually repeated, and until we get an apology for it I will keep making sure that parliament and people like yourselves know that it was a lie.' Last night the corporation stood by its reporter and his 'senior and credible' intelligence source. 'We do not feel the BBC has anything to apologise for,' it said in a statement. It added that other journalists had since been similarly briefed.

An extract from the *Guardian* newspaper, 26 June 2003. The dodgy dossier was the folder of intelligence material which turned out to be largely incorrect.

1 What are the main criticisms of the actions of the British and US governments in Source 14 on page 193?
2 How convincing do you find the arguments in Source 14? Explain your answer.
3 What is the message of the cartoon in Source 16 on page 193?
4 With hindsight, would it be fair to say that the cartoon is harsh on Colin Powell?

Opposition in the USA and the UK

The leaders of Britain and the USA were convinced that the war was right and necessary, but even in these countries there was considerable opposition to the war (see Source 9 on page 190). Many of Tony Blair's own Labour Party MPs were extremely concerned about whether the war was legal, or justified, or even whether it would achieve its aims. The Foreign Secretary Robin Cook and the International Development Minister Clare Short resigned over the war. One MP put forward a motion in Parliament that there was no moral case for the war in Iraq and 139 Labour MPs voted against their own government to support this motion.

SOURCE 14

I applaud the heroic efforts that the Prime Minister has made in trying to secure a second resolution. I do not think that anybody could have done better than the Foreign Secretary in working to get support for a second resolution within the Security Council. But the very intensity of those attempts underlines how important it was to succeed. Now that those attempts have failed, we cannot pretend that getting a second resolution was of no importance.

France has been at the receiving end of bucket loads of commentary in recent days. It is not France alone that wants more time for inspections. Germany wants more time for inspections; Russia wants more time for inspections; indeed, at no time have we signed up even the minimum necessary to carry a second resolution. We delude ourselves if we think that the degree of international hostility is all the result of President Chirac. The reality is that Britain is being asked to embark on a war without agreement in any of the international bodies of which we are a leading partner – not NATO, not the European Union and, now, not the Security Council.

Part of British Foreign Secretary Robin Cook's resignation speech, March 2003.

Focus Task

Why was there opposition to the invasion in many countries?

1 Search through the sources and text on pages 190–193 and list all the different reasons you can find why people opposed the war.
2 **a)** Draw a venn diagram with three circles: political reasons, moral reasons, economic reasons.
  b) Decide in which area of the venn diagram each of your reasons belong.
  c) Which area has the most reasons? Discuss whether that means these are the most important reasons for opposition.
3 Work in small groups. Prepare and role-play a short discussion about whether the war is justified between:
  ◆ a rebel Labour MP
  ◆ a moderate Saudi cleric
  ◆ an opponent of President Bush in the US Senate
  ◆ a French delegate at the UN.
  Try to script your discussion so that the different attitudes of each opponent comes through.

It was a similar story in the USA. Many politicians and officials from the intelligence services and the armed forces had severe doubts about the Iraq War. General Colin Powell tried to make the case for the Iraq War but with hindsight we know that he had major doubts. In a private comment to a British minister, he described Rumsfeld and some of the other neocons as 'crazies'. He resigned in 2004 in order to save the Bush government from embarrassment at the time. Other critics pointed to the links between key figures in the Bush government (including Bush himself) and the big oil companies which had contributed to his election campaign. It was claimed that the war had nothing to do with American security, human rights in Iraq or democracy. It was purely and simply about getting control of one of the largest oil producing regions in the Middle East.

SOURCE 15

A former US diplomat who resigned over the Iraq war on Sunday described US President George W Bush as a 'very weak' man led by the hand into battle by Defence Secretary Donald Rumsfeld. Brady Kiesling, who was political counsellor at the US embassy in Athens at the time of his resignation in February, said in an open letter published in a Greek newspaper that Rumsfeld exploited the war to increase his own power.

Kiesling described Bush as 'a politician who badly wants to appear strong but in reality is very weak'.

He said Rumsfeld led Bush by the hand into war, marginalised the secret services who had doubts about the war, and emerged as the top politician in Washington. 'Easy to convince, (Bush) blindly believed in Rumsfeld's assurances that the occupation of Iraq would pay for itself,' Kiesling said.

From 'Bush a "very weak" man', a report from the South African news service 17 August 2003.

SOURCE 16

A cartoon by Dave Brown from the British newspaper the *Independent* published on 24 January 2003. The main figure is General Colin Powell, who later resigned from the Bush government.

How successful was the invasion?

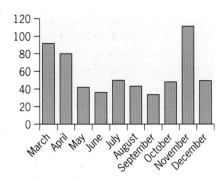

Casualties among coalition forces in Iraq in 2003.

On 17 March 2003 President Bush gave Saddam Hussein two days to leave Iraq. He also told the UNMOVIC teams to leave the country. Two days later he launched 'Operation Iraqi Freedom'. It began with an attempted assassination of Saddam (by bombing) which failed. This was followed by a gigantic air attack using aircraft and missiles. On 21 March 130,000 US troops and around 30,000 other coalition troops (most of them British) invaded Iraq.

Saddam had talked of bitter fighting and huge casualties for the allied forces. In the event, the Iraqi forces were no match for the modern, well equipped coalition forces.

- The coalition had complete air superiority. The Iraqi air force and anti-aircraft capabilities were virtually non-existent. Coalition aircraft and helicopters were able to destroy Iraqi vehicles on the ground with ease.
- The coalition had the latest communications technology including satellites. This allowed them to carry out accurate attacks and also to co-ordinate their advances. Iraqi forces often found themselves surrounded and they simply surrendered or deserted.
- Those who did stand and fight suffered the awesome firepower of a modern army. Estimates suggest that Iraq's armed forces suffered 7,000–12,000 casualties. By comparison the Americans suffered 140 and the British 33. Between 4,000 and 7,000 Iraqi civilians were also killed, mostly by bombing.

By 7 April British forces had taken Basra in the south of Iraq and two days later the Americans took control of Baghdad. Saddam fled into hiding. He was captured in December 2003 and after a long trial he was executed in December 2006. The coalition forces built themselves fortified compounds to protect their troops and equipment. Bewildered Iraqis in Baghdad and other cities simply did not know what to expect next.

From invasion to insurgency

It might seem obvious that the invasion was a stunning success. In terms of defeating Saddam it was, but major problems soon followed. The invasion caused the Iraqi state to collapse. A few days after the Americans captured Baghdad the city descended into anarchy with looting of public buildings on a huge scale. It was partly a form of revenge on the Saddam regime – the hated security forces were gone. It was also an opportunity for impoverished Iraqis to get their hands on anything of value. Government ministries were ransacked, but so were schools, museums, hospitals, universities, libraries, even factories and power stations. Many homes in Baghdad were also looted. At the same time old feuds in Iraq re-emerged. Saddam had exploited the rivalries between different communities in Iraq and with his security forces gone it was not long before they were attacking each other.

An American soldier raises a US flag at a checkpoint in Baghdad on 18 April 2003. The wrecked building nearest to them was a bank.

The coalition troops were completely unprepared and undermanned for this and simply stood by and watched. In the early stages of the invasion there were only 6,000 US troops to control Baghdad, a city of over 5 million people. To most Iraqis it seemed that the US simply did not care that they had plunged Iraq into anarchy. The Americans hoped to depose Saddam and establish a stable, democratic state but this was a poor start and things soon got worse. Thousands of refugees fled across the border into Jordan. Water and electricity supplies began to collapse. Day-to-day life for ordinary Iraqis was soon worse than it had been under Saddam.

1 Look at Source 18. How would you feel about this image if you were an American?
2 Would you feel differently if you were an Iraqi?

SOURCE **19**

SOURCE **19**

On the one hand the US administration seemed determined to set up a fully functioning liberal democracy within a very short space of time, encouraging the development of a market economy and providing a secure environment by reconstructing the Iraqi security establishment, gearing it to police a thriving civil society. Yet the way the US administration set about this ambitious task was at odds with its declared goal. The result was a troubled and increasingly insecure country in which insurgency, lawlessness and sectarian conflict claimed growing numbers of Iraqi lives, in addition to taking a mounting toll of the occupation forces.

An extract from *A History of Iraq* by Professor Charles Tripp of the University of London, published in 2007.

SOURCE **20**

Iraqis waiting for water at a Red Crescent depot in Basra, 11 April 2003.

SOURCE **21**

Local residents in the Karada district of Baghdad take up arms to defend their homes from looters, 11 April 2003. These men risked being shot by coalition forces as they were often mistaken for resistance fighters.

SOURCE **22**

The Iraqi Ministry of Education, 12 April 2003.

In response to this anarchy, Iraqis turned for safety and security to traditional sources of authority such as their family, tribe, local community and sometimes local warlords. Iraq was awash with weapons so it was not difficult for ambitious religious or political leaders to set up a militia and take control of a neighbourhood. A good example of this was the radical Shi'ah cleric Muqtada al Sadr. His father had run a large-scale welfare organisation distributing food and other aid to poor Iraqis. Many poor Iraqis turned to Sadr in the wake of the invasion. He continued to distribute food but he also turned his welfare organisation into a political and military one. By the autumn of 2003 Sadr and his Mahdi Army militia effectively ruled the poor Shi'ah housing estates of east Baghdad and it became known as Sadr City. In time he extended his power and influence over most of Shi'ah southern Iraq.

Many of the men in the various militias had formerly been part of the army or security forces. Before long, these militias were joined by radical Islamic militants who had been trained in al-Qaeda camps in Afghanistan (see page 172). Soon these organisations began to turn their fire on the Americans who they saw as an occupying force who wanted Iraq's oil and did not care at all about its people to whom they could not even supply water and electricity. By July 2003 the US military was forced to admit that they were facing a serious insurgency in Iraq.

Focus Task

How was the invasion completed so quickly?

Invasion news: April 2003
You work for an English newspaper. Your headline is 'Saddam is beaten'. Your editor has asked you for one hundred words and a picture to explain 'How the coalition forces have managed to complete the invasion so quickly'.

Invasion news: May 2003
One month later your editor asks for a new story under the headline: 'Winning the war but losing the peace'. Once again you need to provide one hundred words and an image that explain why the invasion was not as successful as it first appeared.

Who were the insurgents?

In the months which followed the invasion, Iraq descended into chaos and violence. By the time Ayad Allawi became prime minister there was a large-scale insurgency against his new government and the Americans, who were still the main power in Iraq. There were many different groups, some of them attacking each other but the majority wanting to fight the Americans and British. The diagram below summarises the main elements of the insurgency against coalition rule. However, this is rather simplified – the full picture was much more complicated.

Remnants of Saddam's Ba'ath Party

These were men who had lost everything when Saddam fell. They now had very little left to lose and it was very much in their interests for the new Iraq to fail. Many had been part of Saddam's security services so they had experience of underground warfare.

Units of the Iraqi Army

Many army units were recruited from particular villages or areas. Once the army was disbanded, many units reformed as guerrilla bands dominating their locality. They had training and experience. They also had weapons and equipment looted from Saddam's supply dumps.

Shi'ah militant Islamists

Shi'ah militants also wanted the Americans out of Iraq. Probably the most powerful and important Shi'ah leader was Muqtada al-Sadr (see page 195). The Shi'ah militants also received weapons, equipment and training from the Shi'ah government of neighbouring Iran.

Iraqi Nationalist and Islamist groups

These groups saw the coalition forces as enemies invading their lands, just like the Crusaders of many centuries before. Some were fighting for the independence of Iraq, others against the non-Muslim (as they saw it) US and British forces.

Sunni militant Islamists

Saddam was a Sunni Muslim and the Sunnis had dominated Iraq for many years. Sunni militants shared the same dislike of the USA as other Islamic militants. They were also concerned that they would become inferior citizens in an Iraq dominated by the Kurds in the north and the Shi'ah Muslims. One of the leading Shi'ah radicals was the Jordanian, Abu Musab al-Zarqawi. His leadership attracted many young militants because of his links with al-Qaeda.

Islamic militants and al-Qaeda

The US presence in Iraq drew in many Islamic militants, some of whom had been trained in al-Qaeda camps in Afghanistan. Most were from Arab countries. They found it easy to get themselves and weapons into Iraq because there was very little control over Iraq's borders with neighbouring Arab states. They were sometimes able to draw on al-Qaeda's networks of funding and training. They usually joined existing insurgent groups rather than forming their own.

What methods did the insurgents use?

The insurgents used the usual methods of an underground army (or terrorists, depending on your point of view). The main weapons were roadside bomb attacks on military vehicles, sniper attacks and suicide bombs. There were also kidnappings and executions of Westerners in Iraq such as the British engineer Ken Bigley in October 2004. The insurgents were on home ground, many were well trained and they were quite prepared to die for their cause – their casualties were much higher than those of the coalition forces. They were also well equipped. They lived among the population which was generally willing to shelter them, or at least was too afraid to provide the coalition forces with vital intelligence information. The numbers of coalition casualties tell the story of their effectiveness in attacking US and British forces. In a short period the violence also took on the form of a civil war as well as an insurgency against the coalition forces. Bombs set off in Shi'ah areas were usually followed by reprisals against Sunni mosques or civilians. A cycle of reprisals soon followed as old rivalries flared up.

SOURCE 23

US military vehicle burning after a roadside bomb attack in May 2006. British and American forces suffered heavy casualties from these attacks. Civilians were often caught in the blasts from these attacks as well. In this particular attack four Iraqi civilians were wounded.

SOURCE 24

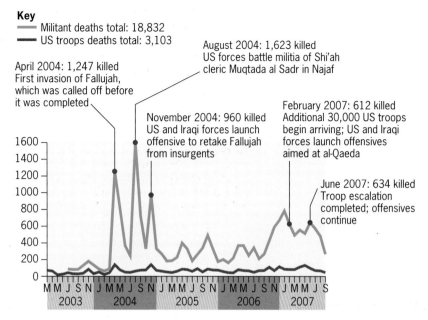

Key
Militant deaths total: 18,832
US troops deaths total: 3,103

April 2004: 1,247 killed
First invasion of Fallujah, which was called off before it was completed

August 2004: 1,623 killed
US forces battle militia of Shi'ah cleric Muqtada al Sadr in Najaf

November 2004: 960 killed
US and Iraqi forces launch offensive to retake Fallujah from insurgents

February 2007: 612 killed
Additional 30,000 US troops begin arriving; US and Iraqi forces launch offensives aimed at al-Qaeda

June 2007: 634 killed
Troop escalation completed; offensives continue

Casualty figures in the insurgency. The numbers of insurgent casualties are estimates.

How did the coalition forces respond?

The coalition forces responded to the insurgency with a range of different tactics. They had some successes. They inflicted much higher casualties than they received. They were able to use their awesome high-tech weaponry to target particular groups and even individuals. For example, Abu Musab al-Zarqawi was killed by laser guided bombs from American aircraft in June 2006. The Americans had received a tip off as to his location. There were also some large scale engagements in the insurgency. In April 2004 US troops, along with the first units of the newly recruited Iraqi armed forces, tried to retake the city of Fallujah from Sunni militants. The civilian casualties and damage to the city were so great that the attack was called off. It was a similar story in Najaf, where US forces tried unsuccessfully to remove Muqtada al-Sadr's Mahdi Army. This attack on Fallujah was resumed in November 2004 after all civilians were warned to leave the city. About 70 per cent of them did but so did many militants, mingling with the civilians. In the fighting which followed, around 5,000 militants and remaining civilians were killed and the town was devastated. There were allegations that US marines executed prisoners and innocent civilians. There was also outrage among Sunnis that the majority of Iraqi troops were Kurds or Shi'ah Muslims.

SOURCE 25

1 Is Source 24 useful for a historian investigating the tactics of the insurgents?
2 Is Source 25 useful as a source of information on the effectiveness of the tactics of the coalition forces?

Damage to a mosque after the US-led offensive on Fallujah, November 2004.

SOURCE 26

	1990	2007
Life expectancy	74 (women) 73 (men)	61 (women) 51 (men)
Annual average salary	$1,000–1,200	$24–60
Child mortality rate	30.5 deaths per 1,000 children (1989)	125 deaths per 1,000 children (2001)
Maternal mortality rate	50 deaths per 100,000 live births (1989)	294 deaths per 100,000 live births (2001)
Access to water	93% of people have access to clean water in towns and 70% in rural areas	30% of people have access to clean water

Statistics relating to health in Iraq before and after the invasion. They have been collected from data published by Oxfam, the World Health Organisation, the United Nations, UNICEF and the UN's Food and Agriculture Organisation.

The impact on civilians

As in most modern conflicts it was the civilian population of Iraq which bore the brunt of the destruction of the invasion and insurgency. Source 26 shows some of the measures of impact. Source 27 summarises the casualties, but these result from a variety of causes. In 2006 there were an average of sixteen civilian deaths every single day just from suicide bomb attacks. One of the insurgent tactics was to attack men wanting to join the new police forces or army. Suicide bombers would simply line up with the other recruits and then detonate their explosives. The casualties from these attacks were appalling, and thousands of civilians lost their lives to them. Law and order had broken down. The prisons had been opened in the invasion and thousands of 'regular' criminals had escaped. The police service ceased to exist and the lack of any border controls meant that smuggling of oil, drugs and other goods was widespread. Kidnapping for profit became common. Even when the new police services were formed they struggled to cope, and there was evidence in many areas that the police were actually involved in many crimes.

Educated Iraqis from the professional classes (such as scientists, teachers and doctors) found themselves targeted by extremist groups. This was probably because they were the people who could have made the reconstruction programme work. The result was that many of Iraq's best qualified people fled the country. Thousands of less qualified people ended up as refugees as well. According to the UN Refugee Agency almost 5 million Iraqis were displaced by violence. Over 2.4 million left their homes for safer areas within Iraq, up to 1.5 million went to Syria, and over 1 million to other states in the Middle East. Those who did remain in Iraq faced shortages of electricity and water. They also faced terrible economic hardships. Unemployment in Iraq after the invasion was running somewhere between 30 per cent and 60 per cent and this was not helped by the fact that insurgent groups attacked oil pipelines, gas depots, power stations and other projects designed to help the economy get back on its feet. These problems led to health problems as well (see Source 26).

SOURCE 27

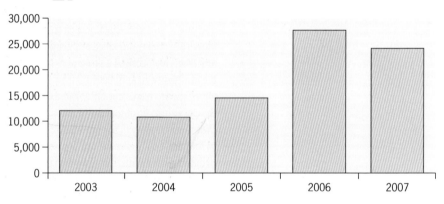

Civilian casualties in Iraq 2003–08. These figures are estimates because no official records have been kept. Casualty numbers are also hotly disputed. The highest estimates put civilian casualties at around 600,000 but these figures are rejected by the USA.

SOURCE 28

Friday, November 12, 2004: These last few days have been explosive – literally.

The sounds seem to be coming from everywhere. I've gotten tired of running upstairs and out on to the roof to find out where it's coming from. It feels like the first days of the war sometimes – planes, explosions, bullets, smoke... roads cut off.

We haven't attempted to leave the house but an uncle who was supposed to visit called to say he wouldn't be able to come because so many roads were blocked. Many people were told not to go to work and students stopped going to college yesterday. It's one of those weeks. Some areas in Baghdad seem to be cut off by armed gangs.

Eid is in a couple of days and that means there's Eid cleaning to do. The water was cut off all day today and the electricity was gone too. This seems to be happening all over Baghdad – we heard about the same situation in several areas.

An extract from *Baghdad Burning*, an internet blog written by 'Riverbend', a 24-year-old woman living in Iraq. Eid is a Muslim holiday.

What went wrong with the invasion?

1 Troop levels too low

Many experts said the coalition would need 300,000-400,000 troops to control Iraq. The US Defence Secretary disagreed and sent in only 130,000 US troops along with 30,000 British troops.

2 Inadequate planning

The US military carried out detailed planning on how to invade Iraq but they did not start planning how to run Iraq afterwards until January 2003. Ten out of thirteen major contracts for reconstruction work were still unsigned by the time the war started in March 2003. When the coalition forces first took over Iraq they set up a temporary government called the Coalition Provisional Authority (CPA). This was headed at first by General Jay Garner but he had no offices, no telephones and no computers.

3 Underestimating the damage to Iraq

The US had underestimated how much damage had been done to Iraq by years of sanctions and war. The invasion destroyed roads, railway lines and other facilities. The looting which followed the invasion also destroyed computer networks and vital records of information. At the simplest level, many government buildings had no desks or chairs. They also underestimated the speed and extent of the collapse of Saddam's regime.

4 Wrong assumptions

The US assumed the Iraqi troops would surrender in large numbers like they had in 1991. In fact they simply took off their uniforms and melded back into the population, often taking their weapons with them. The US also assumed that the Iraqi people would greet the American forces as liberators. Most were happy to see the end of Saddam but they were very unhappy about what they saw as effectively becoming an American colony. Once it became clear that there were no WMDs, Bush and Blair argued that the invasion was justified to improve life for the Iraqi people. These words seemed very hollow as law and order broke down along with crises in electricity, water and food supplies.

5 Wrong people and policies

General Garner was replaced as head of the CPA in May 2003 by Paul Bremer. He was well regarded by the Bush administration in Washington but he and his team had no experience of the Middle East. His role was to run the country until sovereignty was handed over to a new Iraqi government in June 2004. He immediately made two fateful decisions:

- Saddam's Ba'ath Party was banned and all party members above a certain rank were banned from holding a post in public services. Most Party members were not committed to Saddam's regime, they joined the party because it was the only way to get a job. The result of Bremer's first decision was to lose 30,000 experienced administrators who could have helped to establish the new government and make it work.
- The Iraqi armed forces and security services were dissolved. This instantly put 300,000 armed young men out of work. It also cut off the pensions of tens of thousands of ex-army officers. Many of these people became the backbone of the insurgency against coalition rule.

6 Government from the Green Zone

The Americans and their closest Iraqi allies were based in a secure area of Baghdad called the Green Zone. They seemed to be isolated from real life in Iraq. Most of the Iraqis they consulted were exiles who had fled from Saddam. Many of them hoped for positions of power after Saddam, but many Iraqis in Iraq did not know them. The Americans and their friends also seemed to be serving American interests rather than those of Iraqis. Bremer did begin projects to rebuild Iraq, but 75 per cent of the big contracts were awarded to US companies and 2 per cent went to Iraqi firms. Reconstruction was often funded by Iraqi oil money rather than the promised funding from the US Congress. Bremer also tried to start political reconstruction.

1 In what ways was life in the Green Zone different from outside?
2 Why was the writer of Source 29 so upset about the food and drink situation?
3 What were Chandrasekaran's main criticisms of Bremer and his team?
4 In what ways were the Americans disconnected from real life in Iraq according to Source 29?
5 In what ways does Source 30 back up the views expressed in Source 29?

He issued a plan to start drafting a new constitution for Iraq but the way he did this alarmed many Iraqis. Ayatollah Al-Sistani, the most respected Shi'ah cleric in Iraq, issued a decree or fatwa saying that it was unacceptable for a new constitution to be put together by foreigners and Iraqi advisers who were appointed and not elected. Reluctantly, Bremer accepted this. In July 2003 he set up the Iraqi Governing Council (IGC) to voice Iraqi views. The IGC was made up of 25 Iraqis representing the different communities of Iraq. This body then worked on a new draft constitution and the timetable for the handover of power to an Iraqi government. In June 2004 the CPA and IGC were dissolved and a new transitional government was set up under the Iraqi politician Ayad Allawi. He had a massive job on his hands.

SOURCE 29

Life in the Green Zone is thoroughly disconnected from the reality around. Outside, Iraq was in a fair degree of postwar chaos. There wasn't much electricity. There was rampant crime on the streets, traffic jams. Nobody was working. It was just kind of anarchy.

Inside the Green Zone, it was like a different planet inside those 17-foot-high walls. We're in the middle of a Muslim country, right? Muslims don't eat pork. What do they serve at the CPA dining hall for breakfast? Pork bacon. Hotdogs for lunch. They had six or seven bars in the Green Zone where you could get cold beer and wine …

When you got inside that palace – unlike any other building in Iraq, it was chilled to a crisp 68 degrees – you had earnest young Americans who were determined to come fix Iraq. Now mind you, they didn't get out and about that much, but they thought they knew what Iraq needed.

The Iraqis they interfaced with were Iraqis who were either their translators or Iraqis who felt comfortable enough to go through three separate security checks to come into the palace to talk to them. Oftentimes it was Iraqis who wanted to get a contract, who wanted some favourable treatment, who knew that ultimately the Americans were going to devolve some power to the Iraqis, so told their American counterparts what they wanted to hear so they would be seen as trusted partners. And many of the Americans sort of naively said, 'This policy must be just fine, because my Iraqis working for me seem to think it's OK.'

Rajiv Chandrasekaran, the Baghdad correspondent for *The Washington Post* newspaper from April 2003 until October 2004.

SOURCE 30

Monday, August 18, 2003: Normal day today. We were up at early morning, did the usual 'around the house things', you know – check if the water tank is full, try to determine when the electricity will be off, checked if there was enough cooking gas …

… For those who don't know, the interim governing council chosen by Bremer to 'represent' the Iraqi people couldn't decide which of the power-hungry freaks should rule Iraq, so Bremer decided that three people would govern (as temporary presidents) until the Americans could set up elections … Naturally, the other members of the governing council objected … why should Iraq only have three presidents?! And the number became nine. Each of the nine get to 'rule' for a month. You know, Iraq just needs more instability – all we need is a new president each month … The way it will work is that each one will have their chance at governing Iraq, and at the end of the nine month period, Bremer will decide which one of them best represents American assets in the region and he will become 'The Chosen One'. They'll set up some fake elections and 'The Chosen One' will magically be rewarded with … Iraq.

An extract from *Baghdad Burning*, an internet blog written by 'Riverbend', a 24-year-old woman living in Iraq.

SOURCE 31

Wall murals showing torture and abuse of prisoners in the US-run Abu Ghraib camp, June 2004.

7 The problem of hearts and minds

The main problem for the coalition forces was that, just like in the Vietnam War of the 1960s, they had not won over the hearts and minds of the Iraqi people. They were seen as occupiers and invaders. This impression was not helped when it became clear that around 10,000 Iraqis were being held, without trial, in US-run detention camps. Most of these prisoners were arrested on the basis of anonymous tip-offs. To many Iraqis it seemed very similar to the regime of Saddam Hussein. This was especially so when it emerged that many of the prisoners had been tortured and abused at the Abu Ghraib prison camp. It soon became clear that the same thing had happened in other camps and there were accusations that senior commanders knew what was happening.

6 What is happening in Sources 31 and 32?
7 Each source is a form of propaganda. Does that make them untrue?
8 Why are Sources 31 and 32 useful to historians investigating why the Americans failed to win hearts and minds in Iraq?
9 Try to find two or three other sources in this chapter which would also be useful to historians investigating why the Americans failed.

© THE INDEPENDENT

A cartoon from the *Independent* newspaper, 2 April 2003. This paper was a critic of Blair and of the war in Iraq.

SOURCE **33**

November 16th 2004: I'm feeling sick – literally. I can't get the video Al-Jazeera played out of my head:

The American Marines killed a wounded man. It's hard to believe. They killed a man who was completely helpless – like he was some sort of diseased animal. I had read the articles and heard the stories of this happening before – wounded civilians being thrown on the side of the road or shot in cold blood – but to see it happening on television is something else – it makes me crazy with anger.

And what will happen now? A criminal investigation against a single Marine who did the shooting? Just like what happened with the Abu Ghraib atrocities? A couple of people will be blamed and the whole thing will be buried under the rubble of idiotic military psychologists, defence analysts, Pentagon officials and spokespeople and it will be forgotten. It's typical American technique – every single atrocity is lost and covered up by blaming a specific person and getting it over with. What people don't understand is that the whole military is infested with these psychopaths. In this last year we've seen murderers, torturers and xenophobes running around in tanks and guns. I don't care what does it: I don't care if it's the tension, the fear, the 'enemy'... it's murder. We are occupied by murderers.

An extract from *Baghdad Burning*, an internet blog written by 'Riverbend', a 24-year-old woman living in Iraq. Al-Jazeera is an Arabic TV station.

Activity

1 Source 33 is a very powerful source but is it reliable for telling us what actually happened? Evaluate the reliability of the source:
   • What allegations does the source make?
   • How would you describe the language and tone of the source (is it measured? emotional?)? Select words and phrases to support what you say.
   • Do any other sources in this section support or contradict any of the allegations made in the source?
   • Do any facts or figures from the main text in this section support or contradict the source? N.B. Use the internet to research whether any cases were actually brought against US soldiers. A good resource is the BBC news website.
2 Sources 28 and 33 come from the same writer. What do these extracts reveal about the author and her attitudes?
3 Are her views supported by any other sources in this chapter?
4 Make a final decision on whether you accept the allegations in this source.

Focus Task

Why could the invaders not control Iraq?

In this section we have set out seven major reasons why things began to go wrong in Iraq after the successful invasion. Your task is to decide on the order of importance of these factors. Study each one carefully and then complete your own version of this table.

Factor in rank order	Reason(s) for putting it in this place	Worth noting that it is connected to ...
1		
2		
3		
4		
5		
6		
7		

How successful was the transfer to transitional government?

SOURCE **34**

A

B

Two American cartoons from 2005: **A** was published on 26 January 2005, and **B** on 6 April 2005.

Activity

One of the main aims of a political cartoon is to tell as full a story as possible with as few words as possible. How successful do you think Sources 34A and 34B are in this aim? Give each a mark out of 10 and explain your mark by referring to details from each cartoon.

As you have already read, Ayad Allawi was made Prime Minister in June 2004. Allawi made security his top priority, and he was able to rely on US forces to help him with that policy. For ordinary Iraqis this policy did not help much. Allawi targeted the big armed groups like al-Sadr's Mahdi army but the low-level violence, kidnapping and general crime was largely ignored. Allawi's government also suffered from corruption scandals.

Allawi was always seen as a caretaker Prime Minister before Iraqis voted in a new government which would decide what kind of state Iraq would be. The elections took place in January 2005. The overall turnout was around 58 per cent of the electorate, although there were huge variations in turnout from one area to another. Much of the Sunni Arab population boycotted the elections. After the elections there was a lot of negotiation but in April 2005 the new government finally took shape. The Shi'ah politician Ibrahim al-Jafari became the new prime minister. He headed a government of ministers made up of the different Shi'ah, Kurdish and Sunni parties.

In many respects the fact that elections and a government had happened at all was a triumph, but there was still a long way to go and many issues to resolve:

- The constitution of the new Iraq: Many Shi'ah and Sunni Muslims argued that Iraq's new constitution should be based on Islamic shari'ah law. However, the Kurds in the north of Iraq favoured a secular (non-religious) federation of states rather than a single, unified state. Many other Iraqi Muslims were also uneasy about Iraq having a shari'ah based constitution. Educated, professional Iraqis felt that the various religious parties were too traditional and conservative in their views and did not represent them. There were also many educated women who were anxious that the new constitution did not restrict the freedom they had enjoyed under Saddam's secular rule.
- Ministers saw their departments as their own mini-kingdoms and so placed their own loyal followers in positions of power. This increased the divisions and rivalries within the government. It also led to waste and corruption.
- The Iraqi population as a whole, saw the new government as a creation of the Americans so it had little respect in the country.
- Economic recovery continued to be painfully slow and in May 2005 there were protests about food shortages and cuts in water and electricity supplies.
- The new government seemed powerless to contain the insurgency even with American help. Civilian casualties actually rose in 2006–07 (see Source 32). As this book was being printed in 2009 there was no end to the insurgency in sight.

International consequences

There is little doubt that the war in Iraq has had major consequences around the world. It led to deep divisions within the government, armed forces and population of the two main states involved – the USA and the UK. It also soured relations between the USA and many European countries, especially France and Russia. Perhaps the most serious consequence for the USA was the way in which the Iraq war increased support for militant Islam around the world and made the USA and UK particular targets for militant Muslim terrorists (see pages 172–73). This was made more serious by the inability of the armed might of the USA to contain or control the insurgency. It showed that a determined underground movement could effectively oppose even the world's greatest military power.

(see pages 172–73)

SOURCE 35

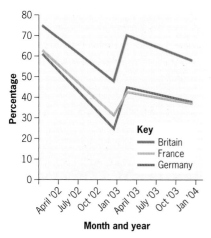

Percentage of people expressing favourable attitudes towards the USA

Key
Britain
France
Germany

Month and year

In the predominantly Muslim countries surveyed, anger toward the United States remains pervasive, although the level of hatred has eased somewhat and support for the war on terrorism has inched up. Osama bin Laden, however, is viewed favourably by large percentages in Pakistan (65 per cent), Jordan (55 per cent) and Morocco (45 per cent). Even in Turkey, where bin Laden is highly unpopular, as many as 31 per cent say that suicide attacks against Americans and other Westerners in Iraq are justifiable. Majorities in all four Muslim nations surveyed doubt the sincerity of the war on terrorism. Instead, most say it is an effort to control Mideast oil and to dominate the world.

Extracts and graph from a research survey carried out 16 March 2004.

SOURCE 36

An authoritative US intelligence report pooling the views of 16 government agencies concludes America's campaign in Iraq has increased the threat of terrorism. The National Intelligence estimate was completed in April but not made public. Its conclusions, which were first reported by the New York Times, *contradict assertions made by President George Bush and White House officials.*

The report, Trends in Global Terrorism: Implications for the United States, *points out the 'centrality' of the US invasion of Iraq in fomenting terrorist cells and attacks. One section of the 30-page report,* Indicators of the Spread of the Global Jihadist Movement, *describes how the American presence in Iraq has helped spread radical Islam by providing a focal point for anti-Americanism.*

While arguing that there has been success in dismantling the leadership of al-Qaeda and its ability to plan major operations, the report says that radical cells have moved to more than 5000 websites to organise and spread their message. CIA chief General Michael Hayden, deputy director of national intelligence, painted an alarming picture. 'New jihadist networks and cells, sometimes united by little more than their anti-western agendas, are increasingly likely to emerge,' Gen Hayden said. 'If this trend continues, threats to the US at home and abroad will become more diverse and that could lead to increasing attacks worldwide.'

A report from the *Guardian* newspaper, 25 September 2006.

SOURCE 37

An alleged bomb plot in Britain that supposedly included plans to attack flights to Canada was a revenge mission for Western-supported military actions in Iraq, Afghanistan and the Palestinian territories, a London court heard on Friday. Prosecutor Peter Wright showed footage from videos alleged to have been made by six of eight British men accused of the massive airline plot, saying the men believed the videos would be discovered following their simultaneous suicide missions.

In the videos the men deliver threats against the West for their actions in 'Muslim lands.'

'This is revenge for the actions of the U.S.A. in Muslim lands, and their accomplices such as the British and the Jews,' says Umar Islam, a convert formerly known as Brian Young. 'If you think you can go into our lands and do what you are doing in Afghanistan, Iraq and Palestine and it will not come back to your doorstep, you have another think coming.'

Report of a court case in London, 2008.

Focus Task

What were the international consequences of the Iraq War?

Fill out your own copy of this table. In column two record the international consequences of the war. In column three record your own opinion as to why this consequence is a particular concern to the leaders who led the invasion.

Source	International consequence	Reasons to be concerned
35		
36		
37		

Was the invasion of Iraq a success?

The table below will help you answer this question by looking at the aims of the USA and its allies in invading Iraq. Look back over pages 194–204 and see how far you think these aims were achieved. You could work in pairs or small groups and research one particular aim or section of the chapter.

Aims	Evidence and examples to support your answer	Location of evidence (page numbers, source numbers,	Overall judgement: 1 stunning success; 5 total disaster
Remove a threat to America and the Western world			
Overthrow Saddam Hussein			
Build a better, safer Iraq for the Iraqi people			
Establish a democracy with an Islamic 'accent'			

What is the significance of the war?

The Iraq war has affected millions of people directly, in Iraq itself and in the region. For the dead, the bereaved, the injured, the homeless, the jobless the war changed their lives, completely and forever. At that important, human level the war was and still is immensely significant.

But there is another side to historical significance. The question of whether a historical event is significant is also about how people in the future will look back and remember this war; what they will learn from it. So the honest answer to 'What is the significance of the Iraq war?' is 'We don't yet know!'

However one thing is very clear from all the writing about the invasion and the war is that politicians and commentators were keenly aware of this war's place in history. On both sides of the conflict, people talked as if they were aware of fighting for a bigger prize than just the future of Iraq. The struggle encompassed and affected many wider issues. Iraq was strategically significant in the Middle East (ie what happened there affected what happened in neighbouring countries) and (so it was claimed) in the battle against international terrorism.

In these final two pages you are going to examine what some of leading figures on the coalition side believed was the historical significance of the war and invasion they launched. You can agree or disagree with them about whether they were right, but it is valuable to understand how they saw the significance of what they were doing. How they learned from history, and how they hoped to change history.

What is the significance of the Iraq war?

1 Work in pairs or small groups. Choose one of Sources 38–40 and explain in detail the comparison which is being made. Imagine your explanation is aimed at an audience which knows little about either the Iraq War or about appeasement in the 1930s (see pages 54–55) or the Vietnam War (see pages 100–123).

2 Study either Source 41 or Source 42 and decide how successful you think your chosen comparison from Part 1 actually is. You need to explain:
   ◆ ways in which it is valid
   ◆ ways in which it is not valid
   ◆ the motives of the person who made the comparison.

3 A British organisation called the History and Policy Unit believes that politicians should develop a better understanding of history in order to guide important decisions they make today. In your group, select three examples of historical events which you think would have been useful for Tony Blair and George Bush to study before they invaded Iraq in 2003. The events can be from any period or place.

SOURCE 38

Listen to this comment from a high-ranking American official: 'It became clear that if we were prepared to stay the course we could lay the cornerstone for a diverse and independent region. If we falter the forces of chaos would smell victory and decades of strife and chaos would stretch endlessly before us. The choice is clear: we shall stay the course.'

That's not President Bush speaking, it's Lyndon Johnson speaking forty years ago, ordering 100,000 more American soldiers to Vietnam. Here's another quotation: 'The big problem is to get territory and to keep it. That is the big problem. You can get territory today and lose it next week. You have to have enough people to clear it and preserve what you have done.'

That is not President Bush on the need for more forces in Iraq. It is President Johnson in 1966 as he doubled our presence in Vietnam. There was no military solution to that war but we kept trying to find one anyway. And in the end 58,000 Americans died in the search for it. Echoes of that disaster are all around us today. Iraq is George Bush's Vietnam.

As with Vietnam, the only rational solution to the crisis is political not military. Injecting more troops into a civil war is not the answer. Our men and women in uniform cannot force the Iraqi people to reconcile their differences. Tens of thousands more American troops will only make the Iraqis more resentful of America's occupation. It will also make the Iraqi government even more dependent on America, not less.

US Senator Edward Kennedy speaking on 9 January 2007. He was commenting on President Bush's increase in troop levels in Iraq in 2007, known as 'the surge'.

SOURCE 39

The 1930s was a time when a certain amount of cynicism and moral confusion set in among Western democracies. When those who warned about a coming crisis, the rise of Fascism and Nazism, were ridiculed or ignored. Indeed, in the decades before World War Two a great many people believed that the Fascist threat was exaggerated. I recount that history, because once again we face similar challenges in our efforts to confront the rising threat of a new type of Fascism. Today a different enemy, a new kind of enemy, has made clear its intentions with attacks in places like New York, Washington DC, Bali, Madrid, Moscow and so many other places. But some seem not to have learned history's lessons. We need to consider the following question: With the growing lethality and the increasing availability of weapons, can we truly afford to believe that somehow, some way, vicious extremists can be appeased?

Donald Rumsfeld, US Secretary of Defence, speaking in August 2006 about the decision to invade Iraq.

SOURCE 40

A cartoon in the US newspaper the *Hartford Courant*, 27 June 2005. The figure on the left is George Bush. The one on the right is Lyndon Johnson, US President 1963–68. You may have already seen this cartoon in Chapter 6, page 123.

SOURCE 41

The true Iraq appeasers

IN HIS MOST recent justification of his Pentagon stewardship, Defense Secretary Donald Rumsfeld reached back to the 1930s, comparing the Bush administration's critics to those who, like US Ambassador to Britain Joseph P. Kennedy, favoured appeasing Adolf Hitler. Rumsfeld avoided a more recent comparison: the appeasement of Saddam Hussein by the Reagan and first Bush administrations. The reasons for selectivity are obvious, since so many of Hussein's appeasers in the 1980s were leading figures in the 2003 Iraq war, including Rumsfeld himself. In 1983, President Reagan initiated a strategic opening to Iraq. Reagan chose Rumsfeld as his emissary to Hussein, whom he visited in December 1983 and March 1984.

… The Reagan and first Bush administrations believed that Hussein could be a strategic partner to the United States. Hussein, having watched the United States gloss over his crimes in the Iran war and at home, concluded he could get away with invading Kuwait. It was a costly error for him, for his country, and eventually for the United States, which now has the largest part of its military bogged down in the Iraqi quagmire. Meanwhile the architects of the earlier appeasement policy now maintain the illusion that they have a path to victory, if only their critics would shut up.

An article from 31 August 2006 by Peter Galbraith, a former US ambassador. The article appeared in *The Boston Globe*, a pro-Democratic party American newspaper.

SOURCE 42

From Ted Kennedy to the cover of Newsweek magazine, we are being warned that Iraq has turned into a quagmire, George W. Bush's Vietnam. Learning from history is well and good, but such talk illustrates the dangers of learning from the wrong history. To understand what is going on in Iraq today, Americans need to go back to 1920, not 1970 …

First, let's dispense with Vietnam. In South Vietnam, the United States was propping up an existing government, whereas in Iraq it has attempted outright 'regime change', just as Britain did at the end of World War One by driving the Ottoman Turks out of the country. 'Our armies do not come into your cities and lands as conquerors or enemies, but as liberators', declared General Frederick Stanley Maude – a line that could equally well have come from Secretary of Defense Donald Rumsfeld this time last year. By the summer of 1920, however, the self-styled liberators faced a full-blown revolt.

… Then, as now, the insurrection had religious origins and leaders, but it soon transcended the country's ancient ethnic and sectarian divisions. The first anti-British demonstrations were in the mosques of Baghdad. But the violence quickly spread to the Shiite holy city of Karbala, where British rule was denounced by Ayatollah Muhammad Taqi al-Shirazi – perhaps the historical counterpart of today's Shiite firebrand, Moktada al-Sadr …

Then, as now, the rebels systematically sought to disrupt the occupiers' communications – then by attacking railways and telegraph lines, today by ambushing convoys. British troops and civilians were besieged, just as hostages are being held today. Then, as now, much of the violence was more symbolic than strategically significant – British bodies were mutilated, much as American bodies were at Falluja.

… There is much, then, to learn from the events of 1920. Yet I'm pessimistic that any senior military commander in Iraq today knows much about it. Late last year, a top American commander in Europe assured me that United States forces would soon be reinforced by Turkish troops; he seemed puzzled when I pointed out that this was unlikely to play well in Baghdad, where there is little nostalgia for the days of Ottoman rule. Few commentators have pointed out that the British at first tried to place disproportionate blame for their troubles on outside agitators. Phantom Bolsheviks then; Al Qaeda interlopers today. But for the most part we get only facile references to Vietnam.

An extract from an article by the British historian Niall Ferguson in the *New York Times*, 4 May 2008.

Paper 1: Core Content

One important thing you can do in your exam preparation is to learn to **spot key words** ('describe', 'explain', 'how far', which examiners call 'command words'), which tell you what they are expecting you to do.

OCR advise you to spend about **15 minutes** on this question. The two parts of the question are worth roughly the same amount so you should aim to spend roughly the same amount of time on each.

DO

- Get **straight to the point**, which is to summarise the message of the cartoon.
- Describe **3–4 features** of the source which help convey this message.
- Use the information in the **caption** and your **background knowledge** to interpret the source.

DON'T

- **Don't describe the cartoon in detail** – only mention details that convey the message.
- **Don't speculate** about things which you can't support from the cartoon or from your own background knowledge. Avoid phrases like 'might show that . . .' or 'could mean . . .'
- **Don't summarise** Hitler's policies in the 1930s.

It's a good idea to **start your answer like this:** 'The message of the cartoon is . . .' It gets you straight to the point.

Notice how this answer uses phrases to **connect** the contents of the cartoon with the message.

'We can see this in the cartoon . . .'

'This shows that Hitler . . .'

'We can tell this from . . .'

Paragraph 1 is good. This answer so far scores 5 out of 7 marks. The candidate clearly understands the source and can use details to support the answer. To reach the top marks the source needs to be **put into context**. This is what paragraph 2 achieves. Successful candidates often end their answers to question 1 with a paragraph which starts: 'The cartoon was published in . . .'

OCR Paper 1 is split into two parts:

1 Core content
2 Your chosen study in depth.

This Exam Focus deals with the Core content. The Core content is split into three sections:

1 The Inter-War Years, 1919–39
2 The Cold War, 1945–75
3 A New World? 1948–2005

The exam will include questions on all aspects but you have to answer questions on **one section only**. Whichever content you choose the format of the questions will be similar. There will be a compulsory question 1 and a choice between questions 2 and 3.

The Compulsory Question 1

The usual pattern is:

1 a) A question that requires you to use your knowledge of the topic to interpret the source. This will typically begin 'What is the message of . . .'
   b) Will be on a closely related topic that asks you to explain a historical event. This question will usually begin: 'Explain why . . .'

Here is an example based on Part 1: The Inter-War Years, 1919–39.

Example Question 1

1 Study the source carefully and then answer the questions which follow.
   a) Study Source A. What is the message of this cartoon? Use details of the cartoon and your knowledge to explain your answer. [7]
   b) Explain why the Nazi–Soviet Pact (1939) was signed. [8]

SOURCE **A**

A cartoon from a British newspaper, 6 September 1939, three days after Britain and France declared war on Germany. It shows Hitler speaking to Mars, the great god of war.

A Good Answer to Question 1a

The message of this cartoon is that Hitler has miscalculated and bitten off more than he can chew. He was expecting a small war but he has ended up with a big war. We can see this in the cartoon as the giant god of war has arrived and he looks very large and threatening. This shows that Hitler now has a large war on his hands. Hitler was expecting a small war. We can tell this from the surprised expression on his face and his body language – backing away from Mars.

The cartoon was published in September 1939. Hitler had taken over Austria and Czechoslovakia in 1938–39 and he did not expect Britain and France to do anything when he launched his small war against Poland in September 1939. However, Britain and France did declare war on him and he now has a bigger war on his hands.

A Good Answer to Question 1b

In 1939 Hitler signed a treaty with Stalin known as the Nazi–Soviet Pact. They agreed not to attack each other. It was surprising because Hitler was anti-Communist and Hitler and Stalin were sworn enemies.

The main reason Hitler made the treaty was that he wanted to take over part of Poland and so retake the last bit of land that Germany lost in the Treaty of Versailles. But Hitler did not think Germany was ready to fight the USSR and without the pact he would have risked a war with Stalin. A second reason Hitler signed the pact was to stop Britain and France becoming allies with the USSR.

Stalin's main reason was that he thought Hitler might attack him. He had tried to get an agreement with Britain and France against Hitler but that had failed. He was not sure he could trust Britain and France particularly because of Appeasement and the Munich Agreement when they basically agreed to give Hitler parts of Czechoslovakia without any resistance at all plus the League of Nations did nothing to stop Hitler expanding German territory in the 1930s. Another reason was that Stalin expected that one day Hitler might invade Russia but the pact gave him more time to build up his army for war.

This paragraph **sets the context** well and shows the examiner that you know what the pact was and why it was surprising. Note that it does not get bogged down in detail – it focuses on the main point.

If an answer has two aspects it is best to deal with **each aspect in a new paragraph** to keep your thinking and writing clear and focused.

DO
• **Use your background knowledge** to support what you have said about the reasons the Pact was signed.

DON'T
• **Don't list all the other events of the 1930s**. There are no marks for mentioning content that is not relevant to your explanation.

Exam Practice

Here are two more examples of compulsory questions based on the other parts of the core content. Have a go and see how you get on.

SOURCE **A**

An American cartoon, 1949.

1 a) Study Source A. What is the message of this cartoon? Use details of the cartoon and your knowledge to explain your answer. [7]
   b) Explain why the Soviet Union blockaded West Berlin in 1948. [8]

• **Write in paragraphs**. As a general guide, aim for no more than eight lines per paragraph – but don't pad your paragraphs out unnecessarily.
• **Keep relating your answer to the question** all the time. For example:
  'The first reason was . . .'
  'Another reason was . . .'
• Remember the value of phrases like: 'This shows that . . .' in order to **connect your evidence with your explanation**.

As with the previous example answer, start by explaining what the Berlin blockade was – briefly! The rest of this answer needs to focus on the actions of the USA and its allies in Germany, BUT **do not just describe** these actions – **you need to explain** why Stalin was threatened by them.

SOURCE **A**

A street cartoon in Prague.

1 a) Study Source A. What is the message of this cartoon? Use details of the cartoon and your knowledge to explain your answer. [7]
   b) Explain why the Soviet Union responded so harshly to the uprisings in Hungary in 1956 and Czechoslovakia in 1968. [8]

Try writing two **themed paragraphs**:
• What were the protests about.
• Why they threatened the Soviet Union.

Paper 1: Core Content

Question 2 or 3

For your core content you will then have a choice of two questions on different topics. Each will follow a similar pattern, typically asking you to:
a) Describe . . .
b) Explain why . . .
c) Evaluate – e.g. 'How far . . .?' or 'Which was more important . . .?'

Example Question

Here is an example drawn from Section 2 of the core.

> **2 a)** Who were the Vietcong? [4]
> **b)** Explain why the USA became involved in Vietnam. [6]
> **c)** Which was more important in bringing about the USA's failure in Vietnam: the military tactics of the North Vietnamese or public opinion in the USA? Explain your answer. [10]

A Good Answer to Question 2a) + b)

> a) The Vietcong was the name given to the Communists who opposed the Americans in the Vietnam War. They used guerrilla tactics against the US forces. They were supported by the North Vietnam leader Ho Chi Minh.
> b) America became involved in Vietnam because of the Domino Theory. This theory said that if one Asian state like Vietnam fell to Communism then all of the other states in the region like Laos, Cambodia or even India would also fall. The USA intervened to prevent this from happening.

Writing Frame for Question 2c

Question 2(c) is the big one. It is a single question but it usually covers two aspects of the topic and the examiner expects you to consider both. Often it gives you a statement to agree or disagree with – in which case the two aspects you have to consider are arguments for the statement or arguments against.

For these long answers it is very important to have a structure in mind before you start. A writing frame helps you do this. This is what your answer should cover.

Paragraph 1: Introduction – explain why the USA failure in Vietnam might be a surprise – i.e. a superpower with such technological superiority fails to defeat a poor peasant army. Say there are a number of reasons but you are going to consider two of them in particular . . .

Paragraph 2: Focus on North Vietnamese tactics – in particular guerrilla warfare. Explain why this was effective against the Americans and how it sapped their morale and led them to conclude they could not win the war.

Paragraph 3: Focus on public opinion. Explain how, to start with, Americans supported the battle against communism, but gradually support leaked away because of American casualties, atrocities such as My Lai, media reports that they could not win, the cost of the war – with the result that an anti-war movement got going which persuaded the politicians they had to get out.

Paragraph 4: Evaluates the relative importance of the two factors. The overall conclusion might be that although they realised they could not win the Americans could have carried on fighting this war for many more years – militarily – if they had kept the American public on side. But they couldn't so it suggests that the public opinion factor was more important than the military tactics but the two worked hand in hand.

OCR **advise** you to spend about **35 minutes** on this question. Look at the marks available. You should spend more time on the later parts.

Question 2(a) is really as **straightforward** as it looks. List three relevant points about the Vietcong.

Question 2(b) is an 'explain why' question. It is very similar to question 1(b) on page 207 and is marked in a similar way. The most important thing is that you have to **explain the reasons and not just list** them.

This answer explains both what the Domino Theory was and why it might lead to American involvement.

To get the full six marks however you should aim to explain **at least two reasons**. But be careful not to OVER ANSWER this question. Examiners will not expect pages of work for six marks.

Finally it would be a good idea in this question to point out how your two reasons were both part of the wider US policy of containment.

It is **not essential** to write an introduction but it helps to get you thinking straight.

Consider **both aspects** fully. You can't ignore the one that you think is less important; you still have to explain why it was important too.

You **can include other aspects** in your answer (e.g. other reasons for American failure if it strengthens your argument) but you won't be penalised if you don't. OCR make it quite clear that candidates only need to consider what is specified in the question.

Give your opinion. Each factor should be evaluated: was it more or less significant than the other factor; did it link to other factors and affect it?

The best answers will **consider the links between the factors**. For example that the effectiveness of US tactics led the Americans to do things that further weakened support for the war at home – such as spraying the jungle with toxic chemicals; or atrocities such as My Lai that were designed to flush out guerrilla fighters but ended up killing innocent people.

Section 2

OCR Paper 1 DEPTH STUDIES

Causes and events of the First World War, 1890–1918

10.1 Why did the First World War break out in 1914?

SOURCE **2**

The Archduke Franz Ferdinand and his wife Sophie arrive in Sarajevo. The Archduke was heir to the throne of Austria, whose powerful empire covered much of central Europe (see page 212).

SOURCE **1**

Sunday 28 June 1914 was a bright and sunny day in Sarajevo. Sarajevo in Bosnia was preparing for a royal visit from Archduke Franz Ferdinand of Austria [see Source 2]. Crowds lined the streets and waited for the procession of cars to appear. Hidden among the crowds, however, were six teenage [Bosnian Serb] terrorists sworn to kill the Archduke. They hated him and they hated Austria. They were stationed at intervals along the riverside route which the cars would follow on their way to the Town Hall. They all had bombs and pistols in their pockets, and phials of poison which they had promised to swallow if they were caught, so that they would not give the others away. It seemed as if the plan could not fail.

Finally, the cavalcade of four large cars came into sight. The Archduke was in a green open-topped car. Beside him sat his wife Sophie, waving politely to the crowd.

At 10.15 the cars passed Mehmedbasic, the first in line of the waiting killers. He took fright, did nothing, and then escaped. The next assassin, Cabriolvic, also lost his nerve and did nothing. But then as the cars passed the Cumurja Bridge, Cabrinovic threw his bomb, swallowed his poison, and jumped into the river. The Archduke saw the bomb coming and threw it off his car, but it exploded under the car behind, injuring several people. Now there was total confusion as the procession accelerated away, fearing more bombs. Meanwhile the police dragged Cabrinovic out of the river. His cyanide was old and had not worked.

The Archduke was driven to the Town Hall, where he demanded to be taken to visit the bomb victims in hospital. Fearing more terrorists, the officials decided to take a new route to avoid the crowds, but this was not properly explained to the driver of the Archduke's car. Moreover, no police guard went with the procession.

Meanwhile the other assassins, on hearing the bomb explode, assumed the Archduke was dead and left – all except Princip, who soon discovered the truth. Miserably he wandered across the street towards Schiller's delicatessen and café.

Princip was standing outside the café when, at 10.45, the Archduke's car suddenly appeared beside him and turned into Franz Josef Street. This was a mistake, for according to the new plan the procession should have continued straight along the Appel Quay. As the driver realised he had taken a wrong turn he stopped and started to reverse. Princip could hardly believe his luck. Pulling an automatic pistol from the right-hand pocket of his coat, he fired two shots at a range of just 3 or 4 metres. He could not miss. One bullet pierced the Archduke's neck and the other ricocheted off the car into Sophie's stomach. Fifteen minutes later she died and the Archduke followed soon after.

Princip was immediately seized. He managed to swallow his poison, but it did not work and he was taken off to prison. All the plotters except Mehmedbasic were eventually caught, but only the organiser, Ilic, was hanged, for the others were too young for the death penalty. Princip died in an Austrian jail, however, in April 1918, aged twenty-three.

Adapted from *Britain at War* by Craig Mair, 1982.

SOURCE **3**

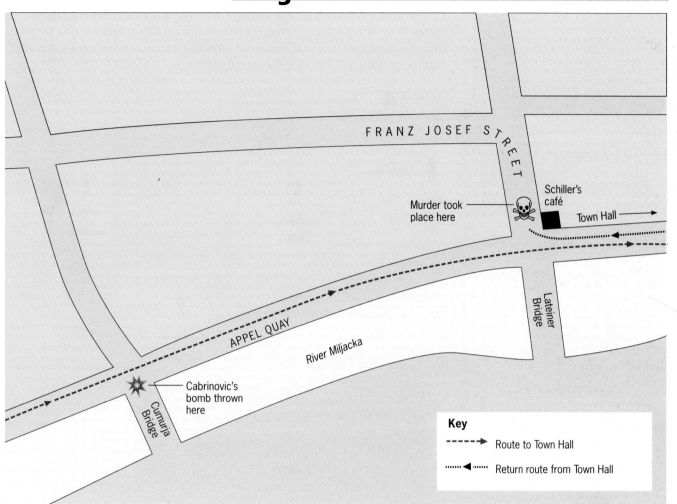

The route taken by Archduke Franz Ferdinand's car in Sarajevo, 28 June 1914.

At his trial, Princip said: 'I am not a criminal, for I destroyed a bad man. I thought I was right.' Two years later he said that if he had known what was to follow he would never have fired the two fatal shots – but his regret was too late. Within six weeks of the Archduke's assassination, almost all of Europe had been dragged into the bloodiest war in history.

On 23 July: Austria blamed Serbia for the death of Franz Ferdinand and sent it an ultimatum.

On 28 July: Austria declared war on Serbia and shelled its capital, Belgrade.

On 29 July: The Russian army got ready to help Serbia defend itself against the Austrian attack.

Germany warned Russia not to help the Serbs.

On 1 August: Germany declared war on Russia. It also began to move its army towards France and Belgium.

On 2 August: The French army was put on a war footing ready to fight any German invasion.

On 3 August: Germany declared war on France and invaded Belgium. Britain ordered Germany to withdraw from Belgium.

On 4 August: With the Germans still in Belgium, Britain declared war on Germany.

On 6 August: Austria declared war on Russia.

To understand **why** the murders in Sarajevo led so quickly to an all-out war involving all the main European powers, we need to find out more about what Europe was like in 1914.

1 There were many moments during 28 June 1914 when events could have turned out differently. Study the account of the murders in Source 1 and list any moments at which a different decision might have saved the lives of the Archduke and his wife.

2 Do you think that if the Archduke had not been shot, the war would not have started? Give your reasons. (These are only your first thoughts. You can revise your opinion later.)

The alliances

In 1914 the six most powerful countries in Europe were divided into two opposing alliances: the Central Powers or Triple Alliance (Germany, Austria–Hungary and Italy), formed in 1882, and the Triple Entente (Britain, France and Russia), formed in 1907. Each country was heavily armed, and each one had reasons for distrusting other countries in Europe.

SOURCE **4**

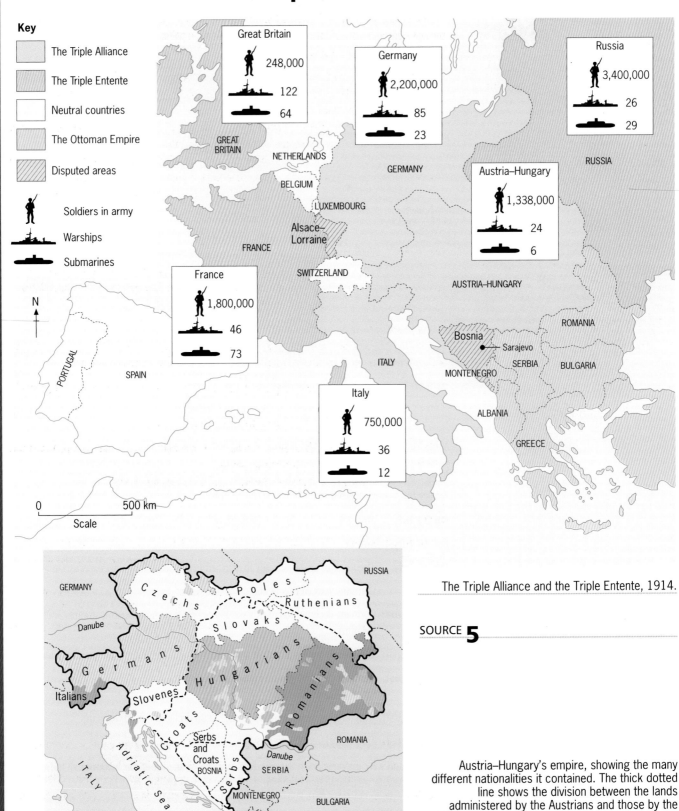

Key

- The Triple Alliance
- The Triple Entente
- Neutral countries
- The Ottoman Empire
- Disputed areas

- Soldiers in army
- Warships
- Submarines

Great Britain
248,000
122
64

Germany
2,200,000
85
23

Russia
3,400,000
26
29

Austria–Hungary
1,338,000
24
6

France
1,800,000
46
73

Italy
750,000
36
12

The Triple Alliance and the Triple Entente, 1914.

SOURCE **5**

Austria–Hungary's empire, showing the many different nationalities it contained. The thick dotted line shows the division between the lands administered by the Austrians and those by the Hungarians.

The Central Powers or the Triple Alliance

Germany

Before 1870 Germany was a collection of small independent states of which Prussia was the most powerful. In 1870 the Prussian statesman Bismarck won a war against France. He then united the many German states into a new and powerful German empire. Germany took the important industrial area of Alsace–Lorraine from France. To guard against a revenge attack from the French he formed an alliance with Austria–Hungary and Italy.

For the next twenty years Bismarck followed a fairly cautious policy. This changed in 1890 when the new German Kaiser, Wilhelm II, took control of German policy from Bismark. Wilhelm took a new more aggressive approach.

- The German Kaiser felt that Germany should be a world power and should have overseas colonies and an empire like France and Britain had (see Source 7). The Germans had established two colonies in Africa, but they wanted more.
- In the 1890s the Kaiser ordered the building of a large navy, which soon became the world's second most powerful fleet. Britain's was the largest and most powerful.
- German leaders were very worried by what they called 'encirclement'. Friendship between Russia to the east and France to the west was seen as an attempt to 'surround' and threaten Germany.
- Germany was also concerned by the huge build-up of arms, especially in Russia, and was itself building up a vast army.

Austria–Hungary

Austria–Hungary was a sprawling empire in central Europe. It was made up of people of different ethnic groups: Germans, Czechs, Slovaks, Serbs and many others. Each group had its own customs and language. Many of these groups wanted independence from Austria–Hungary.

- In the north the Czech people wanted to rule themselves.
- The Slav people in the south-west (especially the Croats) wanted their own state.
- The Serbs living in the south wanted to be joined to the neighbouring state of Serbia.

By 1914 the main concern of the Emperor of Austria–Hungary was how to keep this fragmented empire together.

Austria–Hungary also faced problems from neighbouring states:

- Its newly independent neighbour Serbia was becoming a powerful force in the Balkans. Austria was very anxious that it should not become any stronger.
- Another neighbour, Russia, supported the Serbs, and had a very strong army.

Italy

Like Germany, Italy was formed from a collection of smaller states. At first, its main concern was to get its government established, but by 1914 the country was settled and was looking to 'flex its muscles'.

Like some of the other European powers, Italy wanted to set up colonies and build up an overseas empire. With this aim in mind, Italy joined Germany and Austria in the Triple Alliance. However, there is some evidence that Germany and Austria did not entirely trust their ally. In any case, Italy was not a strong industrial or military power.

The Triple Entente

Britain

In the nineteenth century Britain had tried not to get involved in European politics. Its attitude became known as 'splendid isolation' as it concentrated on its huge overseas empire (see Source on the following page). For most of the nineteenth century, Britain had regarded France and Russia as its two most dangerous rivals. However, by the early 1900s the picture had begun to change.

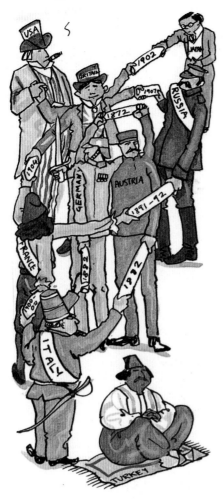

European alliances in 1914.

1 Do you think that preserving peace was a priority for Germany, Austria–Hungary or Italy?

There were three main reasons for this:

- France and Britain had reached a number of agreements about colonies in North Africa in 1904.
- Russia was defeated in a war against Japan in 1904. This weakened Russia so that Britain was less concerned about it.
- Above all, Britain was very worried about Germany. By 1914 Germany's industry had overtaken Britain's. The German Kaiser had made it clear that he wanted Germany to have an empire and a strong navy, which Britain saw as a serious threat to its own empire and navy.

Britain began to co-operate more with France and signed an agreement with it in 1904. Britain signed another agreement with Russia in 1907.

SOURCE 7

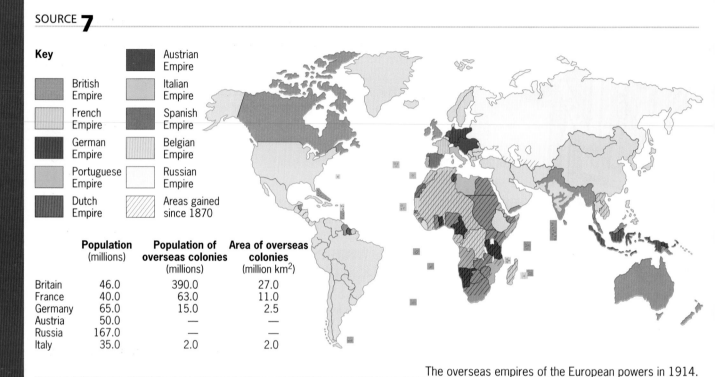

Key

British Empire	Austrian Empire
French Empire	Italian Empire
German Empire	Spanish Empire
Portuguese Empire	Belgian Empire
Dutch Empire	Russian Empire
	Areas gained since 1870

	Population (millions)	Population of overseas colonies (millions)	Area of overseas colonies (million km²)
Britain	46.0	390.0	27.0
France	40.0	63.0	11.0
Germany	65.0	15.0	2.5
Austria	50.0	—	—
Russia	167.0	—	—
Italy	35.0	2.0	2.0

The overseas empires of the European powers in 1914.

France

France had been defeated by Germany in a short war in 1870. Since then, Germany had built up a powerful army and strong industries. It had an ambitious leader in Kaiser Wilhelm. France was worried about the growing power of Germany, so the French had also built up their industries and armies. France had also developed a strong and close friendship with Russia. The main concerns of France were:

- to protect itself against attack by Germany
- to get back the rich industrial region of Alsace–Lorraine which Germany had taken from it in 1870.

Russia

Russia was by far the largest of all the six powers, but was also the most backward. The country was almost entirely agricultural, although loans from France had helped Russia to develop some industries.

Russia shared France's worries about the growing power of Germany.

It also had a long history of rivalry with Austria–Hungary. This was one reason why Russia was so friendly with Serbia. Another reason was that both Russians and Serbs were Slavs. Many other Slavs lived in Austria–Hungary's empire. Russia felt it should have influence over them.

Russia lost a war with Japan in 1905. There was then a revolution against the ruler, Tsar Nicholas II. He survived, but he knew Russia could not afford to lose in any other conflict. The Russians began to build up a large army in case of emergencies in the future.

1 Do you think that preserving peace was a priority for Britain, France or Russia?

Focus Task

1 Draw up a chart like this:

	Germany	Austria–Hungary	Italy
Britain			
France			
Russia			

2 Using the descriptions of the relationships between these countries on pages 213 and 214, complete the chart to show causes of tension between the countries. You may not be able to fill in all the spaces.

3 Which relationship is the greatest source of tension?

4 Explain how each of the following contributed to tensions between the European powers:
   a) colonies   **b)** people wanting independence   **c)** arms build-up.

2 Study the statistics in Source 8. Which country do you think is the strongest? Explain your choice.

3 Which alliance do you think is the strongest? Explain your choice.

SOURCE **8**

		Britain	France	Russia	Germany	Austria–Hungary	Italy
Population (millions)		46	40	167	65	50	35
Steel production (millions of tons)		7.9	4	4	17	2.6	3.9
Merchant ships (millions of tons)		20	2	0.75	5	3	1.75
Foreign trade (£ million per year)		1	0.4	0.2	1	0.2	n/a
Number of soldiers available (in thousands), excluding reserve forces		248	1800	3409	2200	1338	750
Warships (including under construction)		122	46	26	85	24	36
Submarines		64	73	29	23	6	12

Resources of the Great Powers in 1914.

The Balance of Power

Politicians at the time called this system of alliances the 'Balance of Power'. They believed that the size and power of the two alliances would prevent either side from starting a war.

SOURCE **9**

4 Look at Source 9. Did the cartoonist think that the alliances helped to prevent war?

5 Do you think that the alliances made war more likely or less likely?

A modern redrawing of an American cartoon published in the *Brooklyn Eagle*, July 1914. The cartoon was called 'The Chain of Friendship'.

The tension builds, 1900–14

Anglo-German naval rivalry

SOURCE 10

There is no comparison between the importance of the German navy to Germany, and the importance of our navy to us. Our navy is to us what their army is to them. To have a strong navy would increase Germany's prestige and influence, but it is not a matter of life and death to them as it is to us.

Sir Edward Grey, British Foreign Secretary, in a speech to Parliament in 1909.

SOURCE 11

You English are like mad bulls; you see red everywhere! What on earth has come over you, that you should heap on such suspicion? What can I do more? I have always stood up as a friend of England.

Kaiser Wilhelm, speaking in an interview with the *Daily Telegraph* in 1908. The Kaiser liked England and had friends there. He was a cousin of King George V of Britain.

One of the most significant causes of tension in Europe was the naval rivalry which developed after 1900. Ever since the Battle of Trafalgar in 1805, Britain had ruled the seas without any challenge. Its navy was the most powerful in the world. This situation began to change in 1898 when the new Kaiser, Wilhelm, announced his intention to build a powerful German navy.

Britain felt very threatened by this. Germany's navy was much smaller than Britain's but the British navy was spread all over the world, protecting the British Empire. Germany didn't have much of an empire. Why did it need a navy? What was Germany going to do with all of these warships concentrated in the North Sea?

Not surprisingly, Germany did not see things the same way. The Kaiser and his admirals felt that Germany needed a navy to protect its growing trade. They felt that the British were over-reacting to the German naval plans.

Britain was not convinced by what the Germans said. In fact, in 1906 Britain raised the stakes in the naval race by launching HMS *Dreadnought,* the first of a new class of warships. Germany responded by building its own 'Dreadnoughts'. The naval race was well and truly on and both Britain and Germany spent millions on their new ships.

SOURCE 12

Guns on rotating turrets can fire shells over 9 km in any direction

Fast modern turbine engines

Thick armour plating

A British 'Dreadnought', the HMS *Barham*, with the British fleet in Scapa Flow.

SOURCE 13

1906	
1907	
1908	
1909	
1910	
1911	
1912	
1913	
1914	

Britain — Total built by 1914: 29   Germany — Total built by 1914: 17

Number of 'Dreadnoughts' built by Britain and Germany, 1906–14.

1 Why was Britain concerned by Germany's naval plans?
2 How did Germany react to Britain's concerns?
3 Do you think that either country was acting unreasonably? Give your reasons.

Profile

Kaiser Wilhelm II

- Born 1861, with a badly withered left arm. Historians also think he suffered slight brain damage at birth, which affected both his hearing and his attention span.
- He did not have a loving family.
- He became Kaiser at the age of 27 when German industry was growing fast and Germany was becoming a world power.
- He was famous for his energy and enthusiasm, but he was also very unpredictable.
- He was keen on military parades and liked to be photographed wearing his military uniform. He appointed military people to most of the important positions in his government.
- He was very ambitious for Germany. He wanted Germany to be recognised as the greatest power in Europe by the older European states.
- He liked physical exercise, and practical jokes.
- He was very closely involved in Germany's plans for war.
- When Germany was defeated in 1918 he fled into exile. He died in 1941.

The arms race on land

While Britain and Germany built up their navies, the major powers on mainland Europe were also building up their armies.

SOURCE 14

	1900	1910	1914
France	0.7m	0.8m	5.0m
Britain	0.6m	0.55m	0.25m
Russia	1.1m	1.3m	6.0m
Austria–Hungary	0.25m	0.3m	3.0m
Germany	0.5m	0.7m	4.9m
Italy	0.25m	0.3m	0.75m

The arms build-up. Military personnel of the powers, 1900–14 (including trained reserves).

SOURCE 15

The arms race in which all the major powers were involved contributed to the sense that war was bound to come, and soon. Financing it caused serious financial difficulties for all the governments involved in the race; and yet they were convinced there was no way of stopping it.

Although publicly the arms race was justified to prevent war, no government had in fact been deterred from arming by the programmes of their rivals, but rather increased the pace of their own armament production.

James Joll, *Origins of the First World War*, 1992. Joll is a well-respected British historian with an expert knowledge of this topic.

In Germany, in particular, war and militarism were glorified. The Kaiser surrounded himself with military advisers. He staged military rallies and processions. He loved to be photographed in military uniforms. He involved himself closely in Germany's military planning.

Plans for war

Many countries felt so sure that war was 'bound to come' sooner or later that they began to make very detailed plans for what to do if and when it did.

Germany

Germany's army was not the biggest army in Europe but most people agreed it was the best trained and the most powerful.

The problem facing the German commanders was that if a war broke out they would probably have to fight against Russia and France at the same time.

The Germans came up with the Schlieffen Plan. Under this plan they would quickly attack and defeat France, then turn their forces on Russia which (the Germans were sure) would be slow to get its troops ready for war.

SOURCE 16

General von Moltke said: I believe war is unavoidable; war the sooner the better. But we ought to do more through the press to prepare the population for a war against Russia . . . the enemies are arming more strongly than we are.

From the diary of Admiral von Muller, head of the Kaiser's naval cabinet, December 1912.

SOURCE 17

In Moltke's opinion there was no alternative to making preventive war in order to defeat the enemy while we still had a chance of victory . . . I pointed out that the Kaiser . . . would only agree to fight if our enemies forced war upon us . . .

Written by Gottlieb von Jagow, the German Foreign Secretary, May 1914. He was writing this from memory, soon after the end of the war.

1 Read Source 17. What do you think the writer means by 'preventive war'?
2 Does either Source 16 or 17 suggest that people in Germany wanted a war?

SOURCE 18

The remark 'England and Germany are bound to fight' makes war a little more likely each time it is made, and is therefore made more often by the gutter press of each nation.

From *Howard's End*, a widely read novel by EM Forster, published in 1910.

3 Source 18 comes from a novel. In what ways is it useful as evidence about the mood in Britain before the First World War?

Austria–Hungary

Austria–Hungary knew it needed the help of Germany to hold back Russia. It too relied on the success of the Schlieffen Plan so that Germany could help it to defeat Russia.

Russia

The Russian army was badly equipped, but it was huge. Given enough time, Russia could eventually put millions of soldiers into the field. The Russian plan was to overwhelm Germany's and Austria's armies by sheer weight of numbers.

France

France had a large and well-equipped army. Its main plan of attack was known as Plan 17. French troops would charge across the frontier and attack deep into Germany, forcing surrender.

Britain

Britain's military planners had been closely but secretly involved in collaboration with French commanders. This led to Britain setting up the British Expeditionary Force (BEF), consisting of 150,000 highly trained and well-equipped professional soldiers. The BEF could go to France and fight alongside the French at short notice.

One thing that unites all of these plans was the assumption that a war, if and when it came, would be quick. These military plans were designed to achieve a quick victory. No one planned for what to do if the war dragged on. It was almost universally assumed that none of the powers would be able to keep up a long-drawn-out war. The sheer cost of a war would lead to economic collapse (of the enemy only, of course) and so the war would be over in a matter of weeks or months.

With so much talk of war and plans for war, you might think, as many at the time did, that war was inevitable.

Morocco, 1905 and 1911

In 1905 and 1911, two crises in Morocco raised the temperature in Europe.

In 1905 the Kaiser visited Morocco in North Africa. Germany was building up its own African empire and had colonies in central and southern Africa (see Source 7 on page 214). The Kaiser was now keen to show that Germany was an important power in North Africa as well. The French had plans to take control of Morocco so the Kaiser made a speech saying he supported independence for Morocco. The French were furious at his interfering in their affairs. An international conference was held in Algeciras in 1906. But the conference did not cool things down. In fact, it did the opposite: at the conference the Kaiser was humiliated. He had wanted to be seen as a major power in Africa. Instead his views were rejected. He was treated as if he had no right to speak on such matters. This made him bitter. He was also alarmed by the way that Britain and France stuck together at the conference to oppose him. These old rivals now seemed very close.

In 1907, in the wake of the Moroccan crisis, Britain and France formed an alliance with Russia, the Triple Entente. The Entente powers saw their alliance as security against German aggression. The Kaiser and his people saw a threatening policy of encirclement, with hostile powers surrounding Germany.

In 1911 Morocco saw another crisis. The French tried to take over Morocco again. They said they were prepared to compensate Germany if its trade suffered as a result. However, the Kaiser's response was to send a gunboat (the *Panther*) to Agadir. The British feared that the Kaiser wanted to set up a naval base in Agadir, and they did not want German ships in the Mediterranean. Another conference was called. The British and French again stood firm against Germany. France took control of Morocco. Germany was given land in central Africa as compensation. Behind the scenes, Britain and France reached an agreement that the French should patrol the Mediterranean and the Royal Navy should defend France's Atlantic and North Sea coasts.

SOURCE **19**

The Balkans in 1908.

The Balkans: the spark that lit the bonfire

The Balkans were a very unstable area.

- Different nationalities were mixed together.
- The area had been ruled by Turkey for many centuries, but Turkish power was now in decline.
- The new governments which had been set up in place of Turkish rule were regularly in dispute with each other.
- Two great powers, Russia and Austria, bordered the countries in this region. Both wanted to control the area because it gave them access to the Mediterranean.

The first Balkan crisis came in 1908. Austria took over the provinces of Bosnia and Herzegovina. Russia and Serbia protested, but they backed down when Germany made it clear that it supported Austria. Neither Russia nor Serbia was prepared to risk war with Germany over this issue. However, there were some serious consequences. Austria now felt confident that Germany would back it in future disputes. Some historians think that this made Austria too confident, and encouraged it to make trouble with Serbia and Russia. Russia resented being faced down in 1909. It quickened its arms build-up. It was determined not to back down again.

From 1910 to 1911 there was a series of local wars. Serbia emerged from these as the most powerful country in the Balkans. This was very serious for Austria. Serbia had a strong army and it was a close ally of Russia. Austria decided that Serbia would have to be dealt with. By 1914 Austria was looking for a good excuse to crush Serbia.

Austria's opportunity came with the murder of Archduke Franz Ferdinand and his wife Sophie in Sarajevo (see pages 210–211). Although there was no hard evidence that Princip was acting under orders from the Serbian government, Austria blamed Serbia. Frantic diplomatic effort gave Austria a guarantee of German backing (see Witness 9 on page 221). With this support Austria now felt secure enough to deal with the Serbian problem once and for all. It gave Serbia a ten-point ultimatum that would effectively have made Serbia part of the Austrian Empire. The Serbs could not possibly accept it. When the Serbs asked for time to consider, Austria refused and declared war on 28 July 1914. The slide to all-out war had begun.

SOURCE **20**

When I first heard of the assassination [murder] . . . I felt it was a grave matter . . . but my fears were soon calmed . . . the Kaiser left on his yachting holiday and . . . still more reassuring, the head of the German army left for his cure in a foreign spa [health resort] . . .

I remember that an influential Hungarian lady called on me and told me that we were taking the murder of the Grand Duke too quietly . . . it had provoked a storm in Austria . . . and might lead to war with Serbia . . . However, the official reports we had did not seem to justify this alarmist view.

David Lloyd George, *Memoirs*, 1938. David Lloyd George was a government minister in 1914 and became Prime Minister in 1916. His memoirs have a reputation for inconsistency.

4 Look back at your answer to question 2 on page 211. Would you like to change your answer now?

Activity

The atmosphere in Europe between 1900 and 1914 has been likened to a bonfire waiting to be lit.

1 Make your own copy of this bonfire diagram, and add labels to suggest factors that made war possible.
2 Put major factors on big sticks, less important factors on smaller sticks.
3 Add more sticks to the fire if you wish to show more factors.
4 Why do you think the Sarajevo murders 'lit the fire' when previous events such as the Moroccan crisis in 1905 had not? Mention these points in your answer:
   a) Austria's worries about Serbia
   b) the build-up of international problems
   c) the way the alliances worked.

Did Germany cause the war?

SOURCE **21**

The Allied governments affirm, and Germany accepts, the responsibility of Germany and her allies for causing all the loss and damage to which the Allied governments and their peoples have been subjected as a result of the war.

The war guilt clause from the Treaty of Versailles, 1919.

After the war, the victorious Allies forced the defeated Germany to sign the 'war guilt' clause (Source 21). Germany had to accept that it was responsible both for starting the war and for all the damage caused by it. However, as the state 'on trial', Germany refused to accept the sole blame. Historians have argued about this issue ever since. Some have continued to blame Germany. Others have reached different verdicts.

Focus Task

Was Germany to blame for the war?

What do you think? Was Germany to blame?
Your task is to look over the evidence and hold your own retrial, looking back from today.
You will study evidence and hear from witnesses. You must then reach one of four verdicts:

Verdict 1: Germany was rightly blamed for starting the war.

Verdict 2: Germany was mainly responsible for starting the war, but the other powers should accept some of the blame.

Verdict 3: All of the major powers helped to start the war. They should share the blame.

Verdict 4: No one was to blame. The powers were swept along towards an inevitable war. It could not be stopped.

This is how to run the trial. You can work on your own, or in groups.
1 Draw up a table like the one below:

Witness	Which verdict does the witness support?	What evidence does the witness give to support the viewpoint?	Can I trust the witness?

2 Read all the witnesses' statements on page 221 Complete columns 1 and 2.
3 In column 3, note what evidence the witness gives to support his/her viewpoint.
4 In column 4, note what might make the witness reliable or unreliable.
   Think about:
   - the date and origin of each source
   - whether the witness was involved in the events of the time
   - the value and reliability of each witness.
5 Look through the other information in this chapter to see if there are other witnesses you should consider.
6 Choose your verdict from verdicts 1–4.
7 Once you have chosen a verdict, you should sum up the evidence for it in a short explanation.
   Remember to explain why you have chosen your verdict, but also explain why you have rejected the others.
8 Use your table and explanation for a class debate.

The witnesses

WITNESS 1

German militarism, which is the crime of the last fifty years, had been working for this for twenty-five years. It is the logical result of their doctrine. It had to come.

Walter Hines Page, US Ambassador in London, 1914. The USA was an ally of Britain and France during the war, and fought in it against Germany from 1917 to 1918.

WITNESS 2

Bethmann stood in the centre of the room . . . There was a look of anguish in his eyes . . . For an instant neither of us spoke. At last I said to him: 'Well, tell me, at least, how it all happened.' He raised his arms to heaven and answered, 'Oh – if only I knew!'

Prince von Bülow, speaking in 1918, remembers calling on the German Chancellor Bethmann-Hollweg in August 1914.

WITNESS 3

None of the rulers of the Great Powers really knew what they were fighting about in August 1914 . . . the crisis gathered pace and the calculations of statesmen were overwhelmed by the rapid succession of events, the tide of emotion in the various capitals, and the demands of military planning.

The Origins of the First World War by British historian LCF Turner, 1983.

WITNESS 4

The Schlieffen Plan must rank as one of the supreme idiocies of modern times . . . It restricted the actions of the German government disastrously. In July 1914 they had just two choices; either to abandon the only plan they had to win the next war, or to go to war immediately.

Historian DE Marshall in *The Great War: Myth and Reality*, 1988.

WITNESS 5

The World War was directly started by certain officials of the Russian General Staff. But their conduct was caused by the criminal activity of an Austrian Foreign Minister, and this in turn was aided by criminal negligence at Berlin . . .

But they would have been quite unable to start any war, had they not been equally with millions of common people . . . willing agents of forces moving the world towards war . . .

From the *Encyclopaedia Britannica*, 1926.

WITNESS 6

We are being forced to admit that we alone are to blame for the war: such an admission on my lips would be a lie. We are not seeking to absolve [pardon] Germany from all responsibility for this World War, and for the way in which it was fought. However, we do strongly deny that Germany, whose people felt they were fighting a war of defence, should be forced to accept sole responsibility.

Count Brockdorff-Rantzau, head of the German delegates at Versailles, 1919.

WITNESS 7

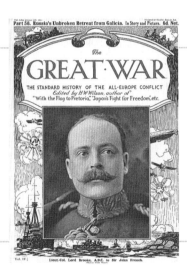

The greatest war of modern times, and perhaps in the whole history of the human race, was begun by Germany using the crime of a schoolboy as an excuse . . . Austria had regarded the growing power of Serbia with concern for many years . . . The situation in Europe seemed to encourage the German peoples in this adventure. England, it was thought, could do nothing . . . with the threats of civil war in Ireland. Russia was in the midst of the reorganisation of her army . . . As for France, Germany believed herself quite competent to deal with her, and sought an opportunity of doing so.

From *The Great War – The Standard History of the All-Europe Conflict*, 1914 (Vol IV). This was a patriotic weekly journal written and published in Britain, describing the war 'as it happened'.

WITNESS 8

German: *I wonder what history will make of all of this?*

Clemenceau: *History will not say that Belgium invaded Germany!*

From a conversation between French Prime Minister Clemenceau and a German representative at the peace conference after the war. Clemenceau was a hard-line anti-German.

WITNESS 9

. . . the Kaiser authorised me to inform our gracious majesty that we might, in this case as in all others, rely upon Germany's full support . . . it was the Kaiser's opinion that this action must not be delayed . . . Russia was in no way prepared for war and would think twice before it appealed to arms . . . If we had really recognised the necessity of warlike action against Serbia, the Kaiser would regret if we did not make use of the present moment which is all in our favour.

Count Szogyeny, the Austrian ambassador in Berlin, reporting a famous conversation with the Kaiser, July 1914. Historians are divided as to whether the Kaiser was making a planned policy statement or was simply giving reassurance on the spur of the moment.

10.2 What happened on the Western Front?

As soon as war was declared Germany's Schlieffen Plan went into operation. The Schlieffen Plan (see page 217) was simple but risky. The idea was to send German forces through Belgium and to quickly knock France out of the war. The theory was that Russia would take a long time to mobilise (get its forces ready for war). It was an all-or-nothing gamble. The Germans had to try to get to Paris and defeat France within six weeks, so that they could then send all their troops to fight against Russia. However, as Source 1 shows, neither the Belgians nor the Russians did what the Schlieffen Plan expected them to do.

1 Explain what Source 2 is saying about Belgium and Germany.

SOURCE 1

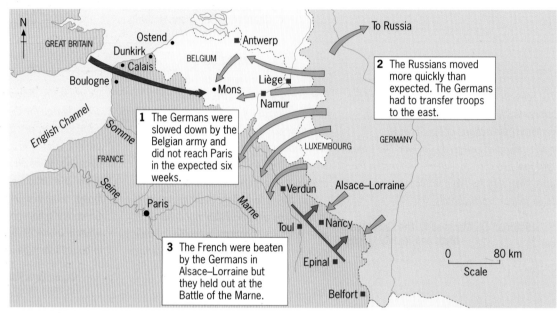

Key
➤ British forces
➤ German forces
➤ French forces
■ Fortress towns

2 The Russians moved more quickly than expected. The Germans had to transfer troops to the east.

1 The Germans were slowed down by the Belgian army and did not reach Paris in the expected six weeks.

3 The French were beaten by the Germans in Alsace–Lorraine but they held out at the Battle of the Marne.

Why the Schlieffen Plan failed.

SOURCE 2

A cartoon from *Punch*, August 1914.

At first, it looked as though the Germans could succeed. The German army invaded Belgium on 4 August. The Belgians put up a heroic resistance from their frontier forts but it did not stop the crushing German advance. Massive German artillery bombardments destroyed the Belgian forts and soon enormous numbers of well-equipped and well-trained German infantry and cavalry were moving ominously towards the French border. Even so, the Belgian resistance won them many friends and bought time for British and French troops to mobilise.

The British Expeditionary Force, led by Sir John French, landed in France and met the advancing Germans at Mons on 23 August. This small but well-trained force of professional soldiers gave the Germans a nasty shock. The troops at Mons were well led by Lieutenant-General Douglas Haig — remember that name, you'll find out a lot more about him later — and were using Lee Enfield .303 bolt action rifles which could fire quickly and accurately. German reports from the time showed that they thought they were up against machine-gun fire.

2 Read Source 3. What factors had influenced Walter Bloem's view of English soldiers?
3 Why was Bloem's first taste of action such a shock to him?

SOURCE **3**

Sunday

Reports were coming back that the English were in front of us. English soldiers? We knew what they looked like from the comics; short scarlet tunics with small caps set at an angle on their heads, or bearskins with the chin-strap under the lip instead of under the chin. There was much joking about this, and also about a remark by Bismarck [the former German leader] about sending the police to arrest the English army.

(The Attack begins . . .)

We had no sooner left the edge of the wood than a volley of bullets whistled past our noses and cracked into the trees behind. Five or six cries near me, five or six of my grey lads collapsed on the grass. Damn it! This was serious . . . ! Forward again – at the double! We crossed the track, jumped the broad ditch full of water, and then on across the squelching meadow. More firing, closer now and tearing into our ranks, more lads falling . . . the 160 men that left the wood with me had shrunk to less than 100 . . .

From now on matters went from bad to worse. Wherever I looked, right or left, there were dead or wounded, quivering in convulsions, groaning terribly, blood oozing from flesh wounds . . .

We had to go back . . . A bad defeat, there could be no gainsaying it; in our first battle we had been badly beaten, and by the English – by the English we had so laughed at a few hours before.

Written by Walter Bloem, a German soldier, about the battle at Mons in Belgium. This was Walter Bloem's first experience of fighting.

Despite their early success, the British were hugely outnumbered. In fact, the best they could do was to organise an orderly retreat. They did slow the Germans down, but only the French had enough forces in the field to stop the German advance. However, the French were facing their own problems.

When war broke out, the French followed their Plan 17 (see page 218) and launched a direct attack on Germany through Alsace–Lorraine. On 20 August the German forces defending the frontier cut the attacking French troops to ribbons with artillery and machine-gun fire. The French lost over 200,000 men in twelve days. They now abandoned Plan 17, and regrouped their forces to defend Paris from the advancing Germans (see Source 4).

SOURCE **4**

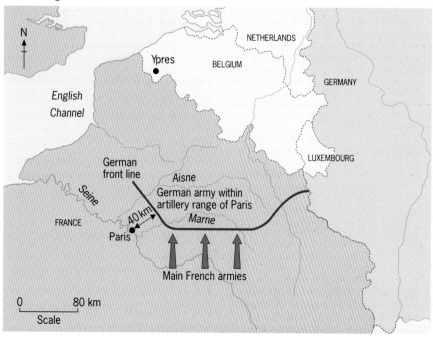

The threat to Paris. The situation in early September 1914.

That [French soldiers] who have retreated for ten days, sleeping on the ground and half dead with fatigue, should be able to take up their rifles when the bugle sounds is a thing which we never expected.

Written by General von Kluck, a German army commander, after the Battle of the Marne.

The Battle of the Marne

The French may have been on the defensive in September 1914, but by this stage things were not going entirely well for the Germans either. The German Supreme Commander Moltke had to pull 100,000 troops out of the army advancing on Paris because the Russians had mobilised far more quickly than expected and had already invaded Germany. This was to prove the break that the British and French needed. The German army also faced another problem. Their advance had been so fast that their supplies of food and ammunition could not keep up. The German soldiers were underfed and exhausted.

Von Kluck, the German commander, decided he could not swing round Paris according to the original plan, so he advanced straight towards it. While the Germans advanced on foot, the French diverted troops to Paris by rail, and then on to the front, transporting some of them there by taxi! The German army was weary and overstretched. The French were fighting to save their country.

SOURCE **6**

The Battle of the Marne, 1914.

The combined British and French forces were able to stop the German advance along the line of the River Marne. They then counter-attacked and pushed the Germans back to the River Aisne. However, they could not drive them out of France entirely.

Neither side could make any progress and by 8 September troops on both sides were digging trenches to protect themselves from snipers and shell fire. Soon after, they added machine guns and barbed wire. Until now, it had been a war of movement, but these were the first signs of the stalemate that was to come.

SOURCE **7**

15 September 1914

We got here pretty beat at 11 pm last night . . . The last part was very tiring to the men and a good many fell out . . . We must have done twenty-five miles yesterday.

October 1914

We can apparently get no further because the Germans have brought up strong reinforcements, and also have a strongly prepared position which we are now up against, so it looks like another siege unless we are reinforced here.

25 October 1914

The last few days have been very busy. Our former forward line was too difficult to hold, we are too weak to shove ahead, so now we are back in a strong position which we dug before withdrawing. The end of our advance was shown by the almost complete loss of the Royal Irish in Le Pilly. Apparently they pushed on too far and were heavily attacked and surrounded. There are only about seventy survivors all told – a bad business.

From the diary of Billy Congreve, a young lieutenant from a soldiering family. He was widely respected and in two years rose to the rank of major. He kept a personal diary from 1914 until he was killed by a sniper at Ypres in 1916.

1 Read Source 7. What do the extracts tell you about how warfare changed on the Western Front between August and November 1914?
2 Is there any evidence that the mood of the soldiers had changed?

SOURCE 8

Key
- British forces
- German forces
- French forces
- Fortress towns
- Front line in early 1915

The race to the sea.

The race to the sea

The Battle of the Marne was a turning point. The Schlieffen Plan had failed. Germany was caught up in a two-front war. Worse still, the German generals realised that they could not break through the enemy lines. Moltke was replaced by a new commander, Falkenhayn, who decided to try to outflank (get round the end of) his enemy's lines. The charge began on 12 October. It became known as 'the race to the sea'.

As the Germans charged west towards the sea, the British and French moved troops to block them whenever it seemed that the Germans were about to break through. One observer at the time called these 'the Railway Battles of Northern France', because both sides moved their troops by rail.

The first Battle of Ypres in Belgium

The key battle in this race to the sea was the first Battle of Ypres (there were two more later in the war) from 12 October to 11 November 1914. The BEF lost around 50,000 men and the Germans probably 100,000, but the British (led by Lt-Gen. Haig in this area) held this important ground. They kept control of the English Channel ports, which meant they could be supplied with equipment and reinforcements.

By November 1914 it was a deadlock. The BEF had been decimated. The French had already suffered around 1 million dead or wounded in just ten weeks. Despite this, the French army tried to break through the German lines in Artois and Champagne in December, but they were beaten back with heavy losses. As 1914 ended, the fighting had reached a stalemate which was to last until 1918. Millions of troops were dug into a line of trenches that stretched from the sea in the west to the Alps in the east. It became known as the 'Western Front'. Over the next pages you will examine the war on the Western Front in detail.

SOURCE 9

A German painting from December 1914. The artist, Alfred Kubin, enthusiastically supported war earlier in 1914. By December, his work had changed to this style in which ghosts and demons often featured. The figure in this painting represents death. The houses represent ordinary life and people.

Focus Task

Why was the war not over by Christmas?

It is Christmas 1914. People were told that the war would be over by Christmas. You have to explain why it isn't.

Work in pairs. You are going to write two reports about the progress of the war from August to December 1914. One of you should write for the British Prime Minister, explaining events as fully as you can. The other should write for the general public back in Britain, trying to give a positive and encouraging message about how the war is going.
   You may wish to mention these points:
- the successes and failures of the various plans
- the important battles that have taken place
- the new lessons being learnt about warfare
- the casualties
- the morale of the troops.

Conclude with:
- your explanation as to why the war is not over by Christmas
- your views on how the war will be fought through 1915.

When you have finished, compare your two reports. Discuss:
1 Are there differences in tone?
2 Have you included different details?
3 Is one more accurate than the other?

How important were new developments in warfare?

You have seen how the war became bogged down in a stalemate of trench warfare by the end of 1914. There is a traditional view of the war which says that the stalemate continued because the commanders were too incompetent and inflexible to try out any new weapons, technology or ideas. In fact, this idea is quite wrong. All the armies on the Western Front constantly improvised new weapons and tried out new tactics, but these measures often cancelled each other out. In this section we are going to look at some of the main developments in warfare on the Western Front.

Artillery

The First World War was an artillery war. Many people think that machine guns caused the most casualties in the war but this is wrong. Artillery bombardments caused more casualties than any other weapon. The artillery had two main jobs – to destroy enemy positions and defences so they could be captured and to destroy enemy guns.

   At the beginning of the war the guns were not very accurate. Firing from well behind their own lines, artillery often bombarded their own forward trenches before they got their range right. By the end of the war, artillery was much more powerful, and it was also more accurate. By 1918 artillery tactics were extremely sophisticated as well (see Source 17 and page 240 – the Hundred Days). Artillery was the key weapon of the Great War. Throughout the war a vast part of European industry was given over to making shells for the artillery. British performance in the war became more effective after 1916 because British industry was supplying enough guns and shells and British forces were using these weapons effectively.

SOURCE **10**

We are the guns, and your masters! Saw ye our flashes?
Heard ye the scream of our shells in the night, and the shuddering crashes?
Saw ye our work by the roadside, the shrouded things lying,
Moaning to God that He made them – the maimed and the dying?
Husbands or sons,
   Fathers or lovers, we break them. We are the guns!

An extract from the poem 'The Voice of the Guns' by Gilbert Frankau. Frankau was an officer in the Royal Artillery.

SOURCE **11**

The bodies of two German soldiers in a trench hit by British artillery at the Battle of the Somme, July 1916.

Activity

A book publisher is producing a book of war poetry and is looking for an image to accompany Source 10. Write a short report explaining whether you think the image in Source 11 is suitable. If you think it is not you could try searching the websites of picture libraries for possible alternatives.

Machine guns

This weapon is the one which most people associate with the appalling casualties of the First World War. Once the war became a stalemate the infantryman became the backbone of the British army. The job of the infantry was to try and capture enemy positions (and hold on to them) or to defend positions they already held.

SOURCE 12

British machine gun crew in 1916.

1. How does Source 12 help to explain why the machine gun was primarily a defensive weapon?
2. Is Source 12 more useful as a source on how the machine gun was used or on how effective it was?
3. Do you think Source 13 or Source 14 is more useful to a historian studying the impact of gas attacks? Explain your answer by referring to both sources.

This is where the machine gun came into its own. Machine guns at the start of the war were very large and heavy so they were not very useful in an attack on an enemy trench. However, they were devastatingly effective as defensive weapons. A machine gun could fire eight bullets a second or more, and each trench would have a number of machine guns. During an infantry charge it could cut down a whole brigade in minutes. The machine gun made it inevitable that any charge on an enemy trench would cost many lives. Machine guns proved to be devastating against British forces in the Battle of the Somme (see page 236). After the war British commanders were often criticised for underestimating the machine gun, and Sir Douglas Haig is said to have believed that it was overrated. However, some officers did have faith in it. At the start of the war British troops had the same ratio of machine guns to troops as the Germans and the British army established its first dedicated Machine Gun Corps in 1915. By 1918 most platoons had their own machine guns and troops even had lightweight sub-machine guns. These guns proved very effective in actions like the capture of the St Quentin Canal in 1918 (see page 240 Hundred Days).

Poison gas

The first poison gas attack was in April 1915. The Germans released chlorine which wafted on the wind across no man's land into the British trenches. There was panic there as the soldiers coughed, retched and struggled to breathe.

From that time gas attacks by both sides became a regular feature of the war. To start with, the aim of a gas attack was to disable enemy troops so that your own infantry charge would be successful. Later, scientists on both sides began to perfect new and more lethal gases such as mustard gas, which had a perfumed smell but which burned, blinded or slowly killed the victims over four to five weeks.

However, scientists also developed very effective gas masks. Soldiers in the trenches would carry their gas masks with them all the time. At the alert they would put them on. As a result only 3,000 British troops died from gas in the whole war. The main significance of gas was its psychological impact. Soldiers who could bear a long bombardment by artillery often lived in fear of a gas attack.

SOURCE 13

GAS! GAS! Quick, boys! – An ecstasy of fumbling.
Fitting the clumsy helmets just in time;
But someone still was yelling out and stumbling
And flound'ring like a man in fire or lime . . .
Dim, through the misty panes and thick green light,
As under a green sea, I saw him drowning.
In all my dreams, before my helpless sight,
He plunges at me, guttering, choking, drowning.
If in some smothering dreams you too could pace
Behind the wagon that we flung him in,

And watch the white eyes writhing in his face,
His hanging face, like a devil's sick of sin;
If you could hear, at every jolt, the blood
Come gargling from the froth-corrupted lungs,
Obscene as cancer, bitter as the cud
Of vile, incurable sores on innocent tongues, –
My friend, you would not tell with such high zest
To children ardent for some desperate glory,
The old Lie: Dulce et decorum est
Pro patria mori.

'Dulce Et Decorum Est' (How right and good it is to die for your country), by Wilfred Owen. Owen was an officer in the British Army. He was killed in 1918, not long before the end of the war.

SOURCE 14

Gassed, a painting by John Singer Sargent. A famous portrait painter, Sargent was commissioned in 1918 to paint a memorial picture of the soldiers killed and injured in the war.

THE TANK
is a travelling fortress
that clears the way for
our soldiers.

It cuts through the wire - under fire
It saves lives
It is *our* War discovery
It is a matter of pride to help to
build Tanks

A poster produced by the government to encourage people to support the building of tanks by buying war bonds and saving scrap metal.

A still of a 'dogfight' (aerial combat). Such battles were often shown in films.

Tanks

The tank was a British invention. Early in the war inventors took the idea of a tank to the army leaders but it was rejected as impractical. However, Winston Churchill, head of the navy, thought that the idea had potential and his department funded its development.

Two years later, the tanks were used for the first time at the Battle of the Somme. They advanced ahead of the infantry, crushing barbed-wire defences and spraying the enemy with machine-gun fire. They caused alarm among the Germans and raised the morale of the British troops. Surely this was the weapon that could achieve a breakthrough!

However, these first machines only moved at walking pace. They were not very manoeuvrable and were very unreliable – more than half of them broke down before they got to the German trenches. It was not until a year later, in November 1917 at Cambrai, that tanks actually achieved great success. Unfortunately they were too successful. They blasted through enemy lines so quickly that the infantry could not keep up.

By 1918, German forces were using armour-piercing machine-gun bullets to deadly effect. They had also learned how to adapt field guns to fire at tanks. Tanks were virtually impossible to miss because they were so large and slow. However, the tank offered a significant boost to British morale.

1 What do you think was the purpose of the poster in Source 15?
2 Does the existence of this poster prove that the tank was a significant weapon? Explain your answer.

Aircraft

One of the few aspects of the fighting in the First World War which gained a glamorous reputation was the war in the air. All countries had brilliant pilots and the thrill of heroic flying in up-to-date machines is easy to understand. The newspapers and journals began to pick up on the story of 'flying aces' from an early stage in the war and moviemakers glamorised them after the war. But were they really important?

In 1914 aeroplanes were extremely primitive. They were also very unreliable and highly dangerous. Losses were very high indeed, especially among new pilots. At the start of the war, planes did the same job as observation balloons.

Soon their speed and mobility meant that commanders used them for detailed reconnaissance work over enemy trenches. The photographs they took were very valuable. At the Battle of the Marne they spotted a potential break in the Allied lines that could have been fatal for the Allies.

Enemy aircraft would be sent to shoot down reconnaissance flights and soon the 'dogfight' had emerged. In these early battles in the air, the pilots used pistols and rifles. It was not until April 1915 that planes were successfully fitted with machine guns. These guns were synchronised so that they did not shoot through their own propeller. By 1918 spectacular aerial battles were common over the Western Front. The rickety early planes had given way to sleek fighters such as the Sopwith Camel and the Fokker Triplane. Planes also played a part in slowing down the German advance in 1918 and in the Allied advances of the Hundred Days (see page 240).

In four years aircraft had changed from string bags to sophisticated machines. In four years the Royal Naval Air Service and Royal Flying Corps had gone from having 37 aeroplanes to 23,000. Even so, aircraft were really only a side show to the land war. Air power was, if anything, more valuable at sea where the aircraft could observe and attack shipping.

Putting it all together

It is important to remember that all of these weapons and developments took place as the war was being fought. They were often the result of ordinary soldiers trying out ideas which officers then recommended for wider use. There was a constant exchange of information and discussion between troops, front-line officers and senior commanders. All of this meant that the British army became increasingly professional as the war went on and that between 1914 and 1918 the way it fought the war was transformed.

SOURCE 17

Look at a photograph of a group of British infantrymen in 1914 … Then look at a photograph from October 1918. The shape and silhouette are different, for the infantryman now resembles not the gamekeeper but the industrial worker. The faces are different, for the average age of senior officers has dropped by about ten years … Half the infantrymen in France are eighteen years old, although all too often young faces frame old eyes. They now wear steel helmet and leather jerkin. It is far more difficult to make out the officers. Even those who are wearing officer style uniforms have moved their badges of rank to their shoulders instead of their chests.

By 1918 some wholly new weapons are in evidence. Pouches bulge with hand grenades and respirators are always handy, for both sides now use gas as a matter of course.

… And the infantry now has its own artillery. Trench mortars are attached to each infantry brigade … In 1914 most artillery was close behind the firing line … In 1918 artillery was tucked into folds of ground behind the infantry, there were far more heavy guns, lurking unseen over the horizon, with a power and range that the men of 1914 could never have dreamt of. Forward observation parties abounded, along with signallers. There were wireless sets at all main headquarters. Even some aircraft were now fitted with wireless to enable them to control the fire of the heavy guns. … By 1918 the air was very busy: one artillery officer reckoned that he could often see fifty aircraft in the sky at any one time.

An extract from *Tommy: The British Soldier on the Western Front* by the British military historian Professor Richard Holmes (2004).

Focus Task

How important were new developments in warfare?

You have been approached by a company designing a new computer game which is set in the First World War. You have been asked to create profiles of some of the weapons and developments which emerged during the war which game players can use for reference. Take all of the developments on pages 226–29 and rate their significance in the following terms:

◆ why it was developed and how it was used
◆ examples of this weapon in action
◆ whether the weapon developed further during the course of the war
◆ the impact of the weapon (for example the casualties caused, the psychological impact)
◆ the reputation of the weapon (think about different groups of people such as the general public, troops, commanders and also the reputation of the weapon at different times)
◆ how each weapon worked with other weapons
◆ your view of its overall significance on a scale of 1–10 (where 10 is high)

You could present these profiles as written reports, presentations or in a format such as Top Trumps cards. You may be able to research these developments further using the internet, or research other weapons and developments such as camouflage or transport.

What was it like to fight in the trenches?

Trench warfare

As the war of movement ended late in 1914 the First World War developed into a stalemate based on trenches. Source 18 shows you a small section of the trench system and Sources 19A and B give a sense of what it was like to be in the different types of trenches at different times. Front-line trenches like 19B were supported by much stronger reserve trenches and linked by communication trenches.

SOURCE **18**

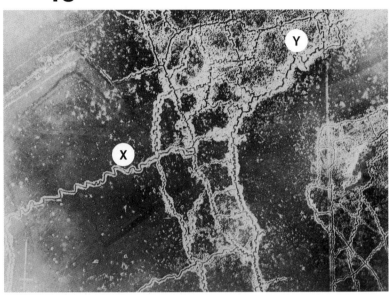

The trench system. This is an aerial photograph taken by British planes. The British trenches are on the right. The main trench area is German.

SOURCE **19**

A A reserve trench in the Somme area, July 1916 and **B** a front-line trench in Guedecourt, December 1916.

Trenches offered the best protection from snipers, shellfire, mines and other dangers for the soldiers who fought in them. But clearly the troops did not hide in the trenches for the whole length of the war. This was where the infantry came in. Before the war, the theory was that an attack on the enemy would be led by a cavalry charge. The infantry's job was to follow the cavalry and take charge of the captured positions. They then had to defend the position against counter-attack. Trench warfare changed the role of the infantry dramatically. The cavalry charge was replaced by the 'infantry charge' which became the main tactic used in the war.

'Over the top'

A major assault would usually proceed like the diagram on the left. The infantry charge was the only attacking strategy the generals had. They thought that if they did it often enough, with enough men, eventually it would wear down the enemy, and they could break through. However, the traditional view that the generals simply threw away lives is not supported by the evidence. As the war continued, the generals tried different ways to make the infantry change more effective and they introduced new tactics, weapons and equipment. Steel helmets giving some protection against shrapnel from enemy shelling became standard equipment in 1916. New camouflage techniques were used to protect troops and guns. Artillery and infantry attacks were better synchronised. Troops were given gas masks. You have already read about these and other developments on page 226–29.

In the front line

The soldiers did not spend all their time charging the enemy trenches. Far from it. Most of the infantry's work was more routine. Infantry soldiers spent much of their time digging new trenches or repairing old ones. They carted supplies and equipment up and down communications trenches. They spent long hours on sentry duty or in secret-listening posts near to enemy trenches. There were also specialist infantry called sappers. Sappers were usually ex-miners who dug tunnels below enemy trenches and placed huge mines there. The infantry also made patrols into no man's land or raided enemy trenches – to capture prisoners or particular positions. Prisoners provided priceless information. If a new enemy unit was in your sector, you could soon be facing an attack.

All of these activities, plus the possibility that death could arrive in the form of a shell at any moment, put inevitable strains on the troops and sometimes generated bitter feelings towards their commanders. Sources 20–22 provide some sense of what they went through.

---

1 The attacking side's artillery bombarded the front-line trenches of the enemy. This was called a 'barrage'.

2 As soon as the barrage stopped, attacking troops would go 'over the top' – that is, climb out of their trenches. It was now a race between them and the defenders, who had to emerge from their shelters and set up their machine guns before the attackers got over the barbed wire of no man's land.

3 The defenders usually had the advantage. They swept the advancing attackers with machine-gun fire, sometimes setting up a cross-fire.

4 If the attackers did capture forward positions, they then had to hold them. This generally proved impossible and they were usually forced back to their original position.

SOURCE **20**

Over the Top, a painting by John Nash. It is based on an attack that he took part in, in 1917, near Cambrai. The soldiers had to climb out of their own trench, charge towards the enemy trench and try to capture it. Of 80 men in his unit, 68 were killed in the first five minutes of the attack.

SOURCE **21**

I do not know why the various occasions on which battalions have fought till there were merely a few score survivors have not been properly chronicled . . . Certain platoons or companies fought shoulder to shoulder till the last man dropped . . . or . . . were shelled to nothingness, or getting over the top went forward till they all withered away under machine gun fire . . . A fortnight after some exploit, a field-marshal or divisional general comes down to a battalion to thank it for its gallant conduct, and fancies for a moment, perchance, that he is looking at the men who did the deed of valour, and not a large draft that has just been brought up from England and the base to fill the gap. He should ask the services of the chaplain and make his congratulations in the graveyard or go to the hospital and make them there.

A private's view of warfare, 1916.

SOURCE **22**

It was just as dangerous to go back as it was to go on. There were machine gun bullets spraying to and fro all the time ... When I reached our trenches I missed my footing and fell on the floor, stunned. When I got up I saw an officer standing on the fire step looking through binoculars at No Man's Land. As I walked down the trench towards the dressing station he stood in my way with a pistol in his hand. He never said a word, but then he just stepped aside and let me pass. When I got to the dressing station I asked someone 'What's that officer doing back there with the gun in his hand?', and they said that his job was to shoot anyone who came back not wounded. I thought to myself, what kind of a job is that? Anyone could have lost his nerve that day.

Memories of the Somme. A British soldier interviewed by the *Sunday Times* for an article published in 1986 – the 70th anniversary of the Battle of the Somme.

Activity

Work in pairs.
1 Each of you write a letter home from the trenches describing exactly what it is like in as much detail as you can. Use all of the information and sources on these two pages to help you. You could even include sketches.
2 Now swap your letters over. Each of you act as censor on the other one's letter and edit out anything which you think is too horrific or which reflects badly on the army.

You may be able to use word processing or email for this task. Make sure you keep a copy of the original.

What was it like to live in the trenches?

Soldiers on the Western Front went through an enormous range of experiences, from extreme boredom to the appalling stress of an enemy bombardment or attack. People often think that soldiers in the trenches spent all their time going over the top, attacking enemy trenches. In fact, such attacks were the exception rather than the rule. Soldiers spent much more time on guard, repairing trenches, or just trying to rest or sleep.

The conditions around them would have seemed very rough by our standards today. Millions of men and thousands of horses lived close together. Sanitation arrangements were makeshift. In the summer the smell of the trenches was appalling owing to a combination of rotting corpses, sewage and unwashed soldiers. The soldiers were also infested with lice, or 'chats' as they called them.

The weather had a marked effect on soldiers' lives. In summer the trenches were hot, dusty and smelly. In wet weather soldiers spent much time up to their ankles or knees in water. Many thousands suffered from 'trench foot', caused by standing in water for hours or days. In winter the trenches offered little protection from the cold. Many soldiers got frostbite.

To add to all of these unpleasant problems the trenches were infested by rats. Many soldiers on all sides described the huge, fat 'corpse rats' which thrived on the dead bodies and the rubbish created by the armies. Some accounts even speak of cats and dogs killed by rats in overwhelming numbers.

So why did the soldiers put up with the conditions?

When people study the First World War they often wonder why British soldiers put up with the conditions they had to endure. Part of the reason for this is that most books and TV programmes only cover the worst aspects of life in the trenches. It probably will not surprise you to know that when we look at a bigger picture a different story emerges about life in the trenches. The diagram opposite summarises this bigger, untold story.

SOURCE 23

You may have seen Captain Bruce Bairnsfather's two pictures showing the hour before going into the trenches and the hour after coming out. Well, they are absolutely IT. Lord, how we laughed over them in the front line … Take it from me he is one of the people who by supplying roars of laughter and joy to the troops are helping to win the war.

A letter to the *Outlook* magazine from a Lieutenant in the British army.

SOURCE 24

In and Out (I)
That last half-hour before "going in" to the same trenches for the 200th time

In and Out (II)
That first half-hour after "coming out" of those same trenches

Two cartoons by Captain Bruce Bairnsfather.

Focus Task

What was it like to live in the trenches?

1 Study Part I of Source 24. Explain what it is trying to say about the feelings of the soldiers by referring to details of the cartoon.
2 Now study Part II of Source 24 and compare it with the diagram on page 233. Which aspects of the soldiers' life are shown in Part II of the cartoon?
3 How does Source 23 help you to decide whether Source 24 is a reliable comment on life in the trenches?
4 'Source 24 is a complete and reliable view of what it was like to serve in the trenches.' How far do you agree with this view? Answer by referring to details from the source.
EXTENSION TASK: Use picture libraries on the internet to see if you can find one or more images which you think provide a better summary of life in the trenches.

Adventure

Travel: most soldiers were ordinary working-class men. They had not travelled much before the war. The fighting took them to France and Belgium, the Middle East and Africa – places they would not otherwise have visited.

Excitement: some men actually enjoyed the risk and the thrill of war.

Challenge: most people like a challenge. War was the ultimate challenge. In war-time, many soldiers achieved things they would never have dreamt possible. It may have been an act of bravery or simply putting up with pain or hardship.

A Soldier's life

Discipline

Soldiers who disobeyed orders, fell asleep on sentry duty or deserted were court martialled and could be executed. A total of 3,080 British soldiers were condemned to death by the army and 346 actually had the sentence carried out.

Humour

We should not underestimate the importance of the British sense of humour in keeping up morale. Bairnsfather's cartoons were a good example but the soldiers produced many humorous news sheets and other publications, often poking fun at the commanders.

Respect

Soldiers had respect for their leaders. There is a widespread modern myth that the generals wined and dined in the officers' mess while the men lived and died in the squalor of the trenches. In fact officers went over the top with their men and suffered higher death rates (around 17 per cent) than the ordinary troops (around 12 per cent). Among senior commanders 78 officers above the rank of brigadier-general from Britain and the British Empire died on active service and 146 were wounded. This is evidence that British generals were often close enough to the front line to be in danger of losing their lives.

Leisure time

The officers worked very hard to organise tours of duty so that the troops got a chance to rest and recuperate. On average a battalion could expect to spend around ten days a month in the trenches, but this included time in the reserve trenches which could be a mile from the front line. Troops would usually spend about three days in the most dangerous sections of the front line before being relieved. However, during a major assault, such as the Battle of the Somme, soldiers could be in the front line for much longer. We also need to remember that soldiers spent about 60 per cent of their time out of the trenches. Many of them took up correspondence courses. Many went sightseeing in France. There were football and other sports teams. There was usually a concert party every week.

Comradeship

Old friends: many battalions were made up of close friends who all joined the army together. Soldiers relied on each other totally. They did not want to let each other down. After the war, many soldiers said they greatly missed the sense of comradeship they had experienced during the war.

New friends: Allied soldiers came from all over the world. British soldiers met Canadian, Australian, South African, New Zealand, Indian, West African and Caribbean soldiers. They also met many other British people.

Patriotism

The soldiers on all sides were generally patriotic. Whatever the horrors of war, most believed they were there to do a job for their country and that the job was worth doing well.

Comforts

Care: Remember this was at a time when civilian life was very hard indeed. Life expectancy was the early 40s for a working-class man. Death and disease were common. So were poverty, hunger, illness and accidents at work. The army looked after its soldiers as well as it could. British forces suffered less from disease than other armies.

Rations: for British troops, food rations were generally good. Soldiers complained about always having tinned beef and jam, but they knew they were better off than French soldiers, and even French civilians, and they were much better fed than the Germans. In fact an average working-class soldier put on around 10 kilos in weight when he joined the army because he was better fed there!

Letters: soldiers received regular letters and parcels from home. The postal service was very efficient and this was a major factor in keeping morale high.

Luxuries: they also received lots of luxuries such as chocolate, cigarettes and alcohol.

Case study: General Haig and the Battle of the Somme

1 Look at Sources 25–27.
   a) Brainstorm a list of ten key words to define the Battle of the Somme that come to mind after looking at the sources.
   b) Compare your ten words with the person sitting next to you.
   c) Agree on the most appropriate five words.

SOURCE 25

A mural, painted in 1936, at Donegall Pass in Belfast. The 36th Ulster Division was one of the few units to achieve its objective on the first day of the Battle of the Somme. It suffered over 5,000 casualties in the battle.

SOURCE 26

There was no lingering about when zero hour came. Our platoon officer blew his whistle and he was the first up the scaling ladder, with his revolver in one hand and cigarette in the other. 'Come on, boys,' he said, and up he went. We went up after him one at a time. I never saw the officer again. His name is on the memorial to the missing which they built after the war at Thiepval. He was only young but he was a very brave man.

The memories of Private George Morgan who took part in the attack on 1 July 1916 at the Battle of the Somme.

SOURCE 27

Reg. No.	Rank.	Name.	Date of Death.
12/288	Pte.	Bagshaw, William	1/7/16
12/289	,,	Bailey, Joseph	1/7/16
12/291	,,	Barlow, Wilfred	16/5/16
12/294	,,	Batley, Edward	1/7/16
12/296	,,	Baylis, Lawrence	1/7/16
12/307	Cpl.	Braham, George	1/7/16
12/310	Pte.	Bramham, George	13/10/18
12/314	C.S.M.	Bright, Arthur Willey	12/4/18
12/318	Pte.	Brookfield, Fredk. Harold	1/7/16
12/591	,,	Bedford, Norman	1/7/16
12/593	,,	Beniston, Aubrey	1/7/16
12/597	L/Cpl.	Blenkarn, William	10/9/16
12/600	Pte.	Bowes, Frank	1/7/16
12/604	,,	Bratley, Clifford William	11/4/18
12/606	,,	Brindley, Charles W.	14/3/17
12/607	,,	Brown, Arthur	1/7/16
12/608	,,	Brown, Samuel	6/12/17
12/611	,,	Busfield, Harry Craven	18/5/17
12/862	L/Cpl.	Barnsley, Frank	1/7/16
12/865	Pte.	Barrott, John Henry	1/7/16
12/867	,,	Barton, John Arthur	1/7/16
12/870	,,	Bennett, Joseph Arnold	1/7/16
12/871	L/Cpl.	Binder, Walter Bertram	1/7/16
12/874	,,	Bland, Ernest	1/7/16

Part of the list of dead and wounded from the Sheffield Pals Battalion on the first day of the Somme. Many soldiers were in 'pals' battalions. If you joined a pals battalion, you would be fighting with men from your local area. The Sheffield Pals suffered 548 casualties on the first day of the battle.

For British history, the Battle of the Somme is one of the most significant events in the war. Sources 25–30 give some idea of why. It was a massive battle. The casualties were horrific. Most casualties were young men in their late teens or early to mid twenties. Many pals battalions (see Source 27) were practically wiped out, and villages in Britain and around the empire lost an entire generation of young men at the Somme. For example, the 11th Cambridgeshire Battalion sent 750 men over the top on 1 July and 691 of them became casualties of war. The casualties alone would qualify this battle for a place in all history books.

But there is more. The Somme has become the focus of debate about leadership. The abiding impression of the war is that the volunteers who made up most of the army followed their orders with enormous courage, but were betrayed by their leaders. It is a popular view. It is also an easy view to support. But in this case study we want to look at the Battle of the Somme more objectively.

What actually went wrong? Was it all the fault of the British commander, General Haig? If it was Haig's fault, why are there military historians who argue that Haig was not a blundering incompetent and why are there also many military historians who believe that the Somme was not a military disaster?

SOURCE 28

General Sir Douglas Haig. He successfully commanded the British troops at Mons and Ypres in 1914. By the end of 1915 he was commanding all the British forces in France.

Activity

Discuss this question as a class:
Is it morally acceptable to make the killing of enemy soldiers an objective for a military operation?

SOURCE 30

Remembering the dissatisfaction displayed by ministers at the end of 1915 because the operations had not come up to their expectations, the General Staff took the precaution to make quite clear beforehand the nature of the success which the Somme campaign might yield. The necessity of relieving pressure on the French Army at Verdun remains, and is more urgent than ever. This is, therefore, the first objective to be obtained by the combined British and French offensive. The second objective is to inflict as heavy losses as possible upon the German armies.

Sir William Robertson, Chief of the Imperial General Staff, commenting on British plans at the Somme after the end of the war.

2 With hindsight, historians know of many errors made by Haig in planning the attack.
  a) List the errors you think he made.
  b) Try to decide how many of these errors can only be seen with the benefit of hindsight.

The plan

The battle was originally planned as an attack by the French army with British support. The British commander, General Haig, actually favoured an attack further north and west in Flanders. The German attack at Verdun altered these plans. By the summer of 1916 it was agreed that Haig would lead a mainly British offensive in the area around the River Somme. The objectives were to gain territory and to draw German troops away from Verdun. Another aim was to kill as many German soldiers as possible as part of the 'war of attrition'.

The tactics

Haig and his deputy, General Rawlinson, worked out the details.

- There would be a huge artillery bombardment, and mines would devastate German positions.
- The enemy's barbed wire would be cut and the German trenches and dug-outs smashed.
- The attacking British troops would be able to walk across no man's land rather than run.
- They would carry heavy packs and trench repair equipment so that they could rebuild and defend the German trenches and so stop the Germans retaking their lost territory.
- British cavalry forces were also kept in readiness to charge into gaps in the German line.

SOURCE 29

A captured German dug-out, 1917.

Were these the right tactics?

Haig certainly knew about the German dug-outs and the masses of barbed wire in front of them. However, Haig overestimated the ability of the artillery to destroy the German defences.

- The defenders were on high ground with a good view of any attacking forces.
- The German defences had been in place since 1914 and the German soldiers had not been idle. Their dug-outs were deep underground and fortified with concrete.
- The Germans had stretched wire like a band more than 30 metres wide all along the front. It was almost impossible to penetrate.
- Many of the shells supplied to the Allied gunners were of poor quality. There was certainly a vast bombardment, but many shells were not powerful enough to destroy the defences or simply failed to go off.

SOURCE 31

Hundreds of dead were strung out like wreckage washed up to a high-water mark. Quite as many died on the enemy wire as on the ground, like fish caught in the net. They hung there in grotesque postures. Some looked as though they were praying; they had died on their knees and the wire had prevented their fall. From the way the dead were equally spread out . . . it was clear that there were no gaps in the wire at the time of the attack.

How did our planners imagine that Tommies, having survived all other hazards . . . would get through the German wire? Had they studied the black density of it through their powerful binoculars? Who told them that artillery fire would pound such wire to pieces, making it possible to get through? Any Tommy could have told them that shell fire lifts wire up and drops it down, often in a worse tangle than before.

An extract from a book written by George Coppard after the war. Coppard was a machine-gunner in the British army and was at the Somme.

SOURCE 33

A *2nd Lieutenant G H Ball, C company, 1/5th South Staffordshires*

I . . . joined this battalion on 13 June 1916. Previous to this attack [1 July] I had only been in the trenches for two days – I am 18 years of age.

B *Caption John Kerr, 5th Sherwood Foresters, whose men in the fourth wave were supposed to carry supplies across to the men who had led the attack at 7.30 a.m.*

The smoke had at that time [approximately 8.10 a.m.] practically disappeared and the enemy's trenches were plainly visible – my men were shot down as soon as they showed themselves and I was unable to get forward beyond 70 or 80 yards.

Extracts from evidence given to the Inquiry into the 46th Division's performance on 1 July 1918.

1 'The key error was overconfidence in the artillery.' Read the section about the events of 1 July 1916 and decide whether you agree with this statement.
2 Read Source 31. Why would a British civilian have found this account shocking if they had seen it in 1916?

The battle

In the last week of June, the British pounded the German lines with 1.7 million shells.

SOURCE 32

French trenches used during the Battle of the Somme.

1 July 1916 . . .

The infantry attack began at 7.30 a.m. on 1 July. Attacks usually began at dawn, but the commanders were confident that there would be little resistance. Two huge mines placed under the German lines by sappers were detonated. The noise could be heard in London.

The assault began. Twenty-seven divisions (about 750,000 men) went over the top against the Germans' 16 divisions.

The French forces made some quick gains. They were more experienced than the British in such battles and they were moving quickly because they were not weighed down by packs. However, the French found themselves isolated and had to withdraw again because most of the British forces were advancing too slowly.

The slow pace of the British advance gave the Germans enough time to emerge from their dug-outs and to set up their machine guns. Some German gunners said that the sheer numbers of British forces would have overwhelmed them, if they had charged more quickly.

The wire was undamaged in many areas, so the British troops were funnelled into areas where there were gaps in the wire. They were sitting targets for German gunners. There were around 57,000 casualties on the first day, about a third of them killed.

At the time it was chaos. No one knew quite what was happening. But the picture soon emerged of a military disaster, the worst in the history of the British army. The ranks of the junior officers were devastated, leaving soldiers confused about what to do – there had been no orders to prepare them for the situation they found themselves in.

and thereafter . . .

Rawlinson was devastated by the events of the first day and expressed doubts about continuing, but Haig insisted that the attacks should continue through July and August – he had to relieve the French at Verdun and he also felt confident that he could win a great victory.

Some lessons were learnt after the initial disaster and some gains were made (for example, the village of Pozieres was captured on 23 July). Haig was bitterly criticised for simply throwing men at massed defences or being obsessed with out-of-date tactics like cavalry charges. This was not entirely fair. For example, on 15 September Haig varied his tactics when British forces attacked in a different part of the Somme area and used tanks for the first time in the war. There were no spectacular breakthroughs as Haig had hoped, but there was a steady grinding capture of territory and a destruction of enemy forces whenever weather conditions allowed.

Haig called off the attack with winter setting in and the battle ended on 18 November. A strip of land about 25 km long and 6 km wide had been taken. These small gains had cost the British casualties of around 420,000, the French around 200,000 and the Germans around 500,000.

The aftermath

Haig was bitterly criticised after the battle by his own soldiers, by politicians and in the newspapers. He gained the unwanted title of 'The Butcher of the Somme'. Was this fair? Haig's interpretation was very different. He had warned the politicians in 1916 that the country needed to be prepared for heavy losses if the war was to be won. Haig believed that the key objectives of the Battle of the Somme were achieved. It saved Verdun – its main objective. And some of Germany's best troops were killed and injured in the battle – a fact that would come back to haunt them in 1918.

This was of little comfort to people in Britain. The Somme changed British attitudes to the war. Until the Somme, people believed that a victorious battle could lead to a breakthrough and thus end the war. The Somme brought home to many people that this would be a long, grim war of attrition.

The battle also damaged confidence in the leaders. In the chaos and confusion of the first days of the battle, many of the reports were misleading and over-optimistic. The high expectations and the confusion about what had happened made the press and public suspicious of their own commanders. Relations between Haig and the British Prime Minister David Lloyd George were particularly poor.

SOURCE 34

Should I have resigned rather than agree to this slaughter of brave men [at the Somme]? I have always felt there are solid grounds for criticism of me in that respect. My sole justification is that Haig promised not to press the attack if it became clear that he could not attain his objectives by continuing the offensive.

An extract from the war memoirs of David Lloyd George, the British Prime Minister during the war.

SOURCE 35

By 1918 the best of the old German army lay dead on the battlefields of Verdun and the Somme . . . As time passed, the picture gradually changed for the worse . . . as the number of old peacetime [1914] officers in a unit grew smaller and were replaced by young fellows of the very best will, but without sufficient knowledge.

A German opinion on the German army of 1918.

SOURCE 36

We may perhaps question whether the four-and-a-half month slog of the Somme was the unmitigated disaster it is usually painted. One voice worth hearing in this context is that of the German supreme commander Field Marshal Paul von Hindenburg, who was sufficiently chastened by the sufferings of his troops during the campaign to state at a conference in January 1917, 'We must save the men from a second Somme battle'. Another notable viewpoint is that of the distinguished soldier-writer Charles Carrington, who would later claim that 'The Somme battle raised the morale of the British Army. Although we did not win a decisive victory there was what matters most, a definite and growing sense of superiority, man to man . . . We were quite sure we had got the Germans beat.'

It is hard now to view this iconic battle through such lenses, but it is vital to remember that between 1918 and the Second World War a cultural transformation took place, associated especially with the tide of disenchantment literature headed by Erich Maria Remarque's All Quiet on the Western Front and Robert Graves' Goodbye to All That (both 1929). Throw in the works of Siegfried Sassoon and Wilfred Owen, and we instantly see in our mind's eye the doomed battalions rising from their trenches to charge the enemy, only to 'die as cattle'. This has probably distorted our ability to view the Somme in its wider historical context.

Malcolm Brown, historian at the Imperial War Museum and an expert on the First World War.

Focus Task

How should we remember the Battle of the Somme?

The Somme is remembered differently by different people. Historians disagree about whether it was a victory or a disaster. Ordinary people are unsure whether their grandfathers and great grandfathers died for a purpose.

Read the information and sources on pages 234–37 and do some research of your own, perhaps using the internet. Decide how you think people in Britain should remember the Battle of the Somme and prepare a presentation on the topic. Here are some descriptions to start your thinking:
- a brutal campaign of attrition that achieved its main objectives
- a crucial battle that saved the French army
- a disaster
- a great victory at a terrible cost
- a shocking case of incompetent leadership on the part of General Haig
- one major step towards the defeat of Germany
- a tribute to the heroism of ordinary soldiers
- an example of cynical political leaders shifting the blame on to military leaders
- an example of society being shocked by the reality of war and looking for someone to blame.

You could present your conclusions as an ICT presentation. Alternatively, you could create a website about the battle.

3 Read Source 34. Is Lloyd George blaming himself or Haig for events at the Somme?

4 Source 36 seems to suggest that the tactics of attrition eventually worked. Does that mean it was morally justifiable? Give reasons.

Why did Germany agree to an armistice in 1918?

The war developed into a stalemate by the end of 1914. Despite the huge efforts of soldiers and civilian populations the war remained a stalemate until the deadlock was finally broken in 1918. In this section you will see how this happened year by year.

SOURCE **37**

Major battles on the Western Front, 1915–17.

1915: The stalemate continues

In 1915 the French, British and Germans all tried and failed to break the deadlock. Early in 1915 the French lost many thousands in an unsuccessful offensive in Champagne (arrow 1 in Source 37). The British gained some ground at Neuve Chapelle in March but at a heavy cost. The Germans were driven back from Ypres in April (arrow 2) with heavy losses and the British suffered a setback at Loos in September.

1916: The year of attrition – Verdun and the Somme

In February 1916 the Germans began a determined battle to capture strategic French forts surrounding Verdun (arrow 4). The Germans recognised that the French were leading the Allied effort at this stage of the war. The German commander, Falkenhayn, came up with a strategy of attrition. His tactic was to 'bleed France white'. The tactic failed, in that both sides suffered roughly equal losses. For six months both sides poured men and resources into this battle. Attacks were followed by counter-attacks and by July 1916 some 700,000 men had fallen. The French, led by General Pétain, held out, but by the summer of 1916 they were close to breaking. The huge losses had weakened both sides, but the Germans had greater resources. The French army was near breaking point.

To relieve the pressure, the British led by Field Marshal Douglas Haig launched their long-planned offensive at the Somme (arrow 5). After a week-long artillery bombardment of German trenches, British troops advanced. On the first day there were 57,000 British casualties. The fighting continued until November 1916 with the loss of 1.25 million men (see pages 234–37).

Back in Britain, politicians and the general public were horrified at the losses. But to the military leaders the nature of the exercise was clear. The war was a contest to see which side could last out the long and dreadful war of attrition. Douglas Haig briefed the government that 'the nation must be taught to bear losses'. The nation did accept them and in doing so played a key role in victory.

For British history, the Somme is one of the most important stories of the war. It tells you a lot about the war in general and reactions to it.

SOURCE 38

German cartoon from 1915 accusing the USA of double standards. The German text means: 'I am neutral'.

1917: The USA in, Russia out

In 1917, the new French General, Nivelle, put forward a plan to break the deadlock. However, the Germans knew of his plans and retreated to their new, stronger positions, called the Hindenburg Line. Nivelle refused to change his plans. By previous standards the Nivelle Offensive (arrow 6) was quite successful, but again the casualties were huge. Nivelle had raised hopes which could not be met, and the French army mutinied. The crisis was resolved by Pétain. By a combination of ruthlessly punishing the leaders of the mutiny yet improving conditions for ordinary soldiers, he regained the confidence of the French troops.

The British and Canadians had some successes. The Canadians in particular enjoyed a spectacular victory, capturing the fortified Vimy Ridge in April 1917 (arrow 3). In July, the third Battle of Ypres began. The British detonated huge mines at Messines which destroyed the German artillery positions, and killed 10,000 German soldiers at a stroke. However, the infantry advance which followed this became hopelessly bogged down. Heavy rain created nightmare conditions, particularly around the ruined village of Passchendaele (arrow 7).

Some successes came at Cambrai in November. The British used over 350 tanks to good effect, but were unable to hold the ground that they had captured. It was the same old story.

These were minor victories in the broader context. The decisive military breakthrough was still elusive. But elsewhere, away from the Western Front, other developments were taking place which might have a more decisive effect on the Western Front.

The British blockade

From the start of the war both sides tried to prevent the other from getting essential supplies to its soldiers. Maybe they could be starved into submission? The British had been blockading German ports since 1914. The blockade was supposed to strangle German industry so that it could not supply the German army. It reduced German trade from $5.9 billion in 1914 to just $0.8 billion in 1917. By 1917 civilians in Germany were experiencing severe shortages (see page 244).

The German U-boat campaign

The Germans tried something similar. They sank British ships supplying Britain. In 1917 they introduced a policy of unrestricted submarine warfare against all ships that they suspected were carrying goods to Britain (see page 243). This caused shortages in Britain but it also had another unintended effect. It helped to bring the USA into the war.

The USA joins the war

The USA was officially neutral but was supplying loans and equipment to the Allies. The Germans attacked and destroyed many American ships which they suspected of carrying supplies to the Allies. They also sank passenger ships, killing many American civilians. When the USA discovered that Germany hoped to ally with Mexico against them it was the final straw and the USA declared war on Germany on 1 April 1917.

SOURCE 39

Month	Number of soldiers in the AEF
June 1917	14,000
January 1918	200,000
May 1918	1,000,000
October 1918	1,800,000

The size of the American Expeditionary Force 1917–18.

The Russian Revolution

The Allies thought that the entry of the USA would turn the tide in their favour, but by late 1917 there was little cause for optimism. The Americans needed time to build up an army. Even worse, the most crushing blow of all, a revolution in Russia had brought in a Communist government and it had made peace with Germany. The Germans could now transfer hundreds of thousands of troops back to the Western Front. It looked as if 1918 could be decisive.

As the fog cleared a little, we saw the Germans for the first time, advancing in thousands. The whole area was darkened by their figures, a moving mass of grey . . . the ground favoured their advance; it was a maze of shell holes and they crawled from one to the other . . . All our Lewis guns, damaged earlier by shell fire, were out of action, and by now German bullets were whistling at us from all directions . . . it was only then that we realised that we were completely surrounded and hopelessly outnumbered. The first breakthrough had apparently come on our right when the enemy had captured our Company Headquarters.

G Wright, a soldier in the North Staffordshire Regiment, remembers the German attack in the Ludendorff Offensive.

Activity

Historians have disagreed as to what were the turning points of the war on the Western Front.
1 Work in groups of three. One of you take 1916, one take 1917, the other take 1918. Each of you write a paragraph explaining why your year saw the turning point in the war. Use the information on pages 338–40 to help you.
2 Show your paragraph to the other members of the group, then take a vote on which year saw the most important turning point.

Focus Task

Why did Germany ask for an armistice in 1918?

The following factors all played a role in forcing Germany to ask for an armistice in 1918. At the moment they are in alphabetical order. Rearrange them in order of importance, with an explanation of your decision:
◆ ability of British and American industry to supply the resources the Allied armies needed
◆ arrival of the USA into the war
◆ British naval blockade
◆ failure of Ludendorff Offensive
◆ German losses in 1916 and 1917
◆ increasing improvements in the effectiveness of the British army, 1917–18.

1918: The Hundred Days – the stalemate is broken

Things may have looked bad for the Allies but the German situation was also desperate in early 1918. Despite the good news of the Russian surrender, the Allies' blockade of German ports had starved the economy of raw materials and the population (including the soldiers) of food. Worse still, the USA was moving troops to France at a rate of 50,000 per month. Above all, the German army was not the quality fighting machine it had been. Germany needed a quick victory and the surrender of Russia gave the Germans one last opportunity to achieve a military breakthrough and end the stalemate.

Through the early months of 1918 Germany transferred troops from the East to the Western Front. In March 1918 the German Commander Ludendorff launched the great gamble to win the war. It started with the typical huge bombardment and gas attacks. However, instead of the usual 'wave' of infantry, he followed up with attacks by smaller bands of specially trained and lightly equipped 'storm troops' (see Source 40) who struck during a heavy fog along the entire front line. The idea was to stop the Allies massing their defence in a single place. It was very effective. The Germans broke through the Allied lines in many places, advanced 64 kilometres and Paris was now in range of heavy gunfire.

The 'Ludendorff Offensive' had so far gone very well. A German victory seemed to be a real possibility. However, the German army lost 400,000 men in making this breakthrough and they had no reserves to call on. The troops of 1918 did not compare well with those of 1914. Their discipline was poor and they were badly fed and supplied. Many of the planned German advances were held up as troops stopped to loot food and supplies from captured trenches or villages. They also came up against well-led and well-equipped Allied forces (see Source 41). The blockades had prevented the Germans from making similar technological improvements.

Between May and August the Germans made no further progress and it was clear that they had run out of time and resources. The Germans had ended trench warfare but it was the Allies who eventually gained the benefit. By now, they had large numbers of well-fed and well-equipped troops. These troops were supported by tanks, aircraft and improved artillery. By 1918 the big guns were capable of hitting targets with impressive accuracy as well as laying down smokescreens or giving covering fire for attackers.

On 8 August the Allies counter-attacked along much of the Western Front. This later became known as the German army's 'Black Day'. It was now just a matter of time before the Allies defeated Germany. By late September they had reached the Hindenburg Line. By October the Germans were in full retreat. This period has become known as the 'Hundred Days'. Finally, on 11 November 1918 the Armistice (ceasefire) came into effect. The Great War was over.

SOURCE **41**

The huge successes under Field Marshal Sir Douglas Haig between 8 August and 11 November 1918 are now largely forgotten by the British public. However, these were the greatest series of victories in the British Army's whole history . . .

Haig's armies took 188,700 prisoners and 2,840 guns – only 7,800 prisoners and 935 guns less than those taken by the French, Belgian and American armies combined. These successes were the result of the courage and endurance of the front-line soldiers. They were also the result of the commanders' tactical and technological improvements. By August 1918, Haig's forces were employing tanks; aircraft; armoured cars; motorised machine-gun units; wireless; and ammunition drops by parachute. They had an excellent communication and transport system that enabled Haig to switch attacks to another sector at short notice – so keeping the Germans off balance.

If we are to criticise Haig and his army commanders for their mistakes in 1916 and 1917, then it is perhaps only fair that, at the same time, they should receive due credit for their decisive, but forgotten victories.

Adapted from an article by Professor Peter Simpkin, senior historian at the Imperial War Museum, London.

10.3 How important were the other fronts?

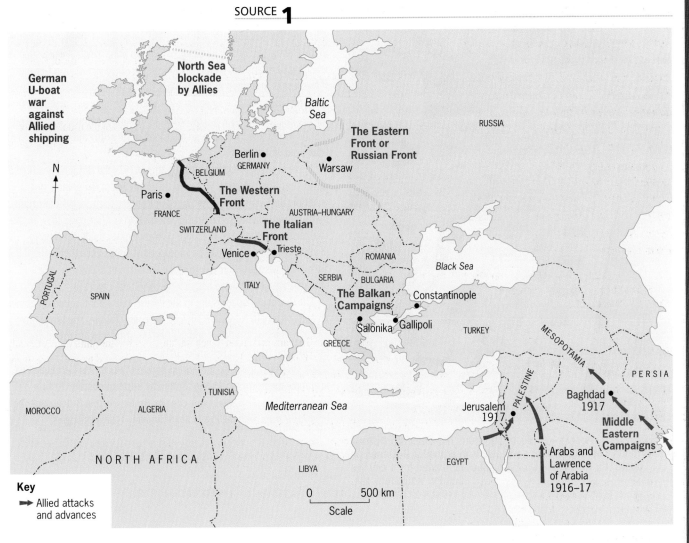

The main fronts of the First World War.

Source 1 shows you the scope of the fighting in the First World War. The Western Front was only part of a war that also caused suffering and destruction in eastern Europe, the Middle East and North Africa. There were spectacular battles in the mountains between Italian and Austrian troops (Italy had entered the war in 1915 on the side of Britain and France). There were tremendous battles on the Eastern Front where Russians fought Germans and Austrians. In the Middle East, Turkish troops with German officers fought British Commonwealth and Empire troops, along with their Arab allies.

Focus Task

1 Draw your own copy of the chart below.

Front	Similarities to the Western Front	Differences from the Western Front

2 Fill it out as you find out about each of the other fronts on pages 245–49.
3 Use your completed table to write an essay comparing the different fronts.

SOURCE 2

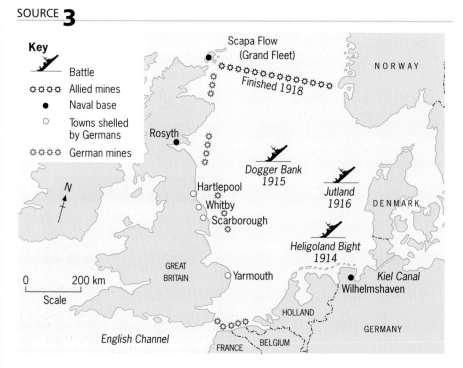

Supplying a warship – an illustration from *The Standard History*. If this much was required for a warship with around 2,000 men on board, try to imagine what the supplies needed for a city like London would look like.

Who won the war at sea?

The sea campaigns of the First World War were unusual in that, although they were vitally important, relatively little fighting took place between the warships. The key objective was to control the seas to stop supplies getting to the enemy. The British blockade of German ports which stopped supplies reaching Germany was a crucial factor in the Allied victory over Germany. It was just as important as any military victory on land.

Both sides knew how important it was to control the sea, and the war at sea became a cautious war. The British Commander Admiral Jellicoe said that he 'could lose the war in an afternoon' if he rashly allowed his fleet to be put out of action.

There were some battles at sea. In August 1914 the Royal Navy scored a clever (but small) tactical victory in the North Sea at Heligoland, but generally the German navy remained in its ports. Early in 1914 German battle cruisers shelled some British east coast towns (see page 405). In the Mediterranean, the German cruiser *Goeben* evaded the Royal Navy to reach Constantinople. This was an important event, since it influenced the Turks, who were pro-German, to make the decision to enter the war – otherwise they would have had to force the *Goeben* to leave.

The Germans had few ships in the Pacific, but a small squadron gained an early victory in November 1914 off the coast of Chile. The Royal Navy set out to remove this threat and the German ships were destroyed around the Falkland Islands in December 1914.

By 1915 only the ships in German ports remained. The Germans tried to enforce their own blockade of Britain by using submarines to sink merchant ships. This was highly effective. In May 1915 a U-boat sank the liner *Lusitania*, with the loss of approximately 1,200 passengers.

Factfile

New weapons in the war at sea

► When the war began, most people expected the war at sea to be a confrontation between the new Dreadnought battleships. In fact, submarines became a key feature of the war at sea.

► Submarines were primitive and inefficient, but they were also very effective.

► It was a new weapon – the torpedo – which made submarine warfare so effective. Even the mightiest battleship was vulnerable to a torpedo from the smallest submarine.

► The mine also came into its own as a devastatingly effective weapon in the war at sea.

► Several ships were lost in the Gallipoli campaign to mines. In the North Sea and the Baltic, minefields were used to protect harbours by both the French and the British.

► Another tactic was for submarines to lay mines in harbours to catch enemy ships by surprise as they set out to sea.

SOURCE 3

Key

- ⚓ Battle
- ✿✿✿✿ Allied mines
- ● Naval base
- ○ Towns shelled by Germans
- ✿✿✿✿ German mines

Scapa Flow (Grand Fleet) — NORWAY

Finished 1918

Rosyth

Dogger Bank 1915

Hartlepool
Whitby
Scarborough

Jutland 1916 — DENMARK

Heligoland Bight 1914

Kiel Canal
Wilhelmshaven

GREAT BRITAIN — Yarmouth

HOLLAND

English Channel

FRANCE BELGIUM — GERMANY

0   200 km
Scale

N

The North Sea blockade.

The Battle of Jutland

The only major sea battle of the war was at Jutland in 1916. In the event, chaos and confusion reigned. The Germans had the best of the exchanges, but the British fleet was simply too large. The Germans sank fourteen British ships and lost eleven themselves but never left their harbours again. Both sides claimed to have won the battle. On the one hand, the Germans caused more damage than they received. On the other, the Battle of Jutland certainly failed to achieve the most important objective for Germany which was to remove the blockade.

The U-boat campaign

In the early stages of the war, German U-boats concentrated their attacks on Allied warships. When the Allies learned to protect their warships the U-boats attacked Allied merchant ships instead.

To start with, the attackers would warn a merchant ship that it was about to be sunk and allow the crew to abandon ship. This 'convention' was abandoned in February 1915 when the Germans began a campaign of unrestricted submarine warfare. All Allied ships were targeted. They could be torpedoed without warning. A notable early casualty of the new campaign was the liner *Lusitania*. British propaganda painted this action as a criminal act, but there was some evidence that the ship was carrying explosives for the war effort.

Over 100 American citizens were killed on the *Lusitania*, causing great tension between the US and German governments. Two years later, in 1917, the USA cited the U-boat campaign as one of its reasons for declaring war on Germany.

After the sinking of the *Lusitania*, Germany called off unrestricted submarine warfare, but in 1916 started it again. The Germans' aim was to prevent essential supplies getting to Britain and they almost succeeded. By June 1917, Britain had lost 500,000 tons of shipping to the U-boats. At one point, it was estimated that London had only six weeks' supply of food remaining.

From 1916 the Allies improved their tactics for dealing with the U-boats (see Source 5). However, two other factors were significant in the fight against submarines: the dedication and heroism of the sailors of the merchant navy and the massive output of shipbuilders. By 1917 Britain and the USA were building so many ships that the U-boats could not possibly sink them all. The Germans simply did not have the resources to sustain their campaign and it was finally called off.

SOURCE **4**

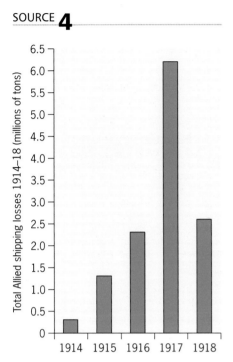

Losses of Allied shipping, 1914–18.

SOURCE **5**

Q ships were decoy ships – merchant ships armed with disguised heavy guns. They were designed to fool U-boats into attacking well-defended targets. The immediate success of the Q ships was one reason why, in 1915, the U-boats stopped warning ships that they were about to be attacked.

Mines destroyed more U-boats than any other weapon. They were particularly effective in preventing U-boats from using the English Channel and sailing into British ports.

Depth charges (bombs set to go off underwater at certain depths) were introduced in 1916 and proved second only to mines as a weapon against the U-boats.

Convoys: From mid-1917 almost all merchant ships travelled in convoys. British and US warships escorted merchant ships in close formation. Allied shipping losses fell by about 20 per cent when the convoy system was introduced in mid-1917. Depth charges became even more effective when used together with the convoy system.

Long-range aircraft: By the end of the war, aircraft technology had developed so much that aircraft could protect convoys.

During the war, new tactics were developed to defend merchant ships against submarine attack.

The British blockade

The British blockade was a key factor in the defeat of Germany. Starved of supplies, the German army was weakened and the German people lost some of their will to support the war. The war at sea was therefore arguably as decisive as the war on land.

SOURCE **6**

300,000 deaths related to malnutrition during 1914–18 among civilian population.

In Germany, the government was forced to slaughter one-third of all pigs in 1915 because the naval blockade had cut off imports of fodder to feed them.

The blockade cut supplies of nitrates to Germany – vital for explosives for the army and fertilisers for the farmers.

In Germany in 1916, the adult meat ration for one week was the equivalent of two burgers in a modern fast-food restaurant.

Effect of Britain's naval blockade on Germany.

Focus Task

Why did Britain win the war at sea?

Draw your own copy of this diagram and label it with details which explain why Britain won the war at sea.

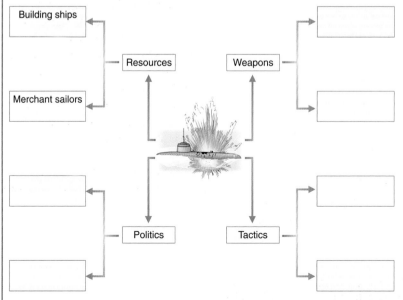

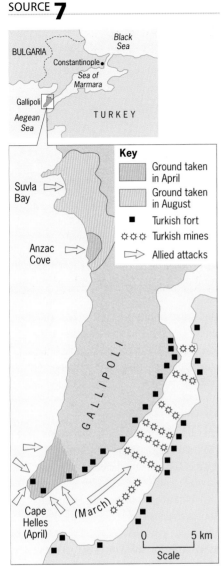

The Dardanelles strait and the Gallipoli campaign.

Gallipoli

In 1915 casualties were mounting on the Western Front and government ministers in London could see no prospect of breaking the stalemate. They began to look for another way to gain a breakthrough in the war. One possibility was to attack one of Germany's allies. Lloyd George described this as 'knocking out the props from under Germany'. However, this was not a very accurate description of Germany's allies. Germany was propping up its allies rather than the other way round.

Nevertheless, the war planners were attracted to the idea of a knock-out blow against Turkey, whom they considered to be one of Germany's more vulnerable allies. Winston Churchill, who was head of the navy, and Lord Kitchener, who was in effect overall commander of the war effort, persuaded the government to attempt an attack on the Dardanelles strait, a narrow stretch of water linking the Aegean Sea and the Sea of Marmara.

The plan

Source 7 shows you what was supposed to happen. British warships were going to sweep through the Dardanelles strait, attack Constantinople and drive Turkey out of the war. This would have three other results:

- It would open up a sea route to the Russian Front so that the Allies could get supplies to the Russians.
- It would establish a new front. Allied troops could march through the Balkans and attack Germany's principal ally, Austria–Hungary.
- It would relieve pressure on the Russian forces by drawing troops away from the Russian Front.

Lord Kitchener even suggested to those who doubted the wisdom of this attack on Constantinople that it was the plan that would win the war.

Britain had the most powerful navy in the world and the plan seemed attractive. There was going to be some infantry in support to attack any land-based guns that might threaten the warships, but they were not going to attempt a land invasion, so there was no danger of troops getting bogged down in trench warfare as they had on the Western Front. Or so they thought!

What actually happened

In March 1915 the warships began their assault. They bombarded the strong forts that lined the strait, then made their advance. As the British and French ships entered the strait, a combination of mines and shell fire from the forts on the shore sank three battle cruisers and damaged others.

The heart of the British navy was thus threatened. The Allied commanders decided that this naval attack would not succeed, and that the risks of the navy's trying to continue towards Constantinople were too great. They decided that after all they would launch a land invasion to capture the peninsula. Once the Turks were driven off Gallipoli, the naval operation could restart.

In April a hastily assembled force of British, French and ANZAC (Australian and New Zealand) troops attacked Helles beach. However, the war commanders had severely underestimated the power of the defending army. The commanders had been refused aid from the Royal Flying Corps, which could have helped a lot in assessing the strength of the Turks.

The Turks had been well aware that an attack was coming. A new German commander Otto Liman von Sanders had doubled the defensive forces, and dug them into strong positions on the hills overlooking the beaches on which the Allies were likely to land. He had given the troops a crash course in defending trench positions – including training in the British speciality, the use of the bayonet.

At four o'clock in the morning on 25 April, in pitch dark, the first troops went ashore and charged up the steep hillsides under a hail of machine-gun fire which continued for most of the day.

Shells were moaning and whining all around us and the noise of gunfire was something terrible. The Fort was firing like Hell. It was one continual deafening roar caused by the firing of our ships and the moaning, hissing noise of the enemy's shells.

Then we saw the Bouvet suddenly keel over and turn upside down. She sank in two and a half minutes taking the best part of her crew with her.

Written by Able Seaman Kemm who was aboard the *Prince George* battleship.

A model showing the landing on Helles beach, 25 April.

SOURCE **10**

It seems that we have finished with general attack and are now reduced to the silly old game of trench warfare. Clearing the Dardanelles at this rate will mean some years' work.

Written by the commander of the naval forces at Gallipoli, Major-General Paris, 13 May.

SOURCE **11**

Disease dominated the whole situation. The latrines were continually thronged with men so that attempts at covering or disinfecting excreta became a farce. Black swarms of flies carried infection warm from the very bowel to the food as it passed the lips.

Written by the official historian of the Australian Medical Services.

By mid-afternoon the beach was strewn with the dead and dying. Despite the massive odds against them, the troops fought very bravely and captured a number of Turkish trenches. However, by the following day it was already clear that the objective of clearing the Turks off the peninsula could not be achieved. Should they dig in or withdraw? The order came through to dig in. 'You have got through the difficult business,' said the commander, 'now you only have to dig, dig, dig, until you are safe.'

Conditions for the troops were awful. In the blistering summer heat, and with decaying corpses strewn along the front line on both sides, disease was rampant. With so many unburied corpses lying in the no man's land between the trenches, on 20 May both sides agreed a one-day truce. They frantically buried the dead. Some Turks and Allied troops met and exchanged greetings. At sunset they returned to their trenches. And the next day the killing started again.

Neither side could break the deadlock and both poured more troops into the area. In August another landing was made at Suvla Bay, but again the troops could not break through the defences of the Turks.

One part of the Allies' campaign in the Dardanelles was successful. Submarines did get through the minefields of the strait to attack Constantinople harbour. Turkish warships, troopships and merchant vessels were sunk in such numbers that the Turkish war effort was seriously affected. But the main fleet never again attempted to get through.

In November the troops at Gallipoli were facing a new problem – frostbite. The hard Turkish winter had closed in. The troops were extremely ill-equipped. In one snowstorm there were 16,000 cases of frostbite and 300 deaths.

In December, eight months after the landing, there was no prospect of success. Tens of thousands of soldiers lay dead around the coasts of Gallipoli. The decision was taken to pull out. The withdrawal was supremely well organised and was a complete success. The campaign, however, was seen as a failure and Churchill was humiliated.

Focus Task

What happened in the Gallipoli campaign of 1915?

Work in pairs. You are historical researchers who have been given two questions to investigate:
◆ Why was the Gallipoli campaign a failure?
◆ Why were the casualties so great?

Take one question each.
As well as the information and sources on pages 245–46, you have Sources 12–18 on page 247 to help you. Taking each source in turn, decide whether it is relevant to your question. If it is, list the reasons it gives you.

Now write a balanced answer to your question, using the sources to support your answer.

SOURCE 12

The expedition was plagued by inadequate resources. The question arose, if Britain lacked the resources to conduct such a campaign, was it wise to attempt it in the first place?

From *The Great War: Myth and Reality* by D Marshall, 1988.

SOURCE 13

The landing place was a difficult one. A narrow, sandy beach backed by a very high intricate mass of hills, those behind the beach being exceedingly steep. The moment the boats landed the men jumped out and rushed straight for the hills rising almost cliff-like only fifty yards or so beyond the beach.

I went ashore there yesterday, into their position, and it seemed almost incredible that any troops could have done it. It is a stiff climb even up the zig-zag path which the Engineers have now built! How they got up fully armed and equipped over the rough scrub-clad hillside one can hardly imagine!

From a letter by Captain Guy Dawnay.

SOURCE 14

A successful military operation against the Gallipoli peninsula must hinge upon the ability of the fleet . . . to dominate the Turkish defences with gunfire and to crush their field troops during that period of helplessness while an army is disembarking, but also to cover the advance of the troops once ashore . . .

From a pre-war report about the strength of the Gallipoli positions, which goes on to say that such an operation would not be possible. The report was not given to the commanders of the Gallipoli campaign.

SOURCE 15

General Hamilton informs me that the army is checked. The help which the navy has been able to give the army in its advance has not been as great as anticipated. Though effective in keeping down the fire of the enemy's batteries, when it is a question of trenches and machine guns the navy is of small assistance.

By the naval commander de Roebeck.

SOURCE 16

When I was there, in every case, attacks were ordered rather lightheartedly and carried out without method. The men on the spot were not listened to when they pointed out steps to be taken before entering on a special task.

The Turks had sited their trenches very cleverly and it was often useless to attack one set before another had been taken. The Turks dig like moles and prepare line after line for defence: seven or eight close behind the other. The great difficulty is in making attacks and supporting them. The trenches become congested: the telephone wires get cut by shrapnel: and the whole show gets out of control.

Almost always in Gallipoli the attacks were made by men in the trenches and not by fresh troops. The men are kept too long and too thick in the trenches: they become stupefied after five days.

Attacks seemed always to be ordered against very long strips of line at once without any weight anywhere. It all seemed very amateur. But I suppose it couldn't be helped, the idea was always to get through with a rush and to disregard losses.

Major H Mynors Farmar, Staff Captain, 86th Brigade, writing about fighting at Gallipoli.

SOURCE 17

At that time there was no centralized organization in Whitehall, and the Admiralty and War Office operated in water-tight compartments. Very little time had been given to combined planning. The navy would follow time-honoured drills for putting small expeditions ashore. Opposed landings on hostile beaches, under heavy close-range fire, do not seem to have entered the syllabuses at any of the service colleges.

It is clear that Kitchener had only a hazy idea of what was entailed, and that he was hoping Hamilton would pick up a multitude of loose ends and come up with a workable plan.

Considering the crucial importance of the operation, this was a hopeless briefing for a newly appointed commander-in-chief. Hamilton was at the outset the victim of gross dereliction of duty on the part of the General Staff.

Hamilton's only intelligence consisted of a 1912 manual on the Turkish army, some old (and inaccurate) maps, a tourist guide-book, and what little could be gleaned from the Turkish desk at the Foreign Office.

From *Gallipoli*, by Michael Hickey, 1995, describing the planning of the campaign in London. General Hamilton was appointed by Kitchener to lead the campaign.

SOURCE 18

[At Gallipoli], the casualties were appalling. Again and again, battalions were all but wiped out; the trauma inflicted on the survivors must have been terrible. Those who were unnerved had to work it out for themselves, helped when necessary by their officers, chaplains and more robust comrades. Those who failed – and there were some – could be court-martialled and shot; the sentence was frequently carried out down on Suvla beach, and in a sinister copse behind the lines at Helles. Gallipoli was not a friendly place.

They had made provision for about 10,000 casualties. However, planning was made on the assumption that there would be an immediate advance off the beaches, leaving room ashore for field ambulances followed rapidly by three stationary hospitals. It was dreadfully flawed.

Hamilton was deprived of the staff who should have been planning casualty evacuation and provision of essential stores. Most of the ships had been loaded so hurriedly that the equipment needed immediately by any force deposited on a hostile shore was buried under tons of less urgent stores.

From *Gallipoli*, as above, describing the arrangements made for the care of the wounded.

The Eastern Front

When war broke out in 1914 it came too soon for Russia. Russia lost a war to Japan in 1905 and was then rocked by revolution. It recovered from these setbacks and between 1905 and 1914 the country began a long, slow process of reform in industry, education, the economy and the military. By 1914 the Russian armed forces had a very effective corps of professional officers and non-commissioned officers (corporals and sergeants). The army had some excellent weapons, including modern rifles, machine guns and artillery. For Russia, the problem was that there were simply not enough of the trained officers and NCOs and nowhere near enough of the modern weapons. Russia was able to put 3.1 million men in the field in

1914 and by the end of the war over 14 million had served in the Russian armed forces. The sheer size of the Russian army overwhelmed the officers and used up the precious weapons and equipment. It also caused huge problems for Russian industry, which could not supply the troops with food, ammunition or even basic items like boots. It also strained the Russian transport system to breaking point. Fighting took place across a vast area of land. There were some trenches, but warfare did not get bogged down in the same way as on the Western Front. Source 19 describes the course of the war on the Eastern Front.

SOURCE 19

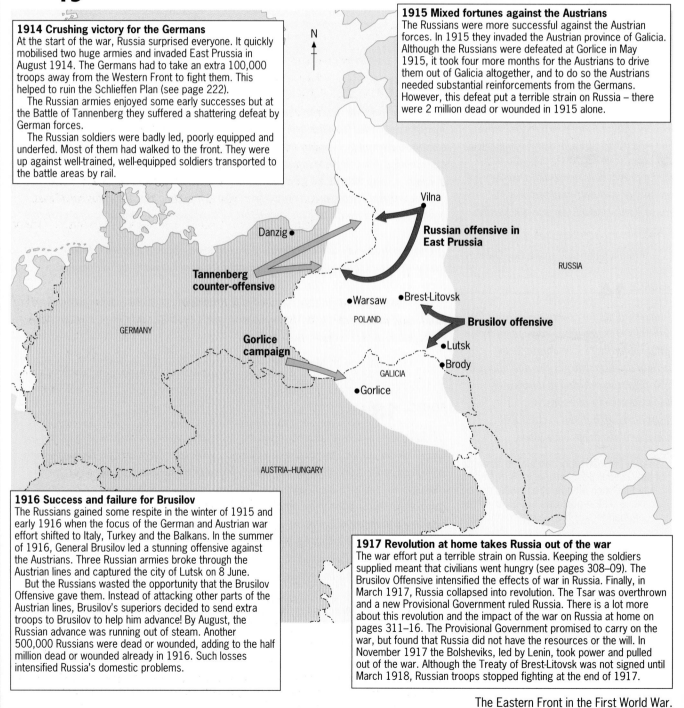

1914 Crushing victory for the Germans
At the start of the war, Russia surprised everyone. It quickly mobilised two huge armies and invaded East Prussia in August 1914. The Germans had to take an extra 100,000 troops away from the Western Front to fight them. This helped to ruin the Schlieffen Plan (see page 222).

The Russian armies enjoyed some early successes but at the Battle of Tannenberg they suffered a shattering defeat by German forces.

The Russian soldiers were badly led, poorly equipped and underfed. Most of them had walked to the front. They were up against well-trained, well-equipped soldiers transported to the battle areas by rail.

1915 Mixed fortunes against the Austrians
The Russians were more successful against the Austrian forces. In 1915 they invaded the Austrian province of Galicia. Although the Russians were defeated at Gorlice in May 1915, it took four more months for the Austrians to drive them out of Galicia altogether, and to do so the Austrians needed substantial reinforcements from the Germans. However, this defeat put a terrible strain on Russia – there were 2 million dead or wounded in 1915 alone.

1916 Success and failure for Brusilov
The Russians gained some respite in the winter of 1915 and early 1916 when the focus of the German and Austrian war effort shifted to Italy, Turkey and the Balkans. In the summer of 1916, General Brusilov led a stunning offensive against the Austrians. Three Russian armies broke through the Austrian lines and captured the city of Lutsk on 8 June.

But the Russians wasted the opportunity that the Brusilov Offensive gave them. Instead of attacking other parts of the Austrian lines, Brusilov's superiors decided to send extra troops to Brusilov to help him advance! By August, the Russian advance was running out of steam. Another 500,000 Russians were dead or wounded, adding to the half million dead or wounded already in 1916. Such losses intensified Russia's domestic problems.

1917 Revolution at home takes Russia out of the war
The war effort put a terrible strain on Russia. Keeping the soldiers supplied meant that civilians went hungry (see pages 308–09). The Brusilov Offensive intensified the effects of war in Russia. Finally, in March 1917, Russia collapsed into revolution. The Tsar was overthrown and a new Provisional Government ruled Russia. There is a lot more about this revolution and the impact of the war on Russia at home on pages 311–16. The Provisional Government promised to carry on the war, but found that Russia did not have the resources or the will. In November 1917 the Bolsheviks, led by Lenin, took power and pulled out of the war. Although the Treaty of Brest-Litovsk was not signed until March 1918, Russian troops stopped fighting at the end of 1917.

The Eastern Front in the First World War.

SOURCE 20

Russian infantry about to attack German positions. The date is not known.

SOURCE 21

Russian prisoners of war captured by the Germans in 1916. Very large numbers of prisoners died from diseases.

SOURCE 22

Russian machine guns and other equipment captured by the Germans in September 1917.

Activity

Study Sources 20–25 carefully. For each source, decide whether you think it supports the view that the Russian defeat was the result of poor leadership, poor supplies or both.

SOURCE 23

The Russian Army of World War One has become notorious for its reputation as a large, ill-equipped force, yet in 1914, Russia's Imperial Troops were actually well trained and equipped. The real problem with the Russian Army lay in its inadequate transportation infrastructure, which was not able to supply and maintain Russian field formations at wartime establishments ... The Russian Army High Command had maintained a lively pre-war debate over what action would be taken in case of war with Germany. By 1910 it was decided to launch major offensive operations immediately upon the outbreak of any war. This decision clearly catered to the 'spirit of the offensive' which was then common in European military thought ... This was to exact a brutal toll in Russian lives, which in turn helped to spur later unrest.

Extract from The War Times Journal, a website for military history enthusiasts.

SOURCE 24

The staff headquarters resembled more a gentlemen's club than it did a military headquarters. The Tsar had appointed a number of his most loyal courtiers as senior army commanders. The general staff headquarters was filled with courtiers. After dinner, they'd have plenty of time for cigars. Most of the generals had plenty of time to write voluminous memoirs. And they had a really rather outdated notion of military strategy. They believed that the bravery of the Russian soldier would be enough to see Russia through, so they commanded vast armies of infantry to charge German artillery positions. As a result of their outdated strategy, there were hundreds of thousands of people needlessly killed. Moreover, there was a careless attitude among many of the general's staff to such losses.

Historian Professor Orlando Figes, an expert on Russian history.

SOURCE 25

Brussilov was the ablest of the army-group commanders. His front was in good order. For that reason we were sent to it. The impression I got in April was the Russian troops, all the men and most of the officers, were magnificent material who were being wasted because of the incompetence, intrigues, and corruption of the men who governed the country.

In June Brussilov's advance showed what they could do, when they were furnished with sufficient weapons and ammunition. But that effort was wasted, too, for want of other blows to supplement it, for want of any definite plan of campaign.

The Russian officers, brutal as they often were to their men (many of them scarcely considered privates to be human), were as a rule friendly and helpful to us. They showed us all we wanted to see. They always cheerfully provided for Arthur Ransome (a fellow journalist), who could not ride owing to some disablement, a cart to get about in.

Report by Hamilton Fyfe, War Correspondent for The Times 1915.

Focus Task

Why was Russia defeated?

Russia was defeated by a combination of military failures and internal problems, but what was the mix? Here is a scale. How should it be divided? Should it be 100 per cent internal problems and 0 per cent military, or 50/50, or something else?

Russia lost because of Military failures	Russia lost because of its own internal problems

Study the information and sources on these two pages (and also pages 308–13), then make your decision. Make sure you can give evidence to support your answer.

11 Germany, 1918–45

Timeline

This timeline shows the period you will be covering in this chapter. Some of the key dates are filled in already.

To help you get a complete picture of the period, you can make your own copy and add other details to it as you work through the chapter.

THE WEIMAR REPUBLIC

- 1918 — The end of the First World War
- 1920
- 1923 — Stresemann becomes Chancellor of Germany
- 1929 — The Wall Street Crash is followed by a worldwide depression
- 1930
- 1933 — Hitler becomes Chancellor of Germany

THE THIRD REICH

- 1939 — The Second World War begins
- 1940
- 1945 — Germany is defeated by the Allies. Hitler kills himself
- 1950

11.1 The Weimar Republic and the rise of the Nazis

Focus

The impact of the First World War on Germany was devastating. The Treaty of Versailles made the country's problems even worse. The Weimar government struggled from crisis to crisis. Out of this conflict Adolf Hitler and the Nazis emerged as the most powerful group in Germany.

In 11.1 you will investigate:
◆ the problems facing the Weimar government in the 1920s
◆ how those problems helped Hitler and the Nazis to take power in 1933.

11.2 you will investigate:
◆ how the Nazis controlled Germany
◆ what it was like to live in Nazi Germany.

The impact of the First World War

In 1914 the Germans were a proud people. Their Kaiser – virtually a dictator – was celebrated for his achievements. Their army was probably the finest in the world. A journey through the streets of Berlin in 1914 would have revealed prospering businesses and a well-educated and well-fed workforce. There was great optimism about the power and strength of Germany.

Four years later a similar journey would have revealed a very different picture. Although little fighting had taken place in Germany itself, the war had still destroyed much of the old Germany. The proud German army was defeated. The German people were surviving on turnips and bread, and even the flour for the bread was mixed with sawdust to make it go further. A flu epidemic was sweeping the country, killing thousands of people already weakened by rations.

This may not surprise you, given the suffering of the First World War. What might surprise you is that five years later the situation for many people in Germany was still very grim indeed.

Whatever had gone wrong in Germany? To find out, you are going to look back at the final stages of the First World War.

SOURCE **1**

German women sell their possessions to buy food in 1922.

SOURCE **2**

National income was about one-third of what it had been in 1913

War left 600,000 widows and 2 million children without fathers – by 1925 the state was spending about one-third of its budget in war pensions

Germany was virtually bankrupt

Industrial production was about two-thirds of what it had been in 1913

The war had deepened divisions in German society

Impact of the war on Germany by 1918

Germany had a revolution and became an unstable democratic republic

There were huge gaps between the living standards of the rich and the poor

Stresses of war led to a revolution in October– November 1918

During the war women were called up to work in the factories. Many people saw this as damaging to traditional family values and society as a whole

Many German workers were bitter at the restrictions placed on their earnings during the war while the factory owners made vast fortunes from the war

Many ex-soldiers and civilians despised the new democratic leaders and came to believe that the heroic leader Field Marshal Hindenburg had been betrayed by weak politicians

The impact of war on Germany by 1918.

Focus Task

How did Germany emerge from defeat in the First World War?

1 Use Source 2 on page 251 and the information on this page to make a list of the challenges facing Ebert when he took over in Germany in 1918. You could organise the list into sections:
   ◆ Political challenges
   ◆ Social challenges
   ◆ Economic challenges.
2 Imagine you are advising Ebert. Explain what you think are the three most serious challenges that need tackling urgently.
3 Take a class vote and see if you can all agree on which are the most serious challenges.

The birth of the Weimar Republic

In autumn 1918 the Allies had clearly won the war. Germany was in a state of chaos, as you can see from Source 2 on page 251. The Allies offered Germany peace, but under strict conditions. One condition was that Germany should become more democratic. When the Kaiser refused, sailors in northern Germany mutinied and took over the town of Kiel. This triggered other revolts. The Kaiser's old enemies, the Socialists, led uprisings of workers and soldiers in other German ports. Soon, other German cities followed. In Bavaria an independent Socialist Republic was declared. On 9 November 1918 the Kaiser abdicated his throne and left Germany for the Netherlands.

The following day, the Socialist leader Friedrich Ebert became the new leader of the Republic of Germany. He immediately signed an armistice with the Allies. The war was over. He also announced to the German people that the new Republic was giving them freedom of speech, freedom of worship and better working conditions. A new constitution was drawn up (see Factfile).

The success of the new government depended on the German people accepting an almost instant change from the traditional, autocratic German system of government to this new democratic system. The prospects for this did not look good.

The reaction of politicians in Germany was unenthusiastic. Ebert had opposition from both right and left. On the right wing, nearly all the Kaiser's former advisers remained in their positions in the army, judiciary, civil service and industry. They restricted what the new government could do. Many still hoped for a return to rule by the Kaiser. A powerful myth developed that men such as Ebert had stabbed Germany in the back and caused the defeat in the war (see page 253). On the left wing there were many Communists who believed that at this stage what Germany actually needed was a Communist revolution just like Russia's in 1917.

Despite this opposition, in January 1919 free elections took place for the first time in Germany's history. Ebert's party won a majority and he became the President of the Weimar Republic. It was called this because, to start with, the new government met in the small town of Weimar (see Source 6) rather than in the German capital, Berlin. Even in February 1919, Berlin was thought to be too violent and unstable.

Factfile

The Weimar Constitution

➤ Before the war Germany had had no real democracy. The Kaiser was virtually a dictator.
➤ The Weimar Constitution, on the other hand, attempted to set up probably the most democratic system in the world where no individual could gain too much power.
➤ All Germans over the age of 20 could vote.
➤ There was a system of proportional representation – if a party gained 20 per cent of the votes, they gained 20 per cent of the seats in the Parliament (Reichstag).
➤ The Chancellor was responsible for day-to-day government, but he needed the support of half the Reichstag.
➤ The Head of State was the President. The President stayed out of day-to-day government. In a crisis he could rule the country directly through Article 48 of the Constitution. This gave him emergency powers, which meant he did not have to consult the Reichstag.

SOURCE **3**

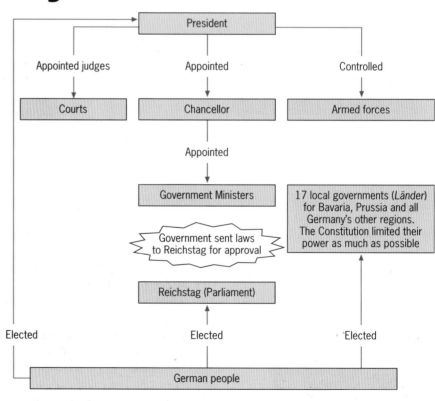

The Weimar Constitution.

The Republic in danger, 1919–24

From the start, Ebert's government faced violent opposition from both left-wing and right-wing opponents.

The threat from the Left

One left-wing group was a Communist party known as the Spartacists. They were led by Karl Liebknecht and Rosa Luxemburg. Their party was much like Lenin's Bolsheviks, who had just taken power in Russia. They argued strongly against Ebert's plans for a democratic Germany (see Factfile). They wanted a Germany ruled by workers' councils or soviets.

Early in 1919 the Spartacists launched their bid for power. Joined by rebel soldiers and sailors, they set up soviets in many towns. Not all soldiers were on the side of the Spartacists, however. Some anti-Communist ex-soldiers had formed themselves into vigilante groups called Freikorps. Ebert made an agreement with the commanders of the army and the Freikorps to put down the rebellion. Bitter street fighting followed between the Spartacists and Freikorps. Both sides were heavily armed. Casualties were high. The Freikorps won. Liebknecht and Luxemburg were murdered and this Communist revolution had failed. However, another one was soon to follow.

It emerged in Bavaria in the south of Germany. Bavaria was still an independent Socialist state led by Kurt Eisner, who was Ebert's ally. In February 1919 he was murdered by political opponents. The Communists in Bavaria seized the opportunity to declare a soviet republic in Bavaria. Ebert used the same tactics as he had against the Spartacists. The Freikorps moved in to crush the revolt in May 1919. Around 600 Communists were killed.

In 1920 there was more Communist agitation in the Ruhr industrial area. Again police, army and Freikorps clashed with Communists. There were 2,000 casualties.

Ebert's ruthless measures against the Communists created lasting bitterness between them and his Socialist Party. However, it gained approval from many in Germany. Ebert was terrified that Germany might go the same way as Russia (at that time rocked by bloody civil war). Many Germans shared his fears. Even so, despite these defeats, the Communists remained a powerful anti-government force in Germany throughout the 1920s.

The Treaty of Versailles

The next crisis to hit the new Republic came in May 1919 when the terms of the Treaty of Versailles were announced. You can read more about this on pages 8–9, but here is a summary. Germany lost:

- 10 per cent of its land
- all of its overseas colonies
- 12.5 per cent of its population
- 16 per cent of its coal and 48 per cent of its iron industry.

In addition:

- its army was reduced to 100,000; it was not allowed to have an air force; its navy was reduced
- Germany had to accept blame for starting the war and was forced to pay reparations.

Most Germans were appalled. Supporters of the Weimar government felt betrayed by the Allies. The Kaiser was gone – why should they be punished for his war and aggression? Opponents of the regime turned their fury on Ebert.

As you read on page 10, Ebert himself was very reluctant to sign the Treaty, but he had no choice. Germany could not go back to war. However, in the minds of many Germans, Ebert and his Weimar Republic were forever to blame for the Treaty. The injustice of the Treaty became a rallying point for all Ebert's opponents. They believed that the German army had been 'stabbed in the back' by the Socialist and Liberal politicians who agreed an armistice in November 1918. They believed not that Germany had been beaten on the battlefield, but that it had been betrayed by its civilian politicians who didn't dare continue the war. The Treaty was still a source of bitterness in Germany when Hitler came to power in 1933.

You can read more about this on pages 8–9

As you read on page 10

SOURCE 4

Spartacists – the Communists who felt that Germany was ready to follow Russia's example of Communist revolution.

SOURCE 5

The Freikorps – ex-servicemen who were totally opposed to Communism.

SOURCE 6

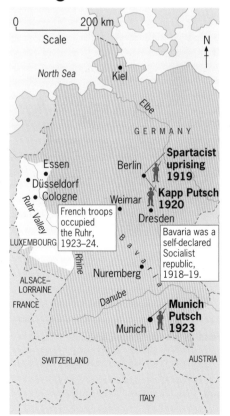

0   200 km
Scale

North Sea   Kiel
                    Elbe
            GERMANY

Essen   Berlin   **Spartacist uprising 1919**
• Düsseldorf
• Cologne   Weimar   **Kapp Putsch 1920**
French troops occupied the Ruhr, 1923–24.   Dresden
LUXEMBOURG   Bavaria was a self-declared Socialist republic, 1918–19.
ALSACE-LORRAINE   Nuremberg
FRANCE   Danube
            Munich Putsch 1923
     Munich
SWITZERLAND   AUSTRIA
        ITALY

Problems for the Weimar Republic, 1919–24.

SOURCE 7

Versailles was a scandal and a disgrace and … the dictate signified an act of highway robbery against our people.

Extract from Hitler's biography *Mein Kampf*, 1924.

SOURCE 8

The majority of the German nation shared the position that Hitler took on the Treaty of Versailles: that it was unfair, and that the imposition on Germany of sole responsibility for the war was wrong.

Professor Jay Winter, an academic historian.

SOURCE 10

Cartoon from the German magazine *Simplicissimus*, June 1919. The caption in the magazine read: 'The Allies are burying Germany with the peace terms'.

German reactions to the Treaty of Versailles

SOURCE 9

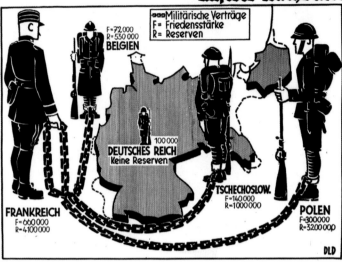

Nazi cartoon commenting on the military terms of the Versailles treaty. The text reads: 'The Mammoth Military superiority of our neighbours'. The Soldier's symbol = military treaties; F = peace time strength; R = reserves; the German Reich is surrounded by Belgium, Czechoslovakia, Poland and France (left to right).

SOURCE 11

A demonstration against the Treaty of Versailles in 1933. The march was organised by the Nazi party. The banners read, 'Day of Versailles, day of dishonour!' and 'We would be free from Versailles!'

1 Work in pairs. One of you study Source 9 and the other Source 10. Explain the message of each source to the other person in your pair. Remember to make a valid inference (for example, the cartoonist is saying …). Then remember to support the inference with a detail from the cartoon (for example this is shown in the cartoon by …).
2 Does Source 11 prove there was long lasting bitterness towards the Treaty?
3 How far do Sources 7 and 9–11 support the views of Professor Winter in Source 8?

Focus Task

What was the impact of the Treaty of Versailles on the Republic?

Which of the following do you think were most damaged by the Treaty of Versailles: Political stability, Economy, Armed forces, Territory, Pride?
Put these points in order of 'most damaged' to 'least damaged':
◆ after reading page 253 (threat from the Left)
◆ after reading this page
◆ after reading page 255 (threat from the Right)
◆ after reading page 256 (Ruhr)
◆ after reading page 258 (hyperinflation)
◆ at the end of this section.

4 Why might the Right dislike the Weimar Constitution (see Factfile, page 252)?
5 For each aspect of the Treaty of Versailles, explain why it would anger Ebert's right-wing opponents.

The threat from the Right

Ebert's government faced violent opposition from the Right. His right-wing opponents were largely people who had grown up in the successful days of the Kaiser's Germany. They had liked the Kaiser's dictatorial style of government. They liked Germany having a strong army. They wanted Germany to expand its territory, and to have an empire. They had been proud of Germany's powerful industry.

In March 1920 Dr Wolfgang Kapp led 5,000 Freikorps into Berlin in a rebellion known as the Kapp Putsch (Putsch means rebellion). The army refused to fire on the Freikorps and it looked as if Ebert's government was doomed. However, it was saved by the German people, especially the industrial workers of Berlin. They declared a general strike which brought the capital to a halt with no transport, power or water (see Source 12). After a few days Kapp realised he could not succeed and left the country. He was hunted down and died while awaiting trial. It seemed that Weimar had support and power after all. Even so, the rest of the rebels went unpunished by the courts and judges.

SOURCE **12**

Berlin während des Verkehrsstreiks.
Kraftwagen nach Halensee.

Original-Aufnahme

Workers being bussed to work privately during the 1920 general strike.

Ebert's government struggled to deal with the political violence in Germany. Political assassinations were frequent. In the summer of 1922 Ebert's foreign minister Walther Rathenau was murdered by extremists. Then in November 1923 Adolf Hitler led an attempted rebellion in Munich, known as the Munich Putsch (see page 265). Both Hitler and the murderers of Rathenau received short prison sentences. Strangely, Hitler's judge at the trial was the same judge who had tried him two years earlier for disorder. Both times he got off very lightly. It seemed that Weimar's right-wing opponents had friends in high places.

6 From reading pages 253 and 255, what differences can you see between the treatment of left-wing and right-wing extremists? Can you explain this?

SOURCE 13

There was a lot of official harassment. There was widespread hunger, squalor and poverty and – what really affected us – there was humiliation. The French ruled with an iron hand. If they disliked you walking on the pavement, for instance, they'd come along with their riding crops and you'd have to walk in the road.

The memories of Jutta Rudiger, a German woman living in the Ruhr during the French occupation.

1 For each of Sources 14 and 15 write an explanation of its message.
2 Is it possible to answer the question 'Could Germany afford the reparations payments?' with a simple yes or no? Explain your answer.

Economic disaster

The Treaty of Versailles destabilised Germany politically, but Germans also blamed it for another problem – economic chaos. See if you agree that the Treaty of Versailles was responsible for economic problems in Germany.

The Treaty of Versailles forced Germany to pay reparations to the Allies. The reparations bill was announced in April 1921. It was set at £6,600 million, to be paid in annual instalments. This was 2 per cent of Germany's annual output. The Germans protested that this was an intolerable strain on the economy which they were struggling to rebuild after the war, but their protests were ignored.

The Ruhr

The first instalment of £50 million was paid in 1921, but in 1922 nothing was paid. Ebert did his best to play for time and to negotiate concessions from the Allies, but the French in particular ran out of patience. They too had war debts to pay to the USA. So in January 1923 French and Belgian troops entered the Ruhr (quite legally under the Treaty of Versailles) and began to take what was owed to them in the form of raw materials and goods.

The results of the occupation of the Ruhr were disastrous for Germany. The government ordered the workers to carry out passive resistance, which meant to go on strike. That way, there would be nothing for the French to take away. The French reacted harshly, killing over 100 workers and expelling over 100,000 protesters from the region. More importantly, the halt in industrial production in Germany's most important region caused the collapse of the German currency.

SOURCE 14

A 1923 German poster discouraging people from buying French and Belgian goods, as long as Germany is under occupation. The poster reads, 'Hands off French and Belgian goods as long as Germany is raped!'.

SOURCE 15

A British cartoon from 1921.

SOURCE 16

A photograph taken in 1923 showing a woman using banknotes to start her fire.

Hyperinflation

Because it had no goods to trade, the government simply printed money. For the government this seemed an attractive solution. It paid off its debts in worthless marks, including war loans of over £2,200 million. The great industrialists were able to pay off all their debts as well.

This set off a chain reaction. With so much money in circulation, prices and wages rocketed, but people soon realised that this money was worthless. Workers needed wheelbarrows to carry home their wages. Wages began to be paid daily instead of weekly. The price of goods could rise between joining the back of a queue in a shop and reaching the front!

Poor people suffered, but the greatest casualties were the richer Germans – those with savings. A prosperous middle-class family would find that their savings in the bank, which might have bought them a house in 1921, by 1923 would not even buy a loaf of bread. Pensioners found that their previously ample monthly pension would not even buy a cup of coffee.

SOURCE 17

	1918	0.63 marks
	1922	163 marks
January	1923	250 marks
July	1923	3465 marks
September	1923	1,512,000 marks
November	1923	201,000,000,000 marks

The rising cost of a loaf of bread in Berlin.

SOURCE 18

1921 £1 = 500 marks
Nov 1923 £1 = 14,000,000,000,000 marks

The exchange rate value of the mark in pounds.

SOURCE 19

A German banknote of 1923 for one billion marks.

SOURCE 20

Billion mark notes were quickly handed on as though they burned one's fingers, for tomorrow one would no longer pay in notes but in bundles of notes . . . One afternoon I rang Aunt Louise's bell. The door was opened merely a crack. From the dark came an odd broken voice: 'I've used 60 billion marks' worth of gas. My milk bill is 1 million. But all I have left is 2000 marks. I don't understand any more.'

E Dobert, *Convert to Freedom*, 1941.

3 Look at Source 19. Use Source 17 to work out how much bread this banknote could buy in July 1923 and November 1923.

4 Use Sources 16–20 to describe in your own words how ordinary Germans were affected by the collapse of the mark.

Focus Task

Was hyperinflation caused by the Treaty of Versailles?

Study Sources 21 and 22 carefully.

1 In what ways do they disagree about the causes of inflation?
2 How does Source 21 support the argument of Source 22?
3 In Source 20 Aunt Louise says 'I don't understand any more.' Imagine that the writer of Source 20 tries to explain the causes of inflation to Aunt Louise. What would they say? Who would they blame?
4 Whom, or what, would you blame for Germany's hyperinflation?

SOURCE 22

. . . the causes of hyperinflation were varied and complex, but the Germans did not see it that way. They blamed reparations and the Weimar Republic which had accepted them and had presided over the chaos of 1923. Many middle-class Germans never forgave the republic for the blow they believed it had dealt to them.

British historian Finlay McKichan, writing in 1992.

1 Read Source 23. Choose two of Sources 16–23 to illustrate a leaflet containing a published version of Hitler's speech. Explain your choice.
2 Explain why people might agree with Hitler that a dictatorship would solve Germany's problems.

SOURCE 23

Believe me, our misery will increase. The State itself has become the biggest swindler . . . Horrified people notice that they can starve on millions . . . we will no longer submit . . . we want a dictatorship!

Adolf Hitler attacks the Weimar government in a speech, 1924.

SOURCE 21

A 1920 German cartoon. Germany complains, 'My sons have taken everything away. All they have left me is a paper mark with which to cover my nakedness.'

It was clear to all, both inside and outside Germany, that the situation needed urgent action. In August 1923 a new government under Gustav Stresemann took over. He called off the passive resistance in the Ruhr. He called in the worthless marks and burned them, replacing them with a new currency called the Rentenmark. He negotiated to receive American loans under the Dawes Plan (see page 32–33). He even renegotiated the reparations payments (see page 260). The economic crisis was solved very quickly. Some historians suggest that this is evidence that Germany's problems were not as severe as its politicians had made out.

It was also increasingly clear, however, that the hyperinflation had done great political damage to the Weimar government. Their right-wing opponents had yet another problem to blame them for, and the government had lost the support of the middle classes.

Focus Task

REVIEW: What was the state of the Weimar Republic in 1924?

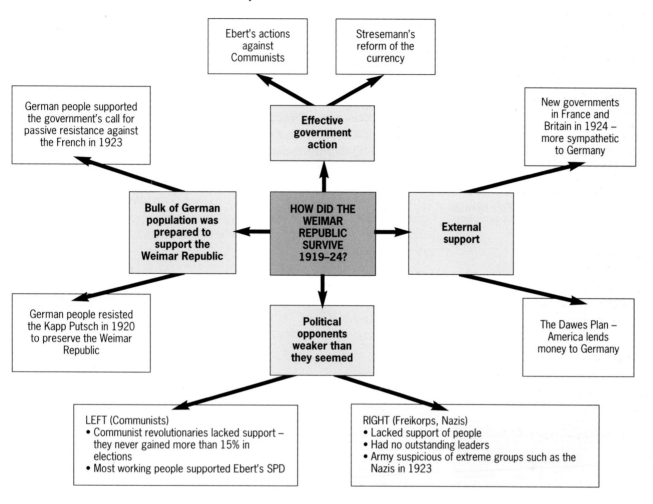

This diagram summarises how the Weimar Republic survived its problems between 1919 and 1924. On its own it presents quite a positive image of the Republic. Is it too positive, or is it about right?

Your task is to write a status report on the Weimar Republic in 1924. You could write your report as though you are advising Ebert or as a modern historian with the benefit of hindsight.

You could divide your report into sections:

a) Political opposition to Weimar
Explain whether you think *all* of the regime's political opponents had been *completely defeated* by 1924.

b) Economic problems
Explain whether you think *all* of the economic problems had been *completely solved* by 1924.

c) Popular support
Explain whether you think the regime had the *complete* support of *all* of the people of Germany.

d) Germany and the wider world
Explain:
- whether you think Germany's relations with other countries had improved in 1924
- whether the problems created by the Treaty of Versailles had been resolved by 1924.

SOURCE 24

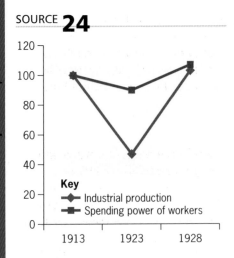

Comparison of aspects of the German economy in 1913, 1923 and 1928.

1 What factors helped Germany's economy to recover?
2 In what ways did economic recovery affect the lives of ordinary Germans?

SOURCE 25

Pillars of Society by George Grosz, 1926. Grosz criticised Weimar Germany because he felt too many leading figures in society still believed in the ideals of the Kaiser's Germany (in this painting you can see the civilians still dream of military glory).

The Weimar Republic under Stresemann

Achievements

The economy

Although Chancellor for only a few months, Stresemann was a leading member of every government from 1923 to 1929. He was a more skilful politician than Ebert, and, as a right-winger, he had wider support. He was also helped by the fact that through the 1920s the rest of Europe was gradually coming out of its post-war depression. Slowly but surely, he built up Germany's prosperity again. Under the Dawes Plan (see page 32–33), reparations payments were spread over a longer period, and 800 million marks in loans from the USA poured into German industry. Some of the money went into German businesses, replacing old equipment with the latest technology. Some of the money went into public works like swimming pools, sports stadia and apartment blocks. As well as providing facilities, these projects created jobs.

By 1927 German industry seemed to have recovered very well. In 1928 Germany finally achieved the same levels of production as before the war and regained its place as the world's second greatest industrial power (behind the USA). Wages for industrial workers rose and for many Germans there was a higher standard of living. Reparations were being paid and exports were on the increase. The government was even able to increase welfare benefits and wages for state employees.

Culture

There was also a cultural revival in Germany. In the Kaiser's time there had been strict censorship, but the Weimar constitution allowed free expression of ideas. Writers and poets flourished, especially in Berlin. Artists in Weimar Germany turned their back on old styles of painting and tried to represent the reality of everyday life, even when that reality was sometimes harsh and shocking. Artists like George Grosz produced powerful paintings like Source 25, which criticised the politicians of the Weimar period. Other paintings of Grosz showed how many soldiers had been traumatised by their experiences in the war.

The famous Bauhaus style of design and architecture developed. Artists such as Walter Gropius, Paul Klee and Wassily Kandinsky taught at the Bauhaus design college in Dessau (Source 26). The Bauhaus architects rejected traditional styles to create new and exciting buildings. They produced designs for anything from houses and shops to art galleries and factories. The first Bauhaus exhibition attracted 15,000 visitors.

SOURCE 26

The Bauhaus design college in Dessau, built 1925–26.

SOURCE 27

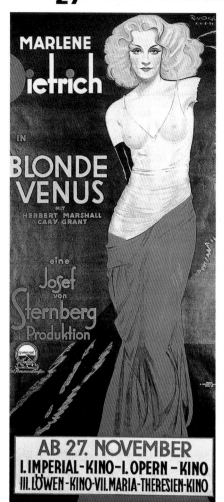

Poster for one of Marlene Dietrich's films.

The 1920s were a golden age for German cinema, producing one of its greatest ever international stars, Marlene Dietrich, and one of its most celebrated directors, Fritz Lang. Berlin was famous for its daring and liberated night life. Going to clubs was a major pastime. In 1927 there were 900 dance bands in Berlin alone. Cabaret artists performed songs criticising political leaders that would have been banned in the Kaiser's days. These included songs about sex that would have shocked an earlier generation of Germans.

Politics

Even politics became more stable. To begin with, there were no more attempted revolutions after 1923 (see page 265). One politician who had been a leading opponent of Ebert in 1923 said that 'the Republic is beginning to settle and the German people are becoming reconciled to the way things are.' Source 28 shows that the parties that supported Weimar democracy did well in these years. By 1928 the moderate parties had 136 more seats in the Reichstag than the radical parties. Hitler's Nazis gained less than 3 per cent of the vote in the 1928 election. Just as importantly, some of the parties who had co-operated in the 'revolution' of 1918 began to co-operate again. The Socialists (SPD), Catholic Centre Party, German Democratic Party (DDP) and the German People's Party (DVP) generally worked well together in the years 1924–29.

SOURCE 28

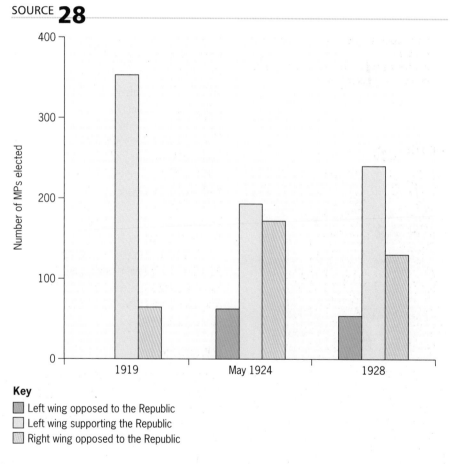

Key
- Left wing opposed to the Republic
- Left wing supporting the Republic
- Right wing opposed to the Republic

Support for the main political parties in Germany, 1919–28.

Activity

Imagine you were interviewing people in the streets of a large German city in 1928. You ask them questions about Culture, Foreign Policy and Politics.
1 For each area, what events or developments do you think most people would know something about?
2 Which area would give Germans most pride?

Foreign policy

Stresemann's greatest triumphs were in foreign policy. In 1925 he signed the Locarno Treaties (see page 32), guaranteeing not to try to change Germany's western borders with France and Belgium. As a result, in 1926 Germany was accepted into the League of Nations. Here Stresemann began to work, quietly but steadily, on reversing some of the terms of the Treaty of Versailles, particularly those concerning reparations and Germany's eastern frontiers. By the time he died in 1929, Stresemann had negotiated the Young Plan, which further lightened the reparations burden on Germany and led to the final removal of British, French and Belgian troops from the Rhineland.

Problems

Economy

The economic boom in Weimar Germany was precarious. The US loans could be called in at short notice, which would cause ruin in Germany.

The main economic winners in Germany were big businesses (such as the steel and chemicals industries) which controlled about half of Germany's industrial production. Other winners were big landowners, particularly if they owned land in towns – the value of land in Berlin rose by 700 per cent in this period. The workers in the big industries gained as well. Most Weimar governments were sympathetic towards the unions, which led to improved pay and conditions. However, even here there were concerns as unemployment began to rise – it was 6 per cent of the working population by 1928.

The main losers were the peasant farmers and sections of the middle classes. The peasant farmers had increased production during the war. In peacetime, they found themselves overproducing. They had mortgages to pay but not enough demand for the food they produced. Many small business owners became disillusioned during this period. Small shopkeepers saw their businesses threatened by large department stores (many of which were owned by Jews). A university lecturer in 1913 earned ten times as much as a coal miner. In the 1920s he only earned twice as much. These people began to feel that the Weimar government offered them little.

Culture

The Weimar culture was colourful and exciting to many. However, in many of Germany's villages and country towns, the culture of the cities seemed to represent a moral decline, made worse by American immigrants and Jewish artists and musicians. As you have read, the Bauhaus design college was in Dessau (Source 26). What you were not told is that it was in Dessau because it was forced out of Weimar by hostile town officials.

Organisations such as the Wandervogel movement were a reaction to Weimar's culture. The Wandervogel wanted a return to simple country values and wanted to see more help for the countryside and less decadence in the towns. It was a powerful feeling which the Nazis successfully harnessed in later years.

SOURCE **29**

A Wandervogel camp in the 1920s.

Politics

Despite the relative stability of Weimar politics in this period, both the Nazis and Communists were building up their party organisations. Even during these stable years there were four different chancellors and it was only the influence of party leaders which held the party coalitions together (see Source 30).

SOURCE 30

What we have today is a coalition of ministers, not a coalition of parties. There are no government parties, only opposition parties. This state of things is a greater danger to the democratic system than ministers and parliamentarians realise.

Gustav Stolper, a Reichstag member for the DDP in 1929.

More worrying for the Republic was that around 30 per cent of the vote regularly went to parties opposed to the Republic. Most serious of all, the right-wing organisations which posed the greatest threat to the Republic were quiet rather than destroyed. The right-wing Nationalist Party (DNVP) and the Nazis began to collaborate closely and make themselves appear more respectable. Another event which would turn out to be very significant was that the German people elected Hindenburg as President in 1926. He was opposed to democracy and wrote to the Kaiser in exile for approval before he took up the post!

Foreign policy

There was also the question of international relations. Nationalists attacked Stresemann for joining the League of Nations and for signing the Locarno Pact, seeing it as an acceptance of the Treaty of Versailles. Communists also attacked Locarno, seeing it as part of a plot against the Communist government in the USSR. Germany was still a troubled place.

Focus Task

How far did the Weimar Republic recover after 1923?

Look back to the Focus Tasks on pages 252 and 259 which examined the state of the Weimar Republic in 1918 and 1924. You are now going to look at the state of the republic in 1928. You have to write or present another report, this time to discuss the question: 'How far has the Weimar Republic recovered?'

You could use the same headings as in 1924:
- Political opposition to Weimar
- Economic problems
- Popular support
- Germany and the wider world.

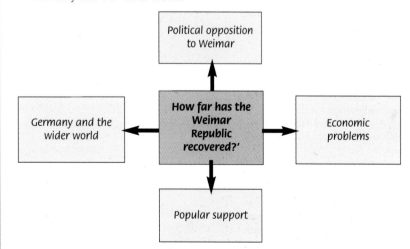

You could also add an additional section about the cultural achievements of the Weimar Republic. Mention failings and achievements in your report. You could give each section a mark out of ten. Finally, you need to decide on an overall judgement: in your opinion, how far had the Weimar Republic recovered? In your answer, do remember that, in the view of many historians, it was probably a major achievement for the Weimar Republic just to have survived.

Profile

Adolf Hitler – the early years, 1889–1919

- ➤ Born in Austria in 1889.
- ➤ He got on badly with his father but was fond of his mother.
- ➤ At the age of 16 he left school and went to Vienna to pursue his ambition of becoming a painter. However, things went wrong for him and between 1909 and 1914 he was virtually a 'down and out' on the streets of Vienna.
- ➤ During this period he developed his hatred of foreigners and Jews.
- ➤ When war broke out in 1914, Hitler joined the German army and served with distinction, winning the Iron Cross.
- ➤ Hitler found it very hard to accept the armistice and was completely unable to accept the Treaty of Versailles.
- ➤ He despised the Weimar democracy and like many Germans looked back to the 'glorious days' of the Kaiser.
- ➤ Hitler stayed in the army after the war, working in Munich for the intelligence services. It was in this job that he came across the DAP or German Workers' Party led by Anton Drexler. He liked the ideas of the party and joined in 1919.

Hitler and the Nazis

Stresemann's government succeeded in stabilising Germany. However, as you have already seen, the extremist opponents of the Weimar government had not disappeared. Through the 1920s they were organising and regrouping, waiting for their chance to win power.

One of the most important of these extremist groups was the Nazi Party. You are now going to look back at what it had been doing since 1919.

The Nazis began as the German Workers' Party, led by Anton Drexler. In 1919 Adolf Hitler joined the party. Drexler soon realised that Hitler had great talent and within months he had put him in charge of propaganda and the political ideas of the party. In 1920 the party announced its Twenty-Five Point Programme (see Factfile), and renamed itself the National Socialist German Workers' Party, or Nazis for short.

SOURCE 31

Hitler's renewed membership card of the German Worker's Party, issued 1 January 1920.

In 1921 Hitler removed Drexler as leader. Hitler's energy, commitment and above all his power as a speaker were soon attracting attention.

SOURCE 32

The most active political force in Bavaria at the present time is the National Socialist Party . . . It has recently acquired a political influence quite disproportionate to its actual numerical strength . . . Adolf Hitler from the very first has been the dominating force in the movement and the personality of this man has undoubtedly been one of the most important factors contributing to its success . . . His ability to influence a popular assembly is uncanny.

American intelligence report on political activities in Germany, 1922.

SOURCE 33

Hitler knew how to whip up those crowds jammed closely in a dense cloud of cigarette smoke – not by argument, but by his manner: the roaring and especially the power of his repetitions delivered in a certain infectious rhythm . . . He would draw up a list of existing evils and imaginary abuses and after listing them, in higher and higher crescendo, he screamed: 'And whose fault is it? It's all . . . the fault . . . of the Jews!'

A person who went to Nazi meetings describes the impact of Hitler's speeches.
From *A Part of Myself: Portrait of an Epoch*, by C Zuckmayer.

SOURCE 34

'Power!' screamed Adolf. 'We must have power!' 'Before we gain it,' I replied firmly, 'let us decide what we propose to do with it.'

Hitler, who even then could hardly bear contradiction, thumped the table and barked: 'Power first – afterwards we can act as circumstances dictate.'

Leading Nazi Otto Strasser recalls a conversation with Hitler in the early 1920s.

SOURCE 35

The Bavarian Ministry is removed. I propose that a Bavarian government be formed consisting of a Regent and a Prime Minister invested with dictatorial powers . . . The government of the November Criminals and the Reich president are declared to be removed . . . I propose that, until accounts have been finally settled with the November Criminals, the direction of policy in the National Government be taken over by me . . .

Hitler declares the revolution, 8 November 1923.

1 Read Source 35. What was Hitler trying to achieve through the Munich Putsch?
2 What impression does Source 36 give of the Putsch and Hitler's role in it?
3 Why would you have concerns about it as a source for finding out what happened?

SOURCE 36

A painting of the Munich Putsch made by one of the Nazis who took part in it. Hitler is in the centre and Ludendorff is in the black hat to Hitler's right.

Hitler had a clear and simple appeal. He stirred nationalist passions in his audiences. He gave them scapegoats to blame for Germany's problems: the Allies, the Versailles Treaty, the 'November Criminals' (the Socialist politicians who signed the Treaty), the Communists and the Jews.

His meetings were so successful that his opponents tried to disrupt them. To counter this, he set up the SA, also known as storm troopers or brownshirts, in 1921. These hired thugs protected Hitler's meetings but also disrupted those of other parties.

By 1923 the Nazis were still very much a minority party, but Hitler had given them a high profile.

Activity

It is 1923. Use the information and sources on pages 264–65 to write a newspaper article about the rise of Hitler and the Nazi Party. Your opening sentences could be:
'In recent months, a new force seems to be arising in German politics. Adolf Hitler and the Nazis have hit the headlines with their meetings, banners and radical ideas. What makes this man successful? . . .'
Your article should tell readers about:
• Hitler's background
• his qualities
• what he and the Nazis believe.

The Munich Putsch, 1923

By November 1923 Hitler believed that the moment had come for him to topple the Weimar government. The government was preoccupied with the economic crisis. Stresemann had just called off Germany's passive resistance in the Ruhr (see pages 256–58). On 8 November, Hitler hijacked a local government meeting and announced he was taking over the government of Bavaria. He was joined by the old war hero Ludendorff.

Nazi storm troopers began taking over official buildings. The next day, however, the Weimar government forces hit back. Police rounded up the storm troopers and in a brief exchange of shots sixteen Nazis were killed by the police. The rebellion broke up in chaos. Hitler escaped in a car, while Ludendorff and others stayed to face the armed police.

Hitler had miscalculated the mood of the German people. In the short term, the Munich Putsch was a disaster for him. People did not rise up to support him. He and other leading Nazis were arrested and charged with treason. At the trial, however, Hitler gained enormous publicity for himself and his ideas, as his every word was reported in the newspapers.

In fact, Hitler so impressed the judges that he and his accomplices got off very lightly. Ludendorff was freed altogether and Hitler was given only five years in prison, even though the legal guidelines said that high treason should carry a life sentence. In the end, Hitler only served nine months of the sentence and did so in great comfort in Landsberg castle. This last point was very significant. It was clear that Hitler had some sympathy and support from important figures in the legal system. Because of his links with Ludendorff, Hitler probably gained the attention of important figures in the army. Time would show that Hitler was down, but not out.

SOURCE 37

I alone bear the responsibility but I am not a criminal because of that . . . There is no such thing as high treason against the traitors of 1918 . . . I feel myself the best of Germans who wanted the best for the German people.

Hitler at his trial.

Focus Task

What did the Nazis stand for in the 1920s?

Imagine the judge at Hitler's trial has asked Hitler the question: 'What do the Nazis really stand for?' Write a reply that Hitler might have given to the judge.
Use sources, the Profile and Factfile as well as the text. Mention:
◆ the Weimar Constitution
◆ the Treaty of Versailles
◆ the German people and anything else that you think Hitler might consider important.

SOURCE 38

When I resume active work, it will be necessary to pursue a new policy. Instead of working to achieve power by armed conspiracy we shall have to take hold of our noses and enter the Reichstag against the Catholic and Marxist deputies. If out-voting them takes longer than out-shooting them, at least the results will be guaranteed by their own constitution. Any lawful process is slow. Sooner or later we shall have a majority and after that we shall have Germany.

Hitler, writing while in prison in 1923.

Factfile

Hitler's views

In 'Mein Kampf' and his later writings, Hitler set out the main Nazi beliefs:

➤ National Socialism: This stood for loyalty to Germany, racial purity, equality and state control of the economy.

➤ Racism: The Aryans (white Europeans) were the Master Race. All other races and especially the Jews were inferior.

➤ Armed force: Hitler believed that war and struggle were an essential part of the development of a healthy Aryan race.

➤ Living space ('Lebensraum'): Germany needed to expand as its people were hemmed in. This expansion would be mainly at the expense of Russia and Poland.

➤ The Führer: Debate and democratic discussion produced weakness. Strength lay in total loyalty to the leader (the Führer).

---

1 Read Source 39. List the five demands made by Goebbels.
2 Would you say this source appeals more to the hearts of German people than to their minds? Support your answer with evidence from the source.

The Nazis in the wilderness, 1924–29

Hitler used his time in prison to write a book, *Mein Kampf* (My Struggle), which clarified and presented his ideas about Germany's future. It was also while in prison that he came to the conclusion that the Nazis would not be able to seize power by force. They would have to work within the democratic system to achieve power but, once in power, they could destroy that system.

As soon as he was released from prison, Hitler set about rebuilding the Nazi Party so that it could take power through democratic means. He saw the Communists building up their strength through youth organisations and recruitment drives. Soon the Nazis were doing the same.

They fought the Reichstag elections for the first time in May 1924 and won 32 seats. Encouraged by this, Hitler created a network of local Nazi parties which in turn set up the Hitler Youth, the Nazi Students' League and similar organisations.

SOURCE 39

The German people is an enslaved people. We have had all our sovereign rights taken from us. We are just good enough that international capital allows us to fill its money sacks with interest payments. That and only that is the result of a centuries-long history of heroism. Have we deserved it? No, and no again! Therefore we demand that a struggle against this condition of shame and misery begin, and that the men in whose hands we put our fate must use every means to break the chain of slavery.

Three million people lack work and sustenance. The officials, it is true, work to conceal the misery. They speak of measures and silver linings. Things are getting steadily better for them, and steadily worse for us. The illusion of freedom, peace and prosperity that we were promised when we wanted to take our fate in our own hands is vanishing. Only complete collapse of our people can follow from these irresponsible policies.

Thus we demand the right of work and a decent living for every working German.

While the front soldier was fighting in the trenches to defend his Fatherland, some Eastern Jewish profiteer robbed him of hearth and home. The Jew lives in palaces and the proletarian, the front soldier, lives in holes that do not deserve to be called 'homes'. That is neither necessary nor unavoidable, rather an injustice that cries out to the heavens. A government that does nothing is useless and must vanish, the sooner the better.

Therefore we demand homes for German soldiers and workers. If there is not enough money to build them, drive the foreigners out so that Germans can live on German soil.

Our people is growing, others diminishing. It will mean the end of our history if a cowardly and lazy policy takes from us the posterity that will one day be called upon to fulfil our historical mission.

Therefore we demand land on which to grow the grain that will feed our children.

While we dreamed and chased strange and unreachable fantasies, others stole our property. Today some say this was an act of God. Not so. Money was transferred from the pockets of the poor to the pockets of the rich. That is cheating, shameless, vile cheating!

A government presides over this misery that in the interests of peace and order one cannot really discuss. We leave it to others to judge whether it represents Germany's interests or those of our capitalist tormentors.

We, however, demand a government of national labour, statesmen who are men and whose aim is the creation of a German state.

These days anyone has the right to speak in Germany – the Jew, the Frenchman, the Englishman, the League of Nations, the conscience of the world and the Devil knows who else. Everyone but the German worker. He has to shut up and work. Every four years he elects a new set of torturers, and everything stays the same. That is unjust and treasonous. We need tolerate it no longer. We have the right to demand that only Germans who build this state may speak, those whose fate is bound to the fate of their Fatherland.

Therefore we demand the annihilation of the system of exploitation! Up with the German worker's state! Germany for the Germans!

A pamphlet called 'We demand', written in 1927 by Nazi propaganda expert Joseph Goebbels.

Focus Task

Why did the Nazis have little success before 1930?

Here are some factors which explain the Nazis' lack of success:
- disastrous Putsch of 1923
- disruption of meetings by political enemies
- lack of support in the police and army
- most industrial workers supported left-wing parties
- Nazi aims were irrelevant to most Germans
- successes of Weimar government (for example in the economy, foreign policy)

At the moment these factors are organised in alphabetical order. Work in groups to rearrange these factors into what you think is their order of importance.

As you can see from Source 39, by 1927 the Nazis were still trying to appeal to German workers, as they had when the party was first founded. The results of the 1928 elections convinced the Nazis that they had to look elsewhere for support. The Nazis gained only twelve Reichstag seats and only a quarter of the Communist vote. Although their anti-semitic policies gained them some support, they had failed to win over the workers. Workers with radical political views were more likely to support the Communists. The great majority of workers supported the socialist Social Democratic Party (SPD), as they had done in every election since 1919. Indeed, despite the Nazis' arguments that workers were exploited, urban industrial workers actually felt that they were doing rather well in Weimar Germany in the years up to 1929.

Other groups in society were doing less well. The Nazis found that they gained more support from groups such as the peasant farmers in northern Germany and middle-class shopkeepers and small business people in country towns. Unlike Britain, Germany still had a large rural population who lived and worked on the land – probably about 35 per cent of the entire population. They were not sharing in Weimar Germany's economic prosperity. The Nazis highlighted the importance of the peasants in their plans for Germany, promising to help agriculture if they came to power. They praised the peasants as racially pure Germans. Nazi propaganda also contrasted the supposedly clean and simple life of the peasants with that of the allegedly corrupt, immoral, crime-ridden cities (for which they blamed the Jews). The fact that the Nazis despised Weimar culture also gained them support among some conservative people in the towns, who saw Weimar's flourishing art, literature and film achievements as immoral.

SOURCE 40

At one of the early congresses I was sitting surrounded by thousands of SA men. As Hitler spoke I was most interested at the shouts and more often the muttered exclamations of the men around me, who were mainly workmen or lower-middle-class types. 'He speaks for me . . . Ach, Gott, he knows how I feel' . . . One man in particular struck me as he leant forward with his head in his hands, and with a sort of convulsive sob said: 'Gott sei Dank [God be thanked], he understands.'

E Amy Buller, *Darkness over Germany*, published in 1943. Buller was an anti-Nazi German teacher.

SOURCE 41

A Nazi election poster from 1928, saying 'Work, freedom and bread! Vote for the National Socialists.'

In 1925 Hitler enlarged the SA. About 55 per cent of the SA came from the ranks of the unemployed. Many were ex-servicemen from the war. He also set up a new group called the SS. The SS were similar to the SA but were fanatically loyal to Hitler personally. Membership of the party rose to over 100,000 by 1928.

Hitler appointed Joseph Goebbels to take charge of Nazi propaganda. Goebbels was highly efficient at spreading the Nazi message. He and Hitler believed that the best way to reach what they called 'the masses' was by appealing to their feelings rather than by rational argument. Goebbels produced posters, leaflets, films and radio broadcasts; he organised rallies; he set up 'photo opportunities'.

Despite these shifting policies and priorities, there was no electoral breakthrough for the Nazis. Even after all their hard work, in 1928 they were still a fringe minority party who had the support of less than 3 per cent of the population. They were the smallest party with fewer seats than the Communists. The prosperity of the Stresemann years and Stresemann's success in foreign policy made Germans uninterested in extreme politics.

Activity

1 Look back at your answer to the Focus Task on page 265. If Hitler had been asked the same question, 'What do the Nazis really stand for?', in 1928, what would have changed?
2 Do you think Hitler would have liked your asking him this question? Explain your answer.

The Depression and the rise of the Nazis

In 1929 the American stock market crashed and sent the USA into a disastrous economic depression. In a very short time, countries around the world began to feel the effects of this depression. Germany was particularly badly affected. American bankers and businessmen lost huge amounts of money in the crash. To pay off their debts they asked German banks to repay the money they had borrowed. The result was economic collapse in Germany. Businesses went bankrupt, workers were laid off and unemployment rocketed.

SOURCE 42

Upper Silesia in 1932: unemployed miners and their families moved into shacks in a shanty town because they had no money to pay their rent.

SOURCE 43

No one knew how many there were of them. They completely filled the streets. They stood or lay about in the streets as if they had taken root there. They sat or lay on the pavements or in the roadway and gravely shared out scraps of newspapers among themselves.

An eyewitness describes the unemployed vagrants in Germany in 1932.

The Depression was a worldwide problem. It was not just Germany that suffered. Nor was the Weimar government the only government having difficulties in solving the problem of unemployment. However, because Germany had been so dependent on American loans, and because it still had to pay reparations to the Allies, the problems were most acute in Germany.

In addition, it seemed that the Weimar Constitution, with its careful balance of power, made firm and decisive action by the government very difficult indeed (see Factfile, page 252).

1 Draw a diagram to show how the Wall Street Crash in New York could lead to miners losing their jobs in Silesia.

Enter the Nazis!

Hitler's ideas now had a special relevance:

- Is the Weimar government indecisive? Then Germany needs a strong leader!
- Are reparations adding to Germany's problems? Then kick out the Treaty of Versailles!
- Is unemployment a problem? Let the unemployed join the army, build Germany's armaments and be used for public works like road building!

The Nazis' Twenty-Five Points (see page 264) were very attractive to those most vulnerable to the Depression: the unemployed, the elderly and the middle classes. Hitler offered them culprits to blame for Germany's troubles – the Allies, the 'November Criminals' and the Jews. None of these messages was new and they had not won support for the Nazis in the Stresemann years. The difference now was that the democratic parties simply could not get Germany back to work.

In the 1930 elections the Nazis got 107 seats. In November 1932 they got nearly 200. They did not yet have an overall majority, but they were the biggest single party.

Why did the Nazis succeed in elections?

When the Nazis were well established in power in Germany in the 1930s, their propaganda chief, Goebbels, created his own version of the events of 1929–33 that brought Hitler to power. In this version, it was Hitler's destiny to become Germany's leader, and the German people finally came to recognise this. How valid was this view? On pages 269–71 you are going to see if you agree with Goebbels.

SOURCE 44

Key
— Unemployed
▨ Communist vote
▥ Nazi vote

Number of seats in the Reichstag (left axis: 0–250)
Unemployed (millions) (right axis: 0–7)

1928 | 1930 | July 1932 | Nov 1932

Support for the Nazis and Communists, and unemployment, 1928–32.

SOURCE **45**

My mother saw a storm trooper parade in the streets of Heidelberg. The sight of discipline in a time of chaos, the impression of energy in an atmosphere of universal hopelessness seems to have won her over.

Albert Speer, writing in 1931. Later, he was to become an important and powerful Nazi leader.

SOURCE **46**

A poster for a 1931 midsummer festival organised by the Nazi Party. The poster proclaims 'Against Versailles'.

SOURCE **48**

A Nazi Party rally in Frankfurt in 1932.

Nazi campaigning

There is no doubt that Nazi campaign methods were modern and effective. They relied on generalised slogans rather than detailed policies. They talked about uniting the people of Germany behind one leader. They also talked about going back to traditional values, though they were never very clear about what this meant in terms of policies. This made it hard to criticise them. When they *were* criticised for a specific policy, they were quite likely to drop it. (For example, when industrialists expressed concern about Nazi plans to nationalise industry, they simply dropped the policy.) The Nazis repeated at every opportunity that they believed Jews, Communists, Weimar politicians and the Treaty of Versailles were the causes of Germany's problems. They expressed contempt for Weimar's democratic system and said that it was unable to solve Germany's economic problems.

Their posters and pamphlets could be found everywhere. Their rallies impressed people with their energy, enthusiasm and sheer size.

At this time, there were frequent street battles between Communist gangs and the police. Everywhere large unruly groups of unemployed workers gathered on street corners. In contrast, the SA and SS gave an impression of discipline and order. Many people felt the country needed this kind of order. They welcomed the fact that the SA were prepared to fight the Communists (page 271). The SA were better organised and usually had the support of the police and army when they beat up opponents and disrupted meetings and rallies.

The Nazis also organised soup kitchens and provided shelter in hostels for the unemployed.

SOURCE **47**

The Duties of German Communist Party volunteers

Unselfishly they help the farmers to dry the harvest.

Particular detachments are responsible for improving transport.

They work nights and overtime getting together useful equipment.

They increase their fitness for the fatherland with target practice.

An English translation of a 1931 Nazi election poster.

The Nazis' greatest campaigning asset was Hitler. He was a powerful speaker. He was years ahead of his time as a communicator. Hitler ran for president in 1932. He got 13 million votes to Hindenburg's 19 million. Despite Hitler's defeat, the campaign raised his profile hugely. Using films, radio and records he brought his message to millions. He travelled by plane on a hectic tour of rallies all over Germany. He appeared as a dynamic man of the moment, the leader of a modern party with modern ideas. At the same time, he was able to appear to be a man of the people, someone who knew and understood the people and their problems.

Nazi support rocketed. For example, in Neidenburg in East Prussia Nazi support rose from 2.3 per cent in 1928 to over 25 per cent in 1931, even though the town had no local Nazi Party and Hitler never went there.

SOURCE 49

Our opponents accuse us National Socialists, and me in particular, of being intolerant and quarrelsome. They say that we don't want to work with other parties. They say the National Socialists are not German at all, because they refuse to work with other political parties. So is it typically German to have thirty political parties? I have to admit one thing – these gentlemen are quite right. We are intolerant. I have given myself this one goal – to sweep these thirty political parties out of Germany.

Hitler speaking at an election rally, July 1932.

Activity

On page 265 you wrote an article about Hitler and the Nazis in 1923. It is now late 1932, almost ten years on. Write a follow-up article explaining what has changed in that time.

SOURCE 50

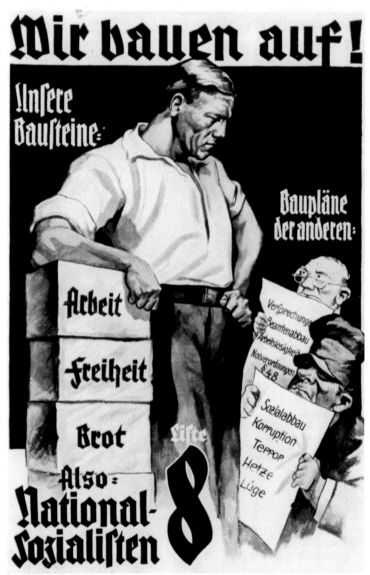

A Nazi election poster from July 1932. The Nazis proclaim 'We build!' and promise to provide work, freedom and bread. They accuse the opposing parties of planning to use terror, corruption, lies and other strategies as the basis for their government.

SOURCE 51

He began to speak and I immediately disliked him. I didn't know then what he would later become. I found him rather comical, with his funny moustache. He had a scratchy voice and a rather strange appearance, and he shouted so much. He was shouting in this small room, and what he was saying was very simplistic. I thought he wasn't quite normal. I found him spooky.

An eyewitness account of one of Hitler's meetings.

'Negative cohesion'

As Source 51 shows, not everyone was taken in by Nazi campaigning methods and Hitler's magnetism. But even some of the sceptics supported the Nazis. The historian Gordon Craig (see Source 63 on page 296) believed that this was because of something he called 'negative cohesion'. This meant that people supported the Nazis not because they shared Nazi views (that would be positive cohesion) but because they shared Nazi fears and dislikes. They cohered (joined together) over negatives not positives: if you hate what I hate, then you can't be all bad!

Disillusionment with democracy

Perhaps the biggest negative factor was a shared dislike of democracy in Weimar Germany. Politicians seemed unable to tackle the problems of the Depression. When the Depression began to bite in 1930 the Chancellor, Heinrich Brüning, pursued a tough economic policy. He cut government spending and welfare benefits. He urged Germans to make sacrifices. Some historians think that he was deliberately making the situation worse in order to get the international community to cancel reparations payments. Other historians think that he was afraid of hyperinflation recurring as in 1923. In protest, the SPD (still the main party in the Reichstag) pulled out of the government. To get his measures passed, Brüning relied on President Hindenburg to use his powers under Article 48 (see Factfile, page 252) to bypass the Reichstag.

Brüning and Hindenburg decided to call new elections in 1930. This was a disastrous decision, as it gave the Nazis the opportunity to exploit the fear and discontent in Germany and make the gains you have seen in Source 44 on page 268. The new elections resulted in another divided Reichstag, and the problems continued into 1931 and 1932. The impression was that democracy involved politicians squabbling over which job they would get in the Cabinet. Meanwhile, they did nothing about the real world, where unemployment was heading towards 6 million and the average German's income had fallen by 40 per cent since 1929. The Reichstag met fewer and fewer times (for only five days in 1932). Brüning had to continue to rely on Hindenburg's using his emergency powers, bypassing the democratic process altogether.

The Communist threat

As the crisis deepened, Communist support was rising too. The Nazis turned this to their advantage. 'Fear of Communism' was another shared negative. The Communist Red Fighting League broke up opposition party meetings, just like the SA. They fought street battles with police. So, out on the streets, the Nazi SA storm troopers met Communist violence with their own violence.

Many middle-class business owners had read about how the Communists in the USSR had discriminated against people like them. The owners of the big industries feared the Communists because of their plans to introduce state control of businesses. The industrialists were also concerned about the growing strength of Germany's trade unions. They felt the Nazis would combat these threats and some began to put money into Nazi campaign funds.

All farmers were alarmed by the Communists. They had read about Communist farming policies in the USSR where the Soviet government had taken over all of the land. Millions of peasants had been killed or imprisoned in the process. In contrast, the Nazis promised to help Germany's desperately struggling small farmers.

Decadence

As for modern decadent Weimar culture – the Nazis could count on all those who felt traditional German values were under threat. The Nazis talked about restoring these old-fashioned values.

The Social Democratic Party made a grave mistake in thinking that German people would not fall for these vague promises and accusations. They underestimated the fear and anger that German people felt towards the Weimar Republic.

SOURCE 52

The so-called race of poets and thinkers is hurrying with flags flying towards dictatorship . . . the radicalism of the Right [Nazis] has unleashed a strong radicalism on the Left [Communists]. The Communists have made gains almost everywhere. The situation is such that half the German people have declared themselves against the present state.

The Reich Interior Minister commenting on the rise of the Nazis and the Communists in 1932.

Focus Task

How did the Depression help the Nazis?

Do you agree with Goebbels' view that people rallied to support Hitler for positive reasons – or do you think that Gordon Craig was right that people supported the Nazis out of fear and disillusionment?

Work through questions 1–4 to help you make up your mind.

1 Look carefully at Sources 44–47 and 50. For each source, write two sentences explaining whether you think it is evidence that:
   ◆ supports the view of Goebbels
   ◆ supports the view of Craig
   ◆ could be used to support either interpretation.
2 Now work through the text and other sources on pages 268–71. Make a list of examples and evidence that seem to support either viewpoint.
3 Decide how far you agree with each of the following statements and give them a score on a scale of 1–5.
   ◆ Very few people fully supported the Nazis.
   ◆ The key factor was the economic depression. Without it, the Nazis would have remained a minority fringe party.
   ◆ The politicians of the Weimar Republic were mainly responsible for the rise of the Nazis.
4 Write a short paragraph explaining your score for each statement.

How did Hitler become Chancellor in 1933?

After the Reichstag elections of July 1932 the Nazis were the largest single party (with 230 seats) but not a majority party. Hitler demanded the post of Chancellor from the President, the old war hero Hindenburg. However, Hindenburg was suspicious of Hitler and refused. He allowed the current Chancellor Franz von Papen (an old friend of Hindenburg) to carry on as Chancellor. He then used his emergency powers to pass the measures that von Papen had hoped would solve the unemployment problem.

However, von Papen was soon in trouble. He had virtually no support at all in the Reichstag and so called yet another election in November 1932. The Nazis again came out as the largest party, although their share of the vote fell.

Hitler regarded the election as a disaster for the Nazis. He had lost more than 2 million votes along with 38 seats in the Reichstag. The signs were that the Hitler flood tide had finally turned. The Nazis started to run out of funds. Hitler is said to have threatened suicide.

Hindenburg again refused to appoint Hitler as Chancellor. In December 1932 he chose Kurt von Schleicher, one of his own advisers and a bitter rival of von Papen. Von Papen remained as an adviser to Hindenburg.

Within a month, however, von Schleicher too was forced to resign. By this time it was clear that the Weimar system of government was not working. In one sense, Hindenburg had already overthrown the principles of democracy by running Germany with emergency powers. If he was to rescue the democratic system, he needed a Chancellor who actually had support in the Reichstag.

Through January 1933 Hindenburg and von Papen met secretly with industrialists, army leaders and politicians. And on 30 January, to everyone's great surprise, they offered Hitler the post of Chancellor. Why did they do this? With only a few Nazis in the Cabinet and von Papen as Vice Chancellor, they were confident that they could limit Hitler's influence and resist his extremist demands. The idea was that the policies would be made by the Cabinet, which was filled with conservatives like von Papen. Hitler would be there to get support in the Reichstag for those policies and to control the Communists. So Hitler ended up as Chancellor not because of the will of the German people, but through a behind-the-scenes deal by some German aristocrats. Both Hindenburg and von Papen were sure that they could control Hitler. Both were very wrong.

SOURCE 53

The majority of Germans never voted for the Nazis.

The Nazis made it clear they would destroy democracy and all who stood in their way. Why then didn't their enemies join together to stop Hitler? . . . Had the Communists and Socialists joined forces they would probably have been strong enough both in the Reichstag and on the streets to have blocked the Nazis. The fact was that by 1932–3 there were simply not enough Germans who believed in democracy and individual freedom to save the Weimar Republic.

S Williams, in *The Rise and Fall of Hitler's Germany*, published in 1986, assesses the reasons for Hitler's success.

SOURCE 54

The Nazis celebrate Hitler's appointment as Chancellor in 1933.

A British cartoonist comments on Hitler's ambitions.

1 Look at Source 55. Do you think Hitler would be pleased by this portrayal of him? Explain your answer.

Focus Task

How did Hitler become Chancellor in 1933?

Here is a list of factors that helped Hitler come to power.

Nazi strengths
◆ Hitler's speaking skills
◆ Propaganda campaigns
◆ Violent treatment of their opponents
◆ Their criticisms of the Weimar system of government
◆ Nazi policies
◆ Support from big business

Opponents' weaknesses
◆ Failure to deal with the Depression
◆ Failure to co-operate with one another
◆ Attitudes of Germans to the democratic parties

Other factors
◆ Weaknesses of the Weimar Republic
◆ Scheming of Hindenburg and von Papen
◆ The impact of the Depression
◆ The Treaty of Versailles
◆ Memories of the problems of 1923

1 For each factor, write down one example of how it helped Hitler.
2 Give each factor a mark out of 10 for its importance in bringing Hitler to power.
3 Choose what you think are the five most important factors and write a short paragraph on each, explaining why you have chosen it.
4 If you took away any of those factors, would Hitler still have become Chancellor?
5 Were any of those five factors also present in the 1920s?
6 If so, explain why the Nazis were not successful in the 1920s.

11.2 Hitler's Germany

Hitler's dictatorship

It is easy to forget, but when Hitler became Chancellor in January 1933 he was in a very precarious position (see Source 1). Few people thought he would hold on to power for long. Even fewer thought that by the summer of 1934 he would be the supreme dictator of Germany. He achieved this through a clever combination of methods – some legal, others dubious. He also managed to defeat or reach agreements with those who could have stopped him.

The Reichstag Fire

Once he was Chancellor, Hitler took steps to complete a Nazi takeover of Germany. He called another election for March 1933 to try to get an overall Nazi majority in the Reichstag. Germany's cities again witnessed speeches, rallies, processions and street fighting. Hitler was using the same tactics as in previous elections, but now he had the resources of state media and control of the streets. Even so, success was in the balance. Then on 27 February there was a dramatic development: the Reichstag building burnt down. Hitler blamed the Communists and declared that the fire was the beginning of a Communist uprising. He demanded special emergency powers to deal with the situation and was given them by President Hindenburg. The Nazis used these powers to arrest Communists, break up meetings and frighten voters.

There have been many theories about what caused the fire, including that it was an accident, the work of a madman, or a Communist plot. Many Germans at the time thought that the Nazis might have started the fire themselves.

SOURCE **1**

THE TEMPORARY TRIANGLE.

A British cartoon from early 1933. Hitler, as Chancellor, is being supported by Hindenburg and Von Papen. He needed their support and, although they were not happy with the idea, they needed his popularity with the masses.

SOURCE **3**

Nazi storm troopers arrest suspected Communists, 1933.

SOURCE **2**

The Reichstag in flames, 1933.

SOURCE **4**

The defeat in 1918 did not depress me as greatly as the present state of affairs. It is shocking how day after day naked acts of violence, breaches of the law, barbaric opinions appear quite undisguised as official decree. The Socialist papers are permanently banned. The 'Liberals' tremble. The Berliner Tageblatt was recently banned for two days; that can't happen to the Dresdener Neueste Nachrichten, it is completely devoted to the government . . . I can no longer get rid of the feeling of disgust and shame. And no one stirs; everyone trembles, keeps out of sight.

An extract for 17 March 1933 from the diary of Victor Klemperer, a Jew who lived in Dresden and recorded his experiences from 1933 to 1941.

1 Some people suggest that the Nazis burnt down the Reichstag themselves. Explain why the Nazis might have wanted to do this.

Factfile

Hitler's consolidation of power

1933

➤ **30 January** Hitler appointed Chancellor; Goering Minister of Interior.

➤ **17 February** Goering ordered local police forces to co-operate with the SA and SS.

➤ **27 February** Reichstag fire. Arrest of 4,000 Communists and other Nazi opponents on the same night.

➤ **28 February** Emergency Decree issued by Hindenburg at Hitler's request. The decree allowed:
  – police to arrest suspects and hold them without trial
  – Hitler to take over regional governments (most were taken over by mid March).

➤ **5 March** Reichstag elections: government used control of radio and police to intimidate opponents. Nazis attracted many new voters with election slogan 'The battle against Marxism'. Won 52 per cent of vote.

➤ **13 March** Goebbels appointed head of new Ministry for Propaganda. Took control of all media.

➤ **24 March** The Enabling Act:
  – allowed Hitler to pass decrees without the President's involvement
  – made Hitler a legal dictator.

➤ **7 April** Civil Service administration, court, and education purged of 'alien elements', i.e. Jews and other opponents of the Nazis.

➤ **1 May** Workers granted May Day holiday.

➤ **2 May** Trade unions banned; all workers to belong to new German Labour Front (DAF).

➤ **9 June** Employment Law: major programme of public works (e.g. road building) to create jobs.

➤ **14 July** Law against the Formation of New Parties: Germany became a one-party state.

➤ **20 July** Concordat (agreement) between the state and the Roman Catholic Church: government protected religious freedom; Church banned from political activity.

1934

➤ **January** All state governments taken over.

➤ **30 June** Night of the Long Knives.

➤ **August** On death of Hindenburg, Hitler became Führer. German armed forces swore oath of loyalty to him.

---

2 Explain why the Enabling Act was so important to Hitler.

3 Why might Hitler have executed people such as von Schleicher who were nothing to do with the SA?

4 Why do you think Hitler chose the support of the army over the support of the SA?

SOURCE 5

Nazi Party	*288 seats*
Social Democrats (SPD)	*120 seats*
Communist Party	*81 seats*
Catholic Centre Party	*73 seats*
Others	*85 seats*

Election results, March 1933.

In the election, the Nazis won their largest-ever share of the votes and, with the support of the smaller Nationalist Party, Hitler had an overall majority. Using the SA and SS, he then intimidated the Reichstag into passing the Enabling Act which allowed him to make laws without consulting the Reichstag. Only the SPD voted against him. Following the election, the Communists had been banned. The Catholic Centre Party decided to co-operate with the Nazis rather than be treated like the Communists. In return, they retained control of Catholic schools. The Enabling Act made Hitler a virtual dictator. For the next four years if he wanted a new law he could just pass it. There was nothing President Hindenburg or anyone else could do.

Even now, Hitler was not secure. He had seen how the Civil Service, the judiciary, the army and other important groups had undermined the Weimar Republic. He was not yet strong enough to remove his opponents, so he set about a clever policy that mixed force, concessions and compromise (see Factfile).

The Night of the Long Knives

Hitler acted quickly. Within a year any opponents (or potential opponents) of the Nazis had either left Germany or been taken to special concentration camps run by the SS. Other political parties were banned.

Hitler was still not entirely secure, however. The leading officers in the army were not impressed by him and were particularly suspicious of Hitler's SA and its leader Ernst Röhm. The SA was a badly disciplined force and, what's more, Röhm talked of making the SA into a second German army. Hitler himself was also suspicious of Röhm. Hitler feared that Röhm's control over the 4 million SA men made him a potentially dangerous rival.

Hitler had to choose between the army and the SA. He made his choice and acted ruthlessly. On the weekend of 29–30 June squads of SS men broke into the homes of Röhm and other leading figures in the SA and arrested them. Hitler accused Röhm of plotting to overthrow and murder him. Over the weekend Röhm and possibly as many as 400 others were executed. These included the former Chancellor von Schleicher, a fierce critic of Hitler, and others who actually had no connection with Röhm. Although the killings took place over the whole weekend, this purge came to be known as the Night of the Long Knives.

Hindenburg thanked Hitler for his 'determined action which has nipped treason in the bud'. The army said it was well satisfied with the events of the weekend.

The SA was not disbanded afterwards. It remained as a Nazi paramilitary organisation, but was very much subordinate to the SS and never regained the influence of 1933. Many of its members were absorbed by the army and the SS.

Der Führer

Soon after the Night of the Long Knives, Hindenburg died and Hitler took over as Supreme Leader (Führer) of Germany. On 2 August 1934 the entire army swore an oath of personal loyalty to Adolf Hitler as Führer of Germany. The army agreed to stay out of politics and to serve Hitler. In return, Hitler spent vast sums on rearmament, brought back conscription and made plans to make Germany a great military power again.

Nazi control of Germany, 1933–45

There was supposed to be no room for opposition of any kind in Nazi Germany. The aim was to create a totalitarian state. In a totalitarian state there can be no rival parties, no political debate. Ordinary citizens must divert their whole energy into serving the state and to doing what its leader wants.

The Nazis had a powerful range of organisations and weapons that they used to control Germany and terrorise Germans into submission.

The SS

SOURCE 6

SS guards after taking over the Berlin broadcasting station in 1933.

SOURCE 7

Order police (Ordinary police)		Himmler (Reichsführer–SS and Head of Germany's police)		Race and resettlement office (Resettlement policy, especially in the occupied territories)	
RHSA (Security head office for the Reich)	General–SS	Death's Head (Concentration camp units)	Waffen–SS (Military branch)	Office for the strengthening of Germanhood (Racial policy, especially in the occupied territories)	

The elements of the SS during wartime.

The SS was formed in 1925 from fanatics loyal to Hitler. After virtually destroying the SA in 1934, it grew into a huge organisation with many different responsibilities. It was led by Heinrich Himmler. SS men were of course Aryans, very highly trained and totally loyal to Hitler. Under Himmler, the SS had primary responsibility for destroying opposition to Nazism and carrying out the racial policies of the Nazis.

Two important sub-divisions of the SS were the Death's Head units and the Waffen-SS. The Death's Head units were responsible for the concentration camps and the slaughter of the Jews. The Waffen-SS were special SS armoured regiments which fought alongside the regular army.

The Gestapo

SOURCE 8

The Gestapo, the German secret state police, in action.

The Gestapo (secret state police) was the force which was perhaps most feared by the ordinary German citizen. Under the command of Reinhard Heydrich, Gestapo agents had sweeping powers. They could arrest citizens on suspicion and send them to concentration camps without trial or even explanation.

Modern research has shown that Germans thought the Gestapo were much more powerful than they actually were. As a result, many ordinary Germans informed on each other because they thought the Gestapo would find out anyway.

This chart gives the impression that Nazi Germany was run like a well-oiled machine: there to do the will of the Führer! Modern research suggests otherwise.

It was, in fact, somewhat chaotic and disorganised. Hitler was not hardworking. He disliked paperwork and decision making. He thought that most things sorted themselves out in time without his intervention. Officials competed with each other to get his approval for particular policies.

The result was often a jumble of different government departments competing with each other and getting in each other's way.

The police and the courts

The police and courts also helped to prop up the Nazi dictatorship. Top jobs in local police forces were given to high-ranking Nazis reporting to Himmler. As a result, the police added political 'snooping' to their normal law and order role. They were, of course, under strict instructions to ignore crimes committed by Nazi agents. Similarly, the Nazis controlled magistrates, judges and the courts, which meant that opponents of Nazism rarely received a fair trial.

SOURCE **9**

German judges swearing their loyalty at the criminal courts in Berlin.

Concentration camps

SOURCE **10**

Political prisoners at the Oranienburg concentration camp near Berlin.

Concentration camps were the Nazis' ultimate sanction against their own people. They were set up almost as soon as Hitler took power. The first concentration camps in 1933 were simply makeshift prisons in disused factories and warehouses. Soon these were purpose-built. These camps were usually in isolated rural areas, and run by SS Death's Head units. Prisoners were forced to do hard labour. Food was very limited and prisoners suffered harsh discipline, beatings and random executions. By the late 1930s, deaths in the camps became increasingly common and very few people emerged alive from them. Jews, Socialists, Communists, trade unionists, churchmen and anyone else brave enough to criticise the Nazis ended up there.

Focus Task

Summarise the information on these two pages in a table with the following headings:
◆ Method of control
◆ Controlled by
◆ Duties
◆ How it helped Hitler to make his position secure.

The average worker is primarily interested in work and not in democracy. People who previously enthusiastically supported democracy showed no interest at all in politics. One must be clear about the fact that in the first instance men are fathers of families and have jobs, and that for them politics takes second place and even then only when they expect to get something out of it.

A report by a Socialist activist in Germany, February 1936.

1 The writer of Source 11 was an opponent of the Nazi regime. Does that affect the value of this source as evidence? Explain your answer.

SOURCE 12

November 1933

Millions of Germans are indeed won over by Hitler and the power and the glory are really his. I hear of some actions by the Communists . . . But what good do such pinpricks do? Less than none, because all Germany prefers Hitler to the Communists.

April 1935

Frau Wilbrandt told us that people complain in Munich when Hitler or Goebbels appear on film but even she (an economist close to the Social Democrats) says: 'Will there not be something even worse, if Hitler is overthrown, Bolshevism?' (That fear keeps Hitler where he is again and again.)

September 1937

On the festival of Yom Kippur the Jews did not attend class. Kufahl, the mathematician, had said to the reduced class: 'Today it's just us.' In my memory these words took on a quite horrible significance: to me it confirms the claim of the Nazis to express the true opinion of the German people. And I believe ever more strongly that Hitler really does embody the soul of the German people, that he really stands for Germany and that he will consequently keep his position. I have not only lost my Fatherland. Even if the government should change one day, my sense of belonging to Germany has gone.

Extracts from the diaries of Victor Klemperer, a Jewish university lecturer in Germany.

Why was there little opposition?

The Nazis faced relatively little open opposition during their twelve years in power. In private, Germans complained about the regime and its actions. Some might refuse to give the Nazi salute. They might pass on anti-Nazi jokes and rude stories about senior Nazis. However, serious criticism was always in private, never in public. Historians have debated why this was so. The main answer they have come up with may seem obvious to you if you've read pages 276–77. It was terror! All the Nazis' main opponents had been killed, exiled or put in prison. The rest had been scared into submission. However, it won't surprise you to learn that historians think the answer is not quite as simple as that. It takes more than just terror to explain why there was so little opposition to the Nazis.

'It's all for the good of Germany' – Nazi successes

Many Germans admired and trusted Hitler. They were prepared to tolerate rule by terror and to trade their rights in political freedom and free speech in return for work, foreign policy success and what they thought was strong government.

- Economic recovery was deeply appreciated.
- Many felt that the Nazis were bringing some much needed discipline back to Germany by restoring traditional values and clamping down on rowdy Communists.
- Between 1933 and 1938 Hitler's success in foreign affairs made Germans feel that their country was a great power again after the humiliations of the First World War and the Treaty of Versailles. For many Germans, the dubious methods of the Nazis may have been regrettable but necessary for the greater good of the country. You will read more about this on pages 288–91.

'I don't want to lose my job' – economic fears

German workers feared losing their jobs if they did express opposition (see Source 11). Germany had been hit so hard by the Depression that many were terrified by the prospect of being out of work again. It was a similar situation for the bosses. Businesses that did not contribute to Nazi Party funds risked losing Nazi business and going bankrupt, and so in self-defence they conformed as well. If you asked no questions and kept your head down, life in Nazi Germany could be comfortable. 'Keeping your head down' became a national obsession. The SS and its special security service the SD went to great lengths to find out what people were saying about the regime, often by listening in on conversations in cafés and bars. Your job could depend on silence.

'Have you heard the good news?' – propaganda

Underlying the whole regime was the propaganda machine. This ensured that many Germans found out very little about the bad things that were happening, or if they did they only heard them with a positive, pro-Nazi slant. You'll study the Nazi use of propaganda in detail on pages 280–82. Propaganda was particularly important in maintaining the image of Hitler. The evidence suggests that personal support for Hitler remained high throughout the 1930s and he was still widely respected even as Germany was losing the war in 1944.

The July bomb plot

In July 1944, some army officers came close to removing Hitler. By this stage of the war, many army officers were sure that the war was lost and that Hitler was leading Germany into ruin. One of these was a colonel in the army, Count von Stauffenberg. On 20 July he left a bomb in Hitler's conference room. The plan was to kill Hitler, close down the radio stations, round up the other leading Nazis and take over Germany. It failed on all counts, for the revolt was poorly planned and organised. Hitler survived and the Nazis took a terrible revenge, killing 5,000 in reprisal.

A parade organised by the German Faith Movement. This movement was a non-Christian movement based on worship of the sun.

Most postwar accounts have concentrated on the few German clerics who did behave bravely . . . But these were few. Most German church leaders were shamefully silent. As late as January 1945, the Catholic bishop of Würzburg was urging his flock to fight on for the Fatherland, saying that 'salvation lies in sacrifice'.

British historian and journalist Charles Wheeler, writing in 1996.

How did the Nazis deal with the Churches?

The relationship between the Churches and the Nazis was complicated. In the early stages of the Nazi regime, there was some co-operation between the Nazis and the Churches. Hitler signed a Concordat with the Catholic Church in 1933. This meant that Hitler agreed to leave the Catholic Church alone and allowed it to keep control of its schools. In return, the Church agreed to stay out of politics.

Hitler tried to get all of the Protestant Churches to come together in one official Reich Church. The Reich Church was headed by the Protestant Bishop Ludwig Müller. However, many Germans still felt that their true loyalties lay with their original Churches in their local areas rather than with this state-approved Church.

Hitler even encouraged an alternative religion to the Churches, the pagan German Faith Movement (see Source 13).

Many churchgoers either supported the Nazis or did little to oppose them. However, there were some very important exceptions. The Catholic Bishop Galen criticised the Nazis throughout the 1930s. In 1941 he led a popular protest against the Nazi policies of killing mentally ill and physically disabled people, forcing the Nazis temporarily to stop. He had such strong support among his followers that the Nazis decided it was too risky to try to silence him because they did not want trouble while Germany was at war.

Protestant ministers also resisted the Nazis. Pastor Martin Niemöller was one of the most high-profile critics of the regime in the 1930s. Along with Dietrich Bonhoeffer, he formed an alternative Protestant Church to the official Reich Church. Niemöller spent the years 1938–45 in a concentration camp for resisting the Nazis. Dietrich Bonhoeffer preached against the Nazis until the Gestapo stopped him in 1937. He then became involved with members of the army's intelligence services who were secretly opposed to Hitler. He helped Jews to escape from Germany. Gradually he increased his activity. In 1942 he contacted the Allied commanders and asked what peace terms they would offer Germany if Hitler were overthrown. He was arrested in October 1942 and hanged shortly before the end of the war in April 1945.

Focus Task

How effectively did the Nazis deal with their opponents?

Work through pages 274–79. Use the information here to complete your own copy of this table.

Opponent	Reasons for opposing the Nazis	Actions	How the Nazis reacted to this opponent	Was the Nazi action effective?
Trade unionists				
Political opponents				
Church leaders				
Army officers				

SOURCE **15**

The Nazis gained 52 per cent of the vote in the March 1933 elections. This government will not be content with 52 per cent behind it and with terrorising the remaining 48 per cent, but will see its most immediate task as winning over that remaining 48 per cent ... It is not enough for people to be more or less reconciled to the regime.

Goebbels at his first press conference on becoming Minister for Propaganda, March 1933.

1 Look at Source 16. How does the rally:
   a) make it clear who the leader is
   b) give people a sense of belonging
   c) provide colour and excitement
   d) show the power of the state
   e) show the Nazis' ability to create order out of chaos?

Propaganda, culture and mass media in Nazi Germany

One reason why opposition to Hitler was so limited was the work of Dr Joseph Goebbels, Minister for Enlightenment and Propaganda. Goebbels passionately believed in Hitler as the saviour of Germany. His mission was to make sure that others believed this too. Throughout the twelve years of Nazi rule Goebbels constantly kept his finger on the pulse of public opinion and decided what the German public should and should not hear. He aimed to use every resource available to him to make people loyal to Hitler and the Nazis.

The Nuremberg rallies

Goebbels organised huge rallies, marches, torchlit processions and meetings. Probably the best example was the Nuremberg rally which took place in the summer each year. There were bands, marches, flying displays and Hitler's brilliant speeches. The rallies brought some colour and excitement into people's lives. They gave them a sense of belonging to a great movement. The rallies also showed the German people the power of the state and convinced them that 'every other German' fully supported the Nazis. Goebbels also recognised that one of the Nazis' main attractions was that they created order out of chaos and so the whole rally was organised to emphasise order.

SOURCE **16**

A Hitler speaks to the assembled Germans.

B A parade through the streets.

C German youth marching with spades.

The annual rally at Nuremberg. The whole town was taken over and the rally dominated radio broadcasts and newsreels.

The 1936 Olympics

One of Goebbels' greatest challenges came with the 1936 Olympic Games in Berlin. Other Nazis were opposed to holding the Games in Berlin, but Goebbels convinced Hitler that this was a great propaganda opportunity both within Germany and internationally.

Goebbels and Hitler also thought that the Olympics could be a showcase for their doctrine that the Aryan race was superior to all other races. However, there was international pressure for nations such as the USA to boycott the Games in protest against the Nazis' repressive regime and anti-Jewish politics. In response the Nazis included one token Jew in their team!

Goebbels built a brand new stadium to hold 100,000 people. It was lit by the most modern electric lighting. He brought in television cameras for the first time. The most sophisticated German photo-electronic timing device was installed. The stadium had the largest stop clock ever built. With guests and competitors from 49 countries coming into the heart of Nazi Germany, it was going to take all Goebbels' talents to show that Germany was a modern, civilised and successful nation. No expense was spared. When the Games opened, the visitors were duly amazed at the scale of the stadium, the wonderful facilities, and the efficiency of the organisation. However, they were also struck, and in some cases appalled, by the almost fanatical devotion of the people to Hitler and by the overt presence of army and SS soldiers who were patrolling or standing guard everywhere.

To the delight of Hitler and Goebbels, Germany came top of the medal table, way ahead of all other countries. However, to their great dismay, a black athlete, Jesse Owens, became the star of the Games. He won four gold medals and broke eleven world records in the process. The ten black members of the American team won thirteen medals between them. So much for Aryan superiority!

To the majority of German people, who had grown used to the Nazi propaganda machine, the Games appeared to present all the qualities they valued in the Nazis – a grand vision, efficiency, power, strength and achievement. However, to many foreign visitors who were not used to such blatant propaganda it backfired on the Nazi regime.

2 Does Source 17 approve or disapprove of the Nazis' use of the Games for propaganda purposes?
3 In what ways was the Berlin Olympics a propaganda success for Goebbels?
4 In what ways was it a failure?
5 Why do you think Nazi propaganda was more successful within Germany than outside it?
6 You have already come across many examples of Nazi propaganda. Choose one example which you think is the clearest piece of propaganda. Explain your choice.

SOURCE **17**

A poster about the 1936 Olympics. The figure on the right is Goebbels. The German text reads 'The purpose of the whole thing – Olympic guests, quick march!'

SOURCE **18**

The stadium built for the 1936 Olympics.

1 Look at Source 19 and explain why Goebbels wanted every German household to have a radio set.

2 Write your own ten-word definition of propaganda.

3 What does Source 20 tell you about the effectiveness of Nazi propaganda?

The media

Less spectacular than the rallies but possibly more important was Goebbels' control of the media. In contrast with the free expression of Weimar Germany, the Nazis controlled the media strictly. No books could be published without Goebbels' permission (not surprisingly the best seller in Nazi Germany was *Mein Kampf*). In 1933 he organised a high-profile 'book-burning'. Nazi students came together publicly to burn any books that included ideas unacceptable to the Nazis.

Artists suffered the same kinds of restriction as writers. Only Nazi-approved painters could show their works. These were usually paintings or sculptures of heroic-looking Aryans, military figures or images of the ideal Aryan family.

Goebbels also controlled the newspapers closely. They were not allowed to print anti-Nazi ideas. Within months of the Nazi takeover, Jewish editors and journalists found themselves out of work and anti-Nazi newspapers were closed down. The German newspapers became very dull reading and Germans bought fewer newspapers as a result – circulation fell by about 10 per cent.

The cinema was also closely controlled. All films – factual or fictional, thrillers or comedies – had to carry a pro-Nazi message. The newsreels which preceded feature films were full of the greatness of Hitler and the massive achievements of Nazi Germany. There is evidence that Germans avoided these productions by arriving late! Goebbels censored all foreign films coming into Germany.

Goebbels plastered Germany with posters proclaiming the successes of Hitler and the Nazis and attacking their opponents.

He banned jazz music, which had been popular in Germany as elsewhere around Europe. He banned it because it was 'Black' music and black people were considered an inferior race.

Goebbels loved new technology and quickly saw the potential of radio broadcasting for spreading the Nazi message. He made cheap radios available so all Germans could buy one and he controlled all the radio stations. Listening to broadcasts from the BBC was punishable by death. Just in case people did not have a radio Goebbels placed loudspeakers in the streets and public bars. Hitler's speeches and those of other Nazi leaders were repeated on the radio over and over again until the ideas expressed in them – German expansion into eastern Europe, the inferiority of the Jews – came to be believed by the German people.

Throughout this period Goebbels was supported in his work by the SS and the Gestapo. When he wanted to close down an anti-Nazi newspaper, silence an anti-Nazi writer, or catch someone listening to a foreign radio station, they were there to do that work for him.

SOURCE **19**

Poster advertising cheap Nazi-produced radios. The text reads 'All Germany hears the Führer on the People's Radio.' The radios had only a short range and were unable to pick up foreign stations.

SOURCE **20**

There are cinema evenings to be caught up with, very enjoyable ones – if only there were not each time the bitterness of the Third Reich's self-adulation and triumphalism. The renewal of German art – recent German history as reflected in postage stamps, youth camp, enthusiastic welcome for the Führer in X or Y. Goebbels' speech on culture to the Germanised theatre people, the biggest lecture theatre in the world, the biggest autobahn in the world, etc. etc. – the biggest lie in the world, the biggest disgrace in the world. It can't be helped . . .

From the diary of Victor Klemperer for 8 August 1937.

SOURCE **21**

Poster for an anti-Jewish exhibition, 1937. The caption reads 'The Eternal Jew'.

Our state is an educational state . . . It does not let a man go free from the cradle to the grave. We begin with the child when he is three years old. As soon as he begins to think, he is made to carry a little flag. Then follows school, the Hitler Youth, the storm troopers and military training. We don't let him go; and when all that is done, comes the Labour Front, which takes possession of him again, and does not let him go till he dies, even if he does not like it.

Dr Robert Ley, who was Chief of the Labour Front and in charge of making 'good citizens' out of the German people.

SOURCE **23**

The Jews are aliens in Germany. In 1933 there were 66,060,000 inhabitants of the German Reich of whom 499,862 were Jews. What is the percentage of aliens in Germany?

A question from a Nazi maths textbook, 1933.

SOURCE **24**

8.00	German (every day)
8.50	Geography, History or Singing (alternate days)
9.40	Race Studies and Ideology (every day)
10.25	Recess, Sports and Special Announcements (every day)
11.00	Domestic Science or Maths (alternate days)
12.10	Eugenics or Health Biology (alternate days)
1.00–6.00	Sport
Evenings	Sex education, Ideology or Domestic Science (one evening each)

The daily timetable for a girls' school in Nazi Germany.

---

4 Read Source 22. Do you think that the speaker is proud of what he is saying?
5 Do you think the real aim of the question in Source 23 is to improve mathematical skills?
6 Read Source 24. Eugenics is the study of how to produce perfect offspring by choosing parents with ideal qualities. How would this help the Nazis?

How did the Nazis deal with young people?

It was Hitler's aim to control every aspect of life in Germany, including the daily life of ordinary people. If you had been a 16-year-old Aryan living in Nazi Germany you would probably have been a strong supporter of Adolf Hitler. The Nazis had reorganised every aspect of the school curriculum to make children loyal to them.

SOURCE **25**

It is my great educative work I am beginning with the young. We older ones are used up . . . We are bearing the burden of a humiliating past . . . But my magnificent youngsters! Are there finer ones in the world? Look at these young men and boys! What material! With them I can make a new world.

Hitler, speaking in 1939.

At school you would have learned about the history of Germany. You would have been outraged to find out how the German army was 'stabbed in the back' by the weak politicians who had made peace. You might well remember the hardships of the 1920s for yourself, but at school you would have been told how these were caused by Jews squeezing profits out of honest Germans. By the time you were a senior pupil, your studies in history would have made you confident that loyalty to the Führer was right and good. Your biology lessons would have informed you that you were special, as one of the Aryan race which was so superior in intelligence and strength to the *Untermenschen* or sub-human Jews and Slavs of eastern Europe. In maths you would have been set questions like the one in Source 23.

SOURCE **26**

All subjects – German language, History, Geography, Chemistry and Mathematics – must concentrate on military subjects, the glorification of military service and of German heroes and leaders and the strength of a rebuilt Germany. Chemistry will develop a knowledge of chemical warfare, explosives, etc, while Mathematics will help the young to understand artillery, calculations, ballistics.

A German newspaper, heavily controlled by the Nazis, approves of the curriculum in 1939.

As a member of the Hitler Youth or League of German Maidens, you would have marched in exciting parades with loud bands. You would probably be physically fit. Your leisure time would also be devoted to Hitler and the Nazis. You would be a strong cross-country runner, and confident at reading maps. After years of summer camps, you would be comfortable camping out of doors and if you were a boy you would know how to clean a rifle and keep it in good condition.

SOURCE **27**

Typical day at a labour camp for 18- to 25-year-olds

6.00	Get up (5.00 in summer)	3.00–4.00	Rest
6.05–6.20	Exercises	4.00–5.00	Sport
6.20–6.40	Washing; bed making	5.00–6.00	Political studies
6.40–6.55	Breakfast	6.00–7.00	Allocation of jobs to be done the next day
7.00–7.30	Flag parade; speech by camp leader	7.00–8.00	Supper
7.30–2.30	March to work; six hours' farm work	8.00–9.00	Songs and dancing; speeches
2.30–3.00	Midday meal	10.00	Lights out

A young person's day in Nazi Germany.

Hitler looked over the stand, and I know he looked into my eyes, and he said: 'You my boys are the standard bearers, you will inherit what we have created.' From that moment there was not any doubt I was bound to Adolf Hitler until long after our defeat. Afterwards I told my friends how Hitler had looked into my eyes, but they all said: 'No! It was my eyes he was looking into.'

A young German describes his feelings after a Hitler Youth rally.

Children have been deliberately taken away from parents who refused to acknowledge their belief in National Socialism . . . The refusal of parents to allow their young children to join the youth organisation is regarded as an adequate reason for taking the children away.

A German teacher writing in 1938.

It was a great feeling. You felt you belonged to a great nation again. Germany was in safe hands and I was going to help to build a strong Germany. But my father of course felt differently about it. [He warned] 'Now Henrik, don't say to them what I am saying to you.' I always argued with my father as I was very much in favour of the Hitler regime which was against his background as a working man.

Henrik Metelmann describes what it was like being a member of the Hitler Youth in the 1930s.

1 Make a list of the main differences between your life and the life of a 16-year-old in Nazi Germany.
2 Totalitarian regimes through history have used children as a way of influencing parents. Why do you think they do this?
3 Read Source 30. Why do you think Henrik's father asks Henrik not to repeat what he says to him?

Members of the Hitler Youth in the 1930s. From a very early age children were encouraged to join the Nazi youth organisations. It was not compulsory, but most young people did join.

As a child in Nazi Germany, you might well feel slightly alienated (estranged) from your parents because they are not as keen on the Nazis as you are. They expect your first loyalty to be to your family, whereas your Hitler Youth leader makes it clear that your first loyalty is to Adolf Hitler. You find it hard to understand why your father grumbles about Nazi regulation of his working practices – surely the Führer (Hitler) is protecting him? Your parents find the idea of Nazi inspectors checking up on the teachers rather strange. For you it is normal.

Illustration from a Nazi children's book. The children are being taught to distrust Jews.

Activity

Draw up two posters summarising the aims and objectives of Nazi youth policy. One poster should be for the young people themselves. The other should be for the parents.

Did all young people support the Nazis?

SOURCE 33

The formation of cliques, i.e. groupings of young people outside the Hitler Youth, has been on the increase before and particularly during the war to such a degree that one must speak of a serious risk of political, moral and criminal subversion of our youth.

From a report by the Nazi youth leadership, 1942.

Many young people were attracted to the Nazi youth movements by the leisure opportunities they offered. There were really no alternatives. All other youth organisations had been either absorbed or made illegal. Even so, only half of all German boys were members in 1933 and only 15 per cent of girls.

In 1939 membership of a Nazi youth movement was made compulsory. But by this time the youth movements were going through a crisis. Many of the experienced leaders had been drafted into the German army. Others – particularly those who had been leaders in the pre-Nazi days – had been replaced by keener Nazis. Many of the movements were now run by older teenagers who rigidly enforced Nazi rules. They even forbade other teenagers to meet informally with their friends.

As the war progressed, the activities of the youth movements focused increasingly on the war effort and military drill. The popularity of the movements decreased and indeed an anti-Hitler Youth movement appeared. The Nazis identified two distinct groups of young people who they were worried about: the Swing movement and the Edelweiss Pirates.

SOURCE 34

The public hanging of twelve Edelweiss Pirates in Cologne in 1944.

The 'Swing' movement

This was made up mainly of middle-class teenagers. They went to parties where they listened to English and American music and sang English songs. They danced American dances such as the 'jitterbug' to banned jazz music. They accepted Jews at their clubs. They talked about and enjoyed sex. They were deliberately 'slovenly'. The Nazis issued a handbook helping the authorities to identify these degenerate types. Some were shown with unkempt, long hair; others with exaggeratedly English clothes.

The Edelweiss Pirates

The Edelweiss Pirates were working-class teenagers. They were not an organised movement, and groups in various cities took different names: 'The Roving Dudes' (Essen); the 'Kittelbach Pirates' (Düsseldorf); the 'Navajos' (Cologne). The Nazis, however, classified all the groups under the single name 'Edelweiss Pirates' and the groups did have a lot in common.

The Pirates were mainly aged between 14 and 17 (Germans could leave school at 14, but they did not have to sign on for military service until they were 17). At the weekends, the Pirates went camping. They sang songs, just like the Hitler Youth, but they changed the lyrics of songs to mock Germany and when they spotted bands of Hitler Youth they taunted and sometimes attacked them. In contrast with the Hitler Youth, the Pirates included boys and girls. The Pirates were also much freer in their attitude towards sex, which was officially frowned upon by the Hitler Youth.

The Pirates' activities caused serious worries to the Nazi authorities in some cities. In December 1942 the Gestapo broke up 28 groups containing 739 adolescents. The Nazi approach to the Pirates was different from their approach to other minorities. As long as they needed future workers for industry and future soldiers they could not simply exterminate all these teenagers or put them in concentration camps (although Himmler did suggest that). They therefore responded uncertainly – sometimes arresting the Pirates, sometimes ignoring them.

In 1944 in Cologne, Pirate activities escalated. They helped to shelter army deserters and escaped prisoners. They stole armaments and took part in an attack on the Gestapo during which its chief was killed. The Nazi response was to round up the so called 'ringleaders'. Twelve were publicly hanged in November 1944.

Neither of the groups described above had strong political views. They were not political opponents of the Nazis. But they resented and resisted Nazi control of their lives.

Focus Task

How did young people react to the Nazi regime?

1 Young people were among the most fanatical supporters of the Nazi regime. Use pages 283–85 to write three paragraphs to explain why the Nazis were successful in winning them over. Include the following points:
   - why the Nazis wanted to control young people
   - how they set about doing it
   - what the attractions of the youth movements were.
2 The Nazi regime was not successful in keeping the loyalty of all young people. Add a fourth paragraph to your essay to explain why some young people rejected the Nazi youth movements.

Women in Nazi Germany

SOURCE **35**

A painting showing the Nazis' view of an ideal German family.

SOURCE **36**

Girls from the German Maidens' League camping. The League offered excitement and escape from boring duties in the home.

All the Nazi leaders were men. The Nazis were a very male-dominated organisation. Hitler had a very traditional view of the role of the German woman as wife and mother. It is worth remembering that many *women* agreed with him. In the traditional rural areas and small towns, many women felt that the proper role of a woman was to support her husband. There was also resentment towards working women in the early 1930s, since they were seen as keeping men out of jobs. It all created a lot of pressure on women to conform to what the Nazis called 'the traditional balance' between men and women. 'No true German woman wears trousers' said a Nazi newspaper headline when the film star Marlene Dietrich appeared wearing trousers in public.

Alarmed at the falling birth rate, Hitler offered tempting financial incentives for married couples to have at least four children. You got a 'Gold Cross' for having eight children, and were given a privileged seat at Nazi meetings. Posters, radio broadcasts and newsreels all celebrated the ideas of motherhood and homebuilding. The German Maidens' League reinforced these ideas, focusing on a combination of good physical health and housekeeping skills. This was reinforced at school (see Source 24 on page 283).

With all these encouragements the birth rate did increase from fifteen per thousand in 1933 to twenty per thousand in 1939. There was also an increase in pregnancies outside marriage. These girls were looked after in state maternity hostels.

SOURCE **37**

Leni Riefenstahl directing the shooting of her film of the 1936 Olympics.

SOURCE 38

Gertrude Scholz-Klink, head of the Nazi Women's Bureau.

SOURCE 39

A German woman and her Jewish boyfriend being publicly humiliated by the SA in 1933.

There were some prominent women in Nazi Germany. Leni Riefenstahl was a high-profile film producer. Gertrude Scholz-Klink was head of the Nazi Women's Bureau, although she was excluded from any important discussions (such as the one to conscript female labour in 1942). Many working-class girls and women gained the chance to travel and meet new people through the Nazi women's organisation. Overall, however, opportunities for women were limited. Married professional women were forced to give up their jobs and stay at home with their families, which many resented as a restriction on their freedom. Discrimination against women applicants for jobs was actually encouraged.

In the late 1930s the Nazis had to do an about-turn as they suddenly needed more women workers because the supply of unemployed men was drying up. Many women had to struggle with both family and work responsibilities. However, even during the crisis years of 1942–45 when German industry was struggling to cope with the demand for war supplies, Nazi policy on women was still torn between their traditional stereotype of the mother, and the actual needs of the workplace. For example, there was no chance for German women to serve in the armed forces, as there was in Allied countries.

SOURCE 40

I went to Sauckel [the Nazi minister in charge of labour] with the proposition that we should recruit our labour from the ranks of German women. He replied brusquely that where to obtain which workers was his business. Moreover, he said, as Gauleiter [a regional governor] he was Hitler's subordinate and responsible to the Führer alone . . . Sauckel offered to put the question to Goering as Commissioner of the Four-Year Plan . . . but I was scarcely allowed to advance my arguments. Sauckel and Goering continually interrupted me. Sauckel laid great weight on the danger that factory work might inflict moral harm on German womanhood; not only might their 'psychic and emotional life' be affected but also their ability to bear children.

Goering totally concurred. But just to be absolutely sure, Sauckel went immediately to Hitler and had him confirm the decision. All my good arguments were therefore blown to the winds.

Albert Speer, *Inside The Third Reich*, 1970. Speer was Minister of Armaments and War Production.

Focus Task

How successful were the Nazi policies for women?

Read these two statements:
- 'Nazi policy for women was confused.'
- 'Nazi policy for women was a failure.'

For each statement explain whether you agree or disagree with it and use examples from the text to support your explanation.

Did Germans gain from Nazi rule?

Economic recovery and rearmament

Hitler and the Nazis came to power because they promised to use radical methods to solve the country's two main problems – desperate unemployment and a crisis in German farming. In return for work and other benefits, the majority of the German people gave up their political freedom. Was it worth it?

At first, many Germans felt it was, particularly the 5 million who were unemployed in 1933. Hitler was fortunate in that by 1933 the worst of the Depression was over. Even so, there is no doubt that the Nazis acted with energy and commitment to solve some of the main problems. The brilliant economist **Dr Hjalmar Schacht** organised Germany's finances to fund a huge programme of work creation. The National Labour Service sent men on **public works projects** and conservation programmes, in particular to build a network of motorways or **autobahns**. Railways were extended or built from scratch. There were major house-building programmes and grandiose new public building projects such as the Reich Chancellery in Berlin.

Other measures brought increasing prosperity. One of Hitler's most cherished plans was **rearmament**. In 1935 he reintroduced **conscription** for the German army. In 1936 he announced a **Four-Year Plan** under the control of **Goering** to get the German economy ready for war (it was one of the very few clear policy documents that Hitler ever wrote).

Activity

As you read through pages 288–91, you will come across a number of individuals, organisations and terms in bold type in the text, **like this**. You could add more of your own if you wish. Draw up a table containing definitions of the words, or explanations of their importance to the Nazi's economic policies. The completed table will help you with your revision. You could organise your table like this:

Key word/term/person	Definition/explanation

SOURCE **42**

A completed autobahn.

SOURCE **41**

Previously unemployed men assemble for the building of the first autobahn, September 1933.

Conscription reduced unemployment. The need for weapons, equipment and uniforms created jobs in the coal mines, steel and textile mills. Engineers and designers gained new opportunities, particularly when Hitler decreed that Germany would have a world-class air force (the Luftwaffe). As well as bringing economic recovery, these measures boosted Hitler's popularity because they boosted **national pride**. Germans began to feel that their country was finally emerging from the humiliation of the Great War and the Treaty of Versailles, and putting itself on an equal footing with the other great powers.

SOURCE **43**

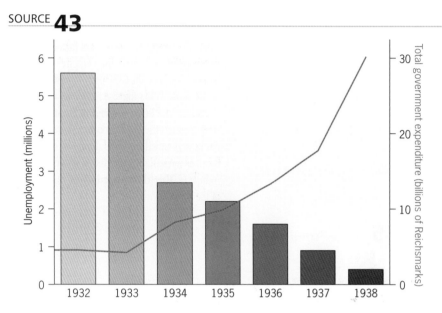

Unemployment and government expenditure in Germany, 1932–38. Economic recovery was almost entirely funded by the state rather than from Germans investing their own savings. Despite this, unemployment fell steadily and Germany was actually running short of workers by 1939.

The Nazis and the workers

Hitler promised (and delivered) lower unemployment which helped to ensure popularity among **industrial workers**. These workers were important to the Nazis: Hitler needed good workers to create the industries that would help to make Germany great and establish a new German empire in eastern Europe. He won the loyalty of industrial workers by a variety of initiatives.

- Propaganda praised the workers and tried to associate them with Hitler.
- Schemes such as **Strength Through Joy (KDF)** gave them cheap theatre and cinema tickets, and organised courses and trips and sports events. Workers were offered cut-price cruises on the latest luxury liners.
- Many thousands of workers saved five marks a week in the state scheme to buy the **Volkswagen Beetle**, the 'people's car'. It was designed by Ferdinand Porsche and became a symbol of the prosperous new Germany, even though no workers ever received a car because all car production was halted by the war in 1939.
- Another important scheme was the **Beauty of Labour** movement. This improved working conditions in factories. It introduced features not seen in many workplaces before, such as washing facilities and low-cost canteens.

What was the price of these advances? Workers lost their main political party, the SDP. They lost their trade unions and for many workers this remained a source of bitter resentment. All workers had to join the **DAF (General Labour Front)** run by **Dr Robert Ley**. This organisation kept strict control of workers. They could not strike for better pay and conditions. In some areas, they were prevented from moving to better-paid jobs. Wages remained comparatively low, although prices were also strictly controlled. Even so, by the late 1930s, many workers were grumbling that their standard of living was still lower than it had been before the Depression (see Source 43).

The Nazis and the farming communities

The **farmers** had been an important factor in the Nazis' rise to power. Hitler did not forget this and introduced a series of measures to help them. In September 1933 he introduced the **Reich Food Estate** under **Richard Darre**. This set up central boards to buy agricultural produce from the farmers and distribute it to markets across Germany. It gave the peasant farmers a guaranteed market for their goods at guaranteed prices. The second main measure was the **Reich Entailed Farm Law**. It gave peasants state protection for their farms: banks could not seize their land if they could not pay loans or mortgages. This ensured that peasants' farms stayed in their hands.

The Reich Entailed Farm Law also had a racial aim. Part of the Nazi philosophy was '**Blood and Soil**', the belief that the peasant farmers were the basis of Germany's master race. They would be the backbone of the new German empire in the east. As a result, their way of life had to be protected. As Source 46 shows, the measures were widely appreciated.

However, rather like the industrial workers, some peasants were not thrilled with the regime's measures. The Reich Food Estate meant that efficient, go-ahead farmers were held back by having to work through the same processes as less efficient farmers. Because of the Reich Entailed Farm Law, banks were unwilling to lend money to farmers. It also meant that only the eldest child inherited the farm. As a result, many children of farmers left the land to work for better pay in Germany's industries. **Rural depopulation** ran at about 3 per cent per year in the 1930s – the exact opposite of the Nazis' aims!

SOURCE **45**

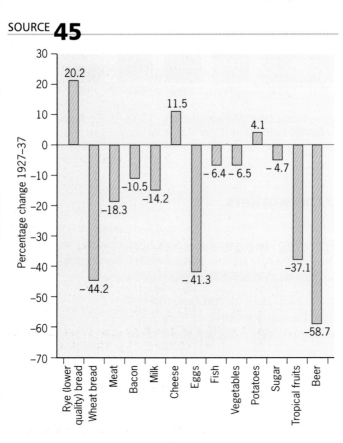

Percentage change 1927–37

Annual food consumption in working class families, 1927–37 (% change).

SOURCE **46**

Thousands of people came from all over Germany to the Harvest Festival celebrations . . . We all felt the same happiness and joy. Harvest festival was the thank you for us farmers having a future again. I believe no statesman has ever been as well loved as Adolf Hitler was at that time. Those were happy times.

Lusse Essig's memories of harvest festivals in the 1930s. Lusse was a farm worker who went on to work for the Agriculture Ministry between 1937 and 1945.

Big business and the middle classes

The record of the Nazis with the **middle classes** was also mixed. Certainly many middle-class business people were grateful to the Nazis for eliminating the Communist threat to their businesses and properties. They also liked the way in which the Nazis seemed to be bringing order to Germany. For the owners of small businesses it was a mixed picture. If you owned a small engineering firm, you were likely to do well from government orders as rearmament spending grew in the 1930s. However, if you produced consumer goods or ran a small shop, you might well struggle. Despite Hitler's promises, the large department stores which were taking business away from local shops were not closed.

It was **big business** that really benefited from Nazi rule. The big companies no longer had to worry about troublesome trade unions and strikes. Companies such as the chemicals giant IG Farben gained huge government contracts to make explosives, fertilisers and even artificial oil from coal. Other household names today, such as Mercedes and Volkswagen, prospered from Nazi policies.

1 On your own copy of Source 47 label the features that are attempting to comment on life in Nazi Germany.

DIE NSDAP SICHERT DIE VOLKS-GEMEINSCHAFT

VOLKSGENOSSEN BRAUCHT IHR RAT UND HILFE SO WENDET EUCH AN DIE ORTSGRUPPE

A Nazi propaganda poster from the 1930s encouraging people to turn to Nazi-led community groups for help and advice.

Focus Task

Did most people in Germany benefit from Nazi rule?

Here are some claims that the Nazi propaganda machine made about how life in Germany had been changed for the better:

♦ 'Germans now have economic security.'
♦ 'Germans no longer need to feel inferior to other states. They can be proud of their country.'
♦ 'The Nazi state looks after its workers very well indeed.'
♦ 'The Nazis are on the side of the farmers and have rescued Germany's farmers from disaster.'
♦ 'The Nazis have made Germany safe from Communism.'

You are now going to decide how truthful these claims actually are.

1 Look back over pages 274–91. Gather evidence that supports or opposes each claim. You could work in groups taking one claim each.
2 For each claim, decide whether, overall, it is totally untrue; a little bit true; mostly true; or totally true.
3 Discuss:
   a) Which of the groups you have studied so far do you think benefited most from Nazi rule: the workers, the farmers, big business or the middle classes?
   b) Did any of these groups not benefit from Nazi rule?

NB. There were some groups of people in Nazi Germany who definitely did not benefit at all. You can return to this final question once you have studied the story of how the Nazis dealt with Jews and other minorities on pages 294–97.

The 'national community' – *Volksgemeinschaft*

We have divided this section by social group, but the Nazis would not want Germans to see their society that way. Hitler wanted all Germans (or more exactly all 'racially pure' Germans) to think of themselves as part of a **national community**, or *Volksgemeinschaft*. Under Nazi rule, workers, farmers, and so on, would no longer see themselves primarily as workers or farmers; they would see themselves as Germans. Their first loyalty would not be to their own social group but to Germany and the Führer. They would be so proud to belong to a great nation that was racially and culturally superior to other nations that they would put the interests of Germany before their own. Hitler's policies towards each group were designed to help win this kind of loyalty to the Nazi state.

The evidence suggests that the Nazis never quite succeeded in this: Germans in the 1930s certainly did not lose their self-interest, nor did they embrace the national community wholeheartedly. However, the Nazis did not totally fail either! In the 1930s Germans did have a strong sense of national pride and loyalty towards Hitler. For the majority of Germans, the benefits of Nazi rule made them willing – on the surface at least – to accept some central control in the interests of making Germany great again.

SOURCE 48

Heinrich Himmler, leader of the SS.

The impact of the Second World War on Germany

In Chapters 1 and 2 of this book you can find out how, through the 1930s, Hitler fulfilled his promises to the German people that he would:

- reverse the Treaty of Versailles
- rebuild Germany's armed forces
- unite Germany and Austria
- extend German territory into eastern Europe.

He fulfilled each of these aims, but started the Second World War in the process.

Germans had no great enthusiasm for war. People still had memories of the First World War. But in war, as in peace time, the Nazis used all methods available to make the German people support the regime.

Food rationing was introduced soon after war began in September 1939. Clothes rationing followed in November 1939. Even so, from 1939 to 1941 it was not difficult to keep up civilian morale because the war went spectacularly well for Germany. Hitler was in control of much of western and eastern Europe and supplies of luxury goods flowed into Germany from captured territories.

However, in 1941 Hitler took the massive gamble of invading the Soviet Union, and for the next three years his troops were engaged in an increasingly expensive war with Russian forces who 'tore the heart out of the German army', as the British war leader, Winston Churchill, put it. As the tide turned against the German armies, civilians found their lives increasingly disrupted. They had to cut back on heating, work longer hours and recycle their rubbish. Goebbels redoubled his censorship efforts. He tried to maintain people's support for the war by involving them in it through asking them to make sacrifices. They donated an estimated 1.5 million fur coats to help to clothe the German army in Russia.

At this stage in the war, the German people began to see and hear less of Hitler. His old speeches were broadcast by Goebbels, but Hitler was increasingly preoccupied with the detail of the war. In 1942 the 'Final Solution' began (see pages 294–97), which was to kill millions of Jewish civilians in German-occupied countries.

From 1942, Albert Speer began to direct Germany's war economy. All effort focused on the armament industries. Postal services were suspended and letter boxes were closed. All places of entertainment were closed, except cinemas – Goebbels needed these to show propaganda films. Women were drafted into the labour force in increasing numbers. Country areas had to take evacuees from the cities and refugees from eastern Europe.

These measures were increasingly carried out by the SS. In fact, the SS became virtually a state within the German state. This SS empire had its own armed forces, armaments industries and labour camps. It developed a business empire that was worth a fortune (see Source 49). However, even the SS could not win the war, or even keep up German morale.

With defeat looming, support for the Nazis weakened. Germans stopped declaring food they had. They stayed away from Nazi rallies. They refused to give the 'Heil Hitler' salute when asked to do so. Himmler even contacted the Allies to ask about possible peace terms.

SOURCE 49

A disused mineshaft at Merkers where, in 1945, US forces found a stash of valuables hidden by the SS. The sacks mainly contained gold.

Goebbels does not always tell you the truth. When he tells you that England is powerless do you believe that? Have you forgotten that our bombers fly over Germany at will? The bombs that fell with these leaflets tell you . . . The war lasts as long as Hitler's regime.

Translation of a leaflet dropped by the Allies on Berlin.

SOURCE **51**

The greatest effect on [civilian] morale will be produced if a new blow of catastrophic force can be struck at a time when the situation already appears desperate.

From a secret report to the British government, 1944.

---

1 What do Sources 50–53 tell you about
   a) the aims of the bombing
   b) the success of the bombing?

The bombing of Dresden

It was the bombing of Germany which had the most dramatic effect on the lives of German civilians. In 1942 the Allies decided on a new policy towards the bombing of Germany. Under Arthur 'Bomber' Harris the British began an all-out assault on both industrial and residential areas of all the major German cities. One of the objectives was to cripple German industry, the other was to lower the morale of civilians and to terrorise them into submission.

The bombing escalated through the next three years, culminating in the bombing of Dresden in February 1945 which killed between 35,000 and 150,000 people in two days. Sources 51–53 tell you more about that bombing.

SOURCE **52**

The centre of Dresden after the bombing in February 1945.

SOURCE **53**

Key

- Totally destroyed
- Badly damaged
- Damaged
- ■ Factory

Military Transport Centre

Air Command HQ

A map showing the destruction of Dresden. Dresden was an industrial city, but the major damage was to civilian areas.

By 1945 the German people were in a desperate state. Food supplies were dwindling. Already 3.5 million German civilians had died. Refugees were fleeing the advancing Russian armies in the east.

Three months after the massive destruction of Dresden, Germany's war was over. Hitler, Goebbels and other Nazi war leaders committed suicide or were captured. Germany surrendered. It was now a shattered country. The Nazi promises lay in tatters and the country was divided up into zones of occupation run by the British, French, US and Soviet forces (see page 70).

Focus Task

How did the war change life in Germany?

1 Draw a timeline from 1939 to 1945 down the middle of a page.
2 On the left, make notes to show how the war was going for Germany's army.
3 On the right, make notes to show how the war affected Germans at home in Germany.
4 Choose one change from the right-hand column that you think had the greatest impact on ordinary Germans and explain your choice.

The persecution of minorities

The Nazis believed in the superiority of the Aryan race. Through their twelve years in power they persecuted members of other races, and many minority groups such as gypsies, homosexuals and mentally handicapped people. They persecuted any group that they thought challenged Nazi ideas. Homosexuals were a threat to Nazi ideas about family life; the mentally handicapped were a threat to Nazi ideas about Germans being a perfect master race; gypsies were thought to be an inferior people.

The persecution of such minorities varied. In families where there were hereditary illnesses, sterilisation was enforced. Over 300,000 men and women were compulsorily sterilised between 1934 and 1945. A so-called 'euthanasia programme' was begun in 1939. At least 5,000 severely mentally handicapped babies and children were killed between 1939 and 1945 either by injection or by starvation. Between 1939 and 1941, 72,000 mentally ill patients were gassed before a public outcry in Germany itself ended the extermination. The extermination of the gypsies, on the other hand, did not cause an outcry. Five out of six gypsies living in Germany in 1939 were killed by the Nazis. Similarly, there was little or no complaint about the treatment of so-called 'asocials' – homosexuals, alcoholics, the homeless, prostitutes, habitual criminals and beggars – who were rounded up off the streets and sent to concentration camps.

You are going to investigate this most disturbing aspect of Nazi Germany by tracing the story of Nazi treatment of the Jewish population in which anti-semitism culminated in the dreadful slaughter of the 'Final Solution'.

SOURCE 54

A poster published in 1920, directed at 'All German mothers'. It explains that over 12,000 German Jews were killed fighting for their country in the First World War.

SOURCE 55

SA and SS men enforcing the boycott of Jewish shops, April 1933.

SOURCE 56

To read the pages [of Hitler's Mein Kampf*] is to enter a world of the insane, a world peopled by hideous and distorted shadows. The Jew is no longer a human being, he has become a mythical figure, a grimacing leering devil invested with infernal powers, the incarnation of evil.*

A Bullock, *Hitler: A Study in Tyranny,* published in 1990.

1 What does Source 54 suggest about attitudes to Jews in 1920?
2 Why did Hitler hate the Jews?

Hitler and the Jews

Anti-semitism means hatred of Jews. Throughout Europe, Jews had experienced discrimination for hundreds of years. They were often treated unjustly in courts or forced to live in ghettos. One reason for this persecution was religious, in that Jews were blamed for the death of Jesus Christ! Another reason was that they tended to be well educated and therefore held well-paid professional jobs or ran successful stores and businesses.

Hitler hated Jews insanely. In his years of poverty in Vienna, he became obsessed by the fact that Jews ran many of the most successful businesses, particularly the large department stores. This offended his idea of the superiority of Aryans. Hitler also blamed Jewish businessmen and bankers for Germany's defeat in the First World War. He thought they had forced the surrender of the German army.

As soon as Hitler took power in 1933 he began to mobilise the full powers of the state against the Jews. They were immediately banned from the Civil Service and a variety of public services such as broadcasting and teaching. At the same time, SA and later SS troopers organised boycotts of Jewish shops and businesses, which were marked with a star of David.

SOURCE 57

A cartoon from the Nazi newspaper *Der Stürmer*, 1935. Jews owned many shops and businesses. These were a constant target for Nazi attacks.

SOURCE 58

[The day after Kristallnacht*] the teachers told us: don't worry about what you see, even if you see some nasty things which you may not understand. Hitler wants a better Germany, a clean Germany. Don't worry, everything will work out fine in the end.*

Henrik Metelmann, member of the Hitler Youth, in 1938.

SOURCE 59

Until Kristallnacht, *many Germans believed Hitler was not engaged in mass murder. [The treatment of the Jews] seemed to be a minor form of harassment of a disliked minority. But after* Kristallnacht *no German could any longer be under any illusion. I believe it was the day that we lost our innocence. But it would be fair to point out that I myself never met even the most fanatic Nazi who wanted the extermination [mass murder] of the Jews. Certainly we wanted the Jews out of Germany, but we did not want them to be killed.*

Alfons Heck, member of the Hitler Youth in 1938, interviewed for a television programme in 1989.

3 Read Sources 58–61. How useful is each source to a historian looking at the German reaction to *Kristallnacht*?
4 Taken together, do they provide a clear picture of how Germans felt about *Kristallnacht*?
5 Could Germans have protested effectively about *Kristallnacht*? Explain your answer with reference to pages 276–82.

In 1935 the Nuremberg Laws took away German citizenship from Jews. Jews were also forbidden to marry or have sex with pure-blooded Germans. Goebbels' propaganda experts bombarded German children and families with anti-Jewish messages. Jews were often refused jobs, and people in shops refused to serve them. In schools, Jewish children were humiliated and then segregated.

Kristallnacht

In November 1938 a young Jew killed a German diplomat in Paris. The Nazis used this as an excuse to launch a violent revenge on Jews. Plain-clothes SS troopers were issued with pickaxes and hammers and the addresses of Jewish businesses. They ran riot, smashing up Jewish shops and workplaces. Ninety-one Jews were murdered. Hundreds of synagogues were burned. Twenty thousand Jews were taken to concentration camps. Thousands more left the country. This event became known as *Kristallnacht* or 'The Night of Broken Glass'. Many Germans watched the events of *Kristallnacht* with alarm and concern. The Nazi-controlled press presented *Kristallnacht* as the spontaneous reaction of ordinary Germans against the Jews. Most Germans did not believe this. However, hardly anyone protested. The few who did were brutally murdered.

SOURCE 60

I hate the treatment of the Jews. I think it is a bad side of the movement and I will have nothing to do with it. I did not join the party to do that sort of thing. I joined the party because I thought and still think that Hitler did the greatest Christian work for twenty-five years. I saw seven million men rotting in the streets, often I was there too, and no one . . . seemed to care . . . Then Hitler came and he took all those men off the streets and gave them health and security and work . . .

H Schmidt, Labour Corps leader, in an interview in 1938.

SOURCE 61

I feel the urge to present to you a true report of the recent riots, plundering and destruction of Jewish property. Despite what the official Nazi account says, the German people have nothing whatever to do with these riots and burnings. The police supplied SS men with axes, house-breaking tools and ladders. A list of the addresses of all Jewish shops and flats was provided and the mob worked under the leadership of the SS men. The police had strict orders to remain neutral.

Anonymous letter from a German civil servant to the British consul, 1938.

The ghettos

The persecution developed in intensity after the outbreak of war in 1939. After defeating Poland in 1939, the Nazis set about 'Germanising' western Poland. This meant transporting Poles from their homes and replacing them with German settlers. Almost one in five Poles died in the fighting and as a result of racial policies of 1939–45. Polish Jews were rounded up and transported to the major cities. Here they were herded into sealed areas, called ghettos. The able-bodied Jews were used for slave labour but the young, the old and the sick were simply left to die from hunger and disease.

Mass murder

In 1941 Germany invaded the USSR. The invasion was a great success at first. However, within weeks the Nazis found themselves in control of 3 million Russian Jews in addition to the Jews in all of the other countries they had invaded. German forces had orders to round up and shoot Communist Party activists and their Jewish supporters. The shooting was carried out by special SS units called *Einsatzgruppen*. By the autumn of 1941, mass shootings were taking place all over occupied eastern Europe. In Germany, all Jews were ordered to wear the star of David on their clothing to mark them out.

SOURCE 62

A drawing by a prisoner in Auschwitz concentration camp. The prisoners are being made to do knee bends to see if they are fit enough to work. If not they will be killed in the gas chambers.

SOURCE 63

The extermination of the Jews is the most dreadful chapter in German history, doubly so because the men who did it closed their senses to the reality of what they were doing by taking pride in the technical efficiency of their actions and, at moments when their conscience threatened to break in, telling themselves that they were doing their duty . . . others took refuge in the enormity of the operation, which lent it a convenient depersonalisation. When they ordered a hundred Jews to get on a train in Paris or Amsterdam, they considered their job accomplished and carefully closed their minds to the thought that eventually those passengers would arrive in front of the ovens of Treblinka.

American historian Gordon Craig, 1978.

1 The systematic killing of the Jews by the Nazis is generally known today as the Holocaust, which means 'sacrifice'. Many people prefer the Jewish term Sho'ah, which means 'destruction'. Why do you think this is?
2 You can see many websites, TV programmes and books about the mass murders. Many of these resources contain terrible scenes showing dead bodies, gas chambers, cremation ovens and other horrors. We have chosen Source 64. Why do you think we did this?

The 'death camps'

In January 1942, senior Nazis met at Wannsee, a suburb of Berlin, for a conference to discuss what they called the 'Final Solution' to the 'Jewish Question'. At the Wannsee Conference, Himmler, head of the SS and Gestapo, was put in charge of the systematic killing of all Jews within Germany and German-occupied territory. Slave labour and death camps were built at Auschwitz, Treblinka, Chelmo and other places. The old, the sick and young children were killed immediately. The able-bodied were first used as slave labour. Some were used for appalling medical experiments. Six million Jews, 500,000 European gypsies and countless political prisoners, Jehovah's Witnesses, homosexuals and Russian and Polish prisoners of war were sent to these camps to be worked to death, gassed or shot.

Was the 'Final Solution' planned from the start?

Historians have debated intensely as to whether or not the 'Final Solution' was the result of a long-term plan of Hitler. Some historians (intentionalists) believe the whole dreadful process was planned. Other historians (structuralists) argue that there was no clear plan and that the policy of mass murder evolved during the war years. Part of the problem is the lack of evidence. Hitler made speeches in which he talked of the annihilation of the Jews, but he never signed any documents or made any recorded orders directly relating to the extermination of the Jews. The Nazis kept the killing programme as secret as they could, so there are relatively few documents.

Although historians disagree about whether there was a plan, they do generally agree that Hitler was ultimately responsible. However, they also point to others who bear some of the responsibility as well. The genocide would not have been possible without:

- The Civil Service bureaucracy – they collected and stored information about Jews.
- Police forces in Germany and the occupied lands – many victims of the Nazis, such as Anne Frank, were actually taken by the police rather than the Gestapo or SS.
- The SS – Adolf Eichmann devised a system of transporting Jews to collection points and then on to the death camps. He was also in charge of looting the possessions of the Jews. The SS Death's Head battalions and *Einsatzgruppen* also carried out many of the killings.
- The Wehrmacht (German armed forces) – the army leaders were fully aware of events.
- Industry – companies such as Volkswagen and Mercedes had their own slave labour camps. The chemicals giant IG Farben competed with other companies for the contract to make the Cyclon B gas which was used in the gas chambers.
- The German people – there was widespread support for anti-semitism, even if these feelings did not include support for mass murder. Many Germans took part in some aspect of the Holocaust, but closed their eyes to the full reality of what was happening (see Source 63).

SOURCE 64

Wedding rings taken from people killed at Buchenwald concentration camp.

SOURCE 65

Dear Teacher,
I am a survivor of a concentration camp.
My eyes saw what no man should witness:
Gas chambers built by learned engineers;
Children poisoned by educated physicians;
Infants killed by trained nurses;
Women and babies shot and burned by
*   high school and college graduates.*
So, I am suspicious of education.
My request is: help your students become
*   human.*
Your efforts must never produce learned
*   monsters, skilled psychopaths, educated*
*   Eichmanns.*
Reading, writing, arithmetic and history
*   are important only if they serve to make*
*   our children more human.*

A letter written by a Holocaust survivor to the United Nations explaining the importance of students studying history.

SOURCE 66

Hitler's dictatorship differed in one
fundamental point from all its predecessors
in history. It was the first dictatorship in the
present period of modern technical
development which made complete use of
all technical means for the domination of
its own country.

Through technical devices like the radio
and loud-speaker, eighty million people
were deprived of independent thought. It
was thereby possible to subject them to the
will of one man . . . The nightmare of
many a man that one day nations could
be ruled by technical means was realised in
Hitler's totalitarian system.

Albert Speer, a leading Nazi, speaking at the Nuremberg war trials.

SOURCE 67

We didn't know much about Nazi ideals.
Nevertheless, we were politically
programmed: to obey orders, to cultivate
the soldierly virtue of standing to attention
and saying 'Yes, Sir' and to stop thinking
when the word Fatherland was uttered and
Germany's honour and greatness were
mentioned.

A former member of the Hitler Youth looks back after the war.

Resistance

Many Jews escaped from Germany before the killing started. Other Jews managed to live under cover in Germany and the occupied territories. Gad Beck, for instance, led the Jewish resistance to the Nazis in Berlin. He was finally captured in April 1945. On the day he was due to be executed, he was rescued by a detachment of troops from the Jewish regiment of the Red Army who had heard of his capture and had been sent to rescue him. There were 28 known groups of Jewish fighters, and there may have been more. Many Jews fought in the resistance movements in the Nazi-occupied lands. In 1945 the Jews in the Warsaw ghetto rose up against the Nazis and held out against them for four weeks. Five concentration camps saw armed uprisings and Greek Jews managed to blow up the gas ovens at Auschwitz.

We know that many Germans and other non-Jews helped Jews by hiding them and smuggling them out of German-held territory. The industrialist Oskar Schindler protected and saved many by getting them on to his 'list' of workers. The Swedish diplomat Raoul Wallenberg worked with other resisters to provide Jews with Swedish and US passports to get them out of the reach of the Nazis in Hungary. He disappeared in mysterious circumstances in 1945. Of course, high-profile individuals such as these were rare. Most of the successful resisters were successful because they kept an extremely low profile and were discovered neither by the Nazis then, nor by historians today.

Activity

Holocaust denial

SOURCE 68

Holocaust-denial activity increased worldwide in 2007, following a temporary lull in 2006 due to the imprisonment of leading denier David Irving, in Austria. In 2007, Irving returned to the lecture circuit, and other deniers continued their efforts in various countries, including holding a conference in Italy to defend Holocaust-denial. At the same time, however, efforts by some European governments, especially Germany and Austria, to prosecute Holocaust-deniers helped curb the extent of denial activity.

In the Middle East, some Arab and Muslim regimes continued to sponsor Holocaust denial and sought to impede UN resolutions opposing denial. The government of Iran went so far as to organise a conference of Holocaust deniers in Teheran. In addition, a poll found a substantial level of Holocaust denial among Israeli Arabs.

There were also several hopeful developments: two prominent Muslims, the former prime minister of Indonesia and the president of the Islamic Society of North America, condemned Holocaust denial; the United Nations General Assembly and UNESCO both passed resolutions opposing Holocaust denial; and the European Union urged all its member-states to adopt legislation prohibiting Holocaust denial.

An extract from *Holocaust Denial – A Global Survey 2007*. This report was published by the David S Wyman Institute for Holocaust Studies, which is based in the USA.

There are many organisations like the David S Wyman Institute which specialise in Holocaust studies. Some of these organisations have been criticised for being too sensitive about the issue. With this in mind, hold a class debate on the issue: Does it matter if people deny that the Holocaust happens? You will need to consider issues such as:
* Who denies the Holocaust?
* Why is it denied?
* What reasons are given?
* How does denial affect present day attitudes?
* Do you think organisations like the David S Wyman Institute harm their own cause by appearing to be too sensitive?
* Should Holocaust denial be a crime?
* Is Holocaust denial really a problem or is the real problem a lack of knowledge about the Holocaust in the first place?

Russia, 1905–41

12.1 Why did the Tsar's regime collapse in 1917?

Timeline

This timeline shows the period you will be covering in this chapter. Some of the key dates are filled in already.

To help you get a complete picture of the period, make your own copy and add other details to it as you work through the chapter.

1900	**TSARIST RUSSIA**
1905	The Tsar survives an attempted revolution
1910	
1914	Russia enters the First World War
1917	Mar The Tsar abdicates. Provisional Government takes power Oct The Bolsheviks take power
1920	**BOLSHEVIK RUSSIA** The Bolsheviks win the Civil War
1924	Lenin dies
	THE USSR
1928	Stalin launches the first Five-Year Plan
1930	
1934	Stalin begins the Purges

The new Tsar

When Nicholas II was crowned Tsar of Russia in 1894, the crowds flocked to St Petersburg to cheer. There were so many people that a police report said 1,200 people were crushed to death as the crowd surged forward to see the new Tsar, whom they called 'the Little Father of Russia'.

Twenty-three years later, he had been removed from power and he and his family were prisoners. They were held under armed guard in a lonely house at Ekaterinburg, far from the Tsar's luxurious palaces. Perhaps the Tsar might have asked himself how this had happened, but commentators were predicting collapse long before 1917.

SOURCE **1**

The coronation of Nicholas II, Tsar of Russia.

Tsar Nicholas II

- ➤ Born 1868.
- ➤ Crowned as Tsar in 1896.
- ➤ Married to Alexandra of Hesse (a granddaughter of Queen Victoria).
- ➤ Both the Tsar and his wife were totally committed to the idea of the Tsar as autocrat – absolute ruler of Russia.
- ➤ Nicholas regularly rejected requests for reform.
- ➤ He was interested in the Far East. This got him into a disastrous war with Japan in 1905.
- ➤ He was not very effective as a ruler, unable to concentrate on the business of being Tsar.
- ➤ He was a kind, loving family man but did not really understand the changes Russia was going through.
- ➤ By 1917 he had lost control of Russia and abdicated.
- ➤ In 1918 he and his family were shot by Bolsheviks during the Russian Civil War.

The Tsar's empire

Russia was a vast empire rather than a single country, and the Tsar was its supreme ruler. It was not an easy job.

Nationalities

The Tsar's empire included many different nationalities. Only 40 per cent of the Tsar's subjects spoke Russian as their first language. Some subjects, for example the Cossacks, were loyal to the Tsar. Others, for example the Poles and Finns, hated Russian rule. Jews often suffered racial prejudice and even vicious attacks, called pogroms, sponsored by the government.

Activity

Look at the profile of Tsar Nicholas II. Read through the information and sources on pages 300–302 and add four more points to the profile. You could work in pairs to draw up a list of points, then narrow them down to just four.

SOURCE 2

Population of the Russian Empire, according to a census in 1897

Russians	55,650,000	Letts	1,400,000
Ukrainians	22,400,000	Georgians	1,350,000
Poles	7,900,000	Armenians	1,150,000
Byelorussians	5,900,000	Romanians	1,110,000
Jews	5,000,000	Caucasians	1,000,000
Kirghiz	4,000,000	Estonians	1,000,000
Tartars	3,700,000	Iranians	1,000,000
Finns	2,500,000	Other Asiatic peoples	5,750,000
Germans	1,800,000	Mongols	500,000
Lithuanians	1,650,000	Others	200,000

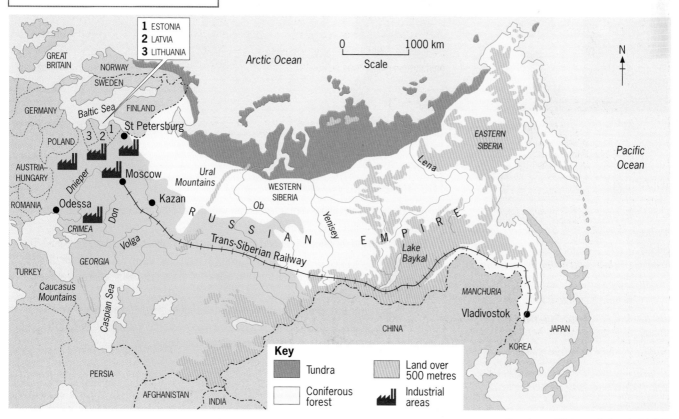

Russia and its population in 1900.

Peasants and the countryside

Around 80 per cent of Russia's population were peasants who lived in communes. There were some prosperous peasant farmers called kulaks, but living and working conditions for most peasants were dreadful. Famine and starvation were common and in some regions the life expectancy of a peasant farmer was only 40 years of age.

Much of Russia's land was unsuitable for farming. As a result, land was in very short supply because, by the early 1900s, the population was growing rapidly. (It increased by 50 per cent between 1860 and 1897.) Russian peasants were still using ancient farming techniques. In most villages, the land was divided into large fields. Each family was allotted a strip of land in one of the fields. This subdivision of the fields was organised by peasant councils called mir. When a peasant had sons, the family plot was subdivided and shared between them.

There was no basic education in Russia and very few peasants could read or write. But, despite all their hardships, many peasants were loyal to the Tsar. This was partly because they were also religious. Every week, they would hear the priest say how wonderful the Tsar was and how they, as peasants, should be loyal subjects. However, not all peasants were loyal or religious. Many supported the opposition, the Social Revolutionaries (see page 303). Their main discontent was over land – they resented the amount of land owned by the aristocracy, the Church and the Tsar.

1   Use Sources 3A and 3B to write a description of peasants' living conditions. Make sure you highlight the contrast with the conditions described in Source 4.

SOURCE **3A**

The interior of a Russian peasant's cottage.

SOURCE **3B**

A typical village in northern Russia.

SOURCE **4**

In the big house the two women hardly manage to wash up all the crockery for the gentlefolk who have just had a meal; and two peasants in dress coats are running up or down stairs serving tea, coffee, wine and water. Upstairs the table is laid; they have just finished one meal and will soon start another that will go on till at least midnight. There are some fifteen healthy men and women here and some thirty able-bodied men and women servants working for them.

Count Leo Tolstoy, writer and improving landlord.

The aristocracy

The peasants' living conditions contrasted sharply with those of the aristocracy, who had vast estates, town and country houses and elegant lifestyles.

The aristocracy were about 1.5 per cent of society but owned about 25 per cent of the land. They were a key part of the Tsar's government, often acting as local officials. In the countryside they dominated the local assemblies or zemstva. Most were loyal to the Tsar and wanted to keep Russian society as it was.

Many of the richer aristocrats lived not on their estates but in the glamorous cities. Some landlords were in financial trouble and had to sell their lands, a piece at a time. Perhaps the greatest fear of the aristocracy was that the peasants would rise up and take their lands.

2 Look at Sources 3 and 5. Were workers in the town any better off than their cousins in the countryside? Explain your answer.

New industries, cities and the working class

From the later nineteenth century, the Tsars had been keen to see Russia become an industrial power. The senior minister Sergei Witte introduced policies that led to rapid industrial growth. Oil and coal production trebled, while iron production quadrupled (see Source 17 on page 306). Some peasants left the land to work in these newly developing industries. However, their living conditions hardly improved.

SOURCE **5A**

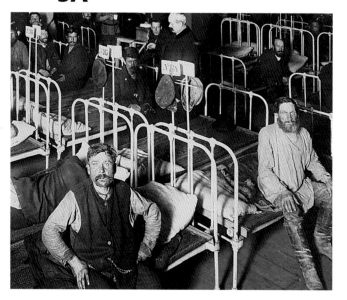

SOURCE **5B**

Workers' living conditions: **A** shows a dormitory and **B** shows a canteen in Moscow. Urban workers made up about 4 per cent of the population in 1900.

The greatest concentrations of these workers were in the capital, St Petersburg, and in Moscow. Here the population was growing fast as peasants arrived looking for a new way of life, or simply trying to earn some extra cash before returning for the harvest. Only a short walk away from the fabulous wealth of the Tsar's Winter Palace in St Petersburg, his subjects lived in filth and squalor. Overcrowding, terrible food, disease and alcoholism were everyday facts of life. The wretchedness of their living conditions was matched by the atrocious working conditions. Unlike every other European power, there were no government regulations on child labour, hours, safety or education. Trade unions were illegal. Low pay, twelve to fifteen-hour days, unguarded machinery and brutal discipline soon made the peasants realise that working in the factories was no better than working on the land.

The middle classes

As a result of industrialisation, a new class began to emerge in Russia – the capitalists. They were landowners, industrialists, bankers, traders and businessmen. Until this time, Russia had had only a small middle class which included people such as shopkeepers, lawyers and university lecturers. The capitalists increased the size of Russia's middle class, particularly in the towns. Their main concerns were the management of the economy, although the capitalists were also concerned about controlling their workforce. Clashes between workers and capitalists were to play an important role in Russia's history in the years up to 1917.

SOURCE **6**

Graph showing the growth of St Petersburg.

(Bar graph. Y-axis: Population in millions, from 0 to 2.5. X-axis years: 1863, 1881, 1897, 1900, 1914 with bars rising approximately 0.5, 0.85, 1.25, 1.45, 2.2 million respectively.)

I am informed that recently in some zemstva, voices have made themselves heard from people carried away by senseless dreams about participation by members of the zemstva in the affairs of internal government: let all know that I, devoting all my strength to the welfare of the people, will uphold the principle of autocracy as firmly and as unflinchingly as my late unforgettable father.

Part of Tsar Nicholas II's coronation speech in 1894. Zemstva were local assemblies dominated by the nobility in the countryside and professionals in the towns.

The Tsar and his government

The huge and diverse empire was ruled by an autocracy. One man, the Tsar, had absolute power to rule Russia. The Tsar believed that God had placed him in that position. The Russian Church supported him in this view. The Tsar could appoint or sack ministers or make any other decisions without consulting anyone else. By the early twentieth century most of the great powers had given their people at least some say in how they were run, but Nicholas was utterly committed to the idea of autocracy and seemed to be obsessed with the great past of his family, the Romanovs (see Source 7). He had many good qualities, such as his loyalty to his family, his willingness to work hard and his attention to detail. However, he was not an able, forceful and imaginative monarch like his predecessors.

Nicholas tended to avoid making important decisions. He did not delegate day-to-day tasks. In a country as vast as Russia, where tasks had to be delegated to officials, this was a major problem. He insisted on getting involved in the tiniest details of government. He personally answered letters from peasants and appointed provincial midwives. He even wrote out the instructions for the royal car to be brought round!

Nicholas also managed his officials poorly. He felt threatened by able and talented ministers, such as Count Witte and Peter Stolypin. He dismissed Witte (see Source 8) in 1906 and was about to sack Stolypin (see page 307) when Stolypin was murdered in 1911. Nicholas refused to chair the Council of Ministers because he disliked confrontation. He insisted on seeing ministers in one-to-one meetings. He encouraged rivalry between them. This caused chaos, as different government departments refused to co-operate with each other.

He also appointed family members and friends from the court to important positions. Many of them were incompetent or even corrupt, making huge fortunes from bribes.

We talked for two solid hours. He shook my hand. He wished me all the luck in the world. I went home beside myself with happiness and found a written order for dismissal lying on my desk.

Count Witte, Russian Prime Minister, 1906.

1 Draw up your own chart to summarise the Tsarist system of government.
2 Look at Sources 7 and 8. What do they suggest about:
 a) the loyalty of the Tsar's ministers
 b) the Tsar as a leader?
3 Describe and explain at least two ways in which Nicholas II made Russia's government weak.
4 Look carefully at Source 9. Would you interpret the contents of this source as:
 a) evidence of the strength of the Tsar's regime
 b) evidence of the weakness of the regime?
 Explain your answer and refer to the information in the text as well.

Control

Despite everything you have read so far, it is important to remember that the Tsar's regime was very strong in some ways. Resistance was limited. At the local level, most peasants had their lives controlled by the mir. The mir could be overruled by land captains. Land captains were usually minor landlords appointed by the Tsar as his officials in local areas. The zemstva or local assemblies also helped to control Russia. They were dominated by the landlords in the countryside and by professional people in the towns. Then there were local governors, appointed by the Tsar from the ranks of the aristocracy. In some areas, Russia was a police state, controlled by local governors. There were special emergency laws that allowed the local governors to:

- order the police to arrest suspected opponents of the regime
- ban individuals from serving in the zemstva, courts or any government organisation
- make suspects pay heavy fines
- introduce censorship of books or leaflets or newspapers.

Local governors controlled the police. The police had a special force with 10,000 officers whose job was to concentrate on political opponents of the regime. There was also the Okhrana, the Tsar's secret police. Finally, if outright rebellion did erupt, there was the army, particularly the Tsar's loyal and terrifying Cossack regiments.

A third of Russia lives under emergency legislation. The numbers of the regular police and of the secret police are continually growing. The prisons are overcrowded with convicts and political prisoners. At no time have religious persecutions [of Jews] been so cruel as they are today. In all cities and industrial centres soldiers are employed and equipped with live ammunition to be sent out against the people. Autocracy is an outdated form of government that may suit the needs of a central African tribe but not those of the Russian people who are increasingly aware of the culture of the rest of the world.

Part of a letter from the landowner and writer Leo Tolstoy to the Tsar in 1902. The letter was an open letter – it was published openly as well as being sent to the Tsar.

Factfile

Marxist theory

➤ Karl Marx was a German writer and political thinker. He believed that history was dominated by class struggle and revolution.
➤ In Marxist theory the first change brought about by the class struggle would be the middle classes taking control from the monarchy and aristocracy.
➤ There would then be a revolution in which the workers (the proletariat) would overthrow the middle classes.
➤ For a short while the Communist Party would rule on behalf of the people, but as selfish desires disappeared there would be no need for any government.
➤ All would live in a peaceful, Communist society.

Activity

Look carefully at Source 10. It was drawn by opponents of the Tsar's regime who had been forced to live in Switzerland to avoid the Tsar's secret police. It is a representation of life in Russia under the rule of the Tsar. Discuss how far you think it is an accurate view of Russian society. Think about:
• ways in which its claims are supported by the information and sources in the text
• ways in which its claims are not supported by the information and sources in the text
• aspects of life in Russia that are not covered by the drawing.

Opposition to the Tsar

The Tsarist government faced opposition from three particular groups. Many middle-class people wanted greater democracy in Russia and pointed out that Britain still had a king but also a powerful parliament. These people were called liberals or 'Cadets'.

Two other groups were more violently opposed to the Tsar. They believed that revolution was the answer to the people's troubles. The Socialist Revolutionaries (SRs) were a radical movement. Their main aim was to carve up the huge estates of the nobility and hand them over to the peasants. They believed in a violent struggle and were responsible for the assassination of two government officials, as well as the murder of a large number of Okhrana (police) agents and spies. They had wide support in the towns and the countryside.

The Social Democratic Party was a smaller but more disciplined party which followed the ideas of Karl Marx. In 1903 the party split itself into Bolsheviks and Mensheviks. The Bolsheviks (led by Lenin) believed it was the job of the party to create a revolution whereas the Mensheviks believed Russia was not ready for revolution. Both of these organisations were illegal and many of their members had been executed or sent in exile to Siberia. Many of the leading Social Democrat leaders were forced to live abroad.

By 1903 the activities of the opposition parties, added to the appalling conditions in the towns and the countryside, led to a wave of strikes, demonstrations and protests. The Tsar's ministers warned him that Russia was getting close to revolution.

SOURCE **10**

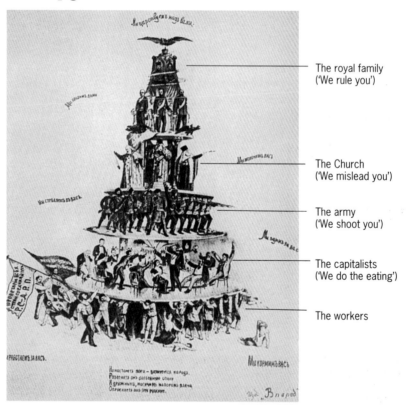

Cartoon showing the Tsarist system. This was published in Switzerland by exiled opponents of the Tsar.

- The royal family ('We rule you')
- The Church ('We mislead you')
- The army ('We shoot you')
- The capitalists ('We do the eating')
- The workers

Focus Task

You are a minister of the Tsar in 1903. Write a report for him, informing him truthfully of the situation in Russia.
Your report should mention:
◆ inefficient and corrupt government
◆ the condition of the peasants
◆ the contrast between rich and poor in Russia
◆ conditions for the workers in the towns
◆ the activities of opposition groups.

5 Read the section headed 'Opposition to the Tsar'. Is there anything the Cadets, the Socialist Revolutionaries, and the Social Democratic Party might agree on?
6 Look again at Source 7. Do you think the Tsar would listen to the ideas of the Cadets?

303

1 Read Source 11. Make two lists:
   a) the petitioners' complaints
   b) their demands.
2 Are these demands revolutionary demands? Explain your answer.
3 Choose two words to sum up the attitude of the petitioners to the Tsar.

SOURCE 11

Lord, we workers, our children, our wives and our old, helpless parents have come, Lord, to seek truth, justice and protection from you.

We are impoverished and oppressed, unbearable work is imposed on us, we are despised and not recognised as human beings. We are treated as slaves, who must bear their fate and be silent. We have suffered terrible things, but we are pressed ever deeper into the abyss of poverty, ignorance and lack of rights.

We ask but little: to reduce the working day to eight hours and to provide a minimum wage of a rouble a day.

Officials have taken the country into a shameful war. We working men have no say in how the taxes we pay are spent.

Do not refuse to help your people. Destroy the wall between yourself and your people.

From the Petition to the Tsar presented by Father Gapon, 1905.

4 a) Compare Sources 12–14. How do these scenes differ in their presentation of Bloody Sunday?
   b) How can you explain these differences?

The 1905 revolution

The government's attempts to deal with its problems failed dramatically. In 1903 it slightly relaxed censorship and other repressive measures. The result was an explosion of anti-government pamphlets, books and newspapers. It also tried to set up government-approved trade unions (free trade unions were illegal), but this simply led to strikes and demands for free unions. In 1904, hoping to unite the country behind him with spectacular victories, the Tsar embarked on a war against Japan. In fact, Russia suffered a series of humiliating defeats.

Bloody Sunday

These tensions all came together on Sunday, 22 January 1905, when a crowd of 200,000 protesters, led by the priest Father Gapon, came to the Winter Palace to give a petition to the Tsar. Many of the marchers carried pictures of the Tsar to show their respect for him.

The Tsar was not in the Winter Palace. He had left St Petersburg when the first signs of trouble appeared. The protesters were met by a regiment of soldiers and mounted Cossacks. Without warning, the soldiers opened fire and the Cossacks charged. It was a decisive day. The Tsar finally lost the respect of Father Gapon and the ordinary people of Russia.

SOURCE 12

Bloody Sunday – as painted in around 1910.

SOURCE 13

Bloody Sunday – as painted in around 1910.

SOURCE 14

Bloody Sunday, reconstructed for a film in the 1920s.

SOURCE 15

A clear, frosty day. There was much activity and many reports. Fredericks came to lunch. Went for a long walk. Since yesterday all the factories and workshops in St Petersburg have been on strike. Troops have been brought in to strengthen the garrison. The workers have conducted themselves calmly hitherto. At the head of the workers is some socialist priest: Gapon.

Sunday 22 January

A painful day. There have been serious disorders in St Petersburg because workmen wanted to come up to the Winter Palace. Troops had to open fire in several places in the city; there were many killed and wounded. God, how painful and sad! Mama arrived from town, straight to church. I lunched with all the others. Went for a walk with Misha. Mama stayed overnight.

From the Tsar's diary, recording the events of Bloody Sunday.

It might appear from Source 15 that the Tsar was out of touch with the seriousness of the situation. For the next ten months it seemed possible that he might lose control of Russia. His uncle was assassinated in Moscow, where striking workers put barricades in the streets. In June, the sailors aboard the battleship *Potemkin* mutinied (revolted). In September a general strike began and paralysed Russian industry. Then revolutionaries, including Lenin and Trotsky, returned from exile to join the revolution. Workers' councils (or soviets) were formed in the towns, while in the countryside peasants murdered landlords and their agents and took over their lands.

How did the Tsar survive?

It took the Tsar some time to respond. In his October Manifesto the Tsar offered the people a Duma (an elected parliament), the right to free speech and the right to form political parties. In November, he announced further concessions and financial help for peasants. This divided his opponents. The middle-class liberals were delighted, but the revolutionary groups were suspicious. In the end, they were proved right in not trusting the Tsar. While his opponents debated what to do next, the Tsar made peace with Japan and brought his best troops back to western Russia to crush the revolt. Rebellions in the countryside were ruthlessly put down (see Source 16).

In December 1905 leaders of the St Petersburg and Moscow soviets were arrested and exiled to Siberia. In Moscow this led to serious fighting in the streets, but the strikers were no match for the army. By March 1906 the revolution had been completely crushed and the revolutionary leaders were either dead, exiled or in hiding abroad. It was clear that no revolution would succeed as long as the army stayed loyal to the Tsar. In May 1906 the Tsar underlined his victory by introducing the Fundamental Laws. These Laws agreed to the existence of the Duma, but they put so many limitations on its powers that it could do virtually nothing.

SOURCE 16

Nightmare: the aftermath of a Cossack punishment expedition: cartoon from the Russian magazine *Leshii*, 1906.

5 Read Source 15. Do you agree that it suggests the Tsar was out of touch? Explain your answer.
6 Do you think 'Nightmare' is a good title for Source 16?

Focus Task

How the Tsar crushed the revolution

How the Tsar kept control

THE TSAR SURVIVES

How did the Tsar survive the 1905 revolution?

1 Copy this diagram.
2 On the left-hand side, list the different steps the Tsar took to crush the revolution in 1905.
3 Explain how each step helped him.
4 As you read the next section of text, list on the right-hand side of your diagram the longer-term measures the Tsar took to keep control after the revolution.
5 Explain how each measure helped him.

SOURCE 17

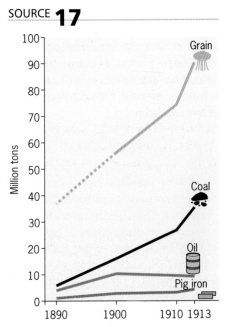

Agricultural and industrial production, 1890–1913.

---

1 What does Source 18 suggest about the attitude of the Tsar and the members of his court to the idea of the 'people' being more involved in running the country?
2 What does Source 19 suggest about working people's attitudes to the Tsar's regime?

SOURCE 19

Year	Strikes	Strikers
1905	13,995	2,863,173
1906	6,114	1,108,406
1907	3,573	740,074
1908	892	176,101
1909	340	64,166
1910	222	46,623
1911	466	105,110
1912	2,032	725,491
1913	2,404	887,096
1914	3,534	1,337,458

These figures were compiled by the Tsar's Ministry of Trade and Industry.

SOURCE 20

Let those in power make no mistake about the mood of the people . . . never were the Russian people . . . so profoundly revolutionised by the actions of the government, for day by day, faith in the government is steadily waning . . .

Guchkov, a Russian conservative in the Duma, 1913. By 1913, even staunch supporters of the Tsar were beginning to want change.

The troubled years, 1905–14

The Tsar survived the 1905 revolution, but some serious questions remained. The most serious was the possibility of another revolution. If he was to prevent this, Nicholas needed to reform Russia and satisfy at least some of the discontented groups that had joined the revolution in 1905. The Duma deputies who gathered for its first meeting in 1906 were hopeful that they could help to steer Russia on a new course. They were soon disappointed (see Source 18). The Tsar continued to rule without taking any serious notice of them. The first and second Dumas were very critical of the Tsar. They lasted less than a year before Nicholas sent them home. In 1907 Tsar Nicholas changed the voting rules so that his opponents were not elected to the Duma. This third Duma lasted until 1912, mainly because it was much less critical of the Tsar than the previous two. But by 1912 even this 'loyal' Duma was becoming critical of the Tsar's ministers and policies. However, it had no power to change the Tsar's policies and criticism alone was not a serious threat to the regime so the Tsar's rule continued.

SOURCE 18

The two hostile sides stood confronting each other. The old and grey court dignitaries, keepers of etiquette and tradition, looked across in a haughty manner, though not without fear and confusion, at 'the people of the street', whom the revolution had swept into the palace, and quietly whispered to one another. The other side looked across at them with no less disdain or contempt.

The court side of the hall resounded with orchestrated cheers as the Tsar approached the throne. But the Duma deputies remained completely silent. It was a natural expression of our feelings towards the monarch, who in the twelve years of his reign had managed to destroy all the prestige of his predecessors. The feeling was mutual: not once did the Tsar glance towards the Duma side of the hall. Sitting on the throne he delivered a short, perfunctory speech in which he promised to uphold the principles of autocracy 'with unwavering firmness' and, in a tone of obvious insincerity, greeted the Duma deputies as 'the best people' of his Empire. With that he got up to leave.

As the royal procession filed out of the hall, tears could be seen on the face of the Tsar's mother, the Dowager Empress. It had been a 'terrible ceremony' she later confided to the Minister of Finance. For several days she had been unable to calm herself from the shock of seeing so many commoners inside the palace.

From the memoirs of Duma deputy Obolensky, published in 1925. He is describing the first session of the Duma in April 1906.

Stolypin

In 1906 the Tsar appointed a tough new Prime Minister – Peter Stolypin. Stolypin used a 'carrot and stick' approach to the problems of Russia.

The stick: He came down hard on strikers, protesters and revolutionaries. Over 20,000 were exiled and over 1,000 hanged (the noose came to be known as 'Stolypin's necktie'). This brutal suppression effectively killed off opposition to the regime in the countryside until after 1914.

The carrot: Stolypin also tried to win over the peasants with the 'carrot' they had always wanted – land. He allowed wealthier peasants, the kulaks, to opt out of the mir communes and buy up land. These kulaks prospered and in the process created larger and more efficient farms. Production did increase significantly (see Source 17). On the other hand, 90 per cent of land in the fertile west of Russia was still run by inefficient communes in 1916. Farm sizes remained small even in Ukraine, Russia's best farmland. Most peasants still lived in the conditions you saw in the sources on page 300.

Stolypin also tried to boost Russia's industries. There was impressive economic growth between 1908 and 1911. But Russia was still far behind modern industrial powers such as Britain, Germany and the USA. Urban workers' wages stayed low and the cost of food and housing stayed high. Living and working conditions remained appalling (see page 301).

3 Make two lists:
  a) Stolypin's achievements
  b) Stolypin's failings.
4 If you were a senior adviser to the Tsar, which of Sources 17–21 would worry you most? Explain your answer.

The profits being made by industry were going to the capitalists, or they were being paid back to banks in France which had loaned the money to pay for much of Russia's industrial growth.

Stolypin was assassinated in 1911, but the Tsar was about to sack him anyway. He worried that Stolypin was trying to change Russia too much. Nicholas had already blocked some of Stolypin's plans for basic education for the people and regulations to protect factory workers. The Tsar was influenced by the landlords and members of the court. They saw Stolypin's reforms as a threat to the traditional Russian society in which everyone knew their place.

Relations between the Tsar and his people became steadily worse. The economy took a downturn in 1912, causing unemployment and hunger. The year 1913 saw huge celebrations for the three hundredth anniversary of the Romanovs' rule in Russia. The celebrations were meant to bring the country together, but enthusiasm was limited.

Focus Task

How well was Russia governed in 1914?

1 Here are five characteristics that you might expect of a good government:
  ◆ trying to improve the lives of all its people
  ◆ building up its agriculture and industry
  ◆ listening to and responding to its population
  ◆ running the country efficiently
  ◆ defending the country from enemies.
On a scale of 1–5, say how well you think the Tsarist government did on each one up to 1914. Explain your reason for giving that score. Your teacher can give you a worksheet to help you.
2 Now make a list of the successes and failures of the Tsarist government up to 1914.
3 Which of the following assessments do you most agree with?
By 1913 the government was:
  ◆ in crisis
  ◆ strong but with some serious weaknesses
  ◆ secure with only minor weaknesses.

SOURCE **21**

Tsar Nicholas at the 1913 celebrations of 300 years of Romanov rule. This was the first time since 1905 that the Tsar had appeared in public.

SOURCE **22**

Russian cartoon. The caption reads: 'The Russian Tsars at home.'

5 Look at Source 22. How does the cartoonist suggest that Rasputin is an evil influence on the Tsar and Tsarina?

The government tried other measures to get the people behind them, such as discrimination and even violence against Jews, Muslims and other minorities. This had little effect, and discontent grew, especially among the growing industrial working class in the cities. Strikes were on the rise (see Source 19), including the highly publicised Lena gold field strike where troops opened fire on striking miners. However, the army and police dealt with these problems and so, to its opponents, the government must have seemed firmly in control.

Strangely, some of the government's supporters were less sure about the government (see Source 20). Industrialists were concerned by the way in which the Tsar preferred to appoint loyal but unimaginative ministers such as Goremykin.

Rasputin

Some of the Tsar's supporters were particularly alarmed about the influence of a strange and dangerous figure – Gregory Yefimovich, generally known as Rasputin. The Tsar's son Alexis was very ill with a blood disease called haemophilia. Through hypnosis, it appeared that Rasputin could control the disease. He was greeted as a miracle worker by the Tsarina (the Tsar's wife). Before long, Rasputin was also giving her and the Tsar advice on how to run the country. People in Russia were very suspicious of Rasputin. He was said to be a drinker and a womaniser. His name means 'disreputable'. The Tsar's opponents seized on Rasputin as a sign of the Tsar's weakness and unfitness to rule Russia. The fact that the Tsar either didn't notice their concern or, worse still, didn't care showed just how out of touch he was.

Focus Task

How did the First World War weaken the Tsar's government?

The First World War had a massive impact on Russia. Your task is to use the material on pages 308–10 to present an overview of how the war affected four different groups of people in Russian society. The groups are:

- the army
- the workers
- the middle classes
- the aristocracy.

1 As you read through pages 308–10 you will find out about the impact of the war on each group. Write a paragraph or series of notes summarising the impact of war on each group.

2 Organise your work as a computer presentation. Do some research to locate pictures that support your presentation.

1 Was the Tsar's decision to take command of the army evidence that he was out of touch with the situation? Explain your answer.
2 Why were the Bolsheviks successful at gaining recruits in the army?

SOURCE 24

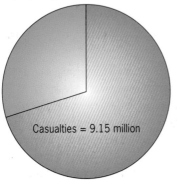

Total soldiers mobilised = 13 million

Casualties = 9.15 million

Russian casualties in the First World War.

SOURCE 25

Again that cursed question of shortage of artillery and rifle ammunition stands in the way of an energetic advance. If we should have three days of serious fighting, we might run out of ammunition altogether. Without new rifles, it is impossible to fill up the gaps.

Tsar Nicholas to his wife Alexandra, July 1915.

War and revolution

In August 1914 Russia entered the First World War. Tensions in the country seemed to disappear. The Tsar seemed genuinely popular with his people and there was an instant display of patriotism. The Tsar's action was applauded. Workers, peasants and aristocrats all joined in the patriotic enthusiasm. Anti-government strikes and demonstrations were abandoned. The good feeling, however, was very short-lived. As the war continued, the Tsar began to lose the support of key sectors of Russian society.

The army

The Russian army was a huge army of conscripts. At first, the soldiers were enthusiastic, as was the rest of society. Even so, many peasants felt that they were fighting to defend their country against the Germans rather than showing any loyalty to the Tsar. You can read about the Russian campaigns in the war on page 249. Russian soldiers fought bravely, but they stood little chance against the German army. They were badly led and treated appallingly by their aristocrat officers. They were also poorly supported by the industries at home. They were short of rifles, ammunition, artillery and shells. Many did not even have boots.

The Tsar took personal command of the armed forces in September 1915. This made little difference to the war, since Nicholas was not a particularly able commander. However, it did mean that people held Nicholas personally responsible for the defeats and the blunders. The defeats and huge losses continued throughout 1916. It is not surprising that by 1917 there was deep discontent in the army and that many soldiers were supporters of the revolutionary Bolshevik Party.

SOURCE 23

The army had neither wagons nor horses nor first aid supplies . . . We visited the Warsaw station where there were about 17,000 men wounded in battle. At the station we found a terrible scene: on the platform in dirt, filth and cold, on the ground, even without straw, wounded men, who filled the air with heart-rending cries, dolefully asked: 'For God's sake order them to dress our wounds. For five days we have not been attended to.'

From a report by Michael Rodzianko, President of the Duma.

Peasants, workers and the ethnic minorities

It did not take long for the strain of war to alienate the peasants and the workers. The huge casualty figures took their toll. In August 1916, the local governor of the village of Grushevka reported that the war had killed 13 per cent of the population of the village. This left many widows and orphans needing state war pensions which they did not always receive.

Despite the losses, food production remained high until 1916. By then, the government could not always be relied on to pay for the food produced. The government planned to take food by force but abandoned the idea because it feared it might spark a widespread revolt. There actually was a revolt in central Asian Russia when the Tsar tried to conscript Muslims into the army. It was brutally suppressed by the army.

By 1916 there was much discontent in the cities. War contracts created an extra 3.5 million industrial jobs between 1914 and 1916. The workers got little in the way of extra wages. They also had to cope with even worse overcrowding than before the war. There were fuel shortages. There were also food shortages. What made it worse was that there was enough food and fuel, but it could not be transported to the cities. The rail network could not cope with the needs of the army, industry and the populations of the cities. As 1916 turned into 1917, many working men and women stood and shivered in bread queues and cursed the Tsar.

SOURCE 26

The average worker's wage in 1917 was
5 roubles a day. This would buy you:

In 1914 | In 1917

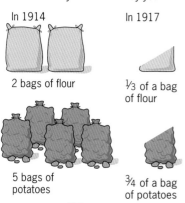

2 bags of flour | ⅓ of a bag of flour

5 bags of potatoes | ¾ of a bag of potatoes

5 kilograms of meat | 0.8 kilograms of meat

Prices in Russia, 1914–17.

SOURCE 27

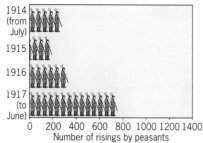

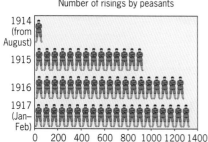

Peasant risings and strikes, 1914–17.

SOURCE 28

Everybody was fed up with the Tsar because they felt he was weak. When he abdicated, there was great rejoicing. Everybody thought things would be much better.

Margot Tracey, the daughter of wealthy Russian capitalists, describing feelings towards the Tsar in 1917.

3 Imagine you are an adviser to the Tsar in 1916. Which of the sources on pages 308–09 would give you most concern? Explain your answer.

The middle classes

The middle classes did not suffer in the same way as the peasants and workers, but they too were unhappy with the Tsar by the end of 1916. Many middle-class activists in the zemstva were appalled by reports such as Source 23. They set up their own medical organisations along the lines of the modern Red Cross, or joined war committees to send other supplies to the troops. These organisations were generally far more effective than the government agencies. By 1916 many industrialists were complaining that they could not fulfil their war contracts because of a shortage of raw materials (especially metals) and fuel. In 1915 an alliance of Duma politicians, the Progressive Bloc, had urged the Tsar to work with them in a more representative style of government that would unite the people. The Tsar dismissed the Duma a month later.

The aristocracy

The situation was so bad by late 1916 that the Council of the United Nobility was calling for the Tsar to step down. The junior officers in the army had suffered devastating losses in the war. Many of these officers were the future of the aristocrat class. The conscription of 13 million peasants also threatened aristocrats' livelihoods, because they had no workers for their estates. Most of all, many of the leading aristocrats were appalled by the influence of Rasputin over the government of Russia. When the Tsar left Petrograd (the new Russian version of the Germanic name St Petersburg) to take charge of the army, he left his wife in control of the country. The fact that she was German started rumours flying in the capital. There were also rumours of an affair between her and Rasputin. Ministers were dismissed and then replaced. The concerns were so serious that a group of leading aristocrats murdered Rasputin in December 1916.

SOURCE 29

I asked for an audience and was received by him [the Tsar] on March 8th. 'I must tell Your Majesty that this cannot continue much longer. No one opens your eyes to the true role which this man is playing. His presence in Your Majesty's court undermines confidence in the Supreme Power and may have an evil effect on the fate of the dynasty and turn the hearts of the people from their Emperor' . . . My report did some good. On March 11th an order was issued sending Rasputin to Tobolsk; but a few days later, at the demand of the Empress, this order was cancelled.

M Rodzianko, President of the Duma, March 1916.

The March revolution

As 1917 dawned, few people had great hopes for the survival of the Tsar's regime. In January strikes broke out all over Russia. In February the strikes spread. They were supported and even joined by members of the army. The Tsar's best troops lay dead on the battlefields. These soldiers were recent conscripts and had more in common with the strikers than their officers. On 7 March workers at the Putilov steelworks in Petrograd went on strike. They joined with thousands of women – it was International Women's Day – and other discontented workers demanding that the government provide bread. From 7 to 10 March the number of striking workers rose to 250,000. Industry came to a standstill. The Duma set up a Provisional Committee to take over the government. The Tsar ordered them to disband. They refused. On 12 March the Tsar ordered his army to put down the revolt by force. They refused. This was the decisive moment. Some soldiers even shot their own officers and joined the demonstrators. They marched to the Duma demanding that they take over the government. Reluctantly, the Duma leaders accepted – they had always wanted reform rather than revolution, but now there seemed no choice.

On the same day, revolutionaries set up the Petrograd Soviet again, and began taking control of food supplies to the city. They set up soldiers' committees, undermining the authority of the officers. It was not clear who was in charge of Russia, but it was obvious that the Tsar was not! On 15 March he issued a statement that he was abdicating. There was an initial plan for his brother Michael to take over, but Michael refused: Russia had finished with Tsars.

Focus Task B

How important was the war in the collapse of the Tsarist regime?

Historians have furiously debated this question since the revolution took place. There are two main views:

> #### View 1
> The Tsar's regime was basically stable up to 1914, even if it had some important problems to deal with. It was making steady progress towards becoming a modern state, but this progress was destroyed by the coming of war. Don't forget that this war was so severe that it also brought Germany, Austria–Hungary and Turkey to their knees as well.

> #### View 2
> The regime in Russia was cursed with a weak Tsar, a backward economy and a class of aristocrats who were not prepared to share their power and privileges with the millions of ordinary Russians. Revolution was only a matter of time. The war did not cause it, although it may have speeded up the process.

Divide the class into two groups.

One group has to find evidence and arguments to support View 1, the other to support View 2.

You could compare notes in a class discussion or organise a formal debate. You may even be able to compare your views with students in other schools using email conferencing.

SOURCE 30

One company of the Pavlovsky Regiment's reserve battalion had declared on 26 February that it would not fire on people . . . We have just received a telegram from the Minister of War stating that the rebels have seized the most important buildings in all parts of the city. Due to fatigue and propaganda the troops have laid down their arms, passed to the side of the rebels or become neutral . . .

General Alekseyev, February 1917.

Focus Task A

Why was the March 1917 revolution successful?

The Tsar faced a major revolution in 1905 but he survived. Why was 1917 different? Why was he not able to survive in 1917?

Failures in the war   The mutiny in the army

Duma setting up alternative parliament   Discontent in the countryside   Formation of soviets

Strikes   Food shortages   The Tsarina and Rasputin

Stage 1

1 Copy the headings in this diagram. They show eight reasons why the Tsar was forced to abdicate in March 1917.
2 For each of the factors, write one or two sentences explaining how it contributed to the fall of the Tsar.
3 Draw lines between any of the factors that seem to be connected. Label your line explaining what the link is.

Stage 2

4 In pairs or small groups, discuss the following points:
   a) Which factors were present in 1905?
   b) Were these same factors more or less serious than in 1905?
   c) Which factors were not present in 1905?
   d) Were the new factors decisive in making the March 1917 revolution successful?

1 Read Source 31. How popular do you think the Provisional Government's policies on
a) the war
b) land
would be with the peasants and the soldiers?

The Provisional Government

Russia's problems were not solved by the abdication of the Tsar. The Duma's Provisional Committee took over government. It faced three overwhelmingly urgent decisions:

- to continue the war or make peace
- to distribute land to the peasants (who had already started taking it) or ask them to wait until elections had been held
- how best to get food to the starving workers in the cities.

The Provisional Government was a mixed group. While it included men such as the lawyer Alexander Kerensky – Justice Minister in the Provisional Government but also a respected member of the Petrograd Soviet – it also included angry revolutionaries who had no experience of government at all. The Provisional Government promised Russia's allies that it would continue the war, while trying to settle the situation in Russia. It also urged the peasants to be restrained and wait for elections before taking any land. The idea was that the Provisional Government could then stand down and allow free elections to take place to elect a new Constituent Assembly that would fairly and democratically represent the people of Russia. It was a very cautious message for a people who had just gone through a revolution.

However, the Provisional Government was not the only possible government. Most workers also paid close attention to the Petrograd Soviet. The Soviet had the support of workers in key industries such as coal mining and water, and the support of much of the army. During the crisis months of spring 1917, the Soviet and Provisional Government worked together.

One man was determined to push the revolution further. He was Lenin, leader of the Bolsheviks (see page 315). When he heard of the March revolution he immediately returned to Russia from exile in Europe. The Germans even provided him with a special train, hoping that he might cause more chaos in Russia!

When Lenin arrived at Petrograd station, he set out the Bolshevik programme in his April Theses. He urged the people to support the Bolsheviks in a second revolution. Lenin's slogans 'Peace, Land and Bread' and 'All power to the soviets' contrasted sharply with the cautious message of the Provisional Government. Support for the Bolsheviks increased quickly (see Sources 32 and 33), particularly in the soviets and in the army.

SOURCE 31

The Provisional Government should do nothing now which would break our ties with the allies. The worst thing that could happen to us would be separate peace. It would be ruinous for the Russian revolution, ruinous for international democracy . . .

As to the land question, we regard it as our duty at the present to prepare the ground for a just solution of the problem by the Constituent Assembly.

A Provisional Government Minister explains why Russia should stay in the war, 1917.

SOURCE 32

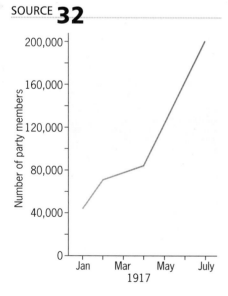

Growth of Bolshevik support, 1917.

SOURCE 33

The Bolshevik speaker would ask the crowd 'Do you need more land?'
Do you have as much land as the landlords do?'
'But will the Kerensky government give you land? No, never. It protects the interests of the landlords. Only our party, the Bolsheviks, will immediately give you land . . .'
Several times I tried to take the floor and explain that the Bolsheviks make promises which they can never fulfil. I used figures from farming statistics to prove my point; but I saw that the crowded square was unsuitable for this kind of discussion.

A Menshevik writer, summer 1917.

In the second half of 1917, the Provisional Government's authority steadily collapsed.

- The war effort was failing. Soldiers had been deserting in thousands from the army. Kerensky became Minister for War and rallied the army for a great offensive in June. It was a disaster. The army began to fall apart in the face of a German counter-attack (see Source 34 on page 312). The deserters decided to come home.
- Desertions were made worse because another element of the Provisional Government's policy had failed. The peasants ignored the orders of the government to wait. They were simply taking control of the countryside. The soldiers, who were mostly peasants, did not want to miss their turn when the land was shared out.

SOURCE 34

The German offensive, which began on 6 July, is turning into an immense catastrophe which may threaten revolutionary Russia with ruin. A sudden and disastrous change has occurred in the attitude of the troops . . . Authority and obedience no longer exist . . . for hundreds of miles one can see deserters, armed and unarmed, in good health and in high spirits, certain they will not be punished.

A Russian officer reporting back to the Provisional Government, 1917.

SOURCE 35

A still from the 1960s film *Doctor Zhivago* showing Russian deserters from the First World War. By the autumn of 1917 discipline among the Russian soldiers who had been fighting the Germans was beginning to collapse.

The Provisional Government's problems got worse in the summer. In July (the 'July Days'), Bolshevik-led protests against the war turned into a rebellion. However, when Kerensky produced evidence that Lenin had been helped by the Germans, support for the rebellion fell. Lenin, in disguise, fled to Finland. Kerensky used troops to crush the rebellion and took over the government.

SOURCE 36

The Provisional Government possesses no real power and its orders are executed only in so far as this is permitted by the Soviet of Workers' and Soldiers' Deputies, which holds in its hands the most important elements of actual power, such as troops, railroads, postal and telegraph service . . .

A letter from Guchkov, Minister for War in the Provisional Government, to General Alekseyev, 22 March 1917.

SOURCE 37

Troops loyal to the Provisional Government fire on Bolshevik demonstrators during the July Days.

Kerensky was in a very difficult situation. The upper and middle classes expected him to restore order. By this time, however, real power lay with the soviets, especially the Petrograd Soviet. It had a Bolshevik majority and a Bolshevik chairman – Leon Trotsky. It also had the support of much of the army and all industrial workers.

Meanwhile, there was little reason for the ordinary people of Russia to be grateful to the Provisional Government (see Sources 38 and 39).

SOURCE **38**

Cabs and horse-drawn carriages began to disappear. Street-car service was erratic. The railway stations filled with tramps and deserting soldiers, often drunk, sometimes threatening. The police force had vanished in the first days of the Revolution. Now 'revolutionary order' was over. Hold-ups and robberies became the order of the day. Politically, signs of chaos were everywhere.

HE Salisbury, *Russia in Revolution.*

SOURCE **39**

Week by week food became scarcer . . . one had to queue for long hours in the chill rain . . . Think of the poorly clad people standing on the streets of Petrograd for whole days in the Russian winter! I have listened in the bread-lines, hearing the bitter discontent which from time to time burst through the miraculous good nature of the Russian crowd.

John Reed, an American writer who lived in Petrograd in 1917.

Others were also fed up with the Provisional Government. In September 1917, the army leader Kornilov marched his troops towards Moscow, intending to get rid of the Bolsheviks and the Provisional Government, and restore order. Kerensky was in an impossible situation. He had some troops who supported him but they were no match for Kornilov's. Kerensky turned to the only group which could save him: his Bolshevik opponents, who dominated the Petrograd Soviet. The Bolsheviks organised themselves into an army which they called the Red Guards. Kornilov's troops refused to fight members of the Soviet so Kornilov's plans collapsed.

But it was hardly a victory for Kerensky. In fact, by October Kerensky's government was doomed. It had tried to carry on the war and failed. It had therefore lost the army's support. It had tried to stop the peasants from taking over the land and so lost their support too. Without peasant support it had failed to bring food into the towns and food prices had spiralled upwards. This had lost the government any support it had from the urban workers.

In contrast, the Bolsheviks were promising what the people wanted most (bread, peace, land). It was the Bolsheviks who had removed the threat of Kornilov. By the end of September 1917, there were Bolshevik majorities in the Petrograd and Moscow Soviets, and in most of Russia's other major towns and cities.

What do you think happened next?

Focus Task

How effective was the Provisional Government?

1 Here is a list of some decisions that faced the Provisional Government when it took over in March 1917:
   a) what to do about the war
   b) what to do about land
   c) what to do about food.
   For each one, say how the government dealt with it, and what the result of the action was.
2 Based on your answers to question 1, how effective do you think the Provisional Government was? Give it a mark out of ten.
3 Read through pages 311–13 again. Look for evidence of how the actions of its opponents harmed the Provisional Government:
   ◆ members of the soviets
   ◆ Bolsheviks
   ◆ General Kornilov.
4 Based on your answers to question 3, would you revise the score you gave the government in question 2?
5 Now reach an overview score. Out of 10, how effective was the Provisional Government? Write a paragraph to explain your score.

SOURCE **1**

The Provisional Government has been overthrown. The cause for which the people have fought has been made safe: the immediate proposal of a democratic peace, the end of land owners' rights, workers' control over production, the creation of a Soviet government. Long live the revolution of workers, soldiers and peasants.

Proclamation of the Petrograd Soviet, 8 November 1917.

1 When the Bolsheviks stormed the Winter Palace, they actually faced very little resistance. Why do you think the artist who painted Source 2 suggests that they did?

12.2 The Bolshevik Revolution

You have seen how Bolshevik support increased throughout 1917. By the end of October 1917, Lenin was convinced that the time was right for the Bolsheviks to seize power. Lenin convinced the other Bolsheviks to act swiftly. It was not easy – leading Bolsheviks like Bukharin felt that Russia was not ready, but neither he nor any other Bolshevik could match Lenin in an argument.

During the night of 6 November, the Red Guards led by Leon Trotsky took control of post offices, bridges and the State Bank. On 7 November, Kerensky awoke to find the Bolsheviks were in control of most of Petrograd. Through the day, with almost no opposition, the Red Guards continued to take over railway stations and other important targets. On the evening of 7 November, they stormed the Winter Palace (again, without much opposition) and arrested the ministers of the Provisional Government. Kerensky managed to escape and tried to rally loyal troops. When this failed, he fled into exile. On 8 November an announcement was made to the Russian people (see Source 1).

SOURCE **2**

The Bolsheviks storm the Winter Palace. A painting from 1937.

Vladimir Ilich Lenin

➤ Born 1870 into a respectable Russian family.
➤ Brother hanged in 1887 for plotting against the Tsar.
➤ Graduated from St Petersburg University after being thrown out of Kazan University for his political beliefs.
➤ One of the largest Okhrana files was about him!
➤ Exiled to Siberia 1897–1900.
➤ 1900–05 lived in various countries writing the revolutionary newspaper 'Iskra' ('The Spark').
➤ Took part in the 1905 revolution but was forced to flee.
➤ Returned to Russia after the first revolution in 1917.
➤ Led the Bolsheviks to power in November 1917.

An analysis of the Bolshevik Revolution

Despite what they claimed, the Bolsheviks did not have the support of the majority of the Russian people. So how were they able to carry out their takeover in November 1917? The unpopularity of the Provisional Government was a critical factor – there were no massive demonstrations demanding the return of Kerensky!

A second factor was that the Bolsheviks were a disciplined party dedicated to revolution, even though not all the Bolshevik leaders believed this was the right way to change Russia. The Bolsheviks had some 800,000 members, and their supporters were also in the right places. At least half of the army supported them, as did the sailors at the important naval base at Kronstadt near Petrograd. (The Bolsheviks were still the only party demanding that Russia should pull out of the war.) The major industrial centres, and the Petrograd and Moscow Soviets especially, were also pro-Bolshevik. The Bolsheviks also had some outstanding personalities in their ranks, particularly Trotsky and their leader Lenin.

Activity

Lenin and Trotsky

Work individually or in pairs, taking one personality each.
1 Using Sources 3–5, add extra details to the profile of Lenin:
   • why Lenin appealed to people
   • his personal qualities
   • his strengths as a leader.
2 Now do the same for Trotsky (see page 316).
3 Finally, write a short report on the contribution of each individual to the Bolsheviks' success in 1917.

SOURCE 3

This extraordinary figure was first and foremost a professional revolutionary. He had no other occupation. A man of iron will and inflexible ambition, he was absolutely ruthless and used human beings as mere material for his purpose. Short and sturdy with a bald head, small beard and deep set eyes, Lenin looked like a small tradesman. When he spoke at meetings his ill-fitting suit, his crooked tie, his ordinary appearance disposed the crowd in his favour. 'He is not one of the gentlefolk, he is one of us', they would say.

The Times, writing about Lenin after his death, 1924.

SOURCE 4

Lenin . . . was the overall planner of the revolution: he also dealt with internal divisions within the party and provided tight control, and a degree of discipline and unity which the other parties lacked.

SJ Lee, The European Dictatorships, 1987.

SOURCE 5

The struggle was headed by Lenin who guided the Party's Central Committee, the editorial board of Pravda, *and who kept in touch with the Party organisations in the provinces . . . He frequently addressed mass rallies and meetings. Lenin's appearance on the platform inevitably triggered off the cheers of the audience. Lenin's brilliant speeches inspired the workers and soldiers to a determined struggle.*

Soviet historian Y Kukushkin, History of the USSR, 1981.

Profile

Leon Trotsky

➤ Born 1879 into a respectable and prosperous Jewish farming family.
➤ Exceptionally bright at school and brilliant at university.
➤ Politically active – arrested in 1900 and deported to Siberia.
➤ Escaped to London in 1902 and met Lenin there.
➤ Joined the Social Democratic Party, but supported the Menshevik wing rather than the Bolsheviks.
➤ Played an important role in organising strikes in the 1905 revolution – imprisoned for his activities.
➤ Escaped in 1907 and became a Bolshevik activist in the years before the First World War.
➤ Published two Bolshevik newspapers, including *Pravda*.
➤ In 1917 he returned to Russia and played a key role in the Bolshevik Revolution.
➤ In 1918 he became the Commissar for War and led the Bolsheviks to victory in the Civil War which broke out in 1918.

SOURCE 6

The Bolshevik party was greatly strengthened by Trotsky's entry into the party. No one else in the leadership came anywhere near him as a public speaker, and for much of the revolutionary period it was this that made Trotsky, perhaps even more so than Lenin, the best known Bolshevik leader in the country. Whereas Lenin remained the master strategist of the party, working mainly behind the scenes, Trotsky became its principal source of public inspiration. During the weeks leading up to the seizure of power he spoke almost every night before a packed house . . .

He was careful always to use examples and comparisons from the real life of the audience. This gave his speeches a familiarity and earned Trotsky the popular reputation of being 'one of us'. It was this that gave him the power to master the crowd, even sometimes when it was extremely hostile.

Historian Orlando Figes, a leading international expert on the Russian Revolution, writing in 1996.

SOURCE 7

Now that the great revolution has come, one feels that however intelligent Lenin may be he begins to fade beside the genius of Trotsky.

Mikhail Uritsky, 1917. Uritsky was a Bolshevik activist and went on to play an important role in Bolshevik governments after 1917.

SOURCE 8

Under the influence of his tremendous activity and blinding success, certain people close to Trotsky were even inclined to see in him the real leader of the Russian revolution . . . It is true that during that period, after the thunderous success of his arrival in Russia and before the July days, Lenin did keep rather in the background, not speaking often, not writing much, but largely engaged in directing organisational work in the Bolshevik camp, whilst Trotsky thundered forth at meetings in Petrograd. Trotsky's most obvious gifts were his talents as an orator and as a writer. I regard Trotsky as probably the greatest orator of our age. In my time I have heard all the greatest parliamentarians and popular tribunes of socialism and very many famous orators of the bourgeois world and I would find it difficult to name any of them whom I could put in the same class as Trotsky.

From *Revolutionary Silhouettes*, by Anatoly Lunacharsky, published in 1918. The book was a series of portraits of leading revolutionaries. The author was a Bolshevik activist and knew Lenin and Trotsky well.

Focus Task

Why were the Bolsheviks successful?

1 Read Source 9.

SOURCE 9

The [November] Revolution has often and widely been held to have been mainly Lenin's revolution. But was it? Certainly Lenin had a heavier impact on the course [of events] than anyone else. The point is, however, that great historical changes are brought about not only by individuals. There were other mighty factors at work as well in Russia in 1917 . . . Lenin simply could not have done or even co-ordinated everything.

Historian Robert Service, writing in 1990.

2 What do you think the writer had in mind when he said there were 'other mighty factors at work'? Make your own list of these factors.
3 Write two or more paragraphs to explain the importance of these factors.

1 Study the Factfile. Which of the Bolshevik decrees would you say aimed to
   a) keep the peasants happy
   b) keep the workers happy
   c) increase Bolshevik control
   d) improve personal freedom in Russia?

Lenin in power

Lenin and the Bolsheviks had promised the people bread, peace and land. Lenin knew that if he failed to deliver, he and the Bolsheviks would suffer the same fate as Kerensky and the Provisional Government.

Lenin immediately set up the Council of People's Commissars (the Sovnarkom). It issued its first decree on 8 November, announcing that Russia was asking for peace with Germany. There followed an enormous number of decrees from the new government that aimed to strengthen the Bolsheviks' hold on power (see Factfile). The peasants were given the Tsar's and the Church's lands. The factories and industries were put into the hands of the workers. The Bolsheviks were given power to deal ruthlessly with their opponents – and they did (see page 319).

The Bolshevik dictatorship

Lenin had also promised free elections to the new Constituent Assembly. Elections were held in late 1917. As Lenin had feared, the Bolsheviks did not gain a majority in the elections. Their rivals, the peasant-based Socialist Revolutionaries, were the biggest party when the Assembly opened on 18 January 1918.

SOURCE **10**

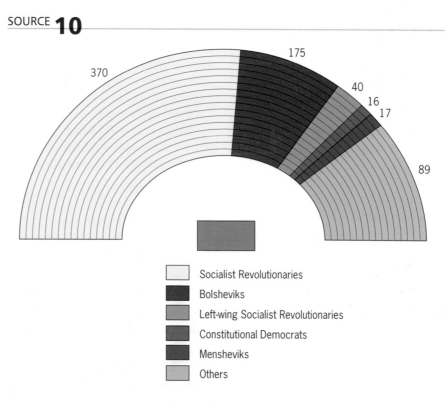

The results of the Constituent Assembly elections, 1917.

Lenin solved this problem in his typically direct style. He sent the Red Guards to close down the Assembly. After brief protests (again put down by the Red Guards) the Assembly was forgotten. Lenin instead used the Congress of Soviets to pass his laws as it did contain a Bolshevik majority.

Russia's democratic experiment therefore lasted less than 24 hours, but this did not trouble Lenin's conscience. He believed he was establishing a dictatorship of the proletariat which in time would give way to true Communism.

SOURCE 11

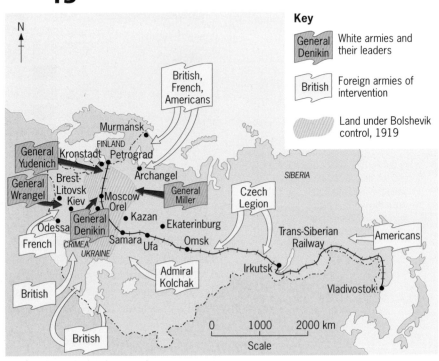

The Treaty of Brest-Litovsk, 1918.

SOURCE 12

The bourgeoisie, landholders, and all wealthy classes are making desperate efforts to undermine the revolution which is aiming to safeguard the interests of the toiling and exploited masses . . . The partisans of the bourgeoisie, especially the higher officials, bank clerks, etc., are sabotaging and organising strikes in order to block the government's efforts to reconstruct the state on a socialistic basis. Sabotage has spread even to the food-supply organisations and millions of people are threatened with famine. Special measures must be taken to fight counter-revolution and sabotage.

From a letter written by Lenin in December 1917.

Factfile

The Whites

'Whites' was a very broad term and was applied to any anti-Bolshevik group(s). Whites were made up of:

➤ Socialist Revolutionaries
➤ Mensheviks
➤ supporters of the Tsar
➤ landlords and capitalists who had lost land or money in the revolution
➤ the Czech Legion (former prisoners of war).

The Whites were also supported for part of the Civil War by foreign troops from the USA, Japan, France and Britain. They were sent by their governments to force Russia back into war against Germany.

Making peace

The next promise that Lenin had to make good was for peace. He put Trotsky in charge of negotiating a peace treaty. He told Trotsky to try to spin out the peace negotiations as long as possible. He hoped that very soon a socialist revolution would break out in Germany as it had in Russia. By February of 1918, however, there was no revolution and the Germans began to advance again. Lenin had to accept their terms in the Treaty of Brest-Litovsk in March 1918.

The Treaty was a severe blow to Russia. You can see how much land was lost in Source 11, but this was not the whole story. Russia's losses included 34 per cent of its population, 32 per cent of its agricultural land, 54 per cent of its industry, 26 per cent of its railways and 89 per cent of its coalmines. A final blow was the imposition of a fine of 300 million gold roubles. It was another example of Lenin's single-minded leadership. If this much had to be sacrificed to safeguard his revolution, then so be it. He may also have had the foresight to know that he would get it back when Germany lost.

Opposition and Civil War

Lenin's activities in 1917–18 were bound to make him enemies. In fact, in August 1918 he was shot three times by a Social Revolutionary agent but had a miraculous escape. In December he set up a secret police force called the Cheka to crush his opponents.

By the end of 1918 an unlikely collection of anti-Bolshevik elements had united in an attempt to crush the Bolsheviks. They became known as the Whites (in contrast to the Bolshevik Reds) and consisted of enemies of the Bolsheviks from inside and outside Russia (see Factfile).

The Bolsheviks' stronghold was in western Russia. Much of the rest of the country was more sympathetic to the Social Revolutionary Party.

In March 1918 the Czech Legion seized control of a large section of the Trans-Siberian Railway.

Soon three separate White armies were marching on Bolshevik-controlled western Russia. Generals Yudenich and Denikin marched towards Petrograd and Moscow, while Admiral Kolchak marched on Moscow from central southern Russia.

SOURCE 13

The main developments of the Civil War.

1 Read Source 12. What evidence does it provide of Lenin's:
   a) political skill
   b) ruthlessness?

The reaction of the Bolsheviks was ruthless and determined. In an amazingly short time, Leon Trotsky created a new Red Army of over 300,000 men. They were led by former Tsarist officers. Trotsky made sure of their loyalty by holding their families hostage and by appointing political commissars to watch over them. The Cheka (secret police) made sure that nobody in Bolshevik territories co-operated with the Whites. There were many beatings, hangings and shootings of opponents or even suspects in what became known as the Red Terror.

Not even the Tsar escaped. In July 1918, White forces were approaching Ekaterinburg where the Tsar was being held. The Bolshevik commander ordered the execution of the Tsar and his family. Lenin could not risk the Tsar's being rescued and returned as leader of the Whites.

The fighting was savage with both sides committing terrible acts of cruelty. The people who suffered most were the ordinary workers and above all the peasants in the areas where the fighting took place.

SOURCE 14

In the villages the peasant will not give grain to the Bolsheviks because he hates them. Armed companies are sent to take grain from the peasant and every day, all over Russia, fights for grain are fought to a finish.

In the Red Army, for any military offence, there is only one punishment, death. If a regiment retreats against orders, machine guns are turned on them. The position of the bourgeoisie [middle class] defies all description. Payments by the banks have been stopped. It is forbidden to sell furniture. All owners and managers of works, offices and shops have been called up for compulsory labour. In Petrograd hundreds of people are dying from hunger. People are arrested daily and kept in prison for months without trial.

The Red Terror, observed by a British businessman in Russia in 1918.

SOURCE 15

Members of the Red Guard requisition grain from peasants during the Civil War.

SOURCE 16

Having surrounded the village [the Whites] fired a couple of volleys in the direction of the village and everyone took cover. Then the mounted soldiers entered the village, met the Bolshevik committee and put the members to death . . . After the execution the houses of the culprits were burned and the male population under forty-five whipped . . . Then the population was ordered to deliver without pay the best cattle, pigs, fowl, forage and bread for the soldiers as well as the best horses.

Diary of Colonel Drozdovsky, from his memoirs written in 1923. He was a White commander during the Civil War.

2 Use Sources 14 and 15 to describe how the Civil War affected ordinary people.
3 Do you think Source 15 was painted by opponents or supporters of the Bolsheviks?

Through harsh discipline and brilliant leadership, Trotsky's Red Army began to turn back the White forces. Admiral Kolchak's forces were destroyed towards the end of 1919 and at the same time the foreign 'armies of intervention' withdrew. The Whites were not really a strong alliance, and their armies were unable to work together. Trotsky defeated them one by one. The last major White army was defeated in the Crimea in November 1920. Although scattered outbreaks of fighting continued, by 1921 the Bolsheviks were securely in control of Russia.

Why did the Bolsheviks win the Civil War?

The advantages of the Reds

The Red Army was no match for the armies that were still fighting on the Western Front in 1918. However, compared to the Whites, the Red Army was united and disciplined. It was also brilliantly led by Trotsky.

SOURCE **17**

Trotsky's war train. For most of the campaign he travelled on an enormous train, giving orders, rallying the troops or transporting essential supplies.

SOURCE **18**

An armoured train in the Civil War. The ability to move troops and supplies securely gave the Bolsheviks a huge advantage.

SOURCE **19**

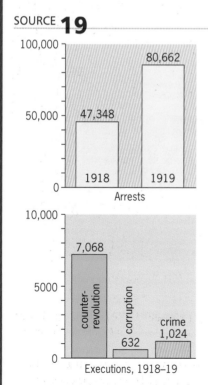

The Red Terror.

SOURCE **20**

We were constructing an army all over again and under fire at that . . . What was needed for this? It needed good commanders – a few dozen experienced fighters, a dozen or so Communists ready to make any sacrifice; boots for the bare-footed, a bath house, propaganda, food, underwear, tobacco, matches.

Trotsky writing about the making of the Red Army.

SOURCE 21

1 *Every food requisition detachment is to consist of not less than 75 men and two or three machine guns.*

2 *The food requisition troop detachments shall be deployed in such a manner as to allow two or three detachments to link up quickly.*

Instructions to Red Army units for requisitioning grain from the peasants.

SOURCE 22

For the first time in history the working people have got control of their country. The workers of all countries are striving to achieve this objective. We in Russia have succeeded. We have thrown off the rule of the Tsar, of landlords and of capitalists. But we still have tremendous difficulties to overcome. We cannot build a new society in a day. We ask you, are you going to crush us? To help give Russia back to the landlords, the capitalists and the Tsar?

Red propaganda leaflet, *Why Have You Come to Murmansk?*

The Bolsheviks also kept strict control over their heartlands in western Russia.

- They made sure that the towns and armies were fed, by forcing peasants to hand over food and by rationing supplies.
- They took over the factories of Moscow and Petrograd so that they were able to supply their armies with equipment and ammunition.
- The Red Terror made sure that the population was kept under strict control (see Source 19).
- The Bolsheviks raised fears about the intentions of the foreign armies in league with the Whites (Source 23). Effective propaganda also made good use of atrocities committed by the Whites and raised fears about the possible return of the Tsar and landlords (see Sources 22–25).

SOURCE 23

ПСЫ АНТАНТЫ.

Bolshevik propaganda cartoon, 1919. The dogs represent the White generals Denikin, Kolchak and Yudenich.

1 Look at Source 23. Who is controlling the White forces?

2 Who do you think Source 22 is talking to?

Finally, the Reds had important territorial advantages. Their enemies were spread around the edge of Russia while they had internal lines of communication. This enabled them to move troops quickly and effectively by rail, while their enemies used less efficient methods.

SOURCE **24**

A Red Army propaganda train in the early 1920s. This is the cinema carriage. The Red Army spread Communist ideas across Russia.

The disadvantages of the Whites

The Whites, in contrast with the Bolsheviks, were not united. They were made up of many different groups, all with different aims. They were also widely spread so they were unable to co-ordinate their campaigns against the Reds. Trotsky was able to defeat them one by one.

They had limited support from the Russian population. Russian peasants did not especially like the Bolsheviks, but they preferred them to the Whites. If the Whites won, the peasants knew the landlords would return.

Both sides were guilty of atrocities, but the Whites in general caused more suffering to the peasants than the Reds.

SOURCE **25**

The Civil War, 1918–1920, was a time of great chaos and estimates of Cheka executions vary from twelve to fifty thousands. But even the highest figure does not compare to the ferocity of the White Terror . . . for instance, in Finland alone, the number of workers executed by the Whites approaches 100,000.

R Appignanesi, *Lenin for Beginners*, 1977.

Focus Task

Why did the Bolsheviks win the Civil War?

Imagine it is the end of the war and you have been asked to make a poster for the Bolsheviks celebrating the victory and showing the main reasons for success.

Design your poster using the information in the text, then write an explanation of your poster to send to Lenin.

1 'Most Russians saw the Bolsheviks as the lesser of two evils.' With reference to Sources 14, 16, 22 and 25 explain whether you agree with this statement or not.

The nature of the Bolsheviks' radical economic policies is a matter of controversy. The name usually given them, 'War Communism', is wrong on several counts . . . the term 'War Communism' was first used – in Lenin's notes – only in 1921. It suggests that the policy was a wartime stopgap . . . My view is that while the civil war deepened an existing crisis, the economic policies later called War Communism – food detachments, nationalisation of industry, restrictions of trade – had been developing . . . since the early winter of 1917–1918. There was no 'normal' period followed by a crisis.

Historian Evan Mawdsley's views on War Communism.

Bolshevik poster, 1920. The sailor is welcoming the dawn of the revolution. The Kronstadt sailors played a key role in the Bolsheviks' original success in 1917–20.

2   Read Source 29. What aspects of War Communism are the sailors most angry about?

3   Would you expect peasants in Russia to feel the same?

4   Why do you think Lenin was more worried about the revolt of the sailors than about starvation among the peasants?

Economic policy

War Communism

War Communism was the name given to the harsh economic measures the Bolsheviks adopted during the Civil War, although the name is misleading in some ways (see Source 26). It had two main aims. The first aim was to put Communist theories into practice by redistributing (sharing out) wealth among the Russian people. The second aim was to help with the Civil War by keeping the towns and the Red Army supplied with food and weapons.

- All large factories were taken over by the government.
- Production was planned and organised by the government.
- Discipline for workers was strict and strikers could be shot.
- Peasants had to hand over surplus food to the government. If they didn't, they could be shot.
- Food was rationed.
- Free enterprise became illegal – all production and trade was controlled by the state.

War Communism achieved its aim of winning the war, but in doing so it caused terrible hardship. (Some historians believe that Lenin's ruthless determination to create a Communist society actually caused the war in the first place.) Peasants refused to co-operate in producing more food because the government simply took it away. This led to food shortages which, along with the bad weather in 1920 and 1921, caused a terrible famine. Some estimates suggest that 7 million Russian people died in this famine. There were even reports of cannibalism.

SOURCE **28**

Children starving during the Russian famine of 1921.

In February 1921 Bolshevik policies sparked a mutiny at Kronstadt naval base.

SOURCE **29**

After carrying out the October Revolution, the working classes hoped for freedom. But the result has been greater slavery. The bayonets, bullets and harsh commands of the Cheka – these are what the working man of Soviet Russia has won. The glorious emblem of the workers' state – the hammer and sickle – has been replaced by the Communist authorities with the bayonet and the barred window. Here in Kronstadt we are making a third revolution which will free the workers and the Soviets from the Communists.

Official statement from the Kronstadt sailors.

Trotsky's troops put down the uprising, but soon afterwards Lenin abandoned the emergency policies of War Communism. Considering the chaos of the Civil War years, it may seem strange that this particular revolt had such a startling effect on Lenin. It did so because the Kronstadt sailors had been among the strongest supporters of Lenin and Bolshevism.

The New Economic Policy

Many thousands of the Kronstadt sailors were killed. The mutiny was crushed. But Lenin recognised that changes were necessary. In March 1921, at the Party Congress, Lenin announced some startling new policies which he called the New Economic Policy (NEP). The NEP effectively brought back capitalism for some sections of Russian society. Peasants were allowed to sell surplus grain for profit and would pay tax on what they produced rather than giving some of it up to the government.

SOURCE **30**

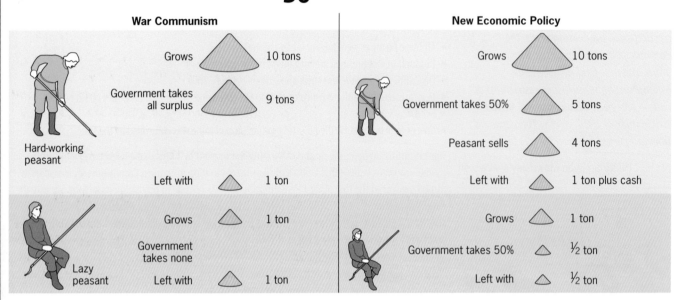

How the NEP differed from War Communism.

In the towns, small factories were handed back into private ownership and private trading of small goods was allowed.

Lenin made it clear that the NEP was temporary and that the vital heavy industries (coal, oil, iron and steel) would remain in state hands. Nevertheless, many Bolsheviks were horrified when the NEP was announced, seeing it as a betrayal of Communism. As always, Lenin won the argument and the NEP went into operation from 1921 onwards. By 1925 there seemed to be strong evidence that it was working, as food production in particular rose steeply. However, as Source 34 suggests, increases in production did not necessarily improve the situation of industrial workers.

SOURCE **31**

Our poverty and ruin are so great that we cannot at one stroke restore large-scale socialist production . . . we must try to satisfy the demands of the peasants who are dissatisfied, discontented and cannot be otherwise . . . there must be a certain amount of freedom to trade, freedom for the small private owner. We are now retreating, but we are doing this so as to then run and leap forward more vigorously.

Lenin, introducing the NEP at the Party Congress, 1921.

SOURCE **32**

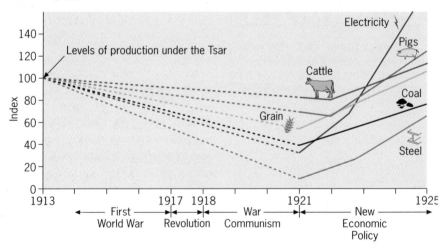

Production under the New Economic Policy, 1921–25.

1 Does the evidence of Source 32 prove that the NEP was a success? Explain your answer with reference to Sources 31, 33 and 34.
2 From all you have found out about Lenin, do you agree with Source 35? (Don't forget to look at Source 36.)

SOURCE **33**

Poor, starving old Russia, Russia of primitive lighting and the meal of a crust of black bread, is going to be covered by a network of electric power stations. The NEP will transform the Russian economy and rebuild a broken nation. The future is endless and beautiful.

Bukharin, speaking in 1922. He was a leading Bolshevik and a strong supporter of the NEP.

SOURCE **34**

In 1925 the Soviet Commissar for Finance admitted that the pay of miners, metal workers and engine drivers was still lower than it had been before 1914. This in turn meant that workers' housing and food were poor. The factory committee of a cement works in Smolensk reported, for example, in 1929: 'Every day there are many complaints about apartments: many workers have families of six and seven people, and live in one room.'

Some problems identified by Soviet observers in the 1920s.

The death of Lenin and the creation of the USSR

Lenin did not live to see the recovery of the Russian economy. He suffered several strokes in 1922 and 1923 which left him paralysed and which led to his death in January 1924. He was a remarkable man by any standards. He led Russia through revolution and civil war and even in 1923 he supervised the drawing up of a new constitution that turned the Russian Empire into the Union of Soviet Socialist Republics. Source 35 gives the opinion of a British historian.

SOURCE **35**

Lenin did more than any other political leader to change the face of the twentieth-century world. The creation of Soviet Russia and its survival were due to him. He was a very great man and even, despite his faults, a very good man.

The British historian AJP Taylor writing in the 1960s.

SOURCE **36**

Lenin had a strong streak of ruthlessness and cruelty. In the late 1980s and 1990s, Soviet archives were opened up as the Communist regime came to an end. These revealed a much harder, more ruthless Lenin than the 'softer' image he had enjoyed amongst left-wing historians and groups. For instance, a memorandum, first published in 1990, reveals his ordering the extermination of the clergy in a place called Shuya after people there fought off officials who had come to raid the church. The Politburo voted to stop further raids on churches but Lenin countermanded them . . . Similarly he was vitriolic about the peasants, ordering the hanging of a hundred kulaks as a lesson to others . . .

Lenin believed that revolutionaries had to be hard to carry out their role, which would inevitably involve spilling the blood of their opponents. Although hard and tough on others, it seems that Lenin was not personally brave. He was not a revolutionary who rushed to the barricades. He left the fighting to others. According to Valentinov, a revolutionary who knew him well, Lenin's rule was 'to get away while the going was good'.

An extract from *Communist Russia under Lenin and Stalin*. This was an A level History textbook published in 2002.

We will never know what policies Lenin would have pursued if he had lived longer – he certainly left no clear plans about how long he wanted the NEP to last. He also left another big unanswered question behind him: who was to be the next leader of the USSR?

Focus Task

How did the Bolsheviks consolidate their rule?

It is January 1924. Lenin is dead. Your task is to look back at the measures he used to consolidate Bolshevik rule.
1 Draw a timeline from 1917 to 1924, and mark on it the events of that period mentioned in the text.
2 Mark on the timeline:
   a) one moment at which you think Bolshevik rule was most threatened
   b) one moment at which you think it was most secure.
3 Write an explanation of how the Bolsheviks made their rule more secure. Mention the following:
   ◆ the power of the Red Army
   ◆ treatment of opposition
   ◆ War Communism
   ◆ the New Economic Policy
   ◆ the Treaty of Brest-Litovsk
   ◆ the victory in the Civil War
   ◆ the promise of a new society
   ◆ propaganda.
4 Is any one of these factors more important than any of the others? Explain your answer.

12.3 Stalin – success or failure?

Stalin or Trotsky?

When Lenin died in 1924 there were several leading Communists who were possible candidates to take his place. There would not be leadership elections. The Communist Party did not work that way. The leader would be the one who showed he had most power within the party. Among the contenders were Kamenev and Zinoviev, leading Bolsheviks who had played important parts in the Bolshevik Revolution of 1917. Bukharin was a more moderate member of the party who favoured the NEP and wanted to introduce Communism gradually to the USSR.

However, the real struggle to succeed Lenin was between two leading figures and bitter rivals in the Communist Party, Joseph Stalin and Leon Trotsky. The struggle between these two was long and hard and it was not until 1929 that Stalin made himself completely secure as the supreme leader of the USSR. Stalin achieved this through a combination of political scheming, the mistakes of his opponents and the clever way in which he built up his power base.

Why did Trotsky lose the leadership contest?

SOURCE **1**

Comrade Stalin, having become Secretary General, has unlimited authority in his hands and I am not sure whether he will always be capable of using that authority with sufficient caution.

Comrade Trotsky, on the other hand, is distinguished not only by his outstanding ability. He is personally probably the most capable man in the present Central Committee, but he has displayed excessive self-assurance and preoccupation with the purely administrative side of the work.

Lenin's Testament. This is often used as evidence that Stalin was an outsider. However, the document contained many remarks critical of other leading Communists as well. It was never published in Russia, although, if it had been, it would certainly have damaged Stalin.

Source 1 shows Lenin's opinions of Trotsky and Stalin. As Lenin lay dying in late 1923 few people in the USSR had any doubts that Trotsky would win. Trotsky was a brilliant speaker and writer, as well as the party's best political thinker, after Lenin. He was also the man who had organised the Bolshevik Revolution and was the hero of the Civil War as leader of the Red Army (see page 319). Finally, he was the man who negotiated peace for Russia with the Treaty of Brest-Litovsk.

So how did Trotsky lose this contest? Much of the blame lies with Trotsky himself. He was brilliant, but also arrogant. He often offended other senior party members. More importantly, he failed to take the opposition seriously. He made little effort to build up any support in the ranks of the party. And he seriously underestimated Stalin.

SOURCE **2**

Trotsky refrained from attacking Stalin because he felt secure. No contemporary, and he least of all, saw in the Stalin of 1923 the menacing and towering figure he was to become. It seemed to Trotsky almost a joke that Stalin, the wilful and sly but shabby and inarticulate man in the background, should be his rival.

Historian I Deutscher in *The Prophet Unarmed, Trotsky 1921–1929*, published in 1959.

Trotsky also frightened many people in the USSR. Trotsky argued that the future security of the USSR lay in trying to spread permanent revolution across the globe until the whole world was Communist. Many people were worried that Trotsky would involve the USSR in new conflicts.

1 Draw up a campaign poster or flier listing Trotsky's qualities for the leadership of the party. Make use of Lenin's Testament (Source 1).
2 Make a list of Trotsky's weaknesses.

Factfile

Stalin's steps to power

➤ **1923** Stalin the outsider – Lenin calls for him to be replaced. Trotsky calls him 'the party's most eminent mediocrity'.

➤ **1924** Lenin's death. Stalin attends funeral as chief mourner. Trotsky does not turn up (tricked by Stalin).

➤ **1924** Stalin, Kamenev and Zinoviev form the triumvirate that dominates the Politburo, the policy-making committee of the Communist Party. Working together, these three cut off their opponents (Trotsky and Bukharin) because between them they control the important posts in the party.

➤ **1925** Trotsky sacked as War Commissar. Stalin introduces his idea of Socialism in One Country.

➤ **1926** Stalin turns against Kamenev and Zinoviev and allies himself with Bukharin.

➤ **1927** Kamenev, Zinoviev and Trotsky all expelled from the Communist Party.

➤ **1928** Trotsky exiled to Siberia. Stalin begins attacking Bukharin.

➤ **1929** Trotsky expelled from USSR and Bukharin expelled from the Communist Party.

SOURCE 3

Lenin and Stalin. Stalin made the most of any opportunity to appear close to Lenin. This photograph is a suspected fake.

3 Draw up a campaign leaflet for Stalin. Remember to mention his strengths and the weaknesses of his opponent.

As it often does in history, chance also played a part. Trotsky was unfortunate in falling ill late in 1923 with a malaria-like infection – just when Lenin was dying, and Trotsky needed to be at his most active.

He was also the victim of a trick by Stalin. Stalin cabled Trotsky to tell him that Lenin's funeral was to be on 26 January, when it was in fact going to be on the 27th. Trotsky was away in the south of Russia and would not have had time to get back for the 26th, although he could have got back for the 27th. As a result, Trotsky did not appear at the funeral whereas Stalin appeared as chief mourner and Lenin's closest friend.

How did Stalin win?

We have already seen that Stalin was a clever politician and he planned his bid for power carefully. He made great efforts to associate himself with Lenin wherever possible and got off to an excellent start at Lenin's funeral.

He was also extremely clever in using his power within the Communist Party. He took on many boring but important jobs such as Commissar for Nationalities and, of course, General Secretary. He used these positions to put his own supporters into important posts and even to transfer supporters of his opponents to remote postings. He was also absolutely ruthless in picking off his rivals one by one. For example he took Bukharin's side in the debate on the NEP in order to help get rid of Trotsky. Once he had got rid of Trotsky, he opposed Bukharin using exactly the same arguments as Trotsky had used before (see Factfile opposite).

Stalin's policies also met with greater favour than Trotsky's. Stalin proposed that in future the party should try to establish 'Socialism in One Country' rather than try to spread revolution worldwide. Finally, Stalin appeared to be a straightforward Georgian peasant – much more a man of the people than his intellectual rivals. To a Soviet people weary of years of war and revolution, Stalin seemed to be the man who understood their feelings.

Profile

Stalin

➤ Born 1879 in Georgia. His father was a shoemaker and an alcoholic. He abandoned the family while Stalin was still a young child.
➤ Original name was Iosif Dzhugashvili but changed his name to Stalin (man of steel).
➤ Twice exiled to Siberia by the Tsarist secret police, he escaped each time.
➤ Made his name in violent bank raids to raise party funds.
➤ He was slow and steady, but very hardworking.
➤ He also held grudges and generally made his enemies suffer.
➤ Became a leading Communist after playing an important role in defending the Bolshevik city of Tsaritsyn (later Stalingrad) during the Civil War.
➤ Had become undisputed party leader by 1929.

Activity

In groups, look at the following statements and decide on a scale of 1–5 how far you agree with them.
• Stalin was a dull and unimaginative politician.
• Stalin appeared to be a dull and unimaginative politician.
• Trotsky lost the contest because of his mistakes.
• Stalin trusted to luck rather than careful planning.
• Stalin was ruthless and devious.
Try to find evidence to back up your judgements.

Focus Task

Why did Stalin win?

Imagine you have to prepare a radio news feature on the reasons why Stalin, not Trotsky, became Lenin's successor.
Your feature should include:
◆ a brief introduction on Lenin's death
◆ profiles of the two main contenders. These could be done as descriptions by people who knew them
◆ an interview with the contenders asking them to state what their aims would be as leader of the USSR. You could also summarise these aims as a slogan
◆ a summary of the key events in their struggle (see Factfile)
◆ a conclusion on the reasons for Stalin's success.
You could work in groups of five and each be responsible for one part of the feature.

Throughout history Russia has been beaten again and again because she was backward . . . All have beaten her because of her military, industrial and agricultural backwardness. She was beaten because people have been able to get away with it. If you are backward and weak, then you are in the wrong and may be beaten and enslaved. But if you are powerful, people must beware of you.

It is sometimes asked whether it is not possible to slow down industrialisation a bit. No, comrades, it is not possible . . . To slacken would mean falling behind. And those who fall behind get beaten . . . That is why Lenin said during the October Revolution: 'Either perish, or overtake and outstrip the advanced capitalist countries.' We are 50 to 100 years behind the advanced countries. Either we make good the difference in ten years or they crush us.

Stalin speaking in 1931.

SOURCE **5**

Key

New industry

0   500 km

Scale

The location of the new industrial centres.

Focus Task

Why did Stalin introduce the Five-Year Plans?

Study Source 4 carefully. In a paragraph, explain whether you think it includes all the reasons why Stalin introduced the Five Year Plans.

Modernising the USSR

Once in power, Stalin was determined to modernise the USSR as quickly as possible, and he had some powerful reasons.

- **To increase the USSR's military strength:** The First World War had shown that a country could only fight a modern war if it had the industries to produce the weapons and other equipment which were needed (see Source 4).
- **To rival the economies of the USA and other capitalist countries:** When Stalin took power, much of Russia's industrial equipment had to be imported. Stalin wanted to make the USSR self-sufficient so that it could make everything it needed for itself. He also wanted to improve standards of living in Russia so that people would value Communist rule.
- **To increase food supplies:** Stalin wanted more workers in industries, towns and cities. He also wanted to sell grain abroad to raise cash to buy industrial equipment. This meant fewer peasants had to produce more food which meant that farming would have to be reorganised.
- **To create a Communist society:** Communist theory said that most of the population had to be workers if Communism was going to work. In 1928 only about one in five Russians were industrial workers.
- **To establish his reputation:** Lenin had made big changes to the USSR. Stalin wanted to prove himself as a great leader by bringing about even greater changes.

Industry and the Five-Year Plans

Stalin ended Lenin's NEP and set about achieving modernisation through a series of Five-Year Plans. These plans were drawn up by GOSPLAN, the state planning organisation that Lenin set up in 1921. They set ambitious targets for production in the vital heavy industries (coal, iron, oil, electricity). The plans were very complex but they were set out in such a way that by 1929 every worker knew what he or she had to achieve.

GOSPLAN set overall targets for an industry.

↓

Each region was told its targets.

↓

The region set targets for each mine, factory, etc.

↓

The manager of each mine, factory, etc. set targets for each foreman.

↓

The foremen set targets for each shift and even for individual workers.

The first Five-Year Plan focused on the major industries and although most targets were not met, the achievements were still staggering. The USSR increased production and created a foundation on which to build the next Five-Year Plans. The USSR was rich in natural resources, but many of them were in remote places such as Siberia. So whole cities were built from nothing and workers taken out to the new industrial centres. Foreign observers marvelled as huge new steel mills appeared at Magnitogorsk in the Urals and Sverdlovsk in central Siberia. New dams and hydro-electric power fed industry's energy requirements. Russian 'experts' flooded into the Muslim republics of central Asia such as Uzbekistan and Kazakhstan (see page 332), creating industry from scratch in previously undeveloped areas.

The second Five-Year Plan (1933–37) built on the achievements of the first. Heavy industry was still a priority, but other areas were also developed. Mining for lead, tin, zinc and other minerals intensified as Stalin further exploited Siberia's rich mineral resources. Transport and communications were also boosted, and new railways and canals were built. The most spectacular showpiece project was the Moscow underground railway.

Stalin also wanted industrialisation to help improve Russia's agriculture. The production of tractors and other farm machinery increased dramatically. In the third Five-Year Plan, which was begun in 1938, some factories were to switch to the production of consumer goods. However, this plan was disrupted by the Second World War.

SOURCE 6

What are the results of the Five-Year Plan in four years?

- *We did not have an iron and steel industry. Now we have one.*
- *We did not have a machine tool industry. Now we have one.*
- *We did not have a modern chemicals industry. Now we have one.*
- *We did not have a big industry for producing agricultural machinery. Now we have one.*

Stalin speaking about the first Five-Year Plan in 1932.

SOURCE 7

		1913	1928	1940
Gas	(billion m³)	0.02	0.3	3.4
Fertilisers	(million tons)	0.07	0.1	3.2
Plastics	(million tons)	–	–	10.9
Tractors	(thousand)	–	1.3	31.6

The growth in the output of the USSR, 1913–40.

SOURCE 8

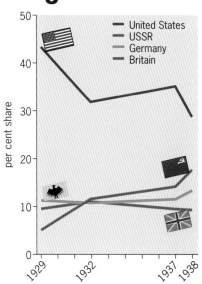

Graph showing share of world manufacturing output, 1929–38.

Were the Five-Year Plans a success?

There is much that could be and was criticised in the Five-Year Plans. Certainly there was a great deal of inefficiency, duplication of effort and waste, although the evidence shows that the Soviets did learn from their mistakes in the second and third Five-Year Plans. There was also an enormous human cost, as you will see on pages 331–33. But the fact remains that by 1937 the USSR was a modern state and it was this that saved it from defeat when Hitler invaded in 1941.

SOURCE 9

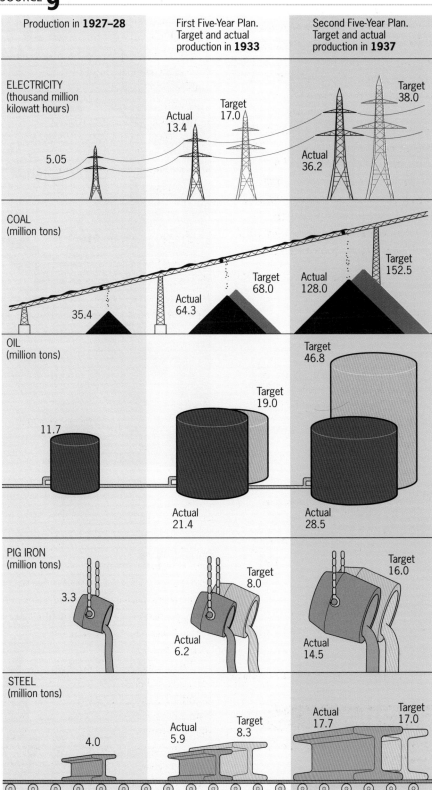

The achievements of the Five-Year Plans.

There is evidence that he [Stalin] exaggerated Russia's industrial deficiency in 1929. The Tsars had developed a considerable industrial capacity . . . in a sense the spadework had already been done and it is not altogether surprising that Stalin should have achieved such rapid results.

Historian SJ Lee, *The European Dictatorships, 1918–1945*, published in 1987.

The Five-Year Plans were used very effectively for propaganda purposes. Stalin had wanted the Soviet Union to be a beacon of socialism and his publicity machine used the successes of industrialisation to further that objective.

SOURCE **11**

Soviet propaganda poster, 1933. In the top half, the hand is holding the first Five-Year Plan. The capitalist is saying (in 1928), 'Fantasy, Lies, Utopia.' The bottom half shows 1933.

1 What is the message of Source 11?
2 How could Stalin use Sources 7 and 8 to support the claims of Source 11?
3 Compare Sources 6 and 10. Do they agree or disagree about the Five-Year Plans? Explain your answer.
4 Which of Sources 6 or 10 do Sources 7, 8 and 9 most support?

SOURCE **12**

A propaganda painting showing Stalin at the Dnieprostroi Dam.

5 Look at Source 12. Stalin felt this project was not a good use of resources when it was begun in 1926. Why do you think he wanted to be shown alongside it?

How was industrialisation achieved?

Any programme as extreme as Stalin's Five-Year Plans was bound to carry a cost. In the USSR this cost was paid by the workers. Many foreign experts and engineers were called in by Stalin to supervise the work and in their letters and reports they marvel at the toughness of the Russian people. The workers were constantly bombarded with propaganda, posters, slogans and radio broadcasts. They all had strict targets to meet and were fined if they did not meet them.

The most famous worker was Alexei Stakhanov. In 1935 with two helpers and an easy coal seam to work on, he managed to cut an amazing 102 tons of coal in one shift. This was fourteen times the average for a shift. Stakhanov became a 'Hero of Socialist Labour' and the propaganda machine encouraged all Soviet workers to be Stakhanovites.

The first Five-Year Plan revealed a shortage of workers, so from 1930 the government concentrated on drafting more women into industry. It set up thousands of new crèches and day-care centres so that mothers could work. By 1937 women were 40 per cent of industrial workers (compared to 28 per cent in 1927), 21 per cent of building workers and 72 per cent of health workers. Four out of five new workers recruited between 1932 and 1937 were women.

SOURCE 13

Propaganda poster showing Stalin as a comrade side by side with Soviet workers. The text means 'It is our workers who make our programme achievable.'

SOURCE 14

We got so dirty and we were such young things, small, slender, fragile. But we had our orders to build the metro and we wanted to do it more than anything else. We wore our miners' overalls with such style. My feet were size four and the boots were elevens. But there was such enthusiasm.

Tatyana Fyodorova, interviewed as an old lady in 1990, remembers building the Moscow underground.

SOURCE 15

Nothing strikes the visitor to the Soviet Union more forcibly than the lack of fear. No fear of not having enough money at the birth of a child. No fear for doctor's fees, school fees or university fees. No fear of underwork, no fear of overwork. No fear of wage reduction in a land where none are unemployed.

Dr Hewlett Johnson, Dean of Canterbury Cathedral, visiting the USSR in 1939.

6 Read Source 15. How can you tell that Dr Johnson was impressed by Stalin's USSR?

By the late 1930s many Soviet workers had improved their conditions by acquiring well-paid skilled jobs and earning bonuses for meeting targets. Unemployment was almost non-existent. In 1940 the USSR had more doctors per head of population than Britain. Education became free and compulsory for all and Stalin invested huge sums in training schemes based in colleges and in the work place.

But, on the other hand, life was very harsh under Stalin. Factory discipline was strict and punishments were severe. Lateness or absences were punished by sacking, and that often meant losing your flat or house as well. To escape the hard work and hard discipline, some workers tried to move to other jobs, so the secret police introduced internal passports which prevented free movement of workers inside the USSR.

On the great engineering projects, such as dams and canals, many of the workers were prisoners who had been sentenced to hard labour for being political opponents, or suspected opponents, of Stalin, or for being kulaks (rich peasants) or Jews. Many other prisoners were simply unfortunate workers who had had accidents or made mistakes in their work but had been found guilty of 'sabotage'.

SOURCE 16

Half a billion cubic feet of excavation work . . . 25,000 tons of structural steel . . . without sufficient labour, without necessary quantities of the most rudimentary materials. Brigades of young enthusiasts arrived in the summer of 1930 and did the groundwork of railroad and dam . . . Later groups of peasants came . . . Many were completely unfamiliar with industrial tools and processes . . .

J Scott, *Behind the Urals*, 1943.

SOURCE 18

We were led down to the communal kitchen in the basement . . . 'My' section consisted of a packing case and two reeking kerosene stoves. On these I was expected to cook, boil up washing and heat water for an occasional bath taken in a basin in the room above . . . The room was good for Moscow we were assured. At least we would not have to share with another family.

Betty Rowland, *Caviar for Breakfast*. The novelist describes her experiences of Russia in the 1930s.

Factfile

Collectivisation

➤ Peasants were to put their lands together to form large joint farms ('kolkhoz') but could keep small plots for personal use.
➤ Animals and tools were to be pooled together.
➤ Motor Tractor Stations (MTS), provided by the government, made tractors available.
➤ Ninety per cent of 'kolkhoz' produce would be sold to the state and the profits shared out.
➤ The remaining 10 per cent of produce was to be used to feed the 'kolkhoz'.

SOURCE 17

As usual, at five o'clock that first morning call was sounded by the blows of a hammer on a length of rail . . . the sound penetrated the window panes on which the frost lay two inches thick . . . [Sukhov] remembered that this morning his fate hung in the balance: they wanted to shift the 104th from the building shops to a new site, the 'Socialist Way of Life' settlement. It lay in open country covered with snowdrifts, and before anything else could be done there they would have to dig pits and put up posts and attach barbed wire to them. Wire themselves in, so they couldn't run away . . .

Alexander Solzhenitsyn, *One Day in the Life of Ivan Denisovich*, published in 1962. Solzhenitsyn was probably the most famous dissident in Stalin's USSR. He spent many years in labour camps. He was exiled in 1974. He lived for the next twenty years in the USA but in 1994 returned to Russia after the fall of Communism.

On these major projects conditions were appalling and there were many deaths and accidents. It is estimated that 100,000 workers died in the construction of the Belomor Canal.

At the same time, the concentration on heavy industry meant that there were few consumer goods (such as clothes or radios) which ordinary people wanted to buy. In the towns and cities, most housing was provided by the state, but overcrowding was a problem. Most families lived in flats and were crowded into two rooms which were used for living, sleeping and eating. What's more, wages actually fell between 1928 and 1937. In 1932 a husband and wife who both worked earned only as much as one man or woman had in 1928.

Stalin was also quite prepared to destroy the way of life of the Soviet people to help industrialisation. For example, in the republics of central Asia the influence of Islam was thought to hold back industrialisation, so between 1928 and 1932 it was repressed. Many Muslim leaders were imprisoned or deported, mosques were closed and pilgrimages to Mecca were forbidden.

Activity

'The Five-Year Plans brought glory to Stalin and misery to his people.' Is that a fair view of Stalin's industrialisation programme?

In pairs or small groups, discuss this question. Make sure you look at all the evidence and information before you make up your mind. You could then write up your conclusions in the form of a letter to Dr Hewlett Johnson, the writer of Source 15. The aim of your letter could be:
• to set him right
• to agree with him.

Modernising agriculture: collectivisation

For the enormous changes of the Five-Year Plan to be successful, Stalin needed to modernise the USSR's agriculture. This was vital because the population of the industrial centres was growing rapidly and yet as early as 1928 the country was already 2 million tons short of the grain it needed to feed its workers. Stalin also wanted to try to raise money for his industrialisation programme by selling exports of surplus food abroad.

The problem was that farming was not organised to do this. Under the NEP, most peasants were either agricultural labourers (with no land) or kulaks – prosperous peasants who owned small farms. These farms were too small to make efficient use of tractors, fertilisers and other modern methods. In addition, most peasants had enough to eat and could see little point in increasing production to feed the towns. To get round these problems, Stalin set out his ideas for collectivisation in 1929.

SOURCE 19

What is the way out [of the food problem]? The way out is to turn the small and scattered peasant farms, gradually but surely, into large farms based on common, co-operative, collective cultivation of the land. There is no other way out.

Stalin in a speech in 1927.

1 Explain why Stalin needed to change farming in the USSR.
2 Why did the peasants resist?

SOURCE 20

In order to turn a peasant society into an industrialised country, countless material and human sacrifices were necessary. The people had to accept this, but it would not be achieved by enthusiasm alone . . . If a few million people had to perish in the process, history would forgive Comrade Stalin . . . The great aim demanded great energy that could be drawn from a backward people only by great harshness.

Anatoli Rybakov, *Children of the Arbat*, 1988. A Russian writer presents Stalin's viewpoint on the modernisation of Russia.

3 Read Source 21. Why do you think the only reports of the famine came from Western journalists?

SOURCE 22

Stalin, ignoring the great cost in human life and misery, claimed that collectivisation was a success; for, after the great famines caused at the time . . . no more famines came to haunt the Russian people. The collective farms, despite their inefficiencies, did grow more food than the tiny, privately owned holdings had done. For example, 30 to 40 million tons of grain were produced every year. Collectivisation also meant the introduction of machines into the countryside. Now 2 million previously backward peasants learned how to drive a tractor. New methods of farming were taught by agricultural experts. The countryside was transformed.

Historian E Roberts, *Stalin, Man of Steel*, published in 1986.

4 According to Source 22, what advantages did collectivisation bring?
5 Do you agree that these advantages outweighed the human cost?

The government tried hard to sell these ideas to the peasants, offering free seed and other perks, but there were soon problems. The peasants, who had always been suspicious of government, whether it was the Tsar, Lenin or Stalin, were concerned about the speed of collectivisation. They disliked the fact that the farms were under the control of the local Communist leader. They were being asked to grow crops such as flax for Russia's industry rather than grain to feed themselves. In short, Stalin was asking the peasants to abandon a way of life that they and their ancestors had led for centuries.

Stalin had a difficult time convincing the peasants about collectivisation, but this was slight compared to the opposition of the kulaks who owned their own land. The kulaks simply refused outright to hand over their land and produce. Within a short time, collectivisation became a grim and bitter struggle. Soviet propaganda tried to turn the people against the kulaks. The war of words soon turned into violence. Requisition parties came and took the food required by the government, often leaving the peasants to starve. Kulaks were arrested and sent by the thousand to labour camps or were forced on to poor-quality land. In revenge, many kulaks burnt their crops and slaughtered their animals so that the Communists could not have them.

The countryside was in chaos. Even where collectivisation had been introduced successfully, peasants were unfamiliar with new ideas and methods. There was much bitterness as starving peasants watched Communist officials sending food for export.

Not surprisingly, food production fell under these conditions and there was a famine in 1932–33. Millions died in Kazakhstan and the Ukraine, Russia's richest agricultural region. When the Germans invaded the Ukraine in 1941, they were at first made welcome for driving out the Communists.

SOURCE 21

'How are things with you?' I asked one old man. He looked around anxiously to see that no soldiers were about. 'We have nothing, absolutely nothing. They have taken everything away.' It was true. The famine is an organised one. Some of the food that has been taken away from them is being exported to foreign countries. It is literally true that whole villages have been exiled. I saw myself a group of some twenty peasants being marched off under escort. This is so common a sight that it no longer arouses even curiosity.

The *Manchester Guardian*, 1933.

Despite the famine, Stalin did not ease off. By 1934 there were no kulaks left. By 1941 almost all agricultural land was organised under the collective system. Stalin had achieved his aim of collectivisation.

Focus Task

Stalin's economic policies: success or failure?

1 Draw up a chart like this:

	Industrialisation	Collectivisation
Reasons the policy was adopted		
Measures taken to enforce the policy		
Successes of the policy		
Failures of the policy		
The human cost of the policy		

2 Working with a partner, fill it out as fully as you can with details from pages 328–33.
3 Then use the chart to write an essay comparing the success of the two policies.

Life under Stalin's rule

One of Stalin's aims was to control his people to such an extent that they would be afraid even to think of opposing him. Throughout his time in power he used the secret police, at first called OGPU and then NKVD, to crush any opponents of his policies.

The Purges

The first signs of the terror which was to come appeared in 1928 when Stalin, without much evidence, accused a number of engineers of sabotage in the important Donbass mining region. In 1931 a number of former Mensheviks (see page 303) were put on trial on charges that were obviously made up.

However, the really terrifying period in Stalin's rule, known as the Purges, began in 1934 when Kirov, the leader of the Leningrad (the new name for Petrograd from 1924) Communist Party, was murdered. Stalin used this murder as an excuse to 'purge' or clear out his opponents in the party. Historians strongly suspect that Stalin arranged for Kirov's murder to give him this excuse. In great 'show trials' loyal Bolsheviks, such as Kamenev (1936), Bukharin (1938) and Zinoviev (1936), confessed to being traitors to the state. It was not only leading figures who were purged. Estimates suggest that around 500,000 party members were arrested on charges of anti-Soviet activities and either executed or sent to labour camps (gulags). In 1940, Trotsky, in exile in Mexico, was murdered by Stalin's agents.

After the trials, Stalin turned his attention to the army, particularly the officers. Approximately 25,000 officers were removed – around one in five – including the Supreme Commander of the Red Army, Marshal Tukhachevsky.

As the Purges were extended, university lecturers and teachers, miners and engineers, factory managers and ordinary workers all disappeared. It is said that every family in the USSR lost someone in the Purges. One of the most frightening aspects was the unpredictability. Arrests would take place in the middle of the night and victims were rarely told what they were accused of. Days of physical and psychological torture would gradually break the victims and they would confess to anything. If the torture failed, the NKVD would threaten the families of those arrested.

By 1937 an estimated 18 million people had been transported to labour camps. Ten million died. Stalin seriously weakened the USSR by removing so many able individuals. The army purges were nearly fatal to the USSR. When Hitler invaded the USSR in 1941, one of the key problems of the Red Army was a lack of good-quality, experienced officers. Stalin had also succeeded in destroying any sense of independent thinking. Everyone who was spared knew that their lives depended on thinking exactly as Stalin did. In the population as a whole, the long-term impact of living with terror and distrust haunted the USSR for a generation.

SOURCE 23

A tribute to Comrade Stalin was called for. Of course, everyone stood up . . . for three minutes, four minutes, the 'stormy applause, rising to an ovation' continued . . . Who would dare to be the first to stop? After all, NKVD men were standing in the hall waiting to see who quit first! After 11 minutes the director [of the factory] . . . sat down . . . To a man, everyone else stopped dead and sat down. They had been saved! . . . That, however, was how they discovered who the independent people were. And that was how they eliminated them. The same night the factory director was arrested.

Alexander Solzhenitsyn, *Gulag Archipelago*, published in 1973. Solzhenitsyn lost his Soviet citizenship as a result of this book.

1 According to Source 23, what sort of people did Stalin want in the USSR?

SOURCE 24

Stalin shown holding a young child, Gelya Markizova, in 1936. Stalin had both of her parents killed. This did not stop him using this image on propaganda leaflets to show him as a kind, fatherly figure.

SOURCE 25

Russian exiles in France made this mock travel poster in the late 1930s. The text says: 'Visit the USSR's pyramids!'

The new constitution

In 1936 Stalin created a new constitution for the USSR. It gave freedom of speech and free elections to the Russian people. This was, of course, a cosmetic measure. Only Communist Party candidates were allowed to stand in elections, and only approved newspapers and magazines could be published.

2 Look at Source 27. Summarise the message of the cartoon in your own words.

SOURCE **26**

One of Stalin's opponents deleted from a photograph, 1935. Techniques of doctoring pictures became far more sophisticated in the 1930s. This allowed Stalin to create the impression that his enemies had never existed.

SOURCE **27**

A cartoon published by Russian exiles in Paris in 1936. The title of the cartoon is 'The Stalinist Constitution' and the text at the bottom reads 'New seating arrangements in the Supreme Soviet'.

The cult of Stalin

Today, Stalin's rule is looked back on as a time of great terror and oppression. However, if you had visited the USSR in the 1930s, you would have found that the average Soviet citizen admired Stalin. Ask about the Purges and people would probably say that they were nothing to do with Stalin himself. For most Soviet citizens, Stalin was not a tyrant dominating an oppressed country. He and his style of government were popular. The Communist Party saw him as a winner and Soviet citizens saw him as a 'dictator of the people'. The Soviet people sincerely believed in Stalin and this belief was built up quite deliberately by Communist leaders and by Stalin himself. It developed into what is known as the Cult of the Personality. The history of the Soviet Union was rewritten so that Lenin and Stalin were the only real heroes of the Revolution.

SOURCE **28**

These men lifted their villainous hands against Comrade Stalin. By lifting their hands against Comrade Stalin, they lifted them against all of us, against the working class . . . against the teaching of Marx, Engels, Lenin . . . Stalin is our hope, Stalin is the beacon which guides all progressive mankind. Stalin is our banner. Stalin is our will. Stalin is our victory.

From a speech made by Communist leader Nikita Khrushchev in 1937, at the height of the Purges. (Khrushchev later became leader of the USSR and in 1956 announced a 'de-Stalinisation' programme – see page 128).

SOURCE **29**

The teacher showed us her school textbooks where the portraits of Party leaders had thick pieces of paper pasted over them as one by one they fell into disgrace – this the children had to do on instructions from their teacher . . . with every new arrest, people went through their books and burned the works of disgraced leaders in their stoves.

A Soviet writer describes how children in Soviet schools had to revise their school history books during the 1930s.

The Soviet education system was geared not to independent thinking but to Stalinist propaganda. Schoolchildren were also expected to join the Young Pioneers (see Source 30).

SOURCE **30**

I, a Young Pioneer of the Soviet Union, in the presence of my comrades, solemnly promise to love my Soviet motherland passionately, and to live, learn and struggle as the great Lenin bade us and the Communist Party teaches us.

The promise made by each member of the Young Pioneers.

Religion, art and culture under Stalin

Stalin understood the power of ideas. After all, Communism was an idea and it had carried him to power. You have seen on page 335 how Stalin kept tight control of the education system. He also kept control of the factors which influenced the way that people thought.

Religious worship was banned. Many churches were closed, priests deported and church buildings pulled down. By 1939 only one in 40 churches were holding regular services and only seven bishops were active in the USSR. Muslim worship was also attacked. In 1917 there were 26,000 mosques in Russia but by 1939 there were only 1,300. Despite this aggressive action, in the 1937 census, around 60 per cent of Russians said that they were Christians and the Church is still a strong force in Russia and the rest of the former USSR today.

SOURCE **31**

A painting showing Soviet officials blowing up a monastery in 1930.

Stalin wanted to be a part of people's daily life. The Soviet people were deluged with portraits, photographs and statues of Stalin. Comrade Stalin appeared everywhere. Every Russian town had a 'Stalin Square' or a 'Stalin Avenue' and a large statue of Stalin in the centre. In Moscow and other big cities, huge building projects were undertaken, including the Palace of the Soviets which was never finished because of war in 1941 and the awesome Moscow metro. Regular processions were organised through the streets of Russian towns and cities praising Stalin and all that he had achieved. There were other high prestige projects but there were also smaller scale ones as well. For example around 70,000 libraries were built across the country.

All music and other arts in the USSR were carefully monitored by the NKVD. Poets and playwrights praised Stalin either directly or indirectly. Composers wrote music praising him. One of the most famous was Dmitri Shostakovich. He studied music in Petrograd in 1919 and his first symphony was performed in 1926. It seemed that he would be a star of the Soviet system, but in 1936 he wrote an opera which met with disapproval from Stalin. He was attacked by the Soviet press and criticised by the Soviet Composers' Union. Shostakovich scrapped his next piece of work and wrote another symphony called 'A Soviet Artist's Practical Creative Reply to Just Criticism'.

1 Why did Stalin try to reduce the influence of religion?
2 How effective were his policies?
3 What changes would ordinary Soviet citizens have noticed as they walked around their towns and cities?
4 What does the story of Shostakovich tell historians about life for musicians under Stalin? Try using the internet to look up other artists or writers such as Maxim Gorky.

SOURCE **32**

A painting from 1937 called *A Collective Farm Feast*, by Alexander Gerasimov.

SOURCE **33**

5 Stalin wanted Socialist Realist art to send out very simple messages which everyone could understand. Do you think Source 33 achieves this aim?
6 Does Source 34 prove that Stalin's policies did not work?

Starting Up, a painting by Soviet artist Alexander Samokhavlov in 1934. It shows a female factory worker starting up her machine.

SOURCE **34**

Whoever said that Soviet literature contains only real images is profoundly mistaken. The themes are dictated by the Party. The Party deals harshly with anybody who tries to depict the real state of affairs in their literature.

Is it not a fact that all of you now reading these lines saw people dying in the streets in 1932? People, swollen with hunger and foaming at the mouth, lying in their death throes in the streets. Is it not a fact that whole villages full of people perished in 1932? Does our literature show any of these horrors, which make your hair stand on end? No. Where will you find such appalling things depicted in Soviet literature? You call it realism?

A protest note pinned on the walls of a college by students in November 1935.

Soviet artists and writers developed a style of art which became known as Socialist Realism. The aim of this style of art was to praise Stalin's rule. It usually involved heroic figures working hard in fields or factories to make the USSR a better place to live. It was certainly Socialist but many people questioned whether it was realism (see Source 34).

Society and people under Stalin

Stalin's rule brought enormous changes to the USSR. As well as the political and economic changes that you have read about there were major social changes too. From 1929 to 1941 around 18.5 million Soviet people left their homes in the agricultural areas to go to the cities and towns to work in the growing industries. This meant a new way of life for these people and it often changed life for their families as well. In many cases a family effectively lost one of its members, often a young son. In the worst cases, we know that many men simply abandoned their families. One effect of this was increasing youth crime. In many areas large numbers of homeless children were surviving on begging or petty crime because they had been abandoned or lost their families.

The Great Retreat

Stalin was concerned about these developments. By the mid 1930s there was a movement to return to traditional family values and discipline, often called 'The Great Retreat'.

- Abortion was made illegal except to protect the health of the mother.
- Divorce was made more difficult. Divorcing couples had to go to court and pay a fee of 50 roubles (more if it was a second or third divorce).
- Divorced fathers had to pay maintenance for their children (although it was often difficult to enforce this).
- Mothers received cash payments of 2,000 roubles per year for each child up to age five.
- A new law in 1935 allowed the NKVD to deal harshly with youth crime. There was even a death sentence introduced for young criminals, although there are no records of it actually being used.
- Parents could be fined if their children caused trouble. Their children could be taken to orphanages and their parents forced to pay for their upkeep.

It is very hard to judge the impact of these measures. The rate of divorce in Leningrad stayed roughly the same (about one in 3.5 marriages). Absent fathers meant women took the major role in holding family life together and became breadwinners as well. Overall, it seems that family life did not decline further in the 1930s and interviews with survivors of the period seem to suggest that most people supported the Great Retreat policies.

Equal society?

One of the main aims of Communist policies was to make life more equal and fair for all members of society. Critics of Communism have usually pointed out that it made life equally bad for everyone in society. There is some evidence to support this.

- The buying power of a worker's wages fell by over 50 per cent during the first Five-Year Plan. The average worker in 1930s Moscow ate only 20 per cent of the meat and fish he ate in 1900 under the Tsar.
- Housing was hard to find. Overcrowding was a major problem and it was almost impossible to get items like paint to keep a house in good condition.
- It was just as difficult to get items like clothing, shoes and boots. Queuing to buy goods became part of life.

On the other hand, there were some positives. Health care improved enormously. Education improved and public libraries became available as literacy became a high priority. Sports facilities were good in most towns and cities.

SOURCE 35

Interviews with Soviet citizens who fled the USSR in the Second World War showed that support for welfare policies, support for strong government and patriotic pride were all robust – and this was from a sample of persons who had shown their hatred of Stalin by leaving the country.

An extract from *A History of Modern Russia* by Robert Conquest, published in 2003. Conquest is a well-known historian in this field.

Despite the ideology a divide in society began to open up. For some, if you were ambitious, you could become part of the new 'class' of skilled workers or a foreman, supervisor or technician. There was an army of managers and bureaucrats, and they created jobs for the secretaries who handled their paperwork. One manager who employed a servant on eighteen roubles a week, while his wife earned 30 roubles a week as a typist. The manager could also get items like clothing and luxuries in the official Party shops.

The nationalities

People often think of Russia and the USSR as the same thing, but this is wrong. Russia was the largest republic in a large collection of republics. As a Georgian, you might think Stalin would sympathise with people who did not want to be part of a Soviet Union dominated by Russia. In fact, Stalin had little time for nationalist feelings. He was much more concerned with control and obedience. Many areas were dramatically changed by the arrival of large numbers of Russian immigrant workers. In some areas whole populations were deported from their homes because Stalin did not trust them. Other groups were persecuted because of long-standing prejudices. For example, Jews still suffered discrimination and the Finnish population in the region around Leningrad fell by one-third during the 1930s.

Activity

How were the Soviet people affected by Stalin's rule?

Many people fled from Stalin's Russia. Some of these reached the USA and were interviewed about life in the USSR. Your task is to work with a partner to role play one of these interviews. Work together to plan out the questions one of you will ask and the answers you will give. You could cover areas such as:
- religion
- how towns and cities looked
- art, music, etc.
- family life
- winners and losers in society
- the nationalities.

REVIEW

Well done! You have now reached the end of this chapter. This is a good point to look back on what you have studied and think about the big questions – the kind of questions an examiner might ask you. Focus Tasks A and B (on page 340) will help you to organise your thoughts about what you have found out.

Focus Task A

How did Stalin control the USSR? Stage 1

This task is in two stages.
1 Draw up a table like this one and fill it out as completely as you can. You may wish to add other subjects in the first column.
2 Now pull your research together in a presentation or a piece of extended writing on the question 'How did Stalin control the USSR?' Use the methods in the first column as headings for slides or paragraphs in your work.

EXTENSION WORK
Add an extra section on how effective you think Stalin's control was.

Method of control	Example
Making people afraid	
Improving living conditions	
Propaganda	
Education	
Control of economy	
Control of mass media	
Cult of the personality	

Focus Task B

How did Stalin control the USSR? Stage 2

SOURCE **36**

The costs of Soviet rule greatly outweighed the advantages. The state of Lenin and Stalin brutalised politics in Russia for decades. It is true that the communists made many social and economic gains beyond those of Tsar Nicholas II's government; but they also reinforced certain features of Tsarism which they had promised to remove. National enmities intensified. Political alienation deepened and respect for law decreased. The dictatorship broke up society and those who obstructed the central state's will were crushed.

An extract from *A History of Modern Russia* by Robert Conquest, published in 2003.
Conquest is a well-known historian in this field.

SOURCE **37**

A poster of Stalin pointing out the achievements of the USSR and its people.

Which of these two views do you think is a fairer summary of the achievements of Stalin and his impact on the Soviet people? Debate this question in class and then hold a vote on it. See if you can compare the results of your class's vote with the results of other classes. You may even be able to debate the issue with other schools using an online discussion forum.

13 The USA, 1919–41

13.1 What was the USA like in the 1920s?

Focus

In the 1920s the USA was the richest and most powerful country in the world. Its industry was booming. Then in 1929 disaster struck. The Wall Street Crash plunged the United States into a deep economic depression – and the rest of the world followed it.

In 13.1 you will study American society in the 1920s. You will investigate:
◆ whether the economic boom in the 1920s was as widespread as it is sometimes made out to be
◆ how and why American society was changing in the 1920s.

In 13.2 you will explore:
◆ the causes and consequences of the Wall Street Crash.

In 13.3 you will examine:
◆ how successfully Roosevelt's New Deal dealt with the problems facing the USA in the 1930s.

Timeline

This timeline shows the period you will be covering in this chapter. Some of the key dates are filled in already.

To help you get a complete picture of the period, you can make your own copy and add other details to it as you work through the chapter.

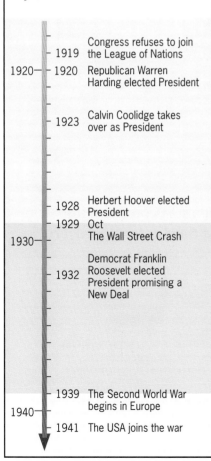

- 1919 — Congress refuses to join the League of Nations
- 1920 — Republican Warren Harding elected President
- 1923 — Calvin Coolidge takes over as President
- 1928 — Herbert Hoover elected President
- 1929 — Oct The Wall Street Crash
- 1932 — Democrat Franklin Roosevelt elected President promising a New Deal
- 1939 — The Second World War begins in Europe
- 1941 — The USA joins the war

Isolationist USA

As you have seen in Chapter 10, President Wilson took the USA into the First World War in 1917. It was a controversial decision. For decades, the USA had deliberately isolated itself from the squabbles of Europe and most Americans thought that was the right policy. But despite their opposition, Wilson took the USA into the war. It was German submarine warfare against US ships that finally forced the USA into the war, but Wilson presented the war to the American people as a struggle to preserve freedom and democracy.

When the war ended in 1918, the divisions in the USA about what its role in the world should be resurfaced. Wilson got hopelessly bogged down in the squabbles of the European states after the war. Some Americans believed, as Wilson did, that the time had come for the USA to take a leading role in world affairs – that there was more chance of peace, if they were involved than if they stayed out. Others felt that Wilson had gone too far already. Thousands of American soldiers had been killed or wounded in a war that they felt was not their concern. US troops were even now involved in a civil war in Russia (see page 318). Now Wilson wanted the USA to take the lead in a League of Nations. Would this mean the USA supplying the troops and resources for this new international police force?

President Wilson travelled the country in 1919 to get the American people – and Congress – to accept the Treaty of Versailles and the League of Nations. The President needed to have the support of Congress (see the Factfile on page 345 to see how the US system of government works). Wilson had many political enemies and eventually they brought him down. In the end, the Isolationists in the USA won the debate. You can read more about this on pages 22–23.

The USA then turned its back on Europe for much of the next twenty years. A new Republican President, Warren Harding, was elected in 1920 promising a return to 'normalcy' – normal life as it had been before the war. Americans turned their energies to what they did best – making money! Over the next ten years the USA, already the richest country in the world, became richer as its economy boomed. The next two pages will give you an idea of what this economic boom was like.

What was the 'boom'?

SOURCE **1**

1919   Cars   1929

9 million   26 million

1920   Radios   1929

60,000   10 million

1915   Telephones   1930

10 million   20 million

1921   Fridges   1929

For every one...   there were 167

Sales of consumer goods, 1915–30. Overall, the output of American industry doubled in the 1920s.

SOURCE **2**

Skyscrapers being built in New York City. There was more building being done in the boom years of the 1920s than at any time in the history of the USA.

SOURCE **3**

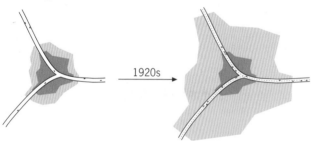

1920s

The car made it possible for more Americans to live in their own houses in the suburbs on the edge of towns. For example, Queens outside New York doubled in size in the 1920s. Grosse Point Park outside Detroit grew by 700 per cent.

SOURCE **4**

Workers on the government's road-building programme. The Federal Road Act of 1916 began a period of intense road building all over the country. Road building employed more people than any other industry in the USA for the next ten years. During the 1920s the total extent of roads in the USA doubled.

SOURCE **5**

For 1927 the most complete line of 4 and 6-cylinder Speed Trucks

KRAFT CHEESE

THE HARVESTER organization announces a complete line of improved Speed Trucks of six distinct chassis designs to meet every requirement for loads up to 1½ tons.

MODEL S is built to carry a 1¼-ton load. It comes equipped with a 4 or 6-cylinder power plant and with any type of body for hauling and delivery.

MODEL SL—safe and low and easy to work with—is a 1½-ton chassis with either a 4 or 6-cylinder engine and has a wheelbase of 160 inches. The top of the frame is only 24 inches from the ground.

MODEL SD is a handy, specially-built 1½-ton chassis with a wheelbase of 110 inches, de-

signed for dump or tractor work. It is ideal for general contracting, road building, and truck hauling.

Every International Speed Truck is a truck from the ground up—not a rebuilt passenger car. Engine, clutch, transmission, axles, springs, frame, and all the other essentials are the result of 22 years of truck building experience.

Whether your loads run to bulk or weight, whether your business calls for style and distinction or plain utility in its hauling equipment—there is a 4 or 6-cylinder Speed Truck in either a 1¼ or 1½-ton chassis made to meet your needs exactly.

For light, quick hauls we suggest our "Special Delivery," a fast and sturdy model for ½-ton loads. Any type of body.

The International line also includes Heavy-Duty Trucks up to 5 tons capacity, Motor Coaches, and the McCormick-Deering Industrial Tractor

INTERNATIONAL HARVESTER COMPANY
OF AMERICA
(INCORPORATED)
606 SO. MICHIGAN AVE.   CHICAGO, ILL.
124 Company-owned Branches in the United States

INTERNATIONAL HARVESTER COMPANY
TRUCKS

The new roads gave rise to a new truck industry. In 1919 there were 1 million trucks in the USA. By 1929 there were 3.5 million.

SOURCE 6

BEFORE YOU LEAVE FOR YOUR VACATION
see that your hosiery wants are supplied in the very newest and most desirable numbers of

"Onyx" Silk Hosiery

With the "POINTEX" Heel

Lord & Taylor New York

Silk stockings had once been a luxury item reserved for the rich. In 1900 only 12,000 pairs had been sold. In the 1920s rayon was invented which was a cheaper substitute for silk. In 1930, 300 million pairs of stockings were sold to a female population of around 100 million.

SOURCE 7

A passenger aircraft in 1927. There were virtually no civilian airlines in 1918. By 1930 the new aircraft companies flew 162,000 flights a year.

SOURCE 8

Workers erecting electricity pylons. In 1918 only a few homes had electricity. By 1929 almost all urban homes had it, although not many farms were on the electricity supply grid.

1 Use Sources 1–9 to make a list of features of the economic boom of the 1920s under the following headings:
- Industry
- Transport
- Home life
- Cities

2 Draw a chart to show connections between any of the features shown in the sources.

3 Using these sources, write a 20-word definition of 'the economic boom of the 1920s'.

SOURCE 9

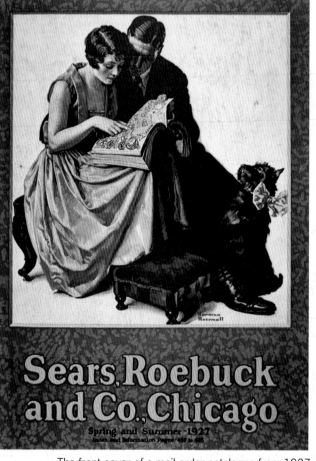

Sears, Roebuck and Co., Chicago

Spring and Summer 1927

The front cover of a mail order catalogue from 1927.

Why was there an economic boom in the 1920s?

As you can see from Sources 1–9, it seemed that everything in the USA was booming in the 1920s. You are now going to investigate the various reasons for that boom.

Industrial strength

The USA was a vast country, rich in natural resources. It had a growing population (123 million by 1923). Most of this population was living in towns and cities. They were working in industry and commerce, usually earning higher wages than in farming. So these new town dwellers became an important market for the USA's new industries. Most US companies had no need to export outside the USA, and most US companies had access to the raw materials they needed in the USA.

SOURCE 10

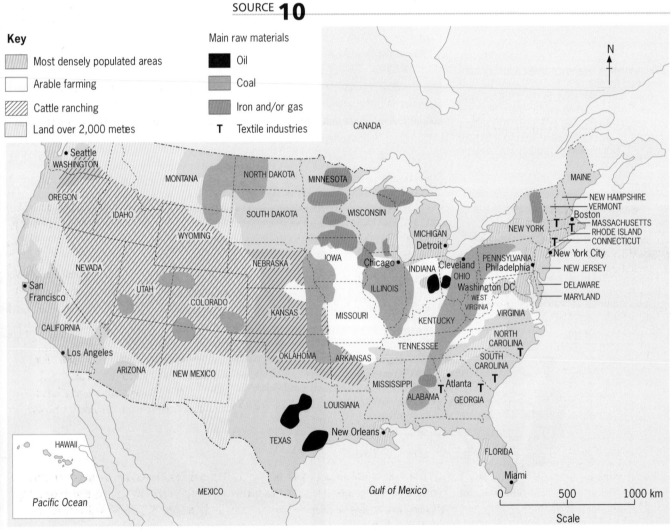

Key

Most densely populated areas	
Arable farming	
Cattle ranching	
Land over 2,000 metes	

Main raw materials

Oil	
Coal	
Iron and/or gas	
T	Textile industries

The USA's main centres of population and main natural resources around 1920.

Ever since the 1860s and 1870s, American industry had been growing vigorously. By the time of the First World War, the USA led the world in most areas of industry. It had massive steel, coal and textile industries. It was the leading oil producer. It was foremost in developing new technology such as motor cars, telephones and electric lighting. In fact, electricity and electrical goods were a key factor in the USA's economic boom. Other new industries such as chemicals were also growing fast. The USA's new film industry already led the world.

The managers of these industries were increasingly skilled and professional, and they were selling more and more of their products not just in the USA but in Europe, Latin America and the Far East.

American agriculture had become the most efficient and productive in the world. In fact, farmers had become so successful that they were producing more than they could sell, which was a very serious problem (see page 349). In 1914, however, most Americans would have confidently stated that American agriculture and industry were going from strength to strength.

The First World War

The Americans tried hard to stay out of the fighting in the First World War. But throughout the war they lent money to the Allies, and sold arms and munitions to Britain and France. They sold massive amounts of foodstuffs as well. This one-way trade gave American industry a real boost. In addition, while the European powers slugged it out in France, the Americans were able to take over Europe's trade around the world. American exports to the areas controlled by European colonial powers increased during the war.

There were other benefits as well. Before the war Germany had had one of the world's most successful chemicals industries. The war stopped it in its tracks. By the end of the war the USA had far outstripped Germany in the supply of chemical products. Explosives manufacture during the war also stimulated a range of by-products which became new American industries in their own right. Plastics and other new materials were produced.

Historians have called the growth and change at this time the USA's second industrial revolution. The war actually helped rather than hindered the 'revolution'.

When the USA joined the fighting it was not in the war long enough for the war to drain American resources in the way it drained Europe's. There was a downturn in the USA when war industries readjusted to peacetime, but it was only a blip. By 1922 the American economy was growing fast once again.

Republican policies

A third factor behind the boom was the policies of the Republican Party. From 1920 to 1932 all the US presidents were Republican, and Republicans also dominated Congress. Here are some of their beliefs.

1 Laissez-faire

Republicans believed that government should interfere as little as possible in the everyday lives of the people. This attitude is called 'laissez-faire'. In their view, the job of the President was to leave the businessman alone – to do his job. That was where prosperity came from.

2 Tariffs

The Republicans believed in import tariffs which made it expensive to import foreign goods. For example, in 1922 Harding introduce the Fordney–McCumber tariff which made imported food expensive in the USA. These tariffs protected businesses against foreign competition and allowed American companies to grow even more rapidly. The USA also began closing its borders to foreign immigrants (see page 358).

3 Low taxation

The Republicans kept taxation as low as possible. This brought some benefits to ordinary working people, but it brought even more to the very wealthy. The Republican thinking was that if people kept their own money, they would spend it on American goods and wealthy people would reinvest their money in industries.

4 Trusts

The Republicans also allowed the development of trusts. These were huge super-corporations, which dominated industry. Woodrow Wilson and the Democrats had fought against trusts because they believed it was unhealthy for men such as Carnegie (steel) and Rockefeller (oil) to have almost complete control of one vital sector of industry. The Republicans allowed the trusts to do what they wanted, believing that the 'captains of industry' knew better than politicians did what was good for the USA.

---

1 List the benefits that the First World War brought to the US economy.

Factfile

US system of government

➤ **The federal system:** The USA's federal system means that all the individual states look after their own internal affairs (such as education). Questions that concern all of the states (such as making treaties with other countries) are dealt with by Congress.

➤ **The Constitution:** The Constitution lays out how the government is supposed to operate and what it is allowed to do.

➤ **The President:** He (or she) is the single most important politician in the USA. He is elected every four years. However, the Constitution of the USA is designed to stop one individual from becoming too powerful. Congress and the Supreme Court both act as 'watchdogs' checking how the President behaves.

➤ **Congress:** Congress is made up of the Senate and the House of Representatives. Congress and the President run the country.

➤ **The Supreme Court:** This is made up of judges, who are usually very experienced lawyers. Their main task is to make sure that American governments do not misuse their power or pass unfair laws. They have the power to say that a law is unconstitutional (against the Constitution), which usually means that they feel the law would harm American citizens.

➤ **Parties:** There are two main political parties, the Republicans and the Democrats. In the 1920s and 1930s, the Republicans were stronger in the industrial north of the USA while the Democrats had more support in the south. On the whole, Republicans in the 1920s and 1930s preferred government to stay out of people's lives if possible. The Democrats were more prepared to intervene in everyday life.

SOURCE 11

Average annual industrial wages	1919:	$1,158
	1927:	$1,304
Number of millionaires	1914:	7,000
	1928:	35,000

Wealth in the USA.

1 How could the Republicans use Sources 11 and 13 to justify their policies?
2 How could critics of Republican policies use Sources 11 and 13 to attack the Republicans?

SOURCE 12

A pre-war anti-trust cartoon. Although there was opposition to trusts, they were so successful and influential that it was difficult to limit their power.

SOURCE 13

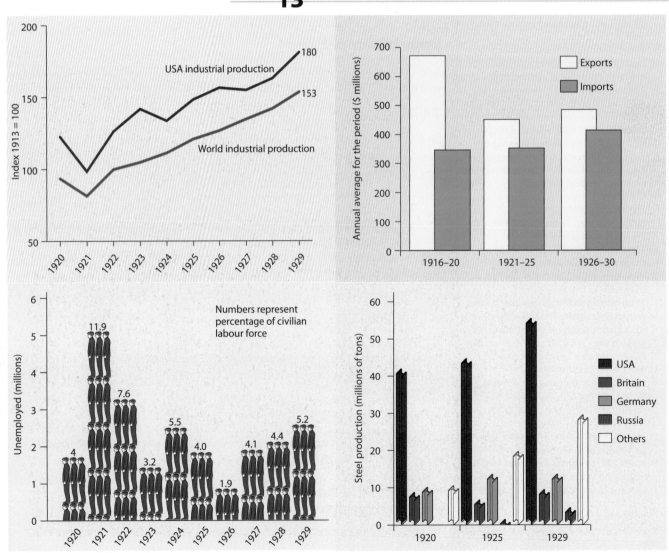

The growth of the US economy in the 1920s.

Activity

Imagine that you are making a radio programme about industry in the USA. Describe the scene in Source 15 for your listeners. Remember you are trying to bring it to life. You could mention:

- the size of the building
- what the workers are doing (you could even 'interview' them)
- the equipment you can see
- how the car develops during the process
- noises and smells
- how and why scenes like this are making the USA rich.

You could present your work as a script, or record your work as a podcast.

New industries, new methods

Through the 1920s new industries and new methods of production were developed in the USA. The country was able to exploit its vast resources of raw materials to produce steel, chemicals, glass and machinery.

These products became the foundation of an enormous boom in consumer goods. Telephones, radios, vacuum cleaners and washing machines were mass-produced on a vast scale, making them cheaper so more people could buy them. New electrical companies such as Hoover became household names. They used the latest, most efficient techniques proposed by the 'Industrial Efficiency Movement'.

At the same time, the big industries used sophisticated sales and marketing techniques to get people to buy their goods. Mass nationwide advertising had been used for the first time in the USA during the war to get Americans to support the war effort. Many of the advertisers who had learned their skills in wartime propaganda now set up agencies to sell cars, cigarettes, clothing and other consumer items. Poster advertisements, radio advertisements and travelling salesmen encouraged Americans to spend. Even if they did not have the money, people could borrow it easily. Or they could take advantage of the new 'Buy now, pay later' hire purchase schemes. Eight out of ten radios and six out of ten cars were bought on credit.

The most important of these new booming industries was the motor-car industry. The motor car had only been developed in the 1890s. The first cars were built by blacksmiths and other skilled craftsmen. They took a long time to make and were very expensive. In 1900 only 4,000 cars were made. Car production was revolutionised by Henry Ford. In 1913 he set up the first moving production line in the world, in a giant shed in Detroit. Each worker on the line had one or two small jobs to do as the skeleton of the car moved past him. At the beginning of the line, a skeleton car went in; at the end of the line was a new car. The most famous of these was the Model T. More than 15 million were produced between 1908 and 1925. In 1927 they came off the production line at a rate of one every ten seconds. In 1929, 4.8 million cars were made.

SOURCE 15

Ford's production line in 1913.

Model Ts in an American high street. In 1925 a Model T cost $290. This was almost three months' wages for an American factory worker.

A state of mind

New industries

Republican policies

The First World War

The USA's industrial strength

By the end of the 1920s the motor industry was the USA's biggest industry. As well as employing hundreds of thousands of workers directly, it also kept workers in other industries in employment. Glass, leather, steel and rubber were all required to build the new vehicles. Automobiles used up 75 per cent of US glass production in the 1920s! Petrol was needed to run them. And a massive army of labourers was busily building roads throughout the country for these cars to drive on. In fact, road construction was the biggest single employer in the 1920s.

Owning a car was not just a rich person's privilege, as it was in Europe. There was one car to five people in the USA compared with one to 43 in Britain, and one to 7,000 in Russia. The car made it possible for people to buy a house in the suburbs, which further boosted house building. It also stimulated the growth of hundreds of other smaller businesses, ranging from hot dog stands and advertising bill boards to petrol stations and holiday resorts.

A state of mind

One thing that runs through all the factors you have looked at so far is an attitude or a state of mind. Most Americans believed that they had a right to 'prosperity'. For many it was a main aim in life to have a nice house, a good job and plenty to eat, and for their home to be filled with the latest consumer goods. Consuming more and more was seen as part of being American.

In earlier decades, thrift (being careful with money and saving 'for a rainy day') had been seen as a good quality. In the 1920s this was replaced by a belief that spending money was a better quality.

Focus Task

What factors caused the economic boom?

1 Make a copy of the diagram on the left. Complete it by adding notes at the right-hand side for each heading. You will need to refer to the information and sources on pages 344–48.

2 One historian has said: 'Without the new automobile industry, the prosperity of the 1920s would scarcely have been possible.'

Explain whether you agree or disagree with this statement. Support your explanation by referring to the sources and information on pages 344–48.

A cartoon showing the situation faced by American farmers in the 1920s.

1 Explain the message of Source 17.

Problems in the farming industry

While so many Americans were enjoying the boom, farmers most definitely were not. Total US farm income dropped from $22 billion in 1919 to just $13 billion in 1928. There were a number of reasons why farming had such problems.

After the war, Europe imported far less food from the USA. This was partly because Europe was poor, and it was partly a response to US tariffs which stopped Europe from exporting to the USA (see page 345).

Farmers were also struggling against competition from the highly efficient Canadian wheat producers. All of this came at a time when the population of the USA was actually falling and there were fewer mouths to feed.

Underlying all these problems was overproduction. From 1900 to 1920, while farming was doing well, more and more land was being farmed. Improved machinery, especially the combine harvester, and improved fertilisers made US agriculture extremely efficient. The result was that by 1920 it was producing surpluses of wheat which nobody wanted.

In the 1920s the average US farmer was each year growing enough to feed his family and fourteen others. Prices plummeted as desperate farmers tried to sell their produce. In 1921 alone, most farm prices fell by 50 per cent (see Source 18). Hundreds of rural banks collapsed in the 1920s and there were five times as many farm bankruptcies as there had been in the 1900s and 1910s.

Not all farmers were affected by these problems. Rich Americans wanted fresh vegetables and fruit throughout the year. Shipments of lettuce to the cities, for example, rose from 14,000 crates in 1920 to 52,000 in 1928. But for most farmers the 1920s were a time of hardship.

This was a serious issue. About half of all Americans lived in rural areas, mostly working on farms or in businesses that sold goods to farmers. Problems in farming therefore directly affected more than 60 million Americans.

Six million rural Americans, mainly farm labourers, were forced off the land in the 1920s. Many of these were unskilled workers who migrated to the cities, where there was little demand for their labour. The African Americans were particularly badly hit. They had always done the least skilled jobs in the rural areas. As they lost their jobs on the farms, three-quarters of a million of them became unemployed.

SOURCE 18

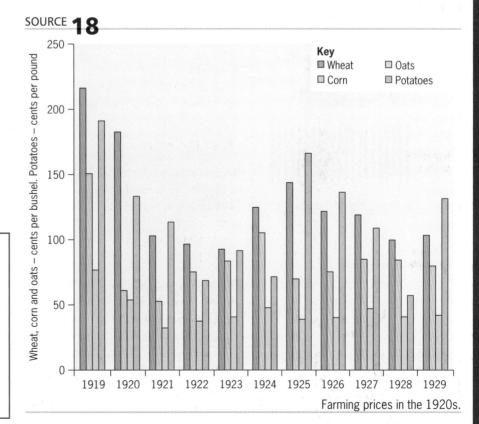

Farming prices in the 1920s.

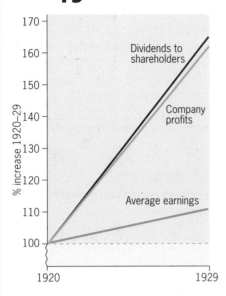

A comparison of the growth of profits and the growth of average earnings.

Did all Americans benefit from the boom?

You have already seen how the farmers – a very large group in American society – did not share in the prosperity of the 1920s. But they were not alone. Workers in many older industries, such as coal, leather and textiles, did not benefit much either. Coal suffered from competition from new industries such as oil and electricity. Leather and textiles were protected from foreign competition, but not from domestic competition. They suffered from the development of new man-made materials. They also struggled to compete with cheap labour in the southern states. Even if workers in these industries did get a pay rise, their wages did not increase on the same scale as company profits or dividends paid to shareholders (see Source 19).

In 1928 there was a strike in the coal industry in North Carolina, where the male workers were paid only $18 and women $9 for a 70-hour week, at a time when $48 per week was considered to be the minimum required for a decent life. In fact, for the majority of Americans wages remained well below that figure. It has been estimated that 42 per cent of Americans lived below the poverty line – they did not have the money needed to pay for essentials such as food, clothing, housing and heating for their families.

What's more, throughout this period unemployment remained a problem. The growth in industry in the 1920s did not create many new jobs. Industries were growing by electrifying or mechanising production. The same number of people (around 5 per cent) were unemployed at the peak of the boom in 1929 as in 1920. Yet the amount of goods produced had doubled. These millions of unemployed Americans were not sharing in the boom. They included many poor whites, but an even greater proportion of African American and Hispanic people and other members of the USA's large immigrant communities.

The plight of the poor was desperate for the individuals concerned. But it was also damaging to American industry. The boom of the 1920s was a consumer-led boom, which means that it was led by ordinary families buying things for their home. But with so many families too poor to buy such goods, the demand for them was likely to begin to tail off. However, Republican policy remained not to interfere, and this included doing nothing about unemployment or poverty.

goes to the richest 5%

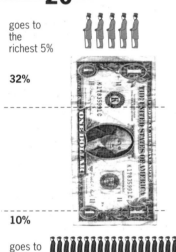

32%

10%

goes to the poorest 42%

The distribution of income in 1925.

A hunger march staged by workers in Washington in the 1920s.

1 Use the text and sources on this page to explain:
   a) why the government should have been concerned about poverty
   b) why, in the event, it did very little to help the poor.

SOURCE 22

The 1922 coal strike.

SOURCE 23

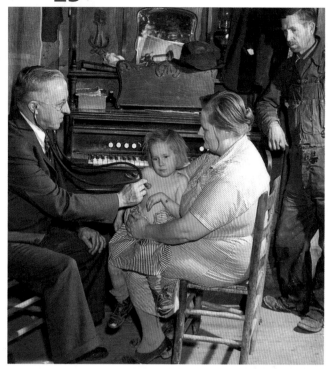

A doctor visiting a poor American family in the 1920s. Doctors' fees were very expensive. They would only be called out if someone was seriously ill.

Focus Task

Did all Americans share in the boom?

In 1928 a new Republican President, Herbert Hoover, was elected. He said:

SOURCE 24

One of the oldest and perhaps the noblest of human activities [aims] has been the abolition of poverty . . . we in America today are nearer to the final triumph over poverty than ever before in the history of any land.

Herbert Hoover.

Your task is to focus on the state of the USA in the 1920s, to assess Hoover's claim.

1 Work in pairs. One of you gather evidence from pages 346–48 to support Hoover's claim. The other gather evidence from pages 349–51 to oppose it.

2 Now, working together as advisers to Hoover, try to use this evidence to present him with a balanced picture. Think carefully about:
 ◆ what evidence you will send him
 ◆ what you will say to put the evidence into context for the President.

Compile the evidence and your explanation as a portfolio for the President's urgent attention.

Chicago in the 1920s

You can find out more about a period by looking at particular places or people. Historians have found out a lot about Chicago in the 1920s. Chicago was one of America's biggest cities. It was the centre of the steel, meat and clothing industries, which employed many unskilled workers. Such industries had busy and slack periods. In slack periods the workers would be 'seasonally unemployed'. Many of these workers were Polish or Italian immigrants, or African American migrants from the southern United States. How far did they share in the prosperity of the 1920s?

Only 3 per cent of semi-skilled workers owned a car. Compare that with richer areas where 29 per cent owned a car. It was the middle classes, not the workers in industry, who bought cars. On the whole, workers in Chicago didn't like to buy large items on credit. They preferred to save for when they might not have a job. Many of them bought smaller items on credit, such as phonographs (record players) and radios. Chicago became the centre of a growing record industry specialising in Polish and Italian records for the immigrant communities.

The poor whites did not benefit much from the new chain stores which had revolutionised shopping in the 1920s. These stores sold the same standard goods all across the country but they mostly served the middle classes. Nearly all of them were in middle-class districts. Poorer white industrial workers preferred to shop at the local grocer's where the owner was more flexible and gave them credit, even though they could have saved money by going to the chain stores.

However, the poor did join the movie craze. There were hundreds of cinemas in Chicago with four performances a day. Working people in Chicago spent more than half of their leisure budget on movies. Even those who were so poor that they were getting Mothers' Aid Assistance went often. It only cost ten or twenty cents to see a movie. Yet even in cinema-going the poor were separated from the rich. They went to the local cinema because they couldn't afford the $1 admission, plus the bus fare, to the more luxurious town-centre cinemas.

By 1930 there was one radio for every two to three households in the poorer districts of Chicago. Those who didn't own a radio set went to shops or to neighbours to listen. It was a communal activity – most families listened to the radio together.

The USA in the Roaring Twenties

The 1920s are often called the Roaring Twenties. The name suggests a time of riotous fun, loud music and wild enjoyment when everyone was having a good time.

You have already found out enough about the USA in the period to know that this is probably not how everyone saw this decade. For example, how do you think the poor farmers described on page 349 would react to the suggestion that the 1920s were one long party?

What is in no doubt is that this was a time of turmoil for many Americans. For those who joined in 'the party', it was a time of liberation and rebellion against traditional values. For those who did not, it was a time of anxiety and worry. For them, the changes taking place were proof that the USA was going down the drain and needed rescuing.

All this combined to make the 1920s a decade of contrasts.

Growing cities

In 1920, for the first time in American history, more Americans lived in towns and cities than in the country. As you can see from Source 25, throughout the 1920s cities were growing fast. People flocked to them from all over the USA. The growing city with its imposing skyline of skyscrapers was one of the most powerful symbols of 1920s USA. In New York, the skyscrapers were built because there was no more land available. But even small cities, where land was not in short supply, wanted skyscrapers to announce to the country that they were sharing in the boom.

Throughout the 1920s there was tension between rural USA and urban USA. Many people in the country thought that their traditional values, which emphasised religion and family life, were under threat from the growing cities, which they thought were full of atheists, drunks and criminals. Certain rural states, particularly in the south, fought a rearguard action against the 'evil' effects of the city throughout the 1920s, as you will see on page 363.

Entertainment

During the 1920s the entertainment industry blossomed. The average working week dropped from 47.4 to 44.2 hours so people had more leisure time. Average wages rose by 11 per cent (in real terms) so workers also had more disposable income. A lot of this spare time and money was channelled into entertainment.

Radio

Almost everyone in the USA listened to the radio. Most households had their own set. People who could not afford to buy one outright, could purchase one in instalments. The choice of programmes grew quickly. In August 1921 there was only one licensed radio station in America. By the end of 1922 there were 508 of them. By 1929 the new network NBC was making $150 million a year.

Jazz

The radio gave much greater access to new music. Jazz music became an obsession among young people. African Americans who moved from the country to the cities had brought jazz and blues music with them. Blues music was particularly popular among the African Americans, while jazz captured the imagination of both young white and African Americans.

Such was the power of jazz music that the 1920s became known as the Jazz Age. Along with jazz went new dances such as the Charleston, and new styles of behaviour which were summed up in the image of the flapper, a woman who wore short dresses and make-up and who smoked in public. One writer said that the ideal flapper was 'expensive and about nineteen'.

The older generation saw jazz and everything associated with it as a corrupting influence on the young people of the USA. The newspapers and magazines printed articles analysing the influence of jazz (see Source 28).

SOURCE **25**

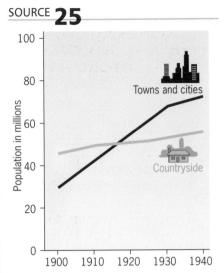

The change in the USA's urban and rural populations, 1900–40.

SOURCE **26**

The Builder, painted by Gerrit A Beneker in the 1920s.

1 Write an advertising slogan to go with Source 26, inviting workers to come to New York City.

SOURCE **27**

King Oliver's Creole Jazz Band, 1920. Louis Armstrong is kneeling at the front.

SOURCE 28

(i) Jazz employs primitive rhythms which excite the baser human instincts.

(ii) Jazz music causes drunkenness. Reason and reflection are lost and the actions of the persons are directed by the stronger animal passions.

Comments on jazz music in articles in the 1920s.

> **2** What do you think the writers in Source 28 mean by 'the baser human instincts' and 'the stronger animal passions'?

SOURCE 29

Crowds queuing for cinema tickets in Chicago. In 1920, 40 million tickets were sold per week and in 1929, 100 million.

SOURCE 30

There was never a time in American history when youth had such a special sense of importance as in the years after the First World War. There was a gulf between the generations like a geological fault. Young men who had fought in the trenches felt that they knew a reality their elders could not even imagine. Young girls no longer consciously modelled themselves on their mothers, whose experience seemed unusable in the 1920s.

William E Leuchtenberg, *The Perils of Prosperity*, 1958.

Sport

Sport was another boom area. Baseball became a big money sport with legendary teams like the New York Yankees and Boston Red Sox. Prominent figures such as Al Capone (see pages 367) were baseball fans. Boxing was also a very popular sport, with heroes like world heavyweight champion Jack Dempsey.

Cinema

In a small suburb outside Los Angeles, called Hollywood, a major film industry was developing. All-year-round sunshine meant that the studios could produce large numbers of films or 'movies'. New stars like Charlie Chaplin and Buster Keaton made audiences roar with laughter, while Douglas Fairbanks thrilled them in daring adventure films. Until 1927 all movies were silent. In 1927 the first 'talkie' was made.

During the 1920s movies became a multi-billion dollar business and it was estimated that, by the end of the decade, a hundred million cinema tickets were being sold each week. That's as many as are sold in a year in Britain today.

Morals

Source 30 is one historian's description of this period. He refers to new attitudes among young women (see pages 354–55). The gulf he mentions was most obvious in sexual morals. In the generation before the war, sex had still been a taboo subject. After the war it became a major concern of tabloid newspapers, Hollywood films, and everyday conversation. Scott Fitzgerald, one of a celebrated new group of young American writers who had served in the First World War, said: 'None of the mothers had any idea how casually their daughters were accustomed to be kissed.'

The cinema quickly discovered the selling power of sex. The first cinema star to be sold on sex appeal was Theda Bara who, without any acting talent, made a string of wildly successful films with titles like *Forbidden Path* and *When a Woman Sins*. Clara Bow was sold as the 'It' girl. Everybody knew that 'It' meant 'sex'. Hollywood turned out dozens of films a month about 'It', such as *Up in Mabel's Room*, *Her Purchase Price* and *A Shocking Night*. Male stars too, such as Rudolph Valentino, were presented as sex symbols. Women were said to faint at the very sight of him as a half-naked Arab prince in *The Sheik* (1921).

Today these films would be considered very tame indeed, but at the time they were considered very daring. The more conservative rural states were worried by the deluge of sex-obsessed films, and 36 states threatened to introduce censorship legislation. Hollywood responded with its own censorship code which ensured that, while films might still be full of sex, at least the sinful characters were not allowed to get away with it!

Meanwhile, in the real world, contraceptive advice was openly available for the first time. Sex outside marriage was much more common than in the past, although probably more people talked about it and went to films about it than actually did it!

The car

The motor car was one factor that tended to make all the other features of the 1920s mentioned above more possible. Cars helped the cities to grow by opening up the suburbs. They carried their owners to and from their entertainments. Cars carried boyfriends and girlfriends beyond the moral gaze of their parents and they took Americans to an increasing range of sporting events, beach holidays, shopping trips, picnics in the country, or simply on visits to their family and friends.

Focus Task

The Roaring Twenties

Draw a diagram to summarise the features of the Roaring Twenties. You can get lots of ideas from the text on these two pages, but remember that other factors may also be relevant: for example, material on the economy (pages 344–48) or on women (pages 354–55). You could also use the internet.

Women in 1920s USA

A school teacher in 1905.

1 Compare the clothes of the women in Sources 31 and 32. Write a detailed description of the differences between them.
2 Flappers were controversial figures in the 1920s. List as many reasons as possible for this.

Women formed half of the population of the USA and their lives were as varied as those of men. It is therefore difficult to generalise. However, before the First World War middle-class women in the USA, like those in Britain, were expected to lead restricted lives. They had to wear very restrictive clothes and behave politely. They were expected not to wear make-up. Their relationships with men were strictly controlled. They had to have a chaperone with them when they went out with a boyfriend. They were expected not to take part in sport or to smoke in public. In most states they could not vote. Most women were expected to be housewives. Very few paid jobs were open to women. Most working women were in lower-paid jobs such as cleaning, dressmaking and secretarial work.

In rural USA there were particularly tight restrictions owing to the Churches' traditional attitude to the role of women. In the 1920s, many of these things began to change, especially for urban women and middle-class women. When the USA joined the war in 1917, some women were taken into the war industries, giving them experience of skilled factory work for the first time. In 1920 they got the vote in all states. Through the 1920s they shared the liberating effects of the car, and their domestic work was made easier (in theory) by new electrical goods such as vacuum cleaners and washing machines.

For younger urban women many of the traditional rules of behaviour were eased as well. Women wore more daring clothes. They smoked in public and drank with men, in public. They went out with men, in cars, without a chaperone. They kissed in public.

In urban areas more women took on jobs – particularly middle-class women. They typically took on jobs created by the new industries. There were 10 million women in jobs in 1929, 24 per cent more than in 1920. With money of their own, working women became the particular target of advertising. Even women who did not earn their own money were increasingly seen as the ones who took decisions about whether to buy new items for the home. There is evidence that women's role in choosing cars triggered Ford, in 1925, to make them available in colours other than black.

Women were less likely to stay in unhappy marriages. In 1914 there were 100,000 divorces; in 1929 there were twice as many.

Films and novels also exposed women to a much wider range of role models. Millions of women a week saw films with sexy or daring heroines as well as other films that showed women in a more traditional role. The newspaper, magazine and film industries found that sex sold much better than anything else.

Limitations

It might seem to you as if everything was changing, and for young, middle-class women living in cities a lot was changing in the 1920s. However, this is only part of the story. Take work, for example. Women were still paid less than men, even when they did the same job. One of the reasons women's employment increased when men's did not was that women were cheaper employees. In politics as well, women in no way achieved equality with men. They may have been given the vote but it did not give them access to political power. Political parties wanted women's votes, but they didn't particularly want women as political candidates as they considered them 'unelectable'. Although many women, such as Eleanor Roosevelt (see Profile), had a high public standing, only a handful of women had been elected by 1929.

Flappers in the 1920s.

Gloria Swanson in *The Trespasser* (1929). Gloria Swanson was one of the most successful film stars of the 1920s and *The Trespasser* was her first 'talkie'.

Were the lives of American women changing?

From films such as Source 33 you would think that all American women were living passionate lives full of steamy romance. However, novels and films of the period can be misleading.

Women certainly did watch such films, in great numbers. But there is no evidence that the majority of women began to copy what they saw in the 1920s. In fact the evidence suggests that the reaction of many women was one of opposition and outrage. There was a strong conservative element in American society. A combination of traditional religion and old country values kept most American women in a much more restricted role than young urban women enjoyed.

SOURCE **34**

It is wholly confusing to read the advertisements in the magazines that feature the enticing qualities of vacuum cleaners, mechanical refrigerators and hundreds of other devices which should lighten the chores of women in the home. On the whole these large middle classes do their own housework with few of the mechanical aids . . .

Women who live on farms – and they form the largest group in the United States – do a great deal of work besides the labour of caring for their children, washing the clothes, caring for the home and cooking . . . thousands still labour in the fields . . . help milk the cows . . .

The other largest group of American women comprises the families of the labourers . . . of the miners, the steel workers . . . the vast army of unskilled, semi-skilled and skilled workers. The wages of these men are on the whole so small [that] wives must do double duty – that is, caring for the children and the home and toil on the outside as wage earners.

Doris E Fleischman, *America as Americans See It*, FJ Ringel (ed.), 1932.

Profile

Eleanor Roosevelt

➤ Born 1884 into a wealthy family.
➤ Married Franklin D Roosevelt in 1905.
➤ Heavily involved in:
  – League of Women Voters
  – Women's Trade Union League
  – Women's City Club (New York)
  – New York State Democratic Party (Women's Division).
➤ Work concentrated on:
  – bringing New York Democrats together
  – public housing for low-income workers
  – birth control information
  – better conditions for women workers.

SOURCE **35**

Though a few young upper middle-class women in the cities talked about throwing off the older conventions – they were the flappers – most women stuck to more traditional attitudes concerning 'their place' . . . most middle-class women concentrated on managing the home . . . Their daughters, far from taking to the streets against sexual discrimination, were more likely to prepare for careers as mothers and housewives. Millions of immigrant women and their daughters . . . also clung to traditions that placed men firmly in control of the family . . . Most American women concentrated on making ends meet or setting aside money to purchase the new gadgets that offered some release from household drudgery.

JT Patterson, *America in the Twentieth Century*, 1999.

Focus Task

Did the role of women change in the 1920s?

It's the Roaring Twenties – life's one big party!

It might be roaring for you, but life's more of a miaow for me!

Work in pairs. Write a script for a story strip to complete this conversation. You will need at least seven more scenes with speech bubbles.

3 How does Source 35 contrast with the image of women given by Sources 32 and 33?

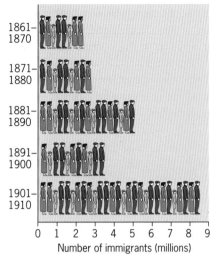

1861–1870

1871–1880

1881–1890

1891–1900

1901–1910

0 1 2 3 4 5 6 7 8 9
Number of immigrants (millions)

Immigration to the USA, 1861–1910.

Prejudice and intolerance

At the same time as some young Americans were experiencing liberation, others were facing intolerance and racism.

The vast majority of Americans were either immigrants or descendants of recent immigrants. Source 37 shows you the ethnic background of the main groups.

As you can see from Source 36, immigration to the USA was at an all-time high from 1901 to 1910. Immigrants were flooding in, particularly Jews from eastern Europe and Russia who were fleeing persecution, and people from Italy who were fleeing poverty. Many Italian immigrants did not intend to settle in the USA, but hoped to make money to take back to their families in Italy.

The United States had always prided itself on being a 'melting pot'. In theory, individual groups lost their ethnic identity and blended together with other groups to become just 'Americans'. In practice, however, this wasn't always the case. In the USA's big cities the more established immigrant groups – Irish Americans, French Canadians and German Americans – competed for the best jobs and the best available housing. These groups tended to look down on the more recent eastern European and Italian immigrants. These in turn had nothing but contempt for African Americans and Mexicans, who were almost at the bottom of the scale.

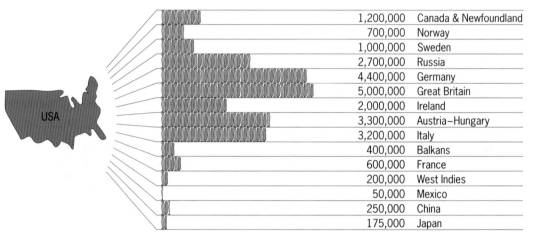

1,200,000	Canada & Newfoundland
700,000	Norway
1,000,000	Sweden
2,700,000	Russia
4,400,000	Germany
5,000,000	Great Britain
2,000,000	Ireland
3,300,000	Austria–Hungary
3,200,000	Italy
400,000	Balkans
600,000	France
200,000	West Indies
50,000	Mexico
250,000	China
175,000	Japan

The ethnic background of Americans.

Italians were reluctant to live alongside people with darker skins and tended to class Mexicans with Negroes. A social worker noted, however, that newly arrived Italians got on well with Mexicans; only after they had been in the United States for some time did they refuse to associate with them. 'In Italy', he said to one Italian, 'you would not be prejudiced against the Mexicans because of their colour.' The reply was 'No, but we are becoming Americanised.'

Maldwyn Jones argues in *Destination America* (published in 1985) that in many ways racist attitudes were more firmly entrenched in America than they had been in Europe.

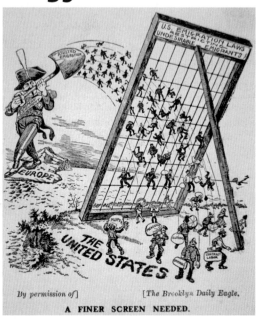

A cartoon from 1904.

SOURCE 40

The blaze of revolution is eating its way into the homes of the American workman, licking at the altars of the churches, leaping into the belfry of the school house, crawling into the sacred corners of American homes, seeking to replace the marriage vows with libertine laws, burning up the foundations of society.

Mitchell Palmer, US Attorney General, speaking in 1920.

SOURCE 41

The steamship companies haul them over to America and as soon as they step off the ships the problem of the steamship companies is settled, but our problem has only begun – Bolshevism, red anarchy, black-handers and kidnappers, challenging the authority and integrity of our flag . . . Thousands come here who will never take the oath to support our constitution and become citizens of the USA. They pay allegiance to some other country while they live upon the substance of our own. They fill places that belong to the wage earning citizens of America . . . They are of no service whatever to our people . . . They constitute a menace and a danger to us every day.

Republican Senator Heflin speaking in 1921 in a debate over whether to limit immigration.

---

1 Look at Sources 40–42. Do they tell historians more about Communists or the enemies of Communism? Explain your answer.

Activity

Work in pairs.
1 One of you collect evidence to show that the Red Scare was the result of fear of Communism.
2 The other collect evidence to show that the Red Scare was the result of prejudice and intolerance.
3 Now try to come up with a definition of the Red Scare that combines both of your views.

The Red Scare

In the 1920s these racist attitudes towards immigrants were made worse by an increased fear of Bolshevism or Communism. The USA watched with alarm as Russia became Communist after the Russian Revolution of 1917 (see pages 314–16). It feared that many of the more recent immigrants from eastern Europe and Russia were bringing similar radical ideas with them to the USA. This reaction was called the Red Scare.

In 1919 Americans saw evidence all around them to confirm their fears. There was a wave of disturbances. Some 400,000 American workers went on strike. Even the police in Boston went on strike and looters and thieves roamed the city. There were race riots in 25 towns.

Today, most historians argue that the strikes were caused by economic hardship. High levels of wartime production were being scaled down – so fewer workers were needed. Most strikers were poorly paid labourers in heavy industry who had been taken on for wartime contracts and then laid off. Many were immigrant workers, since they were usually the first to lose their jobs. Other workers were simply striking for improvements in low pay and appalling working conditions.

However, many prominent Americans in the 1920s saw the strikes as the dangerous signs of Communist interference. Communism meant state control of agriculture and industry, taking it away from its owners, which alarmed Americans. Fear of Communism combined with prejudice against immigrants was a powerful mix.

SOURCE 42

Robert Minor
Apr 26, 1924

A 1924 cartoon showing attitudes to Communism in the USA.

The fears were not totally unjustified. Many immigrants in the USA did hold radical political beliefs. Anarchists published pamphlets and distributed them widely in American cities, calling for the overthrow of the government. In April 1919 a bomb planted in a church in Milwaukee killed ten people. In May, bombs were posted to 36 prominent Americans. In June more bombs went off in seven US cities, and one almost succeeded in killing Mitchell Palmer, the US Attorney General. All those known to have radical political beliefs were rounded up. They were generally immigrants and the evidence against them was often flimsy. The person responsible for this purge was J Edgar Hoover, a young clerk appointed by Palmer. Hoover was to become an immensely important and deeply sinister figure in US history (see page 374). He built up files on 60,000 suspects and in 1919–20 around 10,000 individuals were informed that they were to be deported from the USA.

As Palmer discovered that these purges were popular, he tried to use the fear of revolution to build up his own political support and run for president. Trade unionists, African Americans, Jews, Catholics and almost all minority groups found themselves accused of being Communists. In the end, however, Palmer caused his own downfall. He predicted that a Red Revolution would begin in May 1920. When nothing happened, the papers began to make fun of him and officials in the Justice Department who were sickened by Palmer's actions undermined him. Secretary of Labor Louis Post examined all of the case files prepared by Hoover and found that only 556 out of the thousands of cases brought had any basis in fact.

1 Look again at Sources 38 and 42 on pages 356–57. What problems are associated with immigration?
2 How do you think a supporter of Sacco and Vanzetti would reply to Source 42?
3 Do you think that the US immigration policy was racist? Explain your answer.

Sacco and Vanzetti

Two high-profile victims of the Red Scare were Italian Americans Nicola Sacco and Bartolomeo Vanzetti. They were arrested in 1920 on suspicion of armed robbery and murder. It quickly emerged that they were self-confessed anarchists. Anarchists hated the American system of government and believed in destroying it by creating social disorder. Their trial became less a trial for murder, more a trial of their radical ideas. The case against them was very shaky. The prosecution relied heavily on racist slurs about their Italian origins, and on stirring up fears about their radical beliefs. The judge at the trial said that although Vanzetti 'may not actually have committed the crime attributed to him he is nevertheless morally culpable [to blame] because he is the enemy of our existing institutions'. After the trial, the judge referred to the two as 'those anarchist bastards'.

Sacco and Vanzetti were convicted on flimsy evidence. Explaining the verdict, a leading lawyer of the time said: 'Judge Thayer is narrow minded . . . unintelligent . . . full of prejudice. He has been carried away by fear of Reds which has captured about 90 per cent of the American people.' After six years of legal appeals, Sacco and Vanzetti were eventually executed in 1927, to a storm of protest around the world from both radicals and moderates who saw how unjustly the trial had been conducted.

SOURCE 43

Therefore, I, Michael S Dukakis, Governor of the Commonwealth of Massachusetts . . . hereby proclaim Tuesday, August 23, 1977, Nicola Sacco and Bartolomeo Vanzetti Memorial Day and declare, further, that any stigma and disgrace should be forever removed from the names of Nicola Sacco and Bartolomeo Vanzetti, from the names of their families and descendants, and so . . . call upon all the people of Massachusetts to pause in their daily endeavours to reflect upon these tragic events, and draw from their historic lessons the resolve to prevent the forces of intolerance, fear, and hatred from ever again uniting to overcome the rationality, wisdom, and fairness to which our legal system aspires.

Part of a proclamation by the Governor of Massachusetts, Michael Dukakis, 50 years after the execution of Sacco and Vanzetti.

SOURCE 44

A protest against the execution of Sacco and Vanzetti in 1927.

Activity

Make or design a poster to be displayed in the immigrant reception area on Ellis Island, New York. It should either:
a) warn immigrants of the problems they might face in the USA, or
b) encourage them to see the opportunities that America offers to immigrants.

Immigration quotas

In 1924, in direct response to its fear of radicals, the government took action. It restricted immigration. It introduced a system that ensured that the largest proportion of immigrants was from north-west Europe (mainly British, Irish and German) and that limited immigration from southern and eastern Europe. From a high point of more than a million immigrants a year between 1901 and 1910, by 1929 the number arriving in the USA had fallen to 150,000 per year.

The experience of African Americans

African Americans had long been part of America's history. The first Africans had been brought to the USA as slaves by white settlers in the seventeenth century. By the time slavery was ended in the nineteenth century, there were more African Americans than white people in the southern United States. White governments, fearing the power of African Americans, introduced many laws to control their freedom. They could not vote. They were denied access to good jobs and to worthwhile education, and well into the twentieth century they suffered great poverty.

The Ku Klux Klan

The Ku Klux Klan was a white supremacy movement. It used violence to intimidate African Americans. It had been in decline, but was revived after the release of the film *The Birth of a Nation* in 1915. The film was set in the 1860s, just after the Civil War. It glorified the Klan as defenders of decent American values against renegade African Americans and corrupt white businessmen. President Wilson had it shown in the White House. He said: 'It is like writing history with lightning. And my only regret is that it is all so terribly true.' With such support from prominent figures, the Klan became a powerful political force in the early 1920s.

SOURCE 45

A lad whipped with branches until his back was ribboned flesh . . . a white girl, divorcee, beaten into unconsciousness in her home; a naturalised foreigner flogged until his back was pulp because he married an American woman; a negro lashed until he sold his land to a white man for a fraction of its value.

RA Patton, writing in *Current History* in 1929, describes the victims of Klan violence in Alabama.

African Americans throughout the south faced fierce racism. Source 46 gives you one example. In 1930 James Cameron, aged 16, had been arrested, with two other African American men, on suspicion of the murder of a white man, and the rape of a white woman. The writer survived this attempt to lynch him (hang him without a trial: see Source 47). In his book he vividly describes the fury of the white racists.

SOURCE 46

Little did I dream that one night I would fall into the hands of such a merciless mob of fanatics, that they would attempt to execute me because of the color of my skin. This whole way of life was – and is – a heritage of black slavery in America.

A huge and angry mob were demanding from the sheriff 'those three niggers'. They had gathered from all over the state of Indiana. Ten to fifteen thousand of them at least, against three. Many in the crowd wore the headdress of the Ku Klux Klan.

[The mob broke down the door of the jail, and beat and then hanged his two friends. Source 47 shows you the scene that greeted Cameron as he was dragged out of the jail for his turn.]

The cruel hands that held me were vicelike. Fists, clubs, bricks and rocks found their marks on my body. The weaker ones had to be content with spitting. Little boys and little girls not yet in their teens, but being taught how to treat black people, somehow managed to work their way in close enough to bite and scratch me on the legs.

And over the thunderous din rose the shout of 'Nigger! Nigger! Nigger!'

[Cameron did not know what saved him. The crowd had the rope round his neck before they suddenly stopped and let him limp back to the door of the jail. He called it 'a miraculous intervention'.]

James Cameron, *A Time of Terror*, 1982.

The Ku Klux Klan

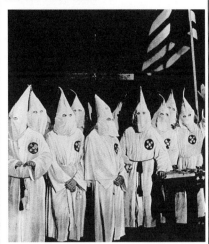

➤ Formed in the 1850s by former soldiers after the American Civil War with the aim of keeping whites in control.

➤ It used parades, beatings, lynchings and other violent methods to intimidate African Americans. It also attacked Jews, Catholics and foreign immigrants.

➤ It was strongest in the midwest and rural south, where working-class whites competed with African Americans for unskilled jobs.

➤ It declined in the late nineteenth century but was started up again in 1915. It spread rapidly in the early 1920s, managing to get Klansmen elected into positions of political power.

➤ By 1924 it had 4.5 million members.

➤ Oregon and Oklahoma had governors who belonged to the Klan. The Klan was especially dominant in Indiana.

➤ The Klan declined after 1925. One of its leaders, Grand Wizard David Stephenson, was convicted of a vicious sexually motivated murder. He turned informer and the corruption of the Klan became common knowledge.

---

4 What does Source 45 tell you about the motives of Klan violence?

5 Explain why the Klan became so powerful.

SOURCE **47**

The scene outside the jail in Marion, Indiana. Abram Smith and Thomas Shipp have already been lynched.

Paul Robeson

➤ Born 1898, son of a church minister who had been a former slave.
➤ Went to Columbia University and passed his law exams with honours in 1923.
➤ As a black lawyer, it was almost impossible for him to find work, so he became an actor – his big break was in the hit musical 'Showboat'.
➤ Visited Moscow in 1934 on a world tour and declared his approval of Communism saying 'Here, for the first time in my life, I walk in dignity.'
➤ As a Communist sympathiser, Robeson suffered in the USA – he was banned from performing, suffered death threats and had his passport confiscated.
➤ He left the USA in 1958 to live in Europe, but returned in 1963.

Activity

Read the profile of Paul Robeson. Imagine you are interviewing him on the radio. Write three questions you'd like to ask him.

Cameron's experience was not unusual. Thousands of African Americans were murdered by lynching in this period. Many reports describe appalling atrocities at which whole families, including young children, clapped and cheered. It is one of the most shameful aspects of the USA at this time.

Faced by such intimidation, discrimination and poverty, many African Americans left the rural south and moved to the cities of the northern USA. Through the 1920s the African American population of both Chicago and New York doubled: New York's from 150,000 to 330,000 and Chicago's from 110,000 to 230,000.

Improvements

In the north, African Americans had a better chance of getting good jobs and a good education. For example, Howard University was an exclusively African American institution for higher education.

In both Chicago and New York, there was a small but growing African American middle class. There was a successful 'black capitalist' movement, encouraging African Americans to set up businesses. In Chicago they ran a successful boycott of the city's chain stores, protesting that they would not shop there unless African American staff were employed. By 1930 almost all the shops in the South Side belt where African Americans lived had black employees.

There were internationally famous African Americans, such as the singer and actor Paul Robeson (see Profile). The popularity of jazz made many African American musicians into high-profile media figures. The African American neighbourhood of Harlem in New York became the centre of the Harlem Renaissance. Here musicians and singers made Harlem a centre of creativity and a magnet for white customers in the bars and clubs. African American artists flourished in this atmosphere, as did African American writers. The poet Langston Hughes wrote about the lives of ordinary working-class African Americans and the poverty and problems they suffered. Countee Cullen was another prominent poet who tried to tackle racism and poverty. In one famous poem ('For A Lady I Know') he tried to sum up attitudes of wealthy white employees to their African American servants:

> She even thinks that up in heaven
> Her class lies late and snores
> While poor black cherubs rise at seven
> To do celestial chores.

African Americans also entered politics. WEB DuBois founded the National Association for the Advancement of Colored People (NAACP). In 1919 it had 300 branches and around 90,000 members. It campaigned to end racial segregation laws and to get laws passed against lynching. It did not make much headway at the time, but the numbers of lynchings did fall.

Another important figure was Marcus Garvey. He founded the Universal Negro Improvement Association (UNIA). Garvey urged African Americans to be proud of their race and colour. He instituted an honours system for African Americans (like the British Empire's honours system of knighthoods). The UNIA helped African Americans to set up their own businesses. By the mid 1920s there were UNIA grocery stores, laundries, restaurants and even a printing workshop.

Garvey set up a shipping line to support both the UNIA businesses and also his scheme of helping African Americans to emigrate to Africa away from white racism. Eventually, his businesses collapsed, partly because he was prosecuted for exaggerating the value of his shares. He was one of very few businessmen to be charged for this offence, and some historians believe that J Edgar Hoover was behind the prosecution. Garvey's movement attracted over 1 million members at its height in 1921. One of these was the Reverend Earl Little. He was beaten to death by Klan thugs in the late 1920s, but his son went on to be the civil rights leader Malcolm X.

Problems

Although important, these movements failed to change the USA dramatically. Life expectancy for African Americans increased from 45 to 48 between 1900 and 1930, but they were still a long way behind the whites, whose life expectancy increased from 54 to 59 over the same period. Many African Americans in the northern cities lived in great poverty. In Harlem in New York they lived in poorer housing than whites, yet paid higher rents. They had poorer education and health services than whites.

In Chicago African Americans suffered great prejudice from longer-established white residents. If they attempted to move out of the African American belt to adjacent neighbourhoods, they got a hostile reception (see Source 50).

SOURCE 48

If I die in Atlanta my work shall only then begin . . . Look for me in the whirlwind or the storm, look for me all around you, for, with God's grace, I shall come and bring with me countless millions of black slaves who have died in America and the West Indies and the millions in Africa to aid you in the fight for Liberty, Freedom and Life.

Marcus Garvey's last word's before going to jail in 1925.

SOURCE 49

Marcus Garvey after his arrest.

SOURCE 50

There is nothing in the make up of a negro, physically or mentally, that should induce anyone to welcome him as a neighbour. The best of them are unsanitary . . . ruin follows in their path. They are as proud as peacocks, but have nothing of the peacock's beauty . . . Niggers are undesirable neighbours and entirely irresponsible and vicious.

From the *Chicago Property Owners' Journal*, 1920.

They got a similarly hostile reception from poor whites. In Chicago when African Americans attempted to use parks, playgrounds and beaches in the Irish and Polish districts, they were set upon by gangs of whites calling themselves 'athletic clubs'. The result was that African American communities in northern areas often became isolated ghettos.

Within the African American communities prejudice was also evident. Middle-class African Americans who were restless in the ghettos tended to blame newly arrived migrants from the south for intensifying white racism. In Harlem, the presence of some 50,000 West Indians was a source of inter-racial tension. Many of them were better educated, more militant and prouder of their colour than the newly arrived African Americans from the south.

Activity

James Cameron, who wrote Source 46 on page 359 went on to found America's Black Holocaust Museum, which records the suffering of black African Americans through American history.

Write a 100-word summary for the museum handbook of the ways in which the 1920s were a time of change for African Americans.

'The vanishing Americans'

The native Americans were the original settlers of the North American continent. They almost disappeared as an ethnic group during the rapid expansion of the USA during the nineteenth century – declining from 1.5 million to around 250,000 in 1920. Those who survived or who chose not to leave their traditional way of life were forced to move to reservations in the mid-west.

SOURCE **51**

Photograph of a native American, Charlie Guardipee, and his family taken for a US government report of 1921. According to the report Charlie Guardipee had twenty horses, ten cattle, no chickens, no wheat, oats or garden, and no sickness in the family.

SOURCE **52**

A scene from the 1925 film *The Vanishing American*. This film was made by Paramount, a big Hollywood studio. It was extremely unusual for its time in having a native American hero – Nophaie, a Navajo warrior who tried to adapt his people's traditional ways to live in peace with the white man. The drama in the film came from an evil and corrupt government agent who managed to stir up a native American revolt which the warrior tried to prevent.

In the 1920s the government became concerned about the treatment of native Americans. Twelve thousand had served in the armed forces in the First World War, which helped to change white attitudes to them. The government did a census in the 1920s and a major survey in the late 1920s which revealed that most lived in extreme poverty, with much lower life expectancy than whites, that they were in worse health and had poorer education and poorly paid jobs (if they were able to get a job at all). They suffered extreme discrimination. They were quickly losing their land. Mining companies were legally able to seize large areas of native American land. Many native Americans who owned land were giving up the struggle to survive in their traditional way and selling up.

They were also losing their culture. Their children were sent to special boarding schools. The aim of the schools was to 'assimilate' them into white American culture. This involved trying to destroy the native Americans' beliefs, traditions, dances and languages. In the 1920s the native Americans were referred to as 'the vanishing Americans'.

However, the 1920s were in some ways a turning point. In 1924 native Americans were granted US citizenship and allowed to vote for the first time. In 1928 the Merriam Report proposed widespread improvement to the laws relating to native Americans, and these reforms were finally introduced under Roosevelt's New Deal in 1934.

SOURCE **53**

. . . for nearly two hours . . . Mr Darrow [lawyer for the defendant] goaded his opponent. [He] asked Mr Bryan if he really believed that the serpent had always crawled on its belly because it tempted Eve, and if he believed Eve was made from Adam's rib . . .

[Bryan's] face flushed under Mr Darrow's searching words, and . . . when one [question] stumped him he took refuge in his faith and either refused to answer directly or said in effect: 'The Bible states it; it must be so.'

From the report of the Monkey Trial in the *Baltimore Evening Sun*, July 1925.

2 Why do you think the trial became known as the Monkey Trial?
3 In what ways did the trial show American intolerance of other points of view?

Activity

The Monkey Trial attracted considerable media attention.
   Draw up an anti-evolution leaflet, to be handed out to journalists at the trial, explaining the views of Fundamentalists. Make your leaflet as convincing as possible. Explain:
a) why you think the theory of evolution is wrong
b) why you think its teaching should be banned.

Focus Task A

How far was American society changing in the 1920s?

At the end of the First World War, one young man said of his war experience: 'The lad from the north was the pal of the lad from the south. Acquaintance meant friendship and what will this friendship mean to America when we return? New bonds will draw us together . . . and the fabric of the nation will be strengthened.'
   As this man looked back in 1929, what comments do you think he might have made about the USA in the 1920s? In your answer you should refer to:
◆ the economic successes of the USA
◆ the economic divisions within the USA
◆ the cultural and social changes of the 1920s
◆ the darker side of the USA in the 1920s.

The Monkey Trial

While the Sacco and Vanzetti trial became a public demonstration of anti-immigrant feelings, another trial in the 1920s – the Monkey Trial – became the focus of ill-feeling between rural and urban USA.

Most urban people in the 1920s would have believed in Charles Darwin's theory of evolution. This said that over millions of years human beings evolved from ape-like ancestors.

Many rural Americans, however, disagreed. They were very religious people. They were mostly Protestants. They went to church regularly and believed in the Bible. When the Bible told them that God made the world in six days, and that on the sixth day He created human beings to be like Him, they took the teachings literally. People with these views were known as Fundamentalists. They were particularly strong in the 'Bible Belt' states such as Tennessee.

At school, however, even in these states, most children were taught evolution. Fundamentalists felt that this was undermining their own religion. It seemed to be yet another example of the USA's abandoning traditional values in the headlong rush to modernise in the 1920s. They decided to roll back the modern ideas and so, in six states, the Fundamentalists led by William Jennings Bryan managed to pass a law banning the teaching of 'evolution'.

A biology teacher called John Scopes deliberately broke the law so that he could be arrested and put his case against Fundamentalism in the courts. The best lawyers were brought in for both sides and in July 1925, in the stifling heat of a Tennessee courtroom, the USA's traditionalists joined battle with its modernists.

The trial captured public imagination and the arguments on both sides were widely reported in the press. Scopes was convicted of breaking the law, but it was really American Fundamentalism itself which was on trial – and it lost! At the trial the anti-evolutionists were subjected to great mockery. Their arguments were publicly ridiculed and their spokesman Bryan, who claimed to be an expert on religion and science, was shown to be ignorant and confused. After the trial, the anti-evolution lobby was weakened.

SOURCE **54**

John Scopes (seated second from the right) surrounded by his lawyers.

Focus Task B

How widespread was intolerance in the 1920s?

You have looked at various examples of intolerance and prejudice in the 1920s. Draw up a chart like this, and fill it in to summarise the various examples.

Group	How did prejudice or intolerance affect them?	How did they react?

Prohibition – did the Americans make a mistake?

Why was prohibition introduced?

In the nineteenth century, in rural areas of the USA there was a very strong 'temperance' movement. Members of temperance movements agreed not to drink alcohol and also campaigned to get others to give up alcohol. Most members of these movements were devout Christians who saw what damage alcohol did to family life. They wanted to stop that damage.

In the nineteenth century the two main movements were the Anti-Saloon League and the Women's Christian Temperance Union (see Sources 55 and 56).

SOURCE 55

A poster issued by the Anti-Saloon League in 1915.

SOURCE 56

A poster issued by the Women's Christian Temperance Union.

SOURCE 57

Our nation can only be saved by turning the pure stream of country sentiment and township morals to flush out the cesspools of cities and so save civilisation from pollution.

A temperance campaigner speaking in 1917.

1. Look at Sources 55 and 56. What do you think the aim of each one is?
2. What is wrong with alcohol according to these sources?
3. Prohibition did not actually make it illegal to drink alcohol. Why not?
4. List all the reasons why prohibition was introduced.
5. Do you think prohibition sounds like a good idea?

The temperance movements were so strong in some of the rural areas that they persuaded their state governments to prohibit the sale of alcohol within the state. Through the early twentieth century the campaign gathered pace. It became a national campaign to prohibit (ban) alcohol throughout the country. It acquired some very powerful supporters. Leading industrialists backed the movement, believing that workers would be more reliable if they did not drink. Politicians backed it because it got them votes in rural areas. By 1916, 21 states had banned saloons.

Supporters of prohibition became known as 'dries'. The dries brought some powerful arguments to their case. They claimed that '3000 infants are smothered yearly in bed, by drunken parents.' The USA's entry into the First World War in 1917 boosted the dries. Drinkers were accused of being unpatriotic cowards. Most of the big breweries were run by German immigrants who were portrayed as the enemy. Drink was linked to other evils as well. After the Russian Revolution, the dries claimed that Bolshevism thrived on drink and that alcohol led to lawlessness in the cities, particularly in immigrant communities. Saloons were seen as dens of vice that destroyed family life. The campaign became one of country values against city values.

In 1917 the movement had enough states on its side to propose the Eighteenth Amendment to the Constitution. This 'prohibited the manufacture, sale or transportation of intoxicating liquors'. It became law in January 1920 and is known as the Volstead Act.

SOURCE 58

35.0
30.0
25.0
20.0
15.0
10.0
5.0
0.0

Gallons of alcohol

1905 1910 1915 1920 1925 1930 1935 1940

Key
— Beer
— Spirits

Period of prohibition

Average alcohol consumption (in US gallons) per year of Americans, 1905–40.

How was prohibition enforced?

SOURCE 59

	1921	*1925*	*1929*
Illegal distilleries seized	*9,746*	*12,023*	*15,794*
Gallons (US) of spirit seized	*414,000*	*11,030,000*	*11,860,000*
Arrests	*34,175*	*62,747*	*66,878*

Activities of federal prohibition agents.

Prohibition lasted from 1920 until 1933. It is often said that prohibition was a total failure. This is not entirely correct. Levels of alcohol consumption fell by about 30 per cent in the early 1920s (see Source 58). Prohibition gained widespread approval in some states, particularly the rural areas in the mid-west, although in urban states it was not popular (Maryland never even introduced prohibition). The government ran information campaigns and prohibition agents arrested offenders (see Source 59). Two of the most famous agents were Isadore Einstein and his deputy Moe Smith. They made 4,392 arrests. Their raids were always low key. They would enter speakeasies (illegal bars) and simply order a drink. Einstein had a special flask hidden inside his waistcoat with a funnel attached. He preserved the evidence by pouring his drink down the funnel and the criminals were caught!

SOURCE 60

Alcohol being tipped down the drain. Vast quantities of bootleg (illegal) liquor were seized, but were only a fraction of the total.

SOURCE 61

Prohibition agents Isadore Einstein and Moe Smith (usually known as Izzy and Moe). They were so successful that speakeasies actually put up posters warning people to watch out for these men.

Supply and demand

Despite the work of the agents, prohibition proved impossible to enforce effectively in the cities. Enforcement was underfinanced. There were not enough agents – each agent was poorly paid and was responsible for a huge area. By far the biggest drawback was that millions of Americans, particularly in urban areas, were simply not prepared to obey this law. So bootleggers (suppliers of illegal alcohol) made vast fortunes. Al Capone (see page 367) made around $60 million a year from his speakeasies. His view was that 'Prohibition is a business. All I do is supply a public demand.' And the demand was huge. By 1925 there were more speakeasies in American cities than there had been saloons in 1919. Izzy Einstein filed a report to his superiors on how easy it was to find alcohol after arriving in a new city. Here are the results:

- Chicago: 21 minutes
- Atlanta: 17 minutes
- Pittsburg: 11 minutes
- New Orleans: 35 seconds (he was offered a bottle of whisky by his taxi driver when he asked where he could get a drink!)

6 Which of Sources 58–61 is the most useful to the historian, or are they more useful when taken together? Explain your answer.

7 Is it possible to enforce any law when the population refuses to obey it? Try to think of laws that affect you today.

A visit to a speakeasy.

Statistics in the Detroit police court of 1924 show 7391 arrests for violations of the prohibition law, but only 458 convictions. Ten years ago a dishonest policeman was a rarity . . . Now the honest ones are pointed out as rarities . . . Their relationship with the bootleggers is perfectly friendly. They have to pinch two out of five once in a while, but they choose the ones who are least willing to pay bribes.

E Mandeville, in *Outlook* magazine, 1925.

> 1   Read Source 64. How has prohibition affected the police in Detroit?

'The National Gesture': a cartoon from the prohibition era.

An illegal still.

Illegal stills (short for distilleries) sprang up all over the USA as people made their own illegal whisky – moonshine. The stills were a major fire hazard and the alcohol they produced was frequently poisonous. Agents seized over 280,000 of these stills, but we have no clear way of knowing how many were not seized. Most Americans had no need for their own still. They simply went to their favourite speakeasy. The speakeasies were well supplied by bootleggers. About two-thirds of the illegal alcohol came from Canada. The vast border between the USA and Canada was virtually impossible to patrol. Other bootleggers brought in alcohol by sea. They would simply wait in the waters outside US control until an opportunity to land their cargo presented itself. One of the most famous was Captain McCoy, who specialised in the finest Scotch whisky. This is where the phrase 'the real McCoy' comes from.

Corruption

Prohibition led to massive corruption. Many of the law enforcement officers were themselves involved with the liquor trade. Big breweries stayed in business throughout the prohibition era. This is not an easy business to hide! But the breweries stayed in operation by bribing local government officials, prohibition agents and the police to leave them alone.

In some cities, police officers were quite prepared to direct people to speakeasies. Even when arrests were made, it was difficult to get convictions because more senior officers or even judges were in the pay of the criminals. One in twelve prohibition agents was dismissed for corruption. The New York FBI boss, Don Chaplin, once ordered his 200 agents: 'Put your hands on the table, both of them. Every son of a bitch wearing a diamond is fired.'

SOURCE 66

TIME

The Weekly Newsmagazine

Volume XV — ALPHONSE ("SCARFACE") CAPONE — Number 12
A pork apiece, a pan of spaghetti.
(See NATIONAL AFFAIRS)

Al Capone in 1930. Everyone knew of his activities, but it was impossible to convict him because of his control of the police.

---

2 Write a definition of the term 'gangster' for an encyclopaedia of American history.

Activity

In other chapters of this book, you have seen profiles of important historical figures.

Use the information and sources to produce two different profiles of Al Capone.
- The first profile is the kind of profile that might appear in this book.
- The second profile is one that might have appeared inside *Time* magazine in 1930 (Source 66).

Make sure you can explain to your teacher why the two profiles are different. These points might be useful to you:
- born in 1889 in New York
- arrived in Chicago in 1919
- took over from Johnny Torio in 1925
- jailed in 1931 for not paying taxes
- released in January 1939
- died in 1947 from syphilis.

Chicago and the gangsters

The most common image people have of the prohibition era is the gangster. Estimates suggest that organised gangs made about $2 billion out of the sale of illegal alcohol. The bootlegger George Remus certainly did well from the trade. He had a huge network of paid officials that allowed him to escape charge after charge against him. At one party he gave a car to each of the women guests, while all the men received diamond cuff links worth $25,000.

The rise of the gangsters tells us a lot about American society at this time. The gangsters generally came from immigrant backgrounds. In the early 1920s the main gangs were Jewish, Polish, Irish and Italian. Gangsters generally came from poorer backgrounds within these communities. They were often poorly educated, but they were also clever and ruthless. Dan O'Banion (Irish gang leader murdered by Capone), Pete and Vince Guizenberg (hired killers who worked for Bugsy Moran and died in the St Valentine's Day Massacre), and Lucky Luciano (Italian killer who spent ten years in prison) were some of the most powerful gangsters. The gangs fought viciously with each other to control the liquor trade and also the prostitution, gambling and protection rackets that were centred on the speakeasies. They made use of new technology, especially automobiles and the Thompson sub-machine gun, which was devastatingly powerful but could be carried around and hidden under an overcoat. In Chicago alone, there were 130 gangland murders in 1926 and 1927 and not one arrest. By the late 1920s fear and bribery made law enforcement ineffective.

The gangsters operated all over the USA, but they were most closely associated with Chicago. Perhaps the best example of the power of the gangsters is Chicago gangster boss Al Capone. He arrived in Chicago in 1919, on the run from a murder investigation in New York. He ran a drinking club for his boss Johnny Torio. In 1925 Torio retired after an assassination attempt by one of his rivals, Bugsy Moran. Capone took over and proved to be a formidable gangland boss. He built up a huge network of corrupt officials among Chicago's police, local government workers, judges, lawyers and prohibition agents. He even controlled Chicago's mayor, William Hale Thompson. Surprisingly, he was a high-profile and even popular figure in the city. He was a regular at baseball and American football games and was cheered by the crowd when he took his seat. He was well known for giving generous tips (over $100) to waiters and shop girls and spent $30,000 on a soup kitchen for the unemployed.

Capone was supported by a ruthless gang, hand picked for their loyalty to him. He killed two of his own men whom he suspected of plotting against him by beating their brains out with a baseball bat. By 1929 he had destroyed the power of the other Chicago gangs, committing at least 300 murders in the process. The peak of his violent reign came with the St Valentine's Day Massacre in 1929. Capone's men murdered seven of his rival Bugsy Moran's gang, using a false police car and two gangsters in police uniform to put Moran's men off their guard.

SOURCE 67

THREE CENTS — THE CHICAGO DAILY NEWS — BLUE STREAK

MASSACRE 7 OF MORAN GANG

HAFFA CHANGES HIS MIND; WILL FIGHT PRISON

TWO OF VICTIMS AND SCENE OF LATEST GANGSTER OUTBREAK

KILLING SCENE TOO GRUESOME FOR ONLOOKERS

VICTIMS ARE LINED AGAINST WALL; ONE VOLLEY KILLS ALL

Assassins Pose as Policemen; Flee in "Squad Car" After Fusillade; Capone Revenge for Murder of Lombardo, Officers Believe.

Newspaper headlines reporting the St Valentine's Day Massacre, 1929.

1 Why do you think the public were so distressed by the St Valentine's Day Massacre?

Why was prohibition ended?

The St Valentine's Day Massacre was a turning point. The papers screamed that the gangsters had graduated from murder to massacre. It seemed that prohibition, often called 'The Noble Experiment', had failed. It had made the USA lawless, the police corrupt and the gangsters rich and powerful. When the Wall Street Crash was followed by the Depression in the early 1930s, there were sound economic arguments for getting rid of it. Legalising alcohol would create jobs, raise tax revenue and free up resources tied up in the impossible task of enforcing prohibition. The Democrat President Franklin D Roosevelt was elected in 1932 and prohibition was repealed in December 1933.

Activity

Why did prohibition fail?

In the end prohibition failed. Here are four groups who could be blamed for the failure of prohibition.

a) the American people who carried on going to illegal speakeasies

b) the law enforcers who were corrupt and ignored the law breakers

c) the bootleggers who continued supplying and selling alcohol

d) the gangsters who controlled the trade through violence

1 For each of the above groups find evidence on pages 364–67 to show that it contributed to the failure of prohibition.
2 Say which group you think played the most important role in the failure. Explain your choice.
3 Draw a diagram to show links between the groups.

Focus Task A

Why was prohibition introduced in 1920 and then abolished in 1933?

Many people who were convinced of the case for prohibition before 1920 were equally convinced that it should be abolished in 1933.

Write two letters.
 The first should be from a supporter of prohibition to his or her Congressman in 1919 explaining why the Congressman should vote for prohibition. In your letter, explain how prohibition could help to solve problems in America.
 The second should be from the same person to the Congressman in 1933 explaining why the Congressman should vote against prohibition. In your letter, explain why prohibition has failed.

Focus Task B

Review of the 1920s

In many democracies today, governments use focus groups to help them work out policies and also to help them keep an eye on how people feel about their policies. The idea of a focus group is that the group represents a broad cross-section of society. It is 1928. President Hoover wants to create a focus group.

1 Your first task is to select for him the members of a focus group to represent American society. The group should contain a minimum of six and a maximum of twelve members. Draw up a list of possible members. They can be actual individuals (e.g. Louis Armstrong) or representative types (e.g. a Detroit car worker). You must be able to explain why you have chosen each member of the group.
2 Your second task is to think of some positive and negative issues for the group to discuss.
  a) Brainstorm the events in 1920s USA that you think a US President would be proud of.
  b) Brainstorm anything that a US President in the 1920s would prefer to keep quiet.
3 Turn these issues into a maximum of four questions for the focus group to discuss.
4 Finally, choose two contrasting members of the group and summarise how they might answer some of the questions.

13.2 The Wall Street Crash

In 1928 there was a presidential election. Herbert Hoover was the Republican candidate. Nobody doubted that the Republicans would win again. The US economy was still booming. After so much success, how could they lose? His opponent Al Smith was an Irish Catholic and a 'wet' – an opponent of prohibition – although he was a highly successful governor of New York.

Hoover did win, by a landslide, and all seemed well. One of his earliest statements as President was: 'We in America today are nearer to the final triumph over poverty than ever before … The poor man is vanishing from among us.' (See Source 24 on page 351.) When Hoover formally moved into the White House in March 1929 the mood of confidence was still there. He pointed out that Americans had more bathtubs, oil furnaces, silk stockings and bank accounts than any other country.

Six months later it was a very different picture. In October 1929 the Wall Street stock market crashed, the American economy collapsed, and the USA entered a long depression that destroyed much of the prosperity of the 1920s.

You are going to investigate what went wrong. Some say that Hoover and the Republicans should have seen what was coming and done something about it. (You have studied some of the USA's economic weaknesses in 13.1.) Others say that at the time no one could really have known how great the problem was or what to do about it. See what you think.

What caused the Wall Street Crash?

To understand the Wall Street Crash you first need to understand how the stock market is supposed to work (see Factfile).

Speculation

You can see that investment on the stock market would be quite attractive during an economic boom. The American economy was doing well throughout the 1920s. Because the economy kept doing well, there were more share buyers than sellers and the value of shares rose (see Source 1).

It seemed to many Americans that the stock market was an easy and quick way to get rich. Anyone could buy shares, watch their value rise and then sell the shares later at a higher price. Many Americans decided to join the stock market. In 1920 there had been only 4 million share owners in America. By 1929 there were 20 million, out of a population of 120 million (although only about 1.5 million were big investors).

Around 600,000 new investors were speculators. Speculation is a form of gambling. Speculators don't intend to keep their shares for long. They borrow money to buy some shares, then sell them again as soon as the price has risen. They pay off their loan and still have a quick profit to show for it. In the 1920s speculators didn't even have to pay the full value of the shares. They could buy 'on the margin', which meant they only had to put down 10 per cent of the cash needed to buy shares and could borrow the rest. Women became heavily involved in speculation. Women speculators owned over 50 per cent of the Pennsylvania Railroad, which became known as the 'petticoat line'. It was not only individuals who speculated. Banks themselves got involved in speculation. And certainly they did nothing to hold it back. American banks lent $9 billion for speculating in 1929.

Through most of the 1920s the rise in share prices was quite steady. There were even some downturns. But in 1928 speculation really took hold. Demand for shares was at an all-time high, and prices were rising at an unheard-of rate. In March, Union Carbide shares stood at $145. By September 1928 they had risen to $413.

One vital ingredient in all this is confidence. If people are confident that prices will keep rising, there will be more buyers than sellers. However, if they think prices might stop rising, all of a sudden there will be more sellers and … crash, the whole structure will come down. This is exactly what happened in 1929.

SOURCE 1

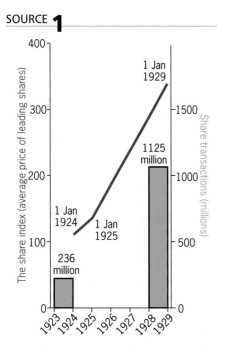

The average price (dollars) of leading shares, and share transactions, 1923–29.

The stock market hysteria reached its apex that year [1929] . . . Everyone was playing the market . . . On my last day in New York, I went down to the barber. As he removed the sheet he said softly, 'Buy Standard Gas. I've doubled . . . It's good for another double.' As I walked upstairs, I reflected that if the hysteria had reached the barber level, something must soon happen.

Cecil Roberts, *The Bright Twenties*, 1938.

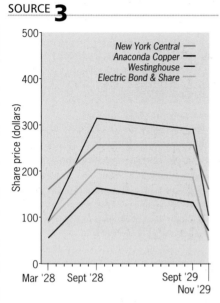

Selected share prices, 1928–29.

Legend:
New York Central
Anaconda Copper
Westinghouse
Electric Bond & Share

Weaknesses in the US economy

The construction industry (one of the leading signs of health in any economy) had actually started its downturn as far back as 1926. You have already seen how farming was in trouble in the 1920s. You have also seen the decline in coal, textile and other traditional trades. There were other concerns, such as the unequal distribution of wealth and the precarious state of some banks. In the decade before the Crash, over 500 banks had failed each year. These were mainly small banks who lent too much.

By 1929 other sectors of the economy were showing signs of strain after the boom years of the 1920s. The boom was based on the increased sale of consumer goods such as cars and electrical appliances. There were signs that American industries were producing more of these goods than they could sell. The market for these goods was largely the rich and the middle classes. By 1929 those who could afford consumer goods had already bought them. The majority of Americans who were poor could not afford to buy them, even on the generous hire purchase and credit schemes on offer.

Companies tried high-pressure advertising. In 1929 American industry spent a staggering $3 billion on magazine advertising. But with workers' wages not rising and prices not falling, demand decreased.

In the past, American industry would have tried to export its surplus goods. But people in Europe could not afford American goods either. In addition, after nine years of American tariffs, Europe had put up its own tariffs to protect its industries.

By the summer of 1929 these weaknesses were beginning to show. Even car sales were slowing, and in June 1929 the official figures for industrial output showed a fall for the first time for four years. Speculators on the American stock exchange became nervous about the value of their shares and began to sell.

As you can see from the Factfile, the slide in share values started slowly. But throughout September and October it gathered pace. Many investors had borrowed money to buy their shares and could not afford to be stuck with shares worth less than the value of their loan. Soon other investors sold their shares and within days panic set in. On Tuesday 29 October 1929 it became clear to the speculators that the banks were not going to intervene to support the price of shares, and so Wall Street had its busiest and its worst day in history as speculators desperately tried to dump 13 million shares at a fraction of the price they had paid for them.

Factfile

The Wall Street Crash, 1929

➤ **June** Factory output starts declining. Steel production starts declining.
➤ **3 Sept** The hottest day of the year. The last day of rising prices.
➤ **5 Sept** 'The Babson Break': Roger Babson, economic forecaster, says 'Sooner or later a crash is coming and it may be terrific.' The index of share prices drops ten points.
➤ **6 Sept** Market recovers.
➤ **Mon 21 Oct** Busy trading. Much selling. So much trading that the 'ticker' which tells people of changes in price falls behind by $1\frac{1}{2}$ hours. Some people don't know they are ruined until after the exchange closes. By then it is too late to do anything about it.
➤ **Thu 24 Oct** Busiest trading yet. Big falls. Banks intervene to buy stock. Confidence returns. Prices stabilise.
➤ **Mon 28 Oct** Massive fall. Index loses 43 points. It is clear that the banks have stopped supporting share prices.
➤ **Tue 29 Oct** Massive fall. People sell for whatever they can get.

Focus Task

How far was speculation responsible for the Wall Street Crash?

Work in groups.
1 Here are five factors that led to the Wall Street Crash. For each one explain how it helped to cause the Crash:
   ◆ poor distribution of income between rich and poor
   ◆ overproduction by American industries
   ◆ the actions of speculators
   ◆ no export market for US goods
   ◆ decision by the banks not to support share prices.
2 If you think other factors are also important, add them to your list and explain why they helped to cause the Crash.
3 Decide whether there is one factor that is more important than any of the others. Explain your choice.

SOURCE 4

- *The Vanderbilt family lost $40 million.*
- *Rockefeller lost 80 per cent of his wealth – but he still had $40 million left.*
- *The British politician Winston Churchill lost $500,000.*
- *The singer Fanny Brice lost $500,000.*
- *Groucho and Harpo Marx (two of the Marx Brothers comedy team) lost $240,000 each.*

Major losers in the crash.

---

1 Look at Source 5. Do you think the cartoonist is sympathetic or critical of the man on the bench? Explain your opinion.

SOURCE 5

A cartoon by American cartoonist John McCutcheon, 1932. The man on the bench has lost all his savings because of a bank failure.

Focus Task

What impact did the crash have on the American economy?

1 Draw a diagram to show how the following were connected to each other:
   - the Wall Street Crash
   - the banking crisis
   - reduced spending
   - unemployment.

Research Task

2 On page 353 you investigated various features of the boom. Try to find out from your own research what happened between 1929 and 1933 to at least two of the industries or activities covered on pages 347–48 and 352–53.

The consequences of the Wall Street Crash

At first, it was not clear what the impact of the Crash would be. In the short term, the large speculators were ruined. The rich lost most because they had invested most (see Source 4). They had always been the main buyers of American goods, so there was an immediate downturn in spending. Many others had borrowed money in order to buy shares that were now worthless. They were unable to pay back their loans to the banks and insurance companies, so they went bankrupt. Some banks themselves also went bankrupt.

At first, however, these seemed like tragic but isolated incidents. President Hoover reassured the nation that prosperity was 'just around the corner'. He cut taxes to help to stimulate people to buy more goods and by mid 1931 production was rising again slightly and there was hope that the situation was more settled.

SOURCE 6

An attempt to make some cash after the Wall Street Crash, 1929.

In fact, it was the worst of the Depression that was 'just around the corner', because the Crash had destroyed the one thing that was crucial to the prosperity of the 1920s: confidence.

This was most marked in the banking crisis. In 1929, 659 banks failed. As banks failed people stopped trusting them and many withdrew their savings. In 1930 another 1,352 went bankrupt. The biggest of these was the Bank of the United States in New York, which went bankrupt in December 1930. It had 400,000 depositors – many of them recent immigrants. Almost one-third of New Yorkers saved with it. This was the worst failure in American history. To make matters worse, 1931 saw escalating problems in European banks, which had a knock-on effect in the USA. Panic set in. Around the country a billion dollars was withdrawn from banks and put in safe deposit boxes, or stored at home. People felt that hard currency was the only security. Another 2,294 banks went under in 1931.

So while Hoover talked optimistically about the return of prosperity, Americans were showing their true feelings. They now kept their money instead of buying new goods or shares. The downward spiral was firmly established. Businesses cut production further and laid off more workers. They reduced the wages of those who still worked for them. Between 1928 and 1933 both industrial and farm production fell by 40 per cent, and average wages by 60 per cent.

As workers were laid off or were paid less, they bought even less. By 1932 the USA was in the grip of the most serious economic depression the world had ever seen. By 1933 there were 14 million unemployed, and 5,000 banks had gone bankrupt. Farm prices had fallen so low that the cost of transporting animals to market was higher than the price of the animals themselves. Total farm income had slipped to just $5 billion. The USA's international trade had also been drastically reduced, falling from $10 billion in 1929 to $3 billion in 1932.

SOURCE **7**

During the last three months I have visited . . . some 20 states of this wonderfully rich and beautiful country. A number of Montana citizens told me of thousands of bushels of wheat left in the fields uncut on account of its low price that hardly paid for the harvesting. In Oregon I saw thousands of bushels of apples rotting in the orchards. At the same time there are millions of children who, on account of the poverty of their parents, will not eat one apple this winter.

. . . I saw men picking for meat scraps in the garbage cans of the cities of New York and Chicago. One man said that he had killed 3,000 sheep this fall and thrown them down the canyon because it cost $1.10 to ship a sheep and then he would get less than a dollar for it.

The farmers are being pauperised [made poor] by the poverty of industrial populations and the industrial populations are being pauperised by the poverty of the farmers. Neither has the money to buy the product of the other; hence we have overproduction and under-consumption at the same time.

Evidence of Oscar Ameringer to a US government committee in 1932.

SOURCE **8**

Unemployed workers queuing for a cheap meal. For Americans used to prosperity and believing in self-help, needing charity was a hard blow to their pride.

The human cost of the Depression

People in agricultural areas were hardest hit by the Depression, because the 1920s had not been kind to them anyway. Huge numbers of farmers were unable to pay their mortgages. Some farmers organised themselves to resist banks seizing their homes. When sheriffs came to seize their property, bands of farmers holding pitch forks and hangman's nooses persuaded the sheriffs to retreat. Others barricaded highways. Most farmers, however, had no choice but to pack their belongings into their trucks and live on the road. They picked up work where they could.

To make matters worse for farmers, overfarming and drought in the central southern states turned millions of acres into a dust bowl and drove farmers off their land. Many of these ruined farmers headed to California looking for labouring work.

SOURCE **9**

A dust bowl farm. Overfarming, drought and poor conservation turned farmland into desert.

In the towns, the story was not much better. For example, in 1932 in the steel city of Cleveland, 50 per cent of workers were now unemployed and in Toledo 80 per cent. At night the parks were full of the homeless and unemployed. In every city, workers who had contributed to the prosperity of the 1920s now queued for bread and soup dished out by charity workers. Every town had a so-called Hooverville. This was a shanty town of ramshackle huts where the migrants lived, while they searched for work. The rubbish tips were crowded with families hoping to scrape a meal from the leftovers of more fortunate people. Through 1931, 238 people were admitted to hospital in New York suffering from malnutrition or starvation. Forty-five of them died.

SOURCE **10**

Last summer, in the hot weather, when the smell was sickening and the flies were thick, there were a hundred people a day coming to the dumps . . . a widow who used to do housework and laundry, but now had no work at all, fed herself and her fourteen-year-old son on garbage. Before she picked up the meat she would always take off her glasses so that she couldn't see the maggots.

From *New Republic* magazine, February 1933.

SOURCE 11

Unemployment in the USA, 1929–33.

Chart data:
- 1929: 1.6 million, 5.2%
- 1930: 4.3 million, 8.7%
- 1931: 8.0 million, 15.9%
- 1932: 12.1 million, 23.6%
- 1933: 14.0 million, 24.9%

Unemployment as a percentage of the labour force is shown in red

Y-axis: Unemployed (millions)

SOURCE 12

A Hooverville shanty town on wasteland in Seattle, Washington.

SOURCE 13

There is not an unemployed man in the country that hasn't contributed to the wealth of every millionaire in America. The working classes didn't bring this on, it was the big boys . . . We've got more wheat, more corn, more food, more cotton, more money in the banks, more everything in the world than any nation that ever lived ever had, yet we are starving to death. We are the first nation in the history of the world to go to the poorhouse in an automobile.

Will Rogers, an American writer, 1931. Rogers had a regular humorous column in an American magazine which was popular with ordinary people.

SOURCE 14

A migrant family.

1 Read Source 13. What do you think Will Rogers means by 'the big boys?'

2 Explain how a writer such as Rogers can be useful to a historian studying the impact of the Depression in the 1930s.

Focus Task

What were the human consequences of the Crash?

You have been asked to prepare an exhibition of photos which compares the life of Americans during the boom times of the 1920s with the depressed years of the 1930s. Choose two pictures from the 1920s and two from the 1930s which you think present the greatest contrast.

Explain your choice.

Do you think everyone suffered equally from the Depression? Explain your answer by referring to Sources 7–14.

The 1932 presidential election

In the 1932 election President Hoover paid the price for being unable to solve the problems of the Depression. It was partly his own fault. Until 1932 he refused to accept that there was a major problem. He insisted that 'prosperity is just around the corner'. This left him open to bitter criticisms such as Source 17. A famous banner carried in a demonstration of Iowa farmers said: 'In Hoover we trusted and now we are busted.'

1 Source 15 had a very powerful effect on Americans. Explain why (refer to Source 19).
2 From Sources 16–18 make a list of criticisms of Hoover and his government.

SOURCE 15

A 1932 Democrat election poster.

SOURCE 16

Never before in this country has a government fallen to so low a place in popular estimation or been so universally an object of cynical contempt. Never before has [a President] given his name so freely to latrines and offal dumps, or had his face banished from the [cinema] screen to avoid the hoots and jeers of children.

Written by a political commentator after the event.

SOURCE 17

Farmers are just ready to do anything to get even with the situation. I almost hate to express it, but I honestly believe that if some of them could buy airplanes they would come down here to Washington to blow you fellows up . . . The farmer is a naturally conservative individual, but you cannot find a conservative farmer today. Any economic system that has in its power to set me and my wife in the streets, at my age what can I see but red?

President of the Farmers' Union of Wisconsin, AN Young, speaking to a Senate committee in 1932.

SOURCE 18

When I think of what has been happening in this country since unemployment began, and when I see the futility of the leaders, I wish we might double the number of Communists in this country, to put the fear, if not of God, then the fear of something else, into the hearts of our leaders.

Written by a Catholic priest, Father J Ryan.

SOURCE 19

In 1929 the Democratic Party hired former newspaperman Charles Michaelson to attack Hoover's image. Backed by a million dollar budget, Michaelson wrote speeches for Democrats on Capitol Hill and distributed a newspaper column . . . Comedian Will Rogers summed up the mood of a nation: 'if someone bit an apple and found a worm in it', he joked, 'Hoover would get the blame'. Desperate encampments of tin and cardboard shacks were dubbed 'Hoovervilles'. There were 'Hoover hogs' (armadillos fit for eating) 'Hoover flags' (empty pockets turned inside out) 'Hoover blankets' (newspapers barely covering the destitute forced to sleep outdoors) and 'Hoover Pullmans' (empty boxcars used by an army of vagabonds escaping from their roots).

An extract from *The Hero to Scapegoat*, the official biography of Hoover by the Hoover Presidential Library and Museum.

Hoover was regarded as a 'do nothing' President. This was not entirely fair on Hoover. He tried to restart the economy in 1930 and 1931 by tax cuts. He tried to persuade business leaders not to cut wages. He set up the Reconstruction Finance Company, which propped up banks to stop them going bankrupt. He tried to protect US industries by introducing tariffs, but this simply strangled international trade and made the Depression worse.

To most observers these measures looked like mere tinkering. Hoover and most Republicans were very reluctant to change their basic policies. They believed that the main cause of the Depression had been economic problems in Europe, not weaknesses in the USA's economy. They said that business should be left alone to bring back prosperity. Government help was not needed. They argued that business went in cycles of boom and bust, and therefore prosperity would soon return. In 1932 Hoover blocked the Garner–Wagner Relief Bill, which would have allowed Congress to provide $2.1 billion to create jobs.

Even more damaging to Hoover's personal reputation, however, was how little he tried to help people who were suffering because of the Depression. He believed that social security was not the responsibility of the government. Relief should be provided by local government or charities. The Republicans were afraid that if the government helped individuals, they would become less independent and less willing to work.

Profile

Franklin D Roosevelt

➤ Born in 1882, into a rich New York family.
➤ He went to university and became a successful lawyer.
➤ In 1910 he entered politics as a Democratic senator for New York.
➤ In 1921 he was paralysed by polio and spent the rest of his life in a wheelchair. He fought bravely against his illness.
➤ He became President in 1933, in the middle of the USA's economic crisis.
➤ Roosevelt was an excellent public speaker, an optimist and a believer in the 'American dream' – that anyone who worked hard enough could become rich.
➤ His policies of providing benefit for the unemployed, and employing men to work on massive state building projects (known as the 'New Deal' – see pages 376–84), made him extremely popular.
➤ He was elected President four times.
➤ He led the USA through the Second World War until his death in April 1945.

SOURCE **21**

Millions of our citizens cherish the hope that their old standards of living have not gone forever. Those millions shall not hope in vain. I pledge you, I pledge myself, to a New Deal for the American people. This is more than a political campaign; it is a call to arms. Give me your help, not to win votes alone, but to win this crusade to restore America . . . I am waging a war against Destruction, Delay, Deceit and Despair . . .

Roosevelt's pre-election speech, 1932.

SOURCE **22**

Roosevelt, the only American president to win four terms in office . . . saw the Democratic Party for what it was: an amorphous association representing a wide variety of competing interests. To win the presidential nomination, he needed to keep on board an improbable mix of Eastern liberals, Western reformers, labour leaders, internationalists, Wall Street financiers and Southern states' rights conservatives and white supremacists. So evasive was he that one columnist dubbed him 'the corkscrew candidate'.

James Macgregor Burns, writing in November 2007. Burns is Professor of Political Science at William College in the USA and is an expert on the methods used by political leaders.

3 Make a list of the differences between the views of Hoover and Roosevelt.

Hoover's reputation was particularly damaged by an event in June 1932. Thousands of servicemen who had fought in the First World War marched on Washington asking for their war bonuses (a kind of pension) to be paid early. The marchers camped peacefully outside the White House and sang patriotic songs. Hoover refused to meet them. He appointed General Douglas MacArthur to handle the situation. MacArthur convinced himself (with little or no evidence) that they were Communist agitators. He ignored Hoover's instructions to treat the marchers with respect. Troops and police used tear gas and burned the marchers' camps. Hoover would not admit he had failed to control MacArthur. He publicly thanked God that the USA still knew how to deal with a mob.

SOURCE **20**

Police attacking the war bonus marchers.

There could be no greater contrast to Hoover than his opponent in the 1932 election, the Democrat candidate, Franklin D Roosevelt. Roosevelt's main characteristics as a politician were:

• He was not a radical, but he believed in 'active government' to improve the lives of ordinary people although only as a last resort if self-help and charity had failed.
• He had plans to spend public money on getting people back to work. As Governor of New York, he had already started doing this in his own state.
• He was not afraid to ask for advice on important issues from a wide range of experts, such as factory owners, union leaders and economists.

The campaign

With such ill-feeling towards Hoover being expressed throughout the country, Roosevelt was confident of victory, but he took no chances. He went on a grand train tour of the USA in the weeks before the election and mercilessly attacked the attitude of Hoover and the Republicans.

Roosevelt's own plans were rather vague and general (see Source 21). But he realised people wanted action, whatever that action was. In a 20,800 km campaign trip he made sixteen major speeches and another 60 from the back of his train. He promised the American people a 'New Deal'.

The election was a landslide victory for Roosevelt. He won by 7 million votes and the Democrats won a majority of seats in Congress. It was the worst defeat the Republicans had ever suffered.

Focus Task

Why did Roosevelt win the 1932 election?

In many ways Roosevelt's victory needs no explanation. Indeed, it would have been very surprising if any President could have been re-elected after the sufferings of 1929–32. But it is important to recognise the range of factors that helped Roosevelt and damaged Hoover.

Write your own account of Roosevelt's success under the following headings:
◆ The experiences of ordinary people, 1929–32
◆ The policies of the Republicans
◆ Actions taken by the Republicans
◆ Roosevelt's election campaign.

SOURCE **1**

This is the time to speak the truth frankly and boldly . . . So let me assert my firm belief that the only thing we have to fear is fear itself – nameless, unreasoning, unjustified terror which paralyses efforts to convert retreat into advance . . . This nation calls for action and action now . . . Our greatest primary task is to put people to work . . . We must act and act quickly.

Roosevelt's inauguration speech, 1933.

---

1 Read Source 1. What do you think Roosevelt means by 'the only thing we have to fear is fear itself'?

SOURCE **2**

The bank rescue of 1933 was probably the turning point of the Depression. When people were able to survive the shock of having all the banks closed, and then see the banks open up again, with their money protected, there began to be confidence. Good times were coming. It marked the revival of hope.

Raymond Moley, one of Roosevelt's advisers during the Hundred Days Congress session.

Factfile

The Hundred Days

- ➤ **4 March** Roosevelt inaugurated.
- ➤ **5 March** Closed banks.
- ➤ **9 March** Selected banks reopened.
- ➤ **12 March** Roosevelt's first radio 'fireside chat'. Encouraged Americans to put their money back into the banks. Many did so.
- ➤ **31 March** The Civilian Conservation Corps set up.
- ➤ **12 May** The Agricultural Adjustment Act passed.
- ➤ **18 May** The Tennessee Valley Authority created.
- ➤ **18 June** The National Industrial Recovery Act passed.

13.3 Franklin D Roosevelt and the New Deal

During his election campaign Roosevelt had promised the American people a New Deal. It was not entirely clear what measures that might include. What was clear was that Franklin D Roosevelt planned to use the full power of the government to get the US out of depression. He set out his priorities as follows:

- getting Americans back to work
- protecting their savings and property
- providing relief for the sick, old and unemployed
- getting American industry and agriculture back on their feet.

The Hundred Days

In the first hundred days of his presidency, Roosevelt worked round the clock with his advisers (who became known as the 'Brains Trust') to produce an enormous range of sweeping measures.

From his first day, Roosevelt went straight into action. One of the many problems affecting the USA was its loss of confidence in the banks. He immediately tackled this banking crisis.

The day after his inauguration Roosevelt ordered all of the banks to close and to remain closed until government officials had checked them over. A few days later 5,000 trustworthy banks were allowed to reopen. They were even supported by government money if necessary. At the same time, Roosevelt's advisers had come up with a set of rules and regulations which would prevent the reckless speculation that had contributed to the Wall Street Crash.

These two measures, the **Emergency Banking Act** and the **Securities Exchange Commission**, gave the American people a taste of what the New Deal was to look like, but there was a lot more to come. One of Roosevelt's advisers at this time said, 'During the whole Hundred Days Congress, people didn't know what was going on, but they knew something was happening, something good for them.' In the Hundred Days, Roosevelt sent fifteen proposals to Congress and all fifteen were adopted. Just as importantly, he took time to explain to the American people what he was doing and why he was doing it. Every Sunday he would broadcast on radio to the nation. An estimated 60 million Americans tuned in to these **'fireside chats'**. Nowadays, we are used to politicians doing this. At that time it was a new development.

The **Federal Emergency Relief Administration** set about meeting the urgent needs of the poor. A sum of $500 million was spent on soup kitchens, blankets, employment schemes and nursery schools.

The **Civilian Conservation Corps** (CCC) was aimed at unemployed young men in particular. They could sign on for periods of six months, which could be renewed if they could still not find work. Most of the work done by the CCC was on environmental projects in national parks. The money earned generally went back to the men's families. Around 2.5 million young men were helped by this scheme.

The **Agricultural Adjustment Administration** (AAA) tried to take a long-term view of the problems facing farmers. It set quotas to reduce farm production in order to force prices gradually upwards. At the same time, the AAA helped farmers to modernise and to use farming methods that would conserve and protect the soil. In cases of extreme hardship, farmers could also receive help with their mortgages. The AAA certainly helped farmers, although modernisation had the unfortunate effect of putting more farm labourers out of work.

The **National Industrial Recovery Act** (NIRA) set up two important organisations:

- The **Public Works Administration** (PWA) used government money to build schools, roads, dams, bridges and airports. These would be vital once the USA had recovered, and in the short term they created millions of jobs.
- The **National Recovery Administration** (NRA) improved working conditions in industry and outlawed child labour. It also set out fair wages and sensible levels of production. The idea was to stimulate the economy by giving workers money to spend, without overproducing and causing a slump. It was voluntary, but firms which joined used the blue eagle as a symbol of presidential approval. Over 2 million employers joined the scheme.

A

B

Two 1933 American cartoons.

2 Look carefully at Source 3. Put the message of each cartoon into your own words.

The Tennessee Valley Authority

As you can see from Source 4, the Tennessee Valley was a huge area that cut across seven states. The area had great physical problems. In the wet season, the Tennessee river would flood. In the dry it would reduce to a trickle. The farming land around the river was a dust bowl. The soil was eroding and turning the land into desert. The area also had great social problems. Within the valley people lived in poverty. The majority of households had no electricity. The problems of the Tennessee Valley were far too large for one state to deal with and it was very difficult for states to co-operate.

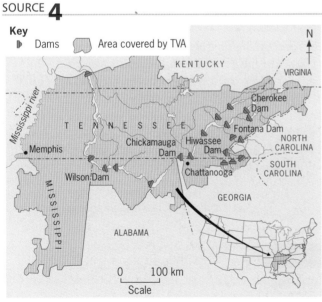

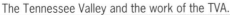

The Tennessee Valley and the work of the TVA.

Effects of erosion in the Tennessee Valley.

Roosevelt therefore set up an independent organisation called the **Tennessee Valley Authority** (TVA), which cut across the powers of the local state governments. The main focus of the TVA's work was to build a series of dams on the Tennessee river. They transformed the region. The dams made it possible to irrigate the dried-out lands. They also provided electricity for this underdeveloped area. Above all, building the dams created thousands of jobs in an area badly hit by the Depression.

Factfile

Achievements of the Hundred Days

➤ Above all, it restored confidence and stopped investors pulling money out of the banks.
➤ Banking measures saved 20 per cent of home owners and farmers from repossession.
➤ Farmers were 50 per cent better off under AAA by 1936.
➤ TVA brought electrical power to underdeveloped areas.
➤ Public Works Administration created 600,000 jobs and built landmarks like San Francisco's Golden Gate Bridge.

1 After reading pages 376–78, add three more bullet points to this Factfile.

SOURCE 7

Wandering around the country with one of New York's baseball teams, I find that [what was] the national road to ruin is now a thriving thoroughfare. It has been redecorated. People have come out of the shell holes. They are working and playing and seem content to let a tribe of professional worriers do their worrying for them.

Rudd Rennie, an American journalist, describes what he saw around the USA in the early days of the New Deal. From *Changing the Tune from Gloom to Cheer*, 1934.

SOURCE 8

The CCC, the PWA, and similar government bodies (the alphabet agencies as Americans called them) made work for millions of people. The money they earned began to bring back life to the nation's trade and businesses. More customers appeared in the shops . . . As people started to buy again, shopkeepers, farmers and manufacturers began to benefit from the money the government was spending on work for the unemployed. This process was described by Roosevelt as 'priming the pump'. By this he meant that the money the Federal Government was spending was like a fuel, flowing into the nation's economic machinery and starting it moving again.

DB O'Callaghan, *Roosevelt and the USA*, published in 1966.

SOURCE 6

The Fontana Dam, one of the TVA's later projects. Dams such as these revitalised farmland, provided jobs and brought electric power to the area.

The measures introduced during the Hundred Days had an immediate effect. They restored confidence in government. Reporters who travelled the country brought back reports of the new spirit to be seen around the USA.

Historians too agree that Roosevelt's bold and decisive action did have a marked effect on the American people.

SOURCE 9

As Roosevelt described it, the 'New Deal' meant that the forgotten man, the little man, the man nobody knew much about, was going to be dealt better cards to play with . . . He understood that the suffering of the Depression had fallen with terrific impact upon the people least able to bear it. He knew that the rich had been hit hard too, but at least they had something left. But the little merchant, the small householder and home owner, the farmer, the man who worked for himself – these people were desperate. And Roosevelt saw them as principal citizens of the United States, numerically and in their importance to the maintenance of the ideals of American democracy.

Frances Perkins, *The Roosevelt I Knew*, 1947. Perkins was Labour Secretary under Roosevelt from 1933.

Focus Task

What was the New Deal of 1933?

Look back over pages 376–78 and complete your own copy of this table.

New Deal measure/agency	Issue/problem it aimed to tackle	Action taken/ powers of agency	Evidence it was/was not effective

The Second New Deal

Workers widening a road under the Works Progress Administration.

SOURCE **11**

Migrant Mother (number 6) by Dorothea Lange, taken in Nipomo, California, March 1936. Many farmers migrated to California where farming had been less badly hit by the Depression.

Despite his achievements, by May 1935 Roosevelt was facing a barrage of criticism Some critics (like Senator Huey Long, see page 380) complained that he was doing too little, others (mainly the wealthy business sector) too much. The USA was recovering less quickly than Europe from Depression. Business was losing its enthusiasm for the NRA (for example Henry Ford had cut wages). Roosevelt was unsure what to do. He had hoped to transform the USA, but it didn't seem to be working.

Tuesday, 14 May 1935 turned out to be a key date. Roosevelt met with a group of senators and close advisers who shared his views and aims. They persuaded him to take radical steps to achieve his vision and make the USA a fairer place for all Americans (see Source 9). One month later, on 14 June, he summoned the leaders of Congress and presented them with a huge range of laws that he wanted passed. This became known as the Second New Deal. The most significant aspects were the following:

- The **Wagner Act** forced all employers to allow trade unions to operate in their companies and to let them negotiate with employers for better pay and conditions. The new Act made it illegal to sack workers for being in a union.
- The **Social Security Act** provided state pensions for the elderly and for widows. It also allowed state governments to work with the federal government to provide help for the sick and the disabled. Most importantly, the Act set up a scheme for unemployment insurance. This meant that employers and workers made a small contribution to a special fund each week. If workers became unemployed, they would receive a small amount of benefit to help them out until they could find work.
- The **Works Progress Administration (WPA)**, later renamed the Works Project Administration, brought together all the organisations whose aim was to create jobs. It also extended this work beyond building projects to create jobs for office workers and even unemployed actors, artists and photographers. The photograph in Source 11 was taken by a photographer working for the New Deal's Farm Security Administration Photographic Project. This project took 80,000 photos of farming areas during the New Deal. Source 12 was produced by an artist working for the Federal Arts Project. The government paid artists to paint pictures to be displayed in the city or town they featured.
- The **Resettlement Administration (RA)** helped smallholders and tenant farmers who had not been helped by the AAA. This organisation moved over 500,000 families to better-quality land and housing. The **Farm Security Administration (FSA)** replaced the RA in 1937. It gave special loans to small farmers to help them buy their land. It also built camps to provide decent living conditions and work for migrant workers.

SOURCE **12**

Steel Industry by Howard Cook, painted for the steel-making town of Pittsburgh, Pennsylvania.

2 What impression of the New Deal does Source 12 attempt to convey?
3 Why do you think Roosevelt wanted artists and photographers to be employed under the New Deal?

Focus Task

Draw up two spider diagrams to compare the objectives and measures of the New Deal and the Second New Deal.

Opposition to the New Deal

A programme such as Roosevelt's New Deal was unheard of in American history. It was bound to attract opposition and it did.

The New Deal isn't doing enough!

A number of high-profile figures raised the complaint that the New Deal was not doing enough to help the poor. Despite the New Deal measures, many Americans remained desperately poor. The hardest hit were African Americans and the poor in farming areas.

SOURCE **13**

A cartoon attacking the New Deal in the mid 1930s. Most newspaper owners were hostile to Roosevelt.

A key figure in arguing on behalf of these people was Huey Long. Long was a remarkable character. He became Governor of Louisiana in 1928 and a senator in 1932. His methods of gaining power were unusual and sometimes illegal (they included intimidation and bribery). However, once he had power he used it to help the poor. He relentlessly taxed big corporations and businesses in Louisiana and used the money to build roads, schools and hospitals. He employed African Americans on the same terms as whites and clashed with the Ku Klux Klan. He supported the New Deal at first, but by 1934 he was criticising it for being too complicated and not doing enough. He put forward a scheme called Share Our Wealth. All personal fortunes would be reduced to $3 million maximum, and maximum income would be $1 million a year. Government taxes would be shared between all Americans. He also proposed pensions for everyone over 60, and free washing machines and radios. Long was an aggressive and forceful character with many friends and many enemies. Roosevelt regarded him as one of the two most dangerous men in the USA until Long was assassinated in 1935.

Others also criticised the New Deal for not doing enough. Dr Francis Townsend founded a number of Townsend Clubs to campaign for a pension of $200 per month for people over 60, providing that they spent it that month, stimulating the economy in the process. A Catholic priest, Father Coughlin, used his own radio programme to attack Roosevelt. He set up the National Union for Social Justice and it had a large membership. However, by the early 1940s the movement had faded in importance.

The New Deal is doing too much!

SOURCE **14**

The New Deal is nothing more or less than an effort to take away from the thrifty what the thrifty and their ancestors have accumulated, or may accumulate, and give it to others who have not earned it and never will earn it, and thus indirectly to destroy the incentive for all future accumulation. Such a purpose is in defiance of all the ideas upon which our civilisation has been founded.

A Republican opponent of the New Deal speaking in 1935.

The New Deal soon came under fire from sections of the business community and from Republicans for doing too much. There was a long list of criticisms:

- The New Deal was complicated and there were too many codes and regulations.
- Government should not support trade unions and it should not support calls for higher wages – the market should deal with these issues.
- Schemes such as the TVA created unfair competition for private companies.
- The New Deal schemes were like the economic plans being carried out in the Communist USSR and unsuitable for the democratic, free-market USA.
- Roosevelt was behaving like a dictator.
- The wealthy were wealthy because they had worked hard and used their abilities. High taxes discouraged people from working hard and gave money to people for doing nothing or doing unnecessary jobs (see Source 14).

Roosevelt was upset by the criticisms, but also by the tactics used against him by big business and the Republicans. They used a smear campaign against him and all connected to him. They said that he was disabled because of a sexually transmitted disease rather than polio. Employers put messages into their workers' pay packets saying that New Deal Schemes would never happen. Roosevelt turned on these enemies bitterly (see Source 16). And it seemed the American people were with him. In the 1936 election, he won 27 million votes – with the highest margin of victory ever achieved by a US president. He was then able to joke triumphantly, 'Everyone is against the New Deal except the voters.'

SOURCE 15

A 1930s cartoon attacking critics of the New Deal.

Opposition from the Supreme Court

Roosevelt's problems were not over with the 1936 election. In fact, he now faced the most powerful opponent of the New Deal – the American Supreme Court. This Court was dominated by Republicans who were opposed to the New Deal. It could overturn laws if those laws were against the terms of the Constitution. In May 1935 a strange case had come before the US Supreme Court. The Schechter Poultry Corporation had been found guilty of breaking NRA regulations because it had:

- sold diseased chickens for human consumption
- filed false sales claims (to make the company worth more)
- exploited workers
- threatened government inspectors.

It appealed to the Supreme Court. The Court ruled that the government had no right to prosecute the company. This was because the NRA was unconstitutional. It undermined too much of the power of the local states.

Roosevelt was angry that this group of old Republicans should deny democracy by throwing out laws that he had been elected to pass. He asked Congress to give him the power to appoint six more Supreme Court judges who were more sympathetic to the New Deal. But Roosevelt misjudged the mood of the American public. They were alarmed at what they saw as Roosevelt's attacking the American system of government. Roosevelt had to back down and his plan was rejected. Even so his actions were not completely pointless. The Supreme Court had been shaken by Roosevelt's actions and was less obstructive in the future. Most of the main measures in Roosevelt's Second New Deal were approved by the Court from 1937 onwards.

SOURCE 16

For twelve years this nation was afflicted with hear-nothing, see-nothing, do-nothing government. The nation looked to government but government looked away. Nine crazy years at the stock market and three long years in the bread-lines! Nine mad years of mirage and three long years of despair! Powerful influences strive today to restore that kind of government with its doctrine that government is best which is most indifferent . . . We know now that government by organised money is just as dangerous as government by organised mob. Never before in all our history have these forces been so united against one candidate – me – as they stand today. They are unanimous in their hate of me – and I welcome their hatred.

A speech by Roosevelt in the 1936 presidential election campaign.

4   What do Sources 15 and 16 suggest about the critics of the New Deal?

SOURCE 17

THE ILLEGAL ACT.
PRESIDENT ROOSEVELT. "I'M SORRY, BUT THE SUPREME COURT SAYS I MUST CHUCK YOU BACK AGAIN."

A *Punch* cartoon, June 1935, attacking the decisions of the Supreme Court.

SOURCE 18

A cartoon from the *Brooklyn Daily Eagle*, February1937, attacking Roosevelt's attempts to 'pack' the Supreme Court.

Focus Task

What were the motives of the opponents of the New Deal?

The thought bubbles below show some of the reasons why people opposed the New Deal. Use the text and sources on these two pages to find examples of individuals who held each belief. Try to find two more reasons why people opposed the New Deal.

It won't work.

It'll harm me.

It'll harm the USA.

Activity

-5 -4 -3 -2 -1 0 1 2 3 4 5

Failure is –5. Success is +5.

Pages 382–84 summarise the impact of the New Deal on various groups.

1 For each of the six aspects of the New Deal, decide where you would place it on the scale. Explain your score and support it with evidence from pages 376–83.

2 Compare your six 'marks' on the scale with those of someone else in your class.

3 Working together, try to come up with an agreed mark for the whole of the New Deal. You will have to think about the relative importance of different issues. For example, you might give more weight to a low mark in an important area than to a high mark in a less important area.

Was the New Deal a success?

The events of 1936 took their toll on Roosevelt and he became more cautious after that. Early in 1937 prosperity seemed to be returning and Roosevelt did what all conservatives had wanted: he cut the New Deal budget. He laid off many workers who had been employed by the New Deal's own organisations and the cut in spending triggered other cuts throughout the economy. This meant that unemployment spiralled upwards once more.

The 1937 recession damaged Roosevelt badly. Middle-class voters lost some confidence in him. As a result, in 1938 the Republicans once again did well in the congressional elections. Now it was much harder for Roosevelt to push his reforms through Congress. However, he was still enormously popular with most ordinary Americans (he was elected again with a big majority in 1940). The problem was that the USA was no longer as united behind his New Deal as it had been in 1933. Indeed, by 1940 Roosevelt and most Americans were focusing more on the outbreak of war in Europe and on Japan's exploits in the Far East (see Chapter 2).

So was the New Deal a success? One of the reasons why this question is hard to answer is that you need to decide what Roosevelt was trying to achieve. We know that by 1940, unemployment was still high and the economy was certainly not booming. On the other hand, economic recovery was not Roosevelt's only aim. In fact it may not have been his main aim. Roosevelt and many of his advisers wanted to reform the USA's economy and society. So when you decide whether the New Deal was a success or not, you will have to decide what you think the aims of the New Deal were, as well as whether you think the aims were achieved.

Aspect 1: A new society?

SOURCE 19

A 1937 cartoon from the *Portland Press Herald* showing Harold Ickes in conflict with big business.

- The New Deal restored the faith of the American people in their government.
- The New Deal was a huge social and economic programme. Government help on this scale would never have been possible before Roosevelt's time. It set the tone for future policies for government to help people.
- The New Deal handled billions of dollars of public money, but there were no corruption scandals. For example, the head of the Civil Works Administration, Harold Hopkins, distributed $10 billion in schemes and programmes, but never earned more than his salary of $15,000. The Secretary of the Interior, Harold Ickes, actually tapped the phones of his own employees to ensure there was no corruption. He also employed African Americans, campaigned against anti-semitism and supported the cause of native Americans.
- The New Deal divided the USA. Roosevelt and his officials were often accused of being Communists and of undermining American values. Ickes and Hopkins were both accused of being anti-business because they supported trade unions.
- The New Deal undermined local government.

Aspect 2: Industrial workers

- The NRA and Second New Deal measures strengthened the position of labour unions against the large American industrial giants.
- Roosevelt's government generally tried to support unions and make large corporations negotiate with them.
- Some labour unions combined forces to form the Committee for Industrial Organisation (CIO) in 1935. This union was large enough to be able to bargain with big corporations.
- The Union of Automobile Workers (UAW) was recognised by the two most anti-union corporations: General Motors (after a major sit-in strike in 1936) and Ford (after a ballot in 1941).
- Big business remained immensely powerful in the USA despite being challenged by the government.
- Unions were treated with suspicion by employers.
- Many strikes were broken up with brutal violence in the 1930s (see Source 22 on page 384).
- Companies such as Ford, Republic Steel and Chrysler employed their own thugs or controlled local police forces.

Aspect 3: Unemployment and the economy

SOURCE 20

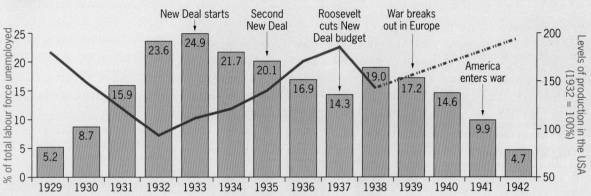

Unemployment, and the performance of the US economy during the 1930s.

- The New Deal created millions of jobs.
- It stabilised the American banking system.
- It cut the number of business failures.
- Projects such as the TVA brought work and an improved standard of living to deprived parts of the USA.
- New Deal projects provided the USA with valuable resources such as schools, roads and power stations.
- The New Deal never solved the underlying economic problems.

- The US economy took longer to recover than that of most European countries.
- Confidence remained low – throughout the 1930s Americans only spent and invested about 75 per cent of what they had before 1929.
- When Roosevelt cut the New Deal budget in 1937, the country went back into recession.
- There were six million unemployed in 1941.
- Only the USA's entry into the war brought an end to unemployment.

Aspect 4: African Americans

- Around 200,000 African Americans gained benefits from the Civilian Conservation Corps and other New Deal agencies.
- Many African Americans benefited from New Deal slum clearance and housing projects.
- Many New Deal agencies discriminated against African Americans. They either got no work or received worse treatment or lower wages.
- Roosevelt failed to pass laws against the lynching of African Americans. He feared that Democrat senators in the southern states would not support him.

SOURCE 21

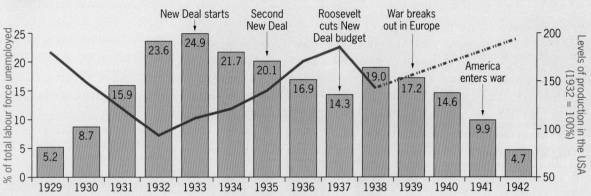

African Americans queuing for government relief in 1937 in front of a famous government poster.

Aspect 5: Women

- The New Deal saw some women achieve prominent positions. Eleanor Roosevelt became an important campaigner on social issues.
- Mary Macleod Bethune, an African American woman, headed the National Youth Administration.
- Frances Perkins was the Secretary of Labor. She removed 59 corrupt officials from the Labor Department and was a key figure in making the Second New Deal work in practice.
- Most of the New Deal programmes were aimed to help male manual workers rather than women (only about 8,000 women were involved in the CCC).
- Local governments tried to avoid paying out social security payments to women by introducing special qualifications and conditions.
- Frances Perkins was viciously attacked in the press as a Jew and a Soviet spy. Even her cabinet colleagues tended to ignore her at social gatherings.

Aspect 6: Native Americans

- The Indian Reorganisation Act 1934 provided money to help native Americans to buy and improve land.
- The Indian Reservation Act 1934 helped native Americans to preserve and practise their traditions, laws and culture.
- Native Americans remained a poor and excluded section of society.

SOURCE **22**

FORD MOTOR COMPANY

A UAW leader Walter Reuther with UAW activists Richard Frankensteen and Robert Kanter. On the left are some of Henry Ford's security men.

B Ford's men beating up Richard Frankensteen.

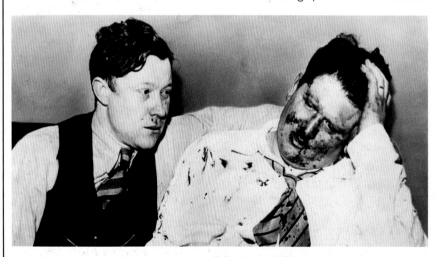

C Reuther and Frankensteen after the attack.

In May 1937 *Detroit News* photographer James Kilpatrick escaped with these pictures only by switching the film he had used with a spare one in his pocket.

SOURCE **23**

Many of Roosevelt's experiments were failures, but that is what experimentation entails. He would be satisfied he said if 75 per cent of them produced beneficial results. Experimentation depended on one of his distinctive characteristics: receptivity to new and untried methods and ideas.

Written by historian Samuel Rosemann.

1 Read Source 23. Explain how this source could be used both to praise and to criticise the New Deal.

Focus Task

How successful was the New Deal?

This is a complicated question. You have already spent time thinking about it; now you are going to prepare to write an essay.

First recap some key points:

Roosevelt's aims

1 Look back at page 376. Make a list of Roosevelt's aims for the First New Deal.
2 What new aims did the Second New Deal have?
3 Which of these aims did Roosevelt succeed in? Which did he fail in?

Unemployment and the economy

4 Explain why unemployment remained high through the 1930s.
5 Does this mean that Roosevelt's New Deal was not a success?

Opposition

6 How far do you think opposition to the New Deal made it hard for the New Deal to work?

Criticisms and achievements

7 Which criticism of the New Deal do you think is the most serious? Why?
8 Which achievement do you think is the most important? Why?
9 Would Roosevelt have agreed with your choice? Why?

Now write your own balanced account of the successes and failures of the New Deal, reaching your own conclusion as to whether it was a success or not. Include:
◆ the nature and scale of the problem facing Roosevelt
◆ the action he took through the 1930s
◆ the impact of the New Deal on Americans
◆ the reasons for opposition to the New Deal
◆ your own judgement on its success.
Include evidence to back up your judgements.

Paper 1: Depth Study

OCR Paper 1 is split into two parts:
1 Core content (Sections A–C)
2 Your chosen study in depth (Section D).

This Exam Focus deals with these part 2 Depth Studies.

Whichever Depth Study you choose the format of the questions will be similar. There will be a compulsory source-based question 4 (usually three sources), followed by a choice between questions 5 and 6.

> The examination paper will only include your **chosen Depth Study**. You can't change your depth study once you get in the exam!

Compulsory Question 4

There will be a compulsory question based on a few sources related to the topic. You may not have seen the sources before but there should be no surprises in the topic – it will be something mainstream from your course. For example, these sources are about Nazi policies towards women and young people.

> OCR advise you to spend **70 minutes** on this section of the paper. You will have to plan your time carefully.

Question 5 or 6

You will then have a choice of questions on two different aspects of the content. Each one will be structured in the same way.

Example Questions

Study the sources carefully and then answer the questions which follow.

SOURCE **B**

A Social Democrat poster published in 1931. It suggests what life will be like for women under the Nazis.

SOURCE **C**

The government has ordered that the Hitler Greeting is to be used in conversation between teachers and pupils. Every day at the beginning of the first lesson, the pupils will get up from their places as soon as the teacher enters the class, stand to attention and each raise their outstretched arm level with their eyes. The teacher will go to the front of the class and offer the same greeting accompanied by the words 'Heil Hitler!' The pupils will reply 'Heil Hitler!'

An extract from a German newspaper published in the mid 1930s.

SOURCE **D**

A photograph of a group of young German boys published in Germany in the late 1930s.

4 a) Study Source B. Why do you think this poster was published in Germany in 1931? Use the source and your knowledge to explain your answer. [7]
  b) Study Source C. How far does this source prove that the Nazis had won the support of young Germans? Use the source and your knowledge to explain your answer. [6]
  c) Study Source D. Why would the Nazi government want to publish photographs like this? Use the source and your knowledge to explain your answer. [6]
5 a) What were the main features of the Weimar Constitution? [4]
  b) Explain why the period from 1924 to 1929 was successful for the Weimar Republic. [6]
  c) 'The main reason for the fall of the Weimar Republic was the economic depression which started in 1929.' How far do you agree with this statement? Explain your answer. [10]

DO

- **Read/look** at all the sources carefully.
- **Refer to the source** in your answer.
- **Refer to the wording** of the question to keep you on the point.
- **Use details** from the source to support your main point(s).
- **Use contextual knowledge** to help you interpret the source.

DON'T

- **Don't simply describe** the picture, or repeat the words. Only include details that help support your point.
- **Don't write everything you know about** Nazi policies towards women, or young people in the 1930s. Only use contextual knowledge that helps you interpret the source.

The key idea in this question is **'purpose'**. It doesn't use the word but that is what they want you to see. Be clear about the difference between a reason and a purpose. A reason is general ('Because they didn't like the Nazi policies on women'). A purpose is specific ('to win women's votes in the elections of 1932'). Someone wanted to achieve something by doing it.

- **Notice the command word** 'How far . . .?' This is an evaluation question.
- The other key word in this question is **'prove'**. This is what you need to evaluate: does this source prove that the Nazis were effective? Make the point that it might 'suggest' or 'imply' but it does not 'prove'.
- To assess whether policies worked, you should look at what the Nazis were trying to do and see whether the evidence suggests that they succeeded.

4 a) Study Source B. Why do you think this poster was published in Germany in 1931? Use the source and your knowledge to explain your answer. [7]

b) Study Source C. How far does this source prove that the Nazis had won the support of young Germans? Use the source and your knowledge to explain your answer. [6]

c) Study Source D. Why would the Nazi government want to publish photographs like this? Use the source and your knowledge to explain your answer. [6]

A Good Answer to Question 4

4 a) This cartoon was designed to get people to vote against the Nazis in elections. It was specifically aimed at women and there was some evidence at the time that women supported traditionalist Nazi views on the role of women, so the Social Democrats were trying to persuade women not to support the Nazis. They did this by showing the woman being treated like a slave. The Nazi has a whip suggesting he might beat her if she ties the laces wrongly. The Social Democrats intended that the people who saw this would think the Nazis were cruel and heartless towards women.

This cartoon was published in 1931. At this time the Social Democrats, the biggest party, had realised how strong the Nazis were becoming – they were now the second biggest party in the Reichstag – and they knew another election was coming soon. They knew that every vote would count.

4 b) The Nazis wanted to win the 'hearts and minds' of all Germans. If you take it at face value this source suggests that they succeeded in schools and got total control over schools and young people. But there are problems with this source.

The first big problem is it comes from a newspaper and the Nazis controlled all the newspapers, so we are likely to be getting a carefully controlled Nazi point of view. The second problem is that this source tells us what the Nazis planned, but not whether it worked. Just because the Nazis had a policy it does not necessarily prove that policy worked.

Other evidence suggests that the Nazis sometimes struggled to get young people to accept Nazi ideas (such as Hitler Youth membership or informing on their parents). Some young people such as the Edelweiss Pirates formed resistance to the Nazis. Many ordinary young Germans who joined the Hitler Youth say they did so because they liked the activities or because their friends joined not because they bought into all the Hitler worship and the political brainwashing.

4 c) The Nazis wanted young Germans to be loyal members of the Hitler Youth, but they were also anxious to show that they respected German traditions like classical music and opera. The Nazis realised the power of photographs to spread their ideas. This photo reflects their ideal. In this image the young Germans are disciplining themselves, practising their music. They are also smart and soldierly in their uniforms and neat hair. The Nazis might want to publish this to persuade people to accept their ideas; or they might publish it to persuade people that their ideas were working so their audience thought that all young Germans were like this.

In reality, the Nazi plans to achieve the loyalty of young people did not always work out. For example, from 1939 onwards the Nazi youth movement was made compulsory and became increasingly strict on Nazi rules and focused on the war effort and military drill. As a result, the popularity of the youth movements decreased and an anti-Hitler Youth movement started – for example, the Edelweiss Pirates who resented Nazi control.

This is a good beginning. Like answer (b) it gets off to a strong, clear start – explaining what the Nazis were trying to achieve which helps you understand their interest in the source.

'Reflects' is a good word too. This image 'reflects' Nazi policies and shows what they want young people to be like. You can then really impress the examiner, when you use the phrase 'In reality . . .' and then go on to explain how Nazi plans for young people did not always work out.

By now you should be getting used to the typical **structure** of an OCR question. This is:

a) Describe . . .

b) Explain . . .

c) Evaluate . . .

Remember all the advice we gave you on this on pages 206–208. You need to use your knowledge – but use it selectively to focus on the question.

5 **a)** What were the main features of the Weimar Constitution? [4]
   b) Explain why the period from 1924 to 1929 was successful for the Weimar Republic. [6]
   c) 'The main reason for the fall of the Weimar Republic was the economic depression which started in 1929.' How far do you agree with this statement? Explain your answer. [10]

Look at the **marks** available. (c) is the big one. Spend most time on that.

a) Is a '**describe**' question so if you simply list features of the Constitution you will only score about half marks. To score higher you also need to **describe any potential weaknesses** or problems in that feature. For example, if you mention that the President had emergency powers, you need to say what those powers were and why that might be a potential problem for a democracy.

General Advice on Paper 1: Depth Studies

As in the Core Content, the Depth Study questions require you to show your knowledge and understanding and communicate what you are trying to say clearly. There are also very specific aims of the Depth Study questions.

- The first is to see how far you understand **the context in which sources were created** and an understanding of **how historians use sources to reach judgements**.
- The second big difference is that you will need to show that you have studied a topic in depth by answering questions which **focus on fairly small areas of the unit** you have followed.

b) is an '**Explain why**' question. So if you only list reasons (such as 'because of The Dawes Plan') you will get a low mark. You will score better if you explain what the Dawes Plan was and how it helped Germany to become prosperous and stable.

You will not have to write longer answers than for questions about the core, it is just that the questions will be on quite narrow areas. This means, there will be big sections of the Depth Study which will not be tested in the examination, so make sure you revise the whole Depth Study!

Paper 1: Depth Study

This is an 'iceberg' question. There is a lot lurking under the surface. Even if you agree with the statement you have to spend part of your answer explaining **the other factors** that contributed to the collapse of the Weimar Republic.

This introduction is not essential but if you have time it helps get you on track if you repeat the question and explain why it matters.

Remember **to explain – don't just list.**

This is where you deal with what is **under the surface** of this question: all the other reasons that contributed to the collapse of the Weimar republic: the role played by Hitler; the Nazi party organisation and tactics; fear of communism; the political manoeuvring.

If you have time and you want to really impress the examiner, add a paragraph that shows how the factors are connected. For example, how economic problems caused unemployment which increased support for Communism which frightened the middle classes and made many of them more likely to support the Nazis.

To score very well, use your conclusion to identify what you regard as 'the main reason'. In this case, would any of the other factors have been important on their own if the Depression had not happened?

5 c) 'The main reason for the fall of the Weimar Republic was the economic depression which started in 1929.' How far do you agree with this statement? Explain your answer. [10]

A Good Answer to Question 5c)

The economic Depression which started in 1929 was certainly one of the main reasons why the Weimar Republic collapsed in 1933. However, there were other important factors as well and it is the way all of these factors combined which caused the Weimar Republic to fall, rather than one single cause.

When the Depression hit Germany in 1929 it caused major economic problems. German businesses suddenly had to pay back loans to American banks. This led to the collapse of many businesses and this soon led to rising unemployment. By 1933 there were over six million unemployed Germans. This helped to cause the collapse of Weimar in two important ways. Firstly, the Depression left many Germans disillusioned with democracy because it could not solve the main challenge facing the German people, which reminded many Germans of the terrible economic problems of hyperinflation in the early 1920s. The democratic parties of the Weimar Republic could not agree on policies to tackle the Depression. For example, when Chancellor Brüning brought in cuts to welfare benefits and public spending, the Social Democrats refused to cooperate with the government. Eventually the President, Hindenburg, effectively took control of the country using Article 48 of the Weimar constitution to pass new measures and it looked like democracy had failed. Secondly, the failure of the Weimar democratic parties to solve the Depression led to support for the Communists and the Nazis, who were both opposed to democracy. The Nazi vote reached its peak in July 1932 with over 200 seats in the Reichstag and it rose in line with unemployment. This was also true of the Communist vote.

At the same time, a range of other factors also played important roles in causing the collapse of the Weimar Republic. The Nazi party would not have benefited from the Depression if it had not been well organised. It had an effective propaganda machine led by Joseph Goebbels and its own private army of Stormtroopers (the SA) to disrupt the meetings of political opponents. The Nazis also had an outstanding leader in Adolf Hitler. He was a brilliant speaker and made effective use of press, radio and film. In the 1932 presidential election he lost but he gained the votes of 13 million Germans. Another important factor was the rivalry between the parties which opposed the Nazis. The Social Democrats and the Communists could have defeated the Nazis in the Reichstag and fought the SA on the streets if they had worked together, but they refused to cooperate with each other. Another important factor was political manoeuvring. Hindenburg, von Papen and von Schleicher gave Hitler the chance to take power in January 1933 because they thought they could control him and that in effect they would be ruling Germany. By January 1933 Nazi support was beginning to drop and without this deal Hitler might not have gained power and overthrown the Weimar Republic.

In conclusion, I do not agree that the Depression was the main reason for the collapse of the Weimar Republic. I believe that it was a combination of the Depression and other factors. Without the Depression, the Communists and Nazis would not have gained strength and support. On the other hand, without the Nazis and the actions of Hindenburg and other politicians the Weimar Republic would not have been overthrown. The Depression and the other factors cannot be separated out.

Section 3

OCR Paper 2 BRITISH DEPTH STUDIES

How was British society changed, 1890–1918?

14.1 How and why did the Liberals help the poor?

For much of the nineteenth century a large proportion of the population lived in poverty and had to endure harsh working conditions. As the century drew to an end conditions for many ordinary working people had improved compared to their parents and grandparents. Wages were higher and they could afford better food along with luxuries like sweets, tea and coffee. Government regulations and inspections began to improve working conditions, pay and safety in factories and other workplaces. However, there was still a large section of society which was extremely poor and had to endure very hard lives indeed. We do not know exactly how many of these people there were, but it is possible that in some areas of the country as many as a third of the population lived in poverty and misery.

The key factor was employment. Very large numbers of workers worked in industries which were unregulated. Dock workers were all employed on a casual basis. They had to wait at the docks each day to see if there was any work. It was common for dock workers and building workers to get only three days work a week. Gas workers worked in horrendous conditions shovelling coal into furnaces. The coal backers (men who carried sacks of coal) could earn fifteen to twenty shillings very quickly but the work was so hard that many of them were unable to work past the age of 40. Some of the worst working conditions could be found in what was known as the Sweated Trades (which today we might call sweatshops). These were trades like making matchboxes or other household goods like pins, chains or shovels. Workers had to work extremely long hours in very poor conditions and they were usually paid a tiny wage for the work they produced – they were certainly not paid by the hour.

SOURCE 1

We saw a double room, perhaps nine by fifteen feet, in which a man, his wife and six children slept and in which same room ten men were usually employed, so that at night eighteen persons would be in that one room . . . with . . . the sanitary condition abominable.

In another tailoring workshop the water-closet is in the shop itself; the females sit within three feet of it . . . There is great want of decency, and it is easy to imagine what follows on such contamination. . . . Three mechanics are at work; there is one fireplace and eight or nine gas jets, also a sky-light, which, when broken, exposes the workers to the rain. On complaints being made, the employer says, 'If you can't work go home.'

. . . [A witness] said that the poor people, who formerly occupied two or three rooms, are now, for the most part, driven to occupy one room. There they live by day and night, and there is to be found all the trade refuse in the room, creating an immense danger not only to themselves but to their neighbours . . .

As the workshops are described by witnesses to be miserable; so is the food stated to be of the poorest description. 'I am almost ashamed to say what my food is . . . I might get meat once in six months.' The work was as uncertain as the wages were meagre and irregular . . . Other witnesses worked for twenty-two hours at a stretch; one had worked for forty. They had 'an hour for dinner, no tea time'. Most of them were paid by the piece – a woman might get 7d for a coat 'and by working fifteen hours she could make four such in the day, earning 2s 6d; but out of this she had to pay 3d for getting the button-holes worked, and 4d for trimmings'. Men made slightly more than women, but frequently had to be content with 1s 6d a day when they were paid at all.

Extracts from a Parliamentary Committee Report on the Sweated Trades in 1890. In 1890 a sum of 2s 6d would have the same buying power as about £10 today.

SOURCE 2

A tailor and his family in the Bethnal Green area of London. This family was making uniforms for the armed forces.

SOURCE 4

We do not say the condition of their homes, for how can those places be called homes, compared with which the lair of a wild beast would be a comfortable and healthy spot? Few who will read these pages have any conception of what these pestilential human rookeries are, where tens of thousands are crowded together amidst horrors which call to mind what we have heard of the middle passage of the slave ship. To get into them you have to penetrate courts reeking with poisonous and malodorous gases arising from accumulations of sewage and refuse scattered in all directions and often flowing beneath your feet . . .

You have to ascend rotten staircases, which threaten to give way beneath every step, . . . that imperil the limbs and lives of the unwary. You have to grope your way along dark and filthy passages swarming with vermin. Then, if you are not driven back by the intolerable stench, you may gain admittance to the dens in which these thousands of beings who belong, as much as you, to the race for whom Christ died, herd together . . . Eight feet square – that is about the average size of very many of these rooms. Walls and ceiling are black with the accretions of filth which have gathered upon them through long years of neglect. It is exuding through cracks in the boards overhead; it is running down the walls; it is everywhere.

An extract from *The Bitter Cry of Outcast London: An Inquiry into the Condition of the Abject Poor* by the Reverend Andrew Mearns, published in 1883.

One of the most infamous Sweated Trades was tailoring. In the 1890s large numbers of Jewish immigrants fleeing persecution in Russia found work in this trade in the East End of London. These new, desperate workers competed with existing workers and drove wages down even further. In 1890 the Anglican Christian Social Union tried to prepare a 'whitelist' of employers who paid and treated their workers well and whose products Christians could buy with a clear conscience. They had to drop the idea because there were so few employers who passed the test. A Parliamentary Report investigated this trade in 1890 (see Source 1).

SOURCE 3

A

B

Drawings of London in the 1870s, by the French artist Gustave Doré. **A** Backstreets of London. **B** Slum Children.

Sources 3A and 3B were published in a book of drawings called *London: A Pilgrimage* in 1872. The book was a commercial success. Many people were gripped with both fascination and terror at the appalling scenes which Doré had depicted. Source 4 was published just over ten years later in 1883. You might think that the images in Source 3 would have sparked outrage, and a determination that something should be done about the plight of the poor – but another ten years on in the 1890s the conditions were still the same for many working people. One reason was that Gustave Doré was best known as an artist with a fantastic imagination who painted weird and wonderful scenes which today we would call science fiction or fantasy. Andrew Mearns' pamphlet caused a sensation but the call for change did not last. Both failed to challenge the view of many people which was that the appalling conditions of the poor were the fault of the poor. It was generally believed that the poor spent most of their money on drink and that if they wanted to lift themselves out of poverty then they could. It was not until the 1890s that these attitudes began to shift, and this was largely because the country became better informed about the incredibly hard lives of the poor both in terms of their living conditions and their working conditions. People became better informed as a result of the work of dedicated social reformers. Two pioneers in this field were Charles Booth and Seebohm Rowntree.

Focus Task

What were working and living conditions like for the poor in the 1890s?

Study Sources 3 and 4 carefully. Prepare a short presentation to convince one of the people who dismissed Source 3 as fantasy that Doré was not using his imagination. You will need to:
◆ select extracts from Source 4 which support Source 3
◆ comment on whether you feel the author of Source 4 is a trustworthy source
◆ comment on how Sources 3 and 4 fit with other information you have come across including Sources 1 and 2.

Focus Task

How were social reformers reacting to the social problems of the 1890s?

You are going to study the work of three social reformers. Choose one reformer and write a profile in the style of page 375 to sum up the key details. Include bullet points on:
◆ background
◆ methods
◆ main findings
◆ impact.

1 Why was Booth's work important in convincing those who were sceptical about poverty?
2 According to Booth, what percentage of the population was poor (see Source 5)?

Charles Booth

Charles Booth was a successful businessman and owner of a Liverpool shipping line which opened a London office in 1880. Booth became interested in social issues as a result of his wife's friendship with the Socialist, Beatrice Webb. Booth had attended lectures and read pamphlets and reports about poverty in London. He had a sneaking suspicion that the reports were exaggerated. Over the following nineteen years Booth collected masses of information on the condition of the poor in London. His findings dismayed him almost from the start. He had been right to think that the estimates about poverty were wrong, but he had not expected them to be underestimates! Like other investigators before him, he found the most appalling conditions and grinding poverty. However, there were certain aspects of Booth's work which were especially important. Because he was a respectable businessman who had set out to show reports as exaggerated, he was taken more seriously. Also he took care to avoid sensational reporting and concentrated on finding out the scale of the problem. The first of seventeen volumes was published in 1889 and it showed that the idle, criminal or undeserving poor only numbered about 1 per cent of the population. His book also showed that about 30 per cent of London's population lived below what he called the poverty line which means being unable to afford decent food, clothing and accommodation. Most importantly of all, he showed that the problems were mainly the result of low wages, casual work, trade depressions and old age or illness.

SOURCE 5

A

BLACK
Class A: The lowest class – loafers, criminals, occasional labourers – $1\frac{1}{4}\%$

DARK BLUE
Class B: Very poor – casual work, widows and deserted women – $11\frac{1}{4}\%$

LIGHT BLUE
Class C: Poor – casual workers, vulnerable to trade conditions – 8%

PURPLE
Class D: Poor – casual and low paid regular workers – $14\frac{1}{2}\%$

PINK
Classes E and F: Regular and reasonably paid working classes

RED
Classes G and H: Middle and upper classes

Booth's classification of London's population.

Extracts from Charles Booth's *Life and Labour of the People of London*, 1889–1901. The figures indicate the percentage of the population each class makes up.

B

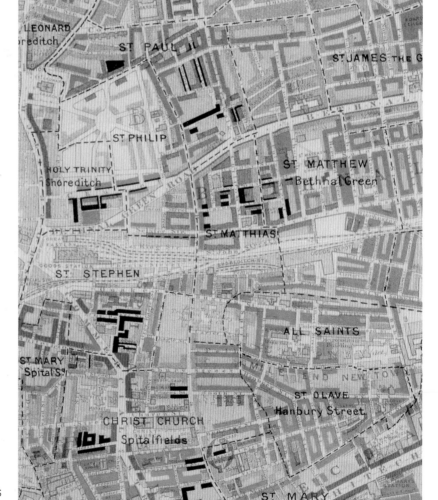

An extract from Booth's poverty map of 1898. One of the many shocking facts about Booth's findings and his maps was how wealth and poverty frequently lived side by side, often only a few yards apart.

Seebohm Rowntree

Rowntree was head of the famous confectionery company in York but he was also a committed social reformer. In 1901 Rowntree published a book called *Poverty: A Study of Town Life*. This book was based on two years' research in his home town of York. It contained a huge amount of statistical and other kinds of evidence on wages, hours of work, diet, health and housing.

SOURCE **6**

Unemployment or partial unemployment: 5 per cent

Death of wage earner: 10 per cent

Illness or old age of wage earner: 5 per cent

Low wages: 22 per cent

Large family: 52 per cent

Other: 6 per cent

Rowntree's findings on the causes of poverty.

SOURCE **7**

A family living on [the poverty line] must never spend a penny on railway fares or the omnibus. They must never go into the country unless they walk . . . They must never contribute anything to their church or chapel, or give any help to a neighbour which costs them money. They cannot save . . . The children must have no pocket money . . . The father must smoke no tobacco . . . The mother must never buy any pretty clothes . . . Should a child fall ill it must be attended by the parish doctor . . . Finally, the wage earner must never be absent from his work for a single day.

An extract from *Poverty: A Study of Town Life* by Seebohm Rowntree, 1901.

As you can see from Source 6, Rowntree's main conclusions were:

- Poverty was generally caused by old age, illness or similar factors. It was not generally the result of the poor being lazy or careless with money.
- The poor often suffered from the ups and downs in Britain's trade cycle. Clearly, ordinary people could not be blamed for these changing circumstances putting them out of work and into poverty.
- In York, 27 per cent of the population lived below the poverty line.
- The state should introduce measures to protect and safeguard the very young, the old, the ill and the unemployed.

Rowntree's work had a particularly powerful impact. Firstly, the figures for York were shocking because York was not a big industrial city with crawling slums. People saw York as a respectable, 'middling' sort of town. Finding such levels of poverty there was totally unexpected.

SOURCE **8**

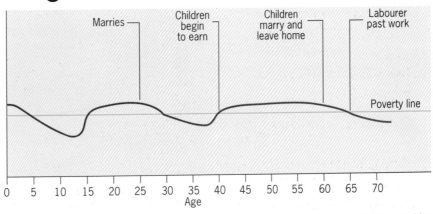

Rowntree's Poverty Line.

 3 Write your own definition of the 'poverty line'.

John Galt

John Galt is not as well known as Rowntree or Booth but as the 1890s gave way to the 1900s he played an important role in raising awareness of the life of the poor in the East End of London. A deeply religious man, Galt worked as a missionary in the East End of London helping the poor there. He was also a keen amateur photographer. He turned his images into a magic lantern show to demonstrate at meetings, mainly of middle-class people. He used his images to show that the majority of the poor lived incredibly hard lives and that they were not sub-human creatures belonging to 'another species' (as some commentators described them). He also used his images to show that far from being lazy, the poor worked incredibly hard at poorly paid jobs which often resulted in their early death. Of course London was not unique in this respect. In Glasgow and Liverpool, for example, dock workers faced the same long hours, dangerous conditions and unpredictable work patterns. So did the millions of home workers in domestic industries around the country.

SOURCE 9

A

B

Examples of John Galt's images: **A** showing workers making firewood from scrap timber and **B** showing people making shovels from scrap metal.

1. What do Sources 9A and 9B reveal about the life and work of the poor around 1900?
2. Why would Sources 9A and 9B be harder to dismiss than the images in Sources 3A and 3B?
3. Would you say that Source 7 was more likely to influence the government than Sources 9A and 9B? Explain your answer.

Activity

A leading newspaper has asked you to write an article for a special feature on poverty. The title of your article is:

'Is it time for a rethink on our attitudes to the poor?'

Your target word limit is 250 words and you can also include three images.

Remember that literacy levels in 1900 are not as high as today, so break up your article into sections, with clear subtitles.

Make sure you include evidence or information taken from the work of Booth, Rowntree or Galt.

Why did the Liberals introduce their welfare reforms?

SOURCE 10

SOURCE **10**

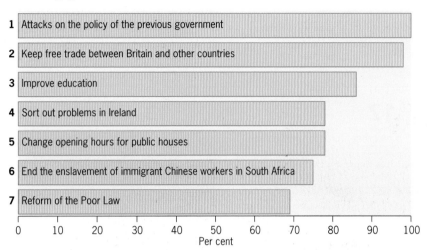

1	Attacks on the policy of the previous government
2	Keep free trade between Britain and other countries
3	Improve education
4	Sort out problems in Ireland
5	Change opening hours for public houses
6	End the enslavement of immigrant Chinese workers in South Africa
7	Reform of the Poor Law

An analysis of the issues covered in speeches by Liberal MPs before the 1906 election.

SOURCE **11**

By the kind permission of the Leeds School Board, and by the help of the schoolmasters, I have examined 100 school children in Leeds; 50 boys and 50 girls, aged 10, 11 and 12 years respectively.

Twenty five boys and twenty five girls were taken indiscriminately from a Board school in a very poor district, and the same number of corresponding age from a district inhabited by working men of the 'well-to-do' class. Each child was examined separately.

Rickets was manifest in 30 out of 50 of the children at the poor-class school; in only 10 out of 50 in the well-to-do.

Teeth – In the poor class they were bad in 27 out of 50; in the well-to-do they were bad in 22.

Weight – In the poor class each child averaged nine pounds less than the well-to-do school child.

As to Height – Each poor child measured on average six inches less than the well-to-do child.

Extract from a letter by Mr William Hall to the *Yorkshire Post* on the health of children, published in 1903.

In 1906 the Liberal Party won a huge victory in the general election in Britain. After reading pages 390–94 you might think that their top priority was to do something about poverty, but as Source 10 shows, this was not the case. Poverty came seventh on the list. It was not that the Liberals did not care, it was just that the other issues listed in Source 10 were seen as much more important. However, within a very short time that view would change and the Liberals would embark on the most ambitious programme of social reform ever seen. Why did they do this?

The social reformers

You have already read about the work of social reformers such as Charles Booth and Seebohm Rowntree. Rowntree's work had a particularly powerful impact on the Liberals. He had wealth and connections and he had been a supporter of the Liberal Party all his life. He was a friend of the leading Liberal MP, David Lloyd George, who became Chancellor of the Exchequer in 1908. His family also owned *The Nation* and the *Daily News*, which between them publicised the issue of poverty among the middle and working classes. Rowntree was asked by the Liberal government to carry out a study into rural poverty in 1913. He was an important influence behind the Old Age Pensions Act and the National Insurance Act (see pages 398–99). The work of Rowntree and others helped to change attitudes towards the poor. The new measures put forward by the Liberals were based on new assumptions:

• It was not always the fault of the poor that they were poor.
• It was the role of government to support the poor when they needed it most.

David Lloyd George even called this new attitude New Liberalism. In the new Edwardian era it was seen as morally wrong that such extreme poverty should be allowed to exist alongside such incredible wealth.

Increasing information about poverty

As well as these high profile reformers, information was being sent to the government from thousands of other sources. The Salvation Army was collecting information as well as running training courses for the unemployed. Many other charities were carrying out similar work. The government's own civil servants were also collecting information. So were officials of the local authorities whose job it was to provide people with sanitation, clean water, education, health care and other essential services.

The scale of the problem

The new evidence built up a picture of the scale of the problem. The poor died at a comparatively early age. Life expectancy for poor men and women was about 45 (today it is in the 70s). In 1900 there were 163 deaths per thousand – much higher than today's figure of 12 per 1,000 in the UK. Even if they made it through to young adulthood, men and women in the poorest areas could easily fall victim to illness or accident. An observer from today would have noticed how small the majority of the poorer classes were. The better off were a similar height and weight to today's average height and weight. In simple terms, there were areas of Britain's towns and cities which resembled parts of the developing world today. This was at a time when Britain had never been richer. There were more millionaires than there had ever been before. However, the top 10 per cent of the population owned 92 per cent of the country's wealth.

SOURCE 12

After 45 it becomes increasingly difficult for a man to obtain employment in most of the skilled trades, and for those over 55 the chances of getting regular work are rare. For the unskilled labourer over the age of 55 there is still less opportunity. The whole tendency of the age is to pay men better but to retire them earlier. Estimates vary as to the extent to which old age is responsible for pauperism. The most reliable figures are to be found in Mr. Burt's Return of the numbers in receipt of Outdoor or Indoor Relief in England and Wales. This showed that in September 1903 the number of paupers 65 years of age and upwards was 284,265, which is equivalent to 18.3 per cent of the total number of persons in that age group.

An extract from a report presented to the Cabinet in 1906.

SOURCE 13

A poor working-class home in Liverpool, 1905. The photograph was taken by the Liverpool City Engineer's department as part of a planning process to map out possible new roads in the city. The photographs were not intended to campaign for social reform.

1 How could you solve the problems described in Source 12?

National efficiency: The Boer War

Between 1899 and 1902, Britain was at war to defend its territory in southern Africa. Half of the recruits who volunteered to fight were found to be unfit for service because of ill health. In some poor areas of Britain, 69 per cent were unfit. The potential recruits were so badly fed that they had not grown properly. The army had to lower its minimum height for a soldier in order to find enough infantrymen. This was alarming for a government that needed to be able to call up a strong army at short notice. The government set up the Committee on Physical Deterioration to investigate the issue, and its recommendations influenced the Liberal programme of reform.

National efficiency: An effective workforce

Britain's military strength was not the only concern. From 1870 onwards, Britain's position as the world's leading industrial power was being challenged by the USA and Germany. By 1900, both countries had overtaken Britain. Lloyd George was extremely impressed with the welfare programme introduced in Germany by Bismarck, the Chancellor. Germany's rapid development appeared to be closely linked to its healthier, better-educated and therefore more efficient workforce. There was also a recognition that some unemployment was caused by foreign competition, not laziness. As a result, government help for the unemployed had widespread support.

SOURCE 14

I warn you about the Labour Party. I warn you it will become a terrifying force that will sweep away Liberalism. We have a Liberal Parliament, but we must act to help the poor. We must get rid of the national disgrace of slums. We must eliminate the widespread poverty which scars this land glittering with wealth, otherwise the working men of Britain will vote Labour instead of Liberal.

Lloyd George speaking to a Liberal Party meeting in Cardiff in 1906.

SOURCE 15

Germany is not as rich as us, yet German social reforms mean they are better organised for peace and also for war. We are organised for nothing! We cannot rely on existing charities and this winter is causing misery. Consequently, there is an urgent need to help the working class and make England a safer and better country for them. When the people begin to feel the benefit of our social reforms they will give solid support to our Liberal Government.

An extract from a letter by Winston Churchill to his leader, Prime Minister Herbert Asquith, in December 1908.

2 Do you agree that the main motivation for reform in Sources 14 and 15 is to help the poor? Explain your answer, using extracts from each source.

Key individuals: David Lloyd George and Winston Churchill

Without doubt, the Liberal politician David Lloyd George had great influence. Lloyd George's father, the head teacher in an elementary school in Manchester, died the year after his son was born. David and his poverty-stricken mother went to live in a Welsh village, where her brother, a shoemaker and Baptist minister, supported the family. With his uncle's help, Lloyd George became a solicitor. Lloyd George hated the way that the English upper classes dominated Welsh life and he sympathised with the ordinary people. He was also a very able politician, and by 1908 he had risen to the post of Chancellor of the Exchequer.

Another key figure was Winston Churchill. He had been a leading Conservative, but switched sides in 1906 when the Liberals started their welfare reforms, supposedly because he supported them, although his enemies said that it was because he did not want to be in the party of opposition. In 1908, Churchill became President of the Board of Trade. These two and other leading Liberals had read the works of Seebohm Rowntree and other social reformers and felt that poverty needed to be tackled. They were aware of the contrast between Britain's vast wealth and its squalid urban slums.

Political rivalry

A final factor was political rivalry. The Liberals' main rivals were the Conservative Party. The Conservatives had introduced welfare measures of their own when they had been in power. In 1905 the Conservatives had introduced the Unemployed Workmen's Act to help fight the effects of high unemployment. This could be a vote-winner among the working classes. The leading figures in the Liberal Party, particularly the Chancellor Herbert Asquith, were also aware that they had won the election in 1906 because the electorate had rejected the Conservatives as much as voting for them. Asquith wanted the Liberal Party to have a big idea which would unite and inspire all Liberals and which would allow them to show how they were different from the Conservatives. Finally, the Liberals also saw welfare reforms as a way of fighting Socialism. If the working classes were healthier and happier, there would be less support for the type of revolutionary Socialist movements that were troubling France, Germany and Russia at this time. It was also hoped that reforms would undermine support for the new Labour Party. Most working-class men could vote in elections by 1906. The new Labour Party was calling for pensions, education and unemployment benefits. The Party was only small in 1906, with 29 seats in Parliament. The Liberals hoped to keep it that way.

Focus Task

Why did the Liberal government introduce reforms to help the young, old and unemployed?

1 Make your own copy of this diagram.

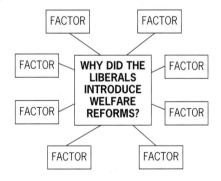

2 Using the text and sources on pages 395–97, complete the diagram to show as many different factors as you can find.
3 Explain how each one helped to influence the Liberals.
4 Once your diagram is completed, see if you can put your factors into categories. Which factors might you put in the following categories:
   ◆ political motives: the desire to get the Liberal government re-elected
   ◆ moral motives: the desire to help and do good
   ◆ nationalistic motives: the desire to make Britain a stronger country?
5 Can you think of other categories into which to organise these factors?

What measures did the Liberals introduce?

1 Children

The Liberals began their programme of reforms almost as soon as they came to power. In 1906, an Act was passed that allowed (but did not force) local authorities to provide free school meals. The new law meant that children would eat at least one decent meal a day. In 1914, 14 million meals were served up, most of which were free. On the other hand, only half of Britain's local authorities actually set up a meals service.

In 1907, attention was turned to medical care. Many parents were not able to afford proper treatment. Now, every local education authority had to set up a school medical service. At first, the service provided only regular medical checks, but from 1912 this was extended to provide treatment in school clinics as well. But it was left to local authorities to make these measures work. As a result, medical care varied widely across the country.

In 1908, the Children and Young Persons Act was inspired by a terrible social evil. In the past, insurance companies had paid out money to parents on the death of their young children, even in suspicious circumstances, with predictable results. The Act gave children special status as protected persons, and their parents could now be prosecuted for neglect. It also made it illegal to insure a child's life.

The Act set up special courts to deal with child crime and also special homes or Borstals to house young offenders so that they did not need to be sent to adult prisons.

2 The old

In 1908, in his first budget as Chancellor of the Exchequer, Lloyd George introduced a government-funded old-age pension. A person over 70 with no other income would receive five shillings per week. Married couples would receive 7s 6d. Anyone who had an income of over £31 per year did not qualify for a state pension. Only British citizens who had been living in Britain for the last twenty years could receive a state pension. Pensions could be refused to people who had failed to work to their best abilities during their working life. Pensions were not new but poor people could not afford private pensions. Many old people had been dependent on poor relief or outdoor relief (handouts of food, clothing or small amounts of cash). Some still lived with the threat of the workhouse. Although the state pension was hardly a generous measure, the effect on the elderly poor was enormous. Their state pensions made them independent for the rest of their lives. In the first year, some 650,000 people collected their pensions. The number of people claiming outdoor relief fell by over 80,000.

As well as helping thousands of old people, the Act established new and important principles. First, it was non-contributory. In other words, people received it without having paid anything towards a pension fund. Second, poverty was being tackled by direct funding from the government, rather than from local rates. It was a small measure but a big step.

Activity 1

Change or continuity?

1 Make your own copy of this table. Fill it in using the information on pages 398–99.

Group	How helped before Liberal reforms	Measures taken by Liberals to tackle problem	Limitations of the reforms
Children	No real system – some charities helped poor families with children; orphans looked after in workhouses		
The old	Charities; family; the workhouse		
The sick	Charities; family; the workhouse		
The unemployed or underemployed	Outdoor relief; voluntary labour exchanges		

Professor Change

These were totally new ideas – very radical – total change.

Professor Continuity

Ah, but look below the surface and the old ideas about poverty are still lurking.

2 The two professors want your help. Find them some evidence on pages 398–99 to back up their viewpoints.

3 The unemployed

Campaigners for social reform had shown how great a problem unemployment and underemployment (irregular work) could be. Labour exchanges run by volunteers had existed for some time. Here, workers could sign on to a register when they were unemployed, and they could find out about available work. In 1909 the government set up its own labour exchanges as part of its campaign against unemployment. By 1913 labour exchanges were putting 3,000 people into jobs every working day.

SOURCE 16

Nothing wearies more than walking about hunting for employment which is not to be had. It is far harder than real work. The uncertainty, the despair, when you reach a place only to discover that the journey is fruitless. I've known a man to say: 'Which way shall I go today?' Having no earthly idea which way to take, he tosses up a button. If the button comes down on one side he treks east; if on the other, he treks west.

Written by William Crooks, a working man who later became a Labour MP.

SOURCE 17

A voluntary labour exchange in Chelsea, 1887.

SOURCE 18

The government labour exchange at Camberwell Green, February 1910.

4 Workers: The National Insurance Act

The National Insurance Act of 1911 was a really important measure. Insurance was not a new idea. It had been the basis of the friendly societies for two centuries or more. Indeed, the Liberals used the friendly societies to administer the national insurance scheme. But Lloyd George's scheme went far beyond any of these private schemes.

Sick pay

The first part of the Act dealt with health insurance. All men and women in lower-paid manual and clerical jobs earning under £160 per year had to join. They then had to pay 4d out of each week's wages. Each payment earned them a 'stamp' on their card. The employer added 3d worth of stamps and the government a further 2d. Liberal posters talked of workers getting 9d for 4d. The money was paid into a friendly society of the worker's choice.

In return, the worker received up to 26 weeks of sick pay at 10 shillings a week from the friendly society. There was also free medical care for the insured.

It was an important boost for low-paid workers, but it did not solve all their problems. The families of workers were not entitled to free treatment, and widows did not receive pensions.

Unemployment benefit

The second part of the Act dealt with unemployment and underemployment. In trades such as building, shipbuilding and engineering, occasional unemployment was common. To cover this, the Act required a further contribution of 2½d per week from the worker, supplemented by 2½d from the employer and 1¾d from the government. These sums paid for 'stamps' on the worker's card. During times of unemployment, a worker would receive seven shillings per week for up to fifteen weeks. It was not much money, certainly not enough to support a working man and his family. This was deliberate, because the government wanted to encourage careful saving and did not want workers to 'sit back and enjoy' the benefits.

Activity 2

You are going to a public meeting in 1914 and Prime Minister Asquith, the Liberal leader since 1908, will be there. You are not a fan of the Prime Minister. Come up with five awkward questions relating to the Liberals' reforms in the period 1906–14.

1 In what ways do Sources 19 and 20 give similar and different impressions of Lloyd George's attitude towards paying for welfare reforms?
2 What is Source 21 trying to say about Lloyd George?
3 Would you agree that Sources 19 and 20 are more sympathetic to Lloyd George than Source 21?
4 Is Source 21 an accurate view of the Liberal welfare reforms? Explain your answer by referring to the details in the image AND by referring to Sources 21–25.
5 The Liberal reforms caused confusion and hostility. How far do these sources support this view?

Reactions to the reforms

The reforms were controversial and were met with enormous opposition. Conservatives opposed the cost and the idea of the 'nanny state'. Doctors were not convinced about health insurance. The friendly societies and insurance companies prevented national insurance benefits being given to widows. Some workers resented the deductions from their wages. The Labour Party criticised the fact that workers had to fund their own benefits. They felt it should come from taxation of the wealthy to help the poor.

Of course the wealthy did not agree. Lloyd George's 1908 Budget (often called the People's Budget) was designed to raise the money for the reforms and it became the centre of a bitter political battle between the Liberal majority in the House of Commons and the Conservative majority in the House of Lords. Lloyd George said that the upper classes inherited much of their wealth and did little work to earn what they had, so they should pay for social reforms to help those who did work and suffered poverty. The House of Lords tried to stop the reforms going through. This major constitutional crisis ended with the reduction of the power of the House of Lords.

Sources 19–25 give a range of viewpoints on the reforms as they were expressed at the time.

SOURCE **19**

The caption read 'Rich fare.' With the 'Giant Lloyd-Gorgibuster' saying, 'Fee, fi, fo, fat, I smell the blood of a plutocrat; Be he alive or be he dead, I'll grind his bones to make my bread.'

SOURCE **21**

A cartoon published by the Conservative Party commenting on the Liberal reforms. Another big issue at this time was trade. Lloyd George favoured free trade between countries but the Conservatives believed in tariffs (taxes) which restricted imports to Britain by making them more expensive.

SOURCE **20**

The title was 'The Philanthropic Highwayman.' With 'Mr Lloyd-George' saying 'I'll make 'em pity the aged poor!'

SOURCE **22**

THE BIG DOG AND THE LITTLE ONE.

LORD HALSBURY: I don't think much of that paltry little thing—it's a mockery of a dog.
AGED PENSIONER: Well, my lord, 'tis only a little 'un, but 'tis a wunnerful comfort to me. Us bain't all blessed wi' big 'uns!

Liberal Party Leaflet, published 1 February 1909

A cartoon from a Liberal Party leaflet, February 1909. Lord Halsbury had criticised the pension for being too small. As a former Conservative Lord Chancellor, his own was £5,000.

SOURCE 23

THE DAWN OF HOPE.

Mr. LLOYD GEORGE'S National Health Insurance Bill provides for the insurance of the Worker in case of Sickness.

Support the Liberal Government
in their policy of
SOCIAL REFORM.

A poster published by the Liberal Party to convince working men of the benefits of the National Insurance Act, 1911.

SOURCE 24

Dear Madam,

My attention has been called to the fact that you [Countess of Desart] and Lady Brassey are organising a mass meeting of women to protest against the inclusion of domestic servants within the scope of the National Insurance Bill.

My motives in this connexion have been subjected to much misrepresentation in irresponsible quarters, but it is not necessary for me to assure you that in wishing to see domestic servants comprised in the Bill I am acting solely by what I believe to be the interests of that class. Let me remind you briefly how the proposal affects them ... every servant will be entitled to free medical care, to the payment of 7/6 a week during sickness for six months, and 5/- thereafter if permanently incapacitated, and to free treatment in a sanatorium if she contracts tuberculosis. These are the minimum benefits under the Bill, but if, as has been said, domestic servants do not require the full sickness benefit, the money thus saved can be used with any other savings to give some other benefit, as, for instance, a pension fund which would provide pensions at an earlier age than 70.

Part of a letter from Lloyd George to the Countess of Desart, November 1911.

SOURCE 25

... now we want to go on living forever, because we give them [his son's family] the 10 shillings a week, and it pays them to have us along with them. I never thought we should be able to pay the boy back for all his goodness to me and the missus.

An old man talks about his pension, 1912.

Focus Task

How effective were the Liberal reforms?

Most historians agree that the Liberal reforms were extremely significant. They marked a change from past attitudes. Here is how Historian Professor Eric Hopkins described them in 1979: *'an impressive body of social legislation, the greatest ever passed by any one government up to that time ... A radical new plan of campaign had been developed to meet the most urgent social needs of the working classes'.*

1 Use Sources 26 and 27 to add some supporting evidence to Hopkins' statement.
2 As well as praising the reforms, Hopkins and other historians have also accepted that they did not eradicate the problems facing the poor. Write a short report explaining the limitations of the reforms. You could organise it into paragraphs:
   ◆ the young   ◆ the sick
   ◆ the old   ◆ the unemployed.
Support your report with evidence from pages 398–401.

SOURCE 26

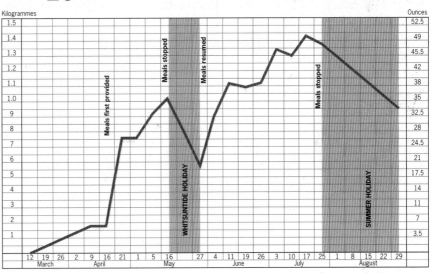

A graph showing the weight gain and loss of schoolchildren in Bradford 1907 (after school meals were introduced in 1906). The information was collected by a schools inspector.

SOURCE 27

The total number of Board of Trade Labour Exchanges open at the end of 1912 was 414, of which 153 were established during the year. The number established during 1911 was 115, and during 1910, was 146. The number on 1st February, 1910, the date of the commencement of operations under the Labour Exchanges Act of 1909, was 61 ...

The number of applicants given work on the General Register in 1912 was 567,790, and the number of situations filled was 785,239, of which 160,428 were temporary in the sense of being known to have been of less than a week's duration. In addition, 266,622 jobs of a casual nature were found for 12,767 individuals.

An extract from an official government report on the work of Labour Exchanges in 1912.

14.2 How and why did women try to win the vote?

Women in society in the late 1800s

By today's standards, women were most definitely second class citizens in Victorian Britain. Of course, people in the 1890s did not see the world through our eyes. Most men and women probably thought that it was perfectly reasonable that women earned less than men, had fewer legal rights than men and lost even more of these rights when they got married. They did not question that the jobs with the longest hours and the lowest pay (particularly domestic service) were overwhelmingly done by women. The majority of people probably did not even think about the issue.

On the other hand, some determined campaigners did think about the issue, and they were encouraged by important changes which took place through the nineteenth century. The growth of shop work brought important new opportunities for women. Shop work was a job which could give a woman a degree of independence and there were also new opportunities in the newly created Post Office. Opportunities also opened up for women in nursing and teaching. For working class women the opportunities were fewer. New laws regulating conditions in factories and other workplaces did bring benefits, but the majority of workers in Sweated Trades (see page 390) were still women.

There were improvements for women in the field of education as well, but again these largely benefited middle-class women from better off homes. One key area was marriage, and the rights of women within marriage. This had been a battleground throughout the nineteenth century. It was far easier for men to divorce women than the other way around, for example, and when a marriage broke down it was assumed that the woman was at fault. In 1882 a Women's Property Act finally gave married women the right to own property on her own, rather than all her property belonging to her husband. In 1884 married women were finally recognised as individuals by the law, rather than being seen as possessions of their husbands.

Through the 1890s there were more important developments:

1889: The Women's Franchise League takes up the rights of married women and campaigns for equality for women in divorce, inheritance and custody of children.

1891: Free and compulsory education is introduced for all working-class children up to the age of twelve. Legal judgement confirms that a man cannot compel his wife to live in the matrimonial home.

1894: Parish Councils Act permits propertied women and ratepayers to serve on urban and parish district councils.

1896: Factory Act bans the employment of children under eleven in factories. Women are not to be employed for four weeks after having a child.

1897: Non-militant National Union of Women's Suffrage Societies (NUWSS) is formed by well-educated middle-class women frustrated with their lives.

1901: Factory Act reduces by one hour the number of hours women work.

So, the advances in work, education and legal rights in this period were real and significant. Women, particularly middle-class women, had gained important rights over their property and new opportunities for education. New jobs and careers were available.

However, one should not overstate the progress made. Women were still very much the inferior partners in marriages. They were barred from most professions. They could not even vote. For many campaigners, this was the most basic injustice of all. To them, it seemed that gaining the right to vote would be a key to many other changes. Yet the evidence of the nineteenth century was that every advance involved an intense struggle. With an all-male Parliament elected by an all-male electorate, women were going to have to fight to move closer to the centre of politics. But how would this be achieved?

Activity

1 Draw up two lists in a copy of the table below.

Ways in which women had achieved greater equality with men in the late 1800s	Ways in which women were treated as second-class citizens' in the late 1800s

2 Highlight two items in each list which women of the time would regard as:
   a) the greatest advance, and
   b) the greatest injustice.

How should citizens campaign for something they believe in?

SOURCE **1**

A

Suffragists begin their six-week pilgrimage to London

B

Suffragettes burn down Rowley Regis church

Newspaper headlines from 18 June 1913.

Compare Sources 1A and 1B. Both events happened on the same day. Both were part of the campaign to win the vote for women – or female suffrage (suffrage means the right to vote).

One protest was staged by the suffragists, who believed in peaceful, law-abiding protest, and the other by the suffragettes, who used violent methods to get their views across. Both groups had the same aim but different methods. Over the next fifteen pages you will be exploring the reasons for these protests and comparing the effectiveness of the two campaigns.

Attitudes towards women

SOURCE **2**

Mr. S. SMITH (Flintshire) said that nothing but a sense of duty caused him to call attention to the disgraceful condition of many of the streets of London at night time … He had travelled in many countries, and he asserted that there was not a heathen country in which there were the open incentives to vice as were to be found in Piccadilly and neighbouring streets at night.

He would naturally be asked how this difficulty could be grappled with. In answer he would point to Liverpool, … they formed a vigilance committee, worked upon public opinion, and at last elected a reforming watch committee to enforce the law; … In the course of ten years the outward aspect of Liverpool was changed … It made a great difference, and it was a great benefit that young men were not assailed on every side by temptation.

Mr SOUTTAR (Dumfriesshire) seconded the motion. He said it was especially on behalf of young men that he pleaded with the Home Secretary.

A discussion by MPs about prostitution and vice generally in British cities, July 1913.

One of the most serious obstacles which women had to face was one of attitudes. Look carefully at Source 2. According to the MPs, who needs protecting? Would we see the men who use prostitutes as people who need protection today? Source 2 shows us different standards being applied to men and women, and that view was at the heart of the campaign for female suffrage.

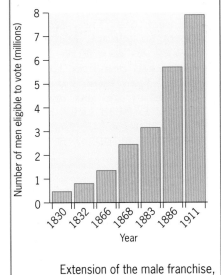

Extension of the male franchise, 1830–1911.

SOURCE **3**

We wish for the vote because there exists a terrible trade of procuring young girls for immoral purposes. Once the girl is seduced it is very difficult for her to return home. She becomes a prostitute. The time has come for women to help and the first step in this lies in winning the vote for without this they have no power. It would be much more difficult for this cruel and wicked traffic to be carried on if it were recognised by the law that women were of the same value and had the same standing as men.

A comment by a member of the National Union of Women's Suffrage Societies (NUWSS).

What were the arguments in favour of votes for women?

In the nineteenth century, new job opportunities for women emerged as teachers, as shop workers or as clerks and secretaries in offices. Many able girls from working-class backgrounds achieved better-paid jobs with higher status than those of their parents. Women gained greater opportunities in education. A few middle-class women won the chance to go to university, to become doctors, for example. By 1900 women could vote in local elections and could take part in local government as councillors. They could also vote in elections for Poor Law Guardians and School Boards. By 1914 over 1,500 women were serving as Poor Law Guardians. Women were also active in national politics. The Labour Party had the Women's Labour League, the Conservatives had the Primrose League and the Liberals had the Women's Liberal Federation. Women activists shared the organisation of election campaigns and often spoke on the same platforms as men in elections. Working-class women were also heavily involved in trade union activities. By 1914 around 20 per cent of all women workers were in a union – a similar rate to male workers. To supporters of female suffrage all of these factors made the restrictions on women look absurd.

SOURCE **4**

Parliament's decisions affect both men and women. So women should be able to vote for the MPs who pass those laws.

LET THE WOMEN HELP! Two heads are better than one.

Women pay taxes just like men.

There are many single women and widows who bear the same responsibilities as men.

Women should be able to influence MPs on how that money is spent.

Women are the spiritual spine of the nation – they are the churchgoers. Give women the vote if you want MPs to show Christian leadership.

A suffragette argues for female suffrage.

Women can already vote in local elections. They serve on local government bodies, such as education committees and Poor Law boards. They have shown that they are able and can be trusted with a vote.

Women have increasing opportunities in education and work – the vote should come next.

Women have special skills and expertise. They can help Parliament make better laws on issues such as education and the home where they are specialists.

Many uneducated working men can vote while well-educated, 'respectable' women can't.

Other arguments for votes for women.

SOURCE 5

'What is it all about?'

Firstly, women need the vote for the protection of themselves under the law and the administration of the country. They point to the unequal treatment of women in the Insurance Act, to the exclusion of women from the better-paid posts in the Civil Service, to the laws relating to divorce, the guardianship of children, inheritance, and many other matters as showing that a voteless section of the population does not obtain fair treatment at the hands of Parliament. In the second place, they claim, that in all legislation affecting the interests of the country as a whole, and the men and women and children in it, the women's point of view is not given adequate weight. The improvement of housing, the better protection of child life, the purification of food, and many other questions do not command the attention they deserve because the women who care most about these things have not the driving power of the vote to force them to the front. And they say that in consequence many thousands of little children die annually from preventable causes, and that the health and life of the country is gravely deteriorated. Lastly, they say that the Parliamentary vote is a symbol of citizenship, that the exclusion from the vote of the whole female sex is a stain on this country which no glib talk about the 'differing spheres of men and women' can obliterate.

An extract from the journal *Votes for Women*, 1913.

SOURCE 6

A cartoon from *Votes for Women* showing how women gained the vote in different countries and states.

SOURCE 7

This Senate is of the opinion that the extension of the Suffrage to the women of Australia on the same terms as men, has had the most beneficial results. It has led to the more orderly conduct of Elections, and at the last Federal Elections, the Women's vote in the majority of the States showed a greater proportionate increase than that cast by men. It has given a greater prominence to legislation, particularly affecting women and children, although the women have not taken up such questions to the exclusion of others of wider significance. In matters of Defence and Imperial concern, they have proved themselves as far-seeing and discriminating as men. Because the reform has brought nothing but good, though disaster was freely prophesied, we respectfully urge that all Nations enjoying Representative Government would be well advised in granting votes to women.

A resolution passed by the Australian Parliament in 1910.

Focus Task

What were the arguments for women's suffrage?

Study the arguments in Source 4 carefully.
1 Reorganise them into categories, such as arguments based on:
  ◆ the principle that men and women should be treated equally
  ◆ the idea that female suffrage would improve everyday life
  ◆ the idea that the country would be run better
  ◆ any other categories you can think of.
2 Read through Sources 3 and 5–7. Are any arguments missing from Source 4? If so, add them in.
3 Reorganise all the arguments one last time, putting what you think are the strongest arguments first and the weakest arguments last.
4 Finally, discuss whether your answer to question 3 would be the same from a 1906 perspective as it would be today.

What were the arguments against votes for women?

The opposition to women's suffrage was strong. Many men and women believed that the two sexes occupied different spheres in life, and that politics belonged in the men's sphere. Many of the strongest opponents were women, who felt that the vote was irrelevant to them or who believed that women getting the vote would upset the traditional balance of relationships in families. Many women felt that their views were represented by their husbands who did have the vote.

Another interesting factor was party politics. By 1900 many backbench Liberal MPs were supporters of votes for women but Liberal leaders were opposed. This was because only better-off, property-owning women would get the vote and these women would vote Conservative. For this reason, some Conservative leaders were quite interested in women's suffrage but they held back because Conservative backbench MPs were completely opposed.

SOURCE 8

Men and women have different interests and responsibilities. Women are home-makers and mothers. It is the role of men to debate and take difficult decisions.

With the vote, women would become the most hateful, heartless and disgusting of human beings. Where would be the protection which man was intended to give to the weaker sex?

Giving respectable women the vote will also encourage them to develop their careers and neglect their family duties. Only the undesirable classes will have children.

It is mainly middle-class women campaigning for the vote. They will have little interest in laws to help ordinary working people.

Giving the vote to women will mean giving it to all men – including layabouts and riffraff.

Women are not rational. They are too emotional to be trusted with the vote.

Queen Victoria commenting on female suffrage.

Women are pure and should be protected from the grubby world of politics.

Women do not fight in wars for their country. So they should not have a say in whether the country should go to war.

Why worry about the vote? There are much more pressing concerns such as Ireland and the trade unions.

Other arguments against votes for women.

SOURCE 9

MR CREMER (Shoreditch, Haggerston), … opposed the motion. He asserted that, if they once admitted any section of females to the right of the Parliamentary vote, it must ultimately lead to adult suffrage. (Hear, hear.) As, according to the last census, there were three quarters of a million more female than male adults, and as, to that number, must be added perhaps a quarter of a million of men who were always unable to record their votes by reason of the nature of their occupations, adult suffrage meant handing the government of the country over to a majority of the electorate who would not be men but women. (Laughter.) He had too great a respect for women to drag them into the political arena and ask them to undertake obligations and discharge duties that they did not understand, and, what was more, that they did not care for. If the women of the country were polled on this question, he believed that the majority would either not vote or would record their vote against it.

An extract from a speech in Parliament by William Cremer, MP.

Focus Task

What were the arguments against women's suffrage?

Study the arguments in Source 8 carefully.

1 Reorganise them into categories, such as arguments based on:
   ◆ the principle that men and women should be treated equally
   ◆ the idea that female suffrage would improve everyday life
   ◆ the idea that the country would be run better
   ◆ any other categories you can think of.
2 Read through Sources 9–11. Are any arguments missing from Source 8? If so, add them in.
3 Reorganise all the arguments one last time putting what you think are the strongest arguments first and the weakest arguments last.
4 Finally, discuss whether your answer to question 3 would be the same from a 1906 perspective as it would today.

SOURCE 10

To the Rt Hon Lloyd George MP
Dear Sir

As a typical women householder and rate and tax payer I beg you – a typical man – to take upon your stronger shoulders the burden of responsibility for the safety of the Empire, the Army, Navy, Trade, Shipping, Mining, Railways etc. I am too thankful to pay my taxes in return for your protection, if only you will leave me to look after my home and my child. It is true that I am in the unfortunate position of having to earn a livelihood as well as perform the duties of a mother, but why, why on that account do you want to add still more to my responsibilities and duties? It would be cruel and cowardly.

Will you not look at this question from our point of view as well as the other and wait until you find out what the majority of women feel.

… If woman suffrage is put into the Reform bill the Liberal Government will be wrecked. Are we to lose the Insurance Bill, Home Rule, Welsh Disestablishment, and Land Reform, for the sake of a mere quarter of a million of misguided women who most of them only want to enfranchise the women of property for the sake of the Conservative Party? Are the other $12\frac{3}{4}$ millions of women to be utterly ignored?

I am
Yours Truly
Gwladys Gladstone Solomon

A letter written to David Lloyd George in June 1912 by a woman from The National League for Opposing Women's Suffrage.

SOURCE 11

"WHAT'S THE DISTURBANCE IN THE MARKET-PLACE?"
"IT'S A MASS MEETING OF THE WOMEN WHO'VE CHANGED THEIR MINDS SINCE THE MORNING AND WANT TO ALTER THEIR VOTING-PAPERS."

Cartoon from *Punch* magazine published in 1918. This cartoon was suggesting what would happen when women were allowed to vote in elections.

How were the suffragist and suffragette campaigns different?

Factfile

Bills for female suffrage, 1906–13

➤ **January 1906** A Liberal government is elected with a massive majority. Four hundred out of 650 MPs are in favour of women's suffrage, including the Prime Minister, Henry Campbell-Bannerman.

➤ **March 1907** A women's suffrage bill is introduced, but opponents delay it so long that it runs out of time.

➤ **February 1908** A new women's suffrage bill is introduced and is passed on a second reading but it gets no further.

➤ **March 1909** The Liberal government introduces a radical Suffrage Bill – giving votes to almost all adult men and women. It wins a majority of 34 on a second reading – but gets no further in Parliament.

➤ **November 1909** A general election is called and the suffrage bill is temporarily dropped.

➤ **June 1910** An all-party committee drafts a Conciliation Bill which gives women the vote and is acceptable to all parties. On a second reading, it is passed by a majority of 110.

➤ **18 November** 1910 Prime Minister Asquith calls another general election and so the bill is abandoned.

➤ **May 1911** The Conciliation Bill is reintroduced. It gets a massive 167 majority. Asquith announces that the government will proceed with the bill in 1912.

➤ **November 1911** The Liberal government will not support the Conciliation Bill. Instead, it wants a male suffrage bill that would widen the vote for men! The bill would not mention women, but Asquith says MPs can amend the bill to include women if they want.

➤ **March 1912** Second reading of the Conciliation Bill. It is defeated by fourteen votes.

➤ **June 1912** Suffrage bill is introduced. Progress is postponed to the following year.

➤ **1913** Attempts are made to include women in the Male Suffrage Bill, but the Speaker announces that the amendments would change the very nature of the bill. As a result, the women's vote amendments are withdrawn.

➤ **May 1913** A new private member's bill to give women the vote is introduced but defeated by a majority of 48.

Who were the suffragists?

The early campaigners for the vote were known as suffragists. They were mainly (though not all) middle-class women. When the MP John Stuart Mill had suggested giving votes to women in 1867, 73 MPs had supported the motion. After so many MPs voted in favour of women's suffrage in 1867, large numbers of local women's suffrage societies were formed. By the time they came together in 1897 to form the National Union of Women's Suffrage Societies (NUWSS), there were over 500 local branches. By 1902, the campaign had gained the support of working-class women as well. In 1901–02, Eva Gore-Booth gathered the signatures of 67,000 textile workers in northern England for a petition to Parliament.

The leader of the movement was Mrs Millicent Fawcett. She believed in constitutional campaigning. She argued her case with MPs, issued leaflets, presented petitions and organised meetings. She thought that it was crucial to keep the issue in the public eye: at every election, suffragists questioned the candidates on their attitudes to women's suffrage. She talked of the suffragist movement as being like a glacier, slow but unstoppable. By 1900 they had achieved some success, gaining the support of many Liberal MPs and some leading Conservative MPs, as well as the new but rather small Labour Party.

However, there was a rather curious situation in Parliament with regard to women's suffrage (as mentioned on page 406). Many backbench Liberal MPs were supporters of votes for women, but the Liberal leaders were opposed to it. This was because they feared that, if only better-off, property-owning women got the vote, these women would vote for their arch rivals, the Conservative Party.

On the other hand, some Conservative leaders, liking the prospect of more Conservative voters, were quite keen on women's suffrage. But they took no action because their backbench MPs were completely opposed, on principle, to changing the role of women.

In addition, both parties had bigger worries than female suffrage. Neither party was prepared to adopt female suffrage as party policy, so it never got priority in Parliament. It was left up to individual MPs to introduce private bills, which were never allowed the time they needed to get through. In the years up to 1900, fifteen times Parliament received a bill to give women the vote; fifteen times the bill failed.

Who were the suffragettes?

This lack of success frustrated many suffragists. As a result, in 1903, Mrs Emmeline Pankhurst founded a new campaigning organisation, the Women's Social and Political Union (WSPU). Mrs Pankhurst thought that the movement had to become more radical and militant if it was to succeed. The *Daily Mail* called these new radicals 'suffragettes', and they soon made the headlines.

The suffragettes disrupted political meetings and harassed ministers. The Liberal Prime Minister, Asquith, who was firmly opposed to women's suffrage, came in for particularly heavy abuse.

1908: Direct action begins

After the latest in a long line of women's suffrage bills ran out of time in 1908, the suffragette campaign intensified and became more vocal. The suffragette Edith New began making speeches in Downing Street; to stop the police from moving her on, she chained herself to the railings and so was arrested. In the same year, some suffragettes threw stones through the windows of 10 Downing Street (the Prime Minister's house). In October, Mrs Pankhurst, her daughter Christabel and 'General' Flora Drummond were sent to prison for inciting a crowd to 'rush' the House of Commons.

SOURCE 12

THE SHRIEKING SISTER.

THE SENSIBLE WOMAN. "*YOU HELP OUR CAUSE? WHY, YOU'RE ITS WORST ENEMY!*"

A 1906 cartoon from *Punch* magazine.

SOURCE 13

Hampstead Women's Social and Political Union,
178, FINCHLEY ROAD, N.W.

WINDOW BREAKING
AND
INCITEMENT
TO
MUTINY.

For Breaking Windows as a Political protest, Women are now in H.M. Gaols serving sentences of **Four and Six months imprisonment.**

For Inciting Soldiers to Disobey Orders, a much more serious crime, known to the law as a felony, and punishable by penal servitude, the Publishers of the "Syndicalist," were sentenced to nine months hard labour, and the Printers of the paper to six months hard labour.

The Government under the pressure of men with votes reduced this sentence on the Publishers to **Six months imprisonment without hard labour,**

and the sentence on the Printers to **One month without hard labour.**

IS THIS JUSTICE TO VOTELESS WOMEN ?

A suffragette handbill.

---

1 a) What is the attitude of the cartoonist in Source 4 to:
  i) the suffragists
  ii) the suffragettes?
  b) How can you tell?
2 Read Source 13 carefully. What point does it make?

There was a logic to the suffragettes' actions. The suffragettes believed that the government did nothing about female suffrage because it did not think that it was a serious issue. The government had more pressing concerns. The suffragettes wanted to make women's suffrage a serious issue – one that the government could not ignore. That was the aim of their militancy: a woman getting arrested for her cause was news. It showed how important the vote was to her. Processions and petitions – however large – were easily ignored.

Reactions to direct action

The reaction of the public was mixed. Some people were sympathetic. Some were worried. Others were scornful. The reaction of the suffragists was also mixed. Many suffragists admired the heroism of the suffragettes – particularly their readiness to go to prison. When the first suffragettes were arrested and imprisoned for staging a protest in Parliament, Mrs Fawcett put on a banquet for them when they were released. However, as the suffragette campaign became more violent, relationships between the suffragists and suffragettes became very strained. The suffragists believed that you could not claim a democratic right (to vote) by undemocratic methods (such as smashing windows). They also believed that militancy would put off the moderate MPs who might otherwise back their cause.

So the two campaigns moved further apart. Both knew that rivalry between the two groups did not help the cause, and Christabel Pankhurst called for the two wings of the movement to join forces. However, Mrs Fawcett did not want her movement to be identified with militancy and so she refused. Even so, her sternest criticism was directed not at the suffragettes but at the inept politicians who had helped to create militancy.

SOURCE 14

Militancy is abhorred by me, and the majority of suffragists. None of the triumphs of the women's movement . . . have been won by physical force: they have been triumphs of moral and spiritual force. But militancy has been brought into existence by the blind blundering of politicians . . . If men had been treated by the House of Commons as women have been treated, there would have been bloody reprisals all over the country.

Millicent Fawcett on the events of 1908.

Opposition intensifies

The suffrage campaigners had always faced opposition, but as suffragette militancy escalated, so did the campaign of their opponents.

SOURCE **15**

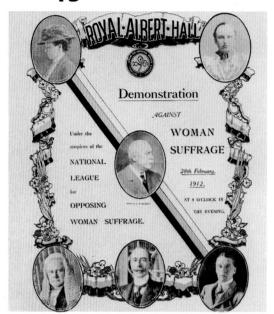

A poster advertising an anti-suffrage demonstration.

1 Do you regard Source 16 as effective propaganda? Explain your answer.
2 Why might a suffragette be more annoyed by Source 16 than Source 15?

SOURCE **16**

An anti-suffragette poster, typical of the sort of attitude suffragettes faced.

SOURCE **17**

VOTES FOR BABIES

Now that it is pretty well assured that women will vote, it is time to arouse public sentiment in favour of Votes for Babies. The awful state of our Government shouts aloud for the infant suffrage . . . Let the babies vote! For that matter let the cows vote.

From the *Gentleman's Journal,* 17 May 1913.

1911: A setback in Parliament

In 1911 the government promised a Conciliation Bill which won all-party support. The suffragettes suspended militant action. The suffragists held an incredible 4,000 meetings (30 per day) to support the bill. It got a majority of 167 – the biggest ever. It looked as if success was just around the corner. Then Asquith dropped the bill! Instead, he announced that he planned to introduce votes for all men, and that an extra clause about women's votes could be tacked on to the bill if MPs wished to add it. Both suffragists and suffragettes were furious.

3 Which of these sources is the most effective piece of propaganda for or against women's suffrage? Explain your choice.
4 Some people say that 'all publicity is good publicity'. Would the Pankhursts agree? Would Mrs Fawcett agree?

The suffragist response

The suffragists' response was to lead a deputation to see the Prime Minister to persuade him to change his mind. They also decided to support the Labour Party at the next election, since it was the only party committed to female suffrage; they organised a peaceful pilgrimage from Carlisle to London involving thousands of suffragists (see Source 1A on page 403). They offered free membership to working women.

SOURCE **18**

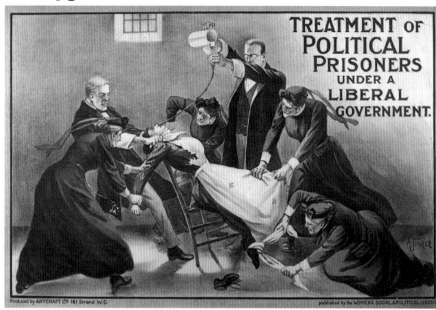

A suffragette poster from 1909, protesting about force feeding.

SOURCE **19**

A suffragette postcard from 1913.

SOURCE **20**

Police arresting a suffragette who has chained herself to the railings of Buckingham Palace, May 1914.

The suffragette response

By contrast, the suffragette response was to escalate their campaign of violence (although usually violence against property not people). They smashed windows, set fire to post boxes, bombed churches (see Source 1B on page 403) and damaged cricket pitches and golf courses. Bombs were placed in warehouses, and telephone wires were cut. Art galleries closed after suffragettes slashed valuable paintings. As a result, more and more suffragettes were sent to prison.

In prison, the suffragettes continued to protest by going on hunger strike. The government responded by ordering the force feeding of protesters. The WPSU made the most of this, with posters such as Source 18, but posters were hardly necessary. Force feeding was brutal and degrading, and it won a good deal of public sympathy for the suffragettes.

In 1913, the government passed a new Act which allowed hunger strikers to leave prison, recover a little and then return to finish their sentence. Campaigners called this the Cat and Mouse Act (see Source 19).

Then in June 1913 came the most publicised protest of all: the death of Emily Davison. You can investigate the death of Emily Davison in the case study on pages 412–13.

Case study: the death of Emily Davison

It was 4 June 1913, the day of the world-famous horse race, the Derby, at Epsom race course. Tens of thousands of spectators were waiting for the big race. Among the crowds were members of the royal family, political leaders and many reporters and photographers. Anything that happened at the Derby was big news.

It was an ideal day for publicising the suffragette cause – or so Emily Davison thought. She was an experienced campaigner. She had been in prison nine times as part of the suffragette campaign. She had set fire to post boxes and even a post office. She had been on hunger strike while in prison.

As the horses rounded Tattenham Corner, Miss Davison rushed out and tried to catch hold of one of the horses. Source 21 shows you what happened next.

SOURCE **21**

A newspaper photograph of the events that led to the death of Emily Davison on 5 June 1913. The *Daily Mail*'s headline in reporting the event was 'Day of Sensations at Epsom'.

Emily Davison was thrown to the ground, her skull fatally fractured by a blow from a horse's hoof. Four days later on 8 June she died of her injuries. At the time, some people thought that Emily Davison had committed suicide, that she intended to kill herself in a most public arena to draw attention to the suffragette cause. The methods of the campaigners had been getting more and more extreme – a martyr might be very useful.

However, a different explanation later emerged. It appeared to be a publicity stunt that had gone terribly wrong. The King's horse, Anmer, was running in the race. Emily Davison thought it would be good publicity to attach a suffragette banner to it as it galloped by. It would enter the finishing straight literally flying the suffragette flag. She had been seen practising stopping horses in a lane near her home in Morpeth for some weeks previously. Sadly, when it came to the real event she misjudged the speed and power of the onrushing racehorses. She was hit and killed.

Was she brave or foolish? Her funeral, ten days later, was attended by thousands of suffragettes. It became a major celebration of her ultimate sacrifice.

SOURCE 22

The woman rushed from the rails as the horses swept round Tattenham Corner. She did not interfere with the racing but she nearly killed the jockey as well as herself and she brought down a valuable horse. A deed of this kind is unlikely to increase the popularity of the women's cause.

The Times, 6 June 1913.

SOURCE 23

Millions of people, not only in our own country but in other countries too, had their attention riveted upon the race. It was an unsurpassable opportunity of proclaiming to a whole world, heedless, perhaps until then, that women claim citizenship and human rights. Miss Davison seized the opportunity, and with an amazing and incredible courage made a protest which has fired the imagination and touched the hearts of the people. Her act has proved to be an appeal infinitely more eloquent than all the words of all the speeches could be . . . She has taught the world that there are women who care so passionately for the vote and all it means that they are willing to die for it.

The Suffragette, 13 June 1913.

SOURCE 24

The Suffragette, 13 June 1913.

SOURCE 25

In some respects it was the most remarkable funeral procession London has ever seen. It was a tribute of women to a woman who, in their eyes at least, had achieved martyrdom for the cause which they all represent . . . No one would grudge to the memory of Emily Wilding Davison any part of that tribute of honour and respect which her fellow women Suffragettes have desired to render at her obsequies [funeral rights] . . . She was herself the most unassuming and the gentlest of creatures, though she possessed a spirit capable of heroic deed and sacrifice.

Sunday Times, 15 June 1913, commenting on Emily Davison's funeral.

SOURCE 26

IMPRESSIVE LONDON PROCESSION

The procession, which was an impressive pageant, was watched by dense crowds . . . Nearly five thousand members from all parts of the country marched in undisturbed quiet and orderliness behind the coffin. Perhaps what impressed the London mind in it all was the note of colour. Among the women who walked there were hundreds dressed in black, but at the head was a young girl in yellow silk carrying a gilt cross.

Manchester Guardian, 16 June 1913, commenting on Davison's funeral.

SOURCE 27

The effect was gracious and dignified. Banners displayed the sentiments of those taking part in the procession who must have numbered some thousands.

Morning Post, 16 June 1913, also commenting on the funeral.

Source Investigation

1 What does Source 22 tell you about the events of 4 June 1913?
2 How do Sources 23 and 24 differ from Source 22 in their attitude to Emily Davison? Explain the contrast.
3 What are the strengths and weaknesses of Sources 23 and 24 for historians investigating reactions to Emily Davison's death?
4 How far do Sources 25–27 agree with each other about Emily Davison's funeral?
5 Would you say there is a change in attitude towards the death of Emily Davison in these sources between 5 and 16 June? Explain your answer.

How effective were the suffragette and suffragist campaigns up to 1914?

Historians have found this a difficult question because it is so difficult to measure effectiveness – you cannot weigh it or use a tape measure! Despite this problem, historians have looked at the impact of the two wings of the movement on areas such as public opinion, the press, politicians. They have also considered the activities and the organisation of the suffragettes and suffragists.

The suffragettes

There is no doubt that in the first instance the suffragettes achieved their aim of gaining maximum publicity for the movement. They were extremely clever propagandists. The suffragette magazine *Votes For Women* had a circulation of around 40,000 in 1914. You will see many sources from *Votes for Women* in this chapter because their articles and illustrations were so clear and effective. The suffragettes also produced striking posters and pamphlets – this was at a time when such methods were relatively new. They even managed to get 'Votes For Women' printed on to the wrapper of one make of bread! One of their most imaginative publicity stunts came in 1908 when the suffragettes publicised a rally in Hyde Park in London by sailing a boat past Parliament flying flags and posters. The importance of this should not be underestimated. One of the greatest frustrations for the suffragists had always been that politicians and the press either ignored them or did not take them seriously.

Of course the aspect of the suffragettes which is generally better known is their violent action. Did this help the cause? At the very least, the campaigns of the suffragettes made it impossible to ignore the fact that female suffrage was an important issue. The bravery and commitment of the suffragettes gained them admiration. The fact that they were often roughly treated also generated sympathy for them. Force feeding created a great deal of sympathy. So did the violence they often suffered at meetings or rallies from male opponents (see Source 29) or even the police.

1 Explain how Source 28 tries to generate sympathy for the suffragettes.

SOURCE **28**

The front page of a suffragette pamphlet from 1908.

414

SOURCE 29

Sir

At the request of some of those who took part in the women's deputation to the House of Commons on November 18 of last year, I have endeavoured to examine the allegations made against the conduct of the police on that occasion. With that object, I have carefully read upwards of one hundred statements made by eye-witnesses, and I have also seen and questioned 10 of the women who were there.

The following facts are either admitted or beyond reasonable dispute:-

1. The women taking part in the deputation collected partly at Caxton Hall and partly at Clement's Inn. They were instructed by their leaders to avoid violence. They were entirely unarmed, even umbrellas or parasols being forbidden. Among them were women of all ages up to 65 or 70.

2. Some of the women, including Mrs Pankhurst, were allowed to approach quite close to St Stephen's entrance. The rest were stopped some distance away. Very few arrests, if any, were made for several hours, and during that time the women suffered every species of indignity and violence.

Apart from the assaults above mentioned, complaints of indignities of a very gross kind have also been made by women, and some of these were repeated in my presence.

In conclusion, may I ask whether anyone thinks that if the deputation had consisted of unarmed men of the same character their demand for an inquiry would have been refused? Are we, then, to take it as officially admitted that in this country there is one law for male electors and another for voteless women?

Yours obediently

Robert Cecil

A letter to the *Times*, March 1911. The *Times* was generally opposed to the Suffragettes. The writer, Robert Cecil, was one of the few Conservative MPs who supported women's suffrage.

---

2 According to Source 29, how were the women treated?
3 What are the main points made in the letter?
4 The writer of Source 29 was a supporter of women's suffrage. Does this mean his letter is worthless as evidence?
5 What does Source 30 reveal about attitudes towards the militants?

SOURCE 30

A hostile crowd gathered, and there were ugly rushes to get at the women speakers. The police had to intervene. Police-Constable Paul said the police had to protect the women as there was an effort on the part of the young men of Streatham to put the militants in the pond. The magistrate said it was impossible to shut one's eyes to the fact that the behaviour of these women had created a strong feeling of resentment and disgust. He would not impose any penalty on that occasion, and in ordering the discharge of the defendants advised them to abstain from any interference in the future.

A Report from the *Morning Post* on the trial of three young men who attacked a suffragette meeting.

SOURCE 31

Haven't the suffragettes the sense to see that the very worst kind of campaigning for the vote is to try to intimidate or blackmail a man into giving them what he would otherwise gladly give?

A comment by Lloyd George, 1913.

Although their courage won them sympathy as individuals, it does appear that it did not win sympathy for their cause (see Source 31). The increasing violence of the suffragettes, especially after 1911, alienated support for the women's cause. Many supporters left the WSPU and transferred to the suffragists. The WSPU had always been a minority organisation anyway. At its peak it had about 2,000 members. It was also very middle class. Its origins lay in the Labour movement but it moved away from these roots and by 1914 it was effectively campaigning in favour of votes for some women — women with property. By 1914 the WSPU had become a smaller movement made up of the more radical elements in the women's suffrage movement. Many suffragettes were in prison, and the Pankhursts were co-ordinating the campaign from exile in Paris. The suffragettes damaged their own cause because they gave their opponents a reason for rejecting women's suffrage. If MPs gave in to violence on this matter, then what hope would they have when the Irish protested violently for home rule, or the dockers or mine workers rioted for higher wages? Even more disturbing was that the suffragettes had lost the goodwill of many of their leading supporters. From 1911 onwards, each time the issue was raised in Parliament there was a bigger majority against women's suffrage.

Focus Task

How effective were the suffragettes up to 1914?

Write a paragraph to explain your views on questions 1–4.
1 What do you think the suffragettes would have been most proud of by 1914?
2 What evidence is there that the suffragettes damaged the cause of votes for women?
3 What do you regard as the greatest single achievement of the suffragettes and what do you think was their greatest single failure?
4 Do you think the suffragette achievements outweighed their failures?

The suffragists

You have already seen in this chapter how the suffragists kept up a campaign of petitions, lobbying and campaigning from the later 1800s right through until some women gained the vote in 1918. However, some historians such as Harold Smith of the University of Houston-Victoria in the USA and Sandra Holton of the University of Adelaide (in Australia) now think that their efforts have been underestimated, mainly because the actions of the suffragettes were more exciting and controversial to study.

These historians argue that the NUWSS was much more important than the WSPU. By 1914 the NUWSS had developed into a very large organisation with over 500 branches and around 100,000 members. It was far larger than the WSPU. The NUWSS also benefited from its moderate approaches and its excellent organisation. Like the WSPU, the NUWSS understood how to use the media of the time. They used posters, pamphlets and the press in the same way as the WSPU. Many of their rallies were filmed. Early film cameras were difficult to set up and use, and suffragist processions were ideal subjects for film cameramen because of the way they filed past the camera. Film shows were very popular in the early 1900s and they would have given a lot of publicity to the movement. Suffragist processions were dignified, organised and impressive – crowds of 20,000 were not unusual. This must have impressed early film audiences. Showing suffragette outrages such as the burning of churches on film probably reflected well on the suffragists as well. In fact, we know from diaries and other evidence that many people supported the NUWSS because WSPU action made them aware of the issue but they did not like the militancy of the WSPU. So, in a strange way, the NUWSS benefited from the actions of the WSPU simply by not being the suffragettes!

SOURCE **32**

A still image from a newsreel showing a suffragist procession 1910.

SOURCE **33**

A still image from a newsreel from 1913 showing a church burned down by suffragettes.

1 Compare the impression given of the suffragists and suffragettes of these two film stills.
2 Write a title to go before each clip as it would have been written at the time. You may be able to check the actual titles on the internet.

SOURCE **34**

The public militancy of the WSPU was complemented by the quieter lobbying of the moderates of the NUWSS, which continued the steady pressure upon politicians and the insertion of women into public life ... For all the tension between the wings of the suffrage movements and the disagreements of historians about them, they are best seen as complementary, the tactics of each assisting achievement of the vote.

Professor Pat Thane of the University of Sussex, writing in 1994.

Another key area of the NUWSS which had a huge impact was the work of their branches. In the early 1900s many of the people who belonged to local NUWSS branches were also interested in other issues such as trade unionism, improving working conditions, charitable work or education. Many activists belonged to more than one organisation. The NUWSS was very effective at meeting up with local activists and explaining their aims and ideas to them. Professor Sandra Holton believes that this work was possibly the single most important factor in achieving votes for women. As you can see from Source 35, the NUWSS were able to convince local branches of the Liberal Party to call on their own leaders to support votes for women. Even more worrying from Prime Minister Asquith's point of view was that the NUWSS were proving very effective at linking up with local Labour Party branches as well. In fact, the NUWSS was beginning to use its powerful campaigning machinery (meetings, rallies, leafleting) to support Labour candidates against Liberal candidates in some elections. Holton believes that this was a potentially serious threat to the Liberal Party. She believes that some measure of female suffrage would have happened if the First World War had not intervened in 1914.

You are now going to leave the story of women to study the war-time developments in detail, but you will return to the final focus points of the specification – how women contributed to the war effort and why they got the vote in 1918 on pages 428–31.

SOURCE 35

An information sheet published in 1912 by the West Lancashire, West Cheshire and North Wales Federation of the NUWSS.

Focus Task

How effective were the suffragists up to 1914?

Write a paragraph to explain your views on questions 1–4.
1 What do you think the suffragists would have been most proud of by 1914?
2 What evidence is there that the suffragettes helped the suffragists?
3 What do you regard as the greatest single achievement of the suffragists?
4 Why do some historians think the suffragettes have received more attention than they deserved and are you convinced by this view?

14.3 The British Home Front during the First World War

The First World War was Britain's first total war. A total war involves or affects all of society – not just the armed forces. It was the first war to deeply affect most people back home in Britain. Previous wars had been remote from everyday life for most ordinary people. They were usually fought far away by small professional armies. All that ordinary people knew about the fighting was what they read in the newspapers or heard from soldiers who had taken part. This war was different. It touched almost everybody's life in one way or another, whether they were soldiers or civilians, men or women, adults or children. Some of this impact was unexpected. Some of it was planned. As you will see from pages 418–19, the government put an enormous effort into planning, organising and controlling life in Britain so that everybody would play their part. You are going to investigate how they did this and what impact it had on the life of ordinary people.

Focus Task

How were civilians affected by the war?

Look carefully at Source 1. This poster shows some of the ways in which the government wanted the people of Britain to be involved in the war effort. Your aim over the next twelve pages is to prepare a short presentation based on this poster. The title of your presentation is: 'How were civilians affected by the war?'

You will use this poster and other evidence on pages 418–19 to help you with your presentation.

1 Start by discussing this poster with the rest of the class. Make notes from the discussion.
   ◆ What impression of wartime Britain does this give?
   ◆ Who do you think the poster is aimed at?
   ◆ What is the purpose of the poster?
   ◆ Do you think it is effective?
   ◆ How might you have responded, if you had seen this poster in 1915?
2 Over the next few pages you will be prompted every now and then to take notes to help you with your presentation.

> **PROMPT 1**
> Read the Factfile on page 419. Make a list of all the ways in which the war affected civilian life.

SOURCE **1**

A government poster published in 1915. It was designed by Sir Robert Baden-Powell, founder of the Scout movement and a former British soldier.

Factfile

The 'Home Front' in the First World War

1914

➤ 2 August — War declared on Germany. Britain needed an army quickly. The government launched a massive recruitment campaign. Half a million joined the army in one month.

➤ 8 August — The Defence of the Realm Act (DORA) was introduced. It gave the government special powers such as the right to take over industries and land which were needed for the war effort, or to censor newspapers.

➤ Autumn — From August to September many different women's organisations were set up, including the Women's Hospital Corps and the Women's Police Volunteers.

➤ 16 December — The first bombing of British civilians. German warships shelled the east coast of Britain. In Scarborough 119 people were killed.

1915

➤ 19 January — First air raids by German Zeppelin airships, dropping bombs on East Anglian towns.

➤ May — It was recognised that the war needed much more careful organisation of all aspects of British life, so a coalition government with politicians from all parties was formed to handle the growing crisis in Britain.

➤ 31 May — The first Zeppelin air raids on London. Air raids by Zeppelins and later by aircraft were a regular feature of the rest of the war.

➤ July — The munitions crisis: British troops were facing a severe shortage of shells and bullets. The government set up the Ministry of Munitions under David Lloyd George to reorganise Britain's munitions supply. Lloyd George and Mrs Pankhurst, a suffragette leader, organised a 'women's march for jobs' to recruit women to work in factories.

➤ Autumn — Many employers refused to take on women, and trade unions refused to allow women workers. The government had to come to an agreement with the trade unions that women would be paid the same as men and would only work 'until sufficient male labour should again be available'. The government also set up its own munitions factories, employing largely women.

1916

➤ 25 January — First Military Service Bill introduced conscription of all single men aged 18–40.

➤ 16 May — Second Military Service Bill extended conscription to married men.

➤ 1 July — The Battle of the Somme began. More British soldiers were killed in this battle than in any previous battle.

➤ August — The British public flocked to cinemas to see the government's new feature film 'The Battle of the Somme', which the 'Evening News' called 'the greatest moving picture in the world'.

➤ 18 November — The Battle of the Somme was called off – with very little gain to show for the half a million British casualties.

➤ November — For the first time there was public criticism of the way the war was being run by the generals.

➤ 7 December — Lloyd George, a critic of the army leadership, became Prime Minister in place of Herbert Asquith. He immediately reorganised the British government to focus all effort on the war. He set up the Ministry of Labour to deal with the labour supply in British industry. He set up the Ministry of Food to deal with the food supply.

1917

➤ February — Germany began its third and most devastating campaign of unrestricted submarine warfare against British merchant ships. The Women's Land Army was formed to recruit women as farm labourers.

➤ April — German U-boats sank one in four British merchant ships in the Atlantic. The food supply was running very low. Under DORA (see page 422) the government took over 2.5 million acres of new farming land to help to feed Britain.

➤ November — A voluntary rationing scheme was introduced. It was a failure. Food prices continued to rise. Food queues got longer.

➤ December — Parliament agreed a law to give all women over 30 who were householders the right to vote in general elections.

1918

➤ 25 February — Compulsory rationing scheme introduced in London and southern Britain with stiff penalties for offenders.

➤ April — Rationing of meat, butter and cheese extended to the entire country.

➤ 11 November — At the eleventh hour of the eleventh day of the eleventh month of 1918 the Armistice was signed. The war was officially over.

➤ 14 December — A general election was held in Britain. Women over 30 voted for the first time.

Recruitment and conscription

When war broke out Britain had only a small professional army. It needed a large one very quickly. The government began a massive recruitment drive, with posters, leaflets, recruitment offices in every town and stirring speeches by government ministers.

There was already a strong anti-German feeling in the country. The press strengthened it further with regular stories of German atrocities – babies butchered in Belgium, nurses murdered and, most famously of all, the German factory where they supposedly made soap out of boiled-up corpses.

The recruitment campaign was highly successful. Half a million signed up in the first month. By 1916 over 2 million had been enlisted (see Source 2).

1 Look at Sources 3–5. Describe the method each poster uses to encourage men to join up.

2 Draw up a list of arguments for and against this statement: 'Conscription was fairer than voluntary recruitment.'

3

> **PROMPT 2**
> Make notes about how recruitment to the army affected civilians. Include notes about:
> • voluntary recruitment
> • conscription
> • conchies
> • family life.

SOURCE **2**

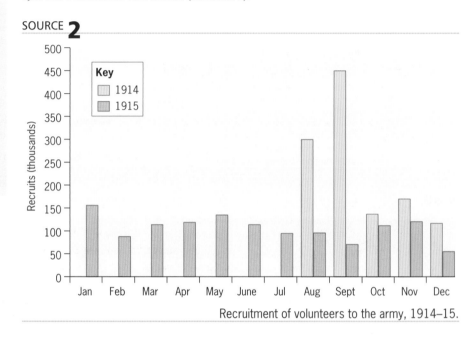

Recruitment of volunteers to the army, 1914–15.

SOURCE **3**

A 1914 recruitment poster. It features Lord Kitchener, a former successful general who became Secretary of State for War and the figurehead of the recruitment campaign.

SOURCE **4**

A 1915 recruitment poster.

SOURCE **5**

A 1915 recruitment poster.

SOURCE 6

COMPULSION BILL

WORKER

"GOT HIM"

A cartoon published in the socialist newspaper the *Workers' Dreadnought* in 1916.

In 1916 the government decided to introduce conscription for the first time. All men aged between 18 and 40 had to register for active service. They could be called up at any time to fight.

The government did this for various reasons. The number of volunteers was falling. As you can see from Source 2, recruitment in December 1915 was the lowest for any month since the start of the war. But the demand for troops was increasing. The dead and wounded needed replacing. Another problem was that the volunteer system was damaging Britain's agriculture and industry. For example, so many miners joined up that there were reports of their having to be sent back to provide essential supplies of coal. The volunteer system was also seen as unfair. Not all parts of society took an equal share of the burden. There was a feeling that some groups avoided the war altogether. Some of the fittest and most able men were not volunteering at all. In the end, many welcomed the government's taking control of the situation and introducing conscription.

SOURCE 9

1 May 1915

William Milton, foreman of Lyons Hall Farm, does not approve of all the recruiting posters on the tree trunks and walls. 'If the government want more men let them take idlers not workmen. Unless the war is over before August there will not be enough men for the harvest.'

The men say 'We will go when we like, or when we are ordered.' Conscription, being just, would be welcome.

The Diary of Rev Andrew Clark, an Essex clergyman.

SOURCE 7

THE HARDEST QUESTION OF ALL

'Then you are willing to see your country defeated?'

That's the question that stops the mouths of many of us when we are trying to explain our position as 'conscientious objectors' . . . There is, I believe, hardly one of us who would, or could, say 'Yes'; but, if we say 'No', we are at once open to the crushing reply, 'Then you are willing to let other men fight and die for you, while you stay quietly and safely at home.'

From the *Friend*, published by the Quakers, a religious group who believed in non-violence, 21 January 1916.

Not everyone welcomed conscription, however. Fifty MPs, including leading Liberals, voted against it in Parliament. Another group who did not welcome it were those who were opposed to the war for religious or political reasons. It would be against their conscience to fight so they were called conscientious objectors or 'conchies'. Conchies had to appear before a tribunal and prove they had a genuine reason for objecting to war and were not just cowards. Some conchies were sent to prison, where they were often badly treated. Others actually went to the front and worked in field hospitals or as stretcher bearers.

SOURCE 8

Sir,

What right have 'conscientious objectors' to live in this country whose existence is only maintained by the fighting men of our Army and Navy?
G Moor,
3 Silverfields,
Harrogate

From the *Daily Mail*, 10 January 1916.

SOURCE 10

Conscientious objectors, 1916. Four of these men, including Mr HHC Marten, second from left in the front row, had been sentenced to death as conchies, but had their sentence reduced to ten years' hard labour. This picture was taken at a granite quarry in Scotland where they were sent to serve their sentence.

DORA

In 1914 the government passed the Defence of the Realm Act which came to be known as DORA. It gave the government unprecedented and wide-ranging powers to control many aspects of people's daily lives. It allowed it to seize any land or buildings it needed, and to take over any industries which were important to the war effort. It allowed the government to control what the public knew about the war through censorship.

The government immediately took control of the coal industry so that the mines could be run to support the war effort rather than for the private profit of the owners.

The munitions crisis

In 1915 the first major problems began to emerge for the government. As the war became bogged down in a stalemate, it became increasingly obvious that planning for such a war was hopelessly inadequate. Most worryingly, there was a chronic shortage of shells, bullets and armaments on the Western Front. New soldiers had to train with wooden sticks instead of rifles as there were not enough rifles to go round. There were reports that soldiers in the front lines were rationed to three rounds of ammunition a day. The artillery were unable to keep up their barrage of enemy trenches because of the shortage of shells. The 'munitions crisis', as it was known, became a national scandal exposed by the *Daily Mail*, which was Britain's highest-circulation newspaper.

As a result of these problems, a coalition government was established – so all parties could work together to support the war effort. Lloyd George was made Minister of Munitions.

SOURCE **11**

A postcard published by the government in 1915.

SOURCE **12**

Details of munitions production, 1915–17.

2 What was the purpose of Source 11?
3 Source 11 shows Lloyd George 'delivering the goods'. Does Source 12 suggest he was successful or not?

Under DORA, Lloyd George introduced a range of measures to 'deliver the goods'. One problem was the shortage of skilled workers in key industries. Lloyd George tried to force skilled workers to stay where the government needed them instead of going to where they could get the best pay. The trade unions protested. Many of the bosses of the firms supplying the government were making huge profits out of the war, so the unions wondered why workers could not do so as well. In fact they often called strikes. During the course of 1916, for example, 235,000 workers went on strike at various times and 2.5 million working days were lost. The engineers won big concessions from the government in May 1917. In 1918 over 900,000 workers went on strike at some stage and over 6 million working days were lost. In many cases the government simply agreed to the demands of the strikers.

One other key element of Lloyd George's programme was to bring women into the workforce (see pages 428–29). Trade unions again resisted this. In 1915, 100,000 women registered for work in industry, yet to start with only 5,000 were given jobs. The trade unions were worried about the effect of women workers on their members' wages. They argued that women worked for lower pay than men, so they 'diluted' men's wages. They refused to co-operate until the government gave a clear promise that women would be paid the same as men and would not be kept on when the men came back. Lloyd George gave them this undertaking. At the same time he also opened the government's own

SOURCE 13

THE KITCHEN IS THE KEY TO VICTORY EAT LESS BREAD

A government poster issued in 1917.

4 Why do you think the government was so concerned about flour and bread?
5 Why was the government reluctant to make rationing compulsory in 1917?
6 Look at Source 14. Why do you think the government published this leaflet?

munitions factories, which employed a large number of women. By the end of 1915 the situation had improved. The British army was well supplied with munitions for the rest of the war, as you can see from Source 12.

Feeding the country

The government also needed to ensure that Britain was fed. Under DORA it was able to take over land and turn it over to farm production. In February 1917 it set up the Women's Land Army to recruit women as farm workers.

By then, however, the food supply in Britain had become quite desperate. In April 1917 German U-boats were sinking one in every four British merchant ships. Britain had only six weeks' supply of wheat left. As food supplies ran short, so prices rose. Wages had hardly risen during the war because people were mostly prepared to sacrifice better pay to support the war effort, but prices were now almost double what they had been in 1914. Richer people bought more than they needed and hoarded it. Poorer people could not afford even basic supplies such as bread. Shops closed early each afternoon as they had run out of goods to sell. In important industrial areas such as South Wales there were serious strikes over poverty-level wages.

The government again responded with a range of measures. Following strikes in 1917, it agreed to raise the wages of industrial workers. In May it started a system of voluntary rationing. The royal family led the way by announcing they were aiming to reduce their consumption of bread by one-quarter, and 'to abstain from the use of flour in pastry and moreover carefully to restrict or wherever possible to abandon the use of flour in all articles other than bread'. They called on all people in Britain to do the same. In November the government introduced laws to control the price of bread – 'The Ninepenny Loaf'. It published many posters encouraging people to be economical with bread. It circulated recipe books with recipes which used less flour.

However, none of these measures was effective in reducing food shortages, so in early 1918 the government introduced compulsory rationing of sugar, butter, meat and beer. Every person had a book of coupons which had to be handed to the shopkeeper when rationed food was bought. There were stiff penalties facing anyone who broke the rationing rules.

On the whole, rationing was widely welcomed as a fairer system of sharing out the available food. By the end of the war, as a result of rationing, the diet and health of many poorer people had actually improved in comparison with pre-war days.

SOURCE 14

DEFENCE OF THE REALM. E.P. 6.
MINISTRY OF FOOD.
BREACHES OF THE RATIONING ORDER

The undermentioned convictions have been recently obtained:—

Court	Date	Nature of Offence	Result
HENDON - -	29th Aug., 1918	Unlawfully obtaining and using ration books -	3 Months' Imprisonment
WEST HAM -	29th Aug., 1918	Being a retailer & failing to detach proper number of coupons	Fined £20
SMETHWICK -	22nd July, 1918	Obtaining meat in excess quantities - - -	Fined £50 & £5 5s. costs
OLD STREET -	4th Sept., 1918	Being a retailer selling to unregistered customer	Fined £72 & £5 5s. costs
OLD STREET -	4th Sept., 1918	Not detaching sufficient coupons for meat sold -	Fined £25 & £2 2s. costs
CHESTER-LE-STREET	4th Sept., 1918	Being a retailer returning number of registered customers in excess of counterfoils deposited - - - -	Fined £50 & £3 3s. costs
HIGH WYCOMBE	7th Sept., 1918	Making false statement on application for and using Ration Books unlawfully - - - - - - -	Fined £40 & £6 4s. costs

Enforcement Branch, Local Authorities Division,
MINISTRY OF FOOD.
September, 1918.

A leaflet produced by the government in 1918.

SOURCE **15**

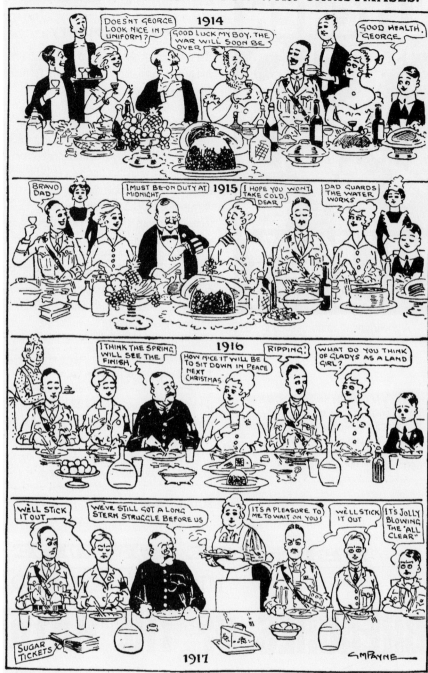

'The Brown Family's Four War Christmases' – a cartoon from 1917.

Activity

Between 1914 and 1918 the war reached into every corner of people's lives. Family members were killed. Food was rationed. Freedom was restricted. Civilians faced danger. Source 15 shows one cartoonist's view of the impact of the war on a British family.

1 Write a detailed description of what each frame shows. Emphasise anything that has changed since the last frame.
2 From what you have found out about life on the Home Front, explain why these changes have taken place.

3 Write a phrase to sum up the family's attitude to the war in each year. You could choose from the following phrases or write your own: Grim determination, War enthusiasm, Let's get organised, Hard times.
4 Do you think this cartoon is an accurate representation of the attitudes of British people during the war? Explain your answer fully.
5 Based on what you have read on pages 418–24, write a description or draw a picture of what the cartoonist might have drawn at the end of 1918.

Propaganda and censorship

The government regarded it as essential that civilians should support the war effort. So DORA also gave the government the right to control the newspapers and other mass media that might influence people's opinions towards the war. On many occasions the government even kept Parliament in the dark about events on the front line.

Good news only

From the start of the war all news, especially bad news, was strictly controlled. Despite the problems of the first few months on the Western Front, the British people were told only of great British victories or heroic resistance. When the British battleship HMS *Audacious* was sunk in October 1914, it was simply not reported.

It was not until November 1916 that the government allowed journalists (and then only approved ones, of course) to be at the front. Reports focused on good news. The newspaper owners and editors themselves were the keenest supporters of the war effort. For example, Lord Beaverbrook, the *Daily Express* owner, was a cabinet minister from 1916, and became Minister for Information in 1918. He and other newspaper barons (as they are known) became an integral part of Britain's war effort. After the war, twelve leading members of the newspaper industry were given knighthoods in recognition of their wartime services.

The government also censored information from the soldiers at the front. The soldiers even censored themselves. There is much evidence that soldiers home on leave chose not to tell relatives the truth about what was going on at the front because they did not want to worry them.

Forced censorship

Some independent papers did publish more balanced news or even anti-war articles. Initially, they were tolerated. However, as the war dragged on papers like the pacifist newspaper *Tribunal* were closed down. Socialist newspapers such as the *Daily Herald* were monitored carefully by the censors.

The censors were also concerned with stopping sensitive information from leaking out to the enemy. In 1916 alone, the government Press Bureau and the Intelligence services examined 38,000 articles, 25,000 photographs and 300,000 private telegrams. Even magazines for railway enthusiasts found themselves in trouble for revealing too much about Britain's transport network.

Books and other publications

Leading authors – HG Wells, Arthur Conan Doyle, Thomas Hardy, Rudyard Kipling – all signed a Declaration by Authors in support of the war. Most of them produced patriotic publications for no fee. The history department at the University of Oxford produced a five-volume explanation of why Britain was justified in going to war (it became known as the Red Book because of its cover). The Red Book sold 50,000 copies.

Propaganda for children

Propaganda was aimed at children too. Toys were made that were intended to encourage support of the war effort, and there were many patriotic books and comics. Needless to say, the German enemy was always cowardly and treacherous and the British Tommy was always modest, brave and successful. We know that these books and magazines sold well because they were regularly reprinted. In fact, many of them were still being reprinted in the 1920s and 1930s and given as school prizes.

SOURCE 16

If the people really knew [the truth about the war] the war would be stopped tomorrow. But of course they don't – and can't – know. The correspondents don't write, and the censors would not pass, the truth.

Prime Minister Lloyd George in a private conversation with the editor of the *Manchester Guardian* in December 1917.

SOURCE 17

It is a domestic tragedy of the war that the country which went out to defend liberty is losing its own liberties one by one, and that the government which began by relying on public opinion as a great help has now come to fear and curtail it.

The *Nation*, May 1916. (This journal was later suppressed under DORA.)

---

1 Effective wartime propaganda aims to:
   a) keep up morale
   b) encourage civilians to support the war effort
   c) create hatred and suspicion of the enemy. Choose one example of each from pages 425–27.

2 **PROMPT 4**
   Make notes for your presentation about how propaganda was used to keep civilian support for the war. Mention:
   • newspapers
   • censorship
   • films and books
   • patriotic organisations.

3 How do Sources 16 and 17 differ in their view of censorship and propaganda?

1 Most historians think that propaganda had more effect on children than any other group in society. Why do you think the toys in Source 18 might be effective?

SOURCE **18**

A selection of toys and games from 1914 to 1918.

Films

The government did not even have to make its own propaganda films. British film makers produced 240 war films between 1915 and 1918, very few of which were actually commissioned by the War Department.

The British Topical Committee for War Films was a group of film companies who got together to make and sell films to the War Department. Their patriotic film *For the Empire* reached an estimated audience of 9 million by the end of 1916. The Committee made some of the most famous films of the war, including *The Battle of the Somme*.

The Battle of the Somme has generally been seen by historians as a propaganda triumph. It showed real scenes from the battle, including real casualties (13 per cent of its running time showed dead or wounded soldiers). It also included 'fake' scenes. The film did not tell its audience which was which.

It was released in August 1916 and was a huge commercial success. Many people talked of it as their first chance to see what conditions were really like in the war – to get closer to the truth. By October 1916 it had been shown in over 2,000 cinemas (out of 4,500 in the country). Some anti-war campaigners approved of the film because it showed the horrors more truly than any previous film. But some people were shocked by its realism. The Dean of Durham Cathedral thought that it was wrong to exploit death and suffering to provide entertainment.

Did the propaganda work?

It is very hard to measure how effective the propaganda was. The ultimate test of the propaganda is whether it helped support for the war to stay firm (and, as you can see on page 427, it mostly did stay firm, despite immense casualties). However, it is almost impossible to judge how far the propaganda was responsible for this.

We can look at numbers: 9 million people saw the film *For the Empire*. Over half the population read a daily newspaper and newspaper circulation increased during the war. The circulation of the *Daily Express* went up from 295,000 in 1914 to 579,000 in 1918. The patriotic weekly journal *John Bull* was selling 2 million copies in 1918 and the *News of the World* was selling even more. These figures give the impression that the ordinary citizen was surrounded by what the government wanted them to hear and see.

In many ways the government did not have to resort to extreme propaganda measures. There is a lot of evidence to suggest that most people mobilised themselves to support the war of their own accord. Many ordinary citizens joined patriotic organisations such as the Fight for Right Movement, the Council of Loyal British Subjects or the Victoria League.

SOURCE **19**

Some scenes from the film *The Battle of the Somme*. **A** and **B** were real. **C** was filmed at a training ground.

Did people support the war?

In the early years of the war the government faced very little opposition to the war. Some Socialists and pacifists protested against the war but they were drowned out by the surge of patriotic feeling. George Bernard Shaw's anti-war pamphlet 'Common Sense About the War' (1914) sold 25,000 copies, but he became the target of much criticism. Ramsay MacDonald had to resign as leader of the Labour Party because he did not support the war while his party did. The headmaster of Eton – an influential figure at the time – was hounded by the press because he simply called on Britain to fight a 'Christian and moral' war. He was eventually forced to take early retirement.

It was a similar story when conscription was introduced in 1916. Fifty MPs, including Liberal leaders, voted against it. The Socialist and pacifist critics of conscription found little sympathy among the general public. Conchies were mostly treated as cowards and shirkers by the press despite considerable evidence that many of them were brave individuals. Perhaps it is not surprising that there were not many conchies. Only 16,000 out of a possible 8 million affected by conscription actually refused to enlist.

From 1914 to 1916, then, the British people were remarkably consistent in their support for the war. However, many historians argue that the Battle of the Somme was a turning point. As the battle dragged on from July to November 1916, half a million soldiers died for just a few square kilometres of gained territory.

In the weeks after the end of the battle, the government faced some serious criticisms as politicians and soldiers questioned publicly for the first time the way the war was being fought. Source 20 is an extract from a letter that Lord Lansdowne, an ex-Cabinet minister, sent to the newspapers. It was debated in Parliament a few days later.

Many people in Britain echoed his feelings. The Battle of the Somme did seem to change the mood in Britain. If you had interviewed a British person about the war in late 1916, you would probably still have found a grim determination to finish the job that had been started, but very little sense of excitement about the war.

Criticism of the war effort left its mark on the government as well. In December the Prime Minister, Asquith, stood down in favour of Lloyd George, who was one of the critics of the army leadership and who was felt to be the only man with the energy and imagination to get Britain through the mounting crisis.

Even so, criticism of the war leadership continued into 1917, as you can see from Source 21 by Siegfried Sassoon. Sassoon was a celebrated war poet. He had been an officer on the Western Front for three years, twice wounded, and decorated for his bravery. In 1917 he wrote a number of poems which accused the generals of being out of touch and incompetent. In July 1917 he went further when he wrote his 'soldier's declaration', which was read out in the House of Commons and was published in the *Daily Mail* and *The Times*.

The government's response was to send Sassoon for psychiatric treatment in a hospital for victims of shell-shock. Sassoon later withdrew his criticism, putting it all down to a nervous breakdown. He returned to France to fight in 1918.

Sassoon was not a lone critic. Many Socialists had criticised the war from the very start, and unions wondered why workers could not do so as well. In fact they often called strikes. During the course of 1916, for example, 235,000 workers went on strike at various times and 2.5 million working days were lost. The engineers won big concessions from the government in May 1917. In 1918 over 900,000 workers went on strike at some stage and over 6 million working days were lost. In many cases the government simply agreed to the demands of the strikers. But Sassoon and the Socialists were in the minority. Even in 1917, when people were prepared to question the war leadership, there was still very little doubt in people's minds that the war against Germany should be pursued to a final victory.

The end of the war in November 1918 was greeted as much with relief as with a sense of triumph. People were all too well aware by then of the human and financial cost of the war in Britain and in other countries, and were desperate to rebuild their lives and their country.

Activity

You are going to compile a class 'propaganda guide' to help you to know how to recognise propaganda and how to use it as historians.

Look through the whole of this chapter and choose five examples of propaganda.

For your guide you should:
- explain how you knew each one was a piece of propaganda
- draw up three rules for your fellow pupils on how to use these sources effectively.

SOURCE 20

We are slowly but surely killing off the best of the male population of these islands. Can we afford to go on paying the same price for the same sort of gain?

From Lord Lansdowne's letter to the press, 29 November 1917.

SOURCE 21

I believe that the war is being prolonged by those who have the power to end it. I believe that this war upon which I entered as a war of defence and liberation has now become a war of conquest and aggression. I have seen and endured the sufferings of the troops and I can no longer be a party to prolonging these sufferings for ends which I believe to be evil and unjust.

'A soldier's declaration' by Siegfried Sassoon, July 1917.

2 Read Source 21. How is this criticism of the war different from Lord Lansdowne's criticism in Source 20?
3 Which criticism would be most troubling to the government?

Focus Task

How effective was government propaganda during the war?

1 On a scale of 1–10, say how effective you think government propaganda was during the war.
2 Write a paragraph to explain your score. Support it with evidence from pages 418–27.
3 Write a paragraph to explain why it is hard to judge clearly whether or not government propaganda was a success.

At this hour of England's grave peril and desperate need, I do hereby pledge myself most solemnly in the name of the King and Country to persuade every man I know to offer his services to the country, and I also pledge myself never to be seen in public with any man who, being in every way fit and free for service, has refused to respond to his country's call.

Part of the oath of the Active Service League.

SOURCE **23**

[The work women are doing] . . . is not of the repetitious type, demanding little or no manipulative ability . . . it taxes the intelligence of the operatives to a high degree. Yet the work turned out has reached a high pitch of excellence.

From the trade journal the *Engineer*, 20 August 1915.

How far did women contribute to the war effort?

As soon as the war broke out in 1914, both the suffragists and the suffragettes suspended their campaigns for the vote. The suffragists, with their formidable publicity machine, worked to persuade the men of Britain to join the army. Meanwhile, Mrs Pankhurst staged a huge demonstration demanding that women be allowed to work in munitions factories. Early in August, all suffragettes were released from prison. Other women's organisations also tried to boost recruitment. The Order of the White Feather encouraged women to give white feathers to young men not in the armed forces. The white feather was a symbol of a coward. The Mothers' Union published posters urging mothers to get their sons to join up. Women members of the Active Service League took an oath to promise to encourage young men to join up (see Source 22).

From an early stage in the war, British industry began to suffer a desperate shortage of labour. By early 1916, Britain had up to 2 million workers fewer than were necessary to keep the country going.

In offices the absence of men did not pose a particular problem. Women were soon employed in place of the male clerks who joined up, and by the end of the war half a million women had replaced men in office jobs. Government departments employed a further 200,000 female clerks.

In manufacturing, however, it was a different story, at least to start with. Employers were very reluctant to take on women to fill men's jobs. They thought that women would not learn the necessary skills, and also feared trouble from the unions. In fact, the unions did resist the employment of women workers, fearing that women would be paid less and that this would be a threat to men's wages. Most unions did not even accept female members.

By 1916, the shortage of engineering workers was desperate, especially as more and more munitions and supplies, and increasing numbers of men, were needed at the front. For practical reasons, employers were persuaded to take on women workers. The government set an example to private industry by employing women almost exclusively in its own munitions factories. By the end of the war, almost 800,000 women had taken up work in engineering industries. The evidence soon showed that even with very little training they were as skilled as men.

Munitions work was tiring and dangerous. As the war went on, shifts got longer and longer. There were disastrous accidents, such as the explosion at Silvertown in the East End of London, in January 1917. In August 1916, medical reports publicised the effects on women of handling TNT explosives. These included breathing difficulties, rashes and yellowing of the skin, digestion problems, blood poisoning and even brain damage.

SOURCE **24**

An official war painting of women at work in a munitions factory.

SOURCE **25**

A photograph taken in a munitions factory in 1917.

SOURCE 26

Women delivering coal in 1917.

As the war took its terrible toll on the male population, more and more women stepped in to fill the gaps. A kind of revolution was taking place. Women gained access to a whole range of jobs that had previously been the preserve of men. They worked as bus conductors, postal workers and farm labourers, and delivered coal. Some 1.6 million extra women workers took part in war work. They became grave diggers, road layers, welders, steel workers and bus drivers. There was a Women's Volunteer Police Service in most of the major cities. Some 260,000 women served in the Women's Land Army. In 1918, the first women's army unit (the Women's Army Auxiliary Corps, or WAAC) was founded, although members were never involved in front-line fighting. There were women nurses in medical stations near the front line. The Salvation Army sent female volunteers as nurses, cooks and helpers to aid soldiers and civilians in France. Women even kept the factory football teams going!

Women workers came from many different backgrounds. Some married women took on their husbands' jobs, but it was mostly unmarried women who took jobs in factories. The government called on middle-class families to do without their servants; with higher wages and preferable conditions in factories, many servants did not need much persuading.

SOURCE 27

Area of work	Women in 1914	Women in 1918	Women replacing men
Metals	170,000	594,000	195,000
Chemicals	40,000	104,000	35,000
Food and drink	196,000	235,000	60,000
Timber	44,000	79,000	23,000
Transport	18,000	117,000	42,000
Government	2,000	225,000	197,000

Women at work, 1914–18.

SOURCE 28

'Palmer's Munitionettes': a women's football team made up of workers from Palmer's Shipbuilding Company.

PROMPT 5
Make notes for your presentation on how the war affected women civilians. Mention:
- their role in recruitment
- job opportunities
- men's attitudes
- working conditions.

Focus Task

How did women contribute to the war effort?

It is 1918. Use the information and sources on pages 428–29 to write a report for the Prime Minister. Your report is designed to convince him that the contribution of women to the war effort means they should get the vote. You should mention the role of women in:
- recruitment
- freeing men to fight
- munitions
- putting up with prejudice
- success at doing 'men's work'.

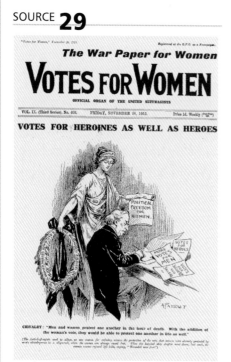

The War Paper for Women

VOTES FOR WOMEN

OFFICIAL ORGAN OF THE UNITED SUFFRAGISTS

VOL. IX. (Third Series), No. 408. FRIDAY, NOVEMBER 26, 1915. Price 1d. Weekly

VOTES FOR HEROINES AS WELL AS HEROES

CHIVALRY: "Men and women protect one another in the hour of death. With the addition of the woman's vote, they would be able to protect one another in life as well."

The front cover of the magazine *Votes for Women*, 26 November 1915.

Former opponents are now declaring themselves on our side, or at any rate withdrawing their opposition. The change of tone in the press is most marked . . . The view has been widely expressed in a great variety of the organs of public opinion that the continued exclusion of women from representation will . . . be an impossibility after the war.

Millicent Fawcett writing in the magazine *Common Cause*, 1916.

I'm against the extension of the franchise to women. I shall always be against the extension of the franchise to women . . . It was in the year 1918, after the war, that the disaster took place. Had it not been for the war, in my judgement we should have continued successfully to resist this measure for an indefinite period of time.

Lord Birkenhead, speaking just before all women gained the vote in 1928.

Why were some women given the vote in 1918?

In 1915, the government began to consider changes to Britain's electoral system. Until then, citizens living outside Britain were not allowed to vote in elections. This was clearly unfair to soldiers who were serving abroad. They wanted to change the voting system to allow the 'hero' soldiers to vote. The campaigners jumped at this chance (see Source 29). The NUWSS had continued to pressure the government quietly and steadily throughout the war. Women had shown themselves to be capable and responsible under the strains of war. By 1916 women were even serving in the armed forces.

Other changes had also taken place. Asquith, one of the main opponents of female suffrage, was no longer Prime Minister. WSPU militancy was a distant memory, so MPs would not be accused of giving in to violence. The country was run by a coalition government of Liberal, Conservative and Labour ministers. This meant that no one party would be seen as the one who gave women the vote. On top of these factors, Millicent Fawcett and the NUWSS communicated closely with the government and agreed the compromise that not all women would get the vote even though all men over 21 would.

The House of Commons passed the Representation of the People Act in 1917 by a massive majority of seven to one. It was given a rougher ride in the Lords, but even so was passed by 63 votes. It became law in 1918. As a result of the Act, all males aged over 21 gained the right to vote. Women over the age of 30 who were householders or married to householders also gained the vote – a total of about 9 million women.

However, you can see from this that the old fears about women having the vote had not entirely disappeared. Although all men now had the vote, MPs were prepared to support votes only for older married women, or women who owned property and were therefore considered more responsible. One leading historian has pointed out that the young, single working-class women who had done most of the war work were the ones who did not gain the vote. MPs were reluctant to enfranchise this new group, whose ideas might be a little too radical.

Women could now also stand for Parliament and in 1919 Nancy Astor became the first woman MP to take her seat in the Commons. (The first woman MP to be elected was Countess Makiewicz, but as an Irish nationalist she refused to sit at Westminster.)

Full voting rights for women were not granted until 1928. Even so, for Millicent Fawcett, the 1918 Act was the fulfilment of a lifetime's work.

The history of the women's movement for the last 50 years is the gradual removal of intolerable grievances. Sometimes the pace was fairly rapid; sometimes it was very slow; but it was always constant, and always in one direction. I have sometimes compared it . . . to the movement of a glacier. But like a glacier it was ceaseless and irresistible. You could not see it move, but if you compared it with a stationary object . . . you had proof positive that it had moved.

Written by Millicent Fawcett in 1918.

Some years ago I used the expression 'Let the women work out their own salvation.' Well, Sir, they had worked it out during the war. How could we have carried on the war without them?

Wherever we turn we see them doing work which three years ago we would have regarded as being exclusively 'men's work'. When the war is over the question will then arise about women's labour and their function in the new order of things. I would find it impossible to withhold from women the power and the right of making their voices directly heard.

From a speech by ex-Prime Minister Asquith in 1917.

Activity

Professor Change

The period 1906 to 1918 saw massive changes in life in Britain.

Professor Continuity

This might look like a period of great change in some ways – but for most people life carried on much as usual.

Professor Evolution

There were undoubtedly important changes in the years 1906 to 1918. However, most of them had already started well before and simply continued to develop during this period.

These three professors all interpret the events in Britain between 1906 and 1918 differently. There is good evidence to support all three views!

1 Using the information over pages 390–431, decide how each of the professors could support his or her view.
2 Then use your evidence to prepare for a class debate on 'Was 1906 to 1918 a time of change in Britain?'

Focus Task

Why were some women given the vote in 1918?

SOURCE **34**

There were three stages in the emancipation of women. The first was the long campaign of propaganda and organisation at the centre of which, patient, unwearying and always hopeful, stood Dame Millicent Fawcett. The second was the campaign of the militants. The third was war.

Had there been no militancy and no war, the emancipation would have come, although more slowly. But without the faithful preparation of the ground over many years by Dame Millicent Fawcett and her colleagues, neither militancy nor the war could have produced the crop.

From the obituary to Millicent Fawcett in the *Manchester Guardian*, 6 August 1929.

Read Source 34. You are now going to consider how far you agree with this analysis.
1 Write each of the following labels on a separate card.
   ◆ Peaceful suffragist campaigning
   ◆ Militant suffragette campaigning
   ◆ Women's support for the war effort
2 On each card, write your own explanation of how this factor helped to lead to women getting the vote.
3 Take one card (any card) away. Explain why women would not have got the vote with just the two remaining factors.
4 Is any one factor more important than the others? Explain your answer carefully.
5 Re-read Source 34, then explain in your own words how these factors are linked together.

How far did British society change, 1939–75?

15.1 What impact did the Second World War have on the British people?

The Second World War was a significant event in world history; it was also a very significant event in British history. You probably already know quite a bit about the impact of the war on British society: the air raids, rationing, evacuation, censorship, propaganda . . . You may be less aware of how significantly the war changed the population of Britain. It brought many newcomers from many different backgrounds. One commentator observed that through the war Britain became like a 'giant tourist camp'. Many areas of the country were more multicultural during the war than they are today.

American GIs

Probably the most high profile arrivals were American soldiers who began arriving in Britain from 1942 onwards. They were known as GIs. During the course of the war around three million were posted all over the UK, often in rural areas. They had a huge impact. Most sources from the time indicate that they were very open and friendly and got on well with local people (see Source 1). British society at that time was divided on class lines. The classes did not mix and working classes were supposed to 'know their place'. America was a much less class-conscious society and the GIs brought these values with them and mixed freely with different classes. The GIs were especially popular with the girls. The GIs were well paid, so they were able to take British girls to the best clubs and restaurants. Around 80,000 British women became 'GI brides' and after the war emigrated to the USA with their new husbands.

Despite their popularity the GIs caused some tensions as well. These mostly arose from cultural differences. To avoid misunderstandings American and British governments even issued films and pamphlets (such as Source 3) to educate the GIs about Britain and the British people.

SOURCE **1**

The white Americans that came into our world shortly afterwards were impressive, but paled into insignificance when compared to our black friends. They were friends despite swarms of children following them, tugging at their clothes and asking, 'Got any gum chum?' They never lost their tempers, were always smiling, and were extremely generous. We loved those first American soldiers and did not even think about colour except that they were black and we were white, a natural state of affairs.

The general resentment felt by local men and British servicemen towards all 'Yanks' led to the saying, 'We don't like Yanks because they are over-sexed, over-paid and over here'. There was a lot of jealousy and resentment amongst them because they were more confident, had more money and were much smarter. The uniforms they wore were beautiful compared to the rough, drab, ill-fitting khaki uniforms of our army. This wasn't the whole story though because the Americans were well-mannered, polite, gregarious and confident. Most of our British counterparts were shy, tongue-tied around women, poor, and felt that they compared badly with the Americans, so resented them even more.

The memories of Ken Clark, who grew up in South Wales during the war.

Focus

This depth study looks at how Britain changed in the period 1939 to 1975. You will start with two contextualising topics:

- In Section 15.1 you will study the **impact of the Second World War** on British society.
- In Section 15.2 you will look at the state of Britain at the end of the war. This will focus on one significant post war development, the **National Health Service**, which affected the lives of almost everyone living in Britain in some way or another.

The rest of the chapter then examines the differing experiences of three different groups of people through this period of change.

- In Section 15.3 you will study the experiences of **immigrants**. You will consider why different people came to Britain; what life was like for them (and why) and the contribution immigrants made to life in Britain.
- In Section 15.4 you will consider how far life for **women** in Britain changed in this period. You will focus on health, work and family and the campaign for equal rights before reaching your own conclusions about how much changed through the period.
- In Section 15.5 you will research at the lives of **young people** in Britain and decide how it was changing in the 1950s and 1960s. The focus will be on health, education and youth culture.

And throughout this chapter your focus will be on sources and evidence. There will be regular Source Investigations such as you will face in an exam, and we will provide plenty of other source material for you to interrogate.

SOURCE 2

GIs dancing with British girls at the US Services club in London, January 1944.

SOURCE 3

GI dancing with a girl in Swansea in 1944.

1 How does Source 1 help historians to understand the appeal of GIs to the British people?

2 Does Source 4 tell historians more about the British or more about the Americans in 1942? Explain your answer.

3 Explain why the picture in Source 3 would have been more acceptable in Britain than in the USA.

African American GIs

A large minority of these GIs were black. One hundred and thirty thousand African American servicemen and women came to Britain. In some respects their experiences were similar to those of their white countrymen. However, while the Americans were not class conscious they were very race conscious. Back in the USA most African Americans suffered from harsh discrimination. Schools, cinemas, restaurants and many other ordinary places were segregated. In Britain the US military was also segregated. The historian Neil Wynn carried out a study on the treatment of African American GIs in the very rural area of Gloucestershire. Wynn found that African American GIs were treated well, and that local people even criticised the white Americans, especially the Military Police, for the way they treated black GIs. After a visit to Britain, Walter White of the US National Association for the Advancement of Colored People (NAACP), concluded that for many African Americans their time in England provided 'Their first experience in being treated as normal human beings and friends by white people'. Despite this, however, Wynn also identified that segregation began to creep into British society as well (see Source 5).

SOURCE 4

SOME IMPORTANT DOS AND DON'TS

- *BE FRIENDLY – but don't intrude anywhere it seems you are not wanted. You will find the British money system easier than you think. A little study beforehand on shipboard will make it still easier.*

- *You are higher paid than the British 'Tommy'. Don't rub it in. Play fair with him. He can be a pal in need.*

- *Don't show off or brag or bluster. If somebody looks in your direction and says, 'He's chucking his weight about', you can be pretty sure you're off base. That's the time to pull in your ears.*

- *If you are invited to eat with a family don't eat too much. Otherwise you may eat up their weekly rations.*

- *Don't make fun of British speech or accents. You sound just as funny to them but they will be too polite to show it.*

- *Avoid comments on the British Government or politics.*

- *Don't try to tell the British that America won the last war or make wise-cracks about the war debts or about British defeats in this war.*

- *NEVER criticise the King or Queen.*

- *Don't criticise the food, beer, or cigarettes to the British. Remember they have been at war since 1939.*

- *Use common sense on all occasions. By your conduct you have great power to bring about a better understanding between the two countries after the war is over.*

- *You will soon find yourself among a kindly, quiet, hard-working people who have been living under a strain such as few people in the world have ever known.*

An extract from 'Instructions for American servicemen in Britain', issued by the US War Department in 1942.

SOURCE 5

Either officially or unofficially, many facilities in Britain became segregated. Thus white troops at camps in Ashchurch were allowed to visit nearby Tewkesbury on Tuesday, Thursday and Saturday; black troops on Monday, Wednesday and Friday. Sundays alternated between the two races. A day club for black servicemen was established in Tewkesbury while whites had similar facilities in Worcester and Cheltenham. In Bristol where initially reports circulated of black soldiers being confined to barracks, two separate Red Cross centres existed in the town, 'one on St George Street for black Americans', and another 'on Byron Corner and Berkeley Square' for whites. Bristol's pubs also became segregated *with some serving whites only and with others, generally the poorer ones, catering only for blacks. As early as 1942 arrangements had also been made to seat the races separately in cinemas in Yeovil and Chard. Even fish and chip shops operated on racial lines or used black Wednesdays and white Thursdays. In the Forest of Dean black troops were excluded from Cinderford 'because it was all whites there'. Provision was made elsewhere, and the Dean Forest Guardian noted that 'Two coloured American girls, well-educated and recruited from the best type' were to run the Red Cross canteen for black troops in Coleford.*

Some findings from *Race War: Black American GIs and West Indians during the Second World War* by Neil Wynn. This was a study of the treatment of African American GIs and West Indian troops in the Gloucestershire area of England during the war. It was published in 2006.

Commonwealth troops

Well before the arrival of the American GIs Britain had already seen an influx of servicemen and women from the Commonwealth and the British Empire. Large numbers of Canadians, Australians, New Zealanders and Indians served in the British forces. There was also a large contingent from the Caribbean, or West Indies as the area was called then. These incomers were usually warmly welcomed. There were over 40,000 marriages between Canadian servicemen and British women. One man, interviewed by the BBC for its People's War website, said that the Canadians stirred up a lot of interest because they seemed to be so tall!

SOURCE **6**

Australian troops queuing to watch a film in London in 1942.

1 Do you agree that Source 7 proves Indian servicemen were welcomed?
2 Study Source 8 carefully. Make a list of all of the positive and negative experiences contained in this source.

SOURCE **9**

Prisoner of War camps in Britain during the Second World War.

SOURCE **7**

An Indian pilot receives a handshake of welcome from a railway police sergeant on his arrival in London on 8 October 1940. The RAF pilots who fought in the Battle of Britain included Indians, Australians, Canadians, Jamaicans and many others.

SOURCE **8**

Most of the good folk I knew were British servicemen, the Jocks and Paddys and Geordies and Taffys, boys who had joined up like me and now had hopes of making a new life out of the mess. We went around together. Sometimes I went home with them . . .

Maybe we had been used. We believed we had been contributing to the war effort, that we had some purpose in being here. We'd been used the world over for centuries . . . I was getting accustomed to being shouted at, insulted, rejected and, sometimes, protected by white people.

An extract from the autobiography of Eric Ferron, a Jamaican who served in the RAF during the Second World War and then settled in Britain after the war.

Prisoners of War

To add to the mix there were also hundreds of thousands of prisoners of war (usually known as POWs). The largest groups of POWs were the German and Italian troops captured in the fighting in North Africa. After 1944 the number of German POWs increased significantly as Allied forces advanced across Europe. Source 9 shows the location of most of the largest camps but there were also many smaller ones. There were over 1,500 facilities which held prisoners. At its highest the POW population numbered 157,000 Italians and 402,000 Germans.

Prisoners of war were generally treated well. They were allocated the same food rations as Allied servicemen, which was actually more than the ordinary civilian population in Britain at the time. They had access to medical care just like Allied troops. They were even paid wages for the work they did, although these wages were very small. The majority of prisoners worked in agriculture, helping to fill the gap left by men who had been called up to serve in the armed forces. In many cases prisoners also had access to a range of educational classes, often run by other prisoners. One of the most popular classes was learning English. The most common complaints were about the food and the weather, but British POWs in Germany generally made exactly the same complaints! At the end of the war a substantial number of prisoners (including around 25,000 German POWs) adopted Britain as their new home, despite the fact that they had been at war with Britain!

3 What does Source 10 tell historians about the treatment of prisoners?
4 Can we assume that all POWs were treated the same way as those described in Source 10?

Activity

The OCR specification says that you should study the experiences of the servicemen and women and POWs who came to Britain in the war and British attitudes towards them. Do you think that Sources 1–11 provide enough material to set a paper on this?

1 Start by looking at the content of each source. What does it say at face value?
2 Now look at each source and see what can be inferred from it.
3 Now look at each source and judge whether you think it is a useful and or reliable source for looking at the experiences of these groups and attitudes towards them.
4 Finally: EITHER
   a) If you think the sources are adequate try to set your own exam paper. Your teacher can show you the typical structure. OR
   b) If you think the sources are inadequate write a short report explaining why Sources 1–11 do not cover the area effectively and explain what other sources they would need.

SOURCE 11

Mr Rogalski, a former Polish servicemen in his new job working for Nutbourne Brickworks Ltd. He was employed building new houses in Godalming, Surrey. He is second on the right in **A** and first on the right in **B**.

SOURCE 10

When potato time came round again Mr Hewitson [the local farmer] employed a gang of Italian prisoners who were stationed at Merelthough Camp nearr Calthwaite. When they came in the morning they were all eating a thick wedge of white bread with a thick spreading of margarine on top, this was to last all day, which was very little considering the hard work. They told me they got one loaf of bread per day which was divided between five men. Years later I discovered that was also the ration our POWs in Germany got for a day.

I was later signed off from work by my Doctor who said I should take up lighter work. I went to work for Major Parkin and his wife at a place called Broomrigg near Ainstable. Mrs Parkin did welfare for the Land Army and POWs through the Red Cross in the area. Mrs Parkin was a Catholic and as most Italians were also she took them to the Catholic church in Warwick Road Carlisle. She also made Christmas parties for them. When they went home the German POWs came and she did the same for them. They were more reserved than the Italians, more like us as many local people used to say.

They, of course, were mostly Protestants so instead of taking them to church she had them singing in German over the telephone to her friends 'Silent Night, Holy Night'. She also made Christmas parties for them too until they finally went home.

In 1949 I married a German ex-POW who stayed on here as his home had been destroyed in the war. He was 21 years old when he left Germany. He lived most of his life here and died in March 1999, his name was Rudi Splinter. We have one daughter and two sons who keep in touch with their German cousins. They stay with each other for holidays. One cousin came with her two daughters this year to go to the Edinburgh Tattoo. Its nice for us older ones who are left to know they visit each other and that some good can come from a past that contained some of the darkest days in the last century.

The memories of one woman who grew up in Cumbria during the Second World War, recorded for the BBC People's War website in 2005.

Poles

One other significant group who settled in Britain during the war were Poles. Poland was invaded by Germany and the USSR in 1939 and many Poles who were able to escape did so. Around 14,000 of them served in the Royal Air Force. Many more served in the other armed forces in Britain and in other parts of the British Empire. At the end of the war Poland was technically free but in reality it was dominated by the USSR and so many Poles chose to settle in Britain – around 120,000 in all.

Prime Minister Winston Churchill had a personal interest in the Poles because Britain went to war in 1939 to save Poland. He was also the leader who had agreed to the USSR having Poland in its sphere of influence (see page 74–76). He was grateful for the Polish contribution to the war effort. The Poles were generally popular in Britain and Britain was suffering from a desperate shortage of workers in the years after the Second World War. As a result Churchill dismissed the concerns of some of his ministers and insisted that Poles should be allowed to stay. A Polish Resettlement Corps was set up to house the Poles and provide training and work for them. The housing was in military camps and former prisoner of war camps and it was very basic indeed. The Poles were also still treated as though they were in military service.

By the end of 1948 there were 65,000 workers in British industry under the Polish Resettlement scheme. The scheme was wound up in 1949 because virtually all Poles had found jobs or had started their own businesses (often providing services like restaurants and shops for other Poles). It was not an easy settlement process, but the Poles generally fared better than other immigrants from Eastern Europe. However, they often found they could be sacked with no compensation because they were not British citizens.

Focus Task

What immigrants were living in Britain in 1945?

Draw up your own spider diagram to record the different groups mentioned on pages 432–35. For each group note the reasons why they came to Britain. Add more groups to your diagram using the map on page 450.

How did the Second World War affect women?

In the First World War it had taken some time to mobilise the full workforce. This time as soon as war broke out the government lost little time. By the summer of 1941, over half of the working population was either employed by the government or was on government schemes related to the war effort. It was not enough, however, and in late 1941 women were conscripted.

'Do your bit for the war effort …'

All women aged twenty or older had to register for war work at a labour exchange. Unless they were ill, pregnant or had small children, they were sent to work in industry or the auxiliary armed forces. By 1945 80 per cent of married women and 90 per cent of single women were either working in industry or in the forces. Some women were reported as working 80–90 hours per week on aeroplane assembly lines. There were 7.5 million women working in 1939, out of a total population of 40 million. Of these, 260,000 women were working in the munitions industry in 1944.

Women took the key role in evacuation. During the war there were 60 million changes of address registered. On the whole it was women who had to administer and cope with this enormous movement of people. It was largely women in the countryside who looked after the young evacuees.

Many became involved in the war effort in other ways, as air-raid wardens, fire officers and so on. Large numbers of women joined the armed services and many served overseas. By 1943 over 443,000 women were in the auxiliary branches of the armed forces (the ATS, WAAF and WRNS). They were involved in a huge range of military activities, including anti-aircraft work (see Source 12).

The mobilisation was so vast that unlike the First World War the novelty of women working in 'men's jobs' quickly wore off. Eight times as many women took on war work in the Second World War as in the First. For example, during the First World War the Women's Land Army had employed only 33,000 women as rural labourers; in 1943, it employed around two million.

The trade unions accepted women workers much more readily than they had done in the previous war. The TUC campaigned to make sure that women were treated the same as men. For example, the TUC successfully complained against the fact that women were paid 25 per cent less and received lower accident compensation than men in the Rolls-Royce armament factories.

SOURCE 12

Key
1938
1944

Manufacture/repair of cars, aircraft
Local government, fire service
Chemicals, explosives
Farming
Banking, insurance
National government service

Per cent
0 10 20 30 40 50 60 70

Proportion of women in different occupations 1938–44.

SOURCE 13

A woman making hand grenades in a munitions factory.

SOURCE 14

Women of the ATS (Auxiliary Territorial Service) on duty as anti-aircraft observers. Their job was to spot enemy aircraft and then track them, relaying information about their movements. They were often targeted by enemy aircraft.

SOURCE 15

British women officers often give orders to men. The men obey smartly and know it is no shame. For British women have proved themselves in this war. They have stuck to their posts near burning ammunition dumps, delivered messages on foot after their motorcycles have been blasted from under them. They have pulled aviators from burning planes . . . There isn't a single record of any British woman in uniformed service quitting her post, or failing in her duty under fire. When you see a girl in uniform with a bit of [medal] ribbon on her tunic, remember she didn't get it for knitting more socks than anyone else in Ipswich.

A US War Department booklet for American soldiers coming to Britain in 1942.

SOURCE 16

Women's Land Army workers in 1942.

SOURCE 17

A woman's life is at least as valuable as a man's and her physical and mental well being are just as important. We do not accept that injured women and girls should receive lower wages than men and boys at government re-training centres.

A statement by the General Council of the TUC relating to compensation for workers killed or injured.

'… but still look after the children!'

One of the biggest challenges for women was juggling work and home. The majority of women had to find time to do their war work AND continue to look after their families as they had always done. Cooking, washing, cleaning, shopping and child care took up enormous amounts of time on top of their long hours at work. Government and employers began to introduce flexible working arrangements to help women workers. Women who had to juggle family and work commitments were allowed shift work and job shares. Nurseries were provided by the government and employers for married workers with babies. This was a major change, considering that before the war women had surrendered their right to work simply by getting married.

SOURCE 18

Women in London in 1942 protesting about a shortage of nusery facilities.

Activity

After the First World War, a leading British politician praised the work of British women in the war. He asked: 'How could we have carried on without them?'
Do you think this comment would have been appropriate at the end of the Second World War? Find evidence to support your view and put your case to the rest of the class in a presentation.

SOURCE 19

Recruitment poster for the Wrens
(Women's Royal Naval Service).

Did the war bring about real change?

Attitudes towards women workers

There is a lot of debate about this between historians. Women clearly got more opportunities to work in a wider range of industries. However, the details of these new jobs are important and reveal much about the attitudes towards women at the time. For example:

- Many skilled jobs in the aircraft industry were broken down into several simpler jobs and allocated to several different women. Managers simply assumed that women could not do these jobs.
- Almost 40 per cent of women employed in 1943 worked in the munitions industry – jobs that were only available in wartime and not 'new jobs' which they could carry on after the war.
- Although government propaganda encouraged women to join the services, the vast majority of women served in the Auxiliary services – 'helping' men rather than replacing them or working as equals. ATS and WRNS women never flew aircraft or sailed on ships.
- The wartime recruitment posters emphasised glamour and being feminine.

SOURCE 20

1939, 7 September: Engaging of females
The following is a guide to the number of female trainees you are to engage for your branch:

Department	Number of females trainees
Cheese	1
Cooked meats	1
Eggs	1
Butter	1 for every two blocks
Bacon	1 or 2
Grocery	1 or 2
Poultry shop	1
Poultry block	1 but realise that rather a different type of women will be required for this work
Meat	None, but they can be very usefully employed assisting the men by wrapping

The women must be made capable to take the place of men, and that can only be done if they are put to work by the side of the men so that they can continually be told and learn.

1943, 22 March: additional duties which can be undertaken by female deputy managers

The Deputy Manager being a woman can obviously most easily assist the Manager, particularly if he is a male, by undertaking on his behalf certain control of the female employees in the following:

- *That each saleswoman seeks authority from the head of her department before leaving the counter: generally reporting to the Manager as to whether or not our instructions regarding leaving the counter are being carried out.*
- *That the female staff cloakroom is kept in proper order.*
- *That hand-bags are kept in the Office or, if there is no Office, in the place fixed by the Manager.*
- *Supervising the general appearance, tidiness, cleanliness, etc. of the female staff, with particular reference to the condition, repair and replacement of overalls, etc.*
- *Acting where necessary as liaison between the Manager and staff on welfare matters. (Managers must remember that in so many matters women will only talk properly to other women).*

Extracts from messages sent by the Head Office of the Sainsburys chain to its branch managers during the war.

1 Study Source 19. What qualities do you think the poster is emphasising? Look at the caption and the way the Wren is represented.
2 Do you agree that the attitude of Source 20 towards women is patronising? Are there any other words you could use to describe its tone instead or as well?

SOURCE 21

A

When you get up in the morning you feel you go out with something in your bag, and something coming in at the end of the week, and it's nice. It's a taste of independence, and you feel a lot happier for it . . . I have everything to do at home, and so all I want is to get on to part-time. It's just what you can imagine nicely when you are middle-age.

B

Of course when we get married I shan't want to work; I shall want to stay at home and have some children. You can't look on anything you do during the war as what you really mean to do; it's just filling in time till you can live your own life again.

Extracts from responses to the Mass Observation Project which monitored the lives of British people from 1937 to the early 1950s.

SOURCE 22

The attitude of the housewife to gainful employment outside the home is not and should not be the same as that of a single woman. She has other duties . . . in the next thirty years housewives and mothers have vital work to do in ensuring the adequate continuance of the British race and of British ideals in the world.

Senior civil servant Sir William Beveridge, 1943.

After the war

Many women liked their war work. When the war did end in 1945 many women feared they would be forced out of work. This had happened in 1918 at the end of the First World War. In fact it was a different story in 1945. The task of rebuilding after the war required a huge labour force, which even the returning soldiers could not fill. The Labour Minister George Isaacs said that, 'in the battle for recovery there are still many front-line jobs for women to do'. Older married women responded quickly to the government's campaign. Their children tended to be at school, and so they were freer to take up part-time jobs. They generally worked in light industry (such as electrical appliances) or shops, or for local authorities. In 1947, 18 per cent of married women were working, as compared with 10 per cent in the 1930s.

In contrast younger married women were more reluctant to continue paid employment. Most women still saw their primary role as having children and raising a family and after the war young women were eager to get on with it. Women's magazines of this period were almost exclusively preoccupied with the image of women as housewives, bringing up children, cooking, washing and looking after the family. After the war, there was a boom in marriages, and women with young families were very unwilling to take jobs.

In response, the government persuaded employers to offer special incentives to attract women back to work. Part-time and shift work helped women cope with the demands of jobs and families. Laundries were installed at places of work. Shops were encouraged to deliver groceries to factories, which eased women's anxieties about not being able to queue for rations (food rationing continued for eight years after the war). The government allocated building materials to nurseries, and asked education authorities to keep schools open late and during holidays to look after the children of working mothers. Women with young children were encouraged to leave their children with relatives or babysitters.

Attitudes of women

There is a great deal of evidence to suggest that many women gained in confidence from their experiences during the war. The government ran a Mass Observation Project which collected a huge amount of data from ordinary people about their experiences during the war. They achieved things they would never have had the chance to do otherwise. The war also gave younger women a degree of freedom to travel and socialise which they would never have had in peacetime. The evidence is that war did change traditional attitudes, relationships and behaviour. Sex outside marriage became much more common, and so did infidelity within marriage. The divorce rate rose and even increased in the years immediately after the war.

So although after the war many women, probably most, wanted to return to a traditional role in which the husband was the breadwinner, they did not want to return to these roles on the same terms as before the war. War had changed their expectations. They expected their marriages to be more like equal partnerships rather than seeing their husband as superior.

Activity

'The war had very little impact on attitudes to women.' How far do you agree with this statement?
1 Find evidence from pages 436–39 of attitudes to women.
2 Place the evidence on a scale like this, then compare your scale with another student in your class and see if you can agree a new position on the scale which you both agree with.
3 Decide where on the scale you belong. Do you think war changed attitudes completely, there was no change or somewhere in between?

War changed attitudes completely   **No change at all**

⬅━━━━━━━━━━━━━━━━━━━━━━━━━➡

			Recruitment posters emphasised glamour	

How did the war affect children and young people?

In many respects young people were affected by the war in much the same way as adults, although they saw events from a different perspective. Source 23 provides some accounts of what it was like to grow up during the war.

SOURCE 23A

The Edwards children in the mid 1930s. This source is based on interviews with some of the surviving members of the Edwards family. Tom and Annie Edwards had seven daughters: Theresa, Pauline, Margie, Geraldine, Eileen, Josephine and Carmel. They were a fairly typical family of the time, although they had more children than most. Annie ran the house. Tom was a qualified nurse. He had served on the Western Front in the Great War. The person we talked to most was Josephine, the second youngest daughter. She was always called Jo.

SOURCE 23B

Jo was only eight when the war started. Her main memory of the war is the air raids. Liverpool was hit hard by the Luftwaffe, especially in the Blitz of 1941. Jo remembers that the council built a brick air-raid shelter on the local playing field. Also it always seemed to be dark everywhere. The blackout curtains were shut tight. You could be fined if lights could be seen from your house.

Even today, Jo gets very upset when she remembers the air raids. During one raid, an incendiary (fire bomb) hit her house. It fell through the roof into her parents' bedroom. Tom and a neighbour managed to put out the fire, but the bed and bedding were ruined. An official came to look at the damage. Within a few days Annie received a slip of paper. She took it to the post office and got money to replace the damaged bed and bedding. Pretty good in the middle of a war, don't you think?

Jo was just a bit too old to be an evacuee, so she doesn't know much about that. However, she heard lots of tales from her friends and sister. Overall, she was glad she did not get evacuated. However, she was jealous of the evacuees in one way. They got beautiful new rucksacks in which to carry their belongings. Jo thought the bags were lovely. They were almost worth getting evacuated for!

Several of Jo's sisters worked during the war. Before the war, it was unusual for many women to work. But during the war, you got some pretty funny looks if you did not work.

- *Pauline worked in the Ministry of Food in the centre of Liverpool.*
- *Theresa worked in a factory on the edge of the city. Conditions there were very bad. Quite a lot of the women caught tuberculosis.*
- *Eileen was one of the first women in Britain to work for the fire service. She was conscripted into the Auxiliary Fire Service in 1941.*

Tom was not conscripted into the army. As a qualified nurse, he was in a reserved occupation. Like most people, he worked very long hours. He would often work a twelve-hour shift, then do his turn as fire warden on the roof of the hospital. This meant watching for incendiary bombs. If one fell, he had to put out the fire with sand.

Jo doesn't remember much about school. She says she remembers being hungry more! In the early years before the Americans arrived, there was little to eat – early 1941 was the worst period. Milk was often in short supply. You had to scrape by – one egg per person every two weeks, for example! The only thing that never seemed to run out was jam.

One of Jo's friends, Frank, remembers the bread and jam as well. Frank's mother had died before the war so he was looked after by his brothers and sister. They often ate bread and jam because their dad was a rotten cook! Frank and his dad had an allotment. They also used all of their garden to grow vegetables and keep chickens. They used to swap the vegetables they grew for things they needed from their neighbours. One man in the street kept pigs. The children collected scraps like potato peelings and gave them to him for the pigs.

The memories of the Edwards family from Liverpool about living through the Second World War.

Activity

Stage 1

Here are some aspects of the war which feature in Source 23:
- air raids and air raid precautions and the Blitz
- food shortages and rationing
- war work
- evacuation.
1 Study Source 23 carefully and see what you can find out about each area from Source 23.
2 Work with a partner and put the different aspects of the war in order of importance in terms of the impact that they had on the Edwards family.

SOURCE 24

The health of Britain's increasingly overweight children would be improved if they were put on a World War Two ration book diet, according to a new study … For a fortnight, a class of eight-year-olds from a London school were fed porridge, stew, steam puddings and other dishes typical of the rationing years. Researchers found that children's concentration levels went up and that they began to stop snacking on sweets after being given a large bowl of porridge for breakfast and a decent-sized lunch. Miss Ursell said: 'It was fascinating how the children adapted and within a couple of days they had forgotten about snacking and junk food.' It went from the children demanding, to parents being back in the driving seat and telling their children what they were having to eat. 'Kids will try it on unless you put your foot down.' Children on a typical diet today consume more than 3,000 calories a day. The wartime menu for the study was drawn up by cookery writer Marguerite Patten, who was an adviser to the Ministry of Food during the war. She said: 'The ration book diet was difficult to follow and was boring and monotonous, but events have proved that it was actually good for you. What we should do now is augment a sensible eating regime with the wealth of good and healthy food we have now.'

An extract from an article in the *Daily Mail* newspaper in 2008.

Activity (continued)

Stage 2

1 Study the information and sources on page 441 and see if there are any other aspects of the war which you could add to the list from the previous stage of the activity.
2 If you have found aspects not mentioned in Source 23, does this mean Source 23 is not a valuable source? Explain your answer.
3 Now take the four points from the previous stage and your new points and put them in order of importance in terms of the impact you think they had on children during wartime.

Source 23 is just one account so of course it cannot tell us everything about the impact of the war on children and young people. We need to look more broadly.

Schooling

Schooling was badly disrupted by the war. Most schools in urban areas were closed. This was because it was expected that most children would be evacuated to the countryside *with* their teachers. In fact, only about 50 per cent of town and city children were evacuated which left large numbers of youngsters, generally from poorer areas, with little to do. Police reports from the time describe many cases of vandalism and petty crime, even to air raid shelters. These poorer children also lost out on services such as school meals and medical inspections. Medical reports from the wartime period show that there was an increase in complaints like head lice and scabies.

For children who were evacuated their schooling did continue, but it was half time. A common arrangement was for the children of a village to be schooled for half a day in the school building and then the evacuees would be schooled for the other half of the day. In some cases local authorities tried to find other suitable buildings such as parish halls, scout huts or warehouses. As the war progressed, the government realised the impact of the disruption to schooling and reopened some of the schools in the industrial towns. However, they then faced a shortage of teachers: many teachers had been conscripted into the armed forces or other areas of war work.

Health

Contrary to what you might expect children's health benefited from war time. Children from the poorest areas of the cities who were evacuated generally ate better food and lived in a healthier environment. Rationing meant people ate less but it actually helped to improve the diet of many of the populations (see Source 24).

Fear and separation

It is harder to measure the emotional impact of war, and of course many children must have suffered greatly. Many lost friends and family as a result of fighting or air raids or even disease and accidents. Even if they did not suffer this kind of loss, many lived in fear that they would. Others were parted for much of the war from fathers who were serving in the armed forces or who were involved in important war work. Thousands of children spent much of the war away from their families as evacuees, which you will investigate in detail on pages 442–45.

SOURCE 25

How did the war affect the family?
I spent a lot of hours on my own, because dad went long distance, and I never knew where he was going, when he was coming back.

He worked for the government, didn't he?
Yes, he took bombs and he had to have special passes to get through. He saw a lot more than I did with going to Liverpool. And he went down to London and Fleet Street was blown up so he set to and helped to clear it. Of course it was all round the village, he was missing.

So after that, did he just used to turn up at home?
Yes, he never announced it.

You never knew when he was coming home or anything?
No. It was a very hard life.

An extract from an interview in 1995 with a woman who lived in Hebden Bridge, near Halifax. Her father was a demolition worker who helped to clear bomb damage safely.

SOURCE **26**

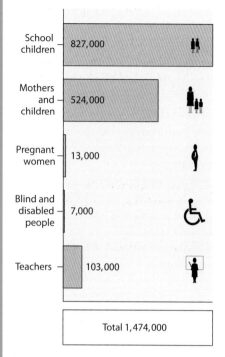

School children	827,000
Mothers and children	524,000
Pregnant women	13,000
Blind and disabled people	7,000
Teachers	103,000

Total 1,474,000

Numbers of evacuees, September 1939.

SOURCE **28**

TAKE THEM BACK! TAKE THEM BACK! TAKE THEM BACK!..

DON'T do it, Mother—

LEAVE THE CHILDREN WHERE THEY ARE

ISSUED BY THE MINISTRY OF HEALTH

A 1942 government poster about evacuation.

Evacuation

The aspect of the war which most obviously affected the largest number of children was evacuation. As soon as war was declared in September 1939, around 1.5 million people, mainly of school age, were moved from areas at high risk of bombing: big cities, industrial areas, ports and villages and towns near to airfields. There were no air raids during the first six months of the war and so many evacuees returned home. Once the Blitz started in 1940 there was a second wave of evacuation and then again in 1944, a third wave, when Germany was bombarding Britain with flying bombs.

The evacuation programme was well planned but there were lots of problems, as you would expect with such a huge migration.

- Evacuees were not used to rural life. There was a clash between city and country values. Many evacuees were from poor families in the inner cities. They often found themselves in much wealthier homes and had to cope with different standards of behaviour. They also had to deal with confusing equipment that many did not have at home such as bathrooms and lavatories!
- Evacuees were usually separated from their families. Some evacuee children were badly treated.
- There was evidence that some people tried to avoid taking evacuees. A report in July 1941 criticised many better-off people for 'shirking their responsibilities'.

SOURCE **27**

Evacuees leaving the East End of London in September 1939.

Understandably many mothers were concerned about sending their children away. Around 50 per cent of children from urban areas were never evacuated at all. Many more were brought back home by their parents because they were homesick or because they were mistreated. The government was anxious to make evacuation work, partly for the safety of the children, but also because it wanted women to be free to work in the war industries and the armed forces. The government censors carefully controlled images and stories about evacuees in newspapers. There was also a propaganda campaign designed to persuade mothers not to bring their children home.

SOURCE **29**

No hitch on great adventure

Evacuation of schoolchildren from London went without a hitch. The children, smiling and cheerful . . . entrained for unknown destinations in the spirit of going on a great adventure.

'I wish all our passengers were as easy to manage,' a railway official said . . .

At Waterloo, 80 per cent of the normal travellers saw nothing of the schoolchildren. After Earl de la Warr, President of the Board of Education, had toured a number of schools in West London, he said, 'If the arrangements at the other end for receiving the children are as good as at this end, it bodes well for the scheme.'

First-aid posts at various stations for the children, were rarely if ever used.

Report from the *Daily Mirror*, 2 September 1939.

SOURCE **30**

The most difficult part of being evacuated is coming home again. It was the worst day of my whole life. When the time came I had completely forgotten my family and London. I was ten years old and suddenly I was to be taken away by this strange lady called Mother, from all these wonderful people I had grown up with and not only from them but the whole village that I knew and loved. I knew every path, track and lane for miles around, every house and cottage, every man, woman and child, every cat, dog, cow and chicken. It was a beautiful world and I had to leave it all behind.

Rene Wingwood, an evacuee from London.

Activity

Look carefully at Source 33. Your task is to explain to a person who knows nothing about the war why this image is a true picture of the experience of evacuees, but it is not a complete picture. Use the other information and sources in this section to support the points you make. You could present your explanation in a talk or using software such as PowerPoint®.

Effects of evacuation

Evacuation saved many lives, but it had other important effects. It did indeed, as the government intended, free up many mothers to take on vital war work. On a personal level, evacuation had a huge impact on many children who were evacuated. Some of these experiences were positive and others were negative. For some children the shock of returning home after the war was the biggest impact of all. Some had been away for six years and felt they had less in common with their home families than they did with the families who had been looking after them. Others were glad to return home but the experience of evacuation left them with psychological scars which lasted for the rest of their lives.

SOURCE **31**

I often wonder what kind of life I would have had if Mrs. Cudd had been allowed to adopt me, because the life I had with my real parents was one of physical and sexual abuse and to this day I am still suffering from the effects.

An evacuee interviewed in 1996 who wished to remain anonymous.

SOURCE **32**

I would never let my children go to camp and they all thought it was unfair, but I could never explain to them why. To put my children in the charge of some stranger was foreign to me – and my husband used to fall out with me over it, not giving them what they should have, but I couldn't … let them … in case some stranger got them.

An extract from an interview with an evacuee in June 1996. The interviewee's sister was abused while she was an evacuee.

SOURCE **33**

Evacuees pictured in July 1944 in a village in Cheshire.

The longer term impact of evacuation

Many of the young evacuees probably did not have a very clear idea of what was happening. The older ones would have known that they were being evacuated because of the war. However, none of these youngsters would have known that evacuation opened up a different kind of campaign. It was a political battle, fought at home. It was a battle over what kind of place Britain would be after the war.

During the 1930s large areas of Britain had suffered from terrible unemployment because of the worldwide economic depression. This in turn led to appalling poverty, ill health and dreadful living conditions in many of the areas which were hardest hit. The war had exposed the problem of poverty in Britain. It also posed three big questions for government, SHOWN ON THE LEFT.

The Labour Party constantly argued that child poverty, disease, slum housing, poor education and other social problems were major problems on a gigantic scale. This was consistently denied by the Conservative dominated National Government which was in power at the time, and the Civil Service supported the government's view. It was a big issue at the start of the twentieth century (see page 390).

You may have come across this debate before in your History studies. Some commentators argued that poverty, ill health and misery were the result of bad decisions and reckless living by the poor – i.e. behavioural issues. Others argued that it was the poverty and terrible living conditions which created most of the social problems – i.e. environmental issues.

The Labour Party and social campaigners argued that the government needed to do far more to tackle poverty, illness, poor education and other social problems. Opponents claimed that this was not necessary and that the problems were being exaggerated.

Throughout the 1930s the Labour Party had been weak and unable to make its voice heard. This affected the Labour leader deeply. The situation changed when the war began. Prime Minister Winston Churchill created a government of national unity involving all the main parties. The Labour ministers supported the war effort totally, but they also used the opportunity to demand that government look at the issue of social conditions. Churchill reluctantly agreed. He needed the support of the Labour ministers for the war effort. Just as importantly, the little evacuees heading from the towns to the countryside had made child poverty an issue the government could not ignore. They were bombarded with letters, reports and recommendations from a range of organisations which were commenting on the health and general well-being of the evacuees from the cities.

> **1 What is the scale of the problem?**

> **2 What causes such social deprivation?**

> **3 What shall we do about poverty?**

SOURCE 34

The experience of evacuation has shattered complacency and has shown that previous standards of medical inspections for children were too low. Only education, better housing and higher wages will solve the problems of poverty and disease.

The Medical Officer, a journal for health professionals, 1940.

SOURCE 35

We have taken in a large number of evacuees from Leeds, Grimsby and Hull. Universally, householders have been shocked by the disgraceful and disgusting conditions in which a certain portion of the population lives.

Yorkshire branch of the Womens Voluntary Service commenting on evacuees in November 1939.

SOURCE 36

[They are] … all filthy, the smell of the room is terrible, they refuse all food except tea and bread, the children have made puddles all over the floor …

Moya Woodside, a middle-class girl in rural Northern Ireland, describes her experience of evacuees from Belfast. When Belfast was bombed in 1941, 6,000 went to Dublin and many thousands more left the dense housing of central Belfast to live in the surrounding countryside.

For the first time, many comfortable people outside the cities learned how bad conditions in the cities were. As well as the health problems and the fact that many of the evacuees clearly lived in terrible housing, people began to realise the effects of poverty. Large numbers of children arrived with no spare clothing because they did not have any. The government initially assumed that charities could help out these children, but by 1940 the scale of the problem was becoming clear. In November 1940 the Ministry of Education agreed to give the London County Council £20,000 (almost £1 million by today's standards) for boots and clothing. It was soon clear that shortages were so great that the government had to step in.

All of this information, and the fact that it came from ordinary people (not from politicians trying to make a point), created a consensus among the political parties that social welfare should become a government priority as well as the war effort. It is probably no understatement to say that the evacuation programme was one of the key driving forces behind the major social changes which were brought in after the Second World War. It was one of the factors which drove the ground breaking Beveridge Report (see pages 446–47).

SOURCE 37

I never knew such conditions existed, and I feel ashamed of having been so ignorant of my neighbours. For the rest of my life I mean to try and make amends by helping such people to live cleaner, healthier lives.

Neville Chamberlain writing to his sister during the war. Before the war the Conservative politician Neville Chamberlain had denied that child poverty existed and that malnutrition among children was not an issue.

SOURCE 39

The experience of evacuation therefore, did not provide any fundamental shift in attitudes towards working class lifestyles. If anything, evacuation confirmed existing prejudices and reaffirmed middle class desires to keep social class boundaries intact. It was also clear that the blame for poverty, poor living standards and hygiene, bad manners and habits, general neglect and ignorance were all laid at the door of parents.

An extract from *Evacuation: The True Story* by Martin Parsons and Penny Starns, published in 1996.

SOURCE 40

A poster promoting the Labour party in the 1945 General election.

On the other hand, there is debate among historians about how far attitudes towards the poor really changed. Some historians argue that although the will existed to improve conditions for the poorest in society, many of the middle classes did not actually want to have anything to do with them.

SOURCE 38

… Evacuation acted as a mirror to society and revealed the blemishes that still remained, so generating an even greater degree of universal agreement that something needed to be done. Evacuation was part of the process by which British society came to know itself as the unkempt, ill-clothed, undernourished and often incontinent children of bombed cities acted as messengers carrying the evidence of the deprivation of urban working-class life into rural homes. Evacuation, which aroused the nation's social conscience in the very first year of war, became the most important subject in the social history of the war because it revealed to the whole people the black spots in its social life.

Evacuation and rationing were twin pillars on which was built a consensus of social democracy. The political unity of wartime, symbolised by the party truce and Labour's entry into Churchill's Coalition, generated an acceptance of progressive welfare objectives across a broad spectrum of opinion. The radicalising effects of total war were reinforced as Labour ministers insisted that domestic social problems were as important as military strategy. A kind of benevolent conspiracy emerged which recognised that the working class had to be offered a new deal if the war was to be won.

An extract from *The evolution of the British Welfare State* by Professor Derek Fraser, an expert on the history of welfare, published in 1984.

Activity

Britain held a General Election in July 1945. The result of the election was a landslide victory for the Labour party. Source 40 shows one of their campaign posters.

1 Write a paragraph to go with Source 36 setting out what reforms you think the new Labour government would put into place to deliver on these promises. (You can check whether your predictions were correct by turning to page 448.)
2 The writers of Sources 34–36 would probably not have been Labour voters. Devise an alternative poster which might persuade these people that they should vote Labour in 1945.
3 Write a paragraph explaining how evacuation played a role in convincing people to vote Labour.

Focus Task

You have investigated four aspects of life in the Second World War, including how it:
◆ changed the ethnic and cultural mix of the British population (pages 432–35)
◆ changed attitudes to and experiences of women (pages 436–39)
◆ affected children (pages 440–43)
◆ changed attitudes to poverty (pages 444–45).

Choose one topic and prepare a PowerPoint® presentation on it. You should include at least three slides (with pictures if possible) summarising:
◆ the situation before the war
◆ the impact of the war
◆ your own assessment of how far these were changes for the better or for the worse.

Indeed let us be frank about it – most of our people have never had it so good. Go around the country, go to the industrial towns, go to the farms and you will see a state of prosperity such as we have never had in my lifetime – nor indeed in the history of this country.

An extract from a speech by Prime Minister Harold Macmillan in July 1957.

	Britain 1924–37	**Britain 1951–73**
Economic growth	1.1% per year	2.8% per year
Unemployment	12.7%	2%

15.2 The post war world: A new age?

Britain emerged from the war in 1945 as a country with major economic problems (it had spent a massive amount on fighting the war) but also a country with a sense of optimism and a determination to improve life for all of its people. It was a country which was about to undergo enormous changes. In Sections 15.3–15.5 we are going to look at some of these changes by focusing on Britain's population and immigration, life for British women and life for children and young people. Before we do that, we are going to look at some of the factors which shaped the changes and developments you are going to study.

Prosperity

Within a relatively short time after the war Britain's economy did begin to recover and there was talk of prosperity. In fact, by the summer of 1957 one politician felt confident enough to make the comment in Source 1.

When Macmillan made the speech in Source 1 he probably had no idea that his statement about life being so good would be quoted in almost every textbook about the period – including this one! In some ways it could be seen as typical of a politician, praising the record of his own government. On the other hand there is a lot of evidence to support what Macmillan was saying, particularly if you compare life in the later 1950s with life in the 1930s or the war years of the 1940s (see the table on the left).

The average male factory worker saw his weekly wage rise from £7.83 in 1950 to £41.52 in 1973 (rising prices took a bite out of this increase but his spending power still tripled). His working hours fell from 47.5 to 44.5 hours per week. The number of people who owned their own homes rose from 30 per cent to 50 per cent. Car ownership rose from 5 per cent to 25 per cent of households. In 1950 around 2 per cent of households had a TV but by 1973 the figure was 90 per cent. It was a similar story for goods like washing machines, refrigerators, vacuum cleaners etc.

Of course not every group in society was enjoying these levels of prosperity, but it is certainly true that for many people prosperity had a big impact on their lives. It was also a key factor in attracting new arrivals to the country who would make a huge contribution to the country and shape the Britain that we live in today. You can find out more about this on pages 450–69.

The Beveridge Report, the Welfare State and the NHS

As you have seen on pages 442–45, the experience of wartime and the hard years of the 1930s brought a determination that post war Britain would be a better place for all to live. The man who was told to research this issue was the senior civil servant Sir William Beveridge. He published his findings in 1942, and the report created a stir which no government or politician would be able to ignore.

Beveridge identified five giant social evils which plagued ordinary working people. These were **Want** (or poverty); **Disease**; **Ignorance**; **Squalor** and **Idleness**. He recommended new principles upon which the relief of poverty was to be based.

- First was the principle of **universality** – all British people would be eligible for benefits.
- Beveridge also recommended a **national system of insurance**. All workers would pay into a National Insurance scheme run by the government. Unemployment or sickness benefits would be high enough, and long-lasting enough, so that there would be no need for charity.
- Beveridge recommended a system of **family allowances** which provided for children and for health care.

The essence of what Beveridge had in mind was Social Security. In return for paying a National Insurance contribution, the citizen gained security against the major ills which had blighted the lives of earlier generations.

SOURCE 2

Family allowances

Cost met by the government

Free health care

THE BEVERIDGE REPORT MAIN PROPOSALS

Flat rate benefits for the unemployed and the sick

National Insurance covering everyone from the cradle to the grave

The new look of government policy on poverty

A summary of Beveridge's proposals.

SOURCE 3

A cartoon from the *Daily Express*, 3 December 1942.

1 What is the cartoonist trying to say in Source 3? Explain your answer by referring to details in the cartoon and the historical context of the cartoon (i.e. what was happening at the time and what had gone before).

Some of Beveridge's proposals were already put into action before the end of the war. The Ministry of National Insurance was set up in 1944 and in 1944 the Education Act was passed which gave free, compulsory education to all children up to the age of 15.

In July 1945 a General Election brought a landslide victory for a new Labour government under Clement Atlee. This government was ready to carry out really radical reforms. It wanted to implement Beveridge's ideas and go further still. From 1945–51 it passed a range of important measures:

- 1945 Family Allowances Act – allowance of 5 shillings per week per child in any family.
- 1946 National Insurance Act – benefits for any worker who was unemployed, injured or sick.
- 1946 National Health Service Act (implemented July 1948) – free health care.
- 1947 Town and Country Planning Act and New Towns Act – clearance of slums and bomb damaged housing and relocation of many of the poorest in Britain's cities to new towns.
- 1948 Children Act – local authorities forced to set up services to protect children.
- 1949 Housing Act – massive programme of building new housing up to the latest specifications.

All of these measures were extremely important and had a big impact on the lives of ordinary people. On the next two pages we are going to look at the impact of just one of them: the National Health Service.

SOURCE 4

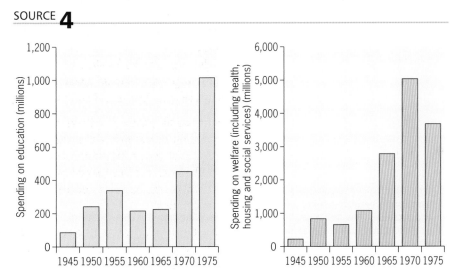

2 Does source 4 prove that governments were committed to improving education and welfare in the period 1945–75? Explain your answer.

These two graphs show government spending on welfare and education, 1945–75.

447

The National Health Service

The introduction of the NHS

The most far-reaching component of the Welfare State was the NHS. As you have seen, most politicians and the majority of the population supported the idea of the Welfare State at the end of the war. Despite this, the Labour Health Minister Aneurin Bevan had to overcome a lot of opposition and a lot of doubters in order to get the NHS set up. However, on 5 July the obstacles were overcome and the NHS opened for business.

SOURCE 5

Commentator: *This new health service will be organised on a national scale as a public responsibility. The cost of the service will be met from rates, taxes and National Insurance – and so everyone will pay for it.*

Charley: *Huh! Thought there was a catch in it.*

Commentator: *And everyone will benefit from it. When you're ill you won't have to pay for treatment.*

Charley: *I don't have to pay the doctor now! I'm on the panel.*

Commentator: *Yes, that's true. But your wife and children aren't. The panel system covers only half the population. And it doesn't cover hospital treatment or a lot of other things, does it? Now suppose – just suppose – you fall off your bike. Suppose your brakes give out. You might have concussion as well. You'd be carted off in an ambulance, which might cost a couple of quid, and then you'd have to pay the hospital too. The new health service would cover all this. Now let's consider it from the family viewpoint. Suppose your wife falls ill suddenly.*

Charley: *But my old woman never is ill – strong as a blooming horse she is!*

Mrs. Charley: *We mothers can't afford to be ill – I am not insured. Just a minute, ducks. And besides I can't take time off from my job!*

Commentator: *Well that's just it. Now let's see how the New Health Act will actually help you. The local council will have a new duty to provide home nursing, health visiting, and home help services. And you'll be able to call on them. Maternity and child welfare services will be improved. And finally, to prevent illness, you'll have the advice of your own doctor. If you are ill, you'll have specialist services if you need them – without worrying about the cost.*

An extract from the script of a public information film broadcast in 1948 to explain the NHS. It was shown in cinemas between the main feature films. In the film the government talks to a character called Charley and his wife.

The impact of the NHS

The demand for health care under the new NHS exceeded all the predictions. What the huge demand really showed was the nation's neglected health in the years which had gone before. In 1947 doctors gave out seven million prescriptions per month. In 1951 that figure rose to 19 million prescriptions per month. Local clinics reported that many women coming in had lost all or half of their teeth. From the 1950s onwards the scale and the quality of the treatment provided by the NHS improved. Between 1948 and 1973 the number of doctors doubled. Anaesthetics continued to advance and this enabled longer and more complex surgery. Spectacular operations were carried out. The bread and butter work of the NHS improved the lives of millions with hip replacement operations, emergency treatment for accident victims or support in pregnancy. The NHS played an important part in prevention as well as cure. By the mid 1960s governments invested in health education. This seemed to have rather mixed success. In general, the majority of the population became healthier and lived longer. On the other hand the Black Report in 1980 reported that for the poorest classes health got worse since the 1960s.

1 What does Source 5 reveal about the limitations of health care before the NHS was introduced?
2 From this source, can you get an impression of what people were expecting from the NHS?

SOURCE 6

This is a photograph of the statue of Aneurin Bevan which is in the middle of Cardiff (he was from South Wales). It commemorates him as the founder of the National Health Service.

The impact of the NHS on women

Since women made up around 50 per cent of the population they naturally benefited from all the advances and developments which we have just described for the population as a whole! However, the NHS also brought improvements which specifically benefited women. Before the NHS many women, probably thousands of them, suffered ill health and could not get treatment because they were not covered by the government's national insurance schemes. The introduction of the NHS changed this situation for women and for children (see Source 5).

The NHS also made high quality maternity care available to many women for the first time. As well as simply improving their quality of life, this type of care also reduced the number of deaths of women in childbirth. It also reduced the number of less serious complications such as infections or post natal depression. In the past, many women had been forced to rely on advice from family and friends rather than from trained medical professionals, sometimes with disastrous consequences. The NHS also provided women with a comprehensive range of services relating to child care, such as midwives and health visitors. The NHS had a considerable impact on the lives of women and the best evidence of this is probably the rising life expectancy for women throughout the century. In 1870 the average age of death for a woman was 45. In 1910 it was not much higher than that. By 1970 the average age of death for women was 76.

The impact of the NHS on children

To begin with, children obviously benefited from the general improvements in health which the whole population were enjoying. They particularly benefited from the fact that mothers were now being cared for better and were enjoying improved health. However, there were also specific aspects of the NHS which were aimed at children. An extensive network of school medical services was set up, including medical inspections carried out by school nurses. These services were more widespread than the medical services available before the war. They were also set up to look for and treat a wider range of illnesses which affected children. One really dramatic development was the introduction of vaccination against some of the main killer diseases. These illnesses were in decline throughout the twentieth century because of generally improving diet, living conditions and prosperity. However, those who were hit by these illnesses were generally the poorest in society, but the free vaccinations under the NHS extended these benefits to the poorest groups. In addition to these other improvements we should remember that the medical professionals of the NHS liaised closely with other professionals such as social workers who were employed as a result of the 1948 Children Act. Perhaps the most telling figure when we look at the impact of the NHS is the fall in infant mortality across the twentieth century (See Source 7).

SOURCE 7

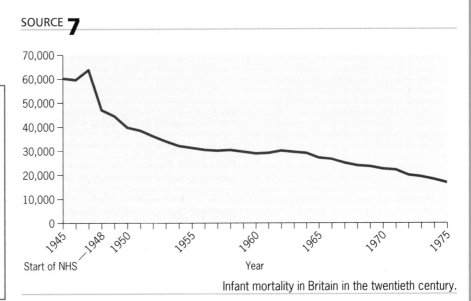

Infant mortality in Britain in the twentieth century.

Focus Task

What was the impact of the National Health Service on people's lives?

Your task is to write three plaques to go on the other three sides of the base of the statue in Source 6.
- One plaque will summarise the impact of the NHS generally
- the second will summarise the impact of the NHS on women
- the third one will summarise the impact on children.

You may be able to use the photograph to create your own virtual statue and add your plaques that way.

15.3 Immigration 1945–75: How did it change Britain?

Britain has always been a country of immigrants and the period 1950–75 was no exception. Immigrants arrived from Eastern Europe, Cyprus, the Old Commonwealth countries (Australia, Canada, New Zealand and South Africa) and the New Commonwealth countries like the Caribbean, India and Pakistan. Source 1 shows some of the main groups who came to settle in Britain in this period.

SOURCE **1**

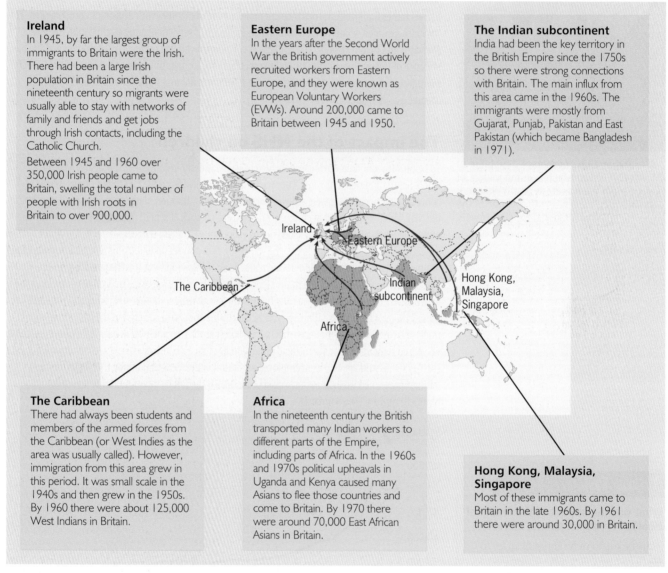

Ireland
In 1945, by far the largest group of immigrants to Britain were the Irish. There had been a large Irish population in Britain since the nineteenth century so migrants were usually able to stay with networks of family and friends and get jobs through Irish contacts, including the Catholic Church.

Between 1945 and 1960 over 350,000 Irish people came to Britain, swelling the total number of people with Irish roots in Britain to over 900,000.

Eastern Europe
In the years after the Second World War the British government actively recruited workers from Eastern Europe, and they were known as European Voluntary Workers (EVWs). Around 200,000 came to Britain between 1945 and 1950.

The Indian subcontinent
India had been the key territory in the British Empire since the 1750s so there were strong connections with Britain. The main influx from this area came in the 1960s. The immigrants were mostly from Gujarat, Punjab, Pakistan and East Pakistan (which became Bangladesh in 1971).

The Caribbean
There had always been students and members of the armed forces from the Caribbean (or West Indies as the area was usually called). However, immigration from this area grew in this period. It was small scale in the 1940s and then grew in the 1950s. By 1960 there were about 125,000 West Indians in Britain.

Africa
In the nineteenth century the British transported many Indian workers to different parts of the Empire, including parts of Africa. In the 1960s and 1970s political upheavals in Uganda and Kenya caused many Asians to flee those countries and come to Britain. By 1970 there were around 70,000 East African Asians in Britain.

Hong Kong, Malaysia, Singapore
Most of these immigrants came to Britain in the late 1960s. By 1961 there were around 30,000 in Britain.

Immigration to Britain, 1950–75.

SOURCE **2**

I soon saw we were all immigrants: it simply depends on how far back you go. A person would have to be part Roman, part German, part Danish, part French, part Jewish, part Irish, part Caribbean, part African, part Indian, part Chinese, part Greek and part every other nationality you can think of. No one person could claim to represent the ethnic or religious strands that twist their way through this story.

An extract from *Bloody Foreigners: A History of Immigration to Britain* by Robert Winder, published in 2004. The writer is explaining why he found it so difficult to write his history of immigration into Britain.

1. What impression do you get of the immigrants from Source 3?
2. What does Source 4 reveal about the type of workers who sailed to Britain on the *Windrush*?
3. 'Sources 3–4 prove that the only explanation for the hostility which faced the *Empire Windrush* immigrants was racial prejudice.' Do you agree?

Immigration from the Caribbean

The arrival of *Empire Windrush* has come to be seen as a key moment in recent British history. It is remembered as the beginning of post war immigration, but why?

- It was not the first ship to carry immigrants from the Caribbean. That was a ship called the *Ormonde* one year earlier in 1947.
- There was no great rush of immigrants from the Caribbean after *Windrush* in 1948. The main migration happened later in the 1950s.
- Immigration from the Caribbean at that time was tiny compared to immigration from Ireland and other parts of Europe.

So these facts would not account for the significance attached to this moment. Nor was this migration controversial. Many of the passengers had served in the armed forces during the war and had contacts in Britain. They were British citizens and had every right to settle in Britain. Britain was short of workers and most were skilled workers who found jobs quickly and easily once they arrived. However there were two things that were special about the *Windrush*:

- *Windrush* was the first ship carrying Caribbean migrants which was met by the newsreel cameras.
- The ship was also met by a small crowd waving placards saying 'Go Home'.

The significance of the *Windrush* was that it first brought to public attention the arrival of immigrants to British shores and also first highlighted how some British people reacted negatively to them.

SOURCE 3

Passengers from the *Empire Windrush* arriving at Tilbury Docks on 22 June 1948.

SOURCE 4

Page from the *Empire Windrush* passenger list, 1948.

SOURCE 5

A school in Jamaica in 1950. Many immigrants wanted to settle in Britain so that their children would be educated in modern British schools.

SOURCE 6

ARE YOU LOOKING FOR EMPLOYMENT?
Take a trip to England
On the Italian Luxury Liners
T.N LUCANIA and SS. AURIGA
Comagnia di navigazione
FRETELLI GRIMALDI

T.N. LUCANIA
Sailing from Barbados 25th January
Tourist Class Passage $322.00
BARBADOS – LONDON

FOR BOOKINGS CONTACT
CARIBBEAN AGENCY
No. 12 Swan Street Bridgetown

A copy of an advertisement from the *Barbados Advocate* newspaper in 1953. This Italian shipping line took passengers from Barbados to Britain. The shipping line opened this service in 1953 and it turned out to be hugely popular and profitable. It was a similar story when a new airfield opened on the island of Montserrat in 1956.

The motives of the Jamaicans on the *Empire Windrush* were rich and varied, as you might expect. Many years later the *Windrush* passengers were asked about their motives and a wide range appeared. Cy Grant was an educated man, a writer. He simply felt that Jamaica was a backwater where nothing was happening. Edwin Ho from Guiana was fleeing from a gambling debt. There were boxers and cricketers hoping to find glory in Britain, but most were respectable young working men. Almost all of them were looking for work but many were also looking for an adventure and planned to return home to the Caribbean.

One common factor was that many people in the Caribbean saw few prospects there. By the late 1940s unemployment in Jamaica and the other islands was a major problem. The sugar trade (the main export) had collapsed. Unlike today there was no tourist trade at this time and most people simply existed, growing food and fishing from the sea. The situation was made worse when hurricanes devastated Jamaica in 1944 and again in 1951. A British government investigation into conditions in the Caribbean found poor housing, poor wages, poor health care and an inadequate education system for the majority of the population.

These problems meant that there was already a long tradition of emigration from the Caribbean. From 1900 to 1950 around one in ten of the population had emigrated to North America to find work. However, in 1952 emigration to the USA was cut back from 65,000 to 800 immigrants a year by the strict controls of the McCarran Walter Act. At the same time, the British government passed the Nationality Act in 1948 which gave all citizens of the British Empire unrestricted access to Britain. It became law at the beginning of 1949.

Britain also looked attractive for other reasons. Most of the peoples of the British Empire admired Britain, despite the faults of imperial rule. The education system had taught them British history and British literature. The Indian nationalist leader Mohandas Gandhi said his education led him to see Britain as 'the land of philosophers and poets, the very centre of civilisation'. Peoples of the Empire were told of wonderful British achievements in business, in engineering and in efficient administration. They were impressed by the ceremony and pageantry which the British did so well. Britain seemed more familiar than many of the other places they could have emigrated to.

Around 10,000 West Indian troops had served in the armed forces during the Second World War. These troops told stories of how Britain seemed like a land of opportunity. On the whole, West Indians in Britain were treated well during the war. They had seen white people working in factories and fields and white children begging in the streets. This was not like home where the whites still dominated and ruled society. There was also the fact that there were more jobs than workers to do the jobs. It was a common saying in the West Indies that there were six jobs to each man. This was something of an exaggeration, but there is no doubt that Britain was facing a labour shortage in the late 1940s and 1950s. Many immigrants later told researchers that they felt they were coming to help the mother country in its time of need as well finding new opportunities for themselves.

SOURCE 7

There were adverts everywhere: 'Come to the mother country! The mother country needs you!' That's how I learned the opportunity was here. I felt stronger loyalty towards England. There was more emphasis there than loyalty to your own island. It really was the mother country and being away from home wouldn't be that terrible because you would belong.

The memories of a West Indian immigrant who settled in Britain in the 1950s.

1 Study Sources 6 and 7 carefully. Did the advertisements create the immigration or simply make it possible. Explain your answer.

SOURCE 9

West Indian immigrants arriving at Victoria train station in 1956.

SOURCE 11

The Dutch Steamship Sibajak *arrived at Southampton at 7.30 am on 22nd September from New York with 683 coloured Jamaicans who all held British passports. 482 were males, of whom 5 were under 12 years of age, and 201 were females, of whom 4 were under 12 years of age.*

The following is a summary of their reasons for coming to the United Kingdom.

Seeking employment	*560*
Employment in prospect	*27*
Nurses and student nurses	*35*
Ordinary students	*7*
Joining relatives in UK	*48*
Accompanying parents	*5*
For marriage	*1*

An extract from a government report on immigration from the West Indies, 1955–56.

The shortages were serious enough to mean that some British organisations were recruiting in the Caribbean in the 1950s. For example:

- Catering: The British Hotels and Restaurants Association launched a recruitment drive.
- The NHS: Sybil Phoenix (Source 8) came to Britain to work in the newly established National Health Service in 1956 after she had been to a talk by a Conservative politician called Enoch Powell about Britain's need for workers. Sybil was one of many who found jobs in the NHS.
- Transport: Another recruiter was London Transport, looking for 4,000 workers to do jobs which British people were refusing to take but which paid good money by Caribbean standards. London Transport even offered to pay the fare to Britain.

SOURCE 8

When I arrived at Paddington train station I was astonished to see a white woman sweeping up dust and rubbish on the platform with a broom. I was only accustomed to seeing white women who were painted devils who did nothing. They never even swept their own homes. They had six of us to do it for them.

Sybil Phoenix, a nurse from British Guiana, commenting on her arrival in Britain in 1956.

A final factor which drew immigrants to Britain was the success of previous immigrants. Most immigrants sent money back to their families. By the late 1950s money from workers in Britain was the second largest source of foreign income for Jamaica after food exports. Having an emigrant worker in Britain was a sign of prestige for a family, especially as they might well be able to buy items such as a fridge or a motorcycle with the money coming home. Returning workers were able to jingle money in their pockets and tell stories about London in the bars at home. All of these factors made emigration look attractive. In 1954 around 24,000 West Indians arrived in Britain. In 1955 it was 26,000. By 1958 there were 115,000 immigrants from the Caribbean in Britain. In the later stages these increases were the result of men bringing their wives and families over to Britain to join them in their new lives.

SOURCE 10

I migrated to Britain in 1954 through the help of a friend from my village. During this period it was termed that 'Migration Fever' had gripped the village and in fact the majority of the Caribbean Islands. People were acquiring their fare by selling whatever they could find in their possession but I had nothing to sell nor did my parents but the Lord opened a way for me to come to England and this was through a neighbour from the village that I had never spoken to.

A younger brother of mine came from the town and he brought a letter addressed to me from England. It was from this boy whom I had never spoken to. He was asking me if I would like to join him in England, be his girlfriend and later his wife. I was so overjoyed at this that I said 'yes'. All around the village was the sound of 'Coming to England' and with me receiving this invite I returned a letter saying 'yes' I would like to come. Arrangements were made and I came to Britain a year after and I'm now here over 51 years. It is a very long story.

A Caribbean immigrant explains why she came to Britain. This story was posted anonymously on a website.

Activity

When they try to explain migration historians often look for push factors which drive people from their home and pull factors which attract people to their new home. Study the information and sources on pages 450–53 and make a list of the push and pull factors for people from the Caribbean at this time.

Push factors	Pull factors

Immigrants from East Africa and the Indian subcontinent

In East Africa many people of Asian origin came to Britain because of persecution. After the abolition of slavery in the 1830s British companies and the British government still needed workers. They transported many labourers from poorer parts of India on schemes which were often not much better than slavery. As a result there were large communities of people in South and East Africa whose roots were in Asia. By the twentieth century there was also a large Asian middle class which had migrated to these British territories to set up businesses or practice as lawyers, doctors and so on. During the 1960s most of Britain's African colonies became independent. The new territories were anxious to build a national identity and Asians sometimes fell foul of this policy. In 1967 President Jomo Kenyatta of Kenya gave all Kenyan Asians two years to become Kenyan citizens or leave. Around 20,000 left and used their British passports to come to Britain because to them, Britain was more home than India. In 1972 the President of Uganda, Idi Amin, simply expelled his country's 50,000 Asians and most of them came to Britain.

SOURCE 12

Q. Can you start by telling me briefly where you are from in India?

A. Originally I came from Punjab, India, in 1955, then went to Kenya, Nairobi. Since then I was working in Civil Service and in Ministry of Tourism precisely and then got the option to retire early because of the Africanisation scheme was introduced by the Kenyan government after the independence.

Q. The Africanisation scheme?

A. Africanisation scheme in the Civil Service, that was the operator after the independence of Kenya, that was thought of, March 1963 and then I stayed on the Civil Service 'til 12th August 1969, then I came to the United Kingdom and I arrived at Gravesend, Kent.

Q. Why did you come to England?

A. Because my father was a British national and on the ground of that I naturally had the passport of British nationality. There was a scope for me to go to India and settle or I can come to United Kingdom. So I have visited India, tried to settle in 1964, but things were not going according to my scheme there so I selected on the later stage I must go to the United Kingdom to get settled with my family, because my children they were very young and it was opportunity to them to study there, an educational opportunity to be grabbed and they have all done so. I selected this country to settle, and my children, I've got five children and …

Transcript of an interview with Maghar Singh Hunjan in 1998.

SOURCE 13

Kenyan Asians arrive in Britain in 1967.

SOURCE 14

Q. What were your initial thoughts when you first heard the news that Asians in Uganda had to leave the country?

A. Well, we thought that when Idi Amin said that all the Asians had to leave from Uganda in three months he was just saying that because Idi Amin never did what he said. But as the time approached, at the end of three months, people started leaving the country and it was dangerous at that time to stay there because Amin said those who stay behind will be killed.

Q. What was the atmosphere like?

A. It was dangerous because the army was all over the town all the time and they were kidnapping people, taking them to the barracks and just killing them. They were putting them in prison. Even my father was put in a car boot and taken away. He came the next day but he was very lucky because some people never came back.

Q. Did you have friends in that country who were from that country?

A. Well, yes, I've got still some friends, native friends, African friends. I went back to Uganda in 1997 and went to see them and they really wanted to say they really missed me.

Q. So what was their reaction to you having to leave Uganda?

A. They never liked us to leave the country because we just became like brothers and sisters even though we were different, but they were very friendly and they really liked us.

Suresh Ruparala, being interviewed in 1998 on his expulsion from Uganda in 1972.

However, the majority of Asian immigrants in Britain had slightly less dramatic stories. For them it was the more familiar factors of poverty at home and the attraction of opportunities in Britain. By 1958 around 58,000 immigrants had arrived from India or Pakistan. There were identifiable phases:

- At first the majority were Eurasians – people from families who had intermarried during Britain's 200 year rule in India. They tended to be educated, middle-class professionals and many were Christians.
- The next wave of immigrants were Sikhs, mainly from the Punjab. For over 100 years Sikhs had been a major part of Britain's armed forces and many Sikh families had at least one son serving in some part of the Empire. As a result, the idea of a son working in the British economy rather than the army fitted in with a traditional way of life. Another incentive for the Sikhs was that they were a minority group in India compared to the Hindus and Muslims. When India became independent in 1947 there had been a lot of violence and disruption in the borderlands between Muslim Pakistan and Hindu India – the territory where most Sikhs lived. The peace and stability of Britain probably appealed to many Sikhs.
- The Sikhs were soon joined by immigrants from elsewhere in India and even more from Pakistan. All were willing and anxious to work hard and take the opportunities on offer. Many worked for themselves as door-to-door salesmen. The majority worked to fill Britain's labour shortages, just like the people from the Caribbean. During the Second World War Indian industry had developed to support the war effort. As a result many immigrants had relevant experience of working in metal, food and especially clothing industries. It is no coincidence that there are large communities of Asians today in Birmingham (which had a large metals industry) and northern towns like Bradford and Oldham (which had strong textile industries).

At first, most immigrants intended to earn money and send it or take it home themselves. However, in time many decided to settle and this in turn stimulated further immigration because new immigrants had contacts in Britain to help them find work and housing.

Focus Task

Why did different groups migrate to Britain between 1948 and 1972?

Look back over pages 450–55 and copy and complete the table below. In each column indicate how important each factor was by rating it 1–5 with 1 being the most important. You could add other groups to this table if you know something about them or would like to research them.

Factor	East Africa	Caribbean	Indian subcontinent
Economic hardship	Rating: Example(s):	Rating: Example(s):	Rating: Example(s):
Persecution or disruption			
Economic opportunity			
Adventure			
Prospect of returning home			
Existing community offering support			
Links with Britain			

What were the experiences of immigrants in Britain?

Over the next 14 pages you are going to examine the experiences of immigrants to Britain between 1950 and 1975. As you read make notes on the following topics.

a) **Experiences:** what happened to immigrants and how did they feel about it?

b) **Changes:** were some periods better or worse than others for immigrants and if so why?

c) **Sources:** what different kinds of evidence you use to find out about these experiences.

d) **Interpretations:** whether people tell this story in different ways and if so why.

On page 469 you will use your notes to draft a presentation.

What were the experiences of immigrants in Britain?

Immigration to Britain was not a planned, official process. Individuals took different approaches to immigration and had different motives and experiences when they arrived here. Many of the early Jamaican immigrants remember being welcomed. One Jamaican nurse remembers that bus conductors would often waive the fare for her and her fellow nurses and, as Source 16 shows, there were other happy experiences too.

SOURCE 15

Father came to Britain in 1948 and then soon after I came with my mother. In London she worked for the first time in her life outside our home, in a sewing workshop with a Jewish refugee from Germany and an Irish woman. The other workers there were among her closest friends all the time she was in England. I used to listen to her talking with a feeling of surprise. Never, in my experience, had she talked so much. She laughed a lot too. I'd probably never seen her so happy as in those times when her life was changing so much.

A West Indian writing in 1999 about his mother's experiences in Britain in the 1950s and 1960s.

Unfortunately, these experiences were the exception rather than the rule. As the number of immigrants grew, the hostility towards them grew as well. Historians now have access to interviews, letters and diaries of immigrants and many of these sources tell a similar story. They found Britain cold, depressing and grey when they arrived. They found the food dull and unappetising. Worst of all, though, was the shock that the British people that they admired so much were unwelcoming and hostile towards them.

SOURCE 16

Reactions to life in Britain in the 1960s. They were collected by the author Daniel Larence, who interviewed immigrants from the West Indies in Nottingham.

1 Is Source 16 or Source 18 more valuable as a source for historians studying the experience of immigrants?

2 In what ways do Sources 17 and 18 support each other as evidence of discrimination?

SOURCE 17

A young Jamaican immigrant looking for accommodation in the later 1950s. The notice reads, 'Rooms to let. No coloured men'.

Almost upon arrival, immigrants found they were up against the 'colour bar'. It was difficult to get accommodation. Signs saying 'No Blacks, No Dogs' were common in the boarding houses where they tried to find a room. Banks and building societies were reluctant to give loans or mortgages to the newcomers. Many local authorities were unhelpful or even obstructive. Generally immigrants had to live in Britain for five years before they could even apply for council accommodation. When they did find accommodation, it was usually a room in a house, often cramped and usually expensive. They therefore had to find whatever accommodation they could, and were open to exploitation. One of the most notorious landlords was Peter Rachman. He owned over 100 properties in west London and most were crammed with immigrants paying high rents for poor accommodation. Anyone who complained faced a beating from Rachman's men.

All of the New Commonwealth immigrants suffered from this discrimination in housing, and there were many other limits on their freedom as well. They would often find that they were not welcome in bars, restaurants and dance halls because the owners of these places feared that trouble would follow. They also faced accusations that they were simply in Britain for the generous benefit system. This was a stupid claim since most of the immigrants were working and therefore not claiming any benefits.

The same prejudices were found in the workplace. The trade unions were extremely unhappy about immigrant workers. They saw immigrants as potential competitors for jobs. In 1955 transport workers in Wolverhampton, West Bromwich and Bristol went on strike to protest about 'increasing numbers of coloured workers' (in the case of West Bromwich this meant one Indian bus conductor). In 1958 the Trades Union Congress passed a resolution calling for an end to all immigrant workers entering the country. In one factory in the Midlands, white workers demanded separate toilet facilities from the Sikh workers. Many Sikhs and other immigrants from the Indian subcontinent worked in the metal industries of the West Midlands and the textile mills of Yorkshire. They almost always got the worst jobs on offer, whether it suited their skills or not. More than half the West Indians in London in the late 1950s were over qualified for the job that they were doing. Immigrant nurses in the NHS were discouraged from taking the SRN (State Registered Nurse) qualifications which would have given them promotion. Source 18 shows that the Asian immigrants suffered similar kinds of discrimination.

SOURCE 18

In 1962 I left Pakistan and went to Nottingham. I knew I wasn't going to get any better job than being a British Railway cleaner. I had seen qualified people from my country who had been teachers and barristers and none of them got proper work. They were labourers, bus conductors and railway cleaners like me. Many times we could read and write much better than the people who were in charge of us. They knew I had been a Customs Inspector in Pakistan, but that didn't matter.

A Pakistani immigrant interviewed in the late 1980s about his experiences in the 1960s.

3 What point is the cartoonist in Source 19 making?

4 Would a cartoon like this be acceptable in a newspaper today? Explain your answer.

Activity

You are an immigrant who has recently arrived in Britain in the 1950s. Write a letter home explaining your disappointment at what you have seen and experienced.

SOURCE 19

A cartoon from the *Daily Mirror*, 3 June 1963. Walsall is in the West Midlands, which was probably the second largest area of New Commonwealth immigrants after London.

Reactions to immigrants

In the face of this hostility it is not surprising that immigrants tended to keep together. At first they could usually only afford to live in the cheapest housing which nobody else wanted. As new immigrants arrived they looked for lodgings with friends and family or other contacts who were already in Britain. As a result, areas like Toxteth in Liverpool, Notting Hill in London, Saint Paul's in Bristol, Handsworth in Birmingham and Moss Side in Manchester became Caribbean communities with a life and a culture of their own. It was a similar story with the other New Commonwealth immigrants. Areas of Birmingham like Smethwick or Alum Rock became the centre of communities from India and Pakistan. The same happened in textile producing towns such as Bradford, Burnley and Oldham. Southall in London became the centre of a thriving Asian community.

SOURCE 20

Contrary to the usual insistence on assimilation as the recipe for successful immigration, a high degree of cultural independence seemed to be more useful. An investigation in Nottingham in the 1960s uncovered a remarkable contrast between two pioneering groups of immigrants. 87 per cent of Jamaicans said that they felt British before they came; while 86 per cent said it was fine by them if their children 'felt' English. In stark contrast, only 2 per cent of Indians and Pakistanis claimed to feel British before their arrival; and only 6 per cent were willing to accept the idea that their children might feel English. So much for the insistence that immigrants should 'fit in' – the common cry of those outraged by foreigners in their midst. In practice, those who tried the hardest to fit in were those most actively discouraged from doing so. Those who were able to form their own communities, develop their own economy and conduct their own affairs – such as Jews, Indians, Pakistanis and Cypriots – found themselves better equipped to advance towards the mainstream.

An extract from *Bloody Foreigners: The Story of Immigration to Britain* by the writer Robert Winder, published in 2004.

In the later 1950s some right-wing activists began a campaign to 'keep Britain white'. The former Fascist leader Oswald Moseley saw an opportunity to make use of the ill feeling towards immigrants and place himself at the head of a protest movement. He set up an organisation called the Union Movement and published anti-immigrant posters and leaflets. He was not the only person saying these things. George Rogers, the Labour MP for North Kensington, urged the government to limit the influx of immigrants into overcrowded areas and claimed that they had a particular taste for crime, drugs and knives. Comments like these increased tensions, especially since Britain's economy was beginning to take a downward turn in 1958 and there was greater competition for jobs.

Activity 1

It could be said that immigrants were stuck in a vicious circle like this one. Use Source 20 and the other information on this page to put more detail on this diagram. You could add extra points on the circle and also add in examples to explain these points.

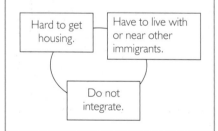

Activity 2

1 Study Source 21 carefully and decide which of these two alternative captions might go better with the image:
Option 1: A group of West Indian men keep together for protection.
Option 2: A group of West Indian men show they are not afraid of intimidation.
2 Can you come up with a better caption?

SOURCE 21

A group of West Indian men in Kensington, London 1956.

SOURCE 22

British Cartoon Archive, University of Kent © Solo Syndication/Associated Newspapers Ltd.

A cartoon from the *Daily Mail*, 3 September 1958.

Summer of violence, 1958

In 1958 there were violent clashes in Nottingham, home to about 2,500 Caribbeans and about 600 Asians. Throughout the summer, white youths had carried out violent attacks on black and Asian people. In August large-scale fighting broke out between black and white youths in the St Ann's Well Road area. Nottingham's two MPs called for an end to immigration and for new laws which allowed deportation.

There was worse to come. In September 1958 gangs of teddy boys and other white youths attacked Caribbean people and their homes in Notting Hill. For three nights around 400 white youths attacked Notting Hill, even using petrol bombs. On the third night the black population fought back, angry that they had received no protection from the police. The press and politicians condemned the attacks but they did little more than that. Public opinion was still anti-immigrant. An opinion poll soon after the riots revealed that 25 per cent of people felt that blacks were to blame for the violence. Another poll showed that 80 per cent of the population favoured controls of some sort. In the spring of 1959 Kelso Cochrane, a carpenter from Antigua, was murdered by six white youths.

SOURCE 23

"THEY JUST AIN'T CIVILISED—LIKE WE ARE . . . !"

British Cartoon Archive, University of Kent © Solo Syndication/Associated Newspapers Ltd.

A cartoon from the *Evening Standard*, 19 May 1959.

Activity 3

1 Work in pairs. Each of you study either Source 22 or 23 and then explain its message to your partner. You may be able to do this using your own copy of the cartoon or a presentation.
2 Now decide which of these two cartoons you think would have had a bigger impact on public opinion. Explain your answer.

Source Investigation

Reactions to immigration in the 1950s

1 What does Source 24 tell you about the attitudes of British people to immigrants in the 1950's?
2 Is Source 24 more useful than Source 25 for an historian investigating why immigrants faced discrimination in the 1950s?
3 Why was Source 27 published in 1958?
4 How reliable is Source 27 as a summary of attitudes in Britain towards the violence of August and September 1958?
5 'The main reason why there were racial tensions in the 1950s was that there were too many immigrants.' Do the sources in this investigation support this view? Use the sources and your own knowledge to answer this question.

SOURCE 24

People talk about a colour problem arising in Britain. How can there be a colour problem here? Even after all the immigration of the past few years, there are only 190,000 people in our population of over 50 million – that is only four out of every 1000. The real problem is not black skins but white prejudice.

Comments by a delegate at the TUC Conference in 1958.

SOURCE 26

Front cover of a pamphlet published by an immigrant organisation in Nottingham in 1958. The pamphlet was supported by the Nottingham trade union branches.

SOURCE 25

I was in love with Britain and that love only grew when I came here from the Caribbean in the1950s. I was employed by the National Health Service as a midwife. I loved the clean hospitals, the efficiency and order. I hated the disorder I had left behind. But my feelings of pride and love were beaten down again and again by racism, ignorance and abuse. There was such unfairness to us Christian people who had fought in the war with the best of them.

A West Indian woman being interviewed in the late 1990s. She was speaking about her experiences in the 1950s and 1960s.

SOURCE 27

You are a minute and insignificant section of the population who have filled the whole nation with horror, indignation and disgust. Everyone, irrespective of the colour of their skin, is entitled to walk through our streets in peace, with their heads held up and free from fear.

Statement by the judge sentencing four white youths convicted of involvement in the Notting Hill violence of September 1958.

SOURCE 28

Though half of Britain's white population had never even met a black person . . . prejudice against black people was widespread. More than two-thirds of Britain's white population, in fact, held a low opinion of black people or disapproved of them . . . Half of this prejudiced two-thirds were . . . only 'mildly' prejudiced. The other half were extremely so.

An extract from *Staying Power: The History of Black People in Britain* by historian Peter Fryer, published in 1984.

SOURCE 29

Race relations problems have never been simply about numbers. Extremists who spoke of Britain being 'swamped' by 'waves of immigrants' were talking nonsense. The proportion of people of non-European origin has never been more than six per cent of the overall population of Britain. Moreover, in every decade of the twentieth century net emigration was greater than net immigration.

An extract from *Modern British History 1900–1999* by Michael Lynch, published in 2001.

Did the politicians help?

When new commonwealth immigrants began arriving in the 1950s and 1960s they received less help than the Poles had received in the 1940s. They received less help even than German prisoners of war had received. They were simply left to find their own way. After the early days of encouraging migrants to work in Britain, the government was now actively discouraging them. One government pamphlet warned people in the Caribbean that British people were not talkative, the food was drab and that if immigrants did come to Britain they should bring hot water bottles. A similar approach was taken to try to discourage immigration from the Indian subcontinent (see Source 30).

1 What was the purpose of Source 30?
2 How did it try to achieve that aim?
3 Sources 31 and 32 are both critical of politicians of the time. What criticisms are they making?

SOURCE 30

Chandra Lal listened to the tales of high wages earned in the factories of Britain. His own uncle regularly sent home money and wrote of life in the industrial Midlands, where the shops were full and nobody went hungry. So, Chandra left his village in India and went to Britain. It was winter when he arrived and the cold wind bit through his thin cotton clothing. Chandra shivered, but found no work because he was not skilled. He went on shivering for four months and at last found a labouring job in Bradford. But Chandra is one of the lucky ones, for there are thousands of other Indians and Pakistanis without work. They think longingly of their villages and the wives and children they left behind.

An extract from a British government leaflet published in India in 1958.

SOURCE 31

The 1964 general election was characterised by an outspoken expression of racist dread. In the Midlands constituency of Smethwick, the Conservative candidate, Peter Griffiths, bucked the national swing against his party and took the seat by brazenly playing what would soon become known as the 'race card'. His supporters told voters: 'If you want a nigger neighbour, vote Labour.' Political analysts noted that such tactics, while disgraceful, were clear vote-winners. By now the term 'immigrants' was fast becoming a polite euphemism for 'coloured people', and a significant proportion of the electorate wanted fewer of them. The fact that in 1964 Britain suffered a net loss of seventeen thousand people – emigration was outstripping immigration for the first time since 1957 – was not much emphasised. Immigration was presented and discussed as if it were a brand-new factor in world affairs. There was wide agreement, even among those who pleaded for tolerance, that the 'problem' could be solved only by having fewer 'coloured people'. It was taken as read that the modern migrants were not properly (i.e. racially) equipped to be British. That the 'problem' had anything to do with the powerful racial prejudices of the British people themselves was rarely allowed to influence either conversation or action.

An extract from *Bloody Foreigners: The Story of Immigration to Britain* by the writer Robert Winder, published in 2004.

SOURCE 32

A cartoon from the *Daily Express*, 21 August 1964. The figure on the left is the Labour leader Harold Wilson and the one on the right is the Conservative leader Sir Alec Douglas-Home.

461

Government action

1959

1959 The violence of 1958 brought the issue of immigration to the forefront of politics. The 1959 election saw the election of a number of MPs determined to raise the issue of immigration, such as Conservative MP Cyril Osborne. He used the slogan 'Keep Britain white' in his campaigning. Other groups such as the Birmingham Immigration Control Association added to the pressure.

1960

1961

1962 The Conservative government listened to the calls and passed the **Commonwealth Immigrants Act**. The Act introduced a voucher system which restricted immigration to people who had a valuable skill or could do a job where there was a shortage of workers. It did not specifically say so, but the Act was aimed at restricting the influx of immigrants from the New Commonwealth because a greater proportion of them tended to be unskilled.

1962

1963

1964 The Labour Party criticised the Act but when it came to power in 1964 Prime Minister Harold Wilson limited the number of immigrants to 8,500 per year. By this time race and immigration were very sensitive issues and were at the forefront of politics in Britain.

1964

1965–66 Wilson passed the **Race Relations Act 1965**. This made it illegal to discriminate against any person because of their colour or race. The government then set up the **Race Relations Board in 1966** to handle complaints about discrimination. Both were steps in the right direction but the 1965 Act failed to prevent discrimination in areas such as housing or employment and in its first year the Race Relations Board dismissed 734 out of 982 complaints received. The Board also lacked legal powers to enforce its decisions and it lacked credibility because it was all white. Neither measure could or did change attitudes.

1965

1966

1967 This year saw the foundation of the National Front. The National Front was a political party which was openly racist. The National Front was partly a response to the arrival of Kenyan Asians in Britain (see page 454). It called for an end to immigration and for immigrants to be sent back to their country of origin. It was also against any kind of mixing between the white and non-white communities.

1967

1968

1969

1970

1971

1972

1973

1974

1975

1976

1968 Following the arrival of Kenyan Asians the government also reacted to this new wave of immigrants with a new Act. Parliament passed the **Commonwealth Immigrants Act in March 1968**. This Act restricted work vouchers further — to 1,500 per year. It also brought in a 'close connection' clause. This restricted entry to Commonwealth citizens who held a British passport and were born in Britain, or whose parents or grandparents were born in Britain. In practice, this Act restricted access to Britain for New Commonwealth immigrants while allowing access to most citizens of white Commonwealth countries such as Canada, Australia or New Zealand.

On 20 April 1968 the senior Conservative MP Enoch Powell made a speech to Conservative Party workers in Birmingham (see next page). Powell claimed that British people were feeling overwhelmed and threatened by immigration and warned that there would be 'rivers of blood' if action was not taken. Action was taken, but not what Powell had in mind. Conservative leader Edward Heath sacked him and the Labour government passed a new Race Relations Act. This Act made discrimination in areas such as housing and employment illegal. It also made it illegal to publish notices like the one in Source 17. It was a step forward but hard to enforce. An employer could discriminate indirectly by claiming another candidate had more relevant experience, for example.

1971 A Conservative government under Edward Heath passed this Act in response to the arrival of Ugandan Asians in the early 1970s (see page 454). In fact most Ugandan Asians were allowed to settle here. The Act kept the same restrictions as the 1968 measure but it allowed patrials (people who had been born in Britain or who had lived in Britain for over five years) the right to settle here.

1976 The government passed the **Racial Equality Act.** This made racially offensive music or publications illegal. It also set up tribunals so that any job applicant who felt that he or she was suffering from discrimination could report the employer. The Act also set up the **Commission for Racial Equality** to investigate racism. On the one hand this was another positive move. On the other hand, it showed that earlier measures had still not eradicated racism from British society.

Focus Task

How well did the government handle immigration in the 1960s?

Historians have generally been critical of the role of politicians in the 1960s. The main accusations are:

◆ They had no clear policies.
◆ They were prepared to exploit the issue to win votes.
◆ All the measures were aimed at non-white Commonwealth immigrants.
◆ They saw the immigrants as the problems rather than those with prejudiced or racist attitudes.

Study the information on these two pages and see which of these three verdicts fits best for each accusation:

◆ guilty
◆ not guilty
◆ too difficult to judge.

You could do this as a written report or in a debate.

Profile

Enoch Powell

- ➤ Born in Birmingham 1912.
- ➤ Brilliant academic career, becoming a professor at Sydney University aged 25.
- ➤ Served with distinction in British Army in the Second World War.
- ➤ Became Conservative MP for Wolverhampton after the war and was soon promoted to the Cabinet.
- ➤ Always a difficult and controversial MP – resigned from the Cabinet in 1958 in protest at high taxes and spending.
- ➤ Had ambitions to lead the Conservative Party but the post went to Edward Heath. Heath and Powell hated each other.
- ➤ Made the Rivers of Blood speech in 1968 (see Source 33). The speech stirred up enormous controversy and he was sacked by Heath.
- ➤ Dockers in London marched to show their support and over 300 of the 412 Conservative Party local branches expressed their approval.
- ➤ Quit the Conservative Party in 1987.
- ➤ Died February 1998.
- ➤ Some historians believe he was insensitive rather than prejudiced. He did get on well with many of the Asians in his constituency and some are said to have agreed with his views.

How significant was Enoch Powell?

SOURCE 33

A week or two ago I fell into conversation with a constituent, a middle-aged, quite ordinary working man employed in one of our nationalised industries. After a sentence or two about the weather, he suddenly said: 'If I had the money to go, I wouldn't stay in this country. I have three children, all of them been through grammar school and two of them married now, with family. I shan't be satisfied till I have seen them all settled overseas. In this country in 15 or 20 years' time the black man will have the whip hand over the white man.'

I can already hear the chorus of criticism. How dare I say such a horrible thing? How dare I stir up trouble and inflame feelings by repeating such a conversation? The answer is that I do not have the right not to do so. Here is a decent, ordinary fellow Englishman, who in broad daylight in my own town says to me, his Member of Parliament, that his country will not be worth living in for his children.

In 15 or 20 years, on present trends, there will be in this country three and a half million Commonwealth immigrants and their descendants. That is not my figure. That is the official figure given to parliament by the spokesman of the Registrar General's Office. Whole areas, towns and parts of towns across England will be occupied by sections of the immigrant and immigrant-descended population.

The natural and rational first question with a nation confronted by such a prospect is to ask: 'How can its dimensions be reduced?' The answers to the simple and rational question are equally simple and rational: by stopping, or virtually stopping, further inflow, and by promoting the maximum outflow.

The sense of being a persecuted minority which is growing among ordinary English people in the areas of the country which are affected is something that those without direct experience can hardly imagine.

. . . As I look ahead, I am filled with foreboding; like the Roman, I seem to see 'the River Tiber foaming with much blood'.

Extracts from Enoch Powell's speech of 22 April 1968. The speech has become known as the Rivers of Blood speech.

SOURCE 34

A photograph published in the *London Evening Standard*, 1 May 1968.

SOURCE 35

I hated Enoch Powell then and I still hate him now.

Roy Hattersley, interviewed in 2008. Hattersley was a Labour MP in 1968 and eventually became Deputy Leader of the Labour Party.

SOURCE 37

'You see, doc, I dropped my "I-back-Enoch" placard on my foot.'

BRITISH CARTOON ARCHIVE, UNIVERSITY OF KENT © SOLO SYNDICATION/ASSOCIATED NEWSPAPERS LTD.

Cartoon published in the *Daily Mail*, 24 April 1968.

SOURCE 36

London dockers march in support of Enoch Powell, 24 April 1968.

Source Investigation

1 Read Source 33. Why did Enoch Powell expect criticism for raising the issue of immigration?
2 What did Powell dare to raise?
3 Do you find his answer convincing?
4 Why did the newspaper publish Sources 34 and 37 in April and May 1968?
5 How useful is Source 36 to a historian assessing the impact of Powell's Rivers of Blood speech?
6 What do Sources 35 and 38 suggest was the impct of Enoch Powell?
7 When they try to assess the significance of an individual, historians look at questions such as:
   • How important was he at the time?
   • How were people affected by him?
   • Was his impact long lasting?
   • How is he remembered today?

Study the profile and all the sources in this investigation and decide how far you think Powell should be regarded as a significant historical individual. You could present your conclusions in a written report, a debate or a presentation.

SOURCE 38

Enoch Powell's 'Rivers of Blood' speech has cast a '40-year shadow' over the immigration debate in Britain, with governments failing to provide articulate leadership on the issue, the head of the country's race watchdog said yesterday.

Trevor Phillips, chairman of the Equality and Human Rights Commission, said the UK was falling behind competitors because of the lack of a coherent immigration strategy. While the issue had led in Britain to a 'creeping resentment which can only be halted by a policy of manifest fairness', other countries were making the most of immigrant talent.

He added: 'Immigration is part of our future. The real question will be whether we can seize the restless tide of talent currently sweeping across the globe. So far we are lagging behind our competitors.' Mr Phillips stressed the need for a renewed debate.

Addressing 200 at the Birmingham hotel where Powell made his speech, Mr Phillips said: 'Many think this is not the time for this debate. If we cannot talk about it now, then when? We cannot allow discussion of race and immigration forever to be seen as playing into the hands of extremists. The 40-year old shockwave of fear has gagged us.'

Powell's speech, with its vision of society disintegrating in racial tension, still bars examination of the subject, said Mr Phillips. 'For 40 years we have sustained a silence on the issue where people most needed articulate political leadership. Powell so discredited talk of planning that we have plunged along with an adhoc approach to immigration.'

Sir Digby Jones, the Business minister, told the conference: 'We are built on immigration. We are a mixed race. This is our country, not mine, and if you are here it's your country, feel you own it.'

An article in the *Independent* newspaper, 21 April 2008.

How have immigrants contributed to British society?

You might be finding this story pretty depressing by now, but there is another side to this story. Most British people were not racist or prejudiced, even if they were not prepared to stand up to the noisy minorities who were. Some individuals and organisations were prepared to show that they welcomed immigrants and that they opposed discrimination.

SOURCE **39**

Photograph taken by a journalist of West Indian immigrants arriving at London's Waterloo station in December 1961.

SOURCE **40**

"While you're at it, put 'Many Happy Returns, Hitler.' It's his birthday today."

A cartoon from the *Daily Express*, April 1967.

BRITISH CARTOON ARCHIVE, UNIVERSITY OF KENT © DAILY EXPRESS

1 From what you have read on pages 456–57, do you think Source 39 shows a typical scene of the time?
2 Does this mean Source 39 is a valid or invalid source?
3 Explain the message of Source 40. You may be able to use a copy of the cartoon and annotate it.

Other people welcomed the immigrants in quiet and purposeful ways. Many people in the more run down areas of Britain's big cities found the new arrivals to be good neighbours and many friendships were made. During the violence in Notting Hill in 1958 we have numerous accounts of local white people protecting their black neighbours. There were thousands of similar events in streets, parks, places of work, pubs and many other places through this period. Trade unions also supported campaigns to stop discrimination in the workplace, although it must be admitted that not all of their members supported these campaigns.

Another group who welcomed the immigrants were employers. In Bradford, for example, many of the textile mills were on the verge of closure because the factory owners could not balance their books. The arrival of a large number of hardworking immigrants mainly from Pakistan who were prepared to work for low wages (by British standards) saved many of these mills.

The contribution of immigrants to Britain

Of course the biggest positive aspect of this story is the immense contribution which individuals have made to Britain's economy and culture since the 1950s. One shining example is Sybil Phoenix. She arrived in Britain in 1956. Her first room was a leaking basement in London (she cooked her first Christmas dinner under an umbrella!). She was an orphan herself and so determined to help other orphans. She became a foster parent and gave a home to over 100 children. She opened a youth group called the Moonshot in Lewisham and helped to found the early race relations groups in the area. In 1971 she was awarded an MBE (Medal of the British Empire) and in 1973 became mayoress of Lewisham. She did not give up her work even when arsonists burnt down her club. You can find out more about her on her website.

SOURCE **41**

Police Constable Harbanna Singh Jabbal. Sikhs won the right to wear their traditional head dress after initial reluctance from the authorities.

Public services

Sybil is an outstanding individual, but like thousands of other immigrants she contributed to a better life for the whole population. Without the contribution of immigrant workers many of Britain's major public services would have ground to a halt. By the mid 1970s the National Health Service was heavily reliant on a huge staff of porters, cleaners, nurses, doctors, surgeons and consultants and a large proportion of these workers were either immigrants or had immigrant roots. It is slightly ironic that it was Enoch Powell, when he was health minister who was one of the biggest recruiters of immigrant doctors. His recruitment campaign in the 1960s led to the arrival of 18,000 Indian doctors and effectively made today's NHS possible. Today over one-third of all doctors in the NHS were born overseas, mostly in the Indian subcontinent. It was not just the NHS of course. London Transport and the London Underground were the first big employers of immigrants but soon many towns and cities also relied on immigrant workers to run essential services like transport and sanitation. Recruits from immigrant backgrounds also play an important role in Britain's armed forces today, especially the army. They are also beginning to establish themselves in the police service although it is true to say that the police would like to recruit larger numbers.

The economy

Immigrants have also played a huge role in Britain's economy. The vast majority of immigrants came to Britain for two main reasons. One was to send money home to their families to improve education, health, general well being and to pay off debts. The other reason, often closely linked to the first, was to better themselves. As a result they were prepared to take any jobs which were offered to them and to work at these jobs until they were successful. Most wanted to gain promotion at work, or start their own businesses. There was also a driving ambition to put enough money together to buy a home in a good area.

4 How could an opponent of Enoch Powell have made use of Source 42?

SOURCE **42**

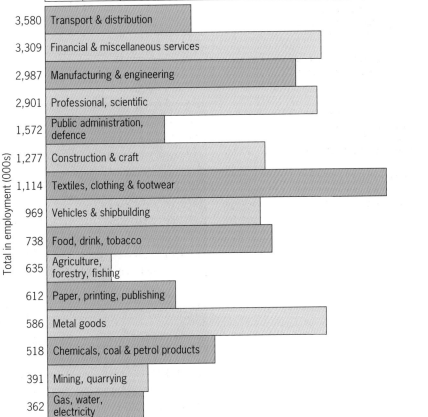

The percentage of immigrant workers in different sectors of the economy as revealed by the census in 1971.

The Asian community in particular has brought to Britain some spectacular success stories. Anwar Perez came from a farming family in Pakistan in 1956. He drove buses in Bradford and saved enough to open a convenience store in London in 1962. He then bought more shops until his Bestway minimarket chain spread across the country and in 1999 he was worth £130 million. Shahad Hussein was a cookery teacher who became the chief adviser to Marks and Spencer on their Asian foods. Perween Warsi set up a business making samosas in Derby. Gulam Kaderbhoy Noon came to Britain in 1969. He built up a business supplying Asian restaurants and supermarkets now estimated to be worth around £480 million. Asians also prospered in the clothing trade. The labels Ciro Citterio and Joe Bloggs were both created by Asian immigrants.

Of course not all Asians became millionaires but many did prosper because they were prepared to work hard and they also understood the value of education. When they arrived in the 1960s many immigrants found they could not get jobs which matched their qualifications, primarily because of prejudice. However, by 1981 the government's Labour Force Survey showed that one-third of Indian men in Britain were highly qualified professionals. This was a higher percentage than white British men and today we can see the impact of this by the number of Asians who are working in high technology industries and also in areas such as banking, insurance, education and the law.

Another key feature of the Asian contribution to the economy has been the corner shop. By the 1960s local stores were closing down because of competition from department stores and supermarkets. Asian entrepreneurs revived this type of business. They provided local communities – Asian and white – with a service which was much appreciated and successful. In Dewsbury (an inner city area of Manchester) in the late 1960s all 37 off-licences were owned by Asian families. In London today around half of the sub-post offices are owned by Asian business people.

Culture

One of the biggest effects of immigration has been on Britain's eating habits. Italian immigrants brought coffee bars, ice cream parlours and Berni Inns to Britain to lighten up the drab post-war years. Immigrants from Cyprus brought exotic food to their restaurants and delicatessens. The British could not get enough of curry in its various forms of course. There were almost 2,000 Indian restaurants in Britain by 1976. It was a similar story with Chinese food and today there is hardly a town or village in the United Kingdom without a Chinese and an Indian takeaway or restaurant. The immigrants showed their business sense by adapting their cuisine to British tastes. For example, Britain's favourite dish, chicken tikka masala, is unheard of in India. It was created specifically because the British like dishes with gravy!

SOURCE 43

A typical Indian restaurant in the 1960s.

Focus Task A

What contribution had immigrants made to Britain by the mid 1970s?

This diagram suggests that the impact of immigrants in these four areas was equal. You have two tasks:

1 Find examples of the impact of immigrants on Britain in each of these areas.
2 Decide whether you agree that all four were equally significant. If you do not, redraw the diagram so that the most significant area is the largest section.

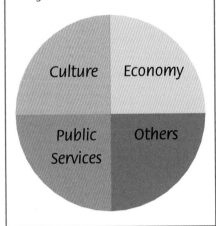

Immigration has also had a huge impact on British music. The Beatles (see page 490) were influenced in the later 1960s by Indian music and instruments. However, the group which had the biggest impact on music and dance was probably the Afro-Caribbean community. They brought colour and style to the music scene of 1950s Britain. The most well-known event was the Notting Hill carnival which introduced British people to reggae music, steel drums, calypso and some truly fabulous costumes and dancing. The first carnival took place in 1958 and was enjoyed by around 7,000 people but today it attracts millions. Reggae music was one of the most important ways in which Caribbean culture became mainstream. As well as being a form of music, reggae was also a powerful vehicle for protest messages, just as Soul and Motown music had been in the civil rights movement in the USA. Reggae was popularised by Jamaican superstar Bob Marley but it also had a big influence on British bands like The Police who brought its rhythms into more mainstream music. The Afro-Caribbean genius for musical invention also developed ska music which was hugely popular with some sections of British youth in the 1950s and 1960s.

Finally, immigration has also brought Britain into close contact with a wide range of world religions. The immigrants from the Indian subcontinent brought their Hindu and Muslim faiths with them and laid the foundations of Britain's modern multicultural society. They have also proved that Enoch Powell was wrong. There are certainly still tensions and difficulties. In Leicester in 1972 the city council warned that 'the entire fabric of our city is at risk' because the immigrant population was beginning to outnumber the white population. Ten years later the city was still standing and it was holding a festival of cultures to celebrate the different peoples in it. The picture is not entirely rosy of course. Discrimination and racism and violence are still major problems. There are also rising tensions in some areas between different groups of immigrants. The big question for the future is what shape multicultural Britain will take.

Focus Task B

What were the experiences of immigrants in Britain?

Over the past 14 pages you have been gathering notes about the experiences of immigrants. You are now going to use those notes to make a presentation on one of these topics. You could work in groups and take one topic each.

Experiences

Think about what it was like to be an immigrant in this period. Ensure you present a range of experiences to show the variety. Include positive and negative experiences. You could turn this into an audio presentation.

Changes

Think about whether there was a harder or an easier time for immigrants? You could prepare a living graph to show the highs and lows along with an explanation of what your graph shows.

Sources

Think about what kind of evidence you have used to research this topic. What else could you use: oral history (interviewing people) or the internet (forums and websites where people share their experiences). Include in your presentation: what evidence is available; and what you have found most useful in understanding these experiences.

Interpretations

Think about ways this story has been interpreted differently by different speakers or writers. Do they interpret it differently because they use different evidence; or because they have a different personal viewpoint which shapes their opinion?

15.4 How far did life change for women in Britain, 1950–75?

It is 1950, the start of a new decade. The Second World War is five years past, and some of the difficult memories of that hard time have started to fade. What can a typical woman look forward to?

How does that sound? Optimistic? Idealistic? Let's look at this period through a different window.

It is 1950. Another woman is thinking about her future:

- She can work if she wants to. The war time experience has mostly ended the taboo against women working, and the shortage of workers means that women are welcome.

- She can look forward to a better home. So many houses were damaged or destroyed in war time that a massive house building programme has started. Smart new council houses and flats are being built. All these new homes have running water, and gas or electricity for fuel. Some even have central heating.

- Better health. Since the start of the National Health Service in 1948 she and her family get their medical care for free. It may not take the pain out of being ill but it takes away some of the anxiety.

- More varied food. Some staple items such as sugar and meat are still rationed but at least there is more food and supplies are reliable.

- If she is married there is free schooling for her children and if they do well enough it could be the grammar school – which is a passport to a better job and a better life.

- There will be lots of good films at the cinema. Hardly anyone has a television. They are still expensive and unreliable. But many women go to the cinema once every week.

- She can't do any job. There are still some areas of work that are regarded as exclusively men's work.

- Wherever she works she will be paid less than a man, even if she is doing similar work to a man.

- Say she gets married and say her husband turns out to have a violent temper and beats her up – she can only get a divorce if she can prove in court that he has been having an affair. And if they divorce he will keep their possessions.

- If she is a young black or Asian woman newly arrived in Britain she may face intimidation and racism and exploitation each time she walks out of the door. And she will be very low on the list of people to receive good housing.

- She wants to plan her life so she has fewer children. She does not want to spend her life as a mother. But there is still no reliable method of family planning.

- If she gets pregnant and does not want a baby she is in trouble. Abortion is illegal and dangerous to the mother.

- All her education to this point, the expectations of her parents, the ideas of her boyfriend or husband, have been pushing her in one direction: that the highest ambition of any woman should be to get married, build a home, raise children and look after the family.

SOURCE 1

The outstanding impression gained from this survey is that women's lives, today as much as ever, are dominated by their role – actual or expected – as wives and mothers. There is no trace of feminist demands for equality, nor do I find that women assume they have a right to work.

An extract from *Britain's Married Women Workers* published by the sociologist Viola Klein in 1957. This was a large scale survey of the attitudes of women workers.

SOURCE 2

- *Have dinner ready. Plan ahead, even the night before, to have a delicious meal ready, on time for his return.*
- *Prepare yourself. Take fifteen minutes to rest so you'll be refreshed when he arrives. Touch up your make-up, put a ribbon in your hair and be fresh-looking.*
- *Be happy to see him. Greet him with a warm smile and show sincerity in your desire to please him.*
- *Your goal: Try to make sure your home is a place of peace, order and tranquillity where your husband can renew himself in body and spirit.*
- *Don't complain if he's late home for dinner or even if he stays out all night. Count this as minor compared to what he might have gone through that day.*
- *Catering for his comfort will provide you with immense personal satisfaction.*

Some extracts from *How To Be A Good Wife*, a book for women published in 1955.

SOURCE 3

- *In 1951 women made up 31 per cent of the labour force.*
- *In 1951 around 36 per cent of adult women were working.*
- *In 1951 only 26 per cent of married women worked.*

Data gathered by the 1951 census. Note – these are the official figures. The numbers of women doing paid work was probably even higher. Many women tended to do casual work such as mending clothes or cleaning and in many cases jobs like these did not feature in the official figures.

SOURCE 4

A typical kitchen in 1950.

SOURCE 5

The front cover of *Woman* magazine from 1956. In the mid 1950s around 58 per cent of all women read weekly magazines and the sales of these magazines reached 11–12 million by about 1960.

SOURCE 6

I was the boss in my kitchen and that is how I liked it. I knew where everything was. My husband never came into the kitchen, so I did all the cooking, all the preparation, all the washing-up. He didn't know the first thing about the washing machine, he didn't know the first thing about ironing, and he didn't know the first thing about the cooker. It was my ambition to run the house to the best of my ability. Being a housewife was a twenty-four hour job so I allotted myself an additional two evenings a week to my home.

A woman teacher from Rotherham interviewed in 1960. This woman was unusual in that she did not give up work when she got married.

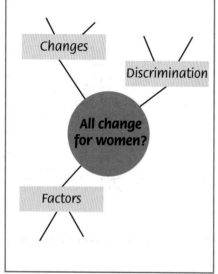
Factfile

Women's rights legislation 1945–75

New measures and laws that affected women's role, rights and status:

➤ Family Allowances introduced in 1945. Mothers got a payment for every child they had.
➤ National Health Service in 1948 introduced free health care for all.
➤ Abortion Act 1967 made abortion legal.
➤ Family Planning Act 1967 (or 1962) allowed the Pill to be dispensed under the National Health Service.
➤ Divorce Reform Act 1969 made divorce easier.
➤ Matrimonial Property Act 1970 meant women kept some of the property if she got divorced.
➤ Equal Pay Act 1970 granting equal wages for women and men doing the same work.
➤ Women's Aid Federation 1974 provided support and refuge for women and children experiencing domestic violence.
➤ Sex Discrimination Act 1975 outlawed sexual discrimination in the workplace.
➤ Domestic Violence Act 1976 enabled married or cohabiting women to obtain a court order aimed at preventing further violence and to exclude her violent partner from the home.

What changed, and why?

The period 1950–1975 saw some great changes in the role of women. This affected their working lives, their home lives, their legal status, their education and many other aspects of life as well. It is a vast subject. The following eight pages look at these changes in overview and the reasons behind them.

Prosperity

As you saw in section 15.2 (page 446) from about 1955–56 Britain's economy finally began to recover from the war. This had two important direct results on women:

• They were more able to get a job if they wanted one. A shortage of workers increased demand for women workers.
• Wages increased faster than prices so there was more spending money available. For the married woman the wages of the main earner in the house could support the whole family.

Working opportunities

In the period 1950–75 more and more women joined the workforce. The official figures show that women made up 31 per cent of the labour force in 1951 but by 1971 it was 38 per cent. It is important to remember that the number of jobs in this period went up dramatically as well, and that many of the new jobs were taken up by women. Many employers liked employing women because they were paid less than men. In 1951 around 36 per cent of adult women were working but in 1971 it was 52 per cent.

The biggest change of all at work was the gradual collapse of the 'marriage bar'. This was the unwritten rule that women should give up their jobs when they got married. In 1951 only 26 per cent of married women worked, but by 1971 it was 49 per cent – almost one in two. This probably reflects the number of married women who returned to the workforce after having children.

So how were these working women treated? There is a lot of evidence to suggest that they were resented by their male colleagues. Working mothers were blamed for crime and unruly behaviour by juveniles, although there was no evidence to show that the children of working mothers behaved worse than non-working mothers. Male colleagues often felt that women were less committed to the job than men, or that they would simply collapse in tears if they faced pressure or confrontation. The result of such negative attitudes was that working women generally took lower paid and lower status jobs than men. In the 1950s eight out of ten women were secretaries, factory workers or shop workers. They rarely gained promotion or management positions. Even when they were doing the same jobs as men they were paid less.

Equal Pay

Some campaigning women's groups allied with trade unions to address the issue of unequal treatment of women in the workplace. The focus of attention was on equal pay. For the largely male-dominated trade unions a key reason for supporting this campaign was to ensure that low-paid women did not replace higher-paid men. For women campaigners themselves the campaign was also about equality and fairness.

In the public sector (i.e. people who were paid directly by the government, such as teachers or civil servants) the equal pay argument was quickly accepted. The government agreed to it in 1955. Equal pay in the public sector was phased in over the next six years. However, outside government, there was little progress. In the 1960s the campaign gathered pace.

There were several strikes for equal pay at some major sector companies, including the huge Ford motor car factory in Dagenham. Women machinists went on strike and car production fell because there were no seats to put in the cars.

Equal Pay Act 1970

Women also voted for the Labour Party in greater numbers when it committed itself to getting rid of sex discrimination. Labour was elected in 1966 and set up a committee to investigate the issue. Significantly Labour appointed a woman, Barbara Castle, as their Minister of Labour. She tried to get employers and unions to negotiate a voluntary scheme for equal treatment but this failed. As a result the government brought in the Equal Pay Act in 1970.

1 In what ways did women face discrimination at work?
2 What does Source 8 reveal about attitudes to women working?
3 Study Sources 7 and 9. How could these sources be used to show that the campaigns of the 1960s and early 1970s were:
   a) successful
   b) unsuccessful?

In many ways the Equal Pay Act was a landmark. Under the Act, women and men had to receive the same pay if they were doing the same jobs. You can see from Source 8 the effect it had on wages for women. It also came at a time when women were campaigning on other issues as well, and therefore helped to create the atmosphere in which other advances towards equality could be made (see pages 476–79). However:

- The Act was not enforced until 1975 (firms could introduce equal pay voluntarily before then).
- The Act did nothing to stop employers paying men more on the grounds of greater experience or training, even if firms only made training available to men.
- The Act also did nothing to address the issue of women being passed over for promotion.

SOURCE 7

A

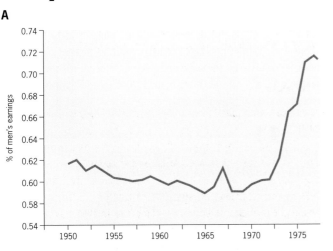

Women's wages as a percentage of men's earnings, 1950–75.

B

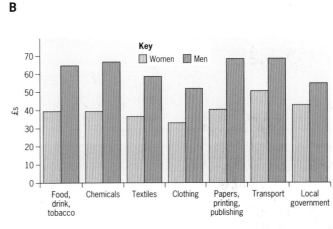

Average weekly earnings for full-time manual workers in 1976.

SOURCE 8

A leaflet published by the Civil Service union NALGO in 1954. You can find more examples at the TUC History website The Union Makes Us Strong.

SOURCE 9

Law: 103 women practising barristers out of a total of 2,073 . . . Just over 400 women were practising solicitors out of a total of 20,250.
Accountants: 11,000 chartered accountants, 82 of them women.
BBC: When the survey was made, women held six of the 150 'top' jobs in the BBC . . .
Journalism: About 2,000 women among the 18,000 members of the National Union of Journalists. There had never been a woman editor of a daily newspaper and even among the magazines which cater especially for women the majority of editors had been male.
Medicine: 17 per cent of those on the Medical Register were women . . . Taking all medical students in all schools, just under 24 per cent were women and about 400 qualified each year . . .
Dentists: 1,446 women out of 16,279 on the Register.
Architects: About 700 women were working as architects, against 16,300 men.
Civil Service: In the Civil Service as a whole there were 189 women in the Administrative class out of a total of 2,482; in the Foreign Service there were 23 out of 750. In the Executive class there were 358 women in the grades of Senior Executive Officer and above, out of a total of 4,326 and 598 out of 19,003 of equivalent level in the Professional, Scientific and Upper Technical classes . . .
Finance and Commerce: Of 40,574 members of the Institute of Directors, only 850 were women.

From a report on discrimination against women, by the National Council for Civil Liberties, 1964.

Home life

While the number of women workers was increasing so too was the number of women marrying. In the first half of the twentieth century around fourteen per cent of women never married and those who did tended to marry in their late twenties. However, in the 1950s and 1960s marriage actually became more common. Women were also marrying younger. As a result, in the late 1950s and early 1960s there was a baby boom. The peak year for births was 1965. What was life like for the married woman at home?

Technology

New technology made a big difference to women's lives in the home. By the 1960s most people lived in homes with gas, electricity and piped water. As a result, back-breaking jobs like bringing in the coal became less of a feature of women's lives. Electricity meant access to a range of labour saving devices which revolutionised housework. Refrigerators kept food fresh, reducing the need for shopping trips. Vacuum cleaners also made household cleaning easier and quicker. Above all, the washing machine removed the back-breaking toil of the weekly wash. In the 1970s these machines became increasingly sophisticated, spinning and drying as well as washing.

SOURCE 10

Washing day around 1900.

> 1 Why are Sources 10 and 11 useful to historians looking at women's domestic lives?

SOURCE 11

THE WASHING MACHINE YOU NEED

doesn't need you!

GO OUT AND FORGET IT! THE AUTOMATED HOOVER KEYMATIC DOES IT ALL!

An advertisement for the Hoover Keymatic washing machine, 1962.

SOURCE 12

No one should waste her life on the treadmill of housework. So decide how much you're prepared to do and when. Four hours a day? One day a week? None? (A high aim, I feel, but good luck to you). Decide how much mechanical help you want, how much it will cost, and how you're going to get the money to pay for it. Don't use that help to raise your housewifely standards. Use it to get more free time to get out and enjoy yourself. Remember that the whole point of housework is to keep the place functioning efficiently as a cheerful background for living – so live!

An extract from *Superwoman* by Shirley Conran, published 1975.

Choice

These machines gave women more time. The average number of minutes per day spent on housework fell from 500 in 1950 to 440 in 1960 to 345 in 1975. There was even some evidence that men were doing some housework (about twenty minutes!). Some women were fortunate enough to be able to use that time on leisure activities, socialising and shopping. Most women used the time to take on part-time work. The important change was not what women chose to do with that extra time, but the fact that the choice was there. It is unthinkable that Source 12 would have been written earlier in the century.

Expectations

The down side of Source 12 is probably clear to you. Superwoman! Many women have commented on how the bar was raised in the 1960s and 1970s. As choices broadened for women the expectations on them as to what they would achieve were also raised. Take childcare for example. Psychological studies suggested that children benefited from spending most of their first five years with their mothers. Traditionally this had been rare. Wealthy mothers usually left their children with nurses, while poorer mothers returned to work leaving the children with family. Some women felt torn between a desire to work and a desire to do right by their children.

SOURCE 13

Women are born to love, born to be partners to the opposite sex and that is the most important thing they can do. To be wives and mothers, to fix their hearts on one man and to love and care for him with all the bounteous unselfishness that love can inspire.

An extract from an article in *Woman's Own* magazine in 1961. The author was Monica Dickens. She was well known as a successful author and broadcaster.

2 Study Source 13. Do you think this view reflects what the writer actually thought or the image she thought women should conform to?

SOURCE 14

British Cartoon Archive, University of Kent © Solo Syndication/Associated Newspapers Ltd.

A cartoon published in the *Daily Mail*, 3 February 1960. The caption reads: 'Every morning when my husband goes to work I hate him . . . because he's going to do things and meet people all day . . . while I'm stuck here . . .'

3 How do the findings of Hannah Gavron help us to understand Source 14?
4 Does Source 16 support Hannah Gavron's conclusions?
5 It would be possible to express the findings of Hannah Gavron to convey a different message. For example: 'Four out of five middle class women felt that they had married at just the right age.' Discuss with a partner the problems of using surveys like this as a historical source.

Magazines and TV

Women were keen magazine readers. More than half read a weekly magazine. In the 1960s the TV began to take over. In 1950 hardly any homes had one. By 1970 almost every home that wanted one had got one. Through magazines and TV women were presented with advice on every conceivable aspect of home life as well as how to look and how to behave. It seems that many women were happy to follow the advice and the pressures which magazines and advertising directed at them.

Magazines did change over the period. You can see examples on page 480. By the 1970s there was less emphasis on being a domestic goddess and more emphasis on film stars and celebrities and also on women as people in their own right rather than as wives and mothers.

How did women feel?

In this situation (increased work opportunities alongside more women becoming wives and mothers) researchers tried to find out what women were now feeling about their roles as mothers. As you would expect they found huge differences between women of different social groups. Women are individuals – think how hard it would be to generalise even about the attitudes of the students in a normal school classroom. They also faced another difficulty. Asking women about such personal and significant issues as their feelings about being a wife or mother was not common at that time. Women were not used to being honest. There was a strong taboo against speaking out about what you really felt. Many women tended to say 'the right thing' – what they thought they were expected to feel rather than what they actually felt.

In the early 1960s the sociologist Hannah Gavron interviewed a number of North London housewives alone, in their own homes. Away from the pressures of families and friends, the women seem to have answered honestly and openly. Here are some of Gavron's findings:

- Thirty-five per cent of working-class wives and 21 per cent of middle-class wives felt they had married too young. They claimed they got married in order to escape their families. Working-class wives also said they married in order to escape dull, low paid jobs.
- Both groups said they were full of regrets for things they had not done, particularly getting training and pursuing a career.
- The majority felt their marriages were more equal partnerships than their parents' marriages but 62 per cent of women did not know what their husband earned.
- Few of the women saw their main role in life as wife and mother.
- Most felt that education and work were totally geared towards men.

Another sociologist from the period, Nancy Sears, drawing on similar findings wondered why, if there was frustration at their role, more women did not 'protest' against such restrictions. She concluded that most women accepted the situation because they could not see any way that they could change it and were afraid to try to do so. Society expected women to be housewives and women who tried to do anything different faced opposition or even ridicule.

SOURCE 15

The biggest obstacle to women is that in subtle and not so subtle ways an atmosphere is created which still makes it appear peculiar or comical for women to be both feminine and use their abilities to the full.

An extract from a survey of women's attitudes by the sociologist Nancy Sears in 1962.

SOURCE 16

There are signs that some girls are tending towards more independence in their dealings with men, and that they will not be content to sign over their lives to their husbands on marriage … They are determined to remain smart and in control of events after they have married; they are not prepared to be bowed down with lots of children, and they will expect their husbands to take a fuller share than their fathers in the running of the home.

An extract from a report by a researcher in Sheffield in 1963.

The women's movement

It seemed clear that emancipation had failed; the number of women in Parliament had settled at a low level; the number of professional women had stabilised as a tiny minority; the pattern of female employment had emerged as underpaid, menial and supportive. The cage door had been opened and the canary had refused to fly out. The conclusion was that the cage door ought never to have been opened because canaries are made for captivity; the suggestion of an alternative had only confused and saddened them.

The feminist Germaine Greer writing about the women's movement before 1970.

The highest value is placed on jobs like designing goods, writing adverts or books, and helping companies to think up new ideas. British trade depends on new ideas and men are no better at thinking up these than women.

Germaine Greer, *The Female Eunuch*, 1970.

What's the matter with women today? Why are they all demanding equal opportunities and equal pay? They do not deserve to be mothers if they cannot sacrifice five years for their children before their children go to school. They are missing the relationship between child and mother. It is no wonder there are so many child delinquents when that relationship is missing. Forget about the money and stay at home until the children go to school.

A delegate at the Labour Women's Conference in 1969.

1 How might the author of Sources 17 and 18 reply to the speech in Source 19?
2 What might the author think of the cartoon Source 20?

In the 1950s the term 'feminism' had been virtually unknown. It was associated with old-fashioned ideas – e.g. the Suffragettes (see section 14.2). Very few people saw the idea of a militant movement to fight for women's rights as being worthwhile or relevant.

There were feminist writers. For example, in 1956 the sociologists Alva Myrdal and Viola Klein published a book called *Woman's Two Roles: Home and Work*. They argued that there should be a fairer distribution of work and leisure between the two sexes. In short they criticised the fact that while men worked and then came home to relaxation and leisure time, women often worked and then had to run the home as well. This book remained in print for ten years. However the great majority of women were not influenced by such books, and may not even have heard of them.

On the other hand, the few women who did think this way turned out to be very influential. Two important organisations were the Fawcett Society and the Six Point Group (their six points were political, occupational, moral, social, economic and legal equality for women). Both these organisations had roots going back to the suffragist campaigns for the vote but by the 1960s they were active in campaigns for equal pay and equal treatment for women under the law. These two groups organised alliances with other organisations such as the National Council for Civil Liberties, trade unions and professional associations such as doctors and lawyers.

Women's liberation

By the late 1960s there were signs that the women's movement was growing in strength and confidence and in some cases it was growing in radicalism. Some women members of organisations like CND (Campaign for Nuclear Disarmament) or even the main political parties began to form parallel women's versions of these movements because they felt they were dominated by men.

Local Women's Groups began to set up all over the country. Was this growing movement because an increasing number were dissatisfied with their role and status, or because an increasing number were feeling more powerful and able to change things? It was probably a combination of both. Certainly such groups made many women feel part of a new movement. The groups talked about liberation and empowerment – making women feel able to change things. They organised 'consciousness raising', which meant making women aware of:

• how discrimination affected them personally
• their own deep-seated ideas about themselves and the role of women
• their own skills and rights so they could seize opportunities which were offered to them.

By 1969 most major British towns had women's liberation groups. Inspired by writers like Germaine Greer (Sources 17 and 18), they questioned what they saw as traditional male assumptions that women were born to be homemakers, leave work when they married and give up their independence on the birth of children. They got involved in very varied issues. They raised awareness of domestic violence against women and gay rights. In Hull the wives of fishermen launched a women's campaign calling for better safety in the industry because accidents affected them as well as their husbands. Women bus conductors in London campaigned for the right to drive buses.

The women's groups came together at a national conference in 1970 to plan an overall programme of action for the women's liberation movement. They agreed four 'demands':

1 equal pay
2 equal education and opportunity
3 twenty-four hour nurseries
4 free contraception and abortion on demand.

This 1970 Conference launched the women's liberation movement on the national scene. Opponents often shortened this to 'Women's Lib'. Over the next two decades its leaders campaigned against discrimination in work and civil rights. They had a major impact on public opinion through magazines, marches and public demonstrations. One of the most famous gestures of protest was the burning of bras, high heels and other clothing which women argued was worn for the benefit of men, not themselves. Sources 21–23 show other examples of their campaign methods.

SOURCE 20

A cartoon published in the *Daily Mail*, 21 June 1968.

Activity

Source 20 is an interesting commentary on how the women's movement was seen in 1968. It is mainly designed to amuse. However cartoons often provide us with lots of useful information without intending to.

- Look at the different array of women who are protesting. They come from different walks of life.
- The banners show what issues campaigners believed important at this time.
- The women look serious and determined while the men seem dismayed.

Of course we cannot take this cartoon to be an accurate representation of what was happening at the time, but it is still extremely useful. On your own copy of Source 20 produce a detailed analysis which explains:
- The message of the source.
- The methods used by the cartoonist to deliver his message.
- The information in the cartoon which is useful to historians.
- Why historians need to be careful with sources like this.

SOURCE 21

Advertisement for a demonstration in 1970. Women protesters had disrupted the 1970 Miss World beauty competition by throwing flour bombs, claiming that the competition treated women like objects. They had been put on trial. This demonstration was in support of the women on trial.

SOURCE 22

A feminist car sticker from the 1970s.

SOURCE 23

Examples of feminist demonstrations in the early 1970s.

Contraception

One central aim of the feminist agenda was free contraception for all women. If women were to be free to make choices then they clearly needed to be free to decide how many children to have and when.

Family planning advice had been available since the 1920s, but thirty years later, methods of contraception were still unreliable and family planning was still something of a taboo subject. Many husbands and wives did not even discuss the subject before they got married. There was misinformation and misunderstanding.

Through the 1950s researchers were working hard on a radical new form of contraception – the combined oral contraceptive pill – which controlled the woman's hormone cycle to prevent conception. The first birth control pill was available in Britain in 1957. By 1961 it was approved for being dispensed under the National Health Service – although you still needed a doctor's prescription to have it. It was a massive breakthrough in contraception. If used properly it was almost 100 per cent effective and it was controlled by the woman. By 1968 there were two million women in Britain taking the pill.

It was also a massive step forward for women's rights. It is hard to overstate the importance of this development for women. There was the obvious consequence: parents could choose how many children to have. Most married couples now had families of two to three children rather than the much larger families of earlier generations. After the peak year of 1965 the birth rate fell dramatically. It also gave unmarried women more sexual freedom. But the most important consequence was that effective family planning increased women's opportunities in all other aspects of life.

SOURCE 24

At the beginning of this century a typical working-class mother devoted some fifteen years of her adult life to begetting and nursing her own children. She would expect to be preoccupied with raising her large family – and supervising her daughters' child-bearing – until she was nearing the end of her active life. Today, by the time a woman approaches forty, her youngest child is going to school; and at this stage she can expect to live for another thirty-six years. She is ready to start a new career . . .

GM Carstairs, *This Island Now*, 1962.

---

1 Make a list of the main changes described in Sources 24 and 25.
2 What is the cartoonist trying to say in source 26?

SOURCE 25

Working women were delaying or curtailing their capacity to bear children, marrying later or perhaps being reluctant to have children at all. The rise of child-minders and crèche facilities . . . was testimony to the wish of women to lead more relaxed, interesting child-free lives . . . The classic working-class mum, living at home to look after her numerous children with the man as the bread-winner . . . conformed less and less to the reality.

Professor Kenneth Morgan, *The People's Peace, British History 1945–1990*, 1992.

SOURCE 26

BRITISH CARTOON ARCHIVE, THE UNIVERSITY OF KENT © THE GUARDIAN

'Of course my husband doesn't agree with Father McMahon!'

A cartoon in the *Guardian* newspaper from 24 February 1965. The Catholic Church (the figure on the right in the cartoon) was opposed to artificial contraception. Father McMahon was a young priest in Birmingham who questioned the Church's position and was disowned by the Church.

Abortion

The women's movement also led the campaign to legalise abortion. Before the arrival of the pill, and as a result of the sexual revolution there were an enormous number of unwanted pregnancies among both unmarried and married women. There were an estimated 200,000 illegal abortions performed each year in Britain in the early 1960s. These were in unregistered premises, often in very unhygienic conditions. The mother's life was at risk. Despite this many women were prepared to take the risk of an illegal, 'backstreet' abortion either because they were desperate not to have a child, or because they could not afford it, or because of the social stigma that still attached to being an unmarried mother.

In 1967 a concerted campaign led to Parliament passing the Abortion Act which became law in 1968. Abortions were available if two doctors agreed it was necessary, it was carried out on registered premises and if the baby was not yet capable of surviving independently.

Divorce

A final key development was the Divorce Reform Act of 1969. Before this Act, a married couple could only get a divorce if there had been some 'matrimonial offence', such as adultery. It was usually seen as the woman's fault when a marriage broke down. The 1969 Act allowed divorce simply on the grounds that the relationship had broken down – it did not have to be the fault of husband or wife.

The Matrimonial Property Act of 1970 recognised that a wife's work was valuable and built up the wealth of the couple. This meant that women usually got a share of the family assets, such as the home, in a divorce. Until this Act many women were left in poverty as a result of a divorce but this was no longer the case.

The divorce rate rose by 3.5 times with over 100,000 divorces per year in the early 1970s.

SOURCE 27

"Don't worry, I'm only taking what's legally mine!"

A cartoon from the *News of The World*, 11 February 1973.

Focus Task A

What factors led to changes in the roles of women?

Over the past eight pages you have been gathering information on a diagram. Have a look at what you have got in the 'factors for change' branch of your diagram and compare it with our list below:

- Affluence
- Work
- Wome's lib stunts
- Pay
- Contraception
- Welfare State
- Feminist writers
- Government legislation
- Domestic technology

1 Write each of these factors, plus your own, on a separate card.
2 On the back of each card summarise how this factor led to changes in the role of women.
3 Now arrange the cards on a large sheet of paper with what you think were the most significant at the top and the least at the bottom.
4 Draw lines and annotations to show how the factors connect with each other.

Focus Task B

How were women discriminated against in the 1960s and early 1970s?

The second strand of your diagram from page 472 should include aspects and examples of discrimination.
1 If you feel that area of discrimination had been dealt with by 1975 then cross it out on your diagram and mark next to it the measure or action that was most influential in overcoming it.
2 Choose an area of discrimination you think was not yet overcome. Use all that you have found out about the women's movement tactics and message to design a leaflet highlighting what is wrong and what should be done about it.

NB. If you chose education you might want to return to this task after you have read pages 494–95.

How much change had taken place between 1950 and 1975?

Magazines are a very useful source for modern social history.
- Weekly magazines were very popular – so they must have reflected something of people's lives or hopes or they would not have bought them.
- They were 'of the moment'. They changed each week according to what was popular at that time.
- They are available! Another good source would have been TV but many of the TV programmes of this period were never recorded so are lost forever.

You have been put in charge of an exhibition of women's magazine covers for the education section at the British Library. Here are the magazine covers you have decided to feature. You have to write a 100-word caption for each one explaining what it tells you about this period. Use your knowledge from the rest of this chapter.

If you don't think these covers tell the whole story you might wish to research alternatives.

SOURCE **28**

Covers of *Woman* and *Woman's Own* magazine, 1956–72.

Activity

1 One of the women's movement aims was equality of education. Compare Source 29 with Source 2 on page 471. These are almost thirty years apart. Does this surprise you? Explain your answer.

2 In 1972, 97 per cent of entries for domestic subjects were girls and 99 per cent of entries for technical drawing were boys.

   a) Does this show change from 1950?

   b) Once you have studied the education section of the next topic (pages 496–97) come back to this question. Do you think that educational opportunity for women was greater in 1975 than it had been in 1950?

   c) From your own experience of education would you say that the gender balance in subjects is any different now from what it was in 1972?

3 What does the writer of Source 30 think is the most significant change in education?

SOURCE 29

Your brother and his friend are arriving home for breakfast after walking all night on a sponsored walk. Iron his shirt that you have previously washed, and press a pair of trousers ready for him to change into. Cook and serve a substantial breakfast for them including toast.

A task from a paper in *Practical Housecraft*, 1982.

SOURCE 30

By having smaller families, expanding into the workforce and asserting their equal status with men, women participated in British national life as never before.

A girl of sixteen in 1970 was far more likely to remain in education than a similar sixteen-year-old in 1956. She was more likely to pursue her own intellectual and cultural interests for as long as she liked, to marry when and whom she wanted, to have children when and if she wanted, and, above all, to choose whether she remained at home as a housewife or pursued her own career. These were not small advances, and they had a profound effect on the way men saw women and women saw themselves. If we are looking for a genuine revolution in the sixties, then perhaps this was it: a revolution with its roots deep in British social history, but a revolution nonetheless.

An extract from *White Heat: A History of Britain in the Swinging Sixties* by Dominic Sandbrook, a historian at Oxford University.

Focus Task

How much change had taken place for women by 1975?

Part A

The final area of your diagram from page 474 should be a record of all the changes that took place. It will probably be a long list, but does that mean there is a lot of change? To answer a 'how much change' question you need also to think about how deeply women were affected by the change; and how widespread and lasting the changes were (did it affect all the social classes, or different racial groups equally?).

1 Look at the changes you have noted on your diagram. For each change decide where you think it should go on the scale below.

2 Decide on your overall judgement bearing in mind all the evidence. Mark your judgement on the scale. Be prepared to justify why you have chosen that position.

3 Compare your scale with a partner's and see if you can agree a new position on the scale which you both agree with.

Major change   No change

Part B

4 A producer of radio programmes for GCSE History has commissioned you to write a short play about women's rights. The opening scene shows a women's rights campaigner in 1975 feeling frustrated because women are still not treated the same as men. She then meets up with her mother, who reminds her how far women have progressed. Write a script for a conversation between these two.

15.5 Was there a youth revolution in the 1960s?

What was it like growing up in Britain in the 1950s?

What impression have you got so far of the 1950s? You may remember from section 15.3 that when Caribbean immigrants came to Britain in the early 1950s many of them found it grey and drab, and they had a point. It was not just the British weather.

Much of the country was still recovering from bomb damage caused by the war. Many other areas of the country resembled building sites as Britain built blocks of new flats and new towns as well as motorways, schools and hospitals. Britain was still recovering from the war economically. Despite its victory against Hitler, Britain felt far from secure and during these early days of the Cold War the government was still spending a lot of the country's wealth on arms. There were still tight controls left over from wartime. Food rationing did not end until 1954 and some items continued to be rationed after that. National service (eighteen months military service for all young men aged 17–21) remained compulsory until 1960. Licensing hours for pubs were still controlled. The shops were not piled high with goods. Shopping was certainly not the leisure pursuit it is today.

In one sense there were no teenagers either. Obviously there were people of that age but they did not behave the way we think of teenagers behaving today. In the early 1950s most young people seemed like younger versions of their parents! They wore similar clothes to their parents, they went to the same schools as their parents had done. They followed many of the same routines, perhaps going to church on Sundays, visiting relatives, listening to the same music at dances. If they had left school they might well go on to work in the same place as their parents.

There was only one TV channel and so, if they had a TV at all, the whole family tended to sit together and watch the same programmes. There was not much choice of listening on the radio either, and again the family tended to listen to the same programmes together. If this sounds a bit dull to you as a teenager then it maybe felt dull for many of them too, although we should never assume that people in the past see things the way we do from the early twenty-first century. Check out the evidence.

SOURCE 1

He's one of the generation that grew up before teenagers existed … in poor Vernon's era there just weren't any: can you believe it? In those days, it seems, you were just an overgrown boy, or an under-grown man, life didn't seem to cater for anything else in between.

Extract from *Absolute Beginners*, a novel published in 1959. Here one character in the novel is talking about his older brother, Vernon.

SOURCE 2

A family in the 1950s.

SOURCE 3

I cannot resist leaping to the defence of the 1950s, since so many people, to my mind, seem to get it wrong. Either they seem to have some kind of a Hovis-ad vision of it, an over-traditional view of little boys in baggy trousers running down country lanes, bumping against the stomach of Dixon of Dock Green, or they think of it as just a damp patch between the battlefield of the 1940s and the fairground of the 1960s. It did not seem like that at all to those of us who were around then. Bar a few fogeys who bemoaned the loss of parlour maids and deference, we thought everything was getting better.

We had the Festival of Britain in 1951, with exhibitions and displays of new materials ... Bits of the empire were getting their freedom, under towering figures such as Kenyatta and Nehru; we had the wildly popular coronation and a new Queen, as young as Princess Diana then. There was plenty of nationalistic feeling still around and much talk of a new Elizabethan age.

This was the decade in which television first hit British homes, and washing machines – think what that did to women's lives.

Rationing ended, though it took its time. The New Look, designed in the 1940s, finally caught up with the dowdiest of us. Council estates weren't seen as crime-ridden badlands then but a wonderful alternative to the slums ...

But weren't we all terribly inhibited and uptight and lacking in sex before the pill? Well, no. There was, for a start, an awful lot of what was known as heavy petting, which took the strain out of a good many situations ... And since in wartime, as everyone knows, morals loosen up all round, it stood to reason that girls didn't suddenly put a padlock on their pants and a lock on their doors on the signing of the Yalta agreement.

And the world was opening up after the war ... We discovered Europe – I could hitch-hike round France by myself for a couple of months without thinking it risky. It was nothing, of course, compared with today's cheap air travel and worldwide backpacking, but heady stuff all the same.

We knew things weren't perfect but we still thought they could be made so.

An extract from an article by the journalist and writer Katharine Whitehorne writing in 2007 about her memories of growing up in the 1950s.

1 Study Source 3. According to this source, what was exciting about being a teenager in the 1950s?
2 Would you regard this source as a balanced view of life in the 1950s?
3 Is it possible to say whether the account in Source 3 is typical of the experience of most teenagers in the 1950s?

Increasing affluence

In the second half of the 1950s an important change was taking place. As you saw in section 15.2, from about 1955–56 Britain's economy finally began to recover from the war and a boom period began. This had two important direct results:

- Unemployment was low so even inexperienced school leavers could usually find a job without much difficulty.
- Wages increased faster than prices so the real value of wages (what your money could buy) was higher than it had ever been. This meant that the wages of the main earner in the house (usually the father) could support the whole family.

At the same time:

- More effective birth control was leading to smaller families, so parents had fewer children to feed and clothe. It also meant that more mothers were able to return to work more quickly after their children went to school (see page 478).
- Young people had more leisure time in which to spend their money. By the late 1950s most working people were working a five-day week rather than five and a half or six which had been more common before the Second World War. The rise of trade unions helped to secure this extra free time, although many businesses already had five day working weeks because it meant a more productive workforce.

The combination of these factors meant that young people who had a job were able to keep most of their wages. In earlier decades they would have had to hand their money to their parents to help keep the family fed and clothed. Now they were able to enjoy the comforts of home while spending their wages on themselves. Parents were mostly happy about this. They had grown up through the hard years of the 1930s Depression and the Second World War. They wanted their children to have a more comfortable life than they had.

It was this disposable cash coupled with sufficient leisure time that most helped change the lives of young people. As the historian Dominic Sandbrook noted in 2005, 'the teenager was a creation of affluence'.

Enter the teenager!

At this point it is important to clarify what the term 'teenager' meant in the context of the 1950s. The term was not new – it was used in the USA and Britain in the 1920s and 1930s, but in the second half of the 1950s the term became widely used to refer to young people aged from fifteen upwards into their early twenties. Teenagers began to be easier to identify. You could tell a teenager by their …

Clothes

They began to wear different styles of clothes from their parents.

Meeting places

Teenagers also began to spend more time with each other than with their families. They gathered in coffee bars and listened to other young people playing music which their parents did not listen to and did not even understand.

SOURCE 4

A

B

Typical teenagers of the 1950s wearing fashions of the day. Nothing too extreme, but very much in fashion with a fair bit of grooming evident.

Note the wonderful layers of net petticoats under Vera's skirt. These male teens are wearing standard male fashions of the day with token attention to small fashion details such as the narrower tie.

It's important to remember that more conventional young men wore this type of clothing than teddy boy gear. Men still did national service and this had an effect of a 'uniform' mentality approach to dress of wearing pressed, neat, clean clothing.

… This basic blazer or jacket look was favoured by the majority of youths and is fairly conventional but was in that era thought quite sharp.

Growing up in the 1950s I recall far more young teen men dressed like those in the picture above, than as the 'typical teddy boy look' so often used as an image of the 50s.

These comments are from Fashion Era, a website on the history of fashion.

Music

In the mid 1950s skiffle bands were very popular (see Source 5), especially the singer Lonnie Donegan. Many skiffle bands developed into rock and roll bands in the later 1950s and early 1960s, partly as a result of the influence of American music.

During the 1950s Rock and Roll music took the USA by storm with stars like Bill Haley and megastars like Elvis Presley. Teenagers in Britain were able to hear these stars on records and see them in films at the cinema. Newspapers started listing the 'Top Twenty' selling singles in the country in the 1950s. Many teenagers also listened to other forms of music, especially African American music like jazz and blues.

Some young musicians in England had a more direct link to the USA. Throughout the 1950s young sailors on Liverpool merchant ships and cruise liners had been using their trips to New York to pick up clothes and music. They were known as Cunard Yanks, after the Cunard shipping line which employed many of them. This was one reason why Liverpool played such a prominent role in the youth culture of the 1960s. Teenagers like John Lennon and Paul McCartney had easy access to a wide range of American music which was hard to find anywhere else in the country. Future Beatle George Harrison got his first electric guitar from a Cunard Yank called Ivan Haywood.

SOURCE 5

Teenagers dancing to skiffle music in London's Soho Square.

Films

American movies were just as influential as American music. One of the most famous movies of all starred James Dean as a rebellious teenager in *Rebel Without A Cause* (1955). His electric performance, along with a plot about a misunderstood teenager, had a huge influence on the youth culture of the 1950s. It also dramatised the gap which seemed to be opening up between the teenage generation and their parents.

SOURCE **6**

Poster from the film *Rebel without a Cause*, starring James Dean.

SOURCE **7**

Teddy Boys in 1957.

Teddy Boys

Distinctive styles of clothing or music began to define the identity of sub–groups. For example, Teddy Boys were so called because the jackets they wore were similar to jackets worn in the Edwardian period (1901–10).

Gangs

Some wilder Teddy Boys acquired a reputation for trouble and violence (see page 459), although the majority of Teddy Boys were simply rebellious rather than deliberately violent.

Diversity

The rise of the teenager makes interesting history. But beware the trap of thinking that people in history are all the same. So when you consider what life was like for young people in the 1950s remember that it all depends on which teenagers, where they lived, their social background, their race, their education and family. Clearly there were huge differences between individuals and within different communities.

Focus Task

Option A: What was it like growing up in the 1950s?

Option B: How much did life for teenagers change in the 1950s?

The examiner for your Paper 2 Depth Study is planning questions for the exam paper but he cannot decide between Option A or B. What do you think?
Work in pairs or small groups. Half of you take Option A and the other one take Option B.
1 What main points would you expect to find in each answer?
2 What information would you expect candidates to use to support their points?
3 Which question would be easier to revise for?
4 Which question do you think would be fairer to all candidates?
5 Which question would be easier to mark?
6 Which question does your pair/group/class recommend and why?
7 Can you suggest a better question?

What did being a teenager mean in the 1960s?

The simplest answer to this question is: much the same as in the late 1950s but more so! The trends from the late 1950s were speeded up and spread more widely. However these combined with some distinctive new influences to make the 1960s a controversial decade.

The teenage consumer

There were about five million teenagers in the early 1960s and they earned about one tenth of the country's personal income. They spent about £800 million per year on themselves – mainly on clothes and entertainment. Cinemas, dance halls, magazine publishers and record shops all depended heavily on teenage customers (see Source 8). Teenagers bought over one-third of all bicycles and motorbikes. They bought one-third of all cosmetics and about one-third of all film tickets.

It is easy to see why companies were keen to pay for advertising slots in new shows like *Ready, Steady, Go!* targeted at teenagers. Record companies, publishers and fashion houses began to target this new and potentially lucrative market. One recent historical study has claimed that pop groups such as the Beatles and the Rolling Stones were not really musicians, they were in fact very successful businessmen who knew how to produce a product which the market wanted to buy.

SOURCE 8

Every week I'd buy at least two or three singles. I had so much money to spend. It's unbelievable looking back. There were so many well-paid jobs for teenagers connected with the car industry. I'd spend £10 every weekend on myself, on clothes, on going out and most of all on music.

Interview from 2005 with a Coventry man who was a teenager in the 1960s.

SOURCE 9

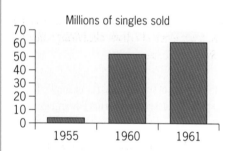

Millions of singles sold

Record sales in Britain, 1955–61.

1 Would you regard Source 8 or Source 9 as more reliable for a historian investigating teenage spending patterns in the 1960s? Explain your answer.

2 Is Source 9 a useful source of information for historians investigating teenagers as consumers?

3 Study Sources 10 and 11. Do you think that Source 11 is a more typical reflection of teenagers in the 1960s than either Source 9 or Source 11? Explain your answer.

SOURCE 10

A young woman shopping for shoes in a London high street in the 1960s.

SOURCE 11

The Sunday Graphic in 1960 found a boy who could hang £127 worth of suits in his parents' back yard to be photographed, another who earned £5 a week and owned: five suits, two pairs of slacks, one pair of jeans, one casual jacket, five white and three coloured shirts, five pairs of shoes, twenty-five ties and an overcoat. A sixteen-year-old typist owned six dresses, seven straight skirts, two pleated ones, one overcoat and a mac, one Italian suit, one pair of boots, one of flat shoes and three of high heels. One eighteen-year-old drove a new car which he had bought for £800; many who earned something under £7 a week had motorbikes at £300. A hire purchase firm said they had 4,000 teenagers on their books and not a single bad debt.

An extract from *The Teenage Revolution*. This was a pioneering study carried out by the journalist Peter Laurie in 1965.

Portable

Radios became small, light and portable thanks to improved batteries and transistors. Young people could now keep up with their favourite radio stations and music while they were 'hanging out' with their friends. Before then radio sets were large and heavy and radio programmes tended to be aimed at the whole family.

It was a similar story with record players. In the 1940s they were large and too expensive for most families. By the 1960s they were made from lightweight plastics and they were cheap enough for the average teenager to have one in his or her bedroom. About half of all record players sold in the 1960s were bought by teenagers.

Sleek

The development of new man-made fabrics contributed to the new fashions of the 1960s and made them cheap enough for teenagers to afford. As with music, this made teenagers a lucrative market for fashion designers and clothing stores. Even if they could not actually afford the clothes, girls in particular could afford the material and often made their own dresses to keep up with the latest fashions.

Wheels

One other practical development which affected teenagers in the 1960s was transport. Public transport improved, especially in the cities. More importantly, many teenagers could afford to buy scooters or motorcycles. This made it easier for them to visit each other, to meet up at the most fashionable places, to take day trips or go to music events which were in another town.

Cool

It was a Friday. It was 9 August 1963 and it was 7 o'clock in the evening. Something new and exciting was about to happen on the TV – if you were a teenager. It was a new ITV show called *Ready, Steady, Go!* and in many ways this new show summed up the Swinging Sixties.

The audience was made up of teenagers, especially selected for their good looks, fashion sense and ability to dance.

The sets changed each week and they were more like art than sets. Trendy posters and bright images were used all over the studio – not like traditional programmes.

All of the huge bands of the 1960s played on *Ready, Steady, Go!* including The Rolling Stones, The Who, The Beach Boys, Cilla Black, Otis Redding and the biggest of them all – The Beatles. One performance on *Ready, Steady Go!* could easily put a band into the Top Ten.

The cameras were positioned at unusual angles and the director switched rapidly from one view to another – not like traditional programmes.

The main presenter was Cathy McGowan. She was a teenager – the same as the audience. She wore the trendiest clothes and used up-to-date slang. She was an office worker and replied to an advertisement from the TV company for a typical teenager to advise them on the show. Then she started presenting it – no need for a smooth talking host like the middle-aged men who presented most programmes.

Music

You are now going to look in more detail at some of the key features of youth culture starting with music.

The most spectacular development of 1960s youth culture was the incredible explosion of musical talent. In the 1940s and 1950s the music scene was dominated by big bands of professional musicians playing music written by professional writers. It was all geared towards whole families listening together on the radio at home. The 1960s changed all that. Small bands of young men and women wrote their own songs and played for people their own age. The Beatles made their reputation playing to teenage audiences in the Cavern Club in Liverpool. They went on to become the biggest band in the 1960s and in British music history. There were other hugely important bands as well, of course. The Who, The Rolling Stones and The Kinks started playing in pubs and clubs in the South of England. The main feature of the music was that it was played by young people for young people. There was often a hard edge to their performances. The Stones openly sang about sex and drugs. The Who regularly smashed up their equipment on stage. At concerts the young teenage fans would go berserk and scream. Bands like The Beatles and The Stones were often trapped in their hotel rooms because they were chased everywhere by screaming girls. Nothing like this had ever been seen before. Some sections of the press liked the new movement. Not surprisingly, there was a good deal of disapproval (see Source 12) but that just made it more appealing to young people.

SOURCE 12

The audience is a bottomless pit of vacuity . . . the huge faces bloated with cheap confectionery and smeared with chain store make-up, the open, sagging mouths and glazed eyes, the hands mindlessly drumming in time to the music, the broken stiletto heels, the shoddy, stereotyped, 'with-it' clothes: here, apparently is a collective portrait of a generation enslaved by a commercial machine.

An extract from an article in *The New Statesman* from February 1964 called The Menace of Beatlism.

SOURCE 14

They're young, new. They're high-spirited, cheerful. What a change from the self-pitying moaners, crooning their lovelorn tunes from the tortured shallows of lukewarm hearts.

The Beatles are whacky. They wear their hair like a mop – but it's WASHED, it's super clean. So is their fresh young act. They don't have to rely on off-colour jokes about homos for their fun . . .

Youngsters like the Beatles are doing a good turn for show business – and the rest of us – with their new sounds, new looks. Good luck Beatles!

The *Daily Mirror*, September 1963.

1 How would you describe the attitude of source 14 towards The Beatles?
2 How does the article describe earlier singers?
3 What caption might the writer of Source 12 put on to the photograph in Source 13?

SOURCE 13

Screaming fans at a Beatles Concert in 1964.

We should also remember that music was big business. The Beatles and the other bands may have felt they were speaking for their generation but the record companies supported them because they sold huge numbers of records and made vast profits. In 1964 for example, The Beatles sold 25 million records worldwide. Just one Rolling Stones single, *Satisfaction*, sold 5 million copies worldwide in 1965. As we have already seen, TV broadcasters recognised that they could attract the high spending teenage market with programmes about the latest music. As well as *Ready, Steady Go!*, teenagers could tune in to *Juke Box Jury* (where the audience commented on new acts). The BBC introduced *Pick of the Pops* in 1962 which eventually developed into *Top Of The Pops* which ran from 1964 until 2006.

Finally, the music boom of the 1960s went hand in hand with an explosion in popular radio. For much of the 1960s the BBC took little notice of youth music and continued to play more family focused material. The demand for the latest music was met by a pirate station called Radio Caroline. It broadcast without a license from a ship in the North Sea and it became the most popular station in Britain. Eventually, the authorities closed the station down, claiming that its broadcasts were a safety threat by interfering with shipping and aircraft communications. The BBC tried to fill the gap left by Radio Caroline by launching Radio 1 in 1967.

Fashion

For much of the 1960s the music and fashion scenes developed hand in hand. Pop stars tried to outdo each other by wearing outrageous clothes. Most teenagers did not go quite this far, but they did spend their money on the new styles being created by talented designers like Mary Quant. In many ways Mary Quant's story sums up the fashion story in the 1960s. She set up a clothes boutique called Bazaar on King's Road in 1955. Within a few years the King's Road became the capital of youth fashion for London and the rest of the world. She and a team of machinists made the clothes and by 1961 she was mass producing her designs in factories. By 1966 she was turning out 500 designs a year and her worldwide sales amounted to over £6 million. As with the music revolution, Mary Quant was making a deliberate break with the past. Her designs were informal and lightweight. The most famous Mary Quant invention was the mini skirt. She used a wide range of different fabrics and colours. She also used models who were very young. The most famous of them all was Lesley Hornby, better known as Twiggy. Fashion became big news and models became big stars. As well as Twiggy there were models like Jean Shrimpton. Photographers like David Bailey became media stars in their own right. There were even celebrity hairdressers like Vidal Sassoon.

SOURCE 15

"Aw! It ain't fair! Someone's getting almost as much publicity as 'me!'"

TWIGGY

Reserved for Victory-over-Smith Bra.

Reserved for Peace-in-Vietnam Panties.

Reserved for Com-market mini-skirt.

BRITISH CARTOON ARCHIVE, UNIVERSITY OF KENT © SOLO SYNDICATION/ASSOCIATED NEWSPAPERS LTD.

A cartoon from the *Daily Express*, 20 February 1967. The small man is the Prime Minster Harold Wilson.

SOURCE 16

I wanted to design clothes that women could put on first thing in the morning and still feel right at midnight; clothes that go happily to the office and equally happily out to dinner. I just happened to start when that something was in the air, was coming to the boil. The clothes I made happened to fit in exactly with the teenage trend, with pop records and expresso bars and music clubs.

Mary Quant commenting on her clothes.

Mary Quant claimed that her clothes were for girls of all classes, but in reality only the better off could afford them. However, her designs were quickly copied and became available at cheaper, but still very trendy shops in areas like London's Carnaby Street. Whatever the designs, the emphasis was on being young and 'with it'. This included designs which tried to tap into the interest and enthusiasm for space age technology, so models were photographed wearing space age dresses and fabrics. Many of the clothes deliberately contrasted with earlier periods by not emphasising female curves. As with the music, what probably made this even more attractive to young people was that most of the older generation did not understand it.

4 Explain what points the cartoonists are making in Sources 15 and 17. Refer to details form the cartoons to support your answer.

SOURCE 17

NEWS
TEENAGERS
SPEND
£3,000,000
A DAY
ON
THEMSELVES

BRITISH CARTOON ARCHIVE, UNIVERSITY OF KENT © DAILY EXPRESS

A cartoon from the *Daily Mail*, 29 January 1960. One policeman is saying to the other, 'Blimey – and look at the result'!

Activity

Today in the early twenty-first century older people often complain that we are obsessed with celebrity culture. Use the information and sources on pages 488–89 to explain (politely!) to one of these older people that being obsessed with celebrities is nothing new. You could record your thoughts as a podcast or video diary or create a presentation.

Rebellion

One theme which has come up several times already in this section is that the youth culture of the 1960s was about being different from your parents' generation. Teenagers had always felt this way, but the difference in the 1960s was that they now had the time, the money and the confidence to express this desire to be different and to rebel a bit.

Traditional figures of authority were questioned. John Lennon got himself into very controversial territory when he said in 1966 that the Beatles were now 'bigger than Jesus'. He did not mean to offend people but he had a point that the influence of some traditional institutions such as the church were declining. However young people were not alone in this. In society as a whole there was a decline in deference. Satirical TV programmes like *That Was The Week That Was* (1962) and magazines like *Private Eye* (also 1962) openly made fun of respectable authority figures. This meant that people were less inclined to see leading figures like politicians or the upper classes as better than themselves.

Films aimed at teenagers challenged traditional views about what was meant by good behaviour. In 1961, for example, *West Side Story* presented an image of cool teenage gangs and a doomed love affair between a girl and a boy from different communities. The film mocked authority figures like the police and social workers and gang loyalty was at the heart of the film. The story was in fact a modern version of the Shakespeare play *Romeo and Juliet* but it sums up the 1960s in which something apparently traditional like Shakespeare was turned into something cool and a bit 'edgy'.

Sex

One form of rebellion which worried most parents were teenager's attitudes to sex. The 1960s is widely seen as a period of sexual revolution. By the 1960s teenagers were bigger and healthier than they had ever been in the twentieth century. As a result they became sexually mature at an earlier age. It was also the period in which the contraceptive pill became available. Improving antibiotics also meant that common sexually-transmitted diseases could be cured relatively easily. At a time when the newspapers and other media were eager to cover the exploits of pop stars and other celebrities it was easy to imagine that all young people were sex mad and outrageously promiscuous.

British films like *Alfie* (1966) showed a promiscuous but likable young man moving from affair to affair with total disregard for the consequences – until an illegal abortion leads him to a breakdown. In the end he asks: 'What's it all about?' This film was enormously successful but very controversial at the time for the way it portrayed the values of the 1960s.

SOURCE 18

It is not only American comics which should be banned but also many other false practices which have been imported into this country. The sooner we return to a sane British way of life based on traditional lines the better for our great nation. We should act now, before the moral values of our young people have become perverted by this degraded and degrading substitute for healthy enjoyment.

An extract from *Picture Post* magazine commenting on American comic books.

SOURCE 19

A poster for the 1966 film *Alfie*, starring Michael Caine.

But were the 60s really sex mad? Sources 20–25 allow you to investigate.

The contraceptive pill was not available on the NHS until 1969. Family Planning Clinics only gave contraception to married women until 1970. It was given to unmarried women at Brooks Clinics from 1964 but by 1966 there were only four of these clinics in the whole country. Other evidence also challenges the traditional view of the sex mad 1960s. In 1965 a researcher called Michael Schofield published a book called *The Sexual Behaviour of Young People* based on interviews with 2,000 teenagers. In 1971 another researcher called Geoffrey Gorer studied a similar number of people aged 16 to 45. Sources 23–24 summarise their findings.

1 What criticisms are made in Source 18 about American influences? Do you think that a) teenagers or b) their parents would agree with these points?

2 Is it possible that Source 18 is exaggerating the impact and potential danger of American comics? Explain your answer.

Source Investigation

Were the Sixties sex-mad?

1 What point is being made in Source 20?
2 Does the tone and language used in Sources 21 and 22 make you think they are reliable sources?
3 How is the tone and content of Sources 21 and 25 different from Sources 23 and 24?
4 Source 25 shows one historian disagreeing with the views of another writer. Which do you find more convincing?
5 Do these sources convince you that there was a sexual revolution in the 1960s?

SOURCE 20

A cartoon from the *Sunday Express*, 8 March 1964.

SOURCE 21

A Worker at a Butlin's holiday camp: I became sickened; the sex was so totally available.

B An actor in his early 20s: The chicks are so cool about sex. At a party you can come up to a girl and say within a couple of minutes of meeting her 'How about coming back to my place?' There'll be no messing about. If she likes you she says 'Sure, let's go'.

Comments on the 1960s sexual revolution.

SOURCE 22

Teenagers in the sixties were the first generation since the war to decide that the mysteries of sex should be explored and discoveries made for the sheer fun of it. People had sex at the slightest excuse after meeting for only ten minutes. Sexual partners were snapped up and discarded without ceremony, provided that they had the newly available contraceptive pill in their pocket or handbag.

An extract from *The Swinging Sixties* by Brian Masters, published in 1985. Masters is a journalist and writer.

SOURCE 23

Most teenagers were still virgins at nineteen. Only one in three boys and one in six girls between seventeen and nineteen had ever had sex. When contrasted with the recurring outcry about teenage immorality, these figures seem low. For younger teenagers, sexual experience was very rare: only 6 per cent of the fifteen-year-old boys and 2 per cent of fifteen-year-old girls had had sex. In almost all cases the first experience of sex had been with a regular boyfriend or girlfriend: this was not random promiscuity, but sex with a steady partner. These results suggest that promiscuity, although it exists, is not a prominent feature of teenage sexual behaviour.

An extract from *The Sexual Behaviour of Young People* by Michael Schofield, published in 1965. It was based on a survey of 2,000 young people.

SOURCE 24

Among the married interviewees, one in four men and two in three women had been virgins on their wedding day, figures that were not radically different from those for earlier periods. The importance of virginity to both sexes was 'remarkably high', but attitudes to pre-marital experience have relaxed since 1950 ... Half the men thought that it was reasonable for women to be sexually experienced but only a third of the female interviewees agreed.

An extract from *Sex and Marriage in England Today* by Geoffrey Gorer based on a survey of 2,000 people aged 16–45 carried out in 1969.

SOURCE 25

Masters says that by the end of the sixties 'people had had sex at the slightest excuse after meeting for only ten minutes'. This seems rather unlikely given what studies said about their behaviour just a few years before ... If wild and abandoned sexual relations suddenly became the norm, why did marriage reach such unprecedented levels of popularity during the sixties?

An extract from *White Heat: A History of Britain in the Swinging Sixties* by historian Dominic Sandbrook, published 2006. Sandbrook is a historian at Oxford University.

Teenage violence

For most teenagers the rebellion was pretty tame – listening to music, or watching films their parents didn't like and maybe staying out a bit longer than they should have. For a few, however, rebellion went further than that and turned to street violence.

Probably the best example of this came in 1964 when there was a series of violent clashes between two rival youth groups, mods and rockers, in a number of seaside towns. Most of these mods and rockers were working-class youth groups. Mods were originally more middle-class, dressing smartly and listening to modern jazz. By 1964 mods had become largely working-class. They kept the smart clothing but they preferred listening to rhythm and blues music. They saw themselves as sophisticated and continental and took great pride in their appearance and also their preferred form of transport, the scooter. By contrast, rockers preferred big motorbikes, leather jackets and a more aggressive appearance.

SOURCE 26

Police separate mods (on the left) and rockers in the seaside town of Margate, May 1964.

1 Write a caption for Source 26 to go on the front page of a national newspaper in 1964.

SOURCE 27

A The Wild Ones invaded a seaside town [Clacton] yesterday – 1,000 fighting, drinking, roaring, rampaging teenagers on scooters and motorcycles … Leather jacketed youths and girls attacked people in the streets, turned over parked cars, broke into beach huts, smashed windows and fought with rival gangs …

B There was Dad asleep in the deckchair and Mum making sandcastles with the children when the 1964 boys took over the beaches at Margate and Brighton yesterday and smeared the traditional postcard scene with blood and violence.

Newspaper headlines, **A** from the *Daily Mirror*, 30 March 1964. In these events there were 97 arrests and about £500 damage caused. **B** is from the *Daily Express*, 19 May 1964. In Brighton there were 76 arrests and £400 damage. In Margate there were 64 arrests and £250 damage.

The newspapers yelled out hysterical headlines in reaction to these clashes. You can see some reports in Source 27 but these were not unusual. Other newspapers described the teenagers as 'marauding Vikings', or 'odious louts' or 'grubby hordes of louts and sluts'. One Margate magistrate described them as 'petty hoodlums' and 'a vicious virus' before sentencing one defendant to three months in prison. The newspapers followed up the story by interviewing the families of some of the youths who had been arrested and found that they were from very respectable families. Parents were mystified by their children's behaviour, except to wonder whether they should have been more strict. Despite the hysteria, recent research suggests that this was all exaggerated (see Source 28). Many of the arrests were for trivial offences, including stealing an ice cream. Youths who were there claimed that there was very little violence and generally a lot more chasing around and being chased.

Activity

Study the reporting of the mod-rocker clashes of 1964. Now think about some recent reporting of youth violence which you may have heard. Has the quality of reporting improved today?

SOURCE 28

In fact most of the reports of violence were wildly exaggerated. Most of the teenagers at Clacton had come not to fight but to hang around, vaguely hoping that they might meet some girls, and they were bored and aimless rather than crazed with bloodlust. Innocent families had not been trampled underfoot on the beaches: the weather was so cold and wet the teenagers had the beach to themselves. There was no evidence of drink or drugs or gang warfare.

An extract from *White Heat: A History of Britain in the Swinging Sixties* by historian Dominic Sandbrook, published 2006.

Focus Task

Why were there changes in the lives of teenagers in the 1960s?

As you have been studying the changes over the past eight pages there have been some recurring factors for change. This diagram summarises them. Make your own copy of this diagram. A very simple one will do with just the titles.

1 Add examples to each point of how this factor affected young people in the 1950s or 1960s.
2 Draw the lines connecting each point to the central question according to how important you think each factor is. A thicker line indicates it is more important.

Television

In the 1950s and 1960s TV moved from nowhere to the number one form of entertainment and the most important the way of communicating ideas. As you saw from page 487, TV spread ideas about style and culture that was never possible before.

Welfare state

The teenagers were the first generation to grow up in the era of the Welfare State and the NHS. Most teenagers were healthier than any generation which had gone before them. They were also better educated and this affected the way they saw the world. There is more on this on the next page.

American influence

This was particularly true of the media industries that were so important in defining youth culture. American films, American comics and American television were very influential.

Affluence

The figures on page 448 show how well the British economy was performing. There was no shortage of jobs. When people today are interviewed about their memories of the 1960s one of the most common points they make is how easy it was to get a job. Even if you walked out of one job you could easily get another one.

Why *did* life for teenagers change during the 1960s?

Consumerism

Previous generations in Britain had grown up with little money and fearful of poverty. This was the first generation that devoted itself so entirely to large-scale consumerism. Business people saw this and built large businesses around selling goods to young consumers.

Attitudes

Society generally was becoming more liberal and this was shown in new laws. A new Obscene Publications Act in 1959 meant that books with sexual content such as Lady Chatterley's Lover could be published without prosecution. The death penalty for murder was abolished in 1957.

Education

Another factor which brought about tremendous change for many teenagers was education. Government spending on education increased throughout the 1950s and 1960s and it was a high priority to prepare young British people for the new world of technology which was emerging. By the 1960s however, the existing education system was facing intense criticism and big changes were made.

Problems with schools

In the 1950s most areas of Britain had grammar schools and secondary modern schools. Grammar school pupils generally went on to university while secondary modern school pupils left at fourteen or fifteen to find work. To get into a grammar school you had to pass the 11+ test.

The aim of the grammar schools was to open up opportunities to the brightest children whatever their social background. There is no doubt that this worked for many children from poor backgrounds. However, it also failed many others. By the 1960s critics, especially left-wing critics in the Labour Party, claimed that the grammar schools were full of middle class children because their parents had the money and the determination to buy private coaching for their children to pass the test. This in turn reinforced class divides. Almost no students who went to a secondary modern school went on to university and so went into relatively low-paid jobs. By contrast almost all grammar school pupils went on to university and went on to better paid jobs in business, the civil service or areas such as teaching or medicine. The grammar schools were also better funded and usually had more qualified teachers. The journalist Peter Laurie commented in 1965 that 'to have been consigned to the secondary modern is to have failed disastrously and very early in life'. Even when working-class children did make it to grammar school many of them found the environment very strange. Many children from that time now describe how they felt grammar school forced them to choose between their own background and the new middle-class society which they were entering.

It was not just left-wing critics and educationalists who had concerns about the existing system. Many middle-class parents were also concerned that their children might fail the 11+.

The solution: Comprehensive schools

In response to this pressure the Education Minister Anthony Crosland issued a document called 10/65 in July 1965 which effectively told local authorities around the country to draw up plans to abolish grammar and secondary modern schools and educate all students together in comprehensive schools. There was a lot of resistance, both from local authorities and from some in the Conservative Party, but by 1970 there were 1,145 comprehensive schools and they were educating one in three school pupils. By the end of the 1970s the vast majority of students were educated in comprehensive schools. One key aim of comprehensives was to get children from different social groups to mix. The comprehensives had mixed success in this respect and the long-term impact of comprehensives is still an issue which historians and educationalists debate. However, there is no doubt that the policy also expanded the number of young people who stayed on longer in education.

SOURCE 29

My old friends dwindled away, until my band of friends only included those from this school and from the church I attended. Problems did not come from my friendships, but from within the family. Quarrels with my parents usually arise from the fact that other children are earning their living at my age – why can't I be more thoughtful. Usually the replies are – you sent me to grammar school and I can't help you a lot because of my homework . . . Grammar school taught me to read widely, yet at the expense of my parents. I thought an evening could not be spent in a pleasanter way than doing my homework and then reading – and not joining in conversation.

Memories of a working-class girl from Huddersfield who went to a grammar school.

1 What does Source 29 reveal about the grammar school system?
2 Was this the main reason why grammar schools were coming under attack in the 1960s?

SOURCE 30

A cartoon from the *Daily Telegraph*, 16 March 1966. The figures on the left are the Labour Party leaders. Those on the right are the leading Conservatives.

3 What is Source 30 trying to say about Labour and its plans for comprehensive schools?
4 Would the Labour leaders be pleased by a cartoon like this?

SOURCE 31

A cartoon from the *Daily Telegraph*, 23 March 1968. The caption read, 'The Labour party has proposed ... the introduction of votes at 18, to add a political dimension to the increasingly important economic and social position of young people. (Labour Manifesto)'

SOURCE 32

Art colleges were therefore perceived as centres of imagination and cultural exchange; the typical art student in the early sixties was thought to be a serious-minded young man in a black polo-neck or duffel coat, perhaps carrying a pile of books or jazz records or CND flyers under his arm, no doubt on his way to the nearest coffee bar for an espresso and a look at some Sartre. In Iris Murdoch's novel The M/ (1958), Dora, the central character, is a typical lower–middle-class art student who spends her meagre pocket money on 'big multi-coloured skirts and jazz records and sandals'. It was in the art schools that relatively uncommercial kinds of music, like modernist jazz or, initially, rhythm and blues, first took hold, and the general ease of art-school life meant that there was plenty of time for aspiring musicians to form and rehearse bands of their own. Indeed, since so many pop musicians, designers and artists of the mid-sixties studied at art colleges, their importance in the youth culture of the sixties can hardly be over-stated.

An extract from *White Heat: A History of Britain in the Swinging Sixties* by Dominic Sandbrook, a historian at Oxford University.

Focus Task

Using these two pages go back to your diagram from page 493 and add extra notes about education.

Problems with universities

An observer of education in the 1960s would probably have concentrated on the incredibly rapid expansion of further and higher education in the 1960s in terms of its impact on young people. In 1939 only 50,000 people studied beyond school. However, just as comprehensive schools attempted to break with Britain's traditional class system, so the 1960s saw an attempt to break with the past in university education. In 1963 the Labour supporting newspaper the Daily Mirror asked 'Where are all the young men going?' in one of its headlines, and went on to claim that 'Young talent has been and is being wasted and frustrated. Brainpower is vital to Britain's future and it is being wasted.'

The solution: New universities and polytechnics

Both Labour and Conservative parties believed in a new, well-educated, democratic Britain, which meant creating a lot more universities and colleges.

- The Conservative governments of the 1950s started the process with **new universities** in Southampton, Staffordshire and Nottingham. During the 1960s the government built eleven more.
- In addition to the universities, the government also introduced 32 new higher education institutions called **polytechnics**. These were supposed to encourage students who wanted to study applied science and technology, essentially a more vocational approach to higher education.
- A third element in the expansion of higher education was the **art colleges**. During the 1960s there were more art colleges per head of population in Britain than in any other country. They tended to attract students from poorer middle-class and working-class backgrounds. These colleges played a major role in introducing a new generation of young people to higher education whose parents almost certainly would not have studied beyond school.
- The final ingredient was **the grant**. To persuade people from poorer backgrounds who could otherwise be working to go to university you had to make it free. So tuition fees were paid by the government. And if you were poor you could also get a grant (it did not need paying back) to cover your living expenses.

The results of this expansion were remarkable. Between 1961 and 1969 the number of young people who were continuing education after school nearly doubled from 200,000 to 390,000.

SOURCE 33

. . . I was a student in London from 1965 to 1968 and received a Local Education Authority grant. I drew out about £7 10s 0d (£7.50) a week from my bank account. I didn't have a current account just a deposit account. My digs (student accommodation with a family) were shared with another student. The digs cost 5 guineas a week (£5–5–0) or £5.25 for which we got bed and breakfast, evening meal and lunch on Saturdays and Sundays. Like most landladies, they only took us in to help pay their mortgage. Rents were always in guineas (£1–1–0d) – £1.05 in modern terms. Meals in the student canteen were 1s–6d (7.5p) for beans and chips, egg and chips, etc. A three-course lunch at the Chinese in Mile End Road was 5 shillings or 25p. Beer was 1s 8d a pint for bitter (about 8 or 9p). I think petrol was about 5s (25p) a gallon. I got a postgrad grant of £512 per year (at least grants existed then for students) . . .

An extract from the BBC's website in which people post up memories of their own lives.

This new generation of young people in higher education had a remarkable and long-lasting impact. Their studies opened their eyes to ideas and insights they had not come across in schools. This extra level of education exposed thousands of young people to new ideas and to new books, films, plays, that they would not have discovered otherwise. They even came across entire new subjects like Sociology, Psychology or Politics, which forced them to think about the world around them and often made them want to change it (see Source 37 and pages 498–99). Even well established subjects like History began to change. The new universities opened up job opportunities for younger lecturers who were interested in new types of History such as the history of women, or slavery, or just ordinary people rather than monarchs and prime ministers. Many of the writers, artists, musicians, politicians and even comedians who went on to challenge the way society worked actually gained their education in the universities of the 1960s. The universities did not just create challenge and protest, but also enormous creativity. As Source 34 shows, the art colleges played a key role in the 1960s youth revolution.

Opting out

A gathering of hippies in a London park in 1968.

During the 1960s young people expressed their views in different ways. One way was to 'opt out' of society. These teenagers and young people were often known as hippies. The hippy movement originated on the west coast of the USA, particularly in San Francisco. Their culture focused on peace and free love and was often associated with the use of drugs, particularly cannabis and LSD. Hippy culture certainly affected the music of the later 1960s. The Beatles produced psychedelic music such as *Lucy in the Sky with Diamonds* and the surreal animated film *Yellow Submarine*. Procul Harum's single *A Whiter Shade of Pale* reminded listeners of a trip on LSD and a new band called Pink Floyd built up a following which would last for many years. The American singer Bob Dylan wrote angry songs which criticised the world which his parents' generation had created. In his famous song *The Times They Are A-Changin'* Dylan said that 'Your sons and your daughters are beyond your command'. The hippies talked of flower power, and carried flowers to show their peaceful beliefs and also that they felt society should be closer to nature. Many of their views were reflected in the hippy underground magazine *Oz* which was originally set up in Australia but moved to the UK in 1966. The movement came to real prominence in 1967 with what became known as the summer of love. In August 1967 around 50,000 young hippies gathered for a three day 'love in'. There was a national petition to legalise cannabis which was signed by The Beatles and some of the Rolling Stones. In 1968 there was a large rally in Hyde Park in London calling for cannabis to be legalised.

As with other areas of youth culture, we need to put this movement into perspective. The great majority of hippies did not really opt out of society. There were a few dozen hippy communes in the whole country. Most hippies had full-time jobs and returned to work in offices, shops and factories after spending the weekend at events like the one in Source 34.

Student protests in the 1960s

Many of the young people who were attracted to the flower power movement also supported the peace movement. The movement itself was not really a single, organised movement. Its origins lay back in the 1950s with the Campaign for Nuclear Disarmament. By the early 1960s many teenagers had joined this movement, especially after the Cuban Missile Crisis of 1962 (see Chapter 5). In 1963 a student organisation called Spies for Peace decided that direct action was needed to influence the government on this issue. They broke into a government bunker and copied top secret documents.

Students also became involved in other protest campaigns. You have seen that some campaigned to legalise cannabis. On many university campuses there were demonstrations against what students saw as old-fashioned and irrelevant university courses. One of the first came at the London School of Economics in 1967. In January 1967 there were demonstrations against the appointment of a new director of the LSE (Walter Adams) because he had worked in Rhodesia (which became Zimbabwe) and was seen by students as a supporter of white rule there. There were other protests and sit-ins throughout 1967 including ones at Essex and Leicester Universities. In May 1968 students at Hull occupied the administrative offices of the university complaining that their examinations were a 'crude qualification which led to money and militarism and poverty'. There were more protests throughout 1968, including a sit-in at Hornsey College of Art in which the students demanded an end to traditional styles of teaching and assessment and the introduction of individual or group research projects. Trouble returned to the LSE in 1969. The director closed the LSE down in response to violent demonstrations and several junior lecturers who supported the students were sacked.

The national press got very excited about the student protests and there were headlines expressing concern at the wave of radicalism in British universities. As so often in the 1960s, however, the press were a long way wide of the mark. Overall, the student demonstrations of the period were very small scale compared to what was happening in the USA and France at the same time. The great majority of students were not involved or even interested. A poll of Leeds university students in 1968 found that 86 per cent of them found student politics boring. A nationwide poll in 1969 found that 80 per cent of students were very happy with their conditions and treatment. The most high profile demonstrations were seen in the later 1960s, particularly in 1968. In Northern Ireland, young people led the protests against the discrimination which many Catholics faced in jobs and housing. These protesters were inspired by the African American campaigns for civil rights led by Martin Luther King in the USA.

SOURCE 35

The 60s is always portrayed mistakenly as the decade of hedonism when, in truth, it was much more the decade of commitment. Forget the free love, the way-out clothes, the hair. They were the superficial externals played up by the media. The strength of the younger generation, the 20-somethings, was that they took on every problem from apartheid to xenophobia and tried to batter through a solution to all of them.

The methods were sometimes ineffective, the results were often inconclusive and yet this generation changed many things forever. Human rights did not exist as a concept before this generation got going with Amnesty International. Nobody questioned the righteousness of any war before this generation sickened everyone with the body bags and the coffins returning from Vietnam. Nobody gave women equal billing or consideration before the Women's Movement got going. Blacks, immigrants, gays and all the others on the margins of society, whatever little ground they may have gained today, they started with the support and help of the younger generation of the 60s.

A comment from a British person now living in Argentina.

The biggest uniting factor for the peace movement was the Vietnam War. The scale of the destruction and the use of chemical weapons by the USA in this war inspired protests from young people and many older political activists as well.

SOURCE 36

Anti-Vietnam War demonstration in London, March 1968.

John Lennon wrote his famous song 'Give Peace a Chance' (1969) as a protest against war in general and the Vietnam War in particular. Many young people were also heavily influenced by left-wing politics and belonged to Socialist or Communist organisations. They were opposed to almost any action by the USA and the security forces thought that many of them were agents of the USSR. With hindsight this was probably part of the general paranoia of the Cold War. Most were simply appalled by what they saw of the Vietnam War and joined the demonstrations outside the American embassy. The first was in March 1968 when 25,000 protesters assembled. Fighting broke out with the police. There were some nasty injuries but it was small scale compared to what was happening in the USA. The next demonstration was in October. This time there were 30,000 demonstrators but they were divided amongst themselves and split into two factions. Around 25,000 marched to Hyde Park for a rally while about 5,000 marched on the American embassy in Grosvenor Square. There were some clashes here but the police were firmly in control. From that point on the movement rapidly ran out of steam, suggesting that the majority of students were not committed political revolutionaries after all.

Focus Task

How did teenagers and students behave in the 1960s and early 1970s?

You have been asked to draw up plans for a new website where people who lived through the 1960s and early 70s can share their memories of what they did and how they lived. You have three big decisions:

1 Whether to have separate areas for university students and others. Were their experiences so different from each other that they need separate forums?
2 Whether to include sections on music, fashion, sex, drugs, violence, protest. You will need to decide how important each of these categories is to life at the time.
3 What other categories you are going to include so that it is a full representation of the different experiences of teenagers and students. You might want to consider some things that we have not even covered in this book. You might also want to come back to this task after you studied the sources on the following page.

Finally:
4 Think about how you are going to get people to contribute their memories. What kind of questions will you ask them? For example, which of these questions will produce the more interesting and useful answers:
   ◆ What bands did you like and why did you like them? Or
   ◆ When you went to a concert what did you do? How did you behave?
You could consult with some people who lived through the 60s and early 70s to help you make your decisions.

Focus Task

How far did the lives of all teenagers change in the 1960s and early 1970s?

It is easy to see why there was talk of a revolution going on in the 1960s. There was undoubtedly a great deal of change taking place. But how significant were the developments of the 1960s? Did they affect most people? Were working-class teenagers involved as well as middle-class ones? The focus of the press and the media tended to be on what was happening to a relatively small number of young people in London and some of the other big cities. Did that reflect the wider picture?

Stage 1

On these two pages are a range of comments on the 1960s.

1 Sort the sources onto a continuum like this.

Lots of change ⟵――――――――――――――⟶ Little change

2 Take the two sources at the extremes of your scale and consider
   a) how useful and
   b) how reliable each one is for telling you about the life of teenagers.
3 Now do the same for the next two sources in.
4 Taking all the sources, which two do you think are
   a) most useful
   b) most reliable for this topic?
   Explain your answer with reference to the content of the source and your own background knowledge.

Stage 2

'In the 1960s there was a Youth Revolution in Britain.' Explain how far you agree or disagree with this statement. Refer to Sources 37–45 in your answer.

SOURCE 37

Front cover of *Time* magazine, April 1966. *Time* was the leading weekly news magazine in the USA, but was mostly read by well-educated people. It was also sold in the UK.

SOURCE 38

This surely was the decade of the greatest contrasts. It began as an extension of what I remember as the austere 50s and ended totally transformed – the so-called 'permissive society' had arrived. It was a good decade in which to become a teenager, as I did. No longer were we girls required to dress as copies of our mothers, but could develop as individuals, able to think for ourselves, dress how we liked and do as we pleased (well, within reason anyway). 'My Generation', as epitomised by The Who, seemed to have it all to look forward to. We have mellowed now, of course, most of us, but I look back on the 60s as a defining decade, a time where everything seemed new, fresh and possible. Hindsight and maturity may cast a different light on it all now, but how privileged we felt to be part of the Swinging Sixties – Carnaby Street, mini-skirts and, not least, the summer of love!

A comment from a person who grew up in Cheshire during the 1960s.

SOURCE 39

The great majority of young people spent more time in their bedrooms or in church youth clubs than they did at rock festivals or on the football terraces.

An extract from *The Rise of Consumer Society in Britain c 1880–1980* by Professor John Benson, published in 1994.

SOURCE 40

It took six months or more for anything fashionable to reach the North-East. London was well into minis, it was splashed everywhere that this revolution in dress had taken place, before any of it reached us . . . It was a long time before minis made it up North. In fact, I think it was about 1966 or 1967 before they reached our village. They may have worn them in Newcastle before that, but not in Sunderland. I don't think the Pill had even reached our village by the mid-sixties. I'd never even heard of a condom.

A Sunderland woman interviewed in 1991.

SOURCE 41

I left school as a real wimp in June 1962 and from October 1962 lived away from home in Liverpool where I was an undergraduate at the university. What perfect timing! My whole world changed. About six weeks after arriving in Liverpool, wet behind the ears, I was at the Silver Blades ice rink and heard 'Love Me Do' playing over the PA. I knew immediately this was very, very different. The rest of the decade was a complete revolution: Profumo scandal, Beatles, Stones, 'different cigarettes', mini-skirts, sex, Vietnam, King's Road, Carnaby Street, and . . . did I say 'mini-skirts'?

A comment from a British person now living in the USA on life in the 1960s.

SOURCE 42

A series of polls in 1969 showed that young and old had strikingly similar hopes for the 1970s: keeping prices and unemployment low, getting the economy sound and improving children's education. This sits uneasily with the notion that young people were a revolutionary vanguard, that their views and values clashed with those of their parents, or that they were always the first to embrace change.

An extract from *White Heat: A History of Britain in the Swinging Sixties* by historian Dominic Sandbrook, published 2006.

SOURCE 43

A large number of middle class students only played at being rebels. They grew their hair, had their sit ins, experimented with drugs and sex, did precious little work – before settling down to the sort of respectability they had formerly scorned. Perhaps, indeed their 'rebellion' had been no more than conformity with their peers.

An extract from *Contemporary Britain 1914–79* by historian Robert Pearce, published in 1996.

SOURCE 44

The old ways have held their ground. There is a suspicion of the new and strange that runs through working-class culture in West Yorkshire. Brass bands are still as prevalent as ever, with thirty-six of them competing for recruits within a fifteen-mile radius, and continuing to attract new blood. Crown Green bowls is easily the most popular participatory sport in the area.

An extract from *Working Class Community* by researcher Brian Jackson, published in 1968.

SOURCE 45

1   Mum
2   Queen Elizabeth II
3   (Famous sailor) Sir Francis Chichester
4   (Prime Minister) Harold Wilson
5   Dad
6   (US President) Lyndon Johnson
7   The typical young husband
8   Elvis Presley
9   U Thant, Secretary General of the United Nations
10 The Duke of Edinburgh and
=   (footballer) Bobby Charlton

The results of a survey of teenagers commissioned by the *Daily Mail* newspaper in 1967. Teenagers were asked which person they most admired.

Your British Depth Study will be either **Britain 1890–1918** or **Britain 1939–75**.

Whichever option you study the questions will be very similar.

- There will be up to eight sources, some pictures and some written.
- They could be drawn from any part of the depth study but they will all be relevant in some way to a focus point: e.g. 'How effective were the Liberal Reforms?' Or 'What was life like for most women in the 1950s?'
- There are no trick sources designed to catch you out, but there will always be disagreement between the sources.
- The questions take you step-by-step through the sources and are carefully designed to help you find out those disagreements or differences, to explain them and to evaluate them.

There is no choice of questions – you have to answer them all. The questions will be designed to test how well you can use historical sources but you will also need to use your historical knowledge as well.

Paper 2 Question types

Type 1   Analysing the message or purpose of a source. For example:
  - What is the message of the cartoon in Source A?
  - Why did the Liberal government publish this poster in 1911?
  - Are you surprised this photograph was published in 1968?

Type 2   Comparing the reliability of two sources. For example:
  - Do you trust Source E more than Source F about the leadership of the WSPU?
  - Does Source C or D give a more accurate view of the reception given to immigrants?

Type 3   Considering the usefulness of sources. For example:
  - How useful is the poster in Source D for finding out about living and working conditions?
  - Is Source A more useful than Source D to historians studying the attitude of women to the suffragettes?

Type 4   The big conclusion question. For example:
  - 'Civilians in Britain suffered during the First World War.' How far do the sources support this statement?
  - 'The British welcomed immigrants in the 1950s and 1960s.' How far do the sources support this statement?
  - 'The suffragettes did more harm than good to the campaign for votes for women.' How far do the sources support this statement?

Ten Tips for Paper 2:

1 **Read through all** the **sources** before you start writing anything.

2 Always **refer to the stated source** when you answer a question.

3 Always **support your answers from the sources**. For written sources use actual words or phrases from the source to support your answer. For visual sources describe relevant features from the source.

4 **Use your background knowledge** whenever it's helpful particularly to:
  - work out if a source is reliable (does it fit what you know about events of the time)
  - explain the purpose of the source (you may know the author or the organisation it comes from).

5 However, **don't include background knowledge just for its own sake** if it's got nothing to do with the source or the question.

6 When you use your own knowledge avoid saying 'my knowledge tells me . . .' Just **state what you know**.

7 **Avoid speculation** – so avoid using words like 'might' and 'could' (such as, 'The author might be a supporter so he could be biased . . .').

8 **Avoid phrases such** as 'we don't know what else . . .' or 'she could have forgotten . . .'. Examiners call this 'stock evaluation' because it could be applied to any source. You will not get any credit for this type of answer.

9 **Cross-referencing is essential** but candidates often fail to do this well. Many candidates could score higher if they cross-referred to other sources to show how they support or contradict the source they are being asked to evaluate.

10 **Don't include your own personal views which are not historical** (such as, 'I think it was awful the way immigrants were treated . . .').

For Type 1

You have already come across these question types on pages 207 and 386. These are marked in the same way.

Many candidates waste time and lose marks describing the source before they actually get to describing the point. So get into the habit of starting your answers with:

'The message of the cartoon is . . . 'The purpose of this cartoon was to . . .'.

For Type 2

In considering reliability the key word is 'trust'. To decide if you trust a source:

- Start with the **authorship** – does that help you to make a decision about reliability? But don't stop there. Go on to . . .
- Look at the **content** of the source. Is there any emotive language or a biased tone?
- Consider whether the source fits with or contradicts your own **knowledge**.
- **Cross-refer**: do any other sources in the paper support or contradict the source? Just because you are comparing two does not mean you can't use the other sources to help you evaluate those two.
- You might conclude sources are **equally trustworthy** or untrustworthy.

For Type 3

Usefulness questions are connected to reliability.

- In a usefulness question the really important part of the question is **'useful for what'**.
- Even if a source is not reliable that does not mean it is not useful. A totally unreliable source can be very useful – it all depends on what you want to use it for. In the first example question the historian is looking for accurate information so an unreliable source would not be very useful. In the second example question the historian is interested in attitudes so **an unreliable source might be very useful** because it will show something about attitudes.

For Type 4

- **Address both sides** of the statement – the yes/no or agree/disagree sides.
- **Use two paragraphs one for each side of the argument**. Start each paragraph clearly.
- **Don't work through source by source**. Group the yes/agree sources together and explain how they support the statement. Then group the no/disagree sources together and explain how they oppose the statement.
- **Refer to at least two sources on each side** and more if you have enough time.
- When you refer to a source – don't only refer to it by letter – **refer to it by content** – and how that content supports or challenges the statement.
- Show awareness that some sources might be **more reliable** than others.
- Add a final paragraph. This is not a time to repeat everything you have just said. **Use your conclusion to say how far you agree** with the statement. One really useful phrase is 'On balance . . .'. The final paragraph can be a good place to make points about reliability as well. That might swing your opinion on the statement one way or the other.

You choose the sources, you set the questions!

It is always a good idea to practice on the types of questions you might meet in the examination. It can sometimes be even more useful to set the question yourself, so you can get into the mind of an examiner. One very effective form of exam preparation is to work with a partner and set questions for each other. For example:

1 Set each other a 'type 1' question (**analysing the message or purpose** of a source).
   - If you are tackling the British Depth Study 1890–1918 one of you could select Source 18 on page 411 and decide whether you think it should have a 'purpose' or a 'message' question. Then set it for your partner and mark his/her response.
   - If you are doing the British Depth Study 1939–75 then you could use Source 22 from page 459.
   - Once you have looked at these examples, look through the relevant chapter and set questions on some other cartoons and posters you find there. What do you think — purpose or message questions? You could even use a rating system for the difficulty of the source.

2 After that you could do the same for 'type 2' questions — **comparing reliability**. With these questions you might even want to edit the source a little. For example, Source 31 on page 461 is rather long. Could you select an extract from it which could be compared with another source?

3 By this stage you should have got the idea, and you can set some 'type 3' questions — **considering the usefulness of a source**. If you are tackling the British Depth Study 1890–1918 then perhaps you could use Sources 27 and 28 on page 429 to compare usefulness. Or if you were studying the British Depth Study 1939–75 you could use Source 8 on page 486.

Now you are the examiner!

Acknowledgements

The text acknowledgements are on page ii.

Photo Credits

p.1 The Art Archive/Imperial War Museum; **p.2** © Hulton Archive/Getty Images; **p.3** *t&l* © Q 29295 & Q 80141 Imperial War Museum, London; **p.4** © Hulton Archive/Getty Images; **p.5** *t&b* © Hulton Archive/Getty Images; **p.6** *t&br&bl* © Punch Ltd; **p.10** © Ullstein Bild/Topfoto; **p.11** *l* © Süddeutscher Verlag Bilderdienst, *r* © Punch Ltd; **p.12** © Akg-images; **p.13** © Mary Evans Picture Library; **p.14** © Cartoon by Will Dyson published by *Daily Herald* on 13 May 1919, British Cartoon Archive, University of Kent © Mirrorpix; **p.15** © The British Library. All rights reserved. Daily Herald 30/06/1919; **p.19** © Corbis; **p.20** © Express Newspapers, London; **p.21** *t* © League of Nations Archives, UNOG Library, *b* © Punch Ltd; **p.22** © The British Library. All rights reserved. Star 11/06/1919; **p.23** *t* © *New York Times* 1920 , *b* © Punch Ltd; **p.24** *t* © Topical Press Agency/Hulton Archive/Getty Images; **p.26** *l&r* © United Nations; **p.27** © United Nations; **p.28** © from Newman: Danger Spots in Europe, Right Book Club, 1939; **p.30** © Punch Ltd; **p.31** © From League of Nations: Greek Refugee Settlement, 1926 II 32; **p.32** *l* © Punch Ltd, *r* © Solo Syndication/Associated Newspapers Ltd; **p.36** © Hulton Archive/Getty Images; **p.37** *l* © Solo Syndication/Associated Newspapers Ltd, *r* © Topham Picturepoint; **p.39** *t* © Solo Syndication/Associated Newspapers Ltd, *r* © Express Newspapers, London; **p.40** © Punch Ltd; **p.41** © Solo Syndication/Associated Newspapers Ltd; **p.42** © Bildarchiv Preussischer Kulturbesitz; **p.43** *l&r* © Punch Ltd; **p.45** *t* ©2003 Credit: Topham Picturepoint/Topfoto, *b* © AKG London; **p.48** © Popperfoto/Getty Images; **p.49** © AKG London; **p.50** *l* © Tribune Media Services, Inc. All Rights Reserved. Reprinted with permission, *r* © The Art Archive; **p.51** © Punch Ltd; **p.52** © Topham Picturepoint/TopFoto; **p.53** *l* © Punch Ltd; **p.55** *t&br* © Solo Syndication/Associated Newspapers Ltd, *bl* © Punch Ltd; **p.57** *t* © Topham Picturepoint/TopFoto, *l* © Popperfoto/Getty Images; **p.58** *t* © Gabriel, *b* © News of the World/NI Syndication; **p.59** *t* © Solo Syndication/Associated Newspapers Ltd, *b* © John Frost Historical Newspapers; **p.60** © 2006 Alinari/TopFoto; **p.61** *l* & **p.62** © Solo Syndication/Associated Newspapers Ltd; **p.63** Muzzy Lane; **p.68** *l* © National Archives c1_s2, *r* © Atlantic Syndication; **p.71** © The Art Archive/Imperial War Museum; **p.74** © Associated Press/Topham/TopFoto; **p.75** © Solo Syndication/Associated Newspapers Ltd; **p.77** © Pravda 1947; **p.78** *l* © French School, (20th century)/Private Collection, Archives Charmet/The Bridgeman Art Library; **p.80** *tl* © Hulton Archive/Getty Images, *b* © Solo Syndication/Associated Newspapers Ltd; **p.81** *bl* © UCL School of Slavonic and East European Studies Library, *br* © Solo Syndication/Associated Newspapers Ltd; **p.82** © Keystone/Hulton/Getty Images; **p.83** © Izvestia 1958; **p.84** *t* © Solo Syndication/Associated Newspapers Ltd, *b* © Izvestia 1963; **p.89** *tl* © Hulton Archive/Getty Images, *tr* © Yale Joel/Life Magazine/Time & Life Pictures/Getty Images, *bl* © Corbis, *br* © Bettmann/Corbis; **p.90** *l* © Pravda 1960, *r* © Bettmann/Corbis; **p.92** © Rolls Press/Popperfoto/Getty Images; **p.96** © Cartoon by Vicky [Victor Weisz] published in *Evening Standard*, 24 October 1962, British Cartoon Archive, University of Kent © Solo Syndication/Associated Newspapers Ltd; **p.100** *l* © Larry Burrows//Time Life Pictures/Getty Images, *r* © Bettmann/Corbis; **p.102** © Associated Press/Topham/Topfoto; **p.107** *t* © Topham Picturepoint/Topfoto, *b* © David King; **p.108** *t* © Rolls Press/Popperfoto/Getty Images, *b* © Nguyen Kong (Nick) Ut/Associated Press/PA Photos; **p.109** © Topham Picturepoint/Topfoto; **p.111** © Larry Burrows/Time Magazine/Time & Life Pictures/Getty Images; **p.113** *tl* © Associated Press/Topham/Topfoto, *tr* © Ronald S. Haeberle//Time Life Pictures/Getty Images, *b* © Cartoon by Leslie Gibbard published in *The Guardian* on 2 April 1971, British Cartoon Archive, University of Kent © Leslie Gibbard, with permission; **p.114** *t* © CBS/Getty Images, *m* © CBS Photo Archive/Getty Images, *b* © Topham Picturepoint/Topfoto; **p.116** © The Herbert Block Foundation; **p.117** *t* © Popperfoto/Getty Images, *b* © Cartoon by Garland published in the *Daily Telegraph* on 11 January 1967, British Cartoon Archive, University of Kent © Daily Telegraph; **p.118** *t* © Bettmann/Corbis, *c* © John Olson/Time & Life Pictures/Getty Images, *b* © Bettmann/Corbis; **p.121** *all* © Bill Mauldin, 1962, 1964, 1966, 1967, 1968, 1970, 1971, 1972. Courtesy of the Bill Mauldin Estate LLC; **p.122** *l* © Jules Feiffer, *r* © Bettmann/Corbis; **p.123** © 2005 Bob Englehart, The Hartford Courant, and PoliticalCartoons.com; **p.124** © Solo Syndication/Associated Newspapers Ltd; **p.126** © Pravda 1949; **p.127** © Pravda 1949; **p.128** © Al Fenn/Time Life Pictures/Getty Images; **p.131** *t* © Jack Esten/Picture Post/Getty Images, *b* © Hulton Archive/Getty Images; **p.133** *t* © Topham/AP/Topfoto, *b* © Josef Koudelka/Magnum Photos; **p.134** *t&b* no credit; **p.135** *t* © From: *In the Name of Peace*, 1959; *m&b* © AP/PA Photos; **p.136** *t* © Topham Picturepoint/Topfoto, *bl* © Ullstein Bild/Topfoto, *br* © Popperfoto/Getty Images; **p.137** *t* © Rolls Press/Popperfoto/Getty Images, *b* © Izvestia 1963; **p.140** © Getty Images; **p.142** © Paul Popper/Popperfoto/Getty Images; **p.144** © 2000 Credit:Topham/AP/Topfoto; **p.147** © Popperfoto/Reuters/TopFoto; **p.148** © DIANE-LU HOVASSE/AFP/Getty Images; **p.149** *t* © Atlantic Syndication, *b* © Novosti/Topham/Topfoto; **p.150** *t* © Spencer Platt/Getty Images, *bl* © PA Photos/TopFoto, *br* © Getty Images; **p.155** *l* © Barry Iverson/Time Life Pictures/Getty Images, *r* © Cartoon by Martin Rowson, published in *The Guardian* on 14 August 2003, British Cartoon Archive, The University of Kent © The Guardian; **p.158** © Claude Salhani/Sygma/Corbis; **p. 159** © CNN via Getty Images; **p.160** *l* © Cartoon by Stanley Franklin, published in *The Sun*, 24 June 1985 © News International, *r* © Cartoon by Stanley Franklin, published in *The Sun*, 23 November 1974 © News International; **p. 164** © AFP/Getty Images; **p.165** *b* © Sinn Fein, *t* © Colman Doyle/Camera Press London; **p.167** *t* © Intelligence & Terrorism Information Center Israel, *b* © Bill Rowton, Source: BW NI book page 100 Ref: *Drawing Support: Murals in the NI Conflict*, Beyond the Pale Publications; **p.170** © 2002 PA/Topham/TopFoto; **p.171** © Rolls Press/Popperfoto/Getty Images; **p.173** *t* © Liz Gilbert/Corbis SYGMA, *b* © Yoni Brook/Corbis; **p.174** *t* © Cartoon by Garland published in the *Daily Telegraph* on 1 February 1994, British Cartoon Archive, University of Kent © Daily Telegraph, *b* © Republican News © Cormac; **p.175** © Shirley Berry/Rex Features; **p.176** © ESAIAS BAITEL/AFP/Getty Images; **p.178** *t* © Tyler Hicks/Getty Images, *b* © Robert Nickelsberg/Getty Images; **p.179** *t* © Joseph Giordono – Pool/Getty Images, *b* © Reuters/Corbis; **p.180** © AFP/AFP/Getty Images; **p.181** *t* © Sean Gallup/Getty Images, *c* © AFP/Getty Images, *b* © Ivan Peredruk/Reuters/Corbis; **p.184** *l* © General Photographic Agency/Getty Images, *r* © ALI AL-SAADI/AFP/Getty Images; **p.185** *l* © Getty Images, *r* © PersianEye/Corbis; **p.186** © Fotoreport Federico Gambarini/dpa/Corbis; **p.187** *l* © AFP/Getty Images, *r* © AP Photo/Jassim Mohammed/PA Photos; **p.189** © Robert Nickelsberg/Getty Images; **p.190** *tl* © Oleg Nikishin/Getty Images, *tr* © Syed Zargham/Getty Images, *cl* © David McNew/Getty Images, *cr* © Pascal Le Segretain/Getty Images, *bl* © Salah Malkawi/Getty Images, *br* © Ian Waldie/Getty Images; **p.192** © Cartoon by Peter Brookes, published in *The Times*, 15 July 2003 © News International; **p.193** © Cartoon by Dave Brown published in *The Independent* on 24 January 2003 © The Independent; **p.194** © Reuters/Corbis; **p.195** *tl* © Reuters/Corbis, *tr* © Patrick Robert/Corbis, *b* © Michael Macor/San Francisco Chronicle/Corbis; **p.197** *t* © Ali Jasim/Reuters/Corbis, *b* © AKRAM SALEH/Reuters/Corbis; **p.200** © epa/Corbis; **p.201** © Cartoon by Dave Brown published in *The Independent* on 2 April 2003 © The Independent; **p.202** *t* © 2005 Sandy Huffaker and PoliticalCartoons.com, *b* © 2005 Bob Englehart, The Hartford Courant, and PoliticalCartoons.com; **p.205** & **p.206** Cartoon by Sidney 'George' Strube published in *Daily Express*, 6 September 1939, British Cartoon Archive, University of Kent © Daily Express; **p.207** Hulton Archive/Getty Images; **p.209** © Mary Evans Picture Library; **p.210** © Time Life Pictures/Mansell/Time Life Pictures/Getty Images; **p.216** SP 1661, © Imperial War Museum, London; **p.217** © Henry Guttmann/Hulton Archive/Getty Images; **p.222** © Punch Ltd; **p.225** © Alfred Kubin/Oberösterreichisches Landesmuseum © DACS 2008; **p.226** © CO 000219, Imperial War Museum; **p.227** *t* © Q 003995 Imperial War Museum, *b* © The Art Archive/Imperial War Museum; **p.228** *t* PST 13305 © Imperial War Museum, London, *b* © Credit:Topham Picturepoint/Topfoto; **p.230** *t* Q45286 © Imperial War Museum, London, *bl* © Print Collector/HIP/TopFoto, *br* © EAU 5575 Imperial War Museum, London; **p.231** © Imperial War Museum, London/Bridgeman Art Library, London; **p.232** *l&r* © Mary Evans Picture Library/Illustrated London News; **p.234** *t* © Bill Rolston, Source, *Drawing Support: Murals in the North of Ireland*, Belfast, Beyond the Pale Publications 1992, p.12, *b* © The Liddell Collection, University of Leeds Library; **p.235** *t* © Hulton Archive/Getty Images, *b* © Q1810 Imperial War Museum, London; **p.236** © Q 49250 Imperial War Museum, London; **p.246** © Q 63667 Imperial War Museum, London; **p.249** *t* © Corbis, *c* © Hulton Archive/Getty Images, *b* © Hulton Archive/Getty Images; **p.250** © Ullstein Bild/Topfoto; **p.253** *t* © Hulton Archive/Getty Images, *b* © Hulton Archive/Getty Images; **p.254** *t* © Graphik: Landesarchiv Berlin/N.N., *bl* © Mary Evans Picture Library, *br* © IMAGNO/Austrian Archives/Getty Images; **p.255** © Bildarchiv Preussischer Kulturbesitz; **p.256** *l* © Ullsteinbild/Topfoto, *r* © Punch Ltd; **p.257** *t* © Bettmann/Corbis, *b* © Akg-images; **p.258** © Süddeutscher Verlag Bilderdienst; **p.260** *l* © *The Pillars of Society*, 1926 (oil on canvas), Grosz, George (1893–1959)/Nationalgalerie, Berlin, Germany, © DACS 2008/The Bridgeman Art Library, *r* © 2004 Credit: Topham Picturepoint/TopFoto; **p.261** © AKG London; **p.262** © Ullstein Bild/Topfoto; **p.264** *l* © Bettmann/Corbis, *r* © AKG London; **p.265** © Sueddeutscher Verlag Bilderdienst; **p.267** © David Crausby/Alamy; **p.268** © Süddeutscher Verlag Bilderdienst; **p.269** *tl* © AKG London, *bl* © AKG London; **p.270** © AKG London; **p.272** © Suddeutscher Verlag Bilderdienst; **p.273** © London Solo Syndication/Associated Newspapers Ltd; **p.274** *tl* © Punch Ltd, *bl* © English School, (20th century)/Private Collection, © Look and Learn/The Bridgeman Art Library; *r* © Bundesarchiv Koblenz; **p.276** *t* © Süddeutscher Verlag Bilderdienst, *b* © Keystone/Hulton Archive/Getty Images; **p.277** *t* © Ullstein Bild/Topfoto, *b* © Ullstein Bild/Topfoto; **p.279** © Wiener Library; **p.280** *tl* © Hulton Archive/Getty Images, *bl* © Hulton Archive/Getty Images, *r* © Süddeutscher Verlag Bilderdienst; **p.281** *l* © Heartfield, John: "Olympic guests, quick march!" © The Heartfield Community of Heirs/VG Bild-Kunst,Bonn and DACS, London/Leonard de Selva/Corbis, *r* © 2003 Credit: Topham Picturepoint/TopFoto; **p.282** *l* © Nazi Poster publicising Hitler's radio broadcasts, 1936 (colour litho), German School, (20th century)/Private Collection, Peter Newark Military Pictures/The Bridgeman Art Library, *r* © AKG London; **p.284** *t* © Süddeutscher Verlag Bilderdienst, *b* © Ben Walsh; **p.285** © Süddeutscher Verlag Bilderdienst; **p.286** *tl* © Bildarchiv Preussischer Kulturbesitz, *bl* © Ullstein Bild/TopFoto, *r* © AKG London; **p.287** *l* © Ullstein Bild/Topfoto, *r* © Ullstein Bild/Topfoto; **p.288** *l* © 2002 Feltz/Topham, *r* © Ullstein Bild/Topfoto; **p.291** © Bundesarchiv Koblenz; **p.292** *t* © Hulton Archive/Getty Images, *b* © Ullstein Bild/TopFoto; **p.293** © Popperfoto/Getty Images; **p.294** *l* © Deutsches Historisches Museum, Berlin, *r* © ullsteinbild/TopFoto; **p.296** *t* © Elek International Rights, NY (photo: Wiener Library), *b* © AKG London; **p.298** © 2005 Roger-Viollet/Topfoto; **p.299** © Hulton Archive/Getty Images; **p.300** *l* © 2006 RIA Novosti/TopFoto, *r* © David King; **p.301** *l&r* ©

David King; **p.303** © RIA Novosti/TopFoto; **p.304** *all* © Novosti/TopFoto; **p.305** © David King; **p.307** *t* © RIA Novosti/TopFoto, *b* © Mary Evans Picture Library; **p.312** *t* © Carlo Ponti/MGM/ALBUM/AKG, *b* © RIA Novosti/TopFoto; **p.314** © Detail from The Storming of the Winter Palace, 7 November 1917 (oil on canvas), Russian School, (20th century)/Private Collection, RIA Novosti/The Bridgeman Art Library; **p.315** © Mary Evans Picture Library; **p.316** © Mary Evans Picture Library; **p.319** © The British Library. All rights reserved. BL063554; **p.320** *t* © David King, *b* © RIA Novosti/TopFoto; **p.321** © David King; **p.322** © David King; **p.323** *l* © David King, *r* © Hulton Archive/Getty Images; **p.327** *t* © Mary Evans Picture Library, *b* © Mary Evans Picture Library; **p.330** *t* © Topham Picturepoint/TopFoto, *b* © Stalin at the hydro-electric complex at Ryon in the Caucasus Mountains, 1935, reproduction of the original in 'Soviet Painting', 1939 (colour litho), Toidze, Irakli Moiseievich (1902–p.1941)/Private Collection, Archives Charmet/The Bridgeman Art Library; **p.331** © David King; **p.334** *l* © RIA Novosti/TopFoto; **p.335** *l* © David King; **p.336** © Mary Evans Picture Library; **p.337** *t* © A Collective Farm Festival, 1937 (oil on canvas), Gerasimov, Sergej Vasilevic (1885–1964)/Tretyakov Gallery, Moscow, Russia, © DACS 2008/Alinari/The Bridgeman Art Library, *b* © Ann Ronan Picture Library/HIP/TopFoto/Samokhvalov, Alexander: "Starting Up" © DACS 2008; **p.340** © David King; **p.342** *t* © Courtesy George Eastman House, New York, *bl* © Culver Pictures; **p.343** *tl* © 'Onyx' Silk Hosiery Advert, 1915 (colour litho) by American School, (20th century) Private Collection/Peter Newark American Pictures/The Bridgeman Art Library, *tr* © MPI/Getty Images, *bl* © Bettmann/Corbis, *br* © Sears, Roebuck & Co. goods catalogue, 1927 (colour litho) by Norman Rockwell (1894–1978) Private Collection/Peter Newark American Pictures/The Bridgeman Art Library. Reproduced by courtesy of the Norman Rockwell Family Agency, Inc; **p.346** © Anti-trust cartoon depicting giant corporations as 'the bosses of the Senate', 1889 (colour litho) by American School, (19th century) Private Collection/Peter Newark American Pictures/The Bridgeman Art Library; **p.347** © Bettmann/Corbis; **p.348** © Topfoto; **p.349** © Cartoon of the 1920's depicting the difficult times of the American Farmers (colour litho) by Fitzpatrick, Daniel Robert (1891–1969) Private Collection/Peter Newark American Pictures/The Bridgeman Art Library; **p.350** © Bettmann/Corbis; **p.351** *l* © Bettmann/Corbis, *r* © Topham Picturepoint/Topfoto; **p.352** *t* © The Builder (colour litho) by Beneker, Gerrit Albertus (1882–1934) Private Collection/Peter Newark American Pictures/The Bridgeman Art Library, *b* © King Oliver's Creole Jazz band, 1920 (b/w photo), American Photographer, (20th century)/Private Collection, Peter Newark American Pictures/The Bridgeman Art Library; **p.353** © Chicago History Museum/Chicago Daily News; **p.354** *t&b* © Bettmann/Corbis; **p.355** *t* © Culver Pictures, *b* © Topham Picturepoint/Topfoto; **p.356** © A Finer Screen Needed, cartoon of the US immigration policy printed in the 'Brooklyn Daily Eagle', 1904 (litho), American School, (20th century)/Private Collection, Peter Newark American Pictures/The Bridgeman Art Library; **p.357** © Communist Party of the United States Photographs Collection, Taiment Library, New York University; **p.358** © Bettmann/Corbis; **p.359** © Mary Evans Picture Library; **p.360** *l* © Hulton Archive/Getty Images, *r* © Bettmann/Corbis; **p.361** © Bettmann/Corbis; **p.362** *t* © US National Archives, Rocky Mountains Division, *b* © Famous Players-Lasky Corporation/Ronald Grant Archive; **p.363** © Bettmann/Corbis; **p.364** *l* © 'Wanted...A father, A little boy's plea', c.1915 (engraving), American School, (20th century)/Private Collection, Peter Newark American Pictures/The Bridgeman Art Library, *r* © Culver Pictures; **p.365** *l&r* © Bettmann/Corbis; **p.366** *tl* © Bettmann/Corbis, *tr* © Making Bootleg Liquor (b/w photo) by American Photographer, (20th century) Private Collection/Peter Newark American Pictures/The Bridgeman Art Library, *b* © Library of Congress; **p.367** *t* © Topham Picturepoint/Topfoto, *b* © The Gusenberg Brothers, St Valentine Day's Massacre, front page of 'The Chicago Daily News', 14 February 1929 (newsprint) by American School, (20th century) Private Collection/Peter Newark American Pictures/The Bridgeman Art Library; **p.371** *l* © Charles Deering McCormick Library of Special Collections, Northwestern University Library, © John T. McCutcheon Jr., *r* © Popperfoto/Getty Images; **p.372** *t* © Car and farm machinery buried by dust and sand, Dallas, South Dakota, 1936 (b/w photo) by American Photographer, (20th century) Private Collection/Peter Newark American Pictures/The Bridgeman Art Library, *b* © Cheap food line at Bryant Park, New York, during the Great Depression, 1931 (b/w photo) by American Photographer, (20th century) Private Collection/Peter Newark American Pictures/The Bridgeman Art Library; **p.373** *t* © Topham Picturepoint/Topfoto, *b* © A Migratory Family from Amarillo, Texas, 1940 (b/w photo) by American Photographer, (20th century) Private Collection/Peter Newark American Pictures/The Bridgeman Art Library; **p.374** © 'Smilette', Democrat Election Poster, 1932 (litho) by American School, (20th century) Private Collection/Peter Newark American Pictures/The Bridgeman Art Library; **p.375** © Culver Pictures; **p.377** *br* © Tennessee Valley Authority; **p.378** © Tennessee Valley Authority; **p.379** *t* © Bettmann/Corbis, *c* © Topham Picturepoint/Topfoto, *b* © National Archives and Records Administration, Washington, D.C.; **p.380** © 'What we need is another pump', Cartoon depicting Franklin D. Roosevelt's (1882–1945) 'Pump Priming Deficits', 1933 (colour litho), American School, (20th century)/Private Collection, Peter Newark American Pictures/The Bridgeman Art Library; **p.381** *t* © Weidenfeld & Nicolson Archives, a division of the Orion Publishing Group, London; *bl* © Punch Ltd; **p.383** © 'World's Highest Standard of Living...', 1937 (litho), American School, (20th century)/Private Collection, Peter Newark American Pictures/The Bridgeman Art Library; **p.384** *t&c* © Walter P. Reuther Library, Wayne State University, *b* © Brown Brothers; **p.385** *l* Bildarchiv Preussischer Kulturbesitz, *r* © 2005 Roger-Viollet/Topfoto; **p.389** © Hulton-Deutsch Collection/Corbis; **p.391** *t* © Illustrated London News Ltd/Mary Evans Picture Library, *bl* © Hulton-Deutsch Collection/Corbis, *br* © Rischgitz/Getty Images; **p.392** London School of Economics; **p.394** *all* © Museum of London/HIP/Topfoto; **p.396** © Liverpool Record Office/Engineer's Collection; **p.399** *t&b* © ILN Pictures/Mary Evans Picture Library; **p.400** *tl* © Mary Evans Picture Library, *tr* © By permission of Llyfrgell Genedlaethol Cymru/The National Library of Wales; *br* © Mary Evans Picture Library; **p.401** © Hulton Archive/Getty Images; **p.405** © The British Library. All rights reserved. Votes for Women 13/06/1913; **p.407** © Punch Limited/TopFoto; **p.409** *l* © Punch Ltd; **p.410** *b* © Mary Evans/Fawcett Library; **p.411** *tl* © Topham Picturepoint/Topfoto, *tr* © Mary Evans Picture Library, *b* © Popperfoto/Getty Images; **p.412** © Popperfoto/Getty Images; **p.413** © Mary Evans Picture Library; **p.414** © National Archives; **p.416** *l* © Topical Press Agency/Getty Images, *r* © Museum of London/HIP/TopFoto; **p.417** © National Archives; **p.418** © 'Are You In This', 1st World War poster (colour litho), English School, (20th century)/Private Collection, Barbara Singer/The Bridgeman Art Library; **p.420** *l* © 'Your Country Needs You', First World War Recruitment Poster, with a Portrait of Field Marshall Earl Kitchener (1850–1916) (see also 65836), / © PST 5089 Imperial War Museum, London, UK,/The Bridgeman Art Library, *c* © ullsteinbild/TopFoto, *r* © Imperial War Museum, London; **p.421** *t* © Mary Evans Picture Library/The Women, *b* © Reproduced with the permission of the Library Committee of the Religious Society of Friends; **p.422** © Weidenfeld & Nicolson Archives, a division of the Orion Publishing Group, London; **p.423** *t* © 'The Kitchen Is The Key To Victory, Eat Less Bread', 1st World War poster, c.1917 (colour litho), English School, (20th century)/Private Collection, Barbara Singer/The Bridgeman Art Library, *b* © Q 56278 Imperial War Museum, London; **p.424** © John Frost Historical Newspapers; **p.426** *t* © The Robert Opie Collection; *b* © A: Q 79520, B: Q 79501, C: Q 70169, Imperial War Museum, London; **p.428** *l* © ART 6513 Imperial War Museum. Gift of Her Majesty the Queen, 1979, *r* © The Print Collector/HIP/Topfoto; **p.429** *t* © Q 30859 Imperial War Museum, London, *b* © Q 110074, Imperial War Museum, London; **p.430** © Mary Evans Picture Library/The Women; **p.433** *t* © Kurt Hutton/Picture Post/Getty Images, *b* © Leonard McCombe/Picture Post/Getty Images; **p.434** *l* © Hulton-Deutsch Collection/Corbis, *r* © Popperfoto/Getty Images; **p.435** © Wieslaw and Zenon Rogalski, www.tweedsmuirmilitarycamp.co.uk; **p.436** *l* © Paul Popper/Popperfoto/Getty Images, *r* © TR 00451, Imperial War Museum, London; **p.437** *t* © Popperfoto/Getty Images, *r* © FPG/Hulton Archive/Getty Images; **p.438** © PST 8286 Imperial War Museum, London; **p.440** © Ben Walsh; **p.442** *l* © PST 3095 and *r* HU 36238 Imperial War Museum, London; **p.443** © Keystone/Getty Images; **p.445** © Topfoto; **p.447** © Cartoon by david low published in the *Evening Standard*, 3 December 1942, British Cartoon Archive, University of Kent © Solo Syndication/Associated Newspapers Ltd.; **p.449** © Alex Ramsay/Alamy; **p.451** *l* © Popperfoto/Getty Images, *r* © The National Archives/HIP/TopFoto; **p.452** © Lisa Larsen//Time Life Pictures/Getty Images; **p.453** © Haywood Magee/Getty Images; **p.454** © Keystone/Getty Images; **p.456** © Hulton-Deutsch Collection/Corbis; **p.457** © Cartoon published in *Daily Mirror*, 3 June 1963; British Cartoon Archive, University of Kent © Mirrorpix; **p.458** © Mary Evans Picture Library/ROGER MAYNE; **p.459** *l* © Cartoon by Emmwood [John Musgrave-Wood] published in *Daily Mail*, 3 September 1958, British Cartoon Archive, University of Kent © Solo Syndication/Associated Newspapers Ltd., *r* © Cartoon by Vicky [Victor Weisz] published in the *Evening Standard* on the 19 May 1959, British Cartoon Archive, University of Kent © Solo Syndication/Associated Newspapers Ltd; **p.461** © Cartoon by Cummings published in *Daily Express*, 21 August 1964, British Cartoon Archive, University of Kent © Daily Express; **p.464** *t* © Aubrey Hart/Evening Standard/Getty Images, *b* © Evening Standard/Getty Images; **p.465** *l* © Cartoon by Jon [William John Philpin Jones] published in *Daily Mail*, 24 April 1968, British Cartoon Archive, University of Kent © Solo Syndication/Associated Newspapers Ltd, *r* © Evening Standard/Getty Images; **p.466** *l* © Central Press/Hulton Archive/Getty Images, *r* © Cartoon by Giles published in *Daily Express*, 20 April 1967, British Cartoon Archive, University of Kent © Daily Express; **p.467** © Central Press/Getty Images; **p.468** © E. Milsom/Evening Standard/Getty Images; **p.471** *l* © Land Lost Content/HIP/TopFoto, with kind permission by IPC Media, *r* © Museum of London/HIP/TopFoto; **p.473** © with kind permission from UNISON; **p.474** *l* © Hulton-Deutsch Collection/Corbis, *r* © Advertising Archives; **p.475** © Cartoon by Emmwood [John Musgrave-Wood] published in *Daily Mail*, 3 February 1960 with the caption "Every morning when my husband goes to work I hate him ... because he's going to do things and meet people all day ... while I'm stuck here ...", British Cartoon Archive, University of Kent © Solo Syndication/Associated Newspapers Ltd; **p.477** *t* © By permission of Llyfrgell Genedlaethol Cymru/The National Library of Wales © Solo Syndication/Associated Newspapers Ltd., *c* © The British Library. All rights reserved. P. 2000/1913, *br* © Rex Features; **p.478** © Cartoon by William Papas published in *The Guardian*, 24 February 1985, British Cartoon Archive, The University of Kent © The Guardian; **p.479** News of the World/NI Syndication; **p.480** *t* Land Lost Content/HIP/Topfoto, with kind permission of IPC Media, *c&b* Advertising Archives, with kind permission by IPC Media; **p.482** © William Gottlieb/Corbis; **p.484** *t* © John Topham/Topfoto, *c* © Meager/Fox Photos/Getty Images, *b* © Hulton-Deutsch Collection/Corbis; **p.485** *t* © Everett Collection/Rex Features, *b* © Edward Miller/Getty Images; **p.486** © Ray Roberts/Hulton Archive/Getty Images; **p.488** © Central Press/Getty Images; **p.489** *t* © Cartoon by Cummings published in *Daily Express*, 20 February 1967, British Cartoon Archive, University of Kent © Daily Express, *b* © Cartoon by Emmwood [John Musgrave-Wood] published in *Daily Mail*, 29 January 1960. Caption: "–And blimey – look at the result", British Cartoon Archive, University of Kent © Solo Syndication/Associated Newspapers Ltd.; **p.490** © Pictorial Press Ltd/Alamy; **p.492** © Keystone/Getty Images; **p.494** © Cartoon by Garland published in the *Daily Telegraph*, 16 March 1966, British Cartoon Archive, University of Kent © Daily Telegraph; **p.495** © Cartoon by Garland published in the *Daily Telegraph* on 23 March 1968, British Cartoon Archive, University of Kent © Daily Telegraph; **p.496** © Bob Aylott/Keystone/Getty Images; **p.497** © Norman Potter/Express/Getty Images; **p.498** © Time Inc./Time Life Pictures/Getty Images; **p.491** © Cartoon by Giles published in *Sunday Express*, 8 March 1964, British Cartoon Archive, University of Kent © Daily Express.

t = top, *b* = bottom, *l* = left, *r* = right, *c* = centre

Every effort has been made to contact copyright holders, and the publishers apologise for any omissions which they will be pleased to rectify at the earliest opportunity.

Index